W9-BXQ-477

"I start my new job tomorrow as Purchasing Manager and am very grateful for the information contained in your books, which was a major contributor to my success."

—*J.F., Racine, Wisconsin*

"In the past two weeks I went on nine interviews and three second interviews. I got the position I wanted! Thank you, thank you, thank you! One person asked me all the questions in your book—I had all the right answers."

—*D.J., Scottsdale, Arizona*

"I read the book cover to cover and then flew to California to complete fourteen intense interviews in a two-day period. Although I was interviewing for an entry-level position with a high-tech firm, I faced few technical questions. Most of them were behavioral questions, exactly the types your book prepared me for. I had the enviable position of making a choice of which job to take!"

—*S.T., San Jose, California*

"I used the techniques you described, received multiple offers, and secured a challenging, satisfying, and well compensated position. Thank you!"

—*G.G., San Francisco, California*

"I've just finished writing my resignation letter to the company from hell, thanks to your *Knock 'em Dead* book."

—*J.W., Pompano Beach, Florida*

"I got two job offers within a twenty-four-hour period. The information provided is as valuable as the air you breathe."

—*J.M., Greensboro, North Carolina*

More Praise from Job Seekers for *Knock 'em Dead*

"I followed your suggestions religiously and now my job search efforts have ended most successfully—and all within a three-week period!"

—*E.V., Miami, FL*

"I read every page of the book and after a two-month search got ten interviews with top-performing companies and six offers (five of which I declined)."

—*M.V., Millington, Tennessee*

"They were downsizing my firm . . . I just had an interview with my manager and our general manager. All the questions they asked were in your book."

—*C.M., Atlanta, Georgia*

"Thank you for writing the best and most logical approach to a job search! After reading the books and following your advice for only two weeks, I have had three interviews."

—*J.K., New Castle, Pennsylvania*

"My best investment ever! Thank you . . . I got a job one month out of college because I *knocked them dead!*"

—*A.J., Passaic, New Jersey*

"I just received the offer of my dreams with an outstanding company. Thank you for your insight. I was prepared!"

—*T.C., San Francisco, California*

"I was sending out hordes of resumes and hardly getting a nibble—and I have top-notch skills and experience in my field. I wasn't prepared for this tough job market. When I read your book, however, I immediately began applying some of your techniques. My few nibbles increased to so many job interviews I could hardly keep up with them!"

—*C.S., Chicago, Illinois*

The Ultimate Job Seeker's Handbook

KNOCK 'EM DEAD

The Ultimate Job Seeker's Handbook

MARTIN YATE

BOB ADAMS, INC.
Holbrook, Massachusetts

Published by
Bob Adams, Inc.
260 Center Street, Holbrook, Massachusetts 02343

ISBN: 1-55850-337-4 (hardcover)
ISBN: 1-55850-287-4 (paperback)

Manufactured in the United States of America.

J   I   H   G   F   E   D   C   B   A   (hardcover)
J   I   H   G   F   E   D   C   B   A   (paperback)

This publication is designed to provide accurate and authoritative information
with regard to the subject matter covered. It is sold with the understanding that the
publisher is not engaged in rendering legal, accounting, or other professional advice. If legal advice or other expert assistance is required, the services of a qualified professional person should be sought.
— From a *Declaration of Principles* jointly adopted by a Committee of the
American Bar Association and a Committee of Publishers and Associations.

REAR COVER PHOTO: Nick Basillion

This book is available at quantity discounts for bulk purchases.
For more information, call 1-800-872-5627.

To your successful job hunt.

Contents

IV Finishing Touches 199

Statistics show that the last person to interview usually gets the job. Here are some steps you can take that will keep your impression strong.

V In Depth 241

Acknowledgments

My thanks to the following people who in different ways have helped this book become what it is today—the only internationally published job-hunting guide of its kind.

I'd like to recognize a couple of people in the media who have given me support and encouragement over an extended period of time. These include Tony Lee and the staff of NBEW at Dow Jones, Bill Thompson of UPI, the Famous Dolans of WOR and CNBC, Fred and the gang at Morning Exchange (for putting me through my paces at the beginning of every tour, every year), and the entire editorial staff at *Working Woman*.

Of course, grateful thanks are also in order to my old friend Gary down in the Lone Star State, to Lisa Fisher, and to research director extraordinaire Karen Galletti.

From the employment services world: Dunhill Personnel System presidents—Brad Brin of Milwaukee, Warren Mahan of Maine, Leo Salzman of Columbus, Dave Bontempo of Southhampton, Paul and Pat Erickson of Shawnee Mission, Jim Fowler of Huntsville (and Ray Johnson), Stan Hart of Troy, Mike Badgett of Cherry Hills Village, and John Webb and everyone in beautiful San Antonio.

Thanks also to Don Kipper of Ernst & Whinney, Dan O'Brien of Grumman Aerospace, Amy Marglis and Kathy Seich of Merrill Lynch, Roger Villanueva of I.M.S., Victor Lindquist of Northwestern University, Ed Fitzpatrick of the University of Michigan, and Mary Giannini of Columbia University.

Gratitude is due to Eric Blume for his editorial assistance in the first three editions, and to my new editor, Brandon Toropov. Thanks go also to that man of vision, my publisher Bob Adams, and the people who got this hot little book into your hands—the tireless sales representatives of Bob Adams, Inc. And special thanks to Jill, for being the brightest star in my firmament.

Why *Knock 'em Dead?*

In 1985, when this book was first published, we began by answering a question: "Why another book about interviewing? Because the others stop at that critical point when the tough questions start flying." Sadly, that critique of the many other books out there is still valid. And with over one million *Knock 'em Dead* books in print worldwide, there seems ample evidence that readers agree with my 1985 assessment.

Still, *Knock 'em Dead* has not stood still. In the years since that first edition, this book has grown in size and scope every year; it has doubled in length and now covers the entire job search process. I am confident that it does so with a broader scope, and with more depth and originality, than any other book in the field.

The ever-expanding page count reflects my responses to the constantly changing realities of the world of work. Although we have revised the work throughout, this flexible approach is perhaps best exemplified by one of the new sections to be found in this year's edition, "When You See Clouds on the Horizon." This new chapter takes into account the sobering reality that you can no longer rely on long years of service to a single company to keep a career in high gear.

I wrote *Knock 'em Dead* because too much of the job search advice I could find on the shelves of my bookstore was infantile at best and detrimental to one's professional health at worst. The vast majority of job-hunting books lack the practical advice of what to do in the heat of battle. *Knock 'em Dead* will take you through the whole process—from putting the paperwork together to negotiating salary to your best advantage. Of course, the core of the book still helps you resolve the job-seeker's most dreaded question: "How on earth do I answer *that* one?"

Here, you'll get hundreds of the tough, sneaky, mean, and low-down questions that interviewers love to throw at you. With each question, I will show you what the interviewer wants to find out about you, and explain how you should reply. After each explanation, you'll get a sample answer and suggestions on how to customize it to your individual circumstances. The examples themselves come from real life, things people like you have done on the job that got them noticed. I'll show you how they packaged those experiences, how they used their practical experience to turn a job interview into a job offer.

Perhaps you are trying to land your first job or are returning to the workplace.

Maybe you are a seasoned executive taking another step up the ladder of success. Whoever you are, this book will help you, because it shows you how to master any interview and succeed with any interviewer. You will learn that every interviewer tries to evaluate each candidate by the same three criteria: Is the candidate *able* to do the job? Is he or she *willing* to put in the effort to make the job a success? And last but not least, is he or she *manageable*? You will learn how to demonstrate your superiority in each of these areas, under all interview conditions.

The job interview is a measured and ritualistic mating dance in which the best partners whirl away with the glittering prizes. The steps of this dance are the give-and-take, question-and-response exchanges that make meaningful business conversation. Learn the steps and you, too, can dance the dance.

Your partner in the dance, obviously, is the interviewer, who will lead with tough questions that carry subtleties hidden from the untrained ear. You will learn how to recognize those questions-within-questions. And with this knowledge, you will be cool, calm, and collected, while other candidates are falling apart with attacks of interview nerves.

How do you discover hidden meanings in questions? I recently heard a story about a young woman who was doing very well on an interview for a high-pressure job in a television studio. The interviewer wanted to know how she would react in the sudden, stressful situations common in TV, and got his answer when he said, "You know, I don't really think you're suitable for the job. Wouldn't you be better off in another company?" With wounded pride, the job-hunter stormed out in a huff. She never knew how close she was, how easy it would have been to land the job. The interviewer smiled: He had caught her with a tough question. Did the interviewer mean what he said? What was really behind the question? How could she have handled it and landed the job? The great answers to tough questions like that and many others are waiting for you in the following pages.

The job interview has many similarities to good social conversation. Job offers always go to the interviewee who can turn a one-sided examination of skills into a dynamic exchange between two professionals. In *Knock 'em Dead*, you will learn the techniques for exciting and holding your interviewer's attention, and at the same time, for promoting yourself as the best candidate for the job.

This book will carry you successfully through the worst interviews and job-hunting scenarios you will ever face. It is written in five interconnected parts. "The Well-Stocked Briefcase" gets you ready for the fray. You will quickly learn to build a resume with broad appeal and to use a unique customizing technique guaranteed to make your application stand out as something special. You will also learn how to tap into thousands of job openings at all levels that never reach the newspapers.

Once you are ready for action, "Getting to Square One" examines all the approaches to getting job interviews and teaches you simple and effective ways to set up multiple interviews. This section ends with techniques to steer you successfully through those increasingly common telephone screening interviews.

"Great Answers to Tough Interview Questions" gives you just that, and teaches you some valuable business lessons that will contribute to your future success. All successful companies look for the same things in their employees, and everything they're looking for you either have or can develop. Sound impossible? I will show you the twenty key personality traits that can convey your potential for success to any interviewer.

"Finishing Touches" assures that out-of-sight-out-of-mind will not apply to you after you leave the interviewer's office. You will even discover how to get a job offer after you have been turned down for the position, and how to negotiate the best salary and package for yourself when a job offer is made. Most important, the sum of those techniques will give you tremendous self-confidence when you go to an interview: No more jitters, no more sweaty palms.

The final section, "In Depth," includes new ideas for long-term career survival, proven tips for jump-starting a stalled job search, and some important advice on keeping your financial boat afloat during tough times.

If you want to know how business works and what savvy businesspeople look for in an employee, if you want to discover how to land the interview and conquer the interviewer, then this book is for you. *Knock 'em Dead* delivers everything you need to win the job of your dreams. Now get to it, step ahead in your career, and knock 'em dead.

—Martin John Yate
New York

I

The Well-Stocked Briefcase

Have you heard the one about the poor man who wanted to become a famous bear-slayer? Once upon a time, in a town plagued by bears, lived a man. The man had always wanted to travel but had neither the right job nor the money. If he could kill a bear, then he could travel to other places plagued with bears and make his living as a bear-slayer. Every day he sat on the porch and waited for a bear to come by. After many weeks of waiting, he thought he might go looking for bears. He didn't know much about them, except that they were out there.

Full of hope, he rose before dawn, loaded his single-shot musket, and headed for the forest. On reaching the edge of the forest, he raised the musket and fired into the dense undergrowth.

Do you think he hit a bear or, for that matter, anything else? Why was he bear-hunting with a single-shot musket, and why did he shoot before seeing a bear? What was his problem? Our hero couldn't tell dreams from reality. He went hunting unprepared and earned what he deserved. The moral of the tale is this: When you look for a job, keep a grip on reality, go loaded for bear, and don't go off half-cocked.

Out there in the forest of your profession hide many companies and countless opportunities. These are major corporations, small family affairs, and some in between. They all have something in common, and that's problems. To solve those problems, companies need people. Think about your present job function: What problems would occur if you weren't there? You were hired to take care of those problems.

Being a problem solver is good, but companies prefer to hire and promote someone who also understands what business is all about. There are three lessons you should remember on this score.

> *Lesson One:* Companies are in business to make money. People have loyalty to companies; companies have loyalty only to the bottom line. They make money by being economical and saving money. They make money by being efficient and saving time. And if they save time, they save money, and have more time to make more money.

Lesson Two: Companies and you are exactly alike. You both want to make as much money as possible in as short a time as possible. That allows you to do the things you really want with the rest of your time.

Lesson Three: There are buyer's markets (advantage: prospective employer) and there are seller's markets (advantage: prospective employee). Job offers put you in a seller's market, and give you the whip hand.

Lesson One tells you the three things every company is interested in. *Lesson Two* says to recognize that you really have the same goals as the company. *Lesson Three* says that anyone with any sense wants to be in a seller's market.

If you look for jobs one at a time, you put yourself in a buyer's market. If you implement my advice in *Knock 'em Dead*, you will have multiple job offers. And job offers, however good or bad they are, will put you in a seller's market, regardless of the economic climate.

Operating in a seller's market requires knowing who, where, and what your buyers are in the market for, then being ready with the properly packaged product.

In this section you will find out how to identify *every* company that could be in need of your services. You will learn how to discover the names of the president, those on the board, and those in management; the company sales volume; complete lines of company services or products; and the size of the outfit. You will evaluate and package your professional skills in a method guaranteed to have appeal to every employer. And you will discover highly desirable professional skills you never knew you had.

It will take a couple of days' work to get you loaded for bear. You are going to need to update your resume (or create a new one), generate some cover letters, research potential employers, and create a comprehensive marketing plan.

While I cover each of these areas in sequence, I recommend that, in the execution, you mix and match the activities. In other words, when the direct research begins to addle the gray matter, switch to resume enhancement, and so on. An hour of one activity followed by an hour of another will keep your mind fresh and your program balanced.

Your first action should be a trip to the library (taking sufficient paper and pens). On the way, purchase some push-pins, a large-scale area map, and some stick-on labels—and rustle up a three-foot piece of string. Take some sandwiches; there is no feeling in the world like eating lunch on the library steps.

1.
All Things to All People

At the library, walk in purposefully and ask for the reference section. When you find it, wander around for a few minutes before staking a claim. You will discover that libraries are a good place to watch the human race, so get the best seat in the house. Make sure you have a clear view of the librarian's desk. When you need a rest, that's where all the comic relief takes place.

Interviewers today are continually asking for detailed examples of your past performance. They safely assume you will do at least as well (or as poorly) on the new job as you did on the old one, and so the examples you give will seal your fate. Therefore you need to examine your past performance in a manner that will empower you to handle these questions in a professional and competent manner.

This chapter will show you how to identify examples of problems solved, projects completed, and contributions made that will impress any interviewer. As you complete the exercises in this chapter and concurrently proceed with your research, your added self-knowledge and confidence could well open your eyes to as-yet-unimagined professional opportunities. You will also get the correctly packaged information for a workmanlike resume. Two birds with one stone.

Resumes, of course, are important, and there are two facts you must know about them. First, you are going to need one. Second, no one will want to read it. The average interviewer has never been trained to interview effectively, probably finds the interview as uncomfortable as you do, and will do everything possible to avoid discomfort. Resumes, therefore, are used more to screen people out than screen them in. So your resume must be all things to all people.

Another hurdle to clear is avoiding too much of your professional jargon in the resume. It is a cold hard fact that the first person to see your resume is often in the personnel department. This office screens for many different jobs and cannot be expected to have an in-depth knowledge of every specialty within the company— or its special language.

For those reasons, your resume must be short, be easy to read and understand, and use words that are familiar to the reader and that have universal appeal. Most important, it should portray you as a problem solver.

While this chapter covers ways to build an effective resume, its main goal is to help you perform better at the interview. You will achieve that as you evaluate your professional skills according to the exercises. In fact, you are likely to discover skills and achievements you didn't even know you had. A few you will use in your resume (merely a preview of coming attractions); the others you will use to knock 'em dead at the interview.

A good starting point is your current or last job title. Write it down. Then, jot down all the other different titles you have heard that describe that job. When you are finished, follow it with a three- or four-sentence description of your job functions. Don't think too hard about it, just do it. The titles and descriptions are not carved in stone—this written description is just the beginning of the resume-building exercises. You'll be surprised at what you've written; it will read better than you had thought.

All attributes that you discover and develop in the following exercises are valuable to an employer. You possess many desirable traits, and these exercises help to reveal and to package them.

☐ **Exercise One**: Reread the written job description, then write down your most important duty/function. Follow that with a list of the skills or special training necessary to perform that duty. Next, list the achievements of which you are most proud in that area. It could look something like this:

> *Duty:* Train and motivate sales staff of six.
>
> *Skills:* Formal training skills. Knowledge of market and ability to make untrained sales staff productive. Ability to keep successful salespeople motivated and tied to the company.
>
> *Achievements:* Reduced turnover 7 percent; increased sales 14 percent.

The potential employer is most interested in the achievements—those things that make you stand out from the crowd. Try to appeal to a company's interests by conservatively estimating what your achievements meant to your employer. If your achievements saved time, estimate how much. If you saved money, how much? If your achievements made money for the company, how much? Beware of exaggeration—if you were part of a team, identify your achievements as such. It will make your claims more believable and will demonstrate your ability to work with others.

Achievements, of course, differ according to your profession. Most of life's jobs fall into one of these broad categories:

- sales and service;
- management and administration;
- technical and production.

While it is usual to cite the differences between those major job functions, at this point it is far more valuable to you to recognize the commonalities. In sales, dollar volume is important. In management or administration, the parallel is time saved, which is money saved; saving money is just the same as making money for your company. In the technical and production areas, increasing production (doing more in less time) accrues exactly the same benefits to the company. Job titles may differ, yet all employees have the same opportunity to benefit their employers, and in turn, themselves.

Today, companies are doing more with less; they are leaner, have higher expectations of their employees, and plan to keep it that way. The people who get hired and get ahead today are those with a basic understanding of business goals. And successful job candidates are those who have the best interests of the company and its profitability constantly in mind.

☐ **Exercise Two**: This simple exercise helps you get a clear picture of your achievements. If you were to meet with your supervisor to discuss a raise, what achievements would you want to discuss? List all you can think of, quickly. Then come back and flesh out the details.

☐ **Exercise Three:** This exercise is particularly valuable if you feel you can't see the forest for the trees.

> Problem: Think of a job-related problem you had to face in the last couple of years. Come on, everyone can remember one.

> Solution: Describe your solution to the problem, step by step. List everything you did.

> Results: Finally, consider the results of your solution in terms that would have value to an employer: money earned or saved; time saved.

☐ **Exercise Four:** Now, a valuable exercise that turns the absence of a negative into a positive. This one helps you look at your job in a different light and accents important but often overlooked areas that help make you special. Begin discovering for yourself some of the key personal traits that all companies look for.

First, consider actions that if not done properly would affect the goal of your job. If that is difficult, remember an incompetent co-worker. What did he or she do wrong? What did he or she do differently from competent employees?

Now, turn the absence of those negatives into positive attributes. For example, think of the employee who never managed to get to work on time. You could honestly say that someone who did come to work on time every day was punctual and reliable, believed in systems and procedures, was efficiency-minded, and cost- and profit-conscious.

If you have witnessed the reprimands and ultimate termination of that tardy employee, you will see the value of the positive traits in the eyes of an employer. The absence of negative traits makes you a desirable employee, but no one will know unless you say. On completion of the exercise, you will be able to make points about your background in a positive fashion. You will set yourself apart from others, if only because others do not understand the benefit of projecting all their positive attributes.

☐ **Exercise Five:** Potential employers and interviewers are always interested in people who:

- are efficiency-minded.
- have an eye for economy.
- follow procedures.
- are profit-oriented.

Proceed through your work history and identify the aspects of your background that exemplify those traits. These newly discovered personal plusses will not only be woven into your resume but will be reflected in the posture of your answers when you get to the interview, and in your performance when you land the right job.

Now you need to take some of that knowledge and package it in a resume. There are three standard types of resumes:

> **Chronological:** The most frequently used format. Use it when your work history is stable and your professional growth is consistent. The chronological format is exactly what it sounds like: It follows your work history backward from the current job, listing companies and dates and responsibilities. Avoid it if you have experienced performance problems, have not grown professionally (but want to), or have made frequent job changes. All those problems will show up in a glaring fashion if you use a chronological resume.

> **Functional:** Use this type if you have been unemployed for long periods of time or have jumped jobs too frequently, or if your career has been stagnant and you want to jump-start it. A functional resume is created without employment dates or company names, and concentrates on skills and responsibilities. It can be useful if you have changed careers, or when current responsibilities don't relate specifically to the job you want. It is written with the most relevant experience to the job you're seeking placed first, and de-emphasizes jobs, employment dates, and job titles by placing them inconspicuously at the end. It allows you to promote specific job skills without emphasizing where or when you developed those skills.

> **Combination:** Use this format if you have a steady work history with demonstrated growth, and if you have nothing you wish to de-emphasize. A combination resume is a combination of chronological and functional resumes. It starts with a brief personal summary, then lists job-specific skills relevant to the objective, and segues into a chronological format that lists the how, where, and when these skills were acquired.

Notice that each style is designed to emphasize strengths and minimize certain undesirable traits. In today's world, all of us need a powerful resume. It is not only a door opener, it is also there long after we are gone and will almost certainly be reviewed just before the choice of the successful candidate is made by the interviewer.

Examples of each style follow; for more detailed information on assembling a winning resume, you may wish to purchase this book's companion volume, *Resumes that Knock 'em Dead*.

If you already have a resume and just want to make sure it measures up, check it against these seven basic rules of resume writing.

☐ **Rule One:** Use the most general of job titles. You are, after all, a hunter of interviews, not of specific titles. Cast your net wide. Use a title that is specific enough to put you in the field, yet vague enough to elicit further questions. One way you can make a job title specifically vague is to add the term "specialist" (e.g., Computer Specialist, Administration Specialist, Production Specialist).

☐ **Rule Two:** If you must state a specific job objective, couch it in terms of contributions you can make in that position. Do not state what you expect of the employer.

☐ **Rule Three:** Do not state your current salary. If you are earning too little or too much, you could rule yourself out before getting your foot in the door. For the same reason, do not mention your desired salary.

☐ **Rule Four:** Remember that people get great joy from getting pleasant surprises. Show a little gold now, but let the interviewer discover the motherlode at the interview.

☐ **Rule Five:** Try to keep your resume to one page; take whatever steps necessary to keep the resume no more than two pages long. No one reads long resumes—they are boring, and every company is frightened that if it lets in a windbag, it will never get him or her out again.

☐ **Rule Six:** Your resume must be typed. As a rule of thumb, three pages of double-spaced, handwritten notes make one typewritten page.

☐ **Rule Seven:** Finally, emphasize your achievements and problem-solving skills. Keep the resume general.

CHRONOLOGICAL RESUME

Jane Swift, 9 Central Avenue, Quincy, MA 02269. (617) 555-1212

SUMMARY: Ten years of increasing responsibilities in the employment services industry. Concentration in the high-technology markets.

EXPERIENCE: Howard Systems International, Inc.   1985-Present
Management Consulting Firm
Personnel Manager

Responsible for recruiting and managing consulting staff of five. Set up office and organized the recruitment, selection and hiring of consultants. Recruited all levels of MIS staff from financial to manufacturing markets.

Additional responsibilities:
* coordinated with outside advertising agencies
* developed P.R. with industry periodicals—placement with over 20 magazines and newsletters
* developed effective referral programs—referrals increased 32%

EXPERIENCE: Technical Aid Corporation   1977-1985
National Consulting Firm. MICRO/TEMPS Division

Division Manager   1983-1985
Area Manager   1980-1983
Branch Manager   1978-1980

As Division Manager, opened additional West Coast offices, staffed and trained all offices with appropriate personnel. Created and implemented all divisional operational policies responsible for P & L. Sales increased to $20 million from $0 in 1978.

* Achieved and maintained 30% annual growth over 7-year period.
* Maintained sales staff turnover at 14%.

As Area Manager opened additional offices, hiring staff, setting up office policies and training sales and recruiting personnel.

Additional responsibilities:
* supervised offices in two states
* developed business relationships with accounts—75% of clients were regular customers
* client base increased 28% per year
* generated over $200,000 worth of free trade-journal publicity

As Branch Manager, hired to establish the new MICRO/TEMPS operation. Recruited and managed consultants. Hired internal staff. Sold service to clients.

EDUCATION: Boston University
B.S. Public Relations, 1977

FUNCTIONAL RESUME

Jane Swift
9 Central Avenue
Quincy, MA 02269
(617) 555-1212

OBJECTIVE: A position in Employment Services where my management, sales and recruiting talents can be effectively utilized to improve operations and contribute to company profits.

SUMMARY: Over ten years of Human Resources experience. Extensive responsibility for multiple branch offices and an internal staff of 40+ employees and 250 consultants.

SALES: Sold high-technology consulting services with consistently profitable margins throughout the United States. Grew sales from $0 to over $20 million a year.

Created training programs and trained salespeople in six metropolitan markets.

RECRUITING: Developed recruiting sourcing methods for multiple branch offices.

Recruited over 25,000 internal and external consultants in the high-technology professions.

MANAGEMENT: Managed up to 40 people in sales, customer service, recruiting, and administration. Turnover maintained below 14% in a "turnover business."

FINANCIAL: Prepared quarterly and yearly forecasts. Presented, reviewed and defended these forecasts to the Board of Directors. Responsible for P & L of $20 million sales operation.

PRODUCTION: Responsible for opening multiple offices and accountable for growth and profitability. 100% success and maintained 30% growth over 7-year period in 10 offices.

**WORK
EXPERIENCE:**

1985 to Present   HOWARD SYSTEMS INTERNATIONAL, Boston, MA
National Consulting Firm
Personnel Manager

1978-1985   TECHNICAL AID CORPORATION, Needham, MA
National Consulting & Search Firm
Division Manager

EDUCATION: B.S., 1977, Boston University

REFERENCES: Available upon request

COMBINATION RESUME

EMPLOYMENT SERVICES MANAGEMENT

Jane Swift
9 Central Avenue
Quincy, MA 02269
(617) 555-1212

OBJECTIVE:

Employment Services Management

SUMMARY:	Ten years of increasing responsibilities in the employment services marketplace. Concentration in the high technology markets.
SALES:	Sold high-technology consulting services with consistently profitable margins throughout the United States. Grew sales from $0 to over $20 million a year.
PRODUCTION:	Responsible for opening multiple offices and accountable for growth and profitability. 100% success and maintained 30% growth over 7-year period in 10 offices.
MANAGEMENT:	Managed up to 40 people in sales, customer service, recruiting, and administration. Turnover maintained below 14% in a "turnover business." Hired branch managers, sales and recruiting staff throughout United States.
FINANCIAL:	Prepared quarterly and yearly forecasts. Presented, reviewed and defended these forecasts to the Board of Directors. Responsible for P & L of $20 million sales operation.
MARKETING:	Performed numerous market studies for multiple branch openings. Resolved feasibility of combining two different sales offices. Study resulted in savings of over $5,000 per month in operating expenses.

COMBINATION RESUME (page 2)

EXPERIENCE:　Howard Systems International, Inc.　　　　1985-Present
Management Consulting Firm
Personnel Manager

Responsible for recruiting and managing consulting staff of five. Set up office and organized the recruitment, selection, and hiring of consultants. Recruited all levels of MIS staff from financial to manufacturing markets.

Additional responsibilities:

- developed P.R. with industry periodicals—placement with over 20 magazines and newsletters
- developed effective referral programs—referrals increased 320%

Technical Aid Corporation　　　　　　　1977-1985
National Consulting Firm. MICRO/TEMPS Division
Division Manager　　　1983-1985
Area Manager　　　　1980-1983
Branch Manager　　　1978-1980

As Division Manager, opened additional West Coast offices, staffed and trained all offices with appropriate personnel. Created and implemented all divisional operational policies. Responsible for P & L. Sales increase to $20 million from $0 in 1978.

- Achieved and maintained 30% annual growth over 7-year period.
- Maintained sales staff turnover at 14%.

As Area Manager opened additional offices, hiring staff, setting up office policies, training sales and recruiting personnel.

Additional responsibilities:

- supervised offices in two states
- developed business relationships with accounts—75% of clients were regular customers
- client base increased 28% per year
- generated over $200,000 worth of free trade-journal publicity

As Branch Manager, hired to establish the new MICRO/TEMPS operation. Recruited and managed consultants. Hired internal staff. Sold service to clients.

EDUCATION:　B.S., 1977, Boston University

2.
The Executive Briefing

A general resume does have drawbacks. First, it is too general to relate your qualifications to each specific job. Second, more than one person will probably be interviewing you, and that is a major stumbling block. While you will ultimately report to one person, you may well be interviewed by other team members. When that happens, the problems begin.

A manager says, "Spend a few minutes with this candidate and tell me what you think." Your general resume may be impressive, but the manager rarely adequately outlines the job being filled or the specific qualifications for which he or she is looking. This means that other interviewers do not have any way to qualify you fairly and specifically. While the manager will be looking for specific skills relating to projects at hand, personnel will be trying to match your skills to the job-description-manual vagaries, and the other interviewers will fumble in the dark because no one told them what to look for. Such problems can reduce your chances of landing a job offer.

A neat trick I helped develop for the executive-search industry is the Executive Briefing. It enables you to customize your resume quickly to each specific job and acts as a focusing device for the person who interviews you.

While the Executive Briefing is only one form of cover letter, I am including it here for one very important reason—namely, that you are, in your research, going to come across "dream opportunities" before your new resume is finished. The Executive Briefing allows you to update and customize that old resume with lightning speed without delaying the rest of your research.

Like many great ideas, the Executive Briefing is beautiful in its simplicity. It is a sheet of paper with the company's requirements for the job opening listed on the left side, and your skills—matching point by point the company's needs—on the right. It looks like this:

Executive Briefing

Dear Sir/Madam:

   While my attached resume will provide you with a general outline of my work history, my problem-solving abilities, and some achievements, I have taken the time to list your current specific requirements and my applicable skills in those areas. I hope this will enable you to use your time effectively today.

Your Requirements:	My Skills:
1. Management of public library service area (for circulation, reference, etc.).	1. Experience as head reference librarian at University of Smithtown.
2. Supervision of 14 full-time support employees	2. Supervised support staff of 17.
3. Ability to work with larger supervisory team in planning, budgeting, and policy formulating.	3. During my last year, I was responsible for budget and reformation of circulation rules.
4. ALA-accredited MLS.	4. ALA-accredited MLS.
5. 3 years' experience.	5. 1 year with public library; 2 with University of Smithtown.

   This briefing assures that each resume you send out addresses the job's specific needs and that every interviewer at that company will be interviewing you for the same job.

   Send an Executive Briefing with every resume; it will substantially increase your chances of obtaining an interview with the company. An Executive Briefing sent with a resume provides a comprehensive picture of a thorough professional, plus a personalized, fast, and easy-to-read synopsis that details exactly how you can help with current needs.

   The use of an Executive Briefing is naturally restricted to jobs that you have discovered through your own efforts or seen advertised. It is obviously not appropriate for sending when the requirements of a specific job are unavailable. Finally, using the Executive Briefing as a cover letter to your resume will greatly increase the chance that your query will be picked out of the pile in the personnel department and hand-carried to the appropriate manager.

3.
The Inside Track

There used to be a stigma about changing jobs or looking for a new one. Today we live in a different climate. Everyone you speak with in your job hunt has been through your experience. Career moves and unemployment are an integral part of our working lives, but how long this phase lasts is entirely up to you.

I recently met an executive who was looking for a job for the first time in twenty years. He had been looking for seven months and wasn't the least bit concerned: "I've been told that it takes a month for every ten thousand dollars of salary, so I really have another eighteen months to go." He seemed to have this mistaken idea that after two years of unemployment, someone would magically appear with another chief executive's job for him.

His method of job hunting was networking "because that is what I've been told is the best way to find jobs." It is if it works, but all too often a single-shot approach misfires.

The employment market varies from year to year. Sometimes it's a buyer's market and sometimes a seller's. But the fact remains that regardless of the state of the economy, there are good jobs out there for the job hunter who employs a systematic and comprehensive approach.

Too many job hunters rely solely on applications to the well-known companies, the IBMs of this world. They forget that the majority of growth in American industry is with small companies with less than fifty employees. Your goal is to land the best possible job for you and your needs. The problem is, you won't have the chance to pick the best opportunity unless you check them all out.

Average employee turnover in the American workplace has remained steady for some years at about 14 percent. In other words, just about every company is looking for someone during the year. What you have to do is to make sure that you are aware of the opportunity and the company, and the company in turn is aware of you when that opportunity arises.

There is a multi-pronged approach that combines active and passive job-hunting strategies that every job hunter can use to cover all the bases and tap the very best opportunities.

> 1. Direct research. Your future could well lie with a company you never dreamed existed.

2. Newspapers. Thousands of overlooked opportunities.

3. Employment agencies. Who you allow to represent you will decide who you get to meet and how seriously your initial candidacy will be considered.

4. References. The references you supply potential employers in the later stages of the job hunt can be effectively utilized at the beginning, too.

5. College placement offices and alumni organizations. Even if you have long since graduated, these organizations can be a big help.

6. Professional associations. It is sometimes said that it is not what you know, but who you know.

7. Job fairs. Home of employers in a feeding frenzy for today and tomorrow.

8. Business and trade publications. These are a much underrated resource for telling you what is happening on your professional main street and who is making it happen.

9. Networking. It is more than an empty phrase. There are numerous networks we can all tap into effectively.

10. Job hunters' networks. If one doesn't exist, create your own.

11. Electronic databases. The newest weapon in your arsenal.

Tapping the hidden job market need not be scary if you follow a sound plan. In the following pages, you'll examine insider tricks to get up to speed and maintain momentum in each of these areas.

4.

The Hidden Job Market

On a radio talk show earlier this year I listened to a problem from a listener. She said, "I'm in the academic field and I've been unemployed for two years, and I don't know what to do." I asked her how many organizations she had contacted, and she said 250. I asked her how many possible employers there were, and she said about 3,000. I said, "Next caller please." The world owes no one a living. You have to go out and find a job.

While I was revising this chapter, I heard from the producer of a national talk show on which I had recently appeared. She told me she used the techniques described in this part of the book to get thirty interviews in three weeks!

1. Direct Research

No job search is going to be truly comprehensive without research. As we have seen, this means visiting the local library with the best research section. It is well worth traveling a few miles to get to a major library.

There are a number of reference books you can consult; they are listed in the bibliography, so I won't waste space teaching you how to use them—the librarian will be happy to do that.

Your goal is to identify and build personalized dossiers on the companies in your chosen geographic area. Do not be judgmental about what and who they might appear to be: You are fishing for possible job openings, so cast your net wide and list them all.

Take a pad of paper, and using a separate sheet for each company, copy all the relevant company information. So that we agree on *relevant*, take a look at the example (page 39).

In the example, you see the names of the company president and chairman of the board, a description of the complete lines of company services or products, the size of the company, and the locations of its various branches. Of course, if you find other interesting information, copy it down, by all means. For instance, you might come across information on growth or shrinkage in a particular area of a company, or you might read about recent acquisitions the company has made. Write it all down.

This information will help you shine at the interview in three ways. Your

```
Corporation, Inc.
Headquarters:
123 Main Street
Boston, MA 01234

Main phone: 617/555-1212
Personnel (Joseph Smith, Director): 617/555-1212

President: Richard Johnson (for 3 yrs.)
COO: William Jones (for 2 yrs.)

Director of Word Processing Services: Peter Lee

Company produces a complete line of office ma-
chines: calculators, adding machines, typewriters
(electric, electronic, manual), telephones, comput-
erized switching systems, and a wide range of pe-
ripheral equipment. Employs 1200, all in
Massachusetts.

This location is primarily an administrative facil-
ity, but it provides all services for the firm (re-
search, repair, operations, word processing).
Manufacturing facilities located in Worcester (cal-
culators, telephone equipment, peripherals) and
Wakefield (typewriters, computers).

Sales (1992): $334.4 million
Profits: +5% over last 5 years

Recently acquired Disko, Inc. (Braintree, MA), a
software firm (looks like it's diversifying ???).
Maybe has something big in the works (possible
merger with The Bigg Corporation).
```

knowledge creates a favorable impression at your first meeting; that you made an effort is noticed. That no one else bothers is a second benefit; you have set yourself apart from the others. And third, you are showing that you respect the company, and therefore, by inference, the interviewer; this sets a favorable tone.

All your effort has an obvious short-term value: It helps you win job offers. It also has long-term value because you are building a personalized reference work of your industry/specialty/profession that will help you throughout your career whenever you wish to make a job change.

Unfortunately, no single reference work you will find at the library is complete. The very size and scope of reference works means that they are just a little out-of-date at publication time. Also, no single reference work lists every company. Because you don't know what company has the very best job for you, you need to research as many businesses in your area as possible, and therefore you will have to look through several reference books.

Be sure to check out any specialized guides mentioned in the bibliography, including the *Standard & Poor's Register* and your state's manufacturing directory. Senior-level executives will be especially interested in volume two of this register, which gives detailed personal histories and contact information about board members and first-rank executives.

Your local Business-to-Business Yellow Pages is also worth a look. Information found here will range from a company name and telephone number to a full-page advertisement providing considerable "insider" data.

If you can get only names and telephone numbers, the directory can still be a valuable resource. While most directories are updated infrequently and tend only to list major players in the field, B-to-B Yellow Pages are updated annually. They are used extensively by growth companies as a marketing tool.

Most of our nation's economic growth (and therefore most of the promising new job opportunities) is with the small-growth companies.

Making the Battle Map

At the end of the day, pack up and head home for some well-deserved troughing and sluicing. Remember to purchase a map of your area, push-pins, and small stick-on labels for implementing the next step of your plan.

Put the map on the wall. Attach the string to a push-pin, stick the pin on the spot where you live, and draw concentric circles at intervals of one mile.

Next, take out the company biographies prepared at the library and write "#1" on the first. Find the firm's location on the map and mark it with a push-pin. Then, mark an adhesive label "#1" and attach it to the head of the pin. As you progress, a dramatic picture of your day's work appears. Each pin-filled circle is a territory that needs to be covered, and each of those pins represents a potential job. In short order you will have defaced a perfectly good map, but you'll have a physical outline of your job-hunting efforts.

It is likely you will return to the library, continuing your research work and preparing your resume. The initial research might take a few days. Your goal in this stage is to generate a couple of hundred sources, enough to get you started. Then, once your campaign is up to speed, you can visit again as prudence dictates.

Try walking to the library the next time, if practical. Not only is it cheaper (a sound reason in itself), but the exercise is important. You are engaged in a battle of wits, and the healthier you are physically, the sharper you will be mentally. You need your wits about you, because there are always well-qualified people looking for the best jobs. Yet it is not the most qualified who always get the job. It is the person who is best prepared who wins every time. Job hunters who knock 'em dead at the interview are those who do their homework. Do a little more walking. Do a little more research.

Purchasing Mailing Lists

Mailing lists can be cheap and effective. With very few exceptions there is a mailing list of exactly the types of movers and shakers you want to work for. Additionally, these lists can be broken down for you by title, geography, zip code—all sorts of ways. They are affordable, too; usually about $100 for a thousand. For a list broker, just look in your Yellow Pages under "Mailing List Brokers/Compilers."

As even the most up-to-date lists are out-of-date by the time they get to you, it is a good investment to call and verify that Joe Schmoe, vice president of engineering, is still there. If Joe is no longer there you can find out where he went, and you will have uncovered another opportunity for yourself.

2. Newspapers

Most people, unfortunately, use either the newspaper or reference books when job hunting, but rarely both. These people run the risk of ending up in a buyer's market. Not a good place to be.

Almost everybody looking for a new job buys the newspaper and then carefully misuses it. A recent story tells of a job hunter who started by waiting for the Sunday paper to be published. He read the paper and circled six jobs. He called about the first only to find it had already been filled, and in the process, got snubbed by someone whose voice had yet to break, requesting that in the future he write and send a resume rather than call. As anything is better than facing telephone conversations like this, the job hunter didn't call the other five companies, but took a week to write a resume that no one would read, let alone understand. He sent it, then waited a week for someone to call. Waited another week. Kicked the cat. Felt bad about that, worse about himself, and had a couple of drinks. Phone rang, someone was interested in the resume but, unfortunately, not in someone who slurred his words at lunchtime. Felt worse, stayed in bed late. Phone rang. An interview! Felt good, went to the interview. They said they'd contact him in a few days. They didn't, and when he called, everybody was mysteriously unavailable. The job hunter begins to feel like a blot on God's landscape.

This is obviously an extreme example, but the story is a little too close to home for many, and it illustrates the wrong way to use the newspaper when you're looking for a job. In today's changing economy it is not unusual for an advertisement in a local paper to draw upwards of 150 responses. I know of ads that have drawn almost 2,000 responses. It is these odds of 1 in 150 or 1 in 2,000 that cause some to reject the want ads as a realistic method for finding employment. There are ways to answer want ads correctly and narrow the odds to 1 in 10 or even 1 in 5. This is exactly what I am going to show you how to do now.

While reference books give you bags of hard information about a company, they tell you little about specific job openings. Newspapers, on the other hand, tell you about specific jobs that need to be filled now, but give you few hard facts about the company. The two types of information complement each other. Often you will find ads in the newspaper for companies you have already researched. What a powerful combination of information this gives you going in the door to the interview!

Use newspaper ads to identify all companies in your field that are currently hiring, not just to identify specific openings. Write down pertinent details about each particular job opening on a separate sheet of paper, as you did earlier when using the reference books. Include the company's name, address, phone number, and contacts.

In addition to finding openings that bear your particular title, look for all the companies that regularly hire in your field. Cross-check the categories. Don't rely solely on those ads advertising for your specific job title. For example, let's say you are a graphic artist looking for a job in advertising. You should flag any advertising or public relations agency with any kind of need. The fact that your job is not being advertised does not mean a company is not looking for you; if a company is in a hiring mode, a position for you might be available. In the instances when a company is active but has not been advertising specifically for your skills, write down all relevant company contact data. Then contact the company. You could be the solution to a problem that has only just arisen or even one they have despaired of ever solving.

Virtually every newspaper has an employment edition each week (in addition to Sunday), when they have their largest selection of help-wanted ads. Make sure you always get this edition of the paper.

It is always a good idea to examine back issues of the newspapers. These can provide a rich source of job opportunities that remain unfilled from previous advertising efforts. I suggest working systematically through the want ads, going back twelve to eighteen months. React to ads as if they were fresh: answer the ones with your job title and contact companies in your field even if they appear to be seeking people with different skills.

When you contact by phone or letter, your opening gambit is not to say, "Gee whiz, Ms. Jones, I'm answering your ad from last July's *Sentinel*." No. You mention that you've "heard through the grapevine that the company might be looking" or that you "have been intrigued by their company and hope they might be looking for . . ."

Sound crazy? That's what a *Knock 'em Dead* reader said to me recently in a letter. He also said this trick landed him a $90,000-a-year job from a seven-month-old want ad. Sometimes the position will never have been filled and the employer simply despaired of getting someone through advertising. Sometimes the person hired left or didn't work out. Or perhaps they are only now starting to look for another person like the one they had advertised for earlier. They might even just be coming off a hiring freeze. Whatever the case, every old ad you follow up on won't result in an opening, but when one does, the odds can be short indeed. Smart money always goes on the short odds.

In addition to your local papers, there are regional, national, and international papers that employers favor to meet their professional needs.

National and International Newspapers:

The Chicago Tribune
The New York Times
The Los Angeles Times
The Financial Times
The San Jose Mercury News (if you are in the high-tech field)
The Wall Street Journal
The National Business Employment Weekly (NBEW)

The NBEW is of special interest to the professional. Published by the *Wall Street Journal*, NBEW is a weekly paper that carries hundreds of higher-level professional positions. It is packed with useful articles on job hunting and entrepreneurship and carries a calendar of support groups activities and employment events around the country. *Of special interest is the weekly profile of salaries by industry and function.* NBEW is available on selected newsstands, or you can subscribe for $35 for eight weeks by calling 1-800-JOB-HUNT.

Regional Newspapers:

Northeast
The New York Times
Newsday
The Washington Post
The Philadelphia Inquirer
The Boston Globe
The Hartford Courant

Midwest
The Chicago Tribune
The Detroit Free Press
The Kansas City Star
Rocky Mountain News
The Denver Post
The St. Louis Post Dispatch

West
The San Francisco Chronicle
The San Francisco Examiner
The San Jose Mercury News
The Sacramento Bee
The Los Angeles Times
The San Diego Union
The Seattle Times

Southwest
The Dallas News
The Dallas Times
The New Orleans Times Picayune

Southeast
The Atlanta Constitution
The Miami Herald

The reason you must use a combination of reference books and advertisements is that companies tend to hire in cycles. When you rely exclusively on newspapers, you miss those companies just about to start or just ending their hiring cycles. Comprehensive research is the way to tap what the business press refers to as the hidden job market. It is paramount that you have as broad a base as possible—people know people who have your special job to fill.

Adding all these companies to your map, you will have a glittering panorama of prospects, the beginnings of a dossier on each one, and an efficient way of finding any company's exact location. This is useful for finding your way to an interview and in evaluating the job offers coming your way.

Box Number Want Ads

Employed professionals are understandably leery of answering ads that give only box numbers. Unemployed professionals wonder whether it is worth the effort. There are many reasons not to answer blind ads, but the two reasons for action far outweigh the negatives.

One, if you don't respond you aren't in the game, and you have to play to win.

Two, you may not be suitable for the job advertised but may be suitable for another position.

If you are employed and skeptical about "blowing your cover," or unemployed and eager to increase your chances, try this technique. Call the main post office in the area and ask for the local office that handles zip code _____. Call the substation and speak to the local post office manager, or P.O. box manager. Introduce yourself as an employed job hunter and ask for the name of the box holder so that you won't jeopardize your current job. If you make your request pleasant and personal enough you might get the information you need. If not, try asking, "Is it my employer, _____?"

Your Own Want Ads

Better use the money to fire up your barbecue.

Consistency

Consistent research is the key to gathering speed and maintaining momentum. Without consistent research your job hunt will stall for lack of people and companies to approach.

A few years ago a neighbor of mine in the airline business found himself looking for a job. At the time, MGM Air, the airline that flies the super-rich between New York and Los Angeles, was just beginning operations. The neighbor had a friend already with the company who was going to get him a job. It took a year of not looking for work before this job hunter realized that things you want to happen often don't . . . unless you make them. Not only did he never work for MGM Air, he never worked in the airline industry again.

When you look like a penguin, act like a penguin, and hide among penguins, don't be surprised if you get lost in the flock. Today's business marketplace demands a different approach. Your career does not take care of itself; you must go out and grab the opportunities.

3. Public and Private Employment Agencies
There are essentially four categories: state employment agencies, private employment agencies and executive recruiters, temporary help organizations, and career counselors.

State Employment Agencies. These are funded by the state labor department and typically carry names like State Division of Employment Security, State Job Service, or Manpower Services. The names vary but the services remain the same. They will make efforts to line you up with appropriate jobs and will mail resumes out on your behalf to interested employers who have jobs listed with them. It is not mandatory for employers to list jobs with state agencies, but more and more are taking advantage of these free services. Once the bastion of minimum-wage jobs, positions listed with these public agencies can reach $50,000–$60,000 a year for some technical positions.

If you are moving across the state or across the country, your local employment office can plug you into what is known as a national job bank, which (theoretically) can give you access to jobs all over the nation. However, insiders agree that it can take up to a month for a particular job from a local office to hit the national system. The most effective way to use the service is to visit your local office and ask for an introduction to the office in your destination area.

Private Employment Agencies. Choose your agent, or headhunter as they are commonly called, with the same care and attention with which you would choose a spouse or an accountant. The caliber of the individual and company you choose could well affect the caliber of the company you ultimately join. Further, if you choose prudently, he or she can become a lifetime counselor who can guide you step by step up the ladder of success.

Understand that there are distinctly different types of employment services.

- Permanent employment agencies where you pay the fee
- Permanent agencies where the employer pays the fee
- Contingency and retained search firms

As this is the for-profit sector of the market place, the question arises: whose pocket is the profit coming from? Employment Agencies in the private sector must be registered as either an Employer Paid Fee (EPF) or an Applicant Paid Fee (APF) agency. To avoid misunderstanding, it is best to confirm which is which before entering into any relationships.

Only employment agencies and certain contingency search firms will actively market you to a large number of companies with whom they may or may not have an existing relationship. A true executive search firm will never market your services. It will only present your credentials on an existing assignment.

So what type of company is best for you? Well, the answer is simple: the one that will get you the right job offer. The problem is there are thousands of companies in each of these broad categories. So how do you choose between the good, the bad, and the ugly?

Fortunately this is not as difficult as it sounds. Let's explode one or two myths. A retained executive search firm is not necessarily any better or more professional than a contingency search firm, which in turn is not necessarily better or more professional than a regular employment agency. Each has its exemplary practitioners and its charlatans. Your goal is to avoid the charlatans and get representation by an exemplary outfit. Make the choice carefully, and having made the choice, stick with it and listen to the advice you are given.

Check on the date of the firm's establishment. If the company has been in town ever since you were in diapers, the chances are good that they are reputable.

A company's involvement in professional associations is always a good sign. It demonstrates commitment and, through extensive professional training programs, an enhanced level of competence. In the employment services industry, the National Association of Personnel Consultants (NAPC) is the premier professional organization, with state associations in all fifty states.

Involvement in independent or franchise networks of firms can also be a powerful plus. For example, an independent network like the National Personnel Associates group has over three hundred member firms around the continental United States and Europe. Membership in one of the leading franchise groups, such as Snelling & Snelling, Sanford Rose, Management Recruiters, Dunhill, or Romac is likewise positive. These networks also have extensive training programs that help assure a high-caliber consultant. Franchise offices can be especially helpful if you are looking to change jobs and move across the country (or further) at the same time, as they tend to have powerful symbiotic relationships with other network members; in fact this is often a primary reason for their being a member of that particular franchise or network. Many of the independent and franchise network members also belong to the NAPC.

To take your evaluation one step further, it is prudent to ask whether your contact has CPC designation. CPC or its international equivalent, CIPC, stands for Certified Personnel Consultant (or Certified International Personnel Consultant). The CPC and CIPC designations are recognized as a standard of excellence and commitment only achieved after rigorous training and study.

CIPC designation requires that the holder already have achieved CPC designation, and it requires adherence to an international code of ethics as designated by the International Personnel Services Association (IPSA).

Although certification can be applied for after two years of experience in the personnel consulting business, the studying involved usually means that even the newest holders of CPC have five years of experience, while your average CPC probably has seven to ten years of experience and contacts with top-notch employers under his or her belt.

Qualified CPCs can also be relied upon to have superior knowledge of the legalities and ethics of the recruitment and hiring process, along with the expertise and tricks of the trade that only come from years of hands-on experience. All of this can be put to work on your behalf.

It makes good sense to have a friend in the business with an ear to the ground on your behalf as you continue your upward climb. If you want my best advice: Find an NAPC member in good standing with CPC designation and listen to what they tell you.

Finally, don't get intimidated, and remember you are not obligated to sign anything. Neither are you obligated to guarantee an agency that you will remain in any employment for any specific length of time. Don't get put in a trick bag by the occasional cowboy in an otherwise exemplary and honored profession.

Executive Recruiters. These people rarely deal at salary levels under $70,000 per year. All the advice I have given you about employment agencies applies here (although you can take it for granted that the executive recruiter will not charge you a fee). They are going to be more interested in your resume for their files than in wanting to see you right then and there, unless you match a specific job they are trying to fill for a client. They are far more interested in the employed than in the unemployed, because an employed person is less of a risk (they often guarantee their finds to the employer for up to a year) and a more desirable commodity. Executive recruiters are there to serve the client, not to find you a job. They neither want nor expect you to rely on them for employment counseling, unless they specifically request that you do—in which case you should listen closely.

Working with a Headhunter

Few people realize it, but symbiotic relationships can be developed with headhunters in all these categories to help you professionally. Their livelihood depends on who and what they know. Perhaps you can exchange mutually beneficial information. But do be circumspect. An unethical headhunter can create further competition for you when you share information about companies you are talking to.

Select two or three firms that work in your field. Do not mass mail your resume to every agent in town. This can lead to multiple submissions of your resume to a single company and a resultant argument over which agency is due a fee. When such a situation arises, companies will sometimes choose to walk away from the candidate in question.

Ascertain network and association membership and how this might help in your job search. Determine who pays the fee and whether any contracts will need to be exchanged. Define titles and the employment levels they represent, along with geographical areas. Know what you want, or ask for assistance in defining your parameters. This will include title, style of company, salary expectations, benefits, and location.

If the professional is interested in representing you, expect a detailed analysis of your background and prepare to be honest. Do not overstate your job duties, accomplishments, or education. If there are employment gaps, explain them.

Find out first what the professional expects of you in the relationship and then explain what you expect. Reach commitments you can both live with and stick with them. If you break those commitments, expect your representative to cease representation and to withdraw your candidacy from potential employers. They are far more interested in long-term relationships than passing nuisances.

Keep the recruiter informed about any and all changes in your status, such as salary increases, promotions, layoffs, or other offers of employment.

Don't consider yourself an employment expert. You get a job for yourself every three or four years. These people do it for a living every day of every week. Ask for their objective input and seek their advice in developing interviewing strategies with their clients.

Always tell the truth.

Temporary Help Companies. There are temporary help companies that provide corporate services to professionals at most levels, from unskilled and semi-skilled labor (referred to as light industrial in the trade) to administration, finance, technical, sales and marketing professionals, doctors, lawyers, and even interim executives up to the levels of CFOs and COOs.

Temporary help services can be a useful resource if you are unemployed. You can get temporary assignments, maintain continuity of employment and skills, and perhaps enhance your marketability in the process.

If you are changing careers or returning to work after an absence, temporary assignments can help get new or rusty skills up to speed and provide you with a current work history in your field. The temporary life can help you break out of your rut as well. It is becoming increasingly common to hear of the career-motivated professional who has been categorized and pigeon-holed in the workplace, but who finds a highly reputable temporary company and subsequently completely overhauls his skills to such an extent that a new career is possible.

In both these situations there are two other benefits.

1. You will get exposure to employers in the community who, if you really shine, could ask you to join the staff full time.

2. You will develop another group of networking contacts.

Working with a Temporary Help Company

Investigate the turnover of the temporary staff. If other temporaries have stayed with the company long term, chances are that company does a good job and has good clients.

Determine whether they are members of the National Association of Temporary Services (NATS), or of NAPC. These are the two leading industry associations.

Select a handful of firms that work in your field; this will increase the odds of suitable assignments appearing quickly.

Define the titles and the employment levels they represent, along with geographical areas they cover.

Do not overstate your job duties, accomplishments, or education.

Find out first what the temporary help professional expects of you in the relationship; then explain what you expect. Reach commitments you can both live with and stick with them.

Judge the assignments not solely on the paycheck (although that can be important) but also on the long-term benefits that will accrue to your job search and ongoing career.

Keep the temporary help counselor informed about any and all changes in your status, such as offers of employment or acquisition of new skills.

Remember that the temporary company is your employer. They will appreciate extra effort when they really need it and will reciprocate.

Resolve key issues ahead of time. Should an employer want to take you on full time, will that employer have to pay a set amount, or will you just stay on as a temporary for a specific period and then go on the employer's payroll?

Career Counselors. Career counselors charge for their services: sometimes as little as $200 for a resume and a half an hour's advice, sometimes up to $10,000. For this you get assistance in your career realignment or job search skill development. What you don't get is a guarantee of employment.

If you consider this route, speak to a number of counselors and check multiple references on all of them. As you are unlikely to be given poor references, you will want to check secondary and tertiary references. This is simple to do. Check the half dozen references you request and then ask each of the referees to refer someone else they know who used the service. Then check that reference as well.

It could also be prudent to check out potential counselors with your local Better Business Bureau to see whether any complaints have been registered against them.

Find out how long the company has been in business; ascertain a complete work history of the individual counselor who is likely to be assisting you. A number of people have been known to slip into this area of the employment services business for a quick buck with little expertise and commitment.

The person who can offer you the best advice in this area is the professional who has both corporate personnel experience *and* employment agency or retained search experience. This exposure should be mandatory for anyone willing to charge you for career and employment assistance.

All the Players

To provide you with the widest possible choice of employment services, here are some contact data for the most comprehensive lists and directories available.

National Association of Personnel Services
3133 Mount Vernon Avenue
Alexandria, VA 22305
703-684-0180
National Directory of Personnel Consultants, $22.95. Identifies companies by

occupational specialization and geographical coverage. Includes employment agencies, contingency and retained search companies, and temporary help organizations in membership. The industry's premier organization. Thousands of reputable contacts. Also available as printed labels and on disk. Price on request.

Directory of Executive Recruiters
Kennedy Publications
Templeton Road
Fitzwilliam, NH 03447
603-585-2200
Directory of Executive Recruiters, $39.95. Details 2,000 retained and contingency firms throughout the USA, Canada, and Mexico. Labels, not available on disk.

National Association of Temporary Services
119 South Saint Asaph Street
Alexandria, VA 22314
703-549-6287
Directory with 7,300 entries by city and state. $135. A SASE with a polite request will get you a free listing of temporary help companies by city for the state of your choice. Disk. Prices on request.

National Job Campaigning Resource Center (NJCRC)
Ken Cole, President
Box 9433
Panama City Beach, FL 32417
904-235-3733
This organization sells data. It should be known as legwork central. The company provides many of the research services offered by the top outplacement firms only for the individual consumer. Among its unique and exciting products for the job hunter:

- Over 100 industry-specific directories of top contingency and retained research firms throughout the United States. Updated quarterly. Provides pinpoint accuracy for $11 per category, with a minimum of three categories. Just specify your industry and get the heavy hitters by return mail. This is a great deal.

- *Executive Research Directory*. $88 (the seventh edition should be available in March of 1994). This is a tremendous resource for the senior-level executive. Perhaps you need contact information for the board members of, say, artificial intelligence's fifty largest firms. Well, here are the researchers who can find this information for you. At the highest levels, it is paramount that your references be sound. This directory provides resources who will check your references for you.

- Senior executive research package. Includes the *Executive Research Directory* and a printout of the four hundred research directors at many of the nation's leading search firms. $125.

- Dun & Bradstreet Database. NJCRC has acquired this database of 230,000 firms. This combined with their state-of-the-art word processing capabilities means that they can offer direct-mail services for specifically targeted markets. Price upon request.
- Labels. Mailing lists customized by geography, occupation, and industry. Price upon request. Disks not available.

Don't restrict yourself to any single category in this area. Executives, especially, should not turn their noses up at local employment agencies. Often that local agency has better rapport and contacts with the local business community than the big-name search firm. I have also known more than one employment agency that regularly placed job candidates earning in excess of $250,000 per year. Don't get hung up on agency versus search firm labels without researching the outfits in question; you could miss some great career opportunities.

4. Your References as a Resource
As a rule, we have faith in ourselves and are confident that our references will speak well of us. The fact is that some will speak well of us, some will speak excellently, and some, we might be surprised to hear, bear us no good will.

The wrong references at a critical juncture could spell disaster. At the very start of your job hunt you need to identify as many potential references as possible. The more options you have, the better your likelihood of coming up with excellent references. When you are currently employed, however, unless you want your employer to know you are actively engaged in making a career move, you will want to avoid using current managers and co-workers as references.

Yet at this point of the job search, excellent references, though important, are simply an added bonus. Your hidden agenda is to use these contacts as job search leads.

The process is simplicity itself, starting with an introduction: "Bob, this is _____. We worked together at Acme between 1985 and 1992. How's it going?" It is appropriate here to catch up on gossip and the like. Then broach the subject of your call.

"John, I wanted to ask your advice." (Everyone loves to be asked for an expert opinion.) "We had some cutbacks at Fly-By-Night Finance, as you probably heard," or "The last five years at Bank of Crooks and Criminals International have been great, and the _____ project we are just winding down has been a fascinating job. Nevertheless, I have decided that this would be a perfect time for a career move to capitalize on my experience."

Then, "John, I realize how important references can be and I was wondering if you would have any reservations about my using you as a reference?" It's better to find out now rather than down the line when it could blow a job offer.

The response will usually be positive, so then you move to the next step. "Thanks, John, I hoped you would feel able to. Let me update you about what I have been doing recently and tell you about the type of opportunity I'm looking for." Then proceed in less than two minutes to give a capsule of what has passed since you worked together and what you are looking for. With co-workers or past managers, be sure to restate why you left your last job, since the reference is likely to be asked.

You can then, if appropriate and time allows, tell the reference some of the questions he might be asked. These might include the time he has known you, your relationship to each other, the title you worked under (be sure to remind your reference of promotions and title changes), your five or six most important duties, the key projects you worked on, your greatest strengths, your greatest weaknesses, your attitude toward your job, your attitude toward your peers, your attitude toward management, the timeliness, quality, and quantity of your work, your willingness to achieve above and beyond the call of duty (remind him of all those weekends you worked), whether he would rehire you (if company policy forbids rehiring, make sure your reference will mention this), your earnings, and any additional comments the reference would like to make.

Once all this has been covered, ask the reference for one further piece of assistance and then recycle the conversation through your networking presentation. (See item #8 below.)

When references are about to be checked for a specific job, get back to your chosen references, reacquaint them with any relevant areas the employer might wish to discuss, and tell them to expect a call. I have even known professionals who, with the approval of the potential employer, have their references call in with recommendations.

Some smart job hunters also take the precaution of having a friend do a dummy check on all references just to confirm what they will say when the occasion arises. This way you can distinguish the excellent references from the merely good. (For guaranteed peace of mind you could call Taylor Review at (313) 651-0286, and have them check your references for you. For a modest fee you'll know in advance just who will be your best spokespeople.)

5. College Placement Offices and Alumni Associations

College Placement Offices. If you are leaving school or college, take advantage of this resource. Remember that the college placement office is not a substitute for your mother; it is not there to provide for you or hand you job offers. Rather, you will find there a wealth of experience that will accelerate the process and aid you in finding your own job.

Placement offices and their staffs are horrendously overworked, and merely keeping pace with the Herculean task of providing assistance to the student body as a whole is more than a full-time job. Take the time to make yourself known here and stress your sincerity and willingness to listen to good advice. Act on it; then, when you come back for more, you will have earned the placement director's respect and as such will begin to earn yourself that extra bit of attention and guidance that winners always manage for themselves.

Don't wait until the last minute, especially if you are hoping to gain your foothold on the ladder of success from on-campus recruiters who represent the big corporations. These recruiters go to society and association meetings on campus all year long. Take an active part in campus affairs and you may well find them coming after you. I know of one campus recruiter for a major accounting firm who swears she has selected all her prime choices before the campus recruiting season even opens. How do such campus recruiters pick the winners from the also-rans? Simple. They all maintain very close working relationships with the placement office, so an endorsement at the right time can mean an important introduction rather than a closed door.

Alumni Associations. Even when your school days are in the misty distant past, this isn't the time to forget the people of the old school tie. People hire people like themselves, people with whom they share something in common. Your school or college alumni association is a complete and valuable network just waiting for you.

As a member of the alumni association you are likely to have access to a membership listing. Additionally, many of the larger schools have alumni placement networks, so you may want to check with the alma mater and tap into the old-boy and -girl network.

6. Professional Associations

Professional associations provide excellent networks for your benefit. Almost all committed professionals are members of at least one or two professional networks. Their membership is based on:

1. Commitment to the profession.

2. The knowledge that people who know people know where the opportunities are hidden.

If you never got around to joining, or your membership has lapsed, it is time to visit the library and check out the *Encyclopedia of Associations* (published by Bowker). It tells you about all known associations for your profession and provides contact information and other relevant data.

You might also check out another important resource: *The Directory of Directories.* This reference work lists all the available directories in the country and details their content. For example, if you are an oil and gas geologist, you'll learn that there is a directory of geologists with 11,000 plus entries that includes full biographical and contact data. *The Directory of Directories* can be a major lead generator and significant professional networking resource for almost anybody.

Some professions have multiple associations, all of which could be of value to the serious job hunter. For example, if you happen to be in retail, you will find thirty national associations and fifty state associations. Together these associations represent one and a half million retailers who provide employment for over fourteen million people. And these are just retail associations that are members of the American Retail Federation. You may well discover even more.

There are two ways to make memberships in professional organizations work. The first is the membership directory, which provides you with a direct networking resource for direct verbal contact and mail campaigns. All associations supply their members with a directory of contact information for all other members. Additionally, all associations schedule regular meetings, which provide further opportunities to mingle with your professional peers on an informal basis, as well as opportunities to get involved on a volunteer basis with organizing such meetings or speaking at a meeting. Networking at the meetings and using an association's directory for contacts are wise and accepted uses of membership.

Professional associations all have newsletters. In addition to using the help-wanted section, you will be able to utilize them in other ways by following the advice on trade and business publications later in this chapter.

It is often one's active membership in professional associations that leads other disgruntled job hunters to mutter, "It's not what you know, it's who you know." (Membership in professional associations is also an excellent way to maintain long-term career stability; see chapter 29.)

7. Job Fairs

Job fairs and career days are occasions on which local or regional companies that are actively hiring get together, usually under the auspices of a job fair promoter or local employment agency to attract large numbers of potential employees.

There aren't many of these occasions, so they won't be taking much of your time, but you shouldn't miss them when they do occur. They are always advertised in the local newspapers and frequently on the radio. Many also appear in the *National Business Employment Weekly's* events calendar.

When the job fair is organized by a promoter, entrance is either free or nominal. When it is organized by a local employment service, it helps to be on their mailing list.

In addition to the exhibit hall, there are likely to be formal group presentations by employers. As all speakers love to get feedback, move in when the crush of presentor groupies has died down; you'll get more time and closer attention. You will also have additional knowledge of the company and the chance to spend a few minutes customizing the emphasis of your skills to meet the stated needs and interests of the employer in question.

When you attend job fairs, go prepared. Take:

- Business cards. (If employed, remember to request the courtesy of confidentiality in calls to the workplace.)
- Resumes—as many as there are exhibitors times two. You'll need one to leave at the exhibit booth and an additional copy for anyone you have a meaningful conversation with.
- Note pad and pen, preferably in a folder.

Go with specific objectives in mind.

- Visit every booth, not just the ones with the flashing lights and professional models stopping traffic.

- Talk to someone at every booth. Since they are the ones who are selling, you have a slight advantage. You can walk up and ask questions about the company, who they are, and what they are doing, before you talk about yourself. This allows you to present yourself in the most relevant light.

- Collect business cards from everyone you speak to so that you can follow up with a letter and a call when they are not so harried. Very few people actually get hired at job fairs. For most companies the exercise is usually one of collecting resumes so that meaningful meetings can take place in the ensuing weeks. But be "on" in case someone wants to sit down and give you a serious interview on the spot. This is most likely to happen when you least expect it, so be prepared.

- Collect company brochures and collateral materials.

- Arrange times and dates to follow up with each employer. "Ms. Jones, I realize you are very busy today, and I would like to speak to you further. Your company sounds very exciting. I should like to set up a time when we could meet to talk further or perhaps set a time to call you in the next few days."

- Dress for business. You may be meeting your new boss, and you don't want the first impression to be less than professional.

Job fairs provide opportunity for administrative, professional, and technical people up to the middle management ranks. However, this doesn't mean that the senior executive should feel such an event beneath her. The opportunity still exists to have meaningful conversations with tens or hundreds of employers in a single day, from which may come further fruitful conversations.

On leaving each booth, and at the end of the day, go through your notes while everything is still fresh in your mind. Review each company and what possibilities it holds for you. Then review all the companies as a whole to see what you might glean about industry needs or marketplace shifts and long-term staffing needs. Make notes.

8. Trade and Business Magazines

This resource includes professional association periodicals, trade magazines, and the general business press. They can all be utilized in a similar fashion: by contacting the individuals and companies mentioned and using the article to begin discussion.

In these publications you may find the following:

- Focus articles about interesting companies, which can alert you to specific growth opportunities.

- Industry overviews and market development pieces, which can tip you off to subtle shifts in your professional marketplace and thereby alert you to opportunities—and provide you with the chance to customize your letters, calls, and resume for specific targets.

- Quotations. "The art of press writing demands frequent quotes, and by necessity, attributions," says Peregrine McCoy, senior partner of Connem, Covertrax and Splitt. Contacting the person quoted is both flattering and shows that you have your finger on the pulse of your profession.

- Articles by industry professionals. When contacting the author of an article, you might include how much you agree with what was said, a little additional information on the subject, or words to the effect that "It's about time someone told it like it is." Never say anything in the vein of, "Hey, the article is great but you missed . . ."

- Opportunities to write the editors of the publication. The editors themselves are always on the lookout for quotable letters, so a flattering note about an article with a line or two about your background in the field may get you some valuable free publicity down the line.

- Columns on promotions, executive moves, and obituaries. If someone has just received a promotion, there are reasonable odds that somewhere in the chain is an opening. If executive A has moved to company B, it could mean the first company is looking for someone. The same applies to obituaries.

- Help-wanted sections. Many employers will give the general newspapers only token attention when it comes to filling hard-to-find professional and trade positions. They will concentrate their advertising budgets instead on the trade press.

- Advertisements for new products can tell you about companies that are making things happen, and that need people who can make things happen.

In all of the above instances it is advisable to clip and keep, in retrievable fashion, all the items that generate leads. There are two reasons for this: You can send a copy to the person you intend to approach, and you will have a copy on file to refresh your memory before any direct communication.

In short, just about every page of your average trade journal holds a valuable job lead. You just need to know how and where to look. Then having found something, you need to take action.

9. Networking

People frequently think networking means annoying the hell out of your friends until they stop taking your calls. What it should mean is using others to assist in your job search. You will find it surprising how willing friends, colleagues, and even strangers are to help you.

The bad news is that networks need nurturing and development. Networking is more than calling your relatives and waiting for them to call back with job offers. People know people, not just in your home town but all over the country and sometimes the world.

I used the word *networks*, not *network*. We all have a number of networks, any of which may produce that all-important job offer. Here are the typical networks we can all tap into.

- Family and relatives. This includes your spouse's family and relatives.
- Friends. This includes neighbors and casual acquaintances.
- Co-workers. This includes professional colleagues past and present. You will especially want to ask about headhunters they know or might hear from, and professional affiliations they have found valuable.
- Managers, past and present. A manager's success depends on tapping good talent. Even if a particular manager can't use you, a judicious referral to a colleague can gain goodwill for the future.
- Service industry acquaintances. This includes your banker, lawyer, insurance agent, realtor, doctors, and dentist.
- Other job hunters.
- Other professionals in your field.

Over a period of a few days you need to develop the most extensive lists you can in each of these categories. Start lists and add to them every day. The experienced professional should be able to come up with a minimum of twenty names for, say, the service industry network list, and upward of a couple of hundred professional colleagues.

Here are some tips for writing networking letters or making calls asking for assistance.

- Establish connectivity. Recall the last memorable contact you had or mention someone you both knew whom you have spoken to recently.
- Tell why you are writing or calling: "It's time for me to make a move. I just got laid off with 1,000 others, and I'm taking a couple of days to catch up with old friends."
- Ask for advice and guidance about your tactics, what the happening companies are, and whether the person can take a look at your resume—because you really need an objective opinion and have always respected his viewpoint. Don't ask specifically, "Can you or your company hire me?" If there is some action available, he will let you know.
- Don't rely on a contact with a particular company to get you into that company. Mount and execute your own plan of attack. No one is as interested as you are to put bread on your table.
- Let contacts know what you are open for. They will usually want to help, but you have to give them a framework within which to target their efforts.
- Discuss the profession, the industry, the areas of opportunity, and the people worthwhile to contact. If you comport yourself in a professional manner most fellow professionals will come up with a lead. If they can't think of a person, back off and ask them about companies. Everyone can think of a company. If they come up with a company, respond, "Hey, that's a great idea. I never thought of those people," even if you have just spoken to that

outfit. Then after a suitable pause, ask for another company. When people see that their advice is appreciated, they will often come up with more. When you have gathered two or three company names, backtrack with, "Do you know of anyone I could speak to _____ company [A, B, C]?" Every time you get a referral be sure to ask whether you can use your contact's name as an introduction. The answer will invariably be yes, but asking demonstrates professionalism and will encourage your contact to come up with more leads.

Remember to ask for information about and specific leads from your targeted companies.

- At the end of the call make sure the contact knows how to get in touch with you. I find the nicest and most effective way of doing this is to say something like, "Mack, I really appreciate your help. I'd like to leave you my name and number in the hope that one day in the future I can return the favor." Not only is this a supremely professional gesture, it ensures that your contact information is available to that individual should openings arise within his sphere of influence. Say you hope you'll get to see each other again soon, that you look forward to doing something together. Invite the contact over for drinks, dinner, or a barbecue.

- When you do get help, say thank you. And if you get it verbally, follow it up in writing. The impression is indelible and just might get you another lead. Include a copy of your resume with the thank-you letter.

- Keep an open mind. You never know who your friends are. You will be surprised at how someone you always regarded as a real pal won't give you the time of day and how someone you never thought of as a friend will go above and beyond the call of duty for you.

- Whether your contacts help you or not, let them know when you get a job and maintain contact at least once a year. A career is a long time. It might be next week or a decade from now when a group of managers (including one from your personal network) are talking about filling a new position and the first thing they'll do is ask "Who do we know?" That could be you. (This topic is discussed in detail in chapter 29.)

Networking is more than one call or letter to each person on your list. Once the first conversation is in the bag, another call in a couple of months won't be taken amiss. For examples of networking cover letters, see the book *Cover Letters that Knock 'em Dead*.

When you get referrals as a result of your networking, use your source as an introduction: "Jane, my name is Martin Yate. Our mutual friend George Smith suggested I call, so before I go any further I must pass on George's regards."

10. The Job Hunter's Network
In your job hunt you will invariably find that companies are looking for everyone but you. The recent graduate is told to come back when she has experience, the ex-

perienced professional is told that only entry-level people are being hired. That's the luck of the draw, but one person's problem is another's opportunity.

The solution is to join or create a support group and job-hunting network of your own with people in the same situation as you are.

Existing Support Groups. In many communities these are sponsored by church or other social organizations. They meet, usually on a weekly basis, to discuss ideas, exchange tips and job leads, and provide encouragement and the opportunity to support and be supported by others in the same situation.

One national organization is known as the 40 Plus Club. The only requirements for membership are that you be a mature professional in your field. The 40 Plus Club has chapters around the country. You can find a comprehensive listing of these, other support groups, and networking opportunities in the weekly edition of the *National Business Employment Weekly*.

Creating Your Own Support Group. All this takes is finding someone in the same situation as yourself. Among your neighbors and friends someone probably knows someone who has the same needs as you do; all it takes is two. Your goals are quite simple: You meet on a regular basis to exchange ideas and tips; review each other's resumes, letters, and verbal presentations; and check on each other's progress. This means that if I tell you that in the last five days I've sent out only three resumes and made only two follow-up calls, you are obliged to get on my case. The purpose of such a group is to provide the pressure to perform that you experience at work.

You can advertise for members in your local penny saver. The paper might even be talked into running the ad for free as a community service.

Once you are involved in a group, you will meet others with different skill levels and areas of expertise. Then when an employer tells you she is hiring only accountants this month, you can offer a referral to the employer or give the lead to your accountant friend. In turn the accountant will be turning up leads in your field. If these openings don't make themselves known during your conversations, you can tag on a question of your own when the conversation is winding down: "John, I'm a member of an informal job-hunting network. If you don't have a need for someone with my background right now, perhaps one of my colleagues could be just what you are looking for. What needs do you have at present and in the forseeable future?"

Becoming an active member in an existing group or creating one of your own can get you leads and provide a forum for you to discuss your fears and hopes with others who understand your concerns.

With all of this chapter's networks working for you, you will have maximum coverage and will have minimized the chances of your exhausting any one member or network through overworking their good will and patience. Do it. You have nothing to lose and everything to gain.

11. The Electronic Job Hunt
There's a new weapon in your arsenal.

You can use your modem and personal computer to access important job information. Savvy job hunters can now tap into huge reservoirs of on-line data before launching a search in earnest or going on an interview. This approach is a new one that may well help you gain an edge over your competition.

There have been many changes recently in the world of on-line information. Gale's *Directory of Databases* indicates that there continues to be strong growth in the database industry; the totals for databases, records, on-line searches, database entries, database producers, and vendors are all up. The industry is showing no signs of leveling off; nor do consumers appear to be at a loss when it comes to finding new ways to use the information available. Using an on-line service is a little like walking into the biggest library in the world and being able to get anything you want without having to walk anywhere (and without having to wait in line). Some services even offer affordable practice forums for developing on-line skills.

The flexibility of on-line services makes them extremely valuable. Through one of the new online database services, you can request a list of all the companies in a certain geographic region; you can specify that you want to see only companies in a certain area that do business in your field of choice; you can further narrow the list by asking to see a list that highlights only firms with a sales level of x dollars or more. It's all up to you. If you need to get a list of all the hospitals in Kansas with five hundred beds or more that boast a state-of-the-art magnetic resonance imaging system, all you have to do is punch in your requirements or explain them to a database representative. The data is all there waiting for you, in over a dozen established business information databases; you'll probably be able to secure names and contact information for key company executives as well.

Many libraries provide walk-in use of on-line fee-based services. Additionally, most will conduct searches for you based on your specific needs. So, if you're a computerphobe, you can get all the benefits without ever touching a keyboard. If your local library doesn't have these services, explain your needs and ask for information on how to contact a library or other database access point that does.

Of course, there is no guarantee that your nearest database access point has the information you want to find. Enter the *Directory of Fee-Based Information Services*, an invaluable resource listing around 440 U.S. and Canadian library systems. This book will provide the details of which library will allow you to access what; you can ask for it at the library or order it direct from the American Library Association at 800-545-2433. Many of the libraries listed in this directory will either conduct a company search for you or provide a full-service business library where you can run your own search for the price of a few photocopies. The retail cost of the most recent edition is $65.00. (*Note:* A much shorter list detailing some of the major databases and the types of data each can generate appears as an appendix at the end of this book.)

Conducting Your Own Search
On-line searching is a tricky task, but one that can open the doors to the employment world in seconds. Even with all the excitement you may feel at the prospect of entering the computer age with your job search, however, a few caveats are in order before you plunge in.

First and foremost, I would issue the warning that time is money when you're on-line; many job seekers, of course, are in short supply of both. If you're one of them, and if you aren't familiar with the sometimes perplexing world of on-line computer searching, *don't take on the job of cruising this ocean of information yourself.* Either have the search conducted for you by a computer-friendly navigator, or use your local library.

If you *are* familiar with both computer procedures and the on-line world, get ready for some exciting news about CompuServe. (And if you aren't, get ready to pass this part of the book on to your navigator.) The Knowledge Index available through CompuServe, offered from 6:00 pm to 6:00 am, contains over a hundred databases—featuring full text, abstracts, or summaries—for only forty cents a minute. Like most databases, this one is word-oriented, but managing the database with CompuServe's menu-assisted windows is pretty easy. This database does *not* charge a "per page" surcharge for the pages of text downloaded. It offers a variety of useful information, including a full-text Standard and Poor's directory of company information, a full-text newspaper database, a full-text *Who's Who* directory, and addresses, phone numbers, and information about key employees of the companies you're searching for. Add to this plenty of data on subsidiaries, financial performance, and any number of other important topics, and you have an avalanche of information that will help you distinguish yourself from the competition.

If you've worked up a little experience with this sort of thing, the average company search will run approximately five minutes on line. That's just $2.00 in database charges per lead. For an additional eighteen minutes of on-line time (read: $7.20), we were able to find and download over a hundred recent news articles about our target company using our 2400-baud modem. In short, we got a small library of invaluable interview-preparation information for under ten bucks. Not a bad value, eh?

Through its BIZ FILE option, CompuServe also offers access to consumer and business phone directories for just twenty-five cents a minute. We searched for the word "resume" and the database prompted us with "resume services." We then asked for a listing of all such companies in twenty major cities across the United States. In about an hour, we had downloaded a fifty-page booklet of names, addresses, and phone numbers; some of the cities had over two hundred resume companies each. Similarly, if you're searching for all the divisions of, say, Ford Motor Company operating in Southern California, you can conduct the same search by going into BIZ FILE and asking the computer to search for all Ford divisions in the applicable regions.

CompuServe, of course, is not the only operation offering such services. Many services do, and there is a bewildering array of access requirements and charges. A good number of the databases are cheaper in the evening; be sure to doublecheck the rates you are quoted for this feature. Some on-line databases are designed to keep professional people informed of developments in their field. These are usually cheaper than other services; typically, they are offered at non-peak hours and are not always available in full-text format. If you find an entry abstract (rather than the material itself) on-line through one of these sources, you can usually do one of two things: build up a bibliography of articles and pop into the full-text index for the article you want, or head to the library, find the right copy of the publication in question, and make a copy of the article for five or ten cents a sheet on the library photocopier. The second option takes more time, but then again, the premium rate for printing an article in some on-line magazine or newspaper databases can run as high as $1.50 per page, plus on-line time and surcharges. Experts may (or may not) be able make the longer searches for articles cost-effective; newcomers are once again advised to avoid paying for a costly—and, often, frustrating—learning-curve experience.

Classifieds on Your Screen

Among the most exciting developments in electronic databases has been E-Span, through which employers are effectively screening out the dinosaurs of the corporate world and zeroing in on the successful professionals of today. E-Span is essentially a national classified help-wanted database; it is also a service tailored to those growth industries of the future where computer literacy is an unspoken requirement for any job.

The ads run from entry-level through senior executive positions, and cover sixteen major professional groupings ranging from accounting to sales. Each of these major groupings has subheadings: the sales grouping, for instance, includes separate sections for advertisings, communications/public relations, customer service, and of course straight sales positions.

A great plus for the job hunter in comparison with a "real" help-wanted section is E-Span's lack of a newspaper's space restrictions. I noticed advertisements running one to two pages in length that gave job requirements in incredible detail. This can give you a substantial edge; it allows you to customize paperwork and focus your expertise in the appropriate direction.

The ads are national in nature, and will not necessarily feature opportunities in your own backyard. By the same token, some of the larger firms may have unadvertised opportunities in your area that you can track through E-Span.

E-Span is available through a number of media, including CompuServe; call 800-682-2901 for more information. This service can be an invaluable aid to your job search. I was able to pick out an ad that profiled a certain company; I then did an article search (through a separate on-line service) to get the latest breaking news on that firm, and I discovered three recent deals it had signed. Finally, I was able to pull up a quarterly interim balance sheet and get a breakdown on the company's worldwide core businesses. I started with nothing, discovered a specific job opening not likely to be advertised in the mainstream press, and gathered eight pages of first-rate analysis of the company.

If you can't get access to a computer, you can still find out what's cooking on E-Span. When we last checked with the service, you could order a disk of the current ads, then take the disk to your local library or copy shop for printout. The last we heard, disks were updated every two weeks. Call the E-Span number above for more information. (Words to the wise: Be sure to specify the working environment in which the disks will be printed out—usually IBM or Macintosh—and the disk size required.)

Close Encounters

As you can see, using on-line research services can do much more than provide extensive contact lists for your mail or phone campaigns. In a tightly run job race, being able to ace the "What do you know about us?" question could make all the differences. On-line services can often yield more detailed information about a specific company than you'd ever imagined possible.

Imagine for a moment that you're a corporate galley slave with an interview slated with 3M in Minneapolis for the day after tomorrow. You decide to call Nexis Express, a service of the Nexis/Lexis databases, both of which are divisions of Mead Data Central. You pick up the phone, dial 800-227-9597, and give them the specifics, asking them to fax the data to a local copy shop for you to pick up.

The total cost is quite reasonable, considering the purpose for which you'll be using the information. The most recent pricing schedules are as follows: $6.00 per minute of on-line search time, four cents per line printing charge, and twenty-five cents per page if the information is faxed to you. If you want the material sent to you by Federal Express, add another fifteen bucks. There is no charge for information sent to you via the U.S. Mail, but you may decide that receiving your data in this way defeats the purpose of *express service*, which is presumably what led you to call in the first place.

What you get for your money is truly remarkable: Over fifteen pages of data providing a complete overview of 3M from its inception to the present day, including contact information, officers and directors, the number of employees, subsidiaries of the company, corporate product lines and services, stock performance records, earnings and finances, and more. And you got it in no time flat. How's that for an advantage to carry into the heat of battle?

But you don't stop there. You call again to take advantage of the service's extensive article search capabilities. You ask for all the business articles run in the past year that featured 3M as the main topic and receive fourteen and a half more pages of material. (If you'd asked for everything about 3M, period, with no restrictions, you could have accessed literally thousands of articles, but you're pressed for time.) The entire process took ninety seconds on the phone and a few minutes of transmission time to your corner copy shop. The total cost for the article search and delivery is the same as for your company search; you can expect to pay $40.00 or a little more for each. Add it all up and you're cruising toward the hundred-dollar line, which is probably a little steep for that practice interview at Last Chance Electronics (where you don't want to work anyway), but may be perfectly appropriate for the Big Interview You've Been Waiting For at 3M.

Within ten minutes the company representative was inviting me in for an interview—and two hours earlier, I could have fit all I knew about microchips on the back of a Doritos package! Imagine what this kind of additional data could do for you if you had some idea what you were talking about in the first place; it would be blindingly obvious at the interview that you were twice as sharp as any other applicant. While this kind of edge is desirable at any level, the seeming omniscience that comes with doing better research than anyone else is all the more important when applying for executive positions. For job seekers at all levels, Nexis gets you what you need—and quick.

Similarly mindboggling is the service available through Standard and Poor's Research Reports, which provides in-depth analyses of specific publicly traded companies. I ran across a job opening at Reebok, the major sports shoe manufacturer, called Standard and Poor's to request a report, and received ten pages of great information guaranteed to knock the socks off any interviewer in the place. You can order through Standard and Poor's Research Reports by calling 800-642-2858. They offer a quick company report for $9.95, plus a $2.50 faxing charge. Within ninety minutes you'll have pages of information on your target company.

The New Resume Databases

Another revolutionary job-hunting technology is emerging: the public resume database. Under this system, you pay a nominal amount (usually between $10 and $30) to have your resume loaded onto a database. Access to this resume bank is then sold to corporations; they pay a few hundred to a few thousand dollars for unlimited access.

The employer logs on, detailing exactly what qualifications are being sought. If the company has asked for someone with four years of experience with Corel desktop publishing software, the computer searches the scanned-in resume text for words such as "Corel" and "four years." (This means that you should check with the database service on guidelines for composing your resume in such a way that it is properly retrieved!) The employer receives hard-copy resumes that exactly meet its criteria. No one in human resources has to scan five hundred resumes; your resume reaches the right person. Everyone benefits.

To the employer, the new system provides a brand-new, cost-effective recruiting and initial screening tool; to the job-hunter, it provides yet another great way to get that resume under the noses of forward-thinking employers. Of course, there is the added benefit that all resumes generated from the search are already perceived to be good matches. Consequently, your candidacy is likely to receive more serious initial evaluation and consideration.

There are currently about a dozen resume database companies in operation. Most claim to be national; none of them really are, at least not by my standards. I don't feel comfortable endorsing any specific companies at this point, but considering the low dollar amounts involved you probably can't go wrong with this method unless you rely on it as your sole means of generating interviews. As one of your many resources, resume banks are certainly worth a shot.

That's the picture now. I predict that by the turn of the century, however, registering one's resume on at least one public database will be a standard component of any professional job search. The savviest job hunters will keep their resumes permanently registered, on the theory that you can only turn down an opportunity if you have heard about it.

Getting the Word Out

So much for the eleven paths most likely to lead you to the hidden job market. Remember, there is no single approach to landing your dream job. Friends may tell you that the only effective way is the way that worked for them. Of course, we are all different people, and some things will be harder for you than others.

Although each of these techniques has proven effective, no single one is guaranteed for any one individual. Your plan of attack must be balanced and comprehensive. It should include elements of every technique discussed in this section. A man who goes fishing and puts one hook in the water has but one chance of catching any one of the millions of fish in the sea; a man with two hooks in the water has double the chances of getting a bite. At this stage of the game you are looking for bites. The more hooks you have in the water, the better your chances.

In the end, of course, you will want to know how to contact the companies you learn about through your various types of research. You have two basic approaches to choose from: the verbal approach, usually by telephone, and the written approach, usually including a letter and resume.

One of these is likely to appeal to you more than the other. However, in execution you will see that they both simply become different steps in the same process. When you send out letters and resumes, you will invariably find yourself following up with phone calls. When you make phone contact, you will inevitably be following up with letters and resumes. Your program needs to maintain a delicate balance between the two, so that your calls force you to follow up in writing and your resumes and letters force you to follow up with phone calls.

The trick is not to overemphasize the approach that is easiest for you (say, networking with friends and colleagues) at the expense of other approaches (say, direct research calls). Now while ultimately it is the conversations, not the letters, that get you interviews, I recommend that you begin your campaign by researching contacts in every single category I have discussed; then begin with a combination of mailings and direct calls, because every letter and every resume and every call is another hook in the water. We will examine the written part of the campaign now; initial phone calls will be the topic of the next few chapters.

Letters

Must you send out hundreds or even thousands of letters in the coming weeks? Yes and no. The goal is to mail as much as you need in your field and no more. Two employer contacts a week will not get you accelerating along that career path again. Only if you approach and establish communication with every possible employer will you create the maximum opportunity for yourself. *Two contacts a week is the behavior of the long-term unemployed.*

On the other hand, I am not recommending that you immediately make up a list of seven hundred companies and mail letters to them today. That isn't the answer either. Your campaign needs strategy. While every job-hunting campaign is unique, you will want to maintain a balance between the *number* of letters you send out on a daily and weekly basis and the *types* of letters you send out. Start off with balanced mailings and your phone contacts will maintain equilibrium, too.

The key is to send out a balanced mailing representing all the different types of leads, and to send them out regularly and in a volume that will allow you to make follow-up calls. Many headhunters manage their time so well that they average over fifty calls per day, year in and year out. While you may aim at building your call volume up to this number, I recommend that you start out with more modest goals. Send five to ten letters per day in each of the following areas:

- In response to newspaper advertisements
- To friends
- To professional colleagues
- To research contacts from reference works, newspapers, etc.
- To headhunters

With adequate research and the resources I have mentioned, there are literally thousands of contacts waiting to be made. So this breakdown of contacts is a daily quota. If it seems a bit steep to begin with, scale down the numbers until they are achievable and gradually build up the volume. But remember, the lower the volume, the longer the job search.

Do you need to write more than one letter? Almost certainly. There is a case to be made for having letters and resumes in more than one format. There is no need to waste precious time crafting your written communication entirely from scratch when templates exist. The key is to do each variation once and to do it right. This means doing your work on a computer if possible and keeping it comprehensively backed up on disk. This way you'll be loaded for bear regardless of when opportunity comes knocking on your door. More information on creating and managing an effective direct-mail campaign can be found in *Cover Letters that Knock 'em Dead.*

Multiple Submissions

You may sometimes find it valuable to send half a dozen contact letters to a given company, to assure that all the important players know of your existence. Let's say you are a young engineer who wants to work for Last Chance Electronics. It is well within the bounds of reason to mail cover or broadcast letters to any or all of the following people (each addressed by name so the letter doesn't end up in the trash): the company president, the vice president of engineering, the chief engineer, the engineering manager, the vice president of human resources, the technical engineering recruitment manager, and the technical recruiter.

A professionally organized and conducted campaign will proceed on two fronts.

Front One. A carefully targeted rifle approach to a select group of companies. You will have first identified these super-desirable places to work when you researched your long list of potential employers. You will continue to add to this primary target list as you unearth fresh opportunities in your day-to-day research efforts.

In this instance you have two choices:

1. Mail to everyone at once, remembering that the letters have to be personalized and followed up.

2. Start your mailings off with one to a line manager and one to a contact in human resources. Follow up in a few days and repeat the process to other names on your list.

Front Two. A carpet bombing approach to every possible employer in the area. After all, you won't know what opportunities exist unless you go find out.

Here you will begin with a mailing to one or two contacts within the company and then repeat the mailings to other contacts when your initial follow-up calls result in referrals or dead ends. Remember, just because Harry in engineering says there are no openings in the company doesn't necessarily make it so. Besides, any one of the additional contacts you make could well be the person *who knows the person* who is just dying to meet you.

Once your campaign is in motion and you have received some responses to your mailings and scheduled some interviews from your calls (how to make the calls is covered in the next chapter), your emphasis will change. Those contacts and interviews will require follow-up letters and conversation. You will be spending time preparing for the interviews.

This is exactly the point at which most job hunts stall. We get so excited about the interview activity that we convince ourselves that "This will be the offer." Experienced headhunters know that the offer that can't fail always will. The offer doesn't materialize, and we are left sitting with absolutely no interview activity. We let the interview funnel empty itself.

The more letters you send out, the more follow-up calls you can make to schedule interviews. The more direct calls you make, the more interviews you will schedule and the more leads you will generate. The more interviews you get, the better you feel and the better you get at interviewing. The better you get at interviewing, the better the offers you get—and the *more* offers you get.

So no matter how good things look, you must continue the campaign. While you have to maintain activity with those companies you are negotiating with, you must also make yourself maintain your daily marketing schedule. Write letters in *each* of the following areas:

- In response to newspaper ads
- To associations, alumni, colleagues
- To direct research contacts
- To headhunters
- Follow-up letters

Small but consistent mailings have many benefits. The balance you maintain is important because most job hunters are tempted to send the easy letters and make the easy calls (networking with old friends). But this will knock your job hunt out of balance and kick you into a tailspin.

Don't stop searching even when an offer is pending, and your potential boss says, "Robin, you've got the job and we're glad you can start on Monday. The offer letter is in the mail." Never accept any "yes" until you have it in writing, you have started work, and the first paycheck has cleared at the bank! Until then keep your momentum building: it is the professional and circumspect thing to do.

It is no use mailing tens or even hundreds of resumes without following up on your efforts. If you are not getting a response with one resume format, you might want to redo it; try changing from a chronological to a functional or combination format, just as you would change the bait if the fish weren't taking what you had on the hook.

Keep things in perspective. Although your 224th contact may not have an opening for you, with a few polite and judicious questions she may well have a good lead. You will learn how to do this in the chapter entitled "Getting Live Leads from Dead Ends."

In the job hunt there are only two yeses: Their "yes-I-want-you-to-work-for-us" and your "yes-I-can-start-on-Monday." Every "no" brings you closer to the big "yes." Never take rejections of your resume or your phone call as rejections of yourself; just as every job is not for you, you aren't right for every job.

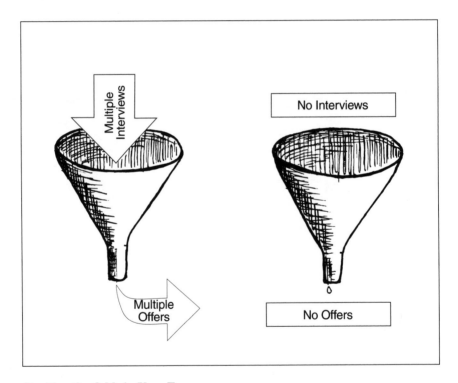

Stacking the Odds in Your Favor
We all have 168 hours a week to become bagmen or billionaires and to make our lives as fulfilling as they can be. For some of us this means a better job, for others it means getting back to work to keep a roof over our heads.

How we manage these hours will determine our success. These Job Hunting Commandments will see you successfully through the job change process or career transition.

- Those in the professional employment field reckon an average of seven hundred fresh contacts is required per job placement. You should anticipate at least this number. In a forty-hour week these professionals average approximately thirty-five to fifty contacts per day. Build to this momentum.

- Work at getting a new job. Work at least forty hours per week at it. Divide your time between contacting potential employers and generating new leads. Never stop the research and job-hunting process until you have a written job offer in hand and you have accepted that job in writing with an agreed-upon start date.

- Research the companies you contact. In a tightly run job race the candidate who is most knowledgeable about the employer has a distinct advantage.

- Contact and recontact your job leads. Follow up on the resumes you send out. Resubmit your resume after six weeks. Change the format of your resume and resubmit yet again. (See my book *Resumes that Knock 'em Dead* for specific ideas on how to do this.)

- Stay in regular telephone contact with your job leads on a monthly basis to maintain top-of-the-mind awareness.

- Take off the blinkers. We all have two specific skills: our professional/technical skills—say, computer programming—and our industry skills—say, banking. Professional/technical skills can be transferable to other industries—say, manufacturing; and industry skills can open up other opportunities in your industry—say, as a technical trainer for programmers and/or technophobes.

- Develop examples of the personality traits that make you special—say, determination. Rehearse building these examples into your interview responses. (See chapter 14.)

- Send follow-up notes with relevant news clippings, cartoons, and so on to those in your networks.

- Work on your self-image. Use this time to get physically fit. Studies show that unfit, overweight people take longer to find suitable work. The more you do today the better you will feel about yourself.

- Maintain a professional demeanor during the work week (clothing, posture, personal hygiene).

- Use regular business hours for making contacts. Use the early morning, lunch time, after 5 p.m., and Saturday for doing the on-going research to maintain momentum.

- Don't feel guilty about taking time off from your job-hunting job. Just do it consciously. If you regularly spend Saturday morning in the library doing research, you can take Wednesday afternoon off.

- Maintain records of your contacts. They will benefit not only this job search but maybe those in the future, too.

- Remember: It's all up to you. There are many excuses not to make calls or send resumes on any given day. There are many excuses to get up later or knock off earlier. There are many excuses to back off because this one's in the bag. There are no real reasons. There are no jobs out there for those who won't look. There are countless opportunities for those who assiduously turn over the stones.

Contact Trackers

Job hunting requires multiple contacts with employers and others. You will call an employer and schedule a follow-up conversation for a specific time and date next week, you will send a resume today, and you need to schedule a follow-up call four to eight days later. When you get up to speed, important opportunities will fall through the cracks unless you maintain a contact tracker like the one on page 72.

How to Use the Contact Tracker

I recommend you make 365 copies of this, date each one, and put them in a ring binder. Once you have been going a couple of weeks, your days will plan themselves. Of course you probably won't use anywhere near all 365, but as we say in New York, "such a problem I should have."

Before making a day's mailing, fill out the contact tracker with the company name, telephone number, and contact name. This will help you structure your job-hunting days. A mailing today will allow you to have a follow-up plan set and ready to go at the appropriate time. As a rule of thumb, a mailing today is ripe for follow-up four to eight days later. Much sooner and you can't guarantee the mail has arrived; much later and it will already be lost in an in-box or passed on.

You will know that your job hunt is on track when you are filling one of these out every day as a result of a mailing, and filling a second one out as a result of your follow-up calls.

Every month I hear from people who use these techniques effectively. Just last week I had a gentleman speak to me on a radio show in Texas who explained that he had been out of work for six months. He said he had bought the *Knock 'em Dead* books just five weeks earlier, had followed my advice to the letter, and had since generated four job offers. Follow my advice in letter and spirit and the same good fortune can be yours.

Network Index Sheets

As you develop your multiple networks, they too will become unwieldy and you will need some form of record keeping. Network index sheets will help you stay on top of the problem. The sheets should be developed on every good contact you make.

Good contacts from the Contact Tracker will be forwarded to a future date for follow up; then, as you develop a history on that person, on a network index sheet you can add a memory jogger to the Contact Tracker.

Follow-up: The Key Ingredient

In theory the perfect letters you send cold or as a result of phone calls will receive a response rate of one hundred percent. Unfortunately there is no perfect letter or call in this less-than-perfect world. If you sit there like some fat Buddha waiting for the world to beat a path to your door, you may wait a long time.

While I was writing this chapter, a pal of mine advertised for a programmer analyst, a two-line ad in the local paper. By Wednesday of the following week he had over one hundred responses. Ten days later he was still plowing through them when he received a follow-up call (the only one he received) from one of the respondents. The job hunter was in the office within two hours, returned the following morning, and was hired before lunchtime.

The story? The candidate's paperwork was simply languishing there in the pile, waiting to be discovered. The follow-up phone call got it discovered. The call made the interviewer sort through the enormous pile of paper, pull out the letter and resume, and act on it. Follow-up calls, and follow-up calls on the follow-up calls, do work.

The best managers maintain a private file of great professionals whom they can't use today but want to keep available. I know of someone who got a top job as a result of being in these files. She got an interview and job offer from a broadcast letter she had sent *three years earlier.*

Grant yourself the right to pick and choose among many job offers with this approach. Because you are in control, it is possible to set your multiple interviews close together. This way your interviewing skills improve from one meeting to the next. And soon, instead of scheduling multiple interviews, you can be weighing multiple job offers.

Date: _____
CONTACT TRACKER

Company	Tel #	Contact Name	Result	F/U Date	Sent Resume
1.					
2.					
3.					
4.					
5.					
6.					
7.					
8.					
9.					
10.					
11.					
12.					
13.					
14.					
15.					
16.					
17.					
18.					
19.					
20.					

NETWORK INDEX SHEET

Name: _____

Relationship: _____

How known: _____

Time known: _____

People in common: _____

_____

Telephone: H# _____, O# _____

Home address: _____

_____

Office address: _____

_____

Secretary: _____

Leads given: _____

_____

_____

BIOGRAPHICAL INFORMATION

Spouse: _____

Children: _____

Interests: _____

_____

Affiliations: _____

_____

Professional experience: _____

_____

_____

Date last contacted: _____

Result: _____

_____

_____

II

Getting to Square One

With the grunt work completed, you are loaded for bear and ready to knock 'em dead. So how do you begin?

It bears repeating that you must take the initiative when it comes to finding a job. You must do so in a distinctive way. What is your first instinct when you must "go look for a job?" Read the want ads? Everybody else does. Apply for jobs listed with the unemployment office? Everybody else does. Send resumes to companies on the off-chance they have a job that fits your resume? Everybody else does. Or, of course, you can wait for someone to call you. Employ those tactics as your main thrust for hunting down the best jobs in town, and you will fail, as do millions of others who fall into the trap of using such outdated job-hunting techniques.

Today's business marketplace demands a different approach. Your career does not take care of itself—you must go out and grab the opportunities.

"Hello, Mr. Smith? My name is Martin Yate. I am an experienced training specialist. . . ."

It's as easy as that.

Guide your destiny by speaking directly to the professionals who make their living in the same way you do. A few minutes spent calling different companies from your research dossier, and you will have an interview. When you get one interview from making a few calls, how many do you think could be arranged with a day's concerted effort?

5.
Painting the Perfect Picture
on the Phone

Before making that first nerve-wracking telephone call, you must be prepared to achieve one of these three goals. They are listed in order of priority.

- I will arrange a meeting.
- I will arrange a time to talk further on the phone.
- I will ask for a lead on a promising job opening elsewhere.

Always keep these goals in mind. By the time you finish the next four chapters, you'll be able to achieve any one of these goals quickly and easily.

To make the initial phone call a success, all you need to do is paint a convincing word picture of yourself. To start, remember the old saying: "No one really listens; we are all just waiting for our turn to speak." With this in mind, you shouldn't expect to hold anyone's attention for an extended period, so the picture you create needs to be brief yet thorough. Most of all, it should be specifically vague: specific enough to arouse interest, to make the company representative prick up his ears and yet vague enough to encourage questions, to make him pursue you. The aim is to paint a representation of your skills in broad brush strokes with examples of the money-making, money-saving, or time-saving accomplishments all companies like to hear about.

A presentation made over the telephone must possess four characteristics to be successful. These can best be remembered by an old acronym from the advertising world: *AIDA*.

A—You must get the company representative's attention.
I—You must get the company representative's interest.
D—You must create a desire to know more about you.
A—You must encourage the company representative to take action.

With AIDA you get noticed. The interest you generate will be displayed by the questions that are being asked: "How much are you making?" "Do you have a degree?" "How much experience do you have?" By giving the appropriate answers to these and other questions (which I will discuss in detail), you will change interest into a desire to know more and then parlay that desire into an interview.

The types of questions you are asked also enable you to identify the company's specific needs, and once they are identified, you can gear the ongoing conversation toward those needs.

Here are the steps in building your AIDA presentation:

Step One: This covers who you are and what you do. It is planned to get the company representative's attention, to give the person a reason to stay on the phone. This introduction will include your job title and a brief generalized description of your duties and responsibilities. Use a nonspecific job title, as you did for your resume. Remember, getting a foot in the door with a generalized title can provide the occasion to sell your superior skills.

Tell just enough about yourself to whet the company's appetite and cause the representative to start asking questions. Again, keep your description a little vague. For example, if you describe yourself as simply experienced, the company representative must try to qualify your statement with a question: "How much experience do you have?" You have established a level of interest. But if you describe yourself as having four years of experience, while the company is looking for seven, you are likely to be ruled out before you are even aware a job exists. Never specify exact experience or list all your accomplishments during the initial presentation. Your aim is just to open a dialogue.

Example:
"Good morning, Mr. Smith. My name is Joan Jones. I am an experienced office equipment salesperson with an in-depth knowledge of the office products industry. Have I caught you at a good time?"

Never ever ask if you have caught someone at a bad time. You are offering your contact an excuse to say yes. By the same token, asking whether you have caught someone at a good time will usually get you a yes. Then you can go directly into the rest of your presentation.

Step Two: Now you are ready to generate interest, and from that, desire; it's time to sell one or two of your accomplishments. You already should have identified these during earlier resume-building exercises. Pull out no more than two items and follow your introductory sentence with them. Keep them brief and to the point, without embellishments.

Example:
"As the #3 salesperson in my company, I increased sales in my territory 15 percent to over $1 million. In the last six months, I won three major accounts from my competitors."

Step Three: You have made the company representative want to know more about you, so now you can make him take action. Include the reason for your call and a request to meet. It should be carefully constructed to finish with a question that will bring a positive response, which will launch the two of you into a nuts-and-bolts discussion.

Example:

"The reason I'm calling, Mr. Smith, is that I'm looking for a new challenge, and having researched your company, I felt we might have some areas for discussion. Are these the types of skills and accomplishments you look for in your staff?"

Your presentation ends with a question that guarantees a positive response, and the conversation gets moving.

□   □   □

Your task before calling is to write out a presentation using these guidelines and your work experience. Knowing exactly what you are going to say and what you wish to achieve is the only way to generate multiple interviews and multiple job offers. When your presentation is prepared and written, read it aloud to yourself, and imagine the faceless company representative on the other end of the line. Practice with a friend or spouse, or use a tape recorder to critique yourself.

After you make the actual presentation on the phone, you'll really begin to work on arranging a meeting, another phone conversation, or establishing a referral. There will likely be a silence on the other end after your initial pitch. Be patient. The company representative needs time to digest your words. If you feel tempted to break the silence, resist; you do not want to break the person's train of thought, nor do you want the ball back in your court.

This contemplative silence may last as long as twenty seconds, but when the company representative responds, only three things can happen.

1. The company representative can agree with you and arrange a meeting.

2. The company representative can ask questions that show interest: "Do you have a degree?" "How much are you earning?"

    (Any question, because it denotes interest, is considered a buy signal. Handled properly, it will enable you to arrange a meeting.)

3. The company representative can raise an objection: "I don't need anyone like that now." "Send me a resume."

These objections, when handled properly, will also result in an interview with the company, or at least a referral to someone else who has job openings. In fact, you will frequently find that objections prove to be terrific opportunities.

□   □   □

I hope you can handle the first option, "I'd like to meet with you," with little assistance; for obvious reasons, it doesn't get its own chapter.

It will sometimes happen that an overly officious receptionist or secretary will try to thwart you in your efforts to present your credentials directly to a potential employer. At least it appears that way to you.

In fact, it is very rare that these corporate gatekeepers, as they are known, are specifically directed to screen calls from professionals seeking employment, as to do so can only increase employment costs to the company. What they are there to do is to screen the nuisance calls from salespeople and the like.

However, to arm you for the occasional objectionable gatekeeper standing between you and making a living, you might try the following techniques used by investigative reporters, private eyes, and headhunters.

Go Up the Ladder

If you can't get through to the person you want to speak to, say the accounting manager, go up the ladder to the controller or the vice president of finance. Interestingly enough, the higher you go, the more accessible people are. In this instance the senior manager may well not schedule an interview with you but instead refer you back down to the appropriate level. Which means that to the pesky gatekeeper you can now say, "Mr. Bigshot, your divisional vice president of finance, asked me to call your Mr. Jones. Is he there?" Or if you didn't get through, and Bigshot's secretary referred you down the ladder, you say, "Mr. Bigshot's office recommended . . ." Then the conversation with your target can begin with your standard introduction, but be sure to mention first that so-and-so suggested you call.

Preempt

Most gatekeepers are trained at most to find out your name and the nature of your business. But when they are asking the questions, they control the conversation. You can remain in control by preempting their standard script. "Hi, I'm Mr. Yate [always use your surname for the intimidation value]. I need to speak to Ms. Jones about an accounting matter. Is she there?" Should a truly obnoxious gatekeeper ask snidely, "Perhaps I can help you?" you can effectively utilize any of the following options: "Thank you, but I'd rather discuss it with Ms. Jones." "It's personal." (Well, it's your livelihood isn't it?) Or you can blind them with science. "Yes, if you can talk to me about the finer points of release 6.2 of Lotus 1-2-3," which invariably they can't, so you're in like Flynn.

When you are clear about who you want to speak to and can predict possible screening devices, you are usually assured of getting through. When you don't have the name, try these techniques.

Explain to gatekeepers that you need to send a letter to (title) and ask for the correct spelling of the name. There is usually more than one person worth speaking to at any company, so ask for more than one name and title. In the finance area, and depending on your title, any or all of the following could provide useful contacts: the accounting supervisor, the accounting manager, the assistant controller, the controller, the vice president of finance, the executive vice president, the COO, the CEO, and the chairman.

Anyone who will give you one name will invariably give you more. Some years ago in Colorado I sat with a job hunter using this technique who gathered 142 names in one hour!

In companies where security is at a premium, the gatekeepers are expressly forbidden to give out names and titles. In this case use some of my blind-siding techniques: There are certain people in every company who by the very nature of their jobs have contacts with people at all levels of the company, and who are not given the responsibility to screen calls. These include people in the mail room, the gate house, guards, shipping and receiving employees, second-, third-, and fourth-shift employees, new or temporary employees, advertising and public relations people, sales and marketing people, travel center, Q/A, or customer service employees.

Automatic Phone Systems

Automatic phone systems are on the increase. If the techniques I've mentioned don't turn the trick for you, these will. When the recorded voice tells you to enter the extension key, keep keying until you hit one that is on the money. It doesn't matter who answers as long as someone does. The conversation goes like this:

"Jack speaking."

"Jack, this is Martin Yate. I'm calling from outside and I'm lost on this damn telephone system." This usually gets a smile. "I'm trying to get hold of (title). Could you check who that would be for me?"

or,

"Jack, this is Martin Yate. I'm lost on this damn telephone system. I need some help. Can you spare me a minute?"

Whichever technique you use, be sensitive to the person in a rush and don't leave numerous messages. Try to get the extension of the person you want, rather than letting yourself be transferred.

6.
Responding to Buy Signals

With just a touch of nervous excitement you finish your presentation: "Are these the types of skills and accomplishments you look for in your staff?" There is silence on the other end. It is broken by a question. You breathe a sigh of relief because you remember that any question denotes interest and is a buy signal.

Now, conversation is a two-way street, and you are most likely to win an interview when you take responsibility for your half. Just as the employer's questions show interest in you, your questions should show your interest in the work done at the company. By asking questions of your own in the normal course of conversation—questions usually tagged on to the end of one of your answers— you will forward the conversation. Also, such questions help you find out what particular skills and qualities are important to the employer. Inquisitiveness will increase your knowledge of the opportunity at hand, and that knowledge will give you the power to arrange a meeting.

The alternative is to leave all the interrogation to the employer. That will place you on the defensive and at the end of the talk, you will be as ignorant of the real parameters of the job as you were at the start. And the employer will know less about you than you might want.

Applying the technique of giving a short answer and finishing that reply with a question will carry your call to its logical conclusion: The interviewer will tell you the job specifics, and as that happens, you will present the relevant skills or attributes. In any conversation, the person who asks the questions controls its outcome. You called the employer to get an interview as the first step in generating a job offer, so take control of your destiny by taking control of the conversation.

Example:
Joan Jones: "Good morning, Mr. Smith. My name is Joan Jones. I am an experienced office equipment salesperson with an in-depth knowledge of the office products industry. Have I caught you at a good time? . . . . As the #3 salesperson in my company, I increased sales in my territory 15 percent to over $1 million. In the last six months, I won three major accounts from my competitors. The reason I'm calling, Mr. Smith, is that I'm looking for a new challenge, and having researched your company, I felt we might have areas for discussion. Are these the types of skills and accomplishments you look for in your staff?"

[Pause.]

Mr. Smith: "Yes, they are. What type of equipment have you been selling?" *[Buy signal!]*

J: "My company carries a comprehensive range, and I sell both the top and bottom of the line, according to my customers' needs. I have been noticing a considerable interest in the latest fax and scanning equipment." *[You've made it a conversation; you further it with the following.]* "Has that been your experience recently?"

S: "Yes, especially in the color and acetate capability machines." *[Useful information for you.]* "Do you have a degree?" *[Buy signal!]*

J: "Yes, I do." *[Just enough information to keep the company representative chasing you.]* "I understand your company prefers degreed salespeople to deal with its more sophisticated clients." *[Your research is paying off.]*

S: "Our customer base is very sophisticated, and they expect a certain professionalism and competence from us." *[An inkling of the kind of person they want to hire.]* "How much experience do you have?" *[Buy signal!]*

J: "Well, I've worked in both operations and sales, so I have a wide experience base." *[General but thorough.]* "How many years of experience are you looking for?" *[Turning it around, but furthering the conversation.]*

S: "Ideally, four or five for the position I have in mind." *[More good information.]* "How many do you have?" *[Buy signal!]*

J: "I have two with this company, and one and a half before that. I fit right in with your needs, don't you agree?" *[How can Mr. Smith say no?]*

S: "Uhmmm . . . What's your territory?" *[Buy signal!]*
J: "I cover the metropolitan area. Mr. Smith, it really does sound as if we might have something to talk about." *[Remember, your first goal is the face-to-face interview.]* "I am planning to take Thursday and Friday off at the end of the week. Can we meet then?" *[Make Mr. Smith decide what day he can see you, rather than whether he will see you at all.]* "Which would be best for you?"

S: "How about Friday morning? Can you bring a resume?"

Your conversation should proceed with that kind of give-and-take. Your questions show interest, carry the conversation forward, and teach you more about the company's needs. By the end of the conversation you have an interview arranged and several key areas to promote when you arrive:

- The company sees growth in the latest fax and scanning equipment, especially those with color and acetate capabilities.
- They want business and personal sophistication.
- They ideally want four or five years' experience.
- They are interested in your metropolitan contacts.

The above is a fairly simple scenario, but even though it is constructive, it doesn't show you the tricky buy signals that can spell disaster in your job hunt. These are questions that appear to be simple buy signals, yet in reality are a part of every interviewer's arsenal called "knock-out" questions—questions that can save the interviewer time by quickly ruling out certain types of candidates. Although these questions most frequently arise during the initial telephone conversation, they can crop up at the face-to-face interview; the answering techniques are applicable throughout the interview cycle.

Note: We all come from different backgrounds and geographical areas. So understand that while my answers cover correct approaches and responses, they do not attempt to capture the regional and personal flavor of conversation. You and I will never talk alike, so don't learn the example answers parrot-fashion. Instead, you should take the essence of the responses and personalize them until the words fall easily from your lips.

Buy Signal:
"How much are you making/do you want?"

This is a direct question looking for a direct answer, yet it is a knock-out question. Earning either too little or too much could ruin your chances before you're given the opportunity to shine in person. There are a number of options that could serve you better than a direct answer. First, you must understand that questions about money at this point in the conversation are being used to screen you in or screen you out of the "ballpark"—the answers you give now should be geared specifically toward getting you in the door and into a face-to-face meeting. (Handling the serious salary negotiations that are attached to a job offer are covered extensively in chapter 23, "Negotiating the Offer.") For now, your main options are as follows.

    ☐ **Put yourself above the money**: "I'm looking for a job and a company to call home. If I am the right person for you, I'm sure you'll make me a fair offer. What is the salary range for the position?"

    ☐ **Give a vague answer**: "The most important things to me are the job itself and the company. What is the salary range for the position?"

☐ **Or you could answer a question with a question:** "How much does the job pay?"

When you are pressed a second time for an exact dollar figure, be as honest and forthright as circumstances permit. Some people (often, unfortunately, women) are underpaid for their jobs when their work is compared to that of others in similar positions. It is not a question of perception; these women in fact make less money than they should. If you have the skills for the job and you are concerned that your current low salary will eliminate you before you have the chance to show your worth, you might want to add into your base salary the dollar value of your benefits. If it turns out to be too much, you can then simply explain that you were including the value of your benefits. Or, you could say, "Mr. Smith, my previous employers felt I am well worth the money I earn due to my skills, dedication, and honesty. Were we to meet, I'm sure I could demonstrate my value and my ability to contribute to your department. You'd like an opportunity to make that evaluation, wouldn't you?"

Notice the "wouldn't you?" at the end of the reply. A reflexive question such as this is a great conversation-forwarding technique because it encourages a positive response. Conservative use of reflexive questions can really help you move things along. Watch the sound of your voice, though. A reflexive question can sound pleasantly conversational or pointed and accusatory; it's not really what you say, but how you say it.

Such questions are easy to create. Just conclude with "wouldn't you?" "didn't you?" "won't you?" "couldn't you?" "shouldn't you?" or "don't you?" as appropriate at the end of virtually any statement, and the interviewer will almost always answer "yes." You have kept the conversation alive, and moved it closer to your goal. Repeat the reflexive questions to yourself. They have a certain rhythm that will help you remember them.

Buy Signal:
"Do you have a degree?"

Always answer the exact question; beware of giving unrequested (and possibly excessive) information. For example, if you have a bachelor's degree in fine arts from New York University, your answer is "Yes," not "Yes, I have a bachelor's degree in fine arts from NYU." Perhaps the company wants an architecture degree. Perhaps the company representative has bad feelings about NYU graduates. You don't want to be knocked out before you've been given the chance to prove yourself.

"Yes, I have a degree. What background are you looking for?" Or, you can always answer a question with a question: "I have a diverse educational background. Ideally, what are you looking for?"

When a degree is perceived as mandatory and you barely scraped through grade school, don't be intimidated. As Calvin Coolidge used to say, "The world is full of educated layabouts." You may want to use the "Life University" answer. For instance: "My education was cut short by the necessity of earning a living at an early age. My past managers have found that my life experience and responsible attitude is a valuable asset to the department. Also, I intend to return to school to continue my education."

A small proportion of the more sensitive employers are verifying educational credentials, and if yours are checked it means the employer takes such matters seriously, so an untruth or an exaggeration could cost you a job. Think hard and long before inflating your educational background.

Buy Signal:

"How much experience do you have?"

Too much or too little could easily rule you out. Be careful how you answer and try to gain time. It is a vague question, and you have a right to ask for qualifications.

"Could you help me with that question?" or, "Are you looking for overall experience or in some specific areas?" or, "Which areas are most important to you?" Again, you answer a question with a question. The employer's response, while gaining you time, tells you what it takes to do the job and therefore what you have to say to get it, so take mental notes—you can even write them down, if you have time. Then give an appropriate response.

You might want to retain control of the conversation by asking another question, for example: "The areas of expertise you require sound very interesting, and it sounds as if you have some exciting projects at hand. Exactly what projects would I be involved with in the first few months?"

After one or two buy signal questions are asked, ask for a meeting. Apart from those just outlined, questions asked over the phone tend not to contain traps. If you simply ask, "Would you like to meet me?" there are only two possible responses: yes or no. Your chances of success are greatly decreased. When you intimate, however, that you will be in the area on a particular date or dates—"I'm going to be in town on Thursday and Friday, Mr. Smith. Which would be better for you?"—you have asked a question that moves the conversation along dramatically. Your question gives the company representative the choice of meeting you on Thursday or Friday, rather than meeting you or not meeting you. By presuming the "yes," you reduce the chances of hearing a negative, and increase the possibility of a face-to-face meeting.

7.
Responding to Objections

Even with the most convincing word picture, the silence may be broken not by a buy signal, but by an objection. An objection is usually a statement, not a question: "Send me a resume," or, "I don't have time to see you," or, "You are earning too much," or, "You'll have to talk to personnel," or, "I don't need anyone like you right now."

Although these seem like brush-off lines, often they are really disguised opportunities to get yourself a job offer—handled properly, almost all objections can be parlayed into interviews. This section will teach you to seize hidden opportunities successfully; notice that all your responses have a commonality with buy-signal responses. They all end with a question, one that will enable you to learn more about the reason for the objection, overcome it, and once again lead the conversation toward a face-to-face interview.

In dealing with objections, as with differences of opinion, nothing is gained by confrontation, though much is to be gained by appreciation of the other's viewpoint. Most objections you hear are best handled by first demonstrating your understanding of the other's viewpoint. Always start your response with "I understand," or, "I can appreciate your position," or, "I see your point," or, "Of course," followed by, "However," or, "Also consider," or a similar line that puts you back into consideration.

Remember, these responses should not be learned merely to be repeated. You need only to understand and implement their meaning, to understand their concept and put the answers in your own words. Personalize all the suggestions to your character and style of speech.

□   □   □

Objection:
"Why don't you send me a resume?"

Danger here. The company representative may be genuinely interested in seeing your resume as a first step in the interview cycle; or it may be a polite way of getting you off the phone. You should identify what the real reason is without causing antagonism. At the same time, you want to open up the conversation. A good reply would be: "Of course, Mr. Smith. Would you give me your exact title and the full address? . . . . Thank you. So that I can be sure that my qualifications fit your needs, what skills are you looking for in this position?"

Notice the steps:

- Apparent agreement to start.
- A show of consideration.
- A question to further the conversation.

Answering in that fashion will open up the conversation. Mr. Smith will relay the aspects of the job that are important to him, and with this knowledge, you can sell Smith on your skills over the phone. Also, you will be able to use the information to draw attention to your skills in the future, in:

- Following conversations.
- The cover letter to your resume.
- Your executive briefing.
- Your face-to-face meeting.
- Your follow-up after the meeting.

The information you glean will give you power and will increase your chances of receiving a job offer.

□   □   □

Objection:

"I don't have time to see you."

If the employer is too busy to see you, he or she has a problem, and by recognizing that, perhaps you can show yourself as the one to solve it. You should avoid confrontation, however—it is important that you demonstrate empathy for the speaker. Agree, empathize, and ask a question that moves the conversation forward.

"I understand how busy you must be; it sounds like a competent, dedicated, and efficient professional [whatever your title is] could be of some assistance. Perhaps I could call you back at a better time, to discuss how I might make you some time. When are you least busy, the morning or afternoon?"

The company representative will either make time to talk now, or will arrange a better time for the two of you to talk further.

Here are some other ideas you could use to phrase the same objection:

"Since you are so busy, what is the best time of day for you? First thing in the morning, or is the afternoon a quieter time?" or, "I will be in your area tomorrow, so why don't I come by and see you?"

Of course, you can combine the two: "I'm going to be in your part of town tomorrow, and I could drop by and see you. What is your quietest time, morning or afternoon?" By presuming the invitation for a meeting, you make it harder for the company representative to object. And if he or she is truly busy, your consideration will be appreciated and will still make it hard to object.

□ □ □

Objection:
"You are earning too much."

You should not have brought up salary in the first place. Go straight to jail. If the company representative brought up the matter, that's a buy signal, which was discussed in the last chapter. If the job really doesn't pay enough, you got (as the carnival barker says) close, but no cigar! How to make a success of this seeming dead-end is handled in the next chapter. You may also refer to helpful information covered in chapter 23, "Negotiating the Offer."

□ □ □

Objection:
"We only promote from within."

Your response could be: "I realize that, Mr. Smith. Your development of employees is a major reason I want to get in! I am bright, conscientious, and motivated. When you do hire from the outside, what assets are you looking for?"

The response finishes with a question designed to carry the conversation forward, and to give you a new opportunity to sell yourself. Notice that the response assumes that the company is hiring from the outside, even though the company representative has said otherwise. You have called his bluff, but in a professional, inoffensive manner.

□ □ □

Objection:
"You'll have to talk to personnel."

Your reply is: "Of course, Mr. Smith. Whom should I speak to in personnel, and what specific position should I mention?"

You cover a good deal of ground with that response. You establish whether there is a job there or whether you are being fobbed off to personnel to waste their time and your own. Also, you move the conversation forward again while changing the thrust of it to your advantage. Develop a specific job-related question to ask while the company representative is answering the first question. It can open a fruitful line for you to pursue. If you receive a nonspecific reply, probe a little deeper. A simple phrase like, "That's interesting, please tell me more," or, "Why's that?" will usually do the trick.

Or you can ask: "When I speak to personnel, will it be about a specific job you have, or is it to see whether I might fill a position elsewhere in the company?"

Armed with the resulting information, you can talk to personnel about your conversation with Mr. Smith. Remember to get the name of a specific person with whom to speak, and to quote the company representative.

Example:
"Good morning, Mr. Johnson. Mr. Smith, the regional sales manager, sug-

gested we should speak to arrange an interview."

That way, you will show personnel that you are not a waste of time; because you know someone in the company, you won't be regarded as one of the frequent "blind" calls they get every day. As the most overworked, understaffed department in a company, they will appreciate that. Most important, you will stand out, be noticed.

Don't look at the personnel department as a roadblock; it may contain a host of opportunities for you. Because a large company may have many different departments that can use your talents, personnel is likely to be the only department that knows all the openings. You might be able to arrange three or four interviews with the same company for three or four different positions!

□ □ □

Objection:

"I really wanted someone with a degree."

You could respond to this by saying: "Mr. Smith, I appreciate your position. It was necessary that I start earning a living early in life. If we meet, I am certain you would recognize the value of my additional practical experience."

You might then wish to ask what the company policy is for support and encouragement of employees taking night classes or continuing-education courses, and will naturally explain how you are hoping to find an employer who encourages employees to further their education. Your response will end with: "If we were to meet, I am certain you would recognize the value of my practical experience. I am going to be in your area next week. When would be the best time of day to get together?"

□ □ □

Objection:

"I don't need anyone like you now."

Short of suggesting that the employer fire someone to make room for you (which, incidentally, has been done successfully on a few occasions), chances of getting an interview with this particular company are slim. With the right question, however, that person will give you a personal introduction to someone else who could use your talents. Asking that right question or series of questions is what networking and the next chapter are all about. So on the occasions when the techniques for answering buy signals or rebutting objections do not get you a meeting, "Getting Live Leads From Dead Ends" will!

8.
Getting Live Leads from Dead Ends

There will be times when you have said all the right things on the phone, but hear, "I can't use anyone like you right now." Not every company has a job opening for you, nor are you right for every job. Sometimes you must accept a temporary setback and understand that the rejection is not one of you as a human being. By using these special interview development questions, though, you will be able to turn those setbacks into job interviews.

The company representative is a professional and knows other professionals in his or her field, in other departments, subsidiaries, even other companies. If you approach the phone presentation in a professional manner, he or she, as a fellow professional, will be glad to advise you on who is looking for someone with your skills. Nearly everyone you call will be pleased to point you in the right direction, but only if you *ask*! And you'll be able to ask as many questions as you wish, because you will be recognized as a colleague intelligently using the professional network. The company representative also knows that his good turn in referring you to a colleague at another company will be returned in the future. And, as a general rule, companies prefer candidates to be referred this way over any other method.

But do not expect people to be clairvoyant. There are two sayings: "You get what you ask for," and "If you don't ask, you don't get." Each is pertinent here.

When you are sure that no job openings exist within a particular department, ask one of these questions:

- "Who else in the company might need someone with my qualifications?"
- "Does your company have any other divisions or subsidiaries that might need someone with my attributes?"
- "Whom do you know in the business community who might have a lead for me?"
- "Which are the most rapidly growing companies in the area?"
- "Whom should I speak to there?"
- "Do you know anyone at the ABC Electronics Company?"
- "When do you anticipate an opening in your company?"

- "Are you planning any expansion or new projects that might create an opening?"
- "When do you anticipate change in your manpower needs?"

Each one of those interview-development questions can gain you an introduction or lead to a fresh opportunity. The questions have not been put in any order of importance—that is for you to do. Take a sheet of paper and, looking at the list, figure out what question you would ask if you had time to ask only one. Write it down. Do that with the remaining questions on the list. As you advance, you will develop a comfortable set of prioritized questions. Add questions of your own. For instance, the type of computer or word-processing equipment a company has might be important to some professions, but not to others, and a company representative might be able to lead you to companies that have your machines. Be sure that any question you add to your list is specific and leads to a job opening. Avoid questions like, "How's business these days?" Time is valuable, and time is money to both of you. When you're satisfied with your list of interview development questions, put them on a fresh sheet of paper and store it safely with your telephone presentation and resume.

Those interview development questions will lead you to a substantial number of jobs in the hidden job market. You are getting referrals from the "in" crowd, who know who is hiring whom long before that news is generally circulated.

By being in with the "in" crowd, you establish a very effective referral network.

When you get leads on companies and specific individuals to talk to, be sure to thank your benefactor and ask to use his or her name as an introduction. The answer, you will find, will always be "yes," but asking shows you to be someone with manners—in this day and age, that alone will set you apart.

You might also suggest to your contact that you leave your telephone number in case he or she runs into someone who can use you. You'll be surprised at how many people call back with a lead.

With personal permission to use someone's name on your next networking call, you have been given the greatest of job-search gifts: a personal introduction. Your call will begin with something like:

"Hello, Ms. Smith. My name is Jack Jones. Joseph McDonald recommended I give you a call. By the way, he sends his regards." [Pause for any response to this.] "He felt we might have something valuable to discuss."

Follow up on every lead you get. Too many people become elated at securing an interview for themselves and then cease all effort to generate additional interviews, believing a job offer is definitely on its way. Your goal is to have a choice of the best jobs in town, and without multiple interviews, there is no way you'll have that choice. Asking interview-development questions ensures that you are tapping all the secret recesses of the hidden job market.

Networking is a continuous cycle:

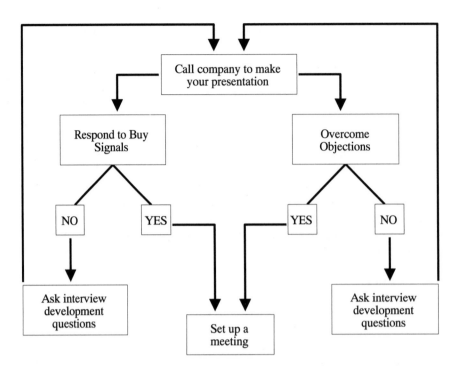

Make a commitment to sell yourself, to make telephone calls, to make a referral network, and to recognize buy signals and objections for what they really are—opportunities to shine. Make a commitment to ask interview development questions at every seeming dead end: They will lead you to all the jobs in town.

9.
The Telephone Interview

In this glorious technological age, the first substantive contact with a potential employer is virtually always by telephone. It's the way business is done today.

It happens in one of three ways:

- You are networking, and the company representative goes into a screening process immediately because you have aroused his or her interest.
- A company calls unexpectedly as a result of a resume you have mailed and catches you off-guard.
- You or a headhunter who has agreed to take you on has set up a specific time for a telephone interview.

Whatever circumstance creates the telephone interview, you must be prepared to handle the questioning and use every means at your disposal to win the real thing—the face-to-face meeting. The telephone interview is the trial run for the face-to-face and is an opportunity you must not bumble; your happiness and prosperity may hinge on it.

This, the first contact with your future employer, will test your mental preparation. Remember: You can plant in your mind any thought, plan, desire, strategy, or purpose, and translate it into reality. Put your goal down on paper and read it aloud to yourself every day, because the constant reiteration will crystallize your aims, and clear goals provide the most solid base of preparation.

Being prepared for a telephone interview takes organization. You never know when a company is going to call once you have started networking and sending your resume out (the word gets around more quickly than you think if it's a resume that knocks 'em dead.). Usually the call comes at the worst of times, such as 8 o'clock Monday morning when you are sleeping late, or 4:56 in the afternoon, just as you return from walking the dog. You can avoid being caught completely off-guard by keeping your resume and alphabetized company dossiers by the telephone.

The most obvious (and often most neglected) point to remember is this: During the interview, the company representative has only ears with which to judge you, and that is something you must overcome. Here are some tips.

- **Take a surprise call in stride.** If you receive a call as a result of a mailed resume or a telephone message you left, and you are unprepared, be calm. Sound positive, friendly, and collected: "Thank you for calling, Mr. Smith. Would you wait just a moment while I close the door?"

  Put the phone down, take three deep breaths to slow your heart down, pull out the appropriate company dossier and your resume, put a smile on your face (it improves the timbre of your voice), and pick up the phone again. Now you are in control of yourself and the situation.

- **Beware of over-familiarity.** You should always refer to the interviewer by his or her surname until invited to do otherwise.

- **Allow the company representative to do most of the talking**—to ask most (but not all) of the questions. Keep up your end of the conversation—this is, after all, a sales presentation, so be sure to ask a few questions of your own that will reveal you as an intelligent person and provide you the opportunity to promote your candidacy. For example, ask what immediate projects the interviewer's department is involved in, or the biggest challenges that are being tackled. When the interviewer answers your question, you will either have a clear picture of how to sell yourself, or you will ask a follow-up question for clarification.

  For example: "What specific skills and personality traits do you think are necessary for a person to succeed with those challenges?" Everyone hires a problem solver—find the problem and you are already halfway toward the offer.

- **Beware of giving yes/no answers.** They give no real information about your abilities.

- **Be factual in your answers.** Brief yet thorough.

- **Speak directly into the telephone.** Keep the mouthpiece about one inch from your mouth. Do not smoke or eat while on the phone. Numbered among the mystical properties of our telephone system is its excellence at picking up and amplifying background music and voices, especially young ones. That is excelled only by its power to transmit the sounds of food or gum being chewed or smoke being inhaled or exhaled. Smokers, take note: there are no laws about discriminating against smokers, and therefore, all nonsmokers naturally discriminate. They will assume that even if you don't actually light up at the interview, you'll have been chain-smoking beforehand and will carry the smell with you as long as you are around. Taking no chances, they probably won't even give you a chance to get through the door once they hear you puffing away over the phone.

- **Take notes.** They will be invaluable to you in preparing for the face-to-face meeting. Were it not for the recent furor over the clandestine use of tape recorders, I would have recommended that you buy a cheap tape recorder and a phone attachment from your local electronics store and tape the whole conversation.

If, for any reason, the company representative is interrupted, jot down the topic under discussion. When he or she gets back on the line, you can helpfully recap: "We were just discussing . . ." That will be appreciated and will set you apart from the others.

The company representative may talk about the corporation, and from the dossier in front of you, you will also know facts about the outfit. A little flattery goes a long way: Admire the company's achievements and you are, in fact, admiring the interviewer. Likewise, if any areas of common interest arise, comment on them, and agree with the interviewer when possible—people hire people like themselves.

If the interviewer does not give you the openings you need to sell yourself, be ready to salvage the situation and turn it to your advantage. Have a few work-related questions prepared—for example, "What exactly will be the three major responsibilities in this job?" or, "What will be the first job I get my teeth into?" While you are getting the explanation, wait for a pause so that you can tell the interviewer your appropriate skills: "Would it be of value if I described my experience in the area of office management?" or, "Then my experience in word processing should be a great help to you," or, "I recently completed an accounting project just like that."

Under no circumstances, though, should you ask about the money you want, or benefits and vacation time; that comes later.

Remember that your single objective at this point is to sell yourself and your skills; if you don't do that, you may never get the face-to-face interview.

The telephone interview has come to an end when you are asked whether you have any questions. Ask any more questions that will improve your understanding of the job requirements. If you haven't asked before, now is the time to establish what projects you would be working on in the first six months. By discovering them now, you will have time before the face-to-face meeting to package your skills to the needs at hand, and to create the appropriate Executive Briefing.

And if you have not already asked or been invited to meet the interviewer, now is the time. Take the initiative.

"It sounds like a very interesting opportunity, Ms. Smith, and a situation where I could definitely make a contribution. The most pressing question I have now is, when can we get together?" [*Note:* Even though the emphasis throughout has been on putting things in your own words, do use "make a contribution." It shows pride in your work—a key personal trait.]

Once the details are confirmed, finish with this request: "If I need any additional information before the interview, I would like to feel free to get back to you." The company representative will naturally agree. No matter how many questions you get answered in the initial conversation, there will always be something you forget. This allows you to call again to satisfy any curiosity—it will also enable you to increase rapport. Don't take too much advantage of it, though: One well-placed phone call that contains two or three considered questions will be appreciated; four or five phone calls will not.

Taking care to ascertain the correct spelling and pronunciation of the interviewer's name shows your concern for the small but important things in life—it will be noticed. This is also a good time to establish who else will be interviewing you, their titles, and how long the meeting is expected to last.

Follow with a casual inquiry as to what direction the meeting will take. You might ask, "Would you tell me some of the critical areas we will discuss on Thursday?" The knowledge gained will help you to package and present yourself, and will allow you time to bone up on any weak or rusty areas.

It is difficult to evaluate an opportunity properly over the telephone. Even if the job doesn't sound right, go to the interview. It will give you practice, and the job may look better when you have more facts. You might even discover a more suitable opening elsewhere within the company when you go to the face-to-face interview.

10.
Dressing for Interview Success

The moment we set eyes on someone, our minds make evaluations and judgments with lightning speed. The same is true for the potential employers who must assess us.

"What you see is what you get!"
"If a candidate can't put himself together in a professional manner, why should you assume he can put it all together on the job? Unless you look the part, don't expect an offer!" It may sound harsh, but that's an accurate summary of most employers' feelings on this issue. It's a fair estimate that nine out of ten of today's employers will reject an unsuitably dressed applicant without a second thought. Similarly dispiriting odds confront those who expect promotions but wear less than appropriate attire on the job. Like it or not, your outward image, your attitude, your confidence level, and your overall delivery are all affected by the clothes you wear.

The respect you receive at the interview is in direct proportion to the respect your visual image earns for you before you have the chance to say a word. If you wear clothes that are generally associated with leisure activities, you may be telling those who see you that you do not take your career seriously, and therefore are not committed to your work. Similarly, if you report for work the first day on a new job wearing clothes that undercut your perceived effectiveness, personal skills, and professionalism, it will be hard for you to be seen as a major contributor—no matter what you do between nine and five.

Employers rarely make overt statements about acceptable dress codes to their employees, much less to interviewees; more often there is an unspoken dictum that those who wish to climb the professional career ladder will dress appropriately . . . and that those who don't, won't.

There are some areas of employment where on-the-job dress (as opposed to interview dress) is somewhat less conservative than in the mainstream: Fashion, entertainment, and advertising are three examples. In these and a few other fields, there is a good deal of leeway with regard to personal expression in workplace attire. But for most of us, our jobs and our employers require a certain minimal level of professionalism in our dress. Interviewees must exceed these standards. This is not to say that you must dress like the chairman of the board (although that probably won't hurt), but you should be aware that dressing for the Friday night Lambada party on the day of your interview is not in your best professional interests.

Dressing Sharp: Your Interviewing Advantage

Our appearance tells people how we feel about ourselves as applicants, as well as how we feel about the interviewer(s), the company, and the process of interviewing itself. By dressing professionally, we tell people that we understand the niceties of corporate life, and we send a subtle "reinforcing" message that we can, for example, be relied upon to deal one-on-one with members of a company's prized client base.

More to the point, the correct image at an interview will give you a real edge over your competition. In fact, your overall appearance and presentation may well leave a more tangible impression than the words you say, since memory is rooted most strongly in pictures and impressions. At the very least, you can expect what you say to be strongly influenced in the mind of your interviewer by the way you present yourself.

Of course, the act of taking time to present an attractive professional image before you interview will add to your own sense of self-esteem and confidence. That is perhaps the greatest advantage of all.

The Look

The safest look for both men and women at interviews is traditional and conservative. This makes life fairly easy for the men: their professional fashions tend not to change much from year to year. A man can usually interview with confidence and poise in his three-year-old Brooks Brothers suit, provided that it isn't worn to a shine.

For women, the matter is a little more complicated. Appropriate female attire for the interview should ideally reflect the current fashion if the applicant is to be taken seriously. Rarely, if ever, can a woman feel comfortable interviewing in something she bought several years ago. Moreover, in selecting her current professional "uniform" the female applicant must walk a thin line, combining elements of both conformity (to show she belongs) and panache (to show a measure of individuality and style).

The key for both sexes is to dress for the position you want, not the one you have. This means that the upwardly mobile professional might need to invest in the clothes that project the desired image. The woman who dresses like a long-term member of the steno pool is unlikely ever to leave the secretarial ranks; the man who dresses like one of the corporate walking wounded will never be invited to move to Mahogany Row. Positions of responsibility are awarded to those who demonstrate that they are able to shoulder the burden. Looking capable will inspire others with the confidence to give you the most visible challenges.

The correct appearance alone probably won't get you a job offer, but it will go a long way toward winning attention and respect. When you know you look right, you can stop worrying about the impression your clothes are making and concentrate on communicating your message.

To be sure, every interview and every interviewer is different; because of this, it isn't possible to set down rigid guidelines for exactly what to wear in each situation. There is, however, relevant broadly based counsel that will help you make the right decision for your interview.

As we have seen, much of what we believe about others is based on our perception of their appearance; this chapter will help you insure that you are perceived as practical, well educated, competent, ethical, and professional.

General Guidelines

Appropriate attire, as we have noted, varies from industry to industry. The college professor can sport tweed jackets with elbow patches on the job, but is nevertheless likely to wear a suit to an interview. The advertising executive may wear wild ties as a badge of creativity (that is what he is being paid for), but he too is likely to dress conservatively for an interview. In all instances, our clothes are sending a message about our image, and the image we want to convey is one of reliability, trustworthiness, and attention to detail.

Most of us are far more adept at recognizing the dress mistakes of others than at spotting our own sartorial failings. When we do look for a second opinion, we often make the mistake of only asking a loved one. It's not that spouses, lovers, and parents lack taste; these people are, however, more in tune with our positive qualities than the rest of the world, and frequently they do not recognize how essential it is to reflect those qualities in our dress. Better candidates for evaluation of your interview attire are trusted friends who have proved their objectivity in such matters, or even a colleague at work.

Whenever possible, find out the dress code of the company you are visiting. For example, if you are an engineer applying for a job at a high-tech company, a blue three-piece suit might be overpowering. It is perfectly acceptable to ask someone in personnel about the dress code (written or informal) of the company. In the example we just used, you might be perfectly comfortable showing up *for work* in a sports coat or blazer; nevertheless, you are advised to wear a suit, at least for the first interview.

You may simply decide to change your look somewhat after learning of a more informal atmosphere with regard to dress at the firm you visit. If you are told that everyone works in shirt-sleeves and that there is never a tie in sight, a prudent and completely acceptable approach is to opt for your less formal brown or beige suit, rather than blues, grays, or pinstripes.

One final piece of advice: Avoid 100% synthetic garments at all costs. Their sheen makes them unattractive and they often retain body odor despite many washings.

Men

Following are the best current dress guidelines for men preparing for a professional interview.

Men's Suits

The most acceptable colors for men's suits are navy through teal blue and charcoal through light gray, followed at some distance by brown and beige. The fabric should be 100% wool; wool looks and wears better than any other material. Stay away from European designer suits, as they tend to be cut tighter and are often too flashy for the conservative world we live in. Two-piece suits are completely acceptable today, whereas only a few years ago one had to wear a three-piece suit to an interview.

The darker the suit, the more authority it carries (but beware: a man should *not* wear a black suit to an interview unless applying for an undertaker's job). Solid colors and pinstripes are both acceptable, so long as the stripes themselves are muted and very narrow. Of the solids, dark gray, navy, or teal blue are equally acceptable. Some feel that a dark solid suit is the best option, because it gives authority to the wearer and is less intimidating than a pinstripe suit.

Men's Shirts

The principles here are simple.

> *Rule One:* Always wear a long-sleeved shirt.
> *Rule Two:* Always wear a white or pale-blue shirt.
> *Rule Three:* Never violate Rules One or Two.

By "white," I do not mean to exclude, for instance, shirts with very thin red or blue pinstripes: these "white" shirts are acceptable, although not really first-rate. There is something about a solid white shirt that conveys honesty, intelligence, and stability; it should be your first choice. It is true that artists, writers, engineers, and other creative types are sometimes known to object to white shirts; for them pale blue may be the best option. Remember that the paler and more subtle the shade, the better the impression you will make.

While monograms are common enough in this country, those who don't accept them usually feel strongly about the implied ostentation of stylized initials on clothing. If you can avoid it, don't take the chance of giving your interviewer the chance to find fault in this area. (On the other hand, if your choice is between wearing your monogrammed shirt or pulling out the old Motley Crue tee-shirt, then your choice should be clear, and so should your conscience.)

Cotton shirts look better and hold up under perspiration more impressively than their synthetic counterparts; if at all possible, opt for a cotton shirt that's been professionally cleaned and starched. A cotton and polyester blend can be an acceptable alternative, but keep in mind that the higher the cotton content, the better the shirt will look. While these blend shirts wrinkle less easily, you are advised to ignore the "wash-and-wear-no-need-to-iron" claims you'll read on the front of the package when you purchase them. Experience has shown that *any* shirt you wear to an interview must be ironed and starched by a professional.

Men's Neckwear: Ties

While an expensive suit can be ruined by a cheap-looking tie, the right tie can do a lot to pull the less-than-perfect suit together for a professional look. When you can't afford a new suit for the interview, you can upgrade your whole look with the right tie.

A pure silk tie makes the most powerful professional impact, has the best finish and feel, and is easiest to tie well. Linen ties are too informal, wrinkle too easily, and may only be worn during warmer weather. (What's more, they can only be tied once between cleanings because they wrinkle so easily.) A wool tie is casual in appearance and has knot problems. Man-made fibers are shiny, make colors look harsh when you want them to look subtle, and may undercut your professional image. A pure silk tie, or a 50-50 wool and silk blend (which is almost wrinkle-proof), should be your choice for the interview.

The tie should complement your suit. This means that there should be a physical balance: the rule of thumb is that the width of your tie should approximate the width of your lapels. The prevailing standard, which has held good for over a decade now, is that ties can range in width between $2\frac{3}{4}$" and $3\frac{1}{2}$". Wearing anything wider may mark you as someone still trapped in the disco era.

While the tie should complement the suit, it should not *match* it. You would never, for instance, wear a navy blue tie with a navy blue suit. Choose an appropriate tie that neither vanishes into nor does battle with your suit pattern; the most popular and safest styles are found within the categories of solids, foulards, stripes, and paisleys.

Do not wear ties with large polka dots, pictures of animals such as leaping trout or soaring mallards, or sporting symbols such as golf clubs or (God forbid) little men on polo ponies. Never wear any piece of apparel that has a manufacturer's symbol emblazoned on the front as part of the decoration. It is difficult to project an image of competent, balanced professionalism when you are acting as a walking billboard for some fashion designer.

Other considerations include the length of the tie (it should, when tied, extend to your trouser belt), the size of the knot (smaller is better), and whether you should wear a bow tie to an interview (you shouldn't).

Men's Shoes

Shoes should be either black leather or brown leather. Stay away from all other materials and colors: They are too risky.

Lace-up wing tips are the most conservative choice and are almost universally acceptable. Slightly less conservative, but equally appropriate, are slip-on dress shoes—not to be confused with boating shoes. The slip-on, with its low, plain vamp or tassel, is versatile enough to be used for both day and evening business wear. (The lace-up wing tip can look a bit cloddish at dinner.)

In certain areas of the South, Southwest, and West, heeled cowboy boots are not at all unusual for business wear neither are those Grand Ole Opry versions of the business suit. But beware: Outside of such specifically defined areas, you will attract only puzzled stares—and few if any professional career opportunities—with these wardrobe selections.

Men's Socks

Socks should complement the suit; accordingly, they are likely to be blue, black, gray, or brown. They should also be long enough for you to cross your legs without showing off lots of bare shin, and should not fall in a bunch toward the ankle as you move. Elastic-reinforced, over-the-calf socks are your best bet.

Men's Accessories

The right accessories can enhance the professional image of any applicant, male or female; the wrong accessories can destroy it.

The guiding principle here is to include nothing that could conceivably be misconstrued or leave a bad impression. Never, for instance, should you wear religious or political insignias in the form of rings, ties, or pins. If you would not initiate a conversation about such topics at a job interview (and you shouldn't), why send smoke signals asking your interviewer to do so?

The watch you wear should be simple and plain. This means Mickey Mouse is out, as are sports-oriented and Swatch-style watches. No one is impressed by digital watches these days; don't be afraid to wear a simple analog model with a leather strap. (Besides, you don't want people wondering whether you can really tell time, do you?) Avoid cheap-looking pseudo-gold watchbands at all costs.

Your briefcase, if you carry one, can make a strong professional statement about you. Leather makes the best impression, while all other materials follow far behind. Brown and burgundy are the colors of choice. The case itself should be plain, although some very expensive models offer a host of embellishments that only detract from the effect you want.

A cotton or linen handkerchief should be part of every job hunter's wardrobe. Plain white is best. Your handkerchief can also be used to relieve the clammy-hands syndrome so common before the interview. Anything to avoid the infamous "wet fish" handshake!

(By the way, avoid the matching-tie-and-pocket-square look at all costs. It's hideous and inappropriate for a professional interview.)

Belts should match or complement the shoes you select. Accordingly, a blue, black, or gray suit will require a black belt and black shoes, while brown, tan, or beige suits will call for brown. With regard to materials, stick with plain leather. The most common mistake made with belts is the buckle: an interview is not the place for your favorite Harley Davidson, Grateful Dead, or Bart Simpson buckle. Select a small, simple buckle that doesn't overwhelm the rest of your look.

Jewelry

Men may wear a wedding band, if applicable, and a small pair of subdued cufflinks (if wearing French cuffs, of course). Anything more is dangerous. Even fraternity rings—much less bracelets, neck chains, or medallions—can send the wrong message.

Overcoats

The safest and most utilitarian colors for overcoats are beige and blue; stick to these two exclusively. If you can avoid wearing an overcoat, do so (it's an encumbrance and adds to clutter).

Makeup

It is inadvisable for a man to wear makeup to an interview or at any other time during his professional life.

Women

Following are the best current dress guidelines for women preparing for a professional interview.

Women's Suits

You have more room for creativity in this area than men do, but also more room for mistakes. Of course, your creativity must stay within certain accepted guidelines created not by me, nor even by the fashion industry, but by the consensus of the business world. And that is a world, alas, that tends to trail behind the rest of us, and so the options for imaginative masterstrokes are limited.

Limit your creativity to materials, patterns, and cuts. A woman's business wardrobe need no longer be simply a pseudo-male selection of drab grey skirts and blouses. (Recent advice that women should avoid pinstripes or ties is probably insecure and dated. With the right cuts, pinstripes and ties can look both stylish and professional.)

Wool and linen are both accepted as the right look for professional women's suits, but there is a problem. Wool wrinkles so quickly that you may feel as though you leave the house dressed for success and arrive at your destination destined for bag-ladyhood. Cotton-polyester blends are great for warm climates: They look like linen but lack the "wrinklability" factor.

Combinations of synthetics and natural fabrics do have their advantages: suits made of such material will certainly retain their shape better. The eye trained to pay attention to detail, however, (read: your interviewers') may well detect the type of fabric, say a cheap polyester blend, and draw unwarranted conclusions about your personality and taste. The choice is up to you; if you do opt for natural fabrics, you will probably want to stay with wool. It provides the smartest look of all, and is most versatile and rugged.

While men are usually limited to either solid or pinstripe suits, a woman can add to this list the varied category of plaids. The Prince of Wales plaid, for instance, is attractive and is utterly acceptable for businesswomen (no doubt because of its regal namesake).

How long a skirt should you wear? Any hard-and-fast rule I could offer here would be in danger of being outdated almost immediately, as the fashion industry demands dramatically different looks every season in order to fuel sales. (After all, keeping the same hemlines would mean that last season's clothes could last another season or two.)

It should go without saying that you don't want to sport something that soars to the upper thigh if you want to be taken seriously as an applicant. Your best bet is to dress somewhat more conservatively than you would if you were simply showing up for work at the organization in question. Hemlines come and go, and while there is some leeway as to what is appropriate for everyday wear on the job, the safest bet is usually to select something that falls just a little below the knee.

Colors most suitable for interview suits include charcoal, medium gray, steel gray, black, and navy blue. All of these look smart with a white blouse. A navy suit can also look good with a gray or beige blouse (but see the notes on blouse color selection below). You may be tempted to select a burgundy blouse with that navy blue outfit, but save it for a dinner date; it is inappropriate at an interview. In the second tier come beige, tan, and camel suits; these look best with blue blouses.

Of all these looks, the cleanest and most professional is the simple solid gray suit (either medium or charcoal) with a white blouse.

Blouses

With regard to blouses, long sleeves will project the authoritative, professional look you desire. Three-quarter-length sleeves are less desirable, and they are followed in turn by short sleeves. *Never* wear a sleeveless blouse to an interview. (You may be confident that there is absolutely no chance that you will be required to remove your jacket, but why take the risk?)

Solid colors and natural fabrics (particularly cotton and silk) are the best selections for blouses. Combinations of natural and synthetic fabrics, while wrinkle-resistant, do not absorb moisture well.

The acceptable color spectrum is wider for blouses than for men's shirts, but it is not limitless. The most prudent choices are still white or pale blue; these offer a universal professional appeal. Pink and gray may also be suitable in certain situations (say, at a "creative" company such as an advertising firm for pink, or at an investment bank in a metropolitan area for gray).

The blouse with a front-tie bow is most acceptable; it always works well with a suit. Asymmetrically-closing blouses, as well as those with the bow at the side, are also good choices for a job interview. The button-down collar always looks great; the more conservative the company/industry, the more positive its impression will be.

Women's Neckwear: Scarves

While a woman might choose to wear a string of pearls instead of a scarf to an interview, the scarf can still serve as a powerful status symbol.

Just as you would expect, a good outfit can be ruined by a cheap-looking scarf. Opting to wear a scarf means that the scarf will be saying something dramatic about you: make sure it's something dramatically positive.

A pure silk scarf will offer a conservative look, a good finish, and ease in tying. Some of the better synthetic blends achieve an overall effect that is almost as good.

While some books on women's clothing will recommend buying blouses that have matching scarves attached to the collar, there is an increasingly vocal lobby of stylish businesswomen who feel this is the equivalent of mandating that a man wear a clip-on bow tie. As with men's ties, the objective is to complement the outfit, not match it. Avoid overly flamboyant styles, and stick with the basics: solids, foulards, small polka dots, or paisleys.

Women's Shoes

Female applicants have a greater color selection in footwear than do their male counterparts. The shoes should still be of leather, but in addition to brown and black a woman is safe in wearing navy, burgundy, black, or even, if circumstances warrant, red.

It is safest to stay away from faddish or multicolored shoes (even such classics as two-toned oxfords). There are two reasons for this: First, all fashion is transitory, and even if you are up-to-date, you cannot assume that your interviewer is; second, many interviewers are male and thus likely to exhibit an inability to appreciate vivid color combinations. As with the rest of your wardrobe, stay away from radical choices and opt for the easily comprehensible professional look.

Heel height is important, as well. Flats are fine; a shoe with a heel of up to about $1\frac{1}{2}$" is perfectly acceptable. Stay away from high heels: At best you will wobble slightly, and at worst you will walk at an angle. Unless you're an Olympic ski jumper, it's hard to maintain an "in-control" image when you are tipped forward at a forty-five degree angle!

The pump or court shoe, with its closed toe and heel, is perhaps the safest and most conservative look. A closed heel with a slightly open toe is acceptable, too, as is the sling-back shoe with a closed toe.

Stockings or Pantyhose

These should not make a statement of their own. Select neutral skintones in most cases. You may be an exception if you are interviewing for a job in the fashion industry, in which case you might coordinate colors with your outfit, but be very sure of the company standard already in place. Even in such an instance, avoid loud or glitzy looks. A bold black, of course, is out entirely.

Pantyhose and stockings are prone to developing runs at the worst possible moment. Keep an extra pair in your purse or briefcase.

Accessories

Because a briefcase is a symbol of authority, it is an excellent choice for the female applicant. Do not, however, bring both your purse and a briefcase to the interview. (You'll look awkward juggling them around.) Instead, transfer essential items to a small clutch bag you can store in the case. In addition to brown and burgundy (recommended colors for the men), you may include blue and black as possible colors for your case, which should be free of expensive and distracting embellishments.

With regard to belts, the advice given for men holds for women as well. Belts should match or complement the shoes you select; a blue, black, or grey suit will require a black belt and black shoes, while brown, tan, or beige suits will call for brown. In addition, women may wear snakeskin, lizard, and the like. Remember that the belt is a functional item; if it is instantly noticeable, it is wrong.

Jewelry

As far as jewelry goes, less is more. A woman should restrict rings to engagement or wedding bands if these are applicable, but she can wear a necklace and earrings, as long as these are subdued and professional-looking. (I should note that some men are put off by earrings of any description in the workplace, so if you wear them keep them small, discreet, and in good taste. Avoid fake or strangely colored pearls, anything with your name or initials on it, and earrings that dangle or jangle.) In addition, a single bracelet on the woman's wrist is acceptable; anything around the ankle is not. Remember, too much of the wrong kind of jewelry can keep a woman from receiving an offer she might otherwise receive, or inhibit her promotional opportunities once on the team.

Makeup

Take care never to appear overly made-up. Natural is the key word; eye makeup should be subtle, so as not to overwhelm the rest of the face. As a general rule, I advise against lipstick at an interview because it can cause negative reactions in some interviewers, and because it can smudge and wear off, as the hours wear on. (Who can say, going in, how long the meeting will last?) However, as women advance into their thirties and beyond, the natural pinkness of the lips can fade; you might feel you look pale and washed out without lipstick. So if you feel "undressed" without your lipstick, use some; but apply it sparingly and carefully, using a subdued color.

For Men and Women: A Note on Personal Hygiene

It should go without saying that bad breath, dandruff, body odor, and dirty nails have the potential to undo all your efforts at putting across a good first impression. These and related problems denote an underlying professional slovenliness, which an interviewer will feel is likely to reflect itself in your work. You want to show yourself to be appealing, self-respecting, and enjoyable to be around. You can't do that if the people you meet with have to call on exceptional powers of self-control in order to stay in the same room with you. (For a more detailed discussion of personal hygiene, see chapter 27.)

Don't ask yourself whether any friend or colleague has actually come out and suggested that you pay more attention to these matters; ask yourself how you felt the last time *you* had to conduct business of any sort with a person who had a hygiene problem. Then resolve never to leave that kind of impression.

11.
Body Language

Given the choice of going blind or going deaf, which would you choose?

If you are like nine out of ten other people, you would choose to go deaf. The vast majority of us rely to a remarkable degree on our ability to gather information visually. This really is not all that surprising: While speech is a comparatively recent development, humans have been sending and receiving nonverbal signals from the dawn of the species.

In fact, body language is one of the earliest methods of communication we learn after birth. We master the spoken word later in life, and in so doing we forget the importance of nonverbal cues. But the signals are still sent and received (usually at a subconscious level), even if most of us discount their importance.

It is common to hear people say of the body language they use, "Take me or leave me as I am." This is all very well if you have no concern for what others think of you. For those seeking professional employment, however, it is of paramount importance that the correct body language be utilized. If your mouth says "Hire me," but your body says something quite different, you are likely to leave the interviewer confused. "Well," he or she will think, "the right answers all came out, but there was something about that candidate that just rubbed me the wrong way." Such misgivings are generally sufficient to keep any candidate from making the short list.

When we are in stressful situations (and a job interview is certainly right there in Stress Hell), our bodies react accordingly. The way they react can send unintentional negative messages. The interviewer may or may not be aware of what causes the concern, but the messages will be sent, and our cause will suffer.

Of course, interviewers can be expected to listen carefully to what we say, too. When our body language doesn't contradict our statements, we will generally be given credence. When our body language complements our verbal statements, our message will gain a great deal of impact. But when our body language *contradicts* what we say, it is human nature for the interviewer to be skeptical. In short, learning to control negative body movements during an interview—and learning to use positive body signals—will greatly increase the chances for job interview success.

Under the Microscope

What is the interviewer watching us for during the interview? The answer is: clues. The mystery for the interviewer is, what kind of an employee would we make? It is incumbent on us to provide not just any old clues but the ones most likely to prompt a decision to hire.

Let's begin at the beginning. When we are invited in to an interview, we are probably safe in assuming that our interviewer believes we meet certain minimum standards, and could conceivably be hired. (Otherwise, why take the time to interview?) Once in the door, we can assume that we will be scrutinized in three main areas:

- Ability (Can we do the job?)
- Willingness (Will we do the job?)
- Manageability (Will we be a pleasure or a pain to have around?)

Appropriate control and use of our gestures can help us emphasize positive features of our personality in these key areas—and also project integrity, honesty, attention to detail, and the like.

The old adage that actions speak louder than words appears to be something we should take quite literally. Studies done at the University of Chicago found that over 50 percent of all effective communication relies on body language. Since we can expect interviewers to respond to the body language we employ at the interview, it is up to us to decide what messages we want them to receive.

There are also studies that suggest that the impression we create in the first few minutes of the interview are the most lasting. Since the first few minutes after we meet the interviewer is a time when he or she is doing the vast majority of the talking, we have very little control over the impression we create with our words: We can't say much of anything! It is up to our bodies, then, to do the job for us.

The Greeting

Giving a "dead fish" handshake will not advance one's candidacy; neither will the opposite extreme, the iron-man bonecrusher grip.

The ideal handshake starts before the meeting actually occurs. Creating the right impression with the handshake is a three-step process. Be sure that:

1. Your hands are clean and adequately manicured.

2. Your hands are warm and reasonably free of perspiration. (There are a number of ways to ensure this, including washing hands in warm water at the interview site, holding one's hand close to the cheek for a few seconds, and even applying a little talcum powder.)

3. The handshake itself is executed professionally and politely, with a firm grip and a warm smile.

Remember that if you initiate the handshake, you may send the message that you have a desire to dominate the interview; this is not a good impression to leave with one's potential boss. Better to wait a moment and allow the interviewer to initiate the shake. (If for any reason you do find yourself initiating the handshake, do not pull back; if you do, you will appear indecisive. Instead, make the best of it, smile confidently, and make good eye contact.)

The handshake should signal cooperation and friendliness. Match the pressure extended by the interviewer—never exceed it. Ideally, the handshake should last for between three and five seconds, and should "pump" for no more than six times. (The parting handshake may last a little longer. Smile and lean forward very slightly as you shake hands before departing.)

Certain cultural and professional differences should be considered with regard to handshakes, as well. Many doctors, artists, and others who do delicate work with their hands can and do give less enthusiastic handshakes than other people. Similarly, the English handshake is considerably less firm than the American, while the German variety is more firm.

Use only one hand; always shake vertically. Do not extend your hand parallel to the floor, with the palm up, as this conveys submissiveness. By the same token, you may be seen as being too aggressive if you extend your flat hand outward with the palm facing down.

Taking Your Seat

> *Some thirty inches from my nose*
> *The frontier of my person goes.*
> *Beware of rudely crossing it;*
> *I have no gun, but I can spit.*
> (With apologies to W.H. Auden.)

Encroaching on another's "personal zone" is a bad idea in any business situation, but it is particularly dangerous in an interview. The thirty-inch standard is a good one to follow: It is the distance that allows you to extend your hand comfortably for a handshake. Maintain this distance throughout the interview, and be particularly watchful of intrusions during the early stages when you meet, greet, and take a seat.

Applying this principle may seem simple enough, but how often have you found yourself dodging awkwardly in front of someone to take a seat before it has been offered? A person's office is an extension of sorts of his personal zone; this is why it is not only polite but also sound business sense to wait until the interviewer offers you a seat.

It is not uncommon to meet with an interviewer in a conference room or other supposedly "neutral" site. Again, wait for the interviewer to motion you to a spot, or, if you feel uncomfortable doing this, tactfully ask the interviewer to take the initiative: "Where would you like me to sit?"

Facial/Head Signals

Once you take your seat, you can expect the interviewer to do most of the talking. You can also probably expect your nervousness to be at its height. Accordingly, you must be particularly careful about the nonverbal messages you send at this stage.

Now, while all parts of the body are capable of sending positive and negative signals, the head (including the eyes and mouth) is under closest scrutiny. Most good interviewers will make an effort to establish and maintain eye contact, and thus you should expect that whatever messages you are sending from the facial region will be picked up, at least on a subliminal level.

Our language is full of expressions testifying to the powerful influence of facial signals. When we say that someone is shifty-eyed, is tight-lipped, has a furrowed brow, flashes bedroom eyes, stares into space, or grins like a Cheshire cat, we are speaking in a kind of shorthand, and using a set of stereotypes that enables us to make judgments—consciously or unconsciously—about the person's abilities and qualities. Those judgments may not be accurate, but they are usually difficult to reverse.

Tight smiles and tension in the facial muscles often bespeak an inability to handle stress; little eye contact can communicate a desire to hide something; pursed lips are often associated with a secretive nature; and frowning, looking sideways, or peering over one's glasses can send signals of haughtiness and arrogance. Hardly the stuff of which winning interviews are made!

The Eyes

Looking at someone means showing interest in that person, and showing interest is a giant step forward in making the right impression. (Remember, each of us is our own favorite subject!)

Your aim should be to stay with a calm, steady, and nonthreatening gaze. It is easy to mismanage this, and so you may have to practice a bit to overcome the common hurdles in this area. Looking away from the interviewer for long periods while he is talking, closing your eyes while being addressed, repeatedly shifting focus from the subject to some other point: These are likely to leave the wrong impression.

Of course, there is a big difference between looking and staring at someone! Rather than looking the speaker straight-on at all times, create a mental triangle incorporating both eyes and the mouth; your eyes will follow a natural, continuous path along the three points. Maintain this approach for roughly three-quarters of the time; you can break your gaze to look at the interviewer's hands as points are emphasized, or to refer to your note pad. These techniques will allow you to leave the impression that you are attentive, sincere, and committed. Staring will only send the message that you are aggressive or belligerent.

Be wary of breaking eye contact too abruptly, and of shifting your focus in ways that will disrupt the atmosphere of professionalism. Examining the interviewer below the head and shoulders, for instance, is a sign of overfamiliarity. (This is an especially important point to keep in mind when being interviewed by someone of the opposite sex.)

The eyebrows send messages as well. Under stress, one's brows may wrinkle; as we have seen, this sends a negative signal about our ability to handle challenges in the business world. The best advice on this score is simply to take a deep breath and collect yourself. Most of the tension that people feel at interviews has to do with anxiety about how to respond to what the interviewer will ask. As a reader of *Knock 'em Dead*, you will be prepared with credible responses for even the toughest queries. Relax.

The Head

Rapidly nodding your head can leave the impression that you are impatient and eager to add something to the conversation—if only the interviewer would let you. Slower nodding, on the other hand, emphasizes interest, shows that you are validating the comments of your interviewer, and subtly encourages him to continue. Tilting the head slightly, when combined with eye contact and a natural smile, demonstrates friendliness and approachability. The tilt should be momentary and not exaggerated, almost like a bob of the head to one side. (Do not overuse this technique!)

The Mouth

One guiding principle of good body language is to turn upward rather than downward. Look at two boxers after a fight: the loser is slumped forward, brows knit and eyes downcast, while the winner's smiling face is thrust upward and outward. The victor's arms are raised high, his back is straight, his shoulders are square. In the first instance the signals we receive are those of anger, frustration, belligerence, and defeat; in the second, happiness, openness, warmth, and confidence.

Your smile is one of the most powerful positive body signals in your arsenal; it best exemplifies the up-is-best principle, as well. Offer an unforced, confident smile as frequently as opportunity and circumstances dictate. *Avoid at all costs* the technique some applicants use: grinning idiotically for the length of the interview, no matter what. This will only communicate that you are either insincere or not quite on the right track.

It's worth remembering that the mouth provides a seemingly limitless supply of opportunities to convey weakness. This may be done by touching the mouth frequently (and, typically, unconsciously); "faking" a cough when confronted with a difficult question; and/or gnawing on one's lips absentmindedly. Employing any of these "insincerity signs" when you are asked about, say, why you lost your last job, will confirm or instill suspicions about your honesty and effectiveness.

Glasses

Those who wear glasses sometimes leave them off when going on an interview in an attempt to project a more favorable image. There are two main difficulties with this. The first is that farsighted people who don't wear their glasses will (unwittingly) seem to stare long and hard at the people they converse with, and this, as we have seen, is a negative signal. The second problem is that leaving the glasses at home—even if you replace them with contacts—will actually undercut your cause in most cases. Many studies have shown that those who wear glasses are perceived as being more intelligent than those who don't. Why not take advantage of this effect? The issue is really not *whether* you should wear your glasses—you should—but how best to make them work for you.

Peering over the top of your glasses—even if you wear reading glasses and have been handed something to read and subsequently asked a question—carries professorial connotations that are frequently interpreted as critical. (If you wear glasses for reading, you should remove them when conversing, replacing them only when appropriate.)

Wearing dark glasses to an interview will paint you as secretive, cold, and devious. Even if your prescription glasses are tinted, the effect will be the same. Try to obtain nontinted glasses for your interview; if you are unable to do so, you are likely to be faced with the only case where contacts are preferable to eyeglasses.

Body-Signal Barricades

Folding or crossing the arms, or holding things in front of the body, is a wonderful way to send negative messages to the interviewer. The signal is, essentially, "I know you're there, but you can't come in. I'm nervous and closed for business."

It is bad enough to feel this way, but worse to express it with blatant signals. Don't fold your arms or "protect" your chest with hands, clipboard, briefcase, or anything else during the interview. (These positions, in fact, should be avoided in any and every business situation.)

Hands

As we have seen, a confident and positive handshake breaks the ice and gets the interview moving in the right direction. Proper use of the hands throughout the rest of the interview will help to convey an above-board, "nothing-to-hide" message.

Watch out for hands and fingers that take on a life of their own, fidgeting with themselves or other objects such as pens, paper, or your hair. Pen tapping is interpreted as the action of an impatient person; this is an example of an otherwise trivial habit that can take on immense significance in an interview situation. (Rarely will an interviewer ask you to stop doing something annoying; instead, he'll simply make a mental note that you are an annoying person, and congratulate himself for picking this up before making the mistake of hiring you.)

Negative hand messages are legion. Some of the most dangerous are listed below.

- You can demonstrate smugness and superiority by clasping your hands behind your head. (You'll also expose any perspiration marks that are under your arms.)

- A man can show insecurity by simply adjusting his tie, and that's not the worst of it: when interviewing with a woman, his gesture will show something other than a businesslike interest in the interviewer.

- Slouching in your chair, with hands in pockets or thumbs in belt, can brand you as insolent and aggressive—and when this error is made in the presence of an interviewer of the opposite sex, it carries sexually aggressive overtones as well. (Beware, too, of sending these signals while you are walking on a tour of the facility.)

- Pulling your collar away from your neck for a moment may seem like an innocent enough reaction to the heat of the day, but the interviewer might assume that you are tense and/or masking an untruth. (The same goes for scratching the neck during, before, or after your response to a question.)
- Moving the hands toward a feature one perceives as deficient is a common unconscious reaction to stress. A man with thinning hair, for example, may thoughtlessly put his hand to his forehead when pondering how to respond to the query, "Why aren't you earning more at your age?" This habit may be extremely difficult for you to detect in the first place, much less reverse, but make the effort. Such protective movements are likely to be perceived—if only on a subliminal level—as acknowledgments of low status.
- Picking at invisible bits of fluff on one's suit looks like what it is: a nervous tic. Keep your focus on the interviewer. (If you do have some bit of lint somewhere on your clothing, the best advice is usually to ignore it rather than call attention to it by brushing it away.)

By contrast, employing the hands in a positive way can further your candidacy. Here are some of the best techniques.

- Subtly exposing your palms now and then as you speak can help to demonstrate that you are open, friendly, and have nothing to hide. (The technique is used to great effect by many politicians and television talk show hosts; watch for it.)
- When considering a question, it can sometimes be beneficial to "steeple" your fingers for a few seconds as you think and when you first start to talk. Unless you hold the gesture for long periods of time, it will be perceived as a neutral demonstration of your thoughtfulness. (Of course, if you overuse this or hold the position for too long, you may be taken as condescending.) Steepling will also give you something constructive to do with your hands; it offers a change from holding your pad and pen.

Seating

The signals you send with your body during an interview can be affected by the type of chair you sit in. If you have a choice, go with an upright chair with arms. Deep armchairs can restrict your ability to send certain positive signals, and encourage the likelihood of negative ones. (They're best suited for watching television, not for projecting the image of a competent professional.)

There is only one way to sit during an interview; bottom well back in the chair and back straight. Slouching, of course, is out, but a slight forward leaning posture will show interest and friendliness toward the interviewer. Keep your hands on the sides of the chair; if there are no arms on the chair, keep your hands in your lap or on your pad of paper.

Crossed legs, in all their many forms, send a mixture of signals; most of them are negative.

- Crossing one ankle over the other knee can show a certain stubborn and recalcitrant outlook (as well as the bottom of your shoe, which is not always a pretty sight). The negative signal is intensified when you grasp the horizontally crossed leg or—worst of all—cross your arms across your chest.

- Crossed ankles have often been assumed to indicate that the person doing the crossing is withholding information. However, some dress fashions encourage decorous ankle crossing. Of course, since the majority of interviews take place across a desk, crossed ankles will often be virtually unnoticeable. The best advice on this body signal is that it is probably the most permissible barrier you can erect; if you must allow yourself one body language vice, this is the one to choose.

- When sitting in armchairs or on sofas, crossing the legs may be necessary to create some stability amid all the plush upholstery. In this instance, the signals you send by crossing your legs will be neutral, as long your crossed legs point toward, rather than away from, the interviewer.

Feet

Some foot signals can have negative connotations. Women and men wearing slip-on shoes should beware of dangling the loose shoe from the toes; this can be quite distracting and, as it is a gesture often used to signal physical attraction, it has no place in a job interview. Likewise, avoid compulsive jabbing of floor, desk, or chair with your foot; this can be perceived as a hostile and angry motion, and is likely to annoy the interviewer.

Walking

Many interviews will require that you walk from point A to point B with the interviewer, either on a guided tour of facilities or to move from one office to another. (Of course, if you are interviewing in a restaurant, you will have to walk with your interviewer to and from the dining facility.) How long these walks last is not as important as how you use them to reinforce positive traits and impressions.

Posture is the first concern. Keep your shoulders back, maintain an erect posture, smile, and make eye contact when appropriate. Avoid fidgeting with your feet as you move, rubbing one shoe against the other, or kicking absentmindedly at the ground as you stand: these signals will lead others to believe that you are anxious and/or insecure. Crossing your arms or legs while standing carries the same negative connotations as it does when you are sitting. Putting your hands in your pockets is less offensive—assuming you don't jangle keys or coins—but men must be careful not to employ the hands-on-hips or thumbs-in-belt postures discussed earlier. These send messages that you are aggressive and dominating.

Seven Signals for Success

So far we have focused primarily on the pitfalls to avoid; but what messages *should* be sent, and how? Here are seven general suggestions on good body language for the interview.

1. Walk slowly, deliberately, and tall upon entering the room.

2. On greeting your interviewer, give (and, hopefully, receive) a friendly "eyebrow flash": that brief, slight raising of the brows that calls attention to the face, encourages eye contact, and (when accompanied by a natural smile) sends a strong positive signal that that interview has gotten off to a good start.

3. Use mirroring techniques. In other words, make an effort—subtly!—to reproduce the positive signals your interviewer sends. (Of course, you should never mirror negative body signals.) Say the interviewer leans forward to make a point; a few moments later, you lean forward slightly in order to hear better. Say the interviewer leans back and laughs; you "laugh beneath" the interviewer's laughter, taking care not to overwhelm your partner by using an inappropriate volume level. This technique may seem contrived at first, but you will learn that it is far from that, if only you experiment a little.

4. Maintain a naturally alert head position; keep your head up and your eyes front at all times.

5. Remember to avert your gaze from time to time so as to avoid the impression that you are staring; when you do so, look confidently and calmly to the right or to the left; never look down.

6. Do not hurry any movement.

7. Relax with every breath.

Putting It All Together

We have discussed the individual gestures that can either improve or diminish your chances of success at the interview. Working in our favor is the fact that positive signals reinforce one another; employing them in combination yields an overwhelming positive message that is truly greater than the sum of its parts. Now it is time to look at how to combine the various positive elements to send a message of competence and professionalism.

Here is the best posture to aim for during the interview.

- Sit well back in the chair; allow the back of it to support you and help you sit upright. Increase the impression of openness ("I have nothing to hide!") by unbuttoning your jacket as you sit down. Keep your head up. Maintain eye contact a good portion of the time, especially when the interviewer begins to speak and when you reply. Smile naturally whenever the opportunity arises. Avoid folding your arms; it is better to keep them on the arms of your chair. Remember to show one or both of your palms occasionally as you make points, but do not overuse this gesture.

Open for Business

The more open your body movements during the interview, the more you will be perceived as open yourself. Understanding and directing your body language will give you added power to turn interviews into cooperative exchanges between two professionals.

Just as you interpret the body language of others, both positive and negative, so your body language makes an indelible impression on those you meet. It tells them whether you like and have confidence in yourself, whether or not you are pleasant to be around, and whether you are more likely to be honest or deceitful. Like it or not, our bodies carry these messages for the world to see.

Job interviews are reliable in one constant: They bring out insecurities in those who must undergo them. All the more reason to consciously manage the impressions the body sends!

12.
The Curtain Goes Up

Backstage in the theater, the announcement "Places, please" is made five minutes before the curtain goes up. It's the performers' signal to psych themselves up, complete final costume adjustments, and make time to reach the stage. They are getting ready to go on stage and knock 'em dead. You should go through a similar process.

Winning that job offer depends not only on the things you do well but also on the absence of things you do poorly. As the interview date approaches, settle down with your resume and the exercises you performed in building it. Immerse yourself in your past successes and strengths. This is a time for building confidence. A little nervousness is perfectly natural and healthy, but channel the extra energy in a positive direction by beginning your physical and mental preparations.

First, you should assemble your interview kit.

- **The company dossier.**
- **Two or three copies of your resume and executive briefing, one for you and one or two for the interviewer.** It is perfectly all right to have your resume in front of you at the interview; it shows that you are organized. It also makes a great cheat sheet (after all, the interviewer is using it for that reason)—you can keep it on your lap during the interview with pad and pencil. It is not unusual to hear, "Mr. Jones wasn't hired because he didn't pay attention to detail and could not even remember his employment dates." And those are just the kinds of things you are likely to forget in the heat of the moment.
- **A pad of paper and writing instruments.** These articles have a twofold purpose. They demonstrate your organization and interest in the job and they give you something constructive to do with your hands during the interview. Bring along a blue or black ballpoint for filling out applications.
- **Contact telephone numbers.** If you get detained on the way to the interview, you can call and let the company representative know.
- **Reference letters**. Take the sensible precaution of gathering these from your employers, on the off-chance they are requested.

- **A list of job-related questions.** During the interview is the time when you gather information to evaluate a job (the actual evaluation comes when you have an offer in hand). At the end of the interview, you will be given the opportunity to ask additional questions. Develop some that help you understand the job's parameters and potential.

     You might ask: "Why is the job open?" "Where does the job lead?" "What is the job's relationship to other departments?" "How do the job and the department relate to the corporate mission?"

For a longer list of questions that might be valuable to ask along those lines, see chapter 23, "Negotiating the Offer." Understand, though, that some of those will obviously only be appropriate in the context of a serious negotiation talk. You can also find good questions to ask in the answer to "Do you have any questions?" at the end of chapter 14.

- **Any additional information you have about the company or the job.** If time permits, ask the interviewer's secretary to send you some company literature. Absorb whatever you can.
- **Directions to the interview.** Decide on your form of transportation and finalize your time of departure. Check the route, distance, and travel time. Write it all down legibly and put it with the rest of your interview kit. If you forget to verify date, time, and place (including floor and suite number), you might not even arrive at the right place, or on the right day, for your interview.

□ □ □

First impressions are the strongest you make, and they are based on your appearance. There is only one way to dress for the first meeting: clean-cut and conservative. You may or may not see yourself that way, but how you see yourself is not important now—your only concern is how others see you. As you could be asked to appear for an interview at a scant couple of hours notice, you must be in a constant state of readiness. Keep your best two suits of clothing freshly cleaned, your shirts or blouses wrinkle-free, and your shoes polished. Never wear these outfits unless you are interviewing.

Here are some more tips:

- Regardless of sex or hairstyle, take it to the lawn doctor once a month.
- While a shower or bath prior to an interview is most desirable, and the use of an unscented deodorant advisable, the wearing of after-shave or perfume should be avoided. You are trying to get hired, not dated.
- You should never drink alcohol the day before an interview. It affects eyes, skin pallor, and your wits.
- Nails should be trimmed and manicured at all times, even if you work with your hands.

□   □   □

To arrive at an interview too early indicates over-anxiousness; to arrive late is inconsiderate. The only sensible solution is to arrive at the interview on time, but at the location early. That allows you time to visit the restroom and make the necessary adjustments to your appearance. Take a couple of minutes in this temporary sanctuary to perform your final mental preparations:

- Review the company dossier.
- Recall the positive things you will say about past employers.
- Breathe deeply and slowly for a minute. This will dispel your natural physical tension.
- Repeat to yourself that the interview will be a success and that afterward the company representatives will wonder how they ever managed without you.
- Smile and head for the interview.

Under no circumstances back out because you do not like the receptionist or the look of the office—that would be allowing interview nerves to get the better of you. As you are shown into the office, you are on!

This potential new employer wants an aggressive and dynamic employee, but someone who is less aggressive and dynamic than he or she is, so take your lead from the interviewer.

Do:

- Give a firm handshake—one shake is enough.
- Make eye contact and smile. Say, "Hello, Ms. Smith. I am John Jones. I have been looking forward to meeting you."

Do not:

- Use first names (unless asked).
- Smoke (even if invited).
- Sit down (until invited).
- Show anxiety or boredom.
- Look at your watch.
- Discuss equal rights, sex, race, national origin, religion, or age.
- Show samples of your work (unless requested).
- Ask about benefits, salary, or vacation.
- Assume a submissive role. Treat the interviewer with respect, but as an equal.

Now you are ready for anything. Except for the tough questions that are going to be thrown at you next.

III

Great Answers
to
Tough
Interview Questions

"**L**ike being on trial for your life" is how many people look at a job interview. They are probably right. With the interviewer as judge and jury, you are at least on trial for your livelihood. Therefore, you must lay the foundation for a winning defense. F. Lee Bailey, America's most celebrated defense attorney, attributes his success in the courtroom to preparation. He likens himself to a magician going into court with fifty rabbits in his hat, not knowing which one he'll really need, but ready to pull out any single one. Bailey is successful because he is ready for any eventuality. He takes the time to analyze every situation and every possible option. He never underestimates his opposition. He is always prepared. F. Lee Bailey usually wins.

Another famous attorney, Louis Nizer, successfully defended all of his fifty-plus capital-offense clients. When lauded as the greatest courtroom performer of his day, Nizer denied the accolade. He claimed for himself the distinction of being the *best prepared*.

You won't win your day in court just based on your skills. As competition for the best jobs increases, employers are comparing more and more applicants for every opening and asking more and more questions. To win against stiff competition, you need more than just your merits. When the race is close, the final winner is often as not picked for a comparative lack of negatives when ranged against the other contenders. Like Bailey and Nizer, you can prove to yourself that the prize always goes to the best prepared.

During an interview, employers may ask you dozens of searching questions. Questions that test your confidence, poise, and desirable personality traits. Questions that trick you into contradicting yourself. Questions that probe your quick thinking and job skills. They are all designed so that the interviewer can make decisions in some critical areas:

- Can you do the job?
- Will you complement or disrupt the department?
- Are you willing to take the extra step?
- Are you manageable?
- Is the money right?

Notice that only one of the critical areas has anything to do with your actual job skills. Being able to do the job is only a small part of getting an offer. Whether you will fit in and make a contribution, and whether you are manageable, are just as important to the interviewer. Those traits the company probes for during the interview are the same that will mark a person for professional growth when on board. In this era of high unemployment and high specialization, companies become more critical in the selection process and look more actively for certain traits, some of which cannot be ascertained by a direct question or answer. Consequently, the interviewer will seek a pattern in your replies that shows your possession of such traits—I discuss them in detail in the next chapter.

The time spent in "court" on trial for your livelihood contains four deadly traps:

- Your failure to listen to the question.
- Annoying the interviewer by answering a question that was not asked.
- Providing superfluous information (you should keep answers brief, thorough, and to the point).
- Attempting to interview without preparation.

The effect of those blunders is cumulative, and each reduces your chances of receiving a job offer.

The number of offers you win in your search for the ideal job depends on your ability to answer a staggering array of questions in terms that have value and relevance to the employer: "Why do you want to work here?" "What are your biggest accomplishments?" "How long will it take you to make a contribution?" "Why should I hire you?" "What can you do for us that someone else cannot do?" "What is your greatest weakness?" "Why aren't you earning more?" and, "What interests you least about this job?" are just some of the questions you will be asked.

The example answers in the following chapters come from across the job spectrum. Though the example answer might come from the mouth of an administrator, while you are a scientist or in one of the service industries, the commonality of all job functions in contributing to the bottom line will help you draw the parallel to your job.

You will also notice that each of the example answers teaches a small yet valuable lesson in good business behavior—something you can use both to get the job and to make a good impression when you are on board.

And remember, the answers provided in the following chapters should not be repeated word for word, exactly as they come off the page. You have your own style of speech (not to mention your own kind of business experience), so try to put the answers in your own words.

13.
The Five Secrets of the Hire

Before we examine the "do's and don'ts" advice on interviewing contained in the next chapter, it's a good idea to review the interview process from the employer's perspective. As we have observed, there is a popular misconception that all that is necessary for success at the interview is for you to show that you have what it takes to do the job. There's a lot more to it than that.

The First Secret: Ability and Suitability
Saying, "Hey, I can do this job—give me a shot and I'll prove it to you" is not enough anymore. Today you have to *prove* ability and suitability.

Every working professional has a combination of skills that broadly define his or her ability and suitability. How well you program that computer, service that client, or sew up that appendix is part of the picture; knowing the steps involved well enough *to be able to explain them clearly and simply to others* is another part.

Itemize your technical/professional skills as they parallel the requirements of the job. Then recall an incident to illustrate each of those skills. When you have done this, and not before, you will be in a position to begin justifying your ability and suitability to an employer.

If you are applying for a job in an industry with which you are familiar, you should also consider highlighting your industry sensibilities. Industry sensibilities means knowing "how we do it here." A good computer programmer working in a bank has technical and professional skills; that is, the ability to program a computer is required by the employer. That same programmer has knowledge of how to get things done *in the industry in which he or she operates*; that is, the ability to work well with bankers, which is quite different than being able to work well with, say, public television fundraisers.

Demonstrating both professional/technical and industry skills will set you apart from the vast majority of candidates. Show that you understand these combinations and you will stand out from the pack.

The Second Secret: Willingness
Ten years ago, if a woman were asked during an interview whether she would be willing to make coffee, she might have experienced some awkwardness in answer-

ing. Nowadays that awkwardness is less common, as she is likely to know that she is within her rights in asking whether the duties were part of her job description. But in doing so, she might be losing an opportunity to demonstrate her readiness to pitch in at any task. This question is being used more and more by potential employers who want to gauge *willingness*—and have no intention of sending applicants off to brew the perfect cup of Good Morning America. Male applicants, too, are well advised to consider an answer along the lines of "Yes, and how would you like your eggs?"

Today, the issue isn't whether you are prepared to do demeaning tasks. It is whether you are the kind of person who is prepared to do whatever it takes to help the team survive and prosper. Can you take the rough with the smooth? Are you prepared to go that extra mile? You are? Great. Think of a time when you did. Figure out how your doing so helped the company. Now rehearse the story until you can tell it in about ninety seconds.

The Third Secret: Manageability and Teamwork

There isn't a manager in the world who enjoys a sleepless night caused by an unmanageable employee. Avoiding such nights is a major concern for managers, who develop, over time, a remarkable sixth sense when it comes to spotting and cutting out mavericks.

Manageability is defined in different ways: the ability to work alone; the ability to work with others; the ability to take direction and criticism when it is carefully and considerately given; and, perhaps dearest to the manager's heart, the ability to take direction when it *isn't* carefully and considerately given, often because of a crisis. Also crucial is a willingness to work with others regardless of their sex, age, religion, physical appearance, abilities or disabilities, skin color, or national origin.

Such "manageability" considerations make a job interview tricky. Yes, you should certainly state your strongly held convictions—after all, you don't want to appear wishy-washy—but you should do so *only as long as they are professional in nature and relate to the job at hand.*

Let me give you an example of what I mean. A number of people have asked me about what they perceive as discrimination as a result of their being born-again Christians. Each discussion invariably ends in the conclusion that a job interview is simply no place to bring up personal beliefs. Today's managers will usually go well out of their way to avoid even the perception of intolerance toward sincerely held spiritual beliefs. Yet, by the same token, they are deeply suspicious of any strident religious rhetoric that surfaces in a professional setting. (This also holds true of political, ethnic, or other inappropriate issues raised by a candidate during an interview.) The potential employer's caution in these circumstances, far from representing discrimination, is a sign of concern that the candidate might not be tolerant of the views of others—and might thereby become an obstacle to a harmonious work group.

The rules here are simple. Don't bring up religious, political, or racial matters during the job interview. Even a casual reference to such topics can put a potential employer on the spot, since he or she could subject the company to a lawsuit if a racial or religious topic is perceived as having influenced a hiring decision. The interview is a potential paycheck; don't mess with it.

You're a team player, someone who gets along well with others and has no problem tolerating other opinions or beliefs. Demonstrate that with your every word and action.

The Fourth Secret: Professional Behavior

I emphasize *professional* behavior throughout this book because, to a large extent, the traits that are most desirable to employers are learned and developed as a result of our experiences in the workplace.

As you will see in the next chapter, there are twenty universally admired behavioral traits common to successful people in all fields. Once you review them, you will no doubt find that they are important to you, too, since just understanding what they are will give you up to twenty unique points to make about your candidacy. But understanding the traits is only part of the secret.

Harry works in Shipping and Receiving. He reads the list of traits, comes across the category labeled "Determination," and thinks, "Yeah, that's me. I'm a determined guy." On its own, though, he knows this is not enough. Then Harry recalls the time he came in over the weekend to clear the warehouse in time to make room for the twenty-ton press due in Monday morning at seven. When he tells this story to the interviewer, he gets a lot further than he would if he simply said, "Hire me; I'm determined." The interviewer, instead of a bland, unsubstantiated claim that would be forgotten almost the instant it left Harry's mouth, gets a mental movie of the event that's hard to forget: Harry coming in on the weekend to make room for that press. Actually, the interviewer *really* sees something much more important, namely Harry applying the same level of determination and extra effort on the behalf of the interviewer's company.

Simple statements don't leave any lasting impression on employers. Anecdotes that prove a point do.

The Fifth Secret: Everyone Hires for the Same Job

Surprised? Here's another, related news flash: No one in the history of industry and commerce has ever been added to a payroll for the love of mankind.

Regardless of job or profession, we are all, at some level, *problem solvers*. That's the first and most important part of the job description for anyone who has ever been hired for any job, at any level, in any organization, anywhere in the world. This fifth secret is absolutely key to job hunting and career success in any field.

Think of your profession in terms of its problem-solving responsibilities. Once you have identified the particular problem-solving business you are in, you will have gone a long way toward isolating what the interviewer will want to talk about. Identify and list for yourself the typical problems you tackle for employers on a daily basis. Come up with plenty of specific examples. Then move on to the *biggest and dirtiest* problems you've been faced with. Again, recall specifically how you solved them.

Here's a technique used by corporate outplacement professionals to help people develop examples of their problem-solving skills and the resulting achievements.

1. *State the problem.* What was the situation? Was it typical of your job, or had something gone wrong? If the latter, be leery of apportioning blame.

2. *Isolate relevant background information.* What special knowledge or education were you armed with to tackle this dilemma?

3. *List your key qualities.* What professional skills and personal behavior traits did you bring into play to solve the problem?

4. *Recall the solution.* How did things turn out in the end? (If the problem did not have a successful resolution, do not use it as an example.)

5. *Determine what the solution was worth.* Quantify the solution in terms of money earned, money saved, or time saved. Specify your role as a team member or as a lone gun, as the facts demand.

With an improved understanding of what employers seek in employees, you will have a better understanding of yourself and what you have to offer in the way of specific problem-solving abilities. If you follow the steps outlined above, you will develop a series of illustrative stories for each key area. Remember, stories help interviewers visualize you solving *their* problems—as a paid member of the team.

Here's a story for you. It's based on a real-life interview pattern, although the names are fictional.

Mr. Wanton Grabbit, eighty-year-old senior partner at the revered Washington law firm of Sue, Grabbit, and Runne, ran a help-wanted advertisement in the Washington *Post* for a word processing specialist. He was looking for someone with five years of experience in W.P. and the same amount working in a legal environment. He also wanted someone with experience in using the office computer system, a Bambleweeney 5000.

Grabbit interviewed ten candidates with exactly the experience the advertisement demanded. Each of them came away from the interview convinced that a job offer was imminent. None of them got the job. The person who did get the job had *three* years of experience and had *never before set foot* inside a law office.

Sue Sharp, the successful candidate, understood the fifth secret and asked a few intelligent questions of her own during the interview. Specifically, she asked, "What are the first projects I will be involved with?" This led Mr. Grabbit to launch into a long discourse on his desire to see the law firm rush headlong into the 20th century by the year 2001. The first project, he explained, would be to load the firm's approximately 4,000 manual files onto the Bambleweeney.

Now, although Sue had never worked in a law firm before, she had, on her last job, automated a cumbersome manual filing system. Having faced the *problem* before, even though she had done so in the "wrong" setting, she was able to demonstrate an understanding of the challenges the position presented. Furthermore, she was able to tell the illustrative stories from her last job that enabled Mr. Grabbit to see her, in his mind's eye, tackling and solving his immediate, specific, short-term problems successfully.

We get two very special benefits when we understand and apply the fifth secret. First, we show that we possess the problem-solving abilities of a first-rate professional in the field. Second, when we ask about the problems, challenges, projects, deadlines, and pressure points that will be tackled in the early months, we show that we will be able to hit the ground running on those first critical projects.

□   □   □

Integrate the five secrets of the hire as you read the rest of this section. You will reap the rewards—while your competition must resign themselves to harvesting sour grapes.

14.
How to Knock 'em Dead

- "Describe a situation where your work or an idea was criticized."
- "Have you done the best work you are capable of doing?"
- "What problems do you have getting along with others?"
- "How long will you stay with the company?"
- "I'm not sure you're suitable for the job."
- "Tell me about something you are not very proud of."
- "What are some of the things your supervisor did that you disliked?"
- "What aspects of your job do you consider most crucial?"

Can you answer all these questions off the top of your head? Can you do it in a way that will set your worth above the other job candidates? I doubt it—they were *designed* to catch you off guard. But they won't after you have read the rest of *Knock 'em Dead*.

Even if you could answer some of them, it would not be enough to assure you of victory: The employer is looking for certain intangible assets as well. Think back to your last job for a moment. Can you recall someone with fewer skills, less professionalism, and less dedication who somehow leveraged his or her career into a position of superiority to you? He or she was able to do that only by cleverly projecting a series of personality traits that are universally sought by all successful companies. Building those key traits into your answers to the interviewer's questions will win you any job and set the stage for your career growth at the new company.

There are twenty universally admired key personality traits; they are your passport to success at any interview. Use them for reference as you customize your answers to the tough questions in the following chapters.

□   □   □

Personal Profile:

The interviewer searches for personal profile keys to determine what type of person you really are. The presence of these keys in your answers tells the company representative how you feel about yourself and your chosen career and what you would be like to work with. Few of them will arise from direct questions—your future employer will search for them in your answers to specific job-performance probes. The following words and phrases are those you will project as part of your successful, healthy personal profile.

- **Drive:** A desire to get things done. Goal-oriented.
- **Motivation:** Enthusiasm and a willingness to ask questions. A company realizes that a motivated person accepts added challenges and does that little bit extra on every job.
- **Communication Skills:** More than ever, the ability to talk and write effectively to people at all levels in a company is a key to success.
- **Chemistry:** The company representative is looking for someone who does not get rattled, wears a smile, is confident without self-importance, gets along with others—who is, in short, a team player.
- **Energy:** Someone who always gives that extra effort in the little things as well as important matters.
- **Determination:** Someone who does not back off when a problem or situation gets tough.
- **Confidence:** Not braggadocio. Poise. Friendly, honest, and open to employees high or low. Not intimidated by the big enchiladas, nor overly familiar.

Professional Profile:

All companies seek employees who respect their profession and employer. Projecting these professional traits will identify you as loyal, reliable, and trustworthy.

- **Reliability:** Following up on yourself, not relying on anyone else to ensure the job is well done, and keeping management informed every step of the way.
- **Honesty/Integrity:** Taking responsibility for your actions, both good and bad. Always making decisions in the best interests of the company, never on whim or personal preference.
- **Pride:** Pride in a job well done. Always taking the extra step to make sure the job is done to the best of your ability. Paying attention to the details.
- **Dedication:** Whatever it takes in time and effort to see a project through to completion, on deadline.
- **Analytical Skills:** Weighing the pros and cons. Not jumping at the first solution to a problem that presents itself. Weighing the short- and long-term benefits of a solution against all its possible negatives.

- **Listening Skills:** Listening and understanding, as opposed to waiting your turn to speak.

Achievement Profile:

Earlier, I discussed that companies have very limited interests: making money, saving money (the same as making money), and saving time (which does both). Projecting your achievement profile, in however humble a fashion, is the key to winning any job.

- **Money Saved:** Every penny saved by your thought and efficiency is a penny earned for the company.
- **Time Saved:** Every moment saved by your thought and efficiency enables your company to save money and make more in the additional time available. Double bonus.
- **Money Earned:** Generating revenue is the goal of every company.

Business Profile:

Projecting your business profile is important on those occasions when you cannot demonstrate ways you have made money, saved money, or saved time for previous employers. These keys demonstrate you are always on the lookout for opportunities to contribute, and that you keep your boss informed when an opportunity arises.

- **Efficiency:** Always keeping an eye open for wastage of time, effort, resources, and money.
- **Economy:** Most problems have two solutions: an expensive one, and the one the company would prefer to implement.
- **Procedures:** Procedures exist to keep the company profitable. Don't work around them. That also means keeping your boss informed. You tell your boss about problems or good ideas, not his or her boss. Follow the chain of command. Do not implement your own "improved" procedures or organize others to do so.
- **Profit:** All the above traits are universally admired in the business world because they relate to profit.

□　□　□

As the requirements of the job are unfolded for you at the interview, meet them point by point with your qualifications. If your experience is limited, stress the appropriate key profile traits (such as energy, determination, motivation), your relevant interests, and your desire to learn. If you are weak in just one particular area, keep your mouth shut—perhaps that dimension will not arise. If the area is probed, be prepared to handle and overcome the negative by stressing skills that compensate and/or demonstrate that you will experience a fast learning curve.

Do not show discouragement if the interview appears to be going poorly. You have nothing to gain by showing defeat, and it could merely be a stress interview tactic to test your self-confidence.

If for any reason you get flustered or lost, keep a straight face and posture; gain time to marshal your thoughts by asking, "Could you help me with that?" or, "Would you run that by me again?" or, "That's a good question; I want to be sure I understand. Could you please explain it again?"

□   □   □

Now it is time for you to study the tough questions. Use the examples and explanations to build answers that reflect your background and promote your skills and attributes.

"What are the reasons for your success in this profession?"

With this question, the interviewer is not so much interested in examples of your success—he or she wants to know what makes you tick. Keep your answers short, general, and to the point. Using your work experience, personalize and use value keys from your personal, professional and business profiles. For example: "I attribute my success to three things: the support I've always received from co-workers, which always encourages me to be cooperative and look at my specific job in terms of what we as a department are trying to achieve. That gives me great pride in my work and its contribution to the department's efforts, which is the second factor. Finally, I find that every job has its problems that need solutions, and while there's always a costly solution, there's usually an economical one as well, whether it's in terms of time or money." Then give an example from your experience that illustrates those points.

"What is your energy level like? Describe a typical day."

You must demonstrate good use of your time, that you believe in planning your day beforehand, and that when it is over, you review your own performance to make sure you are reaching the desired goals. No one wants a part-time employee, so you should sell your energy level. For example, your answer might end with: "At the end of the day when I'm ready to go home, I make a rule always to type one more letter [make one more call, etc.] and clear my desk for the next day."

"Why do you want to work here?"

To answer this question, you must have researched the company and built a dossier. Your research work from chapter 1 is now rewarded. Reply with the company's attributes as you see them. Cap your answer with reference to your belief that the company can provide you with a stable and happy work environment—the company has that reputation—and that such an atmosphere would encourage your best work.

"I'm not looking for just another paycheck. I enjoy my work and am proud of my profession. Your company produces a superior product/provides a superior service. I share the values that make this possible, which should enable me to fit in and complement the team."

"What kind of experience do you have for this job?"

This is a golden opportunity to sell yourself, but before you do, be sure you know what is most critical to the interviewer. The interviewer is not just looking for a competent engineer, typist, or what-have-you—he or she is looking for someone who can contribute quickly to the current projects. When interviewing, companies invariably give everyone a broad picture of the job, but the person they hire will be a problem solver, someone who can contribute to the specific projects in the first six months. Only by asking will you identify the areas of your interviewer's greatest urgency and therefore interest.

If you do not know the projects you will be involved with in the first six months, you must ask. Level-headedness and analytical ability are respected, and the information you get will naturally let you answer the question more appropriately. For example, a company experiencing shipping problems might appreciate this answer: "My high-speed machining background and familiarity with your equipment will allow me to contribute quickly. I understand deadlines, delivery schedules, and the importance of getting the product shipped. Finally, my awareness of economy and profit has always kept reject parts to a bare minimum."

"What are the broad responsibilities of a [e.g.] systems analyst?"

This is suddenly becoming a very popular question with interviewers, and rightly so. There are three layers to it. First, it acknowledges that all employees nowadays are required to be more efficiency- and profit-conscious, and need to know how individual responsibilities fit into the big picture. Second, the answer provides some idea of how much you will have to be taught or reoriented if and when you join the company. Third, it is a very effective knock-out question—if you lack a comprehensive understanding of your job, that's it! You'll be knocked out then and there.

While your answer must reflect an understanding of the responsibilities, be wary of falling afoul of differing corporate jargon. A systems analyst in one company, for instance, may be only a programmer trainee in another. With that in mind, you may wish to preface your answer with, "While the responsibilities of my job title vary somewhat from company to company, at my current/last job, my responsibilities included . . ." Then, in case your background isn't an exact match, ask, "Which areas of relevant expertise haven't I covered?" That will give you the opportunity to recoup.

"Describe how your job relates to the overall goals of your department and company."

This not only probes your understanding of department and corporate missions but also obliquely checks into your ability to function as a team member to get the work done. Consequently, whatever the specifics of your answer, include words to this effect: "The quality of my work directly affects the ability of others to do their work properly. As a team member, one has to be aware of the other players."

"What aspects of your job do you consider most crucial?"

A wrong answer can knock you out of the running in short order. The executive who describes expense reports as the job's most crucial aspect is a case in point. The question is designed to determine time management, prioritization skills, and any inclination for task avoidance.

"Are you willing to go where the company sends you?"

Unfortunately with this one, you are, as the saying goes, damned if you do and damned if you don't. What is the real question? Do they want you to relocate or just travel on business? If you simply answer "no," you will not get the job offer, but if you answer "yes," you could end up in Monkey's Eyebrow, Kentucky. So play for time and ask, "Are you talking about business travel, or is the company relocating?" In the final analysis, your answer should be "yes." You don't have to accept the job, but without the offer you have no decision to make. Your single goal at an interview is to sell yourself and win a job offer. Never forget, only when you have the offer is there a decision to make about that particular job.

"What did you like/dislike about your last job?"

The interviewer is looking for incompatibilities. If a trial lawyer says he or she dislikes arguing a point with colleagues, such a statement will only weaken— if not immediately destroy—his or her candidacy.

Most interviews start with a preamble by the interviewer about the company. Pay attention: That information will help you answer the question. In fact, any statement the interviewer makes about the job or corporation can be used to your advantage.

So, in answer, you liked everything about your last job. You might even say your company taught you the importance of certain keys from the business, achievement, or professional profile. Criticizing a prior employer is a warning flag that you could be a problem employee. No one intentionally hires trouble, and that's what's behind the question. Keep your answer short and positive. You are allowed only one negative about past employers, and then only if your interviewer has a "hot button" about his or her department or company; if so, you will have written it down on your notepad. For example, the only thing your past employer could not offer might be something like "the ability to contribute more in different areas in the smaller environment you have here." You might continue with, "I really liked everything about the job. The reason I want to leave it is to find a position where I can make a greater contribution. You see, I work for a large company that encourages specialization of skills. The smaller environment you have here will, as I said, allow me to contribute far more in different areas." Tell them what they want to hear—replay the hot button.

Of course, if you interview with a large company, turn it around. "I work for a small company and don't get the time to specialize in one or two major areas." Then replay the hot button.

"What is the least relevant job you have held?"

If your least relevant job is not on your resume, it shouldn't be mentioned. Some people skip over those six months between jobs when they worked as soda jerks just to pay the bills, and would rather not talk about it, until they hear a question like this one. But a mention of a job that, according to all chronological records, you never had, will throw your integrity into question and your candidacy out the door.

Apart from that, no job in your profession has been a waste of time if it increases your knowledge about how the business works and makes money. Your answer will include: "Every job I've held has given me new insights into my profession, and the higher one climbs, the more important the understanding of the lower-level, more menial jobs. They all play a role in making the company profitable. And anyway, it's certainly easier to schedule and plan work when you have first-hand knowledge of what others will have to do to complete their tasks."

"What have you learned from jobs you have held?"

Tie your answer to your business and professional profile. The interviewer needs to understand that you seek and can accept constructive advice, and that your business decisions are based on the ultimate good of the company, not your personal whim or preference. "More than anything, I have learned that what is good for the company is good for me. So I listen very carefully to directions and always keep my boss informed of my actions."

"How do you feel about your progress to date?"

This question is not geared solely to rate your progress; it also rates your self-esteem (personal profile keys). Be positive, yet do not give the impression you have already done your best work. Make the interviewer believe you see each day as an opportunity to learn and contribute, and that you see the environment at this company as conducive to your best efforts.

"Given the parameters of my job, my progress has been excellent. I know the work, and I am just reaching that point in my career when I can make significant contributions."

"Have you done the best work you are capable of doing?"

Say "yes," and the interviewer will think you're a has-been. As with all these questions, personalize your work history. For this particular question, include the essence of this reply: "I'm proud of my professional achievements to date, especially [give an example]. But I believe the best is yet to come. I am always motivated to give my best efforts, and in this job there are always opportunities to contribute when you stay alert."

"How long would you stay with the company?"

The interviewer might be thinking of offering you a job. So you must encourage him or her to sell you on the job. With a tricky question like this, end your answer with a question of your own that really puts the ball back in the interviewer's court. Your reply might be: "I would really like to settle down with this company. I take direction well and love to learn. As long as I am growing professionally, there is no reason for me to make a move. How long do you think I would be challenged here?"

"How long would it take you to make a contribution to our company?"

Again, be sure to qualify the question: In what area does the interviewer need rapid contributions? You are best advised to answer this with a question: "That is an excellent question. To help me answer, what do you anticipate my responsibilities will be for the first six or seven months?" or, "What are your greatest areas of need right now?" You give yourself time to think while the interviewer concentrates on images of you working for the company. When your time comes to answer, start with: "Let's say I started on Monday the 17th. It will take me a few weeks to settle down and learn the ropes. I'll be earning my keep very quickly, but making a real contribution . . . [give a hesitant pause] Do you have a special project in mind you will want me to get involved with?" That response could lead directly to a job offer, but if not, you already have the interviewer thinking of you as an employee.

"What would you like to be doing five years from now?"

The safest answer contains a desire to be regarded as a true professional and team player. As far as promotion, that depends on finding a manager with whom you can grow. Of course, you will ask what opportunities exist within the company before being any more specific: "From my research and what you have told me about the growth here, it seems operations is where the heavy emphasis is going to be. It seems that's where you need the effort and where I could contribute toward the company's goals." Or, "I have always felt that first-hand knowledge and experience open up opportunities that one might never have considered, so while at this point in time I plan to be a part of [e.g.] operations, it is reasonable to expect that other exciting opportunities will crop up in the meantime."

"What are your qualifications?"

Be sure you don't answer the wrong question. Does the interviewer want job-related or academic job qualifications? Ask. If the question concerns job-related information, you need to know what problems must be tackled first before you can answer adequately. If you can determine this, you will also know what is causing the manager most concern. Then, if you can show yourself as someone who can contribute to the solution of those projects/problems, you have taken a dramatic step ahead in the race for the job offer. Ask for clarification, then use appropriate value keys from all four categories tied in with relevant skills and achievements. You might say: "I can give you a general answer, but I feel my answer might be more valuable if you could tell me about specific work assignments in the early months."

Or: "If the major task right now is to automate the filing system, I should tell you that in my last job I was responsible for creating a computerized database for a previously uncomputerized firm."

"What are your biggest accomplishments?"

Keep your answers job related; from earlier exercises, a number of achievements should spring to mind. If you exaggerate contributions to major projects, you will be accused of suffering from "coffee machine syndrome," the affliction of a junior clerk who claimed success for an Apollo space mission based on his relationships with certain scientists, established at the coffee machine. You might begin your reply with: "Although I feel my biggest achievements are still ahead of me, I am proud of my involvement with . . . I made my contribution as part of that team and learned a lot in the process. We did it with hard work, concentration, and an eye for the bottom line."

"How do you organize and plan for major projects?"

Effective planning requires both forward thinking ("Who and what am I going to need to get this job done?") and backward thinking ("If this job must be completed by the twentieth, what steps must be made, and at what time, to achieve it?"). Effective planning also includes contingencies and budgets for time and cost overruns. Show that you cover all the bases.

"How many hours a week do you find it necessary to work to get your job done?"

No absolutely correct answer here, so again, you have to cover all the bases. Some managers pride themselves on working nights and weekends, or on never taking their full vacation quota. Others pride themselves on their excellent planning and time management that allows them never to work more than regular office hours. You must pick the best of both worlds: "I try to plan my time effectively and usually can. Our business always has its rushes, though, so I put in whatever effort it takes to get the job finished." It is rare that the interviewer will then come back and ask for a specific number of hours. If that does happen, turn the question around: "It depends on the projects. What is typical in your department?" The answer will give you the right cue, of course.

"Tell me how you moved up through the organization."

A fast-track question, the answer to which tells a lot about your personality, your goals, your past, your future, and whether you still have any steam left in you. The answer might be long, but try to avoid rambling. Include a fair sprinkling of your key personality traits in your stories (because this is the perfect time to do it). As well as listing the promotions, you will want to demonstrate that they came as a result of dedicated, long-term effort, substantial contributions, and flashes of genius.

"Can you work under pressure?"

You might be tempted to give a simple yes or no answer, but don't. It reveals nothing, and you lose the opportunity to sell your skills and value profiles. Actually, this common question often comes from an unskilled interviewer, because it is closed-ended. (How to handle different types of interviewers is covered in chapter 16, "The Other Side of the Desk.") As such, the question does not give you the chance to elaborate. Whenever you are asked a closed-ended question, mentally add: "Please give me a brief yet comprehensive answer." Do that, and you will give the information requested and seize an opportunity to sell yourself. For example, you could say: "Yes, I usually find it stimulating. However, I believe in planning and proper management of my time to reduce panic deadlines within my area of responsibility."

"What is your greatest strength?"

Isolate high points from your background and build in a couple of the key value profiles from different categories. You will want to demonstrate pride, reliability, and the ability to stick with a difficult task yet change course rapidly when required. You can rearrange the previous answer here. Your answer in part might be: "I believe in planning and proper management of my time. And yet I can still work under pressure."

"What are your outstanding qualities?"

This is essentially the same as an interviewer asking you what your greatest strengths are. While in the former question you might choose to pay attention to job-specific skills, this question asks you to talk about your personality profile. Now, although you are fortunate enough to have a list of the business world's most desirable personality traits at the beginning of this chapter, try to do more than just list them. In fact, rather than offering a long "laundry list," you might consider picking out just two or three and giving an illustration of each.

"What interests you most about this job?"

Be straightforward, unless you haven't been given adequate information to determine an answer, in which case you should ask a question of your own to clarify. Perhaps you could say, "Before answering, could I ask you to tell me a little more about the role this job plays in the departmental goals?" or, "Where is the biggest vacuum in your department at the moment?" or, "Could you describe a typical day for me?" The additional information you gather with those questions provides the appropriate slant to your answer—that is, what is of greatest benefit to the department and to the company. Career-wise, that obviously has the greatest benefit to you, too. Your answer then displays the personality traits that support the existing need. Your answer in part might include, "I'm looking for a challenge and an opportunity to make a contribution, so if you feel the biggest challenge in the department is _____, I'm the one for the job." Then include the personality traits and experience that support your statements. Perhaps: "I like a challenge, my background demonstrates excellent problem-solving abilities [give some examples], and I always see a project through to the finish."

"What are you looking for in your next job?"

You want a company where your personal profile keys and professional profile keys will allow you to contribute to business value keys. Avoid saying what you want the company to give you; you must say what you want in terms of what you can give to your employer. The key word in the following example is "contribution": "My experience at the XYZ Corporation has shown me I have a talent for motivating people. That is demonstrated by my team's absenteeism dropping 20 percent, turnover steadying at 10 percent, and production increasing 12 percent. I am looking for an opportunity to continue that kind of contribution, and a company and supervisor who will help me develop in a professional manner."

"Why should I hire you?"

Your answer will be short and to the point. It will highlight areas from your background that relate to current needs and problems. Recap the interviewer's description of the job, meeting it point by point with your skills. Finish your answer with: "I have the qualifications you need [itemize them], I'm a team player, I take direction, and I have the desire to make a thorough success."

"What can you do for us that someone else cannot do?"

This question will come only after a full explanation of the job has been given. If not, qualify the question with: "What voids are you trying to eradicate when you fill this position?" Then recap the interviewer's job description, followed with: "I can bring to this job a determination to see projects through to a proper conclusion. I listen and take direction well. I am analytical and don't jump to conclusions. And finally, I understand we are in business to make a profit, so I keep an eye on cost and return." End with: "How do these qualifications fit your needs?" or, "What else are you looking for?"

You finish with a question that asks for feedback or a powerful answer. If you haven't covered the interviewer's hot buttons, he or she will cover them now, and you can respond accordingly.

"Describe a difficult problem you've had to deal with."

This is a favorite tough question. It is not so much the difficult problem that's important—it's the approach you take to solving problems in general. It is designed to probe your professional profile; specifically, your analytical skills.

"Well, I always follow a five-step format with a difficult problem. One, I stand back and examine the problem. Two, I recognize the problem as the symptom of other, perhaps hidden, factors. Three, I make a list of possible solutions to the problem. Four, I weigh both the consequences and cost of each solution, and determine the best solution. And five, I go to my boss, outline the problem, make my recommendation, and ask for my superior's advice and approval."

Then give an example of a problem and your solution. Here is a thorough example: "When I joined my present company, I filled the shoes of a manager who had been fired. Turnover was very high. My job was to reduce turnover and increase performance. Sales of our new copier had slumped for the fourth quarter in a row, partly due to ineffective customer service. The new employer was very concerned, and he even gave me permission to clean house. The cause of the problem? The customer-service team never had any training. All my people needed was some intensive training. My boss gave me permission to join the American Society for Training and Development, which cost $120. With what I learned there, I turned the department around. Sales continued to slump in my first quarter. Then they sky-rocketed. Management was pleased with the sales and felt my job in customer service had played a real part in the turnaround; my boss was pleased because the solution was effective and cheap. I only had to replace two customer-service people."

"What would your references say?"

You have nothing to lose by being positive. If you demonstrate how well you and your boss got along, the interviewer does not have to ask, "What do you dislike about your current manager?"

It is a good idea to ask past employers to give you a letter of recommendation. That way, you know what is being said. It reduces the chances of the company representative checking up on you, and if you are asked this question, you can pull out a sheaf of rousing accolades and hand them over. If your references are checked by the company, it must by law have your written permission. That permission is usually included in the application form you sign. All that said, never offer references or written recommendations unless they are requested.

"Can we check your references?"

This question is frequently asked as a stress question to catch the too-smooth candidate off guard. It is also occasionally asked in the general course of events. Comparatively few managers or companies ever check references—that astounds me, yet it's a fact of life. On the other hand, the higher up the corporate ladder you go, the more likely it is that your references will be checked.

There is only one answer to this question if you ever expect to get an offer: "Yes."

Your answer may include: "Yes, of course you can check my references. However, at present, I would like to keep matters confidential, until we have established a serious mutual interest [i.e., an offer]. At such time I will be pleased to furnish you with whatever references you need from prior employers. I would expect you to wait to check my current employer's references until you have extended an offer in writing, I have accepted, we have agreed upon a start date, and I have had the opportunity to resign in a professional manner." You are under no obligation to give references of a current employer until you have a written offer in hand. You are also well within your rights to request that reference checks of current employers wait until you have started your new job.

"What type of decisions did you make on your last job?"

Your answer should include reference to the fact that your decisions were all based on appropriate business profile keys. The interviewer may be searching to define your responsibilities, or he or she may want to know that you don't overstep yourself. It is also an opportunity, however humble your position, to show your achievement profile.

For example: "Being in charge of the mailroom, my job is to make sure people get information in a timely manner. The job is well defined, and my decisions aren't that difficult. I noticed a year or two ago that when I took the mail around at

10 a.m., everything stopped for twenty minutes. I had an idea and gave it to my boss. She got it cleared by the president, and ever since, we take the mail around just before lunch. Mr. Gray, the president, told me my idea improved productivity and saved time, and that he wished everyone was as conscientious."

"What was the last book you read (or movie you saw)? How did it affect you?"

It doesn't really matter what you say about the latest book/movie, just as long as you have read/seen it. Don't be like the interviewee who said the name of the first book that came to mind—*In Search of Excellence*—only to be caught by the follow-up, "To what extent do you agree with Peters's simultaneous loose/tight pronouncements?" Also, by naming such a well-known book, you have managed only to say that you are like millions of others, which doesn't make you stand out in the crowd. Better that you should name something less faddish—that helps to avoid nasty follow-up questions. And you needn't mention the most *recent* book or movie you've seen. Your answer must simply make a statement about you as a potential employee. Come up with a response that will set you apart and demonstrate your obvious superiority. Ideally you want to mention a work that in some way has helped you improve yourself; anything that has honed any of the twenty key personality traits will do.

"How do you handle tension?"

This question is different from "Can you handle pressure?"—it asks *how* you handle it. You could reply, "Tension is caused when you let things pile up. It is usually caused by letting other areas of responsibility slip by for an extended period. For instance, if you have a difficult presentation coming up, you may procrastinate in your preparations for it. I've seen lots of people do things like that—a task seems so overwhelming they don't know where to begin. I find that if you break those overwhelming tasks into little pieces, they aren't so overwhelming any more. So I suppose I don't so much handle tension as handle the causes of it, by not letting things slip in the areas that can give rise to it."

"How long have you been looking for another position?"

If you are employed, your answer isn't that important—a short or long time is irrelevant to you in any follow-up probes, because you are just looking for the right job, with the right people and outfit that offers you the right opportunities. If, on the other hand, you are unemployed at the time of the question, how you answer becomes more important. If you say, "Well, I've been looking for two years now," it isn't going to score you any points. The interviewer thinks, "Two years, huh? And no one else wanted him in that time. I wonder what's wrong with him? Well, if no one else is interested, I'm certainly not." So if you must talk of months or more be careful to add something like, "Well, I've been looking for about a year now. I've had a number of offers in that time, but I have determined that as I spend most of my waking hours at work, the job I take and the people I work with have got to be people with values I can identify with. I made the decision that I just wasn't going to suffer clock-watchers and work-to-rule specialists anymore."

"Have you ever been fired?"

Say "no" if you can; if not, act on the advice given to the next question.

"Why were you fired?"

If you were laid off as part of general workforce reduction, be straightforward and move on to the next topic as quickly as possible. If you have been terminated with cause, however, this is a very difficult question to answer. Like it or not, termination with cause is usually justified, because the most loathed responsibility of any manager is to take away someone's livelihood. Virtually no one fires an employee for the heck of it.

Looking at that painful event objectively, you will probably find the cause of your dismissal rooted in the absence of one or more of the twenty profiles. Having been fired also creates instant doubt in the mind of the interviewer, and greatly increases the chances of your references being checked. So if you have been fired, the first thing to do is bite the bullet and call the person who fired you, find out why it happened, and learn what he or she would say about you today.

Your aim is to clear the air, so whatever you do, don't be antagonistic. Reintroduce yourself, explain that you are looking (or, if you have been unemployed for a while, say you are "still looking") for a new job. Say that you appreciate that the manager had to do what was done, and that you learned from the experience. Then ask, "If you were asked as part of a pre- or post-employment reference check, how would you describe my leaving the company? Would you say that I was fired or that I simply resigned? You see, every time I tell someone about my termination, whoosh, there goes another chance of getting another paycheck!" Most managers will plump for the latter option (describing your departure as a resignation). After all, even testy managers tend to be humane after the fact, and such a response saves them potential headaches and even lawsuits.

Whatever you do, don't advertise the fact you were fired. If you are asked, be honest, but make sure you have packaged the reason in the best light possible. Perhaps: "I'm sorry to say, but I deserved it. I was having some personal problems at the time, and I let them affect my work. I was late to work and lost my motivation. My supervisor (whom, by the way, I still speak to) had directions to trim the workforce anyway, and as I was hired only a couple of years ago, I was one of the first to go."

If you can find out the employee turnover figures, voluntary or otherwise, you might add: "Fifteen other people have left so far this year." A combination answer of this nature minimizes the stigma. You have even managed to demonstrate that you take responsibility for your actions, which shows your analytical and listening skills. If one of your past managers will speak well of you, there is nothing to lose and everything to gain by finishing with: "Jill Johnson, at the company, would be a good person to check for a reference on what I have told you."

I would never advise you to be anything but honest in your answers to any interview question. If, however, you have been terminated by a manager who is still vindictive, take heart: Only about 10 percent of all successful job candidates ever get their references checked.

"Have you ever been asked to resign?"

When someone is asked to resign, it is a gesture on the part of the employer: "You can quit, or we will can you, so which do you want it to be?" Because you were given the option, though, that employer cannot later say, "I had to ask him to resign"—that is tantamount to firing and could lead to legal problems. In the final analysis, it is safe to answer "no."

"Were you ever dismissed from your job for a reason that seemed unjustified?"

Another sneaky way of asking, "Were you ever fired?" The sympathetic phrasing is geared to getting you to reveal all the sordid details. The cold hard facts are that hardly anyone is ever fired without cause, and you're kidding yourself if you think otherwise. With that in mind, you can quite honestly say, "No," and move on to the next topic.

"In your last job, what were some of the things you spent most of your time on, and why?"

Employees come in two categories: goal-oriented (those who want to get the job done), and task-oriented (those who believe in "busy" work). You must demonstrate good time management, and that you are, therefore, goal-oriented, for that is what this question probes.

You might reply: "I work on the telephone like a lot of businesspeople; meetings also take up a great deal of time. What is more important to me is effective time management. I find more gets achieved in a shorter time if a meeting is scheduled, say, immediately before lunch or at the close of business. I try to block my time in the morning. At four o'clock, I review what I've achieved, what went right or wrong, and plan adjustments and my main thrust of business for tomorrow."

"In what ways has your job prepared you to take on greater responsibility?"

This is one of the most important questions you will have to answer. The interviewer is looking for examples of your professional development, perhaps to judge your future growth potential, so you must tell a story that demonstrates it. The following example shows growth, listening skills, honesty, and adherence to procedures. Parts of it can be adapted to your personal experience. Notice the then-and-now aspect of the answer.

"When I first started my last job, my boss would brief me morning and evening. I made some mistakes, learned a lot, and got the jobs in on time. As time went by I took on greater responsibilities, [list some of them]. Nowadays, I meet with her every Monday for breakfast to discuss any major directional changes, so that she can keep management informed. I think that demonstrates not only my growth, but also the confidence my management has in my judgment and ability to perform consistently above standard."

"In what ways has your job changed since you originally joined the company?"

You can use the same answer here as for the previous question.

"How does this job compare with others you have applied for?"

This is a variation of more direct questions, such as, "How many other jobs have you applied for?" and "Who else have you applied to?" but it is a slightly more intelligent question and therefore more dangerous. It asks you to compare. Answer the question and sidestep at the same time.

"No two jobs are the same, and this one is certainly unlike any other I have applied for." If you are pressed further, say, "Well, to give you a more detailed answer, I would need to ask you a number of questions about the job and the company. Would now be a good time to do that or would it be better later in the interview process?"

"What makes this job different from your current/last one?"

If you don't have enough information to answer the question, say so, and ask some of your own. Behind the question is the interviewer's desire to uncover experience you are lacking—your answer could be used as evidence against you. Focus on the positive: "From what I know of the job, I seem to have all the experience required to make a thorough success. I would say that the major differences seem to be . . . ." and here you play back the positive attributes of the department and company as the interviewer gave them to you, either in the course of the interview or in answer to your specific questions.

"Do you have any questions?"

A good question. Almost always, this is a sign that the interview is drawing to a close, and that you have one more chance to make an impression. Remember the old adage: People respect what you inspect, not what you expect. Create questions from any of the following.

- Find out why the job is open, who had it last, and what happened to him or her. Did he or she get promoted or fired? How many people have held this position in the last couple of years? What happened to them subsequently?

- Why did the interviewer join the company? How long has he or she been there? What is it about the company that keeps him or her there?

- To whom would you report? Will you get the opportunity to meet that person?

- Where is the job located? What are the travel requirements, if any?

- What type of training is required, and how long is it? What type of training is available?

- What would your first assignment be?

- What are the realistic chances for growth in the job? Where are the opportunities for greatest growth within the company?

- What are the skills and attributes most needed to get ahead in the company?

- Who will be the company's major competitor over the next few years? How does the interviewer feel the company stacks up against them?

- What has been the growth pattern of the company over the last five years? Is it profitable? How profitable? Is the company privately or publicly held?
- If there is a written job description, may you see it?
- How regularly do performance evaluations occur? What model do they follow?

15.

"What Kind of Person Are You Really, Mr. Jones?"

Will you reduce your new employer's life expectancy? The interviewer wants to know! If you are offered the job and accept, you will be working together fifty weeks of the year. Every employer wants to know whether you will fit in with the rest of the staff, whether you are a team player, and most of all: Are you manageable?

There are a number of questions the interviewer might use to probe this area. They will mainly be geared to your behavior and attitudes in the past. Remember: It is universally believed that your past actions predict your future behavior.

"How do you take direction?"

This is really two questions. "How do you take direction?" and, "How do you take criticism?" Your answer will cover both points. "I take direction well and believe there are two types: carefully explained direction, when my boss has time to treat me with honor and respect; then there is the other, a brusque order or correction. While most people get upset with that, personally I always believe the manager is troubled with bigger problems and a tight schedule. As such, I take the direction and get on with the job without taking offense so my boss can get on with her job. It's the only way."

"Would you like to have your boss' job?"

It is a rare boss who wants his or her livelihood taken. On my very first interview, my future boss said, "Mr. Yate, it has been a pleasure to meet you. However, until you walked in, I wasn't looking for a new job."

By the same token, ambition is admired, but mainly by the ambitious. Be cautiously optimistic. Perhaps: "Well, if my boss were promoted over the coming years, I hope to have made a strong enough contribution to warrant his recommendation. I'm looking for a manager who will help me develop my capabilities and grow with him."

"What do you think of your current/last boss?"

Short, sweet, and shut up. People who complain about their employers are recognized to be the same people who cause the most disruption in a department. This question means the interviewer has no desire to hire trouble. "I liked her as a person, respected her professionally, and appreciated her guidance." The question is often followed by one that tries to validate your answer.

"Describe a situation where your work or an idea was criticized."

A doubly dangerous question. You are being asked to say how you handle criticism and to detail your faults. If you are asked this question, describe a poor idea that was criticized, not poor work. Poor work can cost money and is a warning sign, obviously, to the interviewer.

One of the wonderful things about a new job is that you can leave the past entirely behind, so it does not matter how you handled criticism in the past. What does matter is how the interviewer would like you to handle criticism, if and when it becomes his or her unpleasant duty to dish it out; that's what the question is really about. So relate one of those it-seemed-like-a-good-idea-at-the-time ideas, and finish with how you handled the criticism. You could say: "I listened carefully and resisted the temptation to interrupt or defend myself. Then I fed back what I heard to make sure the facts were straight. I asked for advice, we bounced some ideas around, then I came back later and represented the idea in a more viable format. My supervisor's input was invaluable."

"Tell me about yourself."

This is not an invitation to ramble on. You need to know more about the question before giving an answer. "What area of my background would be most relevant to you?" That enables the interviewer to help you with the appropriate focus, so you can avoid discussing irrelevancies. Never answer this question without qualifying whether the interviewer wishes to hear about your business or personal life.

However the interviewer responds to your qualifying question, the tale you tell should demonstrate one or more of the twenty key personality profiles—perhaps honesty, integrity, being a team player, or determination. If you choose "team player," part of your answer might include this: "I put my heart into everything I do, whether it be sports or work. I find that getting along with your peers and being part of the team makes life more enjoyable and productive."

"Rate yourself on a scale of one to ten."

A stupid question. That aside, bear in mind that this is meant to plumb the depths of your self-esteem. If you answer ten, you run the risk of portraying yourself as insufferable; on the other hand, if you say less than seven, you might as well get up and leave. You are probably best claiming to be an eight or nine, saying that you always give of your best, but that in doing so you always increase your skills and therefore always see room for improvement.

"What kinds of things do you worry about?"

Some questions, such as this one, can seem so off-the-wall that you might start treating the interviewer as a father confessor in no time flat. Your private phobias have nothing to do with your job, and revealing them can get you labeled as unbalanced. It is best to confine your answer to the sensible worries of a conscientious professional. "I worry about deadlines, staff turnover, tardiness, back-up plans for when the computer crashes, or that one of my auditors burns out or defects to the competition—just the normal stuff. It goes with the territory, so I don't let it get me down."

"What is the most difficult situation you have faced?"

The question looks for information on two fronts: How do you define difficult? and What was your handling of the situation? You must have a story ready for this one in which the situation both was tough and allowed you to show yourself in a good light. Avoid talking about problems that have to do with co-workers. You can talk about the difficult decision to fire someone, but emphasize that once you had examined the problem and reached a conclusion you acted quickly and professionally, with the best interests of the company at heart.

"What are some of the things that bother you?" "What are your pet hates?" "Tell me about the last time you felt anger on the job."

These questions are so similar that they can be treated as one. It is tremendously important that you show you can remain calm. Most of us have seen a colleague lose his or her cool on occasion—not a pretty sight and one that every sensible employer wants to avoid. This question comes up more and more often the higher up the corporate ladder you climb and the more frequent your contact with clients and the general public. To answer it, find something that angers conscientious workers. "I enjoy my work and believe in giving value to my employer. Dealing with clock-watchers and the ones who regularly get sick on Mondays and Fridays really bothers me, but it's not something that gets me angry or anything like that." An answer of this nature will help you much more than the kind given by a California engineer, who went on for some minutes about how he hated the small-mindedness of people who don't like pet rabbits in the office.

"What have you done that shows initiative?"

The question probes whether you are a doer, someone who will look for ways to increase sales, save time, or save money—the kind of person who gives a manager a pleasant surprise once in a while, who makes life easier for co-workers. Be sure, however, that your example of initiative does not show a disregard for company policies and procedures.

"My boss has to organize a lot of meetings. That means developing agendas, letting employees around the country know the dates well in advance, getting materials printed, etc. Most people in my position would wait for the work to be given them. I don't. Every quarter, I sit down with my boss and find out the dates of all his meetings for the next six months. I immediately make the hotel and flight arrangements and then work backward. I ask myself questions like, 'If the agenda for the July meeting is to reach the field at least six weeks before the meeting, when must it be finished by?' Then I come up with a deadline. I do that for all the major activities for all the meetings. I put the deadlines in his diary; and in mine, only two weeks earlier. That way I can remind the boss that the deadline is getting close. My boss is the best organized, most relaxed manager in the company. None of his colleagues can understand how he does it."

"What are some of the things about which you and your supervisor disagreed?"
It is safest to state that you did not disagree.

"In what areas do you feel your supervisor could have done a better job?"
The same goes for this one. No one admires a Monday-morning quarterback.
You could reply, though: "I have always had the highest respect for my supervisor. I have always been so busy learning from Mr. Jones that I don't think he could have done a better job. He has really brought me to the point where I am ready for greater challenges. That's why I'm here."

"What are some of the things your supervisor did that you disliked?"
If you and the interviewer are both non-smokers, for example, and your boss isn't, use it. Apart from that: "You know, I've never thought of our relationship in terms of like or dislike. I've always thought our role was to get along together and get the job done."

"How well do you feel your boss rated your job performance?"
This is one very sound reason to ask for written evaluations of your work before leaving a company. Some performance-review procedures include a written evaluation of your performance—perhaps your company employs it. If you work for a company that asks you to sign your formal review, you are quite entitled to request a copy of it. You should also ask for a letter of recommendation whenever you leave a job: You have nothing to lose. While I don't recommend thrusting recommendations under unwilling interviewers' noses (they smell a rat when written endorsements of any kind are offered unrequested), the time will come when you are asked and can produce them with a flourish. If you don't have written references, perhaps: "My supervisor always rated my job performance well. In fact, I was always rated as being capable of accepting further responsibilities. The problem was there was nothing available in the company—that's why I'm here."
If your research has been done properly you can also quote verbal appraisals of your performance from prior jobs. "In fact, my boss said only a month ago that I was the most valuable [e.g.] engineer in the workgroup, because . . . ."

"How did your boss get the best out of you?"
This is a manageability question, geared to probing whether you are going to be a pain in the neck or not. Whatever you say, it is important for your ongoing happiness that you make it clear you don't appreciate being treated like a dishrag. You can give a short, general answer: "My last boss got superior effort and performance by treating me like a human being and giving me the same personal respect with which she liked to be treated herself." This book is full of answers that

get you out of tight corners and make you shine, but this is one instance in which you really should tell it like it is. You don't want to work for someone who is going to make life miserable for you.

"How interested are you in sports?"

A recently completed survey of middle- and upper-management personnel found that the executives who listed group sports/activities among their extracurricular activities made an average of $3,000 per year more than their sedentary colleagues. Don't you just love baseball suddenly? The interviewer is looking for your involvement in groups, as a signal that you know how to get along with others and pull together as a team.

"I really enjoy most team sports. Don't get a lot of time to indulge myself, but I am a regular member of my company's softball team." Apart from team sports, endurance sports are seen as a sign of determination: Swimming, running, and cycling are all okay. Games of skill (bridge, chess, and the like) demonstrate analytical skills. Being a Grand Master of Dungeons and Dragons doesn't demonstrate a damned thing.

"What personal characteristics are necessary for success in your field?"

You know the answer to this one: It's a brief recital of key personality profiles.

You might say: "To be successful in my field? Drive, motivation, energy, confidence, determination, good communication, and analytical skills. Combined, of course, with the ability to work with others."

"Do you prefer working with others or alone?"

This question is usually used to determine whether you are a team player. Before answering, however, be sure you know whether the job requires you to work alone. Then answer appropriately. Perhaps: "I'm quite happy working alone when necessary. I don't need constant reassurance. But I prefer to work in a group—so much more gets achieved when people pull together."

"Explain your role as a group/team member."

You are being asked to describe yourself as either a team player or a loner. Most departments depend on harmonious teamwork for their success, so describe yourself as a team player, by all means: "I perform my job in a way that helps others to do theirs in an efficient fashion. Beyond the mechanics, we all have a responsibility to make the workplace a friendly and pleasant place to be. That means everyone working for the common good and making the necessary personal sacrifices toward that good."

"How would you define a conducive work atmosphere?"

This is a tricky question, especially because you probably have no idea what kind of work atmosphere exists in that particular office. So, the longer your answer, the greater your chances of saying the wrong thing. Keep it short and sweet. "One where the team has a genuine interest in its work and desire to turn out a good product/deliver a good service."

"Do you make your opinions known when you disagree with the views of your supervisor?"

If you can, state that you come from an environment where input is encouraged when it helps the team's ability to get the job done efficiently. "If opinions are sought in a meeting, I will give mine, although I am careful to be aware of others' feelings. I will never criticize a co-worker or a superior in an open forum; besides, it is quite possible to disagree without being disagreeable. However, my past manager made it clear that she valued my opinion by asking for it. So, after a while, if there was something I felt strongly about, I would make an appointment to sit down and discuss it one on one." You might choose to end by turning the tables with a question of your own: "Is this a position where we work as a team to solve problems and get the job done, or one where we are meant to be seen and not heard and speak when spoken to?"

"What would you say about a supervisor who was unfair or difficult to work with?"

For this job, you'll definitely want to meet your potential supervisor—just in case you have been earmarked for the company Genghis Khan without warning. The response, "Do you have anyone in particular in mind?" will probably get you off the hook. If you need to elaborate, try: "I would make an appointment to see the supervisor and diplomatically explain that I felt uncomfortable in our relationship, that I felt he or she was not treating me as a professional colleague, and therefore that I might not be performing up to standard in some way—that I wanted to right matters and ask for his or her input as to what I must do to create a professional relationship. I would enter into the discussion in the frame of mind that we were equally responsible for whatever communication problems existed, and that this wasn't just the manager's problem."

"Do you consider yourself a natural leader or a born follower?"

Ow! How you answer depends a lot on the job offer you are chasing. If you are a recent graduate, you are expected to have high aspirations, so go for it. If you are already on the corporate ladder with some practical experience in the school of hard knocks, you might want to be a little more cagey. Assuming you are up for (and want) a leadership position, you might try something like this: "I would be reluctant to regard anyone as a natural leader. Hiring, motivating, and disciplining other adults and at the same time molding them into a cohesive team involves a number of delicately tuned skills that no honest people can say they were born with. Leadership requires first of all the desire; then it is a lifetime learning process. Anyone who reckons they have it all under control and has nothing more to learn isn't doing the employer any favors."

Of course, a little humility is also in order, because just about every leader in every company reports to someone, and there is a good chance that you are talking to such a someone right now. So you might consider including something like, "No matter how well developed any individual's leadership qualities, an integral part of the skills of a leader is to take direction from his or her immediate boss, and also to seek the input of the people being supervised. The wise leader will always follow good advice and sound business judgment wherever it comes from. I would say that given the desire to be a leader, the true leader in the modern business world must embrace both." How can anyone disagree with that kind of wisdom?

"Why do you feel you are a better [e.g.] secretary than some of your co-workers?"

If you speak disparagingly of your co-workers, you will not put yourself in the best light. That is what the question asks you to do, so it poses some difficulties. The trick is to answer the question but not to accept the invitation to show yourself from anything other than a flattering perspective. "I think that question is best answered by a manager. It is so difficult to be objective, and I really don't like to slight my co-workers. I don't spend my time thinking about how superior I am, because that would be detrimental to our working together as a team. I believe, however, some of the qualities that make me an outstanding secretary are . . ." and you go on to illustrate job-related personal qualities that make you a beacon of productivity and a joy to work with.

"You have a doctor's appointment arranged for noon. You've waited two weeks to get in. An urgent meeting is scheduled at the last moment, though. What do you do?"

What a crazy question, you mutter. It's not. It is even more than a question—it is what I call a question shell. The question within the shell—in this instance, "Will you sacrifice the appointment or sacrifice your job?—can be changed at will. This is a situational-interviewing technique, which poses an on-the-job problem to see how the prospective employee will respond. A Chicago company asks this question as part of its initial screening, and if you give the wrong answer, you never even get a face-to-face interview. So what is the right answer to this or any similar shell question?

Fortunately, once you understand the interviewing technique, it is quite easy to handle—all you have to do is turn the question around. "If I were the manager who had to schedule a really important meeting at the last moment, and someone on my staff chose to go to the doctor's instead, how would I feel?"

It is unlikely that you would be an understanding manager unless the visit were for a triple bypass. To answer, you start with an evaluation of the importance of the problem and the responsibility of everyone to make some sacrifices for the organization, and finish with: "The first thing I would do is reschedule the appointment and save the doctor's office inconvenience. Then I would immediately make sure I was properly prepared for the emergency meeting."

"How do you manage to interview while still employed?"

As long as you don't explain that you faked a dentist appointment to make the interview you should be all right. Beware of revealing anything that might make you appear at all underhanded. Best to make the answer short and sweet and let the interviewer move on to richer areas of inquiry. Just explain that you had some vacation time due, or took a day off in lieu of overtime payments. "I had some vacation time, so I went to my boss and explained I needed a couple of days off for some personal business, and asked her what days would be most suitable. Although I plan to change jobs, I don't in any way want to hurt my current employer in the process by being absent during a crunch."

"When do you expect a promotion?"

Tread warily, show you believe in yourself, and have both feet firmly planted on the ground. "That depends on a few criteria. Of course, I cannot expect promotions without the performance that marks me as deserving of promotion. I also need to join a company that has the growth necessary to provide the opportunity. I hope that my manager believes in promoting from within and will help me grow so that I will have the skills necessary to be considered for promotion when the opportunity comes along."

If you are the only one doing a particular job in the company, or you are in management, you need to build another factor into your answer. For example: "As a manager, I realize that part of my job is to have done my succession planning, and that I must have someone trained and ready to step into my shoes before I can expect to step up. That way I play my part in preserving the chain of command." To avoid being caught off guard with queries about your having achieved that in your present job, you can finish with: "Just as I have done in my present job, where I have a couple of people capable of taking over the reins when I leave."

"Tell me a story."

Wow. What on earth does the interviewer mean by that question? You don't know until you get him or her to elaborate. Ask, "What would you like me to tell you a story about?" To make any other response is to risk making a fool of yourself. Very often the question is asked to see how analytical you are: People who answer the question without qualifying show that they do not think things through carefully. The subsequent question will be about either your personal or professional life. If it is about your personal life, tell a story that shows you like people and are determined. Do not discuss your love life. If the subsequent question is about your professional life, tell a story that demonstrates your willingness and manageability.

"What have your other jobs taught you?"

Talk about the professional skills you have learned and the personality traits you have polished. Many interviewees have had success finishing their answer with: "There are two general things I have learned from past jobs. First, if you are confused, ask—it's better to ask a dumb question than make a stupid mistake. Second, it's better to promise less and produce more than to make unrealistic forecasts."

"Define cooperation."

The question asks you to explain how to function as a team player in the workplace. Your answer could be: "Cooperation is a person's ability to sacrifice personal wishes and beliefs whenever necessary to assure the department reaches its goals.

It is also a person's desire to be part of a team, and by hard work and goodwill make the department greater than the sum of its parts."

"What difficulties do you have tolerating people with different backgrounds and interests from yours?"

Another "team player" question with the awkward inference that you do have problems. Give the following answer: "I don't have any."

"In hindsight, what have you done that was a little harebrained?"

You are never harebrained in your business dealings, and you haven't been harebrained in your personal life since graduation, right? The only safe examples to use are ones from your deep past that ultimately turned out well. One of the best to use, if it applies to you, is this one: "Well, I guess the time I bought my house. I had no idea what I was letting myself in for, and at the time, I really couldn't afford it. Still, I managed to make the payments, though I had to work like someone possessed. Yes, my first house—that was a real learning experience." Not only can most people relate to this example, but it also gives you the opportunity to sell one or two of your very positive and endearing traits.

□   □   □

If you think the interview is only tough for the interviewee, it's time to take a look at the other side of the desk. Knowing what's going on behind those Foster Grants can really help you shine.

16.
The Other Side of the Desk

There are two terrible places to be during an interview—sitting in front of the desk wondering what on earth is going to happen next, and sitting behind the desk asking the questions. The average interviewer dreads the meeting almost as much as the interviewee, yet for opposite reasons.

American business frequently yields to the mistaken belief that any person, on being promoted to the ranks of management, becomes mystically endowed with all necessary managerial skills. That is a fallacy. Comparatively few management people have been taught to interview; most just bumble along and pick up a certain proficiency over a period of time.

There are two distinct types of interviewers who can spell disaster for you if you are unprepared. One is the highly skilled interviewer, who has been trained in systematic techniques for probing your past for all the facts and evaluating your potential. The other is the totally incompetent interviewer, who may even lack the ability to phrase a question adequately. Both are equally dangerous when it comes to winning the job offer.

The Skillful Interviewer

Skillful interviewers know exactly what they want to discover. They have taken exhaustive steps to learn the strategies that will help them hire only the best for their company. They follow a set format for the interview process to ensure objectivity in selection and a set sequence of questions to ensure the facts are gathered. They will definitely test your mettle.

There are many ways for a manager to build and conduct a structured interview, but all have the same goals:

- To ensure a systematic coverage of your work history and applicable job-related skills.
- To provide a technique for gathering all the relevant facts.
- To provide a uniform strategy that objectively evaluates all job candidates.
- To determine ability, willingness, and manageability.

Someone using structured interview techniques will usually follow a standard format. The interview will begin with small talk and a brief introduction to relax you. Following close on the heels of that chit-chat comes a statement geared to assure you that baring your faults is the best way to get the job. Your interviewer will then outline the steps in the interview. That will include your giving a chronological description of your work history, and then the interviewer's asking specific questions about your experience. Then, prior to the close of the interview, you will be given an opportunity to ask your own questions.

Sounds pretty simple, huh? Well, watch out! The skilled interviewer knows exactly what questions to ask, why they will be asked, in what order they will be asked, and what the desired responses are. He or she will interview and evaluate every applicant for the job in exactly the same fashion. You are up against a pro.

Like the hunter who learns to think like his or her prey, you will find that the best way to win over the interviewer is to think like the interviewer. In fact, take that idea a little further: You must win, but you don't want the other guys to realize you beat them at their own game. To do that, you must learn how the interviewer has prepared for you; and by going through the same process you will beat out your competitors for the job offer.

The dangerous part of this type of structured interview is called "skills evaluation." The interviewer has analyzed all the different skills it takes to do the job, and all the personality traits that complement those skills. Armed with that data, he or she has developed a series of carefully sequenced questions to draw out your relative merits and weaknesses.

Graphically, it looks like this:

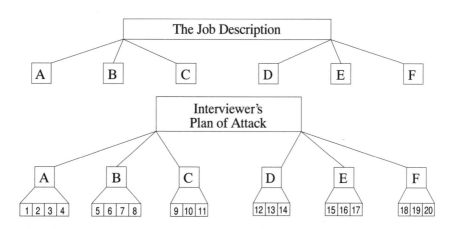

Letters A-F are the separate skills necessary to do the job; numbers 1-20 are questions asked to identify and verify that particular skill. This is where many of the tough questions will arise, and the only way to prepare effectively is to take the interviewer's viewpoint and complete this exercise in its entirety. That effort requires a degree of objectivity, but will generate multiple job offers.

☐ Look at the position you seek. What role does it play in helping the company achieve its corporate mission and make a profit?

☐ What are the five most important duties of that job?

☐ From a management viewpoint, what are the skills and attributes necessary to perform each of these tasks?

Write it all down. Now, put yourself in the interviewer's shoes. What topics would you examine to find out whether a person can really do the job? If for some reason you get stuck in the process, just use your past experience. You have worked with good and bad people, and their work habits and skills will lead you to develop both the potential questions and the correct answers.

Each job skill you identify is fertile ground for the interviewer's questions. Don't forget the intangible skills that are so important to many jobs, like self-confidence and creativity, because the interviewer won't. Develop a number of questions for each job skill you identify.

Again, looking back at co-workers (and still wearing the manager's mask), what are the personal characteristics that would make life more comfortable for you as a manager? Those are also dimensions that are likely to be probed by the interviewer. Once you have identified the questions you would ask in the interviewer's position, the answers should come easily.

That's the way managers are trained to develop structured interview questions—I just gave you the inside track. Complete the exercise by developing the answers you would like to hear as a manager. Take time to complete the exercise conscientiously, writing out both the questions and the appropriate answers.

☐   ☐   ☐

These sharks have some juicy questions to probe your skills, attitude, and personality. Would you like to hear some of them? Notice that these questions tend to lay out a problem for you to solve, but in no way lead you towards the answer. They are often two- and three-part questions as well. The additional question that can be tagged onto them all is, "What did you learn from this experience?" Assume it is included whenever you get one of these questions—you'll be able to sell different aspects of your success profile.

"You have been given a project that requires you to interact with different levels within the company. How do you do this? What levels are you most comfortable with?"
This is a two-part question that probes communication and self-confidence skills. The first part asks how you interact with superiors and motivate those working with and for you on the project. The second part of the question is saying, "Tell me whom you regard as your peer group—help me categorize you." To cover those bases, you will want to include the essence of this: "There are basically two types of people I would interact with on a project of this nature. First, there are those I

report to, who bear the ultimate responsibility for its success. With them, I determine deadlines and how they will evaluate the success of the project. I outline my approach, breaking the project down into component parts, getting approval on both the approach and the costs. I would keep my supervisors up-to-date on a regular basis, and seek input whenever needed. My supervisors would expect three things from me: the facts, an analysis of potential problems, and that I not be intimidated, as that would jeopardize the project's success. I would comfortably satisfy those expectations.

"The other people to interact with on a project like this are those who work with and for me. With those people, I would outline the project and explain how a successful outcome will benefit the company. I would assign the component parts to those best suited to each, and arrange follow-up times to assure completion by deadline. My role here would be to facilitate, motivate, and bring the different personalities together to form a team.

"As for comfort level, I find this type of approach enables me to interact comfortably with all levels and types of people."

"Tell me about an event that really challenged you. How did you meet the challenge? In what way was your approach different from others'?"

This is a straightforward two-part question. The first probes your problem-solving abilities. The second asks you to set yourself apart from the herd. First of all, outline the problem. The blacker you make the situation, the better. Having done that, go ahead and explain your solution, its value to your employer, and how it was different from other approaches.

"My company has offices all around the country; I am responsible for seventy of them. My job is to visit each office on a regular basis and build market-penetration strategies with management, and to train and motivate the sales and customer-service force. When the recession hit, the need to service those offices was more important than ever, yet the traveling costs were getting prohibitive.

"Morale was an especially important factor; you can't let outlying offices feel defeated. I reapportioned my budget and did the following: I dramatically increased telephone contact with the offices. I instituted a monthly sales-technique letter—how to prospect for new clients, how to negotiate difficult sales, and so forth. I bought and rented sales training and motivational tapes and sent them to my managers with instructions on how to use them in a sales meeting. I stopped visiting all the offices. Instead, I scheduled weekend training meetings in central locations throughout my area: one day of sales training and one day of management training, concentrating on how to run sales meetings, early termination of low producers, and so forth.

"While my colleagues complained about the drop in sales, mine increased, albeit a modest 6 percent. After two quarters, my approach was officially adopted by the company."

"Give me an example of a method of working you have used. How did you feel about it?"

You have a choice of giving an example of either good or bad work habits.

Give a good example, one that demonstrates your understanding of corporate goals, your organizational skills, analytical ability, or time management skills.

You could say: "I believe in giving an honest day's work for a day's pay. That requires organization and time management. I do my paperwork at the end of each day, when I review the day's achievements; with this done, I plan for tomorrow. When I come to work in the morning, I'm ready to get going without wasting time. I try to schedule meetings right before lunch; people get to the point more quickly if it's on their time. I feel that is an efficient and organized method of working."

"When you joined your last company and met the group for the first time, how did you feel? How did you get on with them?"

Your answer should include: "I naturally felt a little nervous, but I was excited about the new job. I shared that excitement with my new friends, and told them that I was enthusiastic about learning new skills from them. I was open and friendly, and when given the opportunity to help someone myself, I jumped at it."

"In your last job, how did you plan to interview?"

That's an easy one. Just give a description of how the skilled interviewer prepares.

"How have you benefited from your disappointments?"

Disappointments are different from failures. It is an intelligent—probably trained—interviewer who asks this one; it is also an opportunity for the astute interviewee to shine. The question itself is very positive—it asks you to show how you benefited. Note also that it doesn't ask you to give specific details of specific disappointments, so you don't have to open your mouth and insert your foot. Instead, be general. Edison once explained his success as an inventor by claiming that he knew more ways not to do something than anyone else living; you can do worse than quote him. In any event, sum up your answer with, "I treat disappointments as a learning experience; I look at what happened, why it happened, and how I would do things differently in each stage should the same set of circumstances appear again. That way, I put disappointment behind me and am ready with renewed vigor and understanding to face the new day's problems."

A side note. A person with strong religious beliefs may be tempted to answer a question like this in terms of religious values. If you benefit from disappointments in a spiritual way, remember that not everyone feels the same as you do. More important, the interviewer is, by law, prohibited from talking about religion with you, so you can unwittingly put the interviewer in an awkward position of not knowing how to respond. And making an interviewer feel awkward in any way is not the way to win the job offer.

"What would you do when you have a decision to make and no procedure exists?"

This question probes your analytical skills, integrity, and dedication. Most of all, the interviewer is testing your manageability and adherence to procedures—the "company way of doing things." You need to cover that with: "I would act without my manager's direction only if the situation were urgent and my manager were not available. Then I would take command of the situation, make a decision based on the facts, and implement it. I would update my boss at the earliest opportunity." If possible, tell a story to illustrate.

"That is an excellent answer. Now to give me a balanced view, can you give me an example that didn't work out so well?"

There are two techniques that every skilled interviewer will use, especially if you are giving good answers. In this question, the interviewer looks for negative balance; in the follow-up, the person will look for negative confirmation. Here, you are required to give an example of an inadequacy. The trick is to pull something from the past, not the present, and to finish with what you learned from the experience. For example: "That's easy. When I first joined the workforce, I didn't really understand the importance of systems and procedures. There was one time when I was too anxious to contribute and didn't have the full picture. There was a sales visit report everyone had to fill out after visiting a customer. I always put a lot of effort into it until I realized it was never read; it just went in the files. So I stopped doing it for a few days to see if it made any difference. I thought I was gaining time to make more sales for the company. I was so proud of my extra sales calls I told the boss at the end of the week. My boss explained that the records were for the long term, so that should my job change, the next salesperson would have the benefit of a full client history. It was a long time ago, but I have never forgotten the lesson: There's always a reason for systems and procedures. I've had the best-kept records in the company ever since."

To look for negative confirmation, the interviewer then may say something like, "Thank you. Now can you give me another example?" He or she is trying to confirm a weakness. If you help, you could well do yourself out of a job. Here's your reaction: You sit deep in thought for a good ten seconds, then look up and say firmly, "No, that's the only occasion when anything like that happened." Shut up and refuse to be enticed further.

The Unconscious Incompetent

Now you should be ready for almost anything a professional interviewer could throw at you. Your foresight and strategic planning will generate multiple offers of employment for you in all circumstances except one, and that's when you face the unconsciously incompetent interviewer. He or she is probably more dangerous to your job-offer status than everything else combined.

The problem is embodied in the experienced manager who is a poor interviewer but who does not know it. He or she, consciously or otherwise, bases hiring decisions on "experience" and "knowledge of mankind" and "gut feeling." In any event, he or she is an unconscious incompetent. You have probably been interviewed by one in your time. Remember leaving an interview and, upon reflection, feeling the interviewer knew absolutely nothing about you or your skills? If so, you know how frustrating that can be. Here you'll see how to turn that difficult situation to your advantage. In the future, good managers who are poor interviewers will be offering jobs with far greater frequency than ever before. Understand that a poor interviewer can be a wonderful manager; interviewing skills are learned, not inherited or created as a result of a mystical corporate blessing.

The unconscious incompetents abound. Their heinous crime can only be exceeded by your inability to recognize and take advantage of the proffered opportunity.

As in handling the skilled interviewer, it is necessary to imagine how the unconscious incompetent thinks and feels. There are many manifestations of the poor interviewer. After each of the next examples, follow instructions for appropriate handling of the unique problems each type poses for you.

☐ **Example One:** The interviewer's desk is cluttered, and the resume or application that was handed to him or her a few minutes before cannot be found.

Response: Sit quietly through the bumbling and searching. Check out the surroundings. Breathe deeply and slowly to calm any natural interview nerves. As you bring your adrenaline under control, you bring a certain calming effect to the interviewer and the interview. (This example, by the way, is the most common sign of the unconscious incompetent.)

☐ **Example Two:** The interviewer experiences constant interruptions from the telephone or people walking into the office.

Response: This provides good opportunities for selling yourself. Make note on your pad of where you were in the conversation and refresh the interviewer on the point when you start talking again. He or she will be impressed with your level head and good memory. The interruptions also give time, perhaps, to find something of common interest in the office, something you can compliment. You will also have time to compose the suitable value key follow-up to the point made in the conversation prior to the interruption.

☐ **Example Three:** The interviewer starts with an explanation of why you are both sitting there, and then allows the conversation to degenerate into a lengthy diatribe about the company.

Response: Show interest in the company and the conversation. Sit straight, look attentive (the other applicants probably fall asleep), make appreciative murmurs, and nod at the appropriate times until there is a pause. When that occurs, comment that you appreciate the background on the company, because you can now see more clearly how the job fits into the general scheme of things; that you see, for example, how valuable communication skills would be for the job. Could the interviewer please tell you some of the other job requirements? Then, as the job's functions are described, you can interject appropriate information about your background with: "Would it be of value, Mr. Smith, if I described my experience with . . . ?"

☐ **Example Four:** The interviewer begins with, or quickly breaks into, the drawbacks of the job. The job may even be described in totally negative terms. That is often done without giving a balanced view of the duties and expectations of the position.

Response: An initial negative description often means that the interviewer has had bad experiences hiring for the position. Your course is to empathize (not sympathize) with his or her bad experiences and make it known that you recognize the importance of (for example) reliability, especially in this particular type of job. (You will invariably find in these instances that what your interviewer has lacked in the past is someone with a serious understanding of value keys.) Illustrate your proficiency in that particular aspect of your profession with a short example from your work history. Finish your statements by asking the interviewer what some of the biggest problems to be handled in the job are. The questions demonstrate your understanding, and the interviewer's answers outline the areas from your background and skills to which you should draw attention.

☐ **Example Five:** The interviewer spends considerable time early in the interview describing "the type of people we are here at XYZ Corporation."
Response: Very simple. You have always wanted to work for a company with that atmosphere. It creates the type of work environment that is conducive to a person really giving his or her best efforts.

☐ **Example Six:** The interviewer asks closed-ended questions, ones that demand no more than a yes/no answer (e.g., "Do you pay attention to detail?"). Such questions are hardly adequate to establish your skills, yet you must handle them effectively to secure the job offer.
Response: A yes/no answer to a closed-ended question will not get you that offer. The trick is to treat each closed-ended question as if the interviewer has added, "Please give me a brief yet thorough answer." Closed-ended questions also are often mingled with statements followed by pauses. In those instances, agree with the statement in a way that demonstrates both a grasp of your job and the interviewer's statement. For example: "That's an excellent point, Mr. Smith. I couldn't agree more that the attention to detail you describe naturally affects cost containment. My track record in this area is . . . ."

☐ **Example Seven:** The interviewer asks a continuing stream of negative questions (as described in chapter 17, "The Stress Interview").
Response: Use the techniques and answers described earlier. Give your answers with a smile and do not take the questions as personal insults; they are not intended that way. The more stressful the situations the job is likely to place you in, the greater the likelihood of your having to field negative questions. The interviewer wants to know if you can take the heat.

☐ **Example Eight:** The interviewer has difficulty looking at you while speaking.
Response: The interviewer is someone who finds it uncomfortable being in the spotlight. Try to help him or her to be a good audience. Ask specific questions about the job responsibilities and offer your skills in turn.

☐   ☐   ☐

Often a hiring manager will arrange for you to meet with two or three other people. Frequently, the other interviewers have been neither trained in appropriate interviewing skills nor told the details of the job for which you are interviewing. So you will take additional copies of your executive briefing with you to the interview to aid them in focusing on the appropriate job functions.

When you understand how to recognize and respond to these different types of interviewer, you will leave your interview having made a favorable first impression. No one forgets first impressions.

17.
The Stress Interview

For all intents and purposes, every interview is a stress interview: The interviewer's negative and trick questions can act as the catalyst for your own fear. And the only way to combat that fear is to be prepared, to know what the interviewer is trying to do, to anticipate the various tacks he or she will take. Only preparedness will keep you cool and collected. Whenever you are ill-prepared for an interview, no one will be able to put more pressure on you than yourself. Remember: A stress interview is just a regular interview with the volume turned all the way up—the music's the same, just louder.

You've heard the horror stories. An interviewer demands of a hapless applicant, "Sell me this pen," or asks, "How would you improve the design of a teddy bear?" Or the candidate is faced with a battery of interviewers, all demanding rapid-fire answers to questions like, "You're giving a dinner party. Which ten famous people would you invite and why?" When the interviewee offers evidence of foot-in-mouth disease by asking, "Living or dead?" he receives his just desserts in reply: "Ten of each."

Such awful-sounding questions are thrown in to test your poise, to see how you react under pressure, and to plumb the depths of your confidence. Many people ruin their chances by reacting to them as personal insults rather than the challenge and opportunity to shine that they really represent.

Previously restricted to the executive suite for the selection of high-powered executives, stress interviews are now established throughout the professional world. And they can come complete with all the intimidating and treacherous tricks your worst nightmare can devise. Yet your good performance at a stress interview can mean the difference between a job in the fast lane and a stalled career. The interviewers in a stress interview are invariably experienced and well-organized, with tightly structured procedures and advanced interviewing techniques. The questions and tension they generate have the cumulative effect of throwing you off balance and revealing the "real" you—rather than someone who can respond with last night's rehearsed answers to six or seven stock questions.

Stress questions can be turned to your advantage or merely avoided by your nifty footwork. Whichever, you will be among a select few who understand this line of questioning. As always, remember with the questions in this chapter to build a personalized answer that reflects your experience and profession. Practice them aloud—by doing that, your responses to these interview gambits will become part of you, and that enhancement of your mental attitude will positively affect your confidence during an interview. You might even consider making a tape of tough questions, spacing them at intervals of 30 seconds to two minutes. You can then play the tape back and answer the questions in real time.

As we will see in this chapter, reflexive questions can prove especially useful when the heat is on. Stress questions are designed to sort out the clutch players from those who slow down under pressure. Used with discretion, the reflexives (" . . . don't you think?") will demonstrate to the interviewer that you are able to function well under pressure. At the same time, of course, you put the ball back in the interviewer's court.

One common stress interview technique is to set you up for a fall: A pleasant conversation, one or a series of seemingly innocuous questions to relax your guard, then a dazzling series of jabs and body blows that leave you gibbering. For instance, an interviewer might lull you into a false sense of security by asking some relatively stressless questions: "What was your initial starting salary at your last job?" then, "What is your salary now?" then, "Do you receive bonuses?" etc. To put you on the ropes, he or she then completely surprises you with, "Tell me what sort of troubles you have living within your means," or "Why aren't you earning more at your age?" Such interviewers are using stress in an intelligent fashion, to simulate the unexpected and sometimes tense events of everyday business life. Seeing how you handle simulated pressure gives a fair indication of how you will react to the real thing.

The sophisticated interviewer talks very little, perhaps only twenty percent of the time, and that time is spent asking questions. Few comments, and no editorializing on your answers, means that you get no hint, verbal or otherwise, about your performance.

The questions are planned, targeted, sequenced, and layered. The interviewer covers one subject thoroughly before moving on. Let's take the simple example of "Can you work under pressure?" As a reader of *Knock 'em Dead*, you will know to answer that question with an example, and thereby deflect the main thrust of the stress technique. The interviewer will be prepared for a simple yes/no answer; what follows will keep the unprepared applicant reeling.

☐ *"Can you work under pressure?"* A simple, closed-ended question that requires just a yes/no answer, but you don't get off so easy.

☐ *"Good, I'd be interested to hear about a time when you experienced pressure on your job."* An open-ended request to tell a story about a pressure situation. After this, you will be subjected to the layering technique—six layers in the following instance. Imagine how tangled you could get without preparation.

☐ *"Why do you think this situation arose?"*

☐ *"When exactly did it happen?"* Watch out! Your story of saving thousands from the burning skyscraper may well be checked with your references.

☐ *"What in hindsight were you most dissatisfied with about your performance?"* Here we go. You're trying to show how well you perform under pressure, then suddenly you're telling tales against yourself.

☐ *"How do you feel others involved could have acted more responsibly?"* An open invitation to criticize peers and superiors, which you should diplomatically decline.

☐ *"Who holds the responsibility for the situation?"* Another invitation to point the finger of blame.

☐ *"Where in the chain of command could steps be taken to avoid that sort of thing happening again?"*

You have just been through an old reporters' technique of asking why, when, who, what, how, and where. That technique can be applied to any question you are asked and is frequently used to probe those success stories that sound just too good to be true. You'll find them suddenly tagged on to the simple closed-ended questions, as well as to the open-ended ones, starting, "Share with me," "Tell me about a time when," or, "I'm interested in finding out about," and requesting specific examples from your work history.

After you've survived that barrage, a friendly tone will conceal another zinger: "What did you learn from the experience?" It's a question that is geared to probing your judgment and emotional maturity. Your answer will be to emphasize whichever of the key personality traits your story was illustrating.

When the interviewer feels you were on the edge of revealing something unusual in an answer, you may well encounter "mirror statements." Here, the last key phrase of your answer will be repeated or paraphrased, and followed by a steady gaze and silence: "So, you learned that organization is the key to management." The idea is that the quiet and expectant look will work together to keep you talking. It can give you a most disconcerting feeling to find yourself rambling on without quite knowing why. The trick to that is knowing when to stop. When the interviewer gives you the expectant look, expand your answer (you have to), but by no more than a couple of sentences. Otherwise, you will get that creepy feeling that you're digging yourself into a hole.

There will be times when you face more than one interviewer at a time. When it happens, remember the story of one woman attorney who had five law partners all asking questions at the same time—as the poor interviewee got halfway through one answer, another question would be shot at her. Pausing for breath, she smiled and said, "Hold your horses, ladies and gentlemen. These are all excellent questions, and given time, I'll answer them all. Now who's next?" In so doing, she showed the interviewers exactly what they wanted to see and what, incidentally, is behind every stress interview and every negatively phrased question—finding the presence of poise and calm under fire, combined with a refusal to be intimidated.

You never know when a stress interview will raise its ugly head. Often it can be that rubber-stamp meeting with the senior V.P. at the end of a series of grueling meetings. That is not surprising: While other interviewers are concerned with determining whether you are able, willing, and manageable for the job in question, the senior executive who eventually throws you for a loop is the one who is probing you for potential promotability.

The most intimidating stress interviews are recognizable before the interviewer speaks: no eye contact, no greeting, either silence or a noncommittal grunt, no small talk. You may also recognize such an interviewer by his general air of boredom, lack of interest, or thinly veiled aggression. The first words you hear could well be, "O.K., so go ahead. I don't have all day." In these situations, forewarned is forearmed, so here are some of the questions you can expect to follow such openings.

"What is your greatest weakness?"

This is a direct invitation to put your head in a noose. Decline the invitation.

If there is a minor part of the job at hand where you lack knowledge—but knowledge you will obviously pick up quickly—use that. For instance: "I haven't worked with this type of spreadsheet program before, but given my experience with six other types, I don't think it should take me more than a couple of days to pick it up." Here you remove the emphasis from weakness and put it onto a developmental problem that is easily overcome. Be careful, however: This very effective ploy must be used with discretion.

Another good option is to give a generalized answer that takes advantage of value keys. Design the answer so that your weakness is ultimately a positive characteristic. For example: "I enjoy my work and always give each project my best shot. So when sometimes I don't feel others are pulling their weight, I find it a little frustrating. I am aware of that weakness, and in those situations I try to overcome it with a positive attitude that I hope will catch on."

Also consider the technique of putting a problem in the past. Here you take a weakness from way back when, and show how you overcame it. It answers the question but ends on a positive note. An illustration: "When I first got into this field, I always had problems with my paperwork—you know, leaving an adequate paper trail. And to be honest, I let it slip once or twice. My manager sat me down and explained the potential troubles such behavior could cause. I really took it to heart, and I think you will find my paper trails some of the best around today. You only have to tell me something once." With that kind of answer, you also get the added bonus of showing that you accept and act on criticism.

Congratulations! You have just turned a bear of a question into an opportunity to sell yourself with your professional profile. In deciding on the particular answer you will give, remember that the interviewer isn't really concerned about your general weaknesses—no one is a saint outside of the interview room. He or she is simply concerned about any red flags that might signal your inability to perform the job or be manageable in the performance of your duties.

"With hindsight, how could you have improved your progress?"

Here's a question that demands, "Tell me your mistakes and weaknesses." If you can mention ways of improving your performance without damaging your candidacy, do so. The end of your answer should contain something like: "Other than that, I don't know what to add. I have always given it my best shot." Then shut up.

"What kinds of decisions are most difficult for you?"

You are human, admit it, but be careful what you admit. If you have ever had to fire someone, you are in luck, because no one likes to do that. Emphasize that having reached a logical conclusion, you act. If you are not in management, tie your answer to key profiles: "It's not that I have difficulty making decisions— some just require more consideration than others. A small example might be vacation time. Now, everyone is entitled to it, but I don't believe you should leave your boss in a bind at short notice. I think very carefully at the beginning of the year when I'd like to take my vacation, and then think of alternate dates. I go to my supervisor, tell him what I hope to do, and see whether there is any conflict. I wouldn't want to be out of the office for the two weeks prior to a project deadline, for instance. So by carefully considering things far enough in advance, I don't procrastinate, and I make sure my plans jibe with my boss and the department for the year."

Here you take a trick question and use it to demonstrate your consideration, analytical abilities, and concern for the department—and for the company bottom line.

"Tell me about the problems you have living within your means."

This is a twister to catch you off guard. Your best defense is first of all to know that it exists, and secondly to give it short shrift. "I know few people who are satisfied with their current earnings. As a professional, I am continually striving to improve my skills and to improve my living standard. But my problems are no different from that of this company or any other—making sure all the bills get paid on time and recognizing that every month and year there are some things that are prudent to do and other expenses that are best deferred."

"What area of your skills/professional development do you want to improve at this time?"

Another tell-me-all-your-weaknesses question. You should try to avoid damaging your candidacy by tossing around careless admissions. One effective answer to this is to say, "Well, from what you told me about the job, I seem to have all the necessary skills and background. What I would really find exciting is the opportunity to work on a job where . . ." At this point, you replay the interviewer's hot buttons about the job. You emphasize that you really have all the job-related skills and also tell the interviewer what you find exciting about the job. It works admirably.

Another safe response is to reiterate one or two areas that combine personal strengths and the job's most crucial responsibilities, and finish with saying, "These areas are so important that I don't think anyone can be too good or should ever stop trying to polish skills."

"Your application shows you have been with one company a long time without any appreciable increase in rank or salary. Tell me about this."

Ugh. A toughie. To start with, you should analyze why this state of affairs does exist (assuming the interviewer's assessment is accurate). Then, when you have determined the cause, practice saying it out loud to yourself as you would say it during an actual interview. It may take a few tries. Chances are that no matter how valid your explanation really is, it will come off sounding a little tinny or vindictive without some polishing. Avoid the sour grapes syndrome at all costs.

Here are some tactics you can use. First of all, try to avoid putting your salary history on application forms. No one is going to deny you an interview for lack of a salary history if your skills match those the job requires. Of course, you should never put such trivia on your resume.

If the interviewer is intent, and asks you outright for this information, you'll find a great response in the section on payment histories in chapter 23.

Now then. We address next the delicate matter of "hey-wait-a-minute-why-no-promotions?" This is one case where saying the wrong thing can get you in just as much trouble as failing to say the right thing. The interviewer has posed a truly negative inquiry; the more time either of you spend on it, the more time the interviewer gets to devote to concentrating on negative aspects of your candidacy. Make your answer short and sweet, then shut up. For instance, "My current employer is a stable company with a good working environment, but there's minimal growth there in my area—in fact, there hasn't been any promotion in my area since _____. Your question is the reason I am meeting here with you; I have the skills and ability to take on more responsibility and I'm looking for a place to do that."

"Are you willing to take calculated risks when necessary?"

First, qualify the question: "How do you define calculated risks? What sort of risks? Give me an example of a risk you have in mind; what are the stakes involved?" That will show you exactly the right analytical approach to evaluating a calculated risk, and while the interviewer is rattling on, you have bought time to come up with an answer. Whatever your answer, you will include, "Naturally, I would never take any risk that would in any way jeopardize the safety or reputation of my company or colleagues. In fact, I don't think any employer would appreciate an employee at any level taking risks of any nature without first having a thorough briefing and chance to give input."

"See this pen I'm holding? Sell it to me."

Not a request, as you might think, that would be asked only of a salesperson. In today's business world, everyone is required to sell—sometimes products, but more often ideas, approaches, and concepts. As such, you are being tested to see whether you understand the basic concepts of features-and-benefits selling, how quickly you think on your feet, and how effective your verbal communication is. For example, the interviewer holds up a broad-tip yellow highlighter. You say calmly, "Let me tell you about the special features of this product. First of all, it's a highlighter that will emphasize important points in reports or articles, and that will save you time in recalling the important features. The casing is wide enough to enable you to use it comfortably at your desk or on a flip chart. It has a flat base you can stand it up on. At one dollar, it is disposable—and affordable enough for you to have a handful for your desk, briefcase, car, and at home. And the bright yellow color means you'll never lose it."

Then close with a smile and a question of your own that will bring a smile to your interviewer's face: "How many gross shall we deliver?"

"How will you be able to cope with a change in environment after (e.g.) five years with your current company?"

Another chance to take an implied negative and turn it into a positive. "That's one of the reasons I want to make a change. After five years with my current employer, I felt I was about to get stale. Everyone needs a change of scene once in a while. It's just time for me to make some new friends, face some new challenges, and experience some new approaches; hopefully, I'll have the chance to contribute from my experience."

"Why aren't you earning more at your age?"

Accept this as a compliment to your skills and accomplishments. "I have always felt that solid experience would stand me in good stead in the long run and that earnings would come in due course. Also, I am not the type of person to change jobs just for the money. At this point, I have a solid background that is worth something to a company." Now, to avoid the interviewer putting you on the spot again, finish with a question: "How much should I be earning now?" The figure could be your offer.

"What is the worst thing you have heard about our company?"

This question can come as something of a shock. As with all stress questions, your poise under stress is vital: If you can carry off a halfway decent answer as well, you are a winner. The best response to this question is simple. Just say with a smile: "You're a tough company to get into because your interviews and interviewers are so rigorous." It's true, it's flattering, and it shows that you are not intimidated.

"How would you define your profession?"

With questions that solicit your understanding of a topic, no matter how good your answer, you can expect to be interrupted in mid-reply with "That has nothing to do with it," or, "Whoever put that idea into your head?" While your response is a judgment call, 999 times out of a thousand these comments are not meant to be taken as serious criticisms. Rather, they are tests to see how well you would be able to defend your position in a no-holds-barred conversation with the chairman of the board who says exactly what he or she thinks at all times. So go ahead and defend yourself, without taking or showing offense.

Your first response will be to gain time and get the interviewer talking. "Why do you say that?" you ask, answering a question with a question. And turning the tables on your aggressor displays your poise, calm, and analytical skills better than any other response.

"Why should I hire an outsider when I could fill the job with someone inside the company?"

The question isn't as stupid as it sounds. Obviously, the interviewer has examined existing employees with an eye toward their promotion or reassignment. Just as obviously, the job cannot be filled from within the company. If it could be, it would be, and for two very good reasons: It is cheaper for the company to promote from within, and it is good for employee morale.

Hiding behind this intimidating question is actually a pleasant invitation: "Tell me why I should hire you." Your answer follows two steps. The first is a simple recitation of your skills and personality profile strengths, tailored to the specific requirements of the job.

For the second step, realize first that whenever a manager is filling a position, he or she is looking not only for someone who can do the job, but also for someone who can benefit the department in a larger sense. No department is as good as it could be—each has weaknesses that need strengthening. So in the second part of your answer, include a question of your own: "Those are my general attributes. However, if no one is promotable from inside the company, that means you are looking to add strength to your team in a special way. In what ways do you hope the final candidate will be able to benefit your department?" The answer to this is your cue to sell your applicable qualities.

"Have you ever had any financial difficulties?"

The potential employer wants to know whether you can control not only your own finances, but finances in general. If you are in the insurance field, for example—claims, accounting, supervision, management—you can expect to hear this one. The question, though, is not restricted to insurance: Anyone, especially the person who handles money in day-to-day business, is fair game.

Remember that for someone to check your credit history, he or she must have your written consent. That is required under the 1972 Fair Credit and Reporting Act. When you fill out an application form, sign it, and date it, invariably somewhere on the form is a release permitting the employer to check your credit history. If you have already filled out the form, you might not hear the question, but your creditors might. I should note here that the reader who asked me about this question also described how she'd handled it during the interview: by describing her past problems with bankruptcy in every detail. However, in trying to be open and honest, she had actually done herself a disservice.

The interviewer does not want to hear sob-stories. Concentrate on the information that will damage your candidacy least and enhance it most. You might find it appropriate to bring the matter up yourself if you work in an area where your credit history is likely to be checked. If you choose to wait until the interviewer brings it up, you might say (if you had to file for bankruptcy, for instance), "I should tell you that some years ago, for reasons beyond my control, I was forced into personal bankruptcy. That has been behind me for some time. Today, I have a sound credit rating and no debts. Bankruptcy is not something I'm proud of, but I did learn from the experience, and I feel it has made me a more proficient account supervisor." The answer concentrates on today, not past history.

"How do you handle rejection?"

This question is common if you are applying for a job in sales, including face-to-face sales, telemarketing, public relations, and customer service. If you are after a job in one of these areas and you really don't like the heavy doses of rejection that are any salesperson's lot, consider a new field. The anguish you will experience will not lead to a successful career or a happy life.

With that in mind, let's look behind the question. The interviewer simply wants to know whether you take rejection as rejection of yourself or whether you simply accept it as a temporary rejection of a service or product. Here is a sample answer that you can tailor to your particular needs and background: "I accept rejection as an integral part of the sales process. If everyone said yes to a product, there would be no need for the sales function. As it is, I see every rejection as bringing me closer to the customer who will say yes." Then, if you are encouraged to go on: "I regard rejection as simply a fact of life, that the customer has no need for the product today. I can go on to my next call with the conviction that I am a little closer to my next sale."

"Why were you out of work for so long?"

You must have a sound explanation for any and all gaps in your employment history. If not, you are unlikely to receive a job offer. Emphasize that you were not just looking for another paycheck—you were looking for a company with which to settle and to which to make a long-term contribution.

"I made a decision that I enjoy my work too much just to accept another paycheck. So I determined that the next job I took would be one where I could settle down and do my best to make a solid contribution. From everything I have heard about this company, you are a group that expects people to pull their weight, because you've got a real job to do. I like that, and I would like to be part of the team. What have I got to do to get the job?"

You answer the question, compliment the interviewer, and shift the emphasis from you being unemployed to how you can get the job offer.

"Why have you changed jobs so frequently?"

If you have jumped around, blame it on youth (even the interviewer was young once). Now you realize what a mistake your job-hopping was, and with your added domestic responsibilities you are now much more settled. Or you may wish to impress on the interviewer that your job-hopping was never as a result of poor performance, and that you grew professionally as a result of each job change.

You could reply: "My first job was a very long commute. I soon realized that, but I knew it would give me good experience in a very competitive field. Subsequently, I found a job much closer to home where the commute was only an hour each way. I was very happy at my second job. However, I got an opportunity to really broaden my experience base with a new company that was starting up. With the wisdom of hindsight, I realize that was a mistake; it took me six months to realize I couldn't make a contribution there. I've been with my current company a reasonable length of time. So I have broad experience in different environments. I didn't just job-hop, I have been following a path to gain broad experience. So you see, I have more experience than the average person of my years, and a desire to settle down and make it pay off for me and my employer."

Or you can say: "Now I want to settle down and make all my diverse background pay off in my contributions to my new employer. I have a strong desire to contribute and am looking for an employer that will keep me challenged; I think this might be the company to do that. Am I right?"

"Tell me about a time when you put your foot in your mouth."

Answer this question with caution. The interviewer is examining your ability and willingness to interact pleasantly with others. The question is tricky because it asks you to show yourself in a poor light. Your answer will downplay the negative impact of your action and will end with positive information about your candidacy. The best thing to do is to start with an example outside of the workplace, and show how the experience improved your performance at work.

"About five years ago, I let the cat out of the bag about a surprise birthday party for a friend, a terrific *faux pas*. It was a mortifying experience, and I promised myself not to let anything like that happen again." Then, after this fairly innocuous statement, you can talk about communications in the workplace. "As far as work is concerned, I always regard employer/employee communications on any matter as confidential unless expressly stated otherwise. So, putting my foot in my mouth doesn't happen to me at work."

"Why do you want to leave your current job?" or, *"Why did you leave your last job?"*

This is a common trick question. You should have an acceptable reason for leaving every job you have held, but if you don't, pick one of the six acceptable reasons from the employment industry formula, the acronym for which is CLAMPS:

- **Challenge:** You weren't able to grow professionally in that position.
- **Location:** The commute was unreasonably long.
- **Advancement:** There was nowhere for you to go. You had the talent, but there were too many people ahead of you.
- **Money:** You were underpaid for your skills and contribution.
- **Pride or prestige:** You wanted to be with a better company.
- **Security:** The company was not stable.

For example: "My last company was a family-owned affair. I had gone as far as I was able. It just seemed time for me to join a more prestigious company and accept greater challenges."

"What interests you least about this job?"

This question is potentially explosive, but easily defused. Regardless of your occupation, there is at least one repetitive, mindless duty that everyone groans about and that goes with the territory. Use that as your example in a statement of this nature: "Filing is probably the least demanding part of the job. However, it is important to the overall success of my department, so I try to do it with a smile." This shows that you understand that it is necessary to take the rough with the smooth in any job.

"What was there about your last company that you didn't particularly like or agree with?"

You are being checked out as a potential fly in the ointment. If you have to answer, it might be the way the company policies and/or directives were sometimes consciously misunderstood by some employees who disregard the bottom line— the profitability of the corporation.

Or: "You know how it is sometimes with a big company. People lose awareness of the cost of things. There never seemed to be much concern about economy or efficiency. Everyone wanted his or her year-end bonus, but only worried about it in December. The rest of the year, nobody gave a hoot. I think that's the kind of thing we could be aware of most every day, don't you agree?"

Or: "I didn't like the way some people gave lip-service to 'the customer comes first,' but really didn't go out of their way to keep the customer satisfied. I don't think it was a fault of management, just a general malaise that seemed to affect a lot of people."

"What do you feel is a satisfactory attendance record?"

There are two answers to this question—one if you are in management, one if you are not. As a manager: "I believe attendance is a matter of management, motivation, and psychology. Letting the employees know you expect their best efforts and won't accept half-baked excuses is one thing. The other is to keep your employees motivated by a congenial work environment and the challenge to stretch themselves. Giving people pride in their work and letting them know you respect them as individuals have a lot to do with it, too."

If you are not in management, the answer is even easier: "I've never really considered it. I work for a living, I enjoy my job, and I'm rarely sick."

"What is your general impression of your last company?"

Always answer positively. Keep your real feelings to yourself, whatever they might be. There is a strong belief among the management fraternity that people who complain about past employers will cause problems for their new ones. Your answer is, "Very good" or, "Excellent." Then smile and wait for the next question.

"What are some of the problems you encounter in doing your job, and what do you do about them?"

Note well the old saying, "A poor workman blames his tools." Your awareness that careless mistakes cost the company good money means you are always on the lookout for potential problems. Give an example of a problem you recognized and solved.

For example: "My job is fairly repetitive, so it's easy to overlook problems.

Lots of people do. However, I always look for them; it helps keep me alert and motivated, so I do a better job. To give you an example, we make computer-memory disks. Each one has to be machined by hand, and once completed, the slightest abrasion will turn one into a reject. I have a steady staff and little turnover, and everyone wears cotton gloves to handle the disks. Yet about six months ago, the reject rate suddenly went through the roof. Is that the kind of problem you mean? Well, the cause was one that could have gone unnoticed for ages. Jill, the section head who inspects all the disks, had lost a lot of weight, her diamond engagement ring was slipping around her finger, and it was scratching the disks as she passed them and stacked them to be shipped. Our main client was giving us a big problem over it, so my looking for problems and paying attention to detail really paid off."

The interviewer was trying to get you to reveal weak points; you avoided the trap.

"What are some of the things you find difficult to do? Why do you feel that way?"

This is a variation on a couple of earlier questions. Remember, anything that goes against the best interests of your employer is difficult to do. If you are pressed for a job function you find difficult, answer in the past tense; that way, you show that you recognize the difficulty, but that you obviously handle it well.

"That's a tough question. There are so many things that are difficult to learn in our business if you want to do the job right. I used to have forty clients to sell to every month, and I was so busy touching bases with all of them, I never got a chance to sell to any of them. So I graded them into three groups. I call on the top twenty percent with whom I did business every three weeks. The next group were those I sold to occasionally. I called on them once a month, but with a difference—each month, I marked ten of them to spend time with and really get to know. I still have difficulty reaching all forty of my clients in a month, but my sales have tripled and are still climbing."

"Jobs have pluses and minuses. What were some of the minuses on your last job?"

A variation on the question, "What interests you least about this job?" which was handled earlier. Use the same type of answer. For example, "Like any salesperson, I enjoy selling, not doing the paperwork. But as I cannot expect the customer to get the goods, and me my commission, without following through on this task, I grin and bear it. Besides, if I don't do the paperwork, that holds up other people in the company."

If you are not in sales, use the salesforce as a scapegoat. "In accounts receivable, it's my job to get the money in to make payroll and good things like that. Half the time, the goods get shipped before I get the paperwork because sales says, 'It's a rush order.' That's a real minus to me. It was so bad at my last company, we tried a new approach. We met with sales and explained our problem. The result was that incremental commissions were based on cash in, not on bill date. They saw the connection, and things are much better now."

"What kinds of people do you like to work with?"

This is the easy part of a tricky three-part question. Obviously, you like to work with people who have pride, honesty, integrity, and dedication to their work. Now—

"What kinds of people do you find it difficult to work with?"

The second part of the same question. You could say: "People who don't follow procedures, or slackers—the occasional rotten apples who don't really care about the quality of their work. They're long on complaints, but short on solutions." Which brings us to the third part of the question:

"How have you successfully worked with this difficult type of person?"

This is the most difficult part to answer. You might reply: "I stick to my guns, keep enthusiastic, and hope some of it will rub off. I had a big problem with one guy—all he did was complain and always in my area. Eventually, I told him how I felt. I said if I were a millionaire, I'd have all the answers and wouldn't have to work, but as it was, I wasn't, and had to work for a living. I told him that I really enjoyed his company, but I didn't want to hear it any more. Every time I saw him after that, I presented him with a work problem and asked his advice. In other words I challenged him to come up with positives, not negatives."

You can go on that sometimes you've noticed that such people simply lack enthusiasm and confidence, and that energetic and cheerful co-workers can often change that. If the interviewer follows up with an inquiry about what you would do if no amount of good effort on your part solved the problem, respond, "I would maintain cordial relations, but not go out of my way to seek more than a business-like acquaintance. Life is too short to be demotivated by people who always think their cup is half empty."

"How did you get your last job?"

The interviewer is looking for initiative. If you can, show it. At the least, show determination.

"I was actually turned down for my last job as having too little experience. I asked the manager to give me a trial before she offered it to anyone else. I went in and asked for a list of companies they'd never sold to, picked up the phone, and in that hour I arranged two appointments. How did I get the job? In a word, determination!"

"How would you evaluate me as an interviewer?"

The question is dangerous, maybe more so than the one asking you to criticize your boss. Whatever you do, of course, don't tell the truth if you think the interviewer is an unconscious incompetent. It may be true, but it won't get you a job offer. This is an instance where honesty is not the best policy. It is best to say, "This is one of the toughest interviews I have ever been through, and I don't relish the prospect of going through another. Yet I do realize what you are trying to achieve." Then go on to explain that you understand the interviewer wants to know whether you can think on your feet, that there is pressure on the job, and that he or she is trying to simulate some of that real-life pressure in the interview. You may choose to finish the answer with a question of your own: "How do you think I fit the profile of the person you need?"

"I'm not sure you're suitable for the job."

Don't worry about the tone of the question—the interviewer's "I'm not sure" really means, "I'd like to hire you, so here's a wide-open opportunity to sell me." He or she is probing three areas from your personal profile: your confidence, determination, and listening profiles. Remain calm and put the ball straight back into the interviewer's court: "Why do you say that?" You need both the information and time to think up an appropriate reply, but it is important to show that you are not intimidated. Work out a program of action for this question; even if the interviewer's point regarding your skills is valid, come back with value keys and alternate compatible skills. You counter with other skills that show your competence and learning ability, and use them to show you can pick up the new skills quickly. Tie the two together and demonstrate that with your other attributes you can bring many plusses to the job. Finish your answer with a reflexive question that encourages a "yes" answer.

"I admit my programming skills in that language are a little light. However, all languages have similarities, and my experience demonstrates that with a competence in four other languages, getting up to speed with this one will take only a short while. Plus, I can bring a depth of other experience to the job." Then, after you itemize your experience: "Wouldn't you agree?"

If the reason for the question is not a lack of technical skills, it must be a question about one of your key profile areas. Perhaps the interviewer will say, "You haven't convinced me of your determination." This is an invitation to sell yourself, so tell a story that demonstrates determination.

For example: "It's interesting you should say that. My present boss is convinced of my determination. About a year ago we were having some problems with a union organization in the plant. Management's problem was our 50-percent Spanish monolingual production workforce. Despite the fact that our people had the best working conditions and benefits in the area, they were strongly pro-union. If they were successful, we would be the first unionized division in the company. No one in management spoke Spanish, so I took a crash Berlitz course—two hours at home every night for five weeks. I got one of the maintenance crew to help me with my grammar and diction. Then a number of other production workers started saying simple things to me in Spanish and helping me with the answers. I opened the first meeting with the workforce to discuss the problems. My 'Buenos dias. Me llamo Brandon,' got a few cheers. We had demonstrated that we cared enough to try to communicate. Our division never did unionize, and my determination to take the extra step paid off and allowed my superiors to negotiate from a position of caring and strength. That led to English lessons for the Spanish-speaking, and Spanish classes for the English-speaking. We are now a bilingual company, and I think that shows we care. Wouldn't you agree my work in that instance shows determination?"

"Wouldn't you feel better off in another firm?"

Relax, things aren't as bad as you might assume. This question is usually asked if you are really doing quite well, or if the job involves a certain amount of stress. A lawyer, for example, might well be expected to face this one. The trick is not to be intimidated. Your first step is to qualify the question: Relax, take a breath, sit back, smile, and say, "You surprise me. Why do you say that?" The interviewer must then talk, giving you precious time to collect your wits and come back with a rebuttal.

Then answer "no" and explain why. All the interviewer wants to see is how much you know about the company and how determined you are to join its ranks. Your earlier research and knowledge of personal profile keys (determination) will pay off again. Overcome the objection with an example, and show how that will help you contribute to the company; end with a question of your own. In this instance, the question has a twofold purpose: one, to identify a critical area to sell yourself; and two, to encourage the interviewer to consider an image of you working at the company.

You could reply: "Not at all. My whole experience has been with small companies. I am good at my job and in time could become a big fish in a little pond. But that is not what I want. This corporation is a leader in its business. You have a strong reputation for encouraging skills-development in your employees. This is the type of environment I want to work in. Now, coming from a small company, I have done a little bit of everything. That means that no matter what you throw at me, I will learn it quickly. For example, what would be the first project I would be involved with?"

And you end with a question of your own that gets the interviewer focusing on those immediate problems. You can then explain how your background and experience can help.

"What would you say if I told you your presentation this afternoon was lousy?"

"If" is the key here, with the accusation only there for the terminally neurotic. The question is designed to see how you react to criticism, and so tests manageability. No company can afford the thin-skinned today. You will come back and answer the question with a question of your own.

An appropriate response would be: "First of all, I would ask which aspects of my presentation were lousy. My next step would be to find out where you felt the problem was. If there'd been miscommunication, I'd clear it up. If the problem was elsewhere, I would seek your advice and be sure that the problem was not recurrent." This would show that when it is a manager's duty to criticize performance, you are an employee who will respond in a businesslike and emotionally mature manner.

The Illegal Question

Of course, one of the most stressful—and negative—questions is the illegal one, a question that delves into your private life or personal background. Such a question will make you uncomfortable if it is blatant, and could also make you angry.

Your aim, however, is to overcome the discomfort and to avoid anger: You want to get the job offer, and any self-righteousness or defensive reaction on your part will ensure that you *don't* get it. You may feel angry enough to get up and walk out, or say things like, "These are unfair practices; you'll hear from my lawyer in the morning." But the result will be that you won't get the offer, and therefore won't have the leverage you need. Remember, no one is saying you can't refuse the job once it's offered to you.

But what is an illegal question? Title VII is a federal law that forbids employers from discriminating against any person on the basis of sex, age, race, national origin, or religion. In addition, many states have laws that protect people who fall into other categories, such as the physically challenged. Here are some general guidelines interviewers must follow.

☐ An interviewer may not ask about your religion, church, synagogue, parish, the religious holidays you observe, or your political beliefs or affiliations. He or she may not ask, for instance, "Does your religion allow you to work on Saturdays?" *But*, the interviewer may ask something like, "This job requires work on Saturdays. Is that a problem?"

☐ An interviewer may not ask about your ancestry, national origin, or parentage; in addition, you cannot be asked about the naturalization status of your parents, spouse, or children. The interviewer cannot ask about your birthplace. *But*, the interviewer may ask (and probably will, considering the current immigration laws) whether you are a U.S. citizen or a resident alien with the right to work in the U.S.

☐ An interviewer may not ask about your native language, the language you speak at home, or how you acquired the ability to read, write, or speak a foreign language. *But*, he or she may ask about the languages in which you are fluent, if knowledge of those languages is pertinent to the job.

☐ An interviewer may not ask about your age, your date of birth, or the ages of your children. *But*, he or she may ask you whether you are over eighteen years old.

☐ An interviewer may not ask about maiden names or whether you have changed your name; your marital status, number of children or dependents, or your spouse's occupation; or whether (if you are a woman) you wish to be addressed as Miss, Mrs., or Ms. *But*, the interviewer may ask about how you like to be addressed (a common courtesy) and whether you have ever worked for the company before under a different name. (If you have worked for this company or other companies under a different name, you may want to mention that, in light of the fact that this prospective manager may check your references and additional background information.)

As you consider a question that seems to verge on illegality, you should take into account that the interviewer may be asking it innocently, and may be unaware of the laws on the matter. Your best bet is to be polite and straightforward, as you would in any other social situation. You also want to move the conversation to an examination of your skills and abilities, not your status. Here are some illegal questions—and some possible responses. Remember, your objective is to get job offers; if you later decide that this company is not for you, you are under no obligation to accept the position.

"What religion do you practice?"

If you do practice, you can say, "I attend my church/synagogue/mosque regularly, but I make it my practice not to involve my personal beliefs in my work. The work for the company and my career are too important for that."

If you do not practice a religion, you may want to say something like, "I have a set of personal beliefs that are important to me, but I do not attend any organized services. And I do not mix those beliefs with my work, if that's what you mean."

"How old are you?"

Old-age discrimination is still prevalent, but with older people joining the workforce every day and the increasing need for experienced workers, you will hear this question less and less. Answer the question in terms of your experience. For example: "I'm in my fifties and have more than twenty-five years of experience in this field." Then list your skills as they apply to the job.

"Are you married?"

If you are, the company is concerned with the impact your family duties and future plans will have on your tenure there. Your answer could be, "Yes, I am. Of course, I make a separation between my work life and my family life that allows me to give my all to a job. I have no problem with travel or late hours—those things are part of this line of work. I'm sure my references will confirm this for you."

"Do you plan to have children?"

This isn't any of the interviewer's business, but he or she wants to know whether you will leave the company early to raise a family. You can answer "no," of course. If you answer "yes," you might add, "But those plans are for the future, and they depend on the success of my career. Certainly, I want to do the best, most complete job for this company I can. I consider that my skills are right for the job and that I can make a long-range contribution. I certainly have no plans to leave the company just as I begin to make meaningful contributions."

If the questions become too pointed, you may want to ask—innocently—"Could you explain the relevance of that issue to the position? I'm trying to get a handle on it." That response, however, can seem confrontational; you should only use it if you are *extremely* uncomfortable, or are quite certain you can get away with it. Sometimes, the interviewer will drop the line of questioning.

Illegal questions tend to arise, not out of brazen insensitivity, but rather out of an interest in you. The employer is familiar with your skills and background, feels you can do the job, and wants to get to know you as a person. Outright discrimination these days is really quite rare. With illegal questions, your response must be positive—that's the only way you're going to get the job offer, and getting a job offer allows you to leverage other jobs. You don't have to work for a discriminatory company, but you can certainly use the firm to get to something better.

□   □   □

Interviewers may pull all kinds of tricks on you, but you will come through with flying colors once you realize that they're trying to discover something extremely simple—whether or not you can take the heat. After all, those interviewers are only trying to sort out the good corporate warriors from the walking wounded. If you are asked and successfully handle these trick and negatively phrased questions, the interviewer will end up looking at you favorably. Stay calm, give as good as you get, and take it all in good part. Remember that no one can intimidate you without your permission.

18.
Strange Venues

Why are some interviews conducted in strange places? Are meetings in noisy, distracting hotel lobbies designed as a form of torture? What are the real reasons that an interviewer invites you to eat at a fancy restaurant?

For the most part, these tough-on-the-nerves situations happen because the interviewer is a busy person, fitting you into a busy schedule. Take the case of a woman I know. She had heard stories about tough interview situations but never expected to face one herself. It happened at a retail convention in Arizona, and she had been asked to meet for a final interview by the pool. The interviewer was there, taking a short break between meetings, in his bathing suit. And the first thing the interviewer did was suggest that my friend slip into something comfortable.

That scenario may not lurk in your future, but the chances are that you will face many tough interview situations in your career. They call for a clear head and a little gamesmanship to put you ahead of the competition. The interviewee at the pool used both. She removed her jacket, folded it over the arm of the chair and seated herself, saying pleasantly, "That's much better. Where shall we begin?"

It isn't easy to remain calm at such times. On top of interview nerves, you're worried about being overheard in a public place, or (worse) surprised by the appearance of your current boss. That last item isn't too far-fetched. It actually happened to a reader from San Francisco. He was being interviewed in the departure lounge at the airport when his boss walked through the arrivals door. Oops—he had asked for the day off "to go to the doctor."

Could he have avoided the situation? Certainly, if he had asked about privacy when the meeting was arranged. That would have reminded the interviewer of the need for discretion. The point is to do all you can in advance to make such a meeting as private as possible. Once that's done, you can ignore the rest of the world and concentrate on the interviewer's questions.

Hotel Lobbies and Other Strange Places
Strange interview situations provide other wonderful opportunities to embarrass yourself. You come to a hotel lobby in full corporate battle dress: coat, briefcase, perhaps an umbrella. You sit down to wait for the interviewer. "Aha," you think to

yourself, opening your briefcase, "I'll show him my excellent work habits by delving into this computer printout."

That's not such a great idea. Have you ever tried rising with your lap covered with business papers, then juggling the briefcase from right hand to left to accommodate the ritual handshake? It's quite difficult. Besides, while you are sitting in nervous anticipation, pre-interview tension has no way of dissipating. Your mouth will become dry, and your "Good morning, I'm pleased to meet you" will come out sounding like the cat being strangled.

To avoid such catastrophes in places like hotel lobbies, first remove your coat on arrival. Then, instead of sitting, walk around a little while you wait. Even in a small lobby, a few steps back and forth will help you reduce tension to a manageable level. Keep your briefcase in your left hand at all times—it makes you look purposeful, and you won't trip over it when you meet the interviewer.

If, for any reason, you must sit down, make a conscious effort to breathe deeply and slowly. This will help control the adrenaline that makes you feel jumpy.

A strange setting can actually put you on equal footing with the interviewer. Neither of you is on home turf, so in many cases, the interviewer will feel just as awkward as you do. A little gamesmanship can turn the occasion to your advantage.

To gain the upper hand, get to the meeting site early to scout the territory. By knowing your surroundings, you will feel more relaxed. Early arrival also allows you to control the outcome of the meeting in other subtle ways. You will have time to stake out the most private spot in an otherwise public place. Corners are best. They tend to be quieter, and you can choose the seat that puts your back to the wall (in a practical sense, that is). In this position, you have a clear view of your surroundings and will feel more secure. The fear of being overheard will evaporate.

The situation is now somewhat in your favor. You know the locale, and the meeting place is as much yours as the interviewer's. You will have a clear view of your surroundings, and odds are that you will be more relaxed than the interviewer. When he or she arrives, say, "I arrived a little early to make sure we had some privacy. I think over here is the best spot." With that positive demonstration of your organizational abilities, you give yourself a head start over the competition.

The Meal Meeting

Breakfast, lunch, or dinner are the prime choices for interviewers who want to catch the seasoned professional off guard. In fact, the meal is arguably the toughest of all tough interview situations. The setting offers the interviewer the chance to see you in a nonoffice (and therefore more natural) setting, to observe your social graces, and to consider you as a whole person. Here, topics that would be impossible to address in the traditional office setting will naturally surface, often with virtually no effort on the part of the interviewer. The slightest slip in front of that wily old sea pirate opposite—thinly disguised in a Brooks Brothers suit—could get your candidacy deep-sixed *tout de suite*.

Usually you will not be invited to an "eating meeting" until you have already demonstrated that you are capable of doing the job. It's a good sign, actually: An invitation to a meal means that you are under strong consideration, and, by extension, intense scrutiny.

The meeting is often the final hurdle and could lead directly to the job offer—assuming, of course, that you properly handle the occasional surprises that arise. The interviewer's concern is not whether you can do the job, but whether you have the growth potential that will allow you to fill more senior slots as they become available.

But be careful. Many have fallen at the final hurdle in a close-run race. Being interviewed in front of others is bad enough; eating and drinking in front of them at the same time only makes it worse. If you knock over a glass or dribble spaghetti sauce down your chin, the interviewer will be so busy smirking that he or she won't hear what you have to say.

To be sure that the interviewer remains as attentive to the positive points of your candidacy as possible, let's discuss table manners.

Your social graces and general demeanor at the table can tell as much about you as your answer to a question. For instance, over-ordering food or drink can signal poor self-discipline. At the very least, it will call into question your judgment and maturity. High-handed behavior toward waiters and buspeople could reflect negatively on your ability to get along with subordinates and on your leadership skills. Those concerns are amplified when you return food or complain about the service, actions which, at the very least, find fault with the interviewer's choice of restaurant.

By the same token, you will want to observe how your potential employer behaves. After all, you are likely to become an employee, and the interviewer's behavior to servers in a restaurant can tell you a lot about what it will be like on the job.

☐ **Alcohol:** Soon after being seated, you will be offered a drink—if not by your host, then by the waiter. There are many reasons to avoid alcohol at interview meals. The most important reason is that alcohol fuzzes your mind, and research proves that stress increases the intoxicating effect of alcohol. So, if you order something to drink, try to stick with something nonalcoholic, such as a club soda or simply a glass of water. If pressed, order a white-wine spritzer, a sherry, or a light beer—it depends on the environment and what your host is drinking.

If you do have a drink, never have more than one. If there is a bottle of wine on the table, and the waiter offers you another glass, simply place your hand over the top of your glass. It is a polite way of signifying no.

You may be offered alcohol at the end of the meal. The rule still holds true—turn it down. You need your wits about you even if the interview seems to be drawing to a close. Some interviewers will try to use those moments, when your defenses are at their lowest, to throw in a couple of zingers.

☐ **Smoking:** Smoking is another big problem that is best handled by taking a simple approach. Don't do it unless encouraged. If both of you are smokers, and you are encouraged to smoke, follow a simple rule: Never smoke between courses, only at the end of a meal. Even most confirmed nicotine addicts, like the rest of the population, hate smoke while they are eating.

☐ **Utensils:** Keep all your cups and glasses at the top of your place setting and well away from you. Most glasses are knocked over at a cluttered table when one stretches for the condiments or gesticulates to make a point. Of course, your manners will prevent you from reaching rudely for the pepper-shaker.

When you are faced with an array of knives, forks, and spoons, it is always safe to start at the outside and work your way in as the courses come. Keep your elbows at your sides and don't slouch in the chair. When pausing between mouthfuls (which, if you are promoting yourself properly, should be frequently), rest your knife and fork on the plate this way.

The time to start eating, of course, is when the interviewer does; the time to stop is when he or she does. At the end of a course or the meal, rest your knife and fork together on the plate, at five o'clock.

Here are some other helpful hints:

- Never speak with your mouth full.
- To be on the safe side, eat the same thing, or close to it, as the interviewer. Of course, while this rule makes sense in theory, the fact is that you probably will be asked to order first, so ordering the same thing can become problematic. Solve the problem before you order by complimenting the restaurant during your small talk and then, when the menus arrive, asking, "What do think you will have today?"
- Do not change your order once it is made, and never send the food back.
- Be polite to your waiters, even when they spill soup in your lap.
- Don't order expensive food. Naturally, in our heart of hearts, we all like to eat well, especially on someone else's tab. But don't be tempted. When you come right down to it, you are there to talk and be seen at your best, not to eat.
- Eat what you know. Stay away from awkward, messy, or exotic foods (e.g., artichokes, long pasta, and escargot, respectively). Ignore finger foods, such as lobster or spare ribs. In fact, you should avoid eating with your fingers

altogether, unless you are in a sandwich joint, in which case you should make a point of avoiding the leaky, over-stuffed menu items.

- Don't order salad. The dressing can often get messy. If a salad comes with the meal, request that the dressing be on the side. Then, before pouring it on, cut up the lettuce.

- Don't order anything with bones. Stick with filets; there are few simple, gracious ways to deal with any type of bone.

☐ **Checks and Goodbyes:** I know an interviewer whose favorite test of composure is to have the waiter, by arrangement, put the bill on the interviewee's side of the table. She then chats on, waiting for something interesting to happen. If you ever find yourself in a similar situation, never pick up the check, however long it is left by your plate. When ready, your host will pick it up, because that's the simple protocol of the occasion. By the same token, you should never offer to share payment.

When parting company, always thank the host for his or her hospitality and the wonderful meal. Of course, you should be sure to leave on a positive note by asking good naturedly what you have to do to get the job.

☐   ☐   ☐

Strange interview situations can arise at any time during the interview cycle, and in any public place. Wherever you are asked to go, keep your guard up. Your table manners, listening skills, and overall social graces are being judged. The question on the interviewer's mind is: Can you be trusted to represent the company graciously?

19.
Welcome to the Real World

Of all the steps a recent graduate will take up the ladder of success over the years, none is more important or more difficult than getting a foot on the first rung. And the interviewing process designed for recent graduates is particularly rigorous, because management regards the hiring of entry-level professionals as one of its toughest jobs.

When a company hires experienced people, there is a track record to evaluate. With recent graduates, there is little or nothing. Often, the only solid things an interviewer has to go on are high-school, SAT, and/or college grades. That's not much on which to base a hiring decision—grades don't tell the interviewer whether you will fit in or make a reliable employee. Many recruiters liken the gamble of hiring recent graduates to laying down wines for the future: They know that some will develop into full-bodied, reliable vintages, but that others will be disappointments. So, recruiters have to find different ways to predict your potential accurately.

After relying, as best they can, on school performance to evaluate your ability, interviewers concentrate on questions that reveal how willing you are to learn and get the job done, and how manageable you are likely to be, both on average days and when the going gets rough.

Your goal is to stand out from all the other entry-level candidates as someone altogether different and better. For example, don't be like thousands of others who, in answer to questions about their greatest strength, reply lamely, "I'm good with people," or, "I like working with others." As you know by now, such answers do not separate you from the herd. In fact, they brand you as average. To stand out, a recent graduate must recount a past situation that illustrates how good he or she is with people, or one that demonstrates an ability to be a team player.

Fortunately, the key personality traits discussed throughout the book are just as helpful for getting your foot on the ladder as they are for aiding your climb to the top. They will guide you in choosing what aspects of your personality and background you should promote at the interview.

It isn't necessary to have snap answers ready for every question, because you never will. In fact, it is more important for you to pause after a question and collect your thoughts before answering: You must show that you think before you speak. That way, you will demonstrate your analytical abilities, which age feels youth has in short supply.

By the same token, occasionally asking for a question to be repeated is useful to gain time and is quite acceptable, as long as you don't do it with every question. And if a question stumps you, as sometimes happens, do not stutter incoherently. It is sometimes best to say simply, "I don't know." Or, you might say, "I'd like to come back to that later"—the odds are even that the interviewer will forget to ask again; if he or she doesn't, at least you've had some time to come up with an answer.

Knowing everything about a certain entry-level position is not necessary, because business feels it can teach you most things. But, as a vice president of Merrill Lynch once said, "You must bring to the table the ability to speak clearly." So, knowing what is behind those questions designed especially for recent graduates will give you the time to build informative and understandable answers.

"How did you get your summer jobs?"

All employers look favorably on recent graduates who have any work experience, no matter what it is. "It is far easier to get a fix on someone who has worked while at school," says Dan O'Brien, head of employment at Grumman Aerospace. "They manage their time better, are more realistic, and more mature. Any work experience gives us much more in common." So, as you make your answer, add that you learned that business is about making a profit, doing things more efficiently, adhering to procedures, and putting out whatever effort it takes to get the job done. In short, treat your summer jobs, no matter how humble, as any other business experience.

In this particular question, the interviewer is looking ideally for something that shows initiative, creativity, and flexibility. Here's an example: "In my town, summer jobs were hard to come by, but I applied to each local restaurant for a position waiting tables, called the manager at each one to arrange an interview, and finally landed a job at one of the most prestigious. I was assigned to the afternoon shift, but with my quick work, accurate billing, and ability to keep customers happy, they soon moved me to the evening shift. I worked there for three summers, and by the time I left, I was responsible for the training and management of the night-shift waiters, the allotment of tips, and the evening's final closing and accounting. All in all, my experience showed me the mechanics of a small business and of business in general."

"Which of the jobs you have held have you liked least?"

The interviewer is trying to trip you up. It is likely that your work experience contained a certain amount of repetition and drudgery, as all early jobs in the business world do. So beware of saying that you hated a particular job "because it was boring." Avoid the negative and say something along these lines: "All of my jobs had their good and bad points, but I've always found that if you want to learn, there's plenty to be picked up every day. Each experience was valuable." Then describe a seemingly boring job, but show how it taught you valuable lessons or helped you hone different aspects of your personality profile.

"What are your future vocational plans?"

This is a fancy way of asking, "Where do you want to be five years from now?" The trap all entry-level professionals make is to say, "In management," because they think that shows drive and ambition. It has become such a trite answer, though, that it immediately generates a string of questions that most recent graduates can't answer: What is the definition of management? What is a manager's prime responsibility? A manager in what area? Your safest answer identifies you with the profession you are trying to break into, and shows you have your feet on the ground. "My vocational plans are that I want to get ahead. To do that I must be able to channel my energies and expertise into those areas my industry and employer need. So given a couple of years I hope to have become a thorough professional with a clear understanding of the company, the industry, and where the biggest challenges, and therefore opportunities, lie. By that time, my goals for the future should be sharply defined." An answer like that will set you far apart from your contemporaries.

"What college did you attend, and why did you choose it?"

The college you attended isn't as important as your reasons for choosing it—the question is trying to examine your reasoning processes. Emphasize that it was your choice, and that you didn't go there as a result of your parents' desires or because generations of your family have always attended the Acme School of Welding. Focus on the practical. "I went to Greenbriar State—it was a choice based on practicality. I wanted a school that would give me a good education and prepare me for the real world. State has a good record for turning out students fully prepared to take on responsibilities in the real world. It is (or isn't) a big school, but/and it has certainly taught me some big lessons about the value of (whatever personality values apply) in the real world of business."

If the interviewer has a follow-up question about the role your parents played in selection of your school, be wary—he or she is plumbing your maturity. It is best to reply that the choice of the school was yours, though you did seek the advice of your parents once you had made your selection, and that they supported your decision.

"Are you looking for a permanent or temporary job?"

The interviewer wants reassurance that you are genuinely interested in the position and won't disappear in a few months to pursue post-doctoral studies in St. Tropez. Try to go beyond saying simply yes: Explain why you want the job. You might say, "Of course, I am looking for a permanent job. I intend to make my career in this field, and I want the opportunity to learn the business, face new challenges, and learn from experienced professionals." You will also want to qualify the question with one of your own at the end of your answer: "Is this a permanent or a temporary position you are trying to fill?" And don't be scared to ask. The occasional unscrupulous employer will hire someone fresh out of school for a short period of time—say, for one particular project—and then lay them off.

"How did you pay for college?"

Avoid saying "Oh, Daddy handled all of that," as it probably won't create quite the impression you'd like. Your parents may well have helped you out, but you should explain, if it's appropriate, that you worked part-time and took out loans (as most of us must during college).

"We have tried to hire people from your school/your major before, and they never seem to work out. What makes you different?"

Here's a stress question to test your poise and analytical skills. You can shout that, yes, of course you are different and can prove it. So far, though, all you know is that there was a problem, not what caused the problem. Respond this way: "First, may I ask you exactly what problems you've had with people from this background?" Once you know what the problem is (if one really exists at all—it may just be a curve ball to test your poise) then you can illustrate how you are different. But only then. Otherwise, you run the risk of your answer being interrupted with, "Well, that's what everyone else said before I hired them. You haven't shown me that you are different."

"I'd be interested to hear about some things you learned in school that could be used on the job."

While specific job-related courses could form part of your answer, they cannot be all of it. The interviewer wants to hear about "real-world" skills, so oblige by explaining what the experience of college taught you rather than a specific course. In other words, explain how the experience honed your relevant personality profiles. "Within my major and minor I tried to pursue those courses that had most practical relevance, such as . . . However, the greatest lessons I learned were the importance of . . ." and then list your personality profile strengths.

"Do you like routine tasks/regular hours?"

A trick question. The interviewer knows from bitter experience that most recent graduates hate routine and are hopeless as employees until they come to an acceptance of such facts of life. Explain that, yes, you appreciate the need for routine, that you expect a fair amount of routine assignments before you are entrusted with the more responsible ones, and that that is why you are prepared to accept it as necessary. As far as regular hours go you could say, "No, there's no problem there. A company expects to make a profit, so the doors have to be open for business on a regular basis."

"What have you done that shows initiative and willingness to work?"

Again, tell a story about how you landed or created a job for yourself, or even got involved in some volunteer work. Your answer should show initiative in that you both handled unexpected problems calmly and anticipated others. Your willingness is demonstrated by the ways you overcame obstacles. For example: "I worked for a summer in a small warehouse. I found out that a large shipment was due in a couple of weeks, and I knew that room had to be made. The inventory system was outdated, and the rear of the warehouse was disorganized, so I came in on a Saturday, figured out how much room I needed, cleaned up the mess in the rear, and catalogued it all on the new inventory forms. When the shipment arrived, the truck just backed in. There was even room to spare."

Often after an effort above and beyond the call of duty, a manager might congratulate you, and if it had happened to you in this instance, you might conclude your answer with the verbal endorsement. "The divisional manager happened along just when I was finishing the job, and said he wished he had more people who took such pride in their work."

"Can you take instructions without feeling upset or hurt?"

This is a manageability question. If you take offense easily or bristle when your mistakes are pointed out, you won't last long with any company. Competition is fierce at the entry level, so take this as another chance to set yourself apart. "Yes, I can take instructions—and more important, I can take constructive criticism without feeling hurt. Even with the best intent, I will still make mistakes, and at times someone will have to put me back on the right track. I know that if I ever expect to rise in the company, I must first prove myself to be manageable."

"Have you ever had difficulties getting along with others?"

This is a combination question, probing willingness and manageability. Are you a team player or are you going to disrupt the department and make the interviewer's life miserable? This is a closed-ended question that requires only a yes/no answer, so give one and shut up.

"What type of position are you interested in?"

This again is one of those questions that tempts you to mention management. Don't. Say you are interested in what you will be offered anyway, which is an entry-level job. "I am interested in an entry-level position that will enable me to learn this business inside and out, and will give me the opportunity to grow when I prove myself, either on a professional or a managerial ladder."

"What qualifications do you have that will make you successful in this field?"

There is more to answering this question than reeling off your academic qualifications. In addition you will want to stress relevant work experience and illustrate your strong points as they match the key personality traits as they apply to the position you seek. It's a simple, wide-open question that says, "Hey, we're looking for an excuse to hire you. Give us some help."

"Why do you think you would like this type of work?"

This is a deceptively simple question because there is no pat answer. It is usually asked to see whether you really understand what the specific job and profession entails on a day-to-day basis. So, to answer it requires you to have researched the company and job functions as carefully as possible. Preparation for this should include a call to another company in the field and a request to speak to someone doing the job you hope to get. Ask what the job is like and what that person does day to day. How does the job fit into the department? What contribution does it make to the overall efforts of the company? Why does he or she like that type of work? Armed with that information, you will show that you understand what you are getting into; most recent graduates do not.

"What's your idea of how industry works?"

The interviewer does not want a long dissertation, just the reassurance that you don't think it works along the same lines as a registered charity. Your understanding should be something like this: "The role of any company is to make as much money as possible, as quickly and efficiently as possible, and in a manner that will encourage repeat business from the existing client base and new business from word of mouth and reputation." Finish with the observation that it is every employee's role to play as a team member in order to achieve those goals.

"What do you know about our company?"

You can't answer this question unless you have enough interest to research the company thoroughly. If you don't have that interest, you should expect someone who has made the effort to get the job.

"What do you think determines progress in a good company?"

Your answer will include all the positive personality traits you have been illustrating throughout the interview. Include allusions to the listening profile, determination, ability to take the rough with the smooth, adherence to systems and procedures, and the good fortune to have a manager who wants you to grow.

"Do you think grades should be considered by first employers?"

If your grades were good, the answer is obviously yes. If they weren't, your answer needs a little more thought. "Of course, an employer should take everything into consideration, and along with grades will be an evaluation of willingness and manageability, an understanding of how business works, and actual work experience. Combined, such experience and professional skills can be more valuable than grades alone."

□   □   □

Many virtuous candidates are called for entry-level interviews, but only those who prepare themselves to answer the tough questions will be chosen. Interviews for recent graduates are partly sales presentations. And the more you interview, the better you get, so don't leave preparing for them until the last minute. Start now and hone your skills to get a headstart on your peers. Finally, here's what a professor from a top-notch business school once told me: "You are taking a new product to market. Accordingly, you've got to analyze what it can do, who is likely to be interested, and how you are going to sell it to them." Take some time to get to know yourself and your particular values as they will be perceived in the world of business.

20.
The Graceful Exit

To paraphrase Shakespeare, all the employment world's a stage, and all the people on it merely players making their entrances and exits. Curtains rise and fall, and your powerful performance must be capped with a professional and memorable exit. To ensure you leave the right impression, this chapter will review the do's and don'ts of leaving an interview.

A signal that the interview is drawing to a close comes when you are asked whether you have any questions. Ask questions, and by doing so, highlight your strengths and show your enthusiasm. Your goal at the interview is to generate a job offer, so you should find it easy to avoid the crimes that damage your case.

Don'ts:

1. **Don't discuss salary, vacation, or benefits.** It is not that the questions are invalid, just that the timing is wrong. Bringing such topics up before you have an offer is asking what the company can do for you—instead, you should be saying what you can do for the company. Those topics are part of the negotiation (handled in chapter 23, "Negotiating the Offer"); remember, without an offer you have nothing to negotiate.

2. **Don't press for an early decision.** Of course you should ask, "When will I know your decision?" But don't press it. And don't try to use the "other-opportunities-I-have-to-consider" gambit as leverage when no such offers exist—that annoys the interviewer, makes you look foolish, and may even force you to negotiate from a position of weakness. Timing is everything; the issue of how to handle other opportunities as leverage is explored in detail later.

3. **Don't show discouragement.** Sometimes a job offer can occur on the spot. Usually it does not. So don't show discouragement if you are not offered the job at the interview, because discouragement shows a lack of self-esteem and determination. Avoiding a bad impression is merely the foundation of leaving a good one, and the right image to leave is one of enthusiasm, guts, and openness—just the traits you have been projecting throughout the interview.

4. **Don't ask for an evaluation of your interview performance.** That forces the issue and puts the interviewer in an awkward position. You *can* say that you want the job, and ask what you have to do to get it.

Dos:

1. **Ask appropriate job-related questions.** When the opportunity comes to ask any final questions, review your notes. Bring up any relevant strengths that haven't been addressed.

2. **Show decisiveness.** If you are offered the job, react with enthusiasm. Then sleep on it. If it's possible to do so without making a formal acceptance, lock the job up now and put yourself in control; you can always change your mind later. But before you make any commitment with regard to compensation, see chapter 23, "Negotiating the Offer."

3. **When you are interviewed by more than one person, be sure you have the correct spelling of their names.** "I enjoyed meeting your colleagues, Ms. Smith. Could you give me the correct spelling of their names, please?" This question will give you the names you forgot in the heat of battle and will demonstrate your consideration.

4. **Review the job's requirements with the interviewer.** Match them point by point with your skills and attributes.

5. **Find out whether this is the only interview.** If so, you must ask for the job in a positive and enthusiastic manner. Find out the time frame for a decision and finish with: "I am very enthusiastic about the job and the contributions I can make. If your decision will be made by the fifteenth, what must I do in the meantime to assure I get the job?"

6. **Ask for the next interview.** When there are subsequent interviews in the hiring procedure, ask for the next interview in the same honest and forthright manner. "Is now a good time to schedule our next meeting?" If you do not ask, you do not get.

7. **Keep yourself in contention.** A good leading question to ask is, "Until I hear from you again, what particular aspects of the job and this interview should I be considering?"

8. **Always depart in the same polite and assured manner you entered.** Look the interviewer in the eye, put on a smile (there's no need to grin), give a firm handshake, and say, "This has been an exciting meeting for me. This is a job I can do, and I feel I can contribute to your goals, because the atmosphere here seems conducive to doing my very best work. When will we speak again?"

IV

Finishing Touches

The successful completion of every interview is a big stride toward getting job offers, yet it is not the end of your job hunt.

A company rarely hires the first competent person it sees. A hiring manager will sometimes interview as many as fifteen people for a particular job, but the strain and pace of conducting interviews naturally dim the memory of each applicant. Unless you are the last person to be interviewed, the impression you make will fade with each subsequent interview the interviewer undertakes. And if you are not remembered, you will not be offered the job. You must develop a strategy to keep your name and skills constantly in the forefront of the interviewer's mind. These finishing touches often make all the difference.

Some of the suggestions here may not seem earth-shattering, just simple, sensible demonstrations of your manners, enthusiasm, and determination. But remember that today all employers are looking for people with that extra little something. You can avoid the negative or merely indifferent impression and be certain of creating a positive one by following these guidelines.

21.
Out of Sight, Out of Mind

The first thing you do on leaving the interview is breathe a sigh of relief. The second is to make sure that "out of sight, out of mind" will not apply to you. You do this by starting a follow-up procedure immediately after the interview.

Sitting in your car, on the bus, train, or plane, do a written recap of the interview while it's still fresh in your mind. Answer these questions.

- Whom did you meet? (Names and titles.)
- What does the job entail?
- What are the first projects/biggest challenges?
- Why can you do the job?
- What aspects of the interview went poorly? Why?
- What is the agreed-upon next step?
- What was said during the last few minutes of the interview?

Probably the most difficult—and most important—thing to do is to analyze what aspects of the interview went poorly. A person does not get offered a job based solely on strength. On the contrary, many people get new jobs based on their relative lack of negatives as compared to the other applicants. So it is mandatory that you look for and recognize any negatives from your performance. That is the only way you will have an opportunity to package and overcome those negatives in your follow-up procedure and during subsequent interviews.

The next step is to write the follow-up letter to the interviewer to acknowledge the meeting and to keep you fresh in his or her mind. Writing a follow-up letter also shows that you are both appreciative and organized, and it refreshes the urgency of your candidacy at the expense of other candidates. But remember that a canned follow-up form letter could hurt your candidacy.

☐ **1. Type the letter.** It exhibits greater professionalism. If you don't own a typewriter, the local library will frequently allow the use of theirs. If not, a typing service will do it for a nominal fee. If, for any reason, the letter cannot be typed, make sure it is legibly and neatly written. The letter should make four points clear to the company representative:

- You paid attention to what was being said.
- You understood the importance of the interviewer's comments.
- You are excited about the job, can do it, and want it.
- You can contribute to those first major projects.

☐ **2. Use the right words and phrases in your letter.** Here are some you might want to use.

- "Upon reflection," or, "Having thought about our meeting . . ."
- Recognize—"I recognize the importance of . . ."
- Listen—"Listening to the points you made . . ."
- Enthusiasm—Let the interviewer catch your enthusiasm. It is very effective, especially as your letter will arrive while other applicants are nervously sweating their way through the interview.
- Impressed—Let the interviewer know you were impressed with the people/product/service/facility/market/position, but do not overdo it.
- Challenge—Show that you feel you would be challenged to do your best work in this environment.
- Confidence—There is a job to be done and a challenge to be met. Let the interviewer know you are confident of doing both well.
- Interest—If you want the job (or next interview), say so. At this stage, the company is buying and you are selling. Ask for the job in a positive and enthusiastic manner.
- Appreciation—As a courtesy and mark of professional manners, you must express appreciation for the time the interviewer took out of his or her busy schedule.

☐ **3. Whenever possible and appropriate, mention the names of the people you met at the interview.** Draw attention to one of the topics that was of general interest to the interviewers.

☐ **4. Address the follow-up letter to the main interviewer.** Send a copy to personnel with a note of thanks as a courtesy.

☐ **5. Don't gild the lily.** Keep it short—less than one page—and don't make any wild claims that might not withstand close scrutiny.

☐ **6. Mail the letter within twenty-four hours of the interview.** If the decision is going to be made in the next couple of days, hand-deliver the letter or make a strong point by sending a mailgram. The follow-up letter will help to set you apart from other applicants and will refresh your image in the mind of the interviewer just when it would normally be starting to dim.

☐ **7. If you do not hear anything after five days (which is quite normal), put in a telephone call to the company representative.** Reiterate the points made in the letter, saying that you want the job (or next interview), and finish your statements with a question: "Mr. Smith, I feel confident about my ability to contribute to your department's efforts, and I really want the job. Could you tell me what I have to do to get it?" Then be quiet and wait for the answer.

☐   ☐   ☐

Of course, you may be told you are no longer in the running. The next chapter will show you that that is a great opportunity to snatch victory from the jaws of defeat.

22.
Snatching Victory from the Jaws of Defeat

During the interviewing process, there are bound to be interviewers who erroneously come to the conclusion that you are not the right person for the job they need to fill. When that happens, you will be turned down. Such an absurd travesty of justice can occur in different ways:

- At the interview.
- In a letter of rejection.
- During your follow-up telephone call.

Whenever the turn-down comes, you must be emotionally and intellectually prepared to take advantage of the opportunity being offered to you.

When you get turned down for the only opportunity you have going, the rejection can be devastating to your ego. That is why I have stressed the wisdom of having at least a few interviews in process at the same time.

You will get turned down. No one can be right for every job. The right person for a job doesn't always get it, however—the best prepared and most determined often does. While you may be responsible in part for the initial rejection, you still have the power to correct the situation and win the job offer. What you do with the claimed victory is a different matter—you will then be in a seller's market with choice and control of your situation.

To turn around a turn-down often requires only willpower and determination. Almost every job you desire is obtainable once you understand the hiring process from the interviewer's side of the desk. Your initial—and temporary—rejection is attributable to one of these reasons:

- The interviewer does not feel you can do the job.
- The interviewer feels you lack a successful profile.
- The interviewer did not feel your personality would contribute to the smooth functioning of the department—perhaps you didn't portray yourself as either a team player, or as someone willing to take the extra step.

With belief in yourself, you can still succeed. Repeat to yourself constantly through the interview cycle: "I will get this job, because no one else can give as much to this company as I can!" Do that and implement the following plan immediately when you hear of rejection, whether in person, via mail, or over the telephone.

☐ **Step One:** Thank the interviewer for the time and consideration. Then ask politely: "To help my future job search, why wasn't I chosen for the position?" Assure the interviewer that you would truly appreciate an honest, objective analysis. Listen to the reply and do not interrupt regardless of the comments. Use your time constructively and take notes furiously. When the company representative finishes speaking, show you understood the comments. (Remember, understanding and agreeing are different animals.)

"Thank you, Mr. Smith, now I can understand the way you feel. Because I am not a professional interviewer, I'm afraid my interview nerves got in the way. I'm very interested in working for your company" [use an enthusiastic tone] "and am determined to get the job. Let me meet with you once again. This time, when I'm not so nervous, I am confident you will see I really do have the skills you require" [then provide an example of a skill you have in the questionable area]. "You name the time and the place, and I will be there. What's best for you, Mr. Smith?"

End with a question, of course. An enthusiastic request like that is very difficult to refuse and will usually get you another interview. An interview, of course, at which you must shine.

☐ **Step Two:** Check your notes and accept the company representative's concerns. Their validity is irrelevant; the important point is that the negative points represent the problem areas in the interviewer's perception of you. List the negative perceptions, and using the techniques, exercises, and value keys discussed throughout the book, develop different ways to overcome or compensate for every negative perception.

☐ **Step Three:** Reread part 3 of this book.

☐ **Step Four:** Practice aloud the statements and responses you will use at the interview. If you can practice with someone who plays the part of the interviewer, so much the better. That will create a real interview atmosphere and be helpful to your success. Lacking a role-play partner, you can create that live answer by putting the anticipated objections and questions on a tape and responding to them.

☐ **Step Five:** Study all available information on the company.

☐ **Step Six:** Congratulate yourself continually for getting another interview after initial rejection. This is proof of your self-worth, ability, and tenacity. You have nothing to lose and everything to gain, having already risen phoenix-like from the ashes of temporary defeat.

☐ **Step Seven:** During the interview, ask for the job in a positive and enthusiastic manner. Your drive and staying power will impress the interviewer. All you must do to win the job is overcome the perceived negatives, and you have been given the time to prepare. Go for it.

☐ **Step Eight:** Even when all has failed at the subsequent interview, do not leave without a final request for the job. Play your trump card: "Mr. Smith, I respect the fact that you allowed me the opportunity to prove myself here today. I am convinced I am the best person for the job. I want you to give me a trial, and I will prove on the job that I am the best hiring decision you have made this year. Will you give us both the opportunity?"

A reader once wrote to me as I was revising *Knock 'em Dead*. The letter read in part, "I read the chapter entitled 'Snatching Victory from the Jaws of Defeat' and did everything you said to salvage what appeared to be a losing interview. My efforts did make a very good impression on the interviewer, but as it was finally explained to me, I really did not have equal qualifications for the job, and finally came in a close second. I really want to work for this growing company, and they say they have another position coming up in six months. What should I do?"

I know of someone in the airline business who wanted a job working on that most prestigious of aircraft, the Concorde. He had been recently laid off and had high hopes for a successful interview. As it happened, he came in second for the Concorde position. He was told that the firm would speak to him again in the near future. So he waited—for eight months. Finally, he realized that waiting for the job could only leave him unemployed. The moral of the story is that you must be brutally objective when you come out second-best, and whatever the interviewer says, you must sometimes assume that you are getting the polite brush-off.

With that in mind, let's see what can be done on the positive side. First of all, send a thank-you note to the interviewer, acknowledging your understanding of the state of affairs and reaffirming your desire to work for the company. Conclude with a polite request to bear you in mind for the future.

Then, keep an eye out for any news item about the company in the press. Whenever you see something, cut it out and mail it to the interviewer with a very brief note that says something like: "I came across this in *Forbes* and thought you might find it interesting. I am still determined to be your next account manager, so please keep me in mind when the next opening occurs."

You can also call the interviewer once every couple of months, just to check in. Remember, of course, to keep the phone call brief and polite—you simply want to keep your name at the top of the interviewer's mind.

And maybe something will come of it. Ultimately, however, your only choice is to move on. There is no gain waiting on an interviewer's word. Go out and keep looking, because chances are that you will come up with an even better job. Then, if you still want to work for that company that gave you the brush-off, you will have some leverage.

Most people fail in their endeavors by quitting just before the dawn of success.

Follow these directions and you can win the job. You have proved yourself to be a fighter, and that is universally admired. The company representative will want you to succeed because you are made of stuff that is rarely seen today. You are a person of guts, drive, and endurance—the hallmarks of a winner. Job turn-downs are an opportunity to exercise and build your strengths, and by persisting, you may well add to your growing number of job offers, now and in the future.

23.
Negotiating the Offer

The crucial period after you have received a formal offer and before you accept is probably the one point in your relationship with an employer at which you can say with any accuracy that you have the whip hand. The advantage, for now, is yours. They want you but don't have you; and their wanting something they don't have gives you a negotiating edge. An employer is also more inclined to respect and honor a person who has a clear understanding of his or her worth in the marketplace—they want a savvy and businesslike person.

You don't have to accept or reject the first offer, whatever it is. In most instances you can improve the initial offer in a number of ways, but you have to know something about the existing market conditions for those employed in your area of endeavor. If you are female, bear in mind that simply settling for a few points above your current rate of pay is bad advice for anyone and downright crazy for you. A word or two on the sober topic of pay discrimination is in order here.

The Women's Bureau of the U.S. Department of Labor tells us that men outearn women in nearly every field. (For what it's worth, my research could not turn up a single industry in which this was not the case.) Even if a woman's responsibilities, background, and accomplishments are exactly the same as those of her male colleague, she is statistically unlikely to take home a paycheck equal to his.

According to the Women's Bureau, male engineers make 14.3 percent more than their female counterparts. Male mathematicians make 16.3 percent more. Male advertising and public relations professionals make 28 percent more. Male lawyers and judges make 28 percent more. And male editors and reporters make a whopping 43 percent more than women performing the same or comparable work.

Those are big discrepancies, and they're just the tip of the iceberg. On average, a woman earns seventy cents for every dollar a man performing the same work earns. That's up from fifty-nine cents, which was the figure back in 1981, but it's still a depressing figure for women in the workplace today. At this rate, American industry will not be able to reach gender-based pay equity until the year 2020.

Is this a conscious male conspiracy against women? I think not. My personal belief is that much of the gap can be attributed to a simple lack of knowledge of professional negotiating skills, and that women in the workplace are picking these skills up fast. A recent Industry Week survey showed that 75 percent of men believe their firms pay men and women equally, even though only a little over half of all American corporations have standardized pay scales. This indicates that qualified female hires are now in a position, at least at the majority of firms, to receive fair consideration of their requests for equitable pay rates. But they have to ask.

Man or woman, there is no guarantee that you are being paid what you are worth. The simple facts are these: If you don't get it while they want you and don't have you, you sure as shootin' can't count on getting it once they do have you. When a thirty-year-old undernegotiates his or her salary by just $2,000 on a new job, it will cost that person a minimum of $70,000 over the course of a career. And remember, every subsequent raise will come from a proportionately lower base; real dollars lost over an entire career span could actually be double this figure.

To get what you have coming at the negotiating table, you must take the time to understand what you have achieved, what you have to offer, and what you are worth to the employer. You should be able to get a better handle on that final item by doing good research, but remember that regional influences can affect pay levels, as can current business conditions.

Everything in this book has been written toward maximizing your professional worth, and salary negotiation is certainly no exception. Please bear in mind that there are no shortcuts. The ideas presented in this chapter will be helpful to you if they represent the culmination of your successful campaign to set yourself apart from the competition, but you cannot negotiate a terrific salary package if an employer is not convinced that you are in the top tier of applicants.

Follow this three-step procedure in planning your salary discussions with employers.

☐ **Step One:** Before getting into negotiation with any employer, work out your minimum cash requirements for any job; you must know what it is going to take to keep a roof over your head and bread on the table. It's necessary to know this figure, but you need never discuss it with anyone—knowing it is the foundation of getting both what you need and what you are worth.

☐ **Step Two:** Get a grip on what your skills are worth in the current market. There are a number of ways to do that. Consider the resources and methods outlined below.

- You may be able to find out the salary range for the level above you and the level beneath you at the company in question.

- You can get information from the Bureau of Labor Statistics in Washington, DC, which keeps stats on hundreds of job titles. Be warned, however, that those titles are often a little out of date.

- Your state labor office may have salary ranges available for you to review.

- Ask headhunters—they know better than anyone what the market will bear. You should, as a matter of career prudence, establish an ongoing relationship with a reputable headhunter, because you never know when his or her services will come in handy.

- Many professional journals publish annual salary surveys you can consult.
- *The National Business Employment Weekly*, a magazine published by *The Wall Street Journal*, runs ongoing salary surveys by profession; back issues are available.

☐ **Step Three:** This is the fun part. Come up with the figure that would make you smile, drop dead, and go to heaven on the spot. (But try to keep it somewhere within the bounds of reality—multimillion-dollar offers with stock options being in relatively short supply for most of us.)

☐　☐　☐

You now have three figures: a minimum, a realistic midpoint desired salary, and a dream salary.

Your minimum is, as I have said, for personal consumption—never discuss it with anyone. Put it aside, and what do you have left? A salary range, just like the one every employer has for every interview you attend. Yours extends from your midpoint to your dream salary. Yes, that range represents the "top half" of what you want or, more accurately, could conceivably accept—but there's a reason for that. In the event, you will find that it is far easier to negotiate down than it is to negotiate up, and you must find a starting point that gives you every possible advantage.

Negotiate When You Can

I have said throughout *Knock 'em Dead* that your sole aim at the interview is to get the job offer, because without it you have nothing to negotiate. Once the offer is extended, the time to negotiate has arrived, and there will never be a more opportune time. Your relationship with the potential employer has gone through a number of distinct changes—from, "Perhaps we should speak to this one," to, "Yes, he might be able to do the job," through, "This is the top candidate, we really like him and want to have him on board." But now is the only point in the relationship when you will have the upper hand. Enjoy it while you can.

Although questions of salary are usually brought up after you are under serious consideration, you must be careful to avoid painting yourself into a corner when you fill out the initial company application form that contains a request for required salary. Usually you can get away with "open" as a response; sometimes the form will instruct you not to write "open," in which case you can write "negotiable," or "competitive."

☐　☐　☐

So much for basic considerations. Let's move on to the money questions that are likely to be flying around the room.

The salary/job negotiation begins in earnest in two ways. The interviewer can bring up the topic with statements like:

- "How do you think you would like working here?"

- "People with your background always fit in well with us."
- "You could make a real contribution here."
- "Well, you certainly seem to have what it takes."

Or, if it is clearly appropriate to do so, you can bring on the negotiating stage. In that case, you can make mirror images of the above, which make the interviewer face the fact that you certainly are able to do the job, and that the time has therefore come to talk turkey:

- "How do you think I would fit in with the group?"
- "I feel my background and experience would definitely complement the workgroup, don't you?"
- "I think I could make a real contribution here. What do you think?"
- "I know I have what it takes to do this job. What questions are lingering in your mind?"

Now then. What do you do when the question of money is brought up before you have enough details about the job to negotiate from a position of knowledge and strength? Postpone money talk until you have the facts in hand. Do that by asking something like: "I still have one or two questions about my responsibilities, and it will be easier for me to talk about money when I have cleared them up. Could I first ask you a few questions about . . . ?"

Then proceed to clarify duties and responsibilities, being careful to weigh the relative importance of the position and the individual duties to the success of the department you may join.

The employer is duty-bound to get your services as reasonably as possible, while you have an equal responsibility to do the best you can for yourself. Your goal is not to settle for less than will enable you to be happy on the job—unhappiness at work can taint the rest of your life. It is far easier to negotiate down than it is to negotiate up. The value of the offer you accept depends on your performance throughout the interview and hiring cycle, and especially the finesse you display in the final negotiations. The rest of the chapter is going to address the many questions that might be asked, or that you might ask, to bring matters to a successful conclusion.

"What is an adequate reward for your efforts?"

A glaring manageability question and money probe all in one. The interviewer probably already has a typist on staff who expects a Nobel Prize each time he or she gets out a faultless letter. Your answer should be honest and cover all bases. "My primary satisfaction and reward comes from a job well done and completed on time. The occasional good word from my boss is always welcome. Last but not least, I think everyone looks forward to a salary review."

"What is your salary history?" or, *"What was your salary progress on your last job?"*

The interviewer is looking for a couple of things here. First, he or she is looking for the frequency, percentage, and dollar-value of your raises, which in turn tell him or her about your performance and the relative value of the offer that is about to be made. What you want to avoid is tying the potential offer to your salary history—the offer you negotiate should be based solely on the value of the job in hand. Again, this is even more important if you are a woman.

Your answer needs to be specifically vague. Perhaps: "My salary history has followed a steady upward path, and I have never failed to receive merit increases. I would be glad to give you the specific numbers if needed, but I shall have to sit down and give it some thought with a pencil and paper." The odds are that the interviewer will not ask you to do that; if he or she does, nod in agreement and say that you'll get right to it when you get home. Don't begin the task until you are requested a second time, which is unlikely.

If for any reason you do get your back against the wall with this one, be sure to include in the specifics of your answer that "one of the reasons I am leaving my current job is that raises were standard for all levels of employees, so that despite my superior contributions, I got the same percentage raise as the tardy employee. I want to work in an environment where I will be recognized and rewarded for my contributions." Then end with a question: "Is this the sort of company where I can expect that?"

"What were you making on your last job?"

A similar but different question. It could also be phrased, "What are you making now?" or, "What is your current salary?"

While I have said that your current earnings should bear no relation to your starting salary on the new job, it can be difficult to make that statement clear to the interviewer without appearing objectionable. Although the question asks you to be specific, you needn't get too specific. Instead, you should try to draw attention to the fact that the two jobs are different. A short answer might include: "I am earning $X, although I'm not sure how that will help you in your evaluation of my worth for this job, because the two jobs are somewhat different."

It is important to understand the "areas of allowable fudge." For instance, if you are considerably underpaid, you may want to weigh the dollar-value of such perks as medical and dental plans, pay in lieu of vacation, profit-sharing and pension plans, bonuses, stock options, and other incentives. For many people, those can add between 20 to 35 percent to their base salary—you might honestly be able to mention a higher figure than you at first thought possible. Also, if you are due for a raise imminently, you are justified in adding it in.

It isn't common for current or previous salaries to be verified by employers, although certain industries, because of legal requirements, check more than others do (for instance, the stock market or the liquor business). Before your "current salary" disappears through the roof, however, you should know that the interviewer can ask to see a payroll stub or W2 form at the time you start work, or could make the offer dependent on verification of salary. After you are hired, the new employer may request verbal or written confirmation from previous employers, or might use an outside verification agency. In any instance where the employer contacts someone verbally or in writing, the employer must by law have your written permission to do so. That small print on the bottom of the job application form followed by a request for your signature usually authorizes the employer to do just that.

"Have you ever been refused a salary increase?"

This implies that you asked. An example of your justifiable request might parallel the following true story. An accountant in a tire distributorship made changes to an accounting system that saved $65,000 a year, plus thirty staff hours a week. Six months after the methods were obviously working smoothly, he requested a salary review, was refused, but was told he would receive a year-end bonus. He did: $75. If you can tell a story like that, by all means tell how you were turned down for a raise. If not, it is best to play it safe and explain that your work and salary history showed a steady and marked continual improvement over the years.

"How much do you need to support your family?"

As we have seen, your best advice is to find some way to sidestep this by discussing your midpoint desired salary.

This question is sometimes asked of people who will be working in a sales job, where remuneration is based upon a draw against forthcoming commissions. If this scenario describes your income patterns, be sure you have a firm handle on your basic needs before you accept the position.

For salaried positions, this question is of questionable relevance. It implies the employer will try to get you at a subsistence salary, which is not why you are there. In this instance, give a range from your desired high-end salary down to your desired mid-point salary.

"How much will it take to get you?" "How much are you looking for?" "What are your salary expectations?" "What are your salary requirements?"

You are being asked to name a figure here. Give the wrong answer and you can get eliminated. It is always a temptation to ask for the moon, knowing you can come down later, but there are better approaches. It is wise to confirm your understanding of the job and its importance before you start throwing numbers around, because you will have to live with the consequences. You need the best possible offer without pricing yourself out of the market, so it's time to dance with one of the following responses.

"Well, let's see if I understand the responsibilities fully . . ." You then proceed to itemize exactly what you will be doing on a daily basis and the parameters of your responsibilities and authority. Once that is done you will seek agreement: "Is this the job as you see it or have I missed anything?" Remember to describe the job in its most flattering and challenging light, paying special attention to the way you see it fitting into the overall picture and contributing to the success of department, workgroup, and company. You can then finish your response with a question of your own: "What figure did you have in mind for someone with my track record?" or, "What range has been authorized for this position?" Your answer will include, in part, something along the lines of, "I believe my skills and experience will warrant a starting salary between _____ and _____."

You also could ask, "What would be the salary range for someone with my experience and skills?" or, "I naturally want to make as much as my background and skills will allow. If I am right for the job, and I think my credentials demonstrate that I am, I am sure you will make me a fair offer. What figure do you have in mind?"

Another good response is: "I would expect a salary appropriate to my experience and ability to do the job successfully. What range do you have in mind?"

Such questions will get the interviewer to reveal the salary range, and concentrate his or her attention on the challenges of the job and your ability to accept and work with those challenges.

When you are given a range, you can adjust your money requirements appropriately, latching on to the upper part of the range. For example, if the range is $30,000–$35,000 a year, you can come back with a range of $34,000–$37,000.

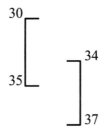

Consequently, your response will include: "That certainly means we have something to talk about. While your range is $30,000-$35,000, I am looking for a minimum of $34,000 with an ideal of $37,000. Tell me, what flexibility is there at the top of your salary range?" You need to know to put yourself in the strongest negotiating position, and this is the perfect time and opportunity to gain the information and the advantage.

All this fencing is aimed at getting the interviewer to show his or her hand first. Ask for too much, and it's "Oh dear, I'm afraid you're overqualified"—to which you can reply, "So overpay me." (Actually, that works when you can carry it off with an ingratiating smile.) If your request is too low, you are likely to be ruled out as lacking the appropriate experience.

When you have tried to get the interviewer to name a range and failed, you must come up with specific dollars and cents. At this point, the key is to understand that all jobs have salary ranges attached to them. Consequently, the last thing you will ever do is come back with a specific dollar figure—that traps you. Instead, you will mention your own range, which will not be from your minimum to your maximum but rather from your midpoint to your maximum. Remember, you can always negotiate down, but can rarely negotiate up.

"What kind of salary are you worth?"
This is a how-much-do-you-want question with a slight twist. It is asking you to name a desired figure, but the twist is that it also asks you to justify that figure.

It requires that you demonstrate careful analysis of your worth, industry norms, and job requirements. You are recommended to try for a higher figure rather than a lower one. "Having compared my background and experience with industry norms and salary surveys, I feel my general worth is in the region of $X to $Y. My general background and credentials fit your needs, and my first-hand knowledge of the specific challenges and projects I would face in this job are an exact match, so I feel worthy of justifying an offer toward the top of this range. Don't you agree?"

After your response to a salary question, you can expect to hear, "That's too much," or, "Oh, that is more than we were hoping to pay," or, "That would be stretching the budget to the breaking point." When that happens, accept it as no more than a negotiating gambit and come back with your own calm rebuttal: "What did you have in mind?"

"What do you hope to be earning two to five years from now?"

A difficult question. The interviewer is probing your desired career and earning path and is trying to see whether you have your sights set high enough—or too high. Perhaps a jocular tone doesn't hurt here: "I'd like to be earning just about as much as my boss and I can work out!" Then, throw the ball back with your own question: "How much is it possible to make here?"

If you give a specific figure, the interviewer is going to want justification. If you come up with a salary range, you are advised also to have a justified career path to go along with it.

You could also say, "In two years, I will have finished my C.P.A. requirements, so with that plus my additional experience, industry norms say I should be earning between $X and $Y. I would hope to be earning at least within that range, but hopefully with a proven track record of contributions, I would be making above the norm." The trick is to use industry statistics as the backbone of your argument, express confidence in doing better than the norm, and whenever possible stay away from specific job titles unless pressed.

"Do you think people in your occupation should be paid more?"

This one can be used prior to serious salary negotiation to probe your awareness of how your job really contributes to the bottom line. Or it can occur in the middle of salary negotiations to throw you off balance. The safe and correct answer is to straddle the fence. "Most jobs have salary ranges that reflect the job's relative importance and contribution to a company. And those salary ranges reflect the norm for the great majority of people within that profession. That does not mean, however, that the extraordinary people in such a group are not recognized for the extra performance and skills. There are always exceptions to the rule."

Good Offers, Poor Offers
After a period of bantering back and forth like this, the interviewer names a figure, hopefully meant as a legitimate offer. If you aren't sure, qualify it: "Let me see if I understand you correctly: Are you formally offering me the position at $X a year?"

The formal offer can fall into one of two categories.

☐ **It sounds fair and equitable:** In that case, you still want to negotiate for a little more—employers almost expect it of you, so don't disappoint them. Mention a salary range again, the low end of which comes at about the level of their offer and the high end somewhat above it. You can say, "Well it certainly seems that we are close. I was hoping for something more in the range of $X to $Y. How much room do we have for negotiation here?"

No one will withdraw an offer because you say you feel you are worth more. After all, the interviewer thinks you are the best person for the job, and has extended a formal offer, and the last thing he or she needs now is to start from square one again. The employer has a vested interest in bringing the negotiation to a satisfactory conclusion. In a worst-case scenario, the interviewer can stick to the original offer.

☐ **It isn't quite what you expected:** Even if the offer isn't what you thought it would be, you still have options other than accepting or rejecting the offer as it stands. But your strategy for now is to run the money topic as far as you can in a calm and businesslike way; then once you have gone that far, you can back off and examine the other potential benefits of the job. That way you will leave yourself with an opening, if you need it, to hit the money topic once more at the close of negotiations.

If you feel the salary could do with a boost, say so. "I like the job, and I know I have what it takes to be successful in it. I would also be prepared to give you a start date of [e.g.] March 1 to show my sincerity. But quite honestly, I couldn't justify it with your initial salary offer. I just hope that we have some room for negotiation here."

Or you can say, "I could start on March 1, and I do feel I could make a contribution here and become an integral part of the team. The only thing standing in the way is my inability to make ends meet based on your initial offer. I am sincerely interested in the opportunity and flattered by your interest in me. If we could just solve this money problem, I'm sure we could come to terms. What do you think can be done about it?"

The interviewer will probably come back with a question asking how much you want. "What is the minimum you would be prepared to work for?" he or she might ask. Respond with your range again—with your minimum really your midpoint—and the interviewer may well then come back with a higher offer and ask for your concurrence. This is the time to be noncommittal but encouraged, and to move on to the benefits included with the position: "Well, yes, that is a little better. Perhaps we should talk about the benefits."

Alternatively, the interviewer may come back with another question: "That's beyond our salary range for this job title. How far can you reduce your salary needs to fit our range?"

That question shows good faith and a desire to close the deal, but don't give in too easily—the interviewer is never going to want you as much as he or she does now. Your first response might be: "I appreciate that, but if it is the job title and its accompanying range that is causing the problem, couldn't we upgrade the title, thereby putting me near the bottom of the next range?" Try it—it often works. If is doesn't, it is probably time to move to other negotiable aspects of the job offer.

But not before one last try. You can take that final stab by asking, "Is that the best you can do?" With this question, you must look the interviewer directly in the eye, ask the question, and maintain eye contact. It works surprisingly well. You should also remember to try it as a closing gambit *at the very end of negotiations* when you have received everything you can hope for. You may get a surprise.

Negotiating Your Future Salary

At this point, you have probably ridden present salary as hard as you reasonably can (for a while, anyway)—so the time has come to shift the conversation to future remuneration.

"Even though the offer isn't quite what I'd hoped for to start the job, I am still interested. Can we talk about the future for a while?" Then you move the conversation to an on-the-job focus. Here are a few arrangements corporate headhunters frequently negotiate for their recruits.

☐ **A single, lump-sum signing bonus.** Nice to have, though it is money here today and gone tomorrow. Don't make the mistake of adding it onto the base. If you get a $2,500 signing bonus, that money won't be figured in for your year-end review—your raise will be based on your actual salary, so the bonus is a little less meaningful than it appears.

☐ **A 60-, 90-, or 120-day performance review with raise attached.** You can frequently negotiate a minimum percentage increase here, if you have confidence in your abilities.

☐ **A title promotion and raise** after two, three, or four months.

☐ **Bonus.** When you hear talk about a year-end bonus, don't rely on "what it's going to be this year" or "what it was last year," because the actual bonus will never bear any resemblance to either figure. Base the realism of any bonus expectations on a five-year performance history.

☐ **Things other than cash.** Also in the realm of real disposable income are things like a company car, gas, maintenance, and insurance. They represent hard dollars you would not have to spend. It's not unusual to hear of employers paying car or insurance allowances, picking up servicing bills for your personal automobile, or paying gas up to a certain amount each month. But if you don't ask, you can never expect an employer to offer. What have you got to lose? Remember, though, to get any of those unusual goodies in writing—even respectable managers in respected companies can suffer amnesia.

Questions to Leverage and Evaluate the Offer

No two negotiations are going to be alike, so there is no absolute model you can follow.

Nevertheless, when you have addressed present and future remuneration, this might be the time to get some more information on the company and the job itself.

Even if you haven't agreed on money, you are probably beginning to get a feeling as to whether or not you can put the deal together; you know the employer wants to. Many of the following questions will be appropriate here; some might even be appropriate at other times during the interview cycle.

Full knowledge of all the relevant facts is critical to your successful final negotiation of money and benefits. Your prudent selection of questions from this list will help you negotiate the best offers and choose the right job for you. (At this point, asking some pertinent questions from the following list also serves as a decompression device of sorts for both parties.)

□   □   □

The questions come in these categories:

- Nuts-and-bolts job clarification.
- Job and department growth.
- Corporate culture.
- Company growth and direction.

The following section is also worth reading between first and second interviews.

Nuts and Bolts
First, if you have career aspirations, you want to land in an outfit that believes in promoting from within. To find out, ask a few of these questions.

How long has the job been open? Why is it open? Who held the job last? What is he doing now? Promoted, fired, quit? How long was he in that job? How many people have held this job in the last three years? Where are they now? How often and how many people have been promoted from this position—and to where?

Other questions that might follow would include . . .

"What is the timetable for filling the position?"
The longer the job has been open and the tighter the timeframe for filling it, the better your leverage. That can also be determined by asking, "When do you need me to start? Why on that date particularly?"

"What are the first projects to be addressed?" or, *"What are the major problems to be tackled and conquered?"*

"What do you consider the five most important day-to-day responsibilities of this job? Why?"

"What personality traits do you consider critical to success in this job?"

"How do you see me complementing the existing group?"

"Will I be working with a team, or on my own? What will be my responsibilities as a team member? What will be my leadership responsibilities?"

"How much overtime is involved?"

"How much travel is involved?" and, *"How much overnight travel?"*

With overnight travel you need to find out the number of days per week and month; and more important, whether you will be paid for weekend days or given comp time. I have known companies who regularly expect you to get home from a long weekend trip at one o'clock in the morning and be at work at 8:30 on Monday—all without extra pay or comp time.

"How frequent are performance and salary reviews? And what are they based on—standard raises for all, or are they weighted toward merit and performance?

How does the performance appraisal and reward system work? Exactly how are outstanding employees recognized, judged, and rewarded?"

"What is the complete financial package for someone at my level?"

Job and Department Growth

Not everyone wants a career path—in fact, careers and career paths are fairly new to business and are a phenomenon of the latter part of the twentieth century. The fast track may or may not be for you. Gauging the potential for professional growth in a job is very important for some; for others, it comes slightly lower down the list. Even if you aren't striving to head the corporation in the next few years, you will still want to know what the promotional and growth expectations are so that you don't end up with a company expecting you to scale the heights.

"To what extent are the functions of the department recognized as important and worthy of review by upper management?"

If upper management takes an interest in the doings of your workgroup, rest assured you are in a visible position for recognition and reward.

"Where and how does my department fit into the company pecking order?"

"What does the department hope to achieve in the next two to three years? How will that help the company? How will it be recognized by the company?"

"What do you see as the strengths of the department? What do you see as weaknesses that you are looking to turn into strengths?"

"What role would you hope I would play in these goals?"

"What informal/formal benchmarks will you use to measure my effectiveness and contributions?"

"Based on my effectiveness, how long would you anticipate me holding this position? When my position and responsibilities change, what are the possible titles and responsibilities I might grow into?"

"What is the official corporate policy on internal promotion? How many people in this department have been promoted from their original positions since joining the company?"

"How do you determine when a person is ready for promotion?"

"What training and professional development programs are available to help me grow professionally?"

"Does the company encourage outside professional development training? Does the company sponsor all or part of any costs?"

"What are my potential career paths within the company?"

"To what jobs have people with my title risen in the company?"

"Who in the company was in this position the shortest length of time? Why? Who has remained in this position the longest? Why?"

Corporate Culture
All companies have their own way of doing things—that's corporate culture. Not every corporate culture is for you.

"What is the company's mission? What are the company's goals?"

"What approach does this company take to its marketplace?"

"What is unique about the way this company operates?"

"What is the best thing you know about this company? What is the worst thing you know about this company?"

"How does the reporting structure work? What are the accepted channels of communication and how do they work?"

"What kinds of checks and balances, reports, or other work-measurement tools are used in the department and company?"

"What do you and the company consider important in my fitting into the corporate culture—the way of doing things around here?"

"Will I be encouraged or discouraged from learning about the company beyond my own department?"

Company Growth and Direction

For those concerned about career growth, a healthy company is mandatory; for those concerned about stability of employment, the same applies.

"What expansion is planned for this department, division, or facility?"

"What markets does the company anticipate developing?"

"Does the company have plans for mergers or acquisitions?"

"Currently, what new endeavors is the company actively pursuing?"

"How do market trends affect company growth and progress? What is being done about them?"

"What production and employee layoffs and cutbacks have you experienced in the last three years?"

"What production and employee layoffs and cutbacks do you anticipate? How are they likely to affect this department, division, or facility?"

"When was the last corporate reorganization? How did it affect this department? When will the next corporate reorganization occur? How will it affect this department?"

"Is this department a profit center? How does that affect remuneration?"

The Package

Take-home pay is the most important part of your package. (You'll probably feel that the only thing wrong with your pay is that it gets taxed before you get to take it home!) That means you must carefully negotiate any possible benefits accruing to the job that have a monetary value but are nontaxable, and/or add to your physical and mental happiness. The list is almost endless, but here is a comprehensive listing of commonly available benefits. Although many of these benefits are available to all employees at some companies, you should know that, as a rule of thumb, the higher up the ladder you climb, the more benefits you can expect. Because the corporate world and its concepts of creating a motivated and committed workforce are constantly in flux, you should never assume that a particular benefit will not be available to you.

The basic rule is to ask—if you don't ask, there is no way you will get. A few years ago, it would have been unthinkable that anyone but an executive could expect something as glamorous as an athletic-club membership in a benefits package. In the 1990s, however, more companies have a membership as a standard benefit; an increasing number are even building their own health-club facilities. In New York you can easily pay between $250 and $700 for membership in a good club. What's this benefit worth in your area? Call a club and find out.

Benefits Your Package May Include

- 401K and other investment matching programs.
- "Cafeteria" insurance plans—you pick the insurance benefits you want.
- Car allowance.
- Car insurance or an allowance.
- Car maintenance and gas or an allowance.
- Car.
- Compensation days—for unpaid overtime/business travel time.
- Country club or health club membership.
- Accidental death insurance.
- Deferred compensation.
- Dental insurance—note deductibles and the percentage that is employer-paid.
- Employment contract and/or termination contract.
- Expense account.
- Financial planning help and tax assistance.
- Life insurance.
- Medical insurance—note deductibles and percentage that is employer-paid.
- Optical insurance—note deductibles and percentage that is employer-paid.
- Paid sick leave.
- Pension plans.
- Personal days off.
- Profit sharing.
- Short- or long-term disability compensation plans.
- Stock options.
- Vacation.

Evaluating the Offer

Once the offer has been negotiated to the best of your ability, you need to evaluate it—and that doesn't have to be done on the spot. Some of your requests and questions will take time to get answered, and very often the final parts of negotiation—"Yes, Mr. Jones, we can give you the extra $20,000 and six months of vacation you requested"—will take place over the telephone. Regardless of where the final negotiations are completed, never accept or reject the offer on the spot.

Be positive, say how excited you are about the prospect and that you would like a little time (overnight, a day, two days) to think it over, discuss it with your spouse, consult your tarot cards, whatever. Not only is this delay standard practice, but it will also give you the opportunity to leverage other offers, as discussed in the next chapter.

Use the time you gain to speak to your mentors or advisors. But a word of caution: In asking advice from those close to you, be sure you know exactly where that advice is coming from—you need clear-headed objectivity at this time.

Once the advice is in, and not before, weigh it along with your own observations—no one knows your needs and aspirations better than you do. While there are many ways of doing that, a simple line down the middle of a sheet of paper, with the reasons to take the job written on one side and the reasons to turn it down on the other, is about as straightforward and objective as you can get.

You will weigh salary, future earnings and career prospects, benefits, commute, lifestyle, and stability of the company, along with all those intangibles that are summed up in the term "gut feelings." Make sure you answer these questions for yourself:

- Do you like the work?
- Can you be trained in a reasonable period of time, thus having a realistic chance of success on the job?
- Are the title and responsibilities likely to provide you with challenge?
- Is the opportunity for growth in the job compatible with your needs and desires?
- Are the company's location, stability, and reputation in line with your needs?
- Is the atmosphere/culture of the company conducive to your enjoying working at the company?
- Can you get along with your new manager and immediate workgroup?
- Is the money offer and total compensation package the best you can get?

Notice that money is but one aspect of the evaluation process. There are many other factors to take into account as well. Even a high-paying job can be less advantageous than you think. For instance, you should be careful not to be foxed by the gross figure. It really is important that you get a firm handle on those actual, spendable, after-tax dollars—the ones with which you pay the rent. Always look at an offer in the light of how many more spendable dollars a week it will put in your pocket.

Evaluating the New Boss

When all that is done, you must make a final but immensely important determination—whether or not you will be happy with your future manager. Remember, you are going to spend the majority of your waking hours at work, and the new job can only be as good as your relationship with your new boss. If you felt uncomfortable with the person after an interview or two, you need to evaluate carefully the kind of discomfort and unhappiness it could generate over the coming months and years.

You'll want to know about the manager's personal style: Is he or she confrontational, authoritarian, democratic, hands-off? How would reprimands or differing viewpoints be handled? Does he or she share information on a need-to-know basis, the old military-management style of keep-'em-in-the-dark? When a group member makes a significant contribution, who gets the credit as far as senior management is concerned—the person, the manager, or the group? You can find out some of that information from the manager; other aspects you'll need to review when you meet team members, or the people from personnel.

Accepting New Jobs, Resigning from Others

Once your decision is made, you should accept the job verbally. Spell out exactly what you are accepting: "Mr. Smith, I'd like to accept the position of engineer at a starting salary of $42,000. I will be able to start work on March 1. And I understand my package will include life, health, and dental insurance, a 401K plan, and a company car." Then you finish with: "I will be glad to start on the above date pending a written offer received in time to give my present employer adequate notice of my departure. I'm sure that's acceptable to you."

Until you have the offer in writing, you have nothing. A verbal offer can be withdrawn—it happens all the time. That's not because the employer suddenly doesn't like you, but because of reasons that affect, but bear no real relationship to, your candidacy. I have known of countless careers that have stalled through reneged verbal offers—they lead to unemployment, bitterness, and even lawsuits. So avoid the headaches and play it by the numbers.

Once you have the offer in writing, notify your current employer in the same fashion. Quitting is difficult for almost everyone, so you can write a pleasant resignation letter, walk into your boss's office, hand it to him or her, then discuss things calmly and pleasantly once he or she has read it.

You will also want to notify any other companies who have been in negotiation with you that you are no longer on the market, but that you were most impressed with meeting them and would like to keep communications open for the future. (Again, see the next chapter for details on how to handle—and encourage— multiple job offers.)

24.
Multiple Interviews, Multiple Offers

False optimism and laziness lead many job hunters to be content with only one interview in process at any given time. That severely reduces the odds of landing the best job in town within your chosen time frame. Complacency guarantees that you will continue to operate in a buyer's market.

The recommended approach is to generate as many interviews as possible in a two- to three-week period. Interviewing skills are learned and consequently improve with practice. With the improved skills comes a greater confidence, and those natural interview nerves disperse. Your confidence shows through to potential employers, and you are perceived in a positive light. And because other companies are interested in you, everyone will move more quickly to secure your services. That is especially important if you are unfortunate enough to be unemployed. Being out of work is when you need money the most and is the time when the salary you can command on the open market is substantially reduced. The interview activity you generate will help offset this.

By generating multiple interviews, you bring the time of the first job offer closer and closer. That one job offer can be quickly parlayed into a number of others. And with a single job offer, your unemployed status has, to all intents and purposes, passed.

Immediately, you can call every company with whom you've met, and explain the situation. "Mr. Johnson, I'm calling because while still under consideration with your company I have received a job offer from one of your competitors. I would hate to make a decision without the chance of speaking with you again. I was very impressed by my meeting with you. Can we get together in the next couple of days?" End, of course, with a question that carries the conversation forward.

If you were in the running at all, your call will usually generate another interview; Mr. Johnson does not want to miss out on a suddenly prized commodity. Remember: It is human nature to want the very things one is about to lose. So you see, your simple offer can be multiplied almost by the number of interviews you have in process at the time.

A single job offer can also be used to generate interviews with new firms. It is as simple as making your usual telephone networking presentation, but you end it differently. You would be very interested in meeting with them because of your knowledge of the company/product/service, but also because you have just received a job offer—would it be possible to get together in the next couple of days?

Relying on one interview at a time can only lead to prolonged anxiety, disappointment, and possibly unemployment. That reliance is due to the combination of false optimism, laziness, and fear of rejection. Those are traits that cannot be tolerated except by confirmed defeatists, for defeat is the inevitable result of those traits. As Heraclitus said, "Character is destiny." Headhunters say, "The job offer that cannot fail will."

Self-esteem, on the other hand, is vital to your success, and happiness is found with it. And with it you will begin to awake each day with a vitality previously unknown. Vigor will increase, your enthusiasm will rise, and desire to achieve will burn within. The more you do today, the better you will feel tomorrow.

Even when you follow this plan to the letter, not every interview will result in an offer. But with many irons in the fire, an occasional firm "no" should not affect your morale. It won't be the first or last time you face rejection. Be persistent, and above all, close your mind to all negative and discouraging influences. The success you experience from implementing this plan will increase your store of willpower and determination, affect the successful outcome of your job hunt, and enrich your whole life. Start today.

The key to your success is preparation. Remember, it is necessary to plan and organize in order to succeed. Failing is easy—it requires no effort. It is the achievement of success that requires effort; and that means effort today, not tomorrow, for tomorrow never comes. So start building that well-stocked briefcase today.

25.

What If I Am Asked to Take a Drug Test?

"*W*ould you be willing to take a drug test as a condition of employment?"

Rightly or wrongly, drug testing as a condition of employment is much more common than in years past; it is likely to remain part of the job-search landscape for the foreseeable future. We can reasonably expect that by the mid-nineties, up to one out of every three jobs will require some form of drug testing as part of the selection process.

The Supreme Court has upheld drug testing programs for federal employees holding law enforcement positions and for customs personnel involved in drug interdiction activities. While there is no direct link between these governmental policies and private industry hiring, the rulings have been interpreted as reflecting our society's general acceptance of drug testing.

Recently, the U.S. Chamber of Commerce estimated that half of all Fortune 500 companies engage in some form of drug testing, either in the selection process or as part of random testing programs subsequent to hiring. As it turns out, the vast majority of testing is done to screen potential employees; the Employment Management Association has concluded that once hired, you are less likely to be subjected to drug testing than you were as an applicant (unless, of course, you exhibit signs of drug abuse on the job).

Perhaps you are reading this section out of curiosity, because drugs and drug testing are in the news these days. You may even think to yourself, "Well, this is all very interesting, but *I* don't take drugs; none of this applies to me." Unfortunately, you couldn't be more wrong.

Drug testing is everyone's business, because even those who have no problem with abusing controlled substances can be maligned by a false reading on a drug test. Such readings are, alas, all too common. Drug testing as it is practiced in today's workplace is rife with false positives, or, stated somewhat less clinically, mistakes. These mistakes provide seemingly authoritative "evidence" that you use illicit drugs when you do not.

What causes false positives? There are a number of factors, but of greatest interest here is the way many everyday foods, liquids, and over-the-counter drugs can set off alarms meant to identify serious drug abuse. By taking a pain reliever that contains ibuprofen, for instance—as millions do for relief of any number of aches and pains—you are increasing the risk that you will test positive for marijuana use. If you suffer from a cold and want to be sure to get the sleep necessary to put in a good day at work tomorrow, you may decide to take a nighttime cold medication; but if there is a surprise drug test the next day, you may learn to your surprise that you are an abuser of amphetamines!

False positives can occur as the result of asthma medications you receive on prescription, or because of cross-reacting chemicals in that doctor-prescribed and controlled diet plan. Has your physician instructed you to take the sedative Valium? If you do, a drug test could earn you a reputation as an angel dust fan. You are likely to show up as a morphine addict if you've suffered a bad cold or cough and have been prescribed codeine or certain other medications. This may also happen if you indulge in that most wicked of all addictions: lust for poppy seed bagels. That's what two bagel-hefting Navy doctors discovered recently: their careers nearly ran aground when two consecutive tests branded them as users of morphine. A few weeks later, however, the Navy discovered the error and traced it to the ship's commissary. The consumption levels of the bagels in question, the Navy eventually admitted, were well within the range of "normal dietary use."

The pharmaceutical companies that sell the tests list the *known* substances that are *proven* to cross-react, but that doesn't mean that those administering the tests can always be depended upon to possess this information or use it wisely. It should be noted, too, that the test manufacturers admit the tests are sometimes just plain wrong, poppy seeds or no poppy seeds; currently, the line is that urinalysis carries no more than a 5-percent inaccuracy rate. (This is misleading, however, as we shall see.)

Five percent doesn't seem like much, does it? Many businesses and organizations seem to have deemed that error rate to be an acceptable level of risk. Stop for a moment, though, and ask yourself this: What happens if you are the unlucky one out of twenty wrongly identified as a drug abuser? Remember, the mere presence of a positive on your test is usually enough to brand you as a person with a drug problem. By contrast, a breathalyzer test for alcohol is designed to determine whether you have consumed *too much* liquor. Drug testing recognizes no such niceties: If the buzzer goes off, you're one of the bad guys.

A little background is probably in order here. Drug testing recognizes (or, at any rate, is meant to recognize) whether miniscule traces of a certain substance are present in the urine. While marijuana, which accounts for over 90 percent of all positive findings, stays in an average-sized body for about three weeks, the length of time any substance stays in your system is affected by your actual body weight.

Now then. Since the question is not whether you *decided* to put a substance in your body, but whether it is *present*, an interesting set of issues arises. We are all well aware of the ongoing conflict over second-hand cigarette smoke; current evidence indicates that even those who don't smoke tobacco can, if they breathe air polluted by cigarette smoke, suffer adverse health effects as a result. The smoke still enters the body, even if you don't have a cigarette between your lips. Well, marijuana makes smoke, too. And you don't have to smoke it for it to show up in your system; just go to a party where someone else is smoking it, or sit next to a puffing Wall Streeter at a Grateful Dead concert, and you could have your professional reputation destroyed by an "accurate" drug test the next day!

What's more, the 5-percent accuracy rate claimed by the manufacturers of urinalysis tests is, while true in the strict sense, not meaningful in practical terms. In clinical testing conditions, these tests have indeed been shown to perform at or under 5 percent where errors are concerned. But your drug test will not be conducted in clinical testing conditions. It will be conducted "in the field"—out in the real world, where things aren't monitored quite so closely. When the lab's emphasis is on weeding out drug users (rather than on research), the error rate can be expected to balloon to 14 percent, according to estimates made in the Journal of Analytic Toxicology.

But why should we rely on estimates? The Center for Disease Control (CDC) and the National Institute on Drug Abuse (NIDA) ran a nine-year study on the accuracy of private-sector laboratories. Private-sector labs, where your specimen is most likely to be handled, hardly inspire confidence: they don't have to be licensed, they usually operate under no legislated employee training requirements, and they are often staffed by workers receiving only minimum wage. The results of the study? Brace yourself.

When the labs knew the specimens in question came from the CDC and the NIDA, the results were extremely impressive and could serve as a model for any testing program. But when the labs did not know who the specimens were coming from—when the specimen, in other words, could have been yours—a very different picture emerged. Up to sixty-six out of a hundred samples showed false positives. That translates to two-thirds of a given group of people having their reputations and careers destroyed for no particular reason. At the same time, the inaccuracy rate for screening known abusers under these "blind" conditions was shown to rise to as high as 100 percent! Translation: the labs gave a clean bill of health to up to 100 percent of the sample specimens *known* to contain traces of illegal drugs.

It's quite clear, then, that the claims of the pharmaceutical industry notwithstanding, there is cause for considerable concern when it comes to accuracy in urinalysis testing. In theory, the numbers may border on acceptable (though they are not iron-clad by any means); in practice, however, the record is horrendous.

What causes the inaccuracy? First of all, juggling urine specimens all day long is not exactly everyone's idea of ultimate career fulfillment; it is not surprising that the quality of work is less than exemplary. Second, urine testing is easy to do incorrectly. The specimens go stale quickly and react poorly to extremes of heat and cold. In addition, urine that is too acidic or too alkaline can skew the test results; these problems can be caused simply by the subject's eating spicy foods.

Bearing all of this depressing news in mind, then, how are you supposed to answer when asked whether you would submit to a drug test?

If you want the job offer—and at the early stage of the game the offer is all that's important—your short answer is "Yes." There is nothing at all wrong with answering in this way and using whatever offer may arise to negotiate with other employers, as outlined earlier in this book. Remember that being asked *whether* you would take a test is not the same thing as being asked *when* you would take a test. Initially, the question is invariably placed on a hypothetical footing: "Would you have any problem with taking a drug test?" And once you assent to the testing, you have about a fifty-fifty chance of making it through without actually being asked to provide a specimen.

When it appears that the drug test is about to move from the hypothetical into the realm of stark reality, though, you will need to protect yourself. Your good reputation could be in jeopardy.

Prior to the testing, an ethical company will give you a form to read, fill in, and sign. This formalizes your permission to conduct the test, and affirms your willingness to comply with company policies on the matter. The form should also list all the over-the-counter and prescription drugs—and other ingestible substances—known to cross-react with the test that will be used. Be sure to indicate on the form any of these substances and all drugs and medications you have taken recently. (The form often asks you to note what has been taken "within the week," but you should also list any medications you have taken in the past few weeks. Depending on your body weight, one week may not be enough to flush the residues from your system.)

Do not fail to note *every* applicable item! Five minutes ago you had no idea that a bagel or a cold medication could earn you a reputation as a lowlife; nothing is "innocent" when it comes to cross-reaction with drug tests. And all tests cross-react with something!

If the above-mentioned ethical courtesies are not extended to you prior to the test, cover yourself by saying something along the following lines.

> "Yes, I would of course be willing to take a drug test as part of the condition of employment. However, I have seen some reliable reporting that says many of these tests could show me to be a drug abuser if I have taken something as innocuous as a headache pill. I have been assured that you will not take offense if I ask what medications the test is known to cross-react with."

Again, if you are provided with the list, you should add whatever medications you have been taking, whether or not they appear on the list. If the company is unable or unwilling to give you the list you will be faced with a judgment call. Only you can say how important your good name is. In this case, you might ask whether, under the circumstances, the company would be willing to have your personal physician administer the test.

If the test should show a positive result, ethical organizations will agree to guarantee you a backup test *of another type* because of the chance of a false reading. Reputable pharmaceutical companies and laboratories recommend an additional test upon the first occurrence of a positive; you are well within your rights to ask whether you will be given this basic consideration. If the company in question refuses to offer you a backup test, there is a good chance it is because they are costly and the company is short-sighted enough to want to scrimp in this area. It is your decision whether or not to interview or work at such a firm.

There is, unfortunately, more bad news you should be aware of when it comes to corporate drug-testing policies. A number of companies have shown themselves to be less than ethical in their handling of samples received as a result of drug testing; people have unwittingly been tested for asthma, diabetes, epilepsy, and even pregnancy. Check the form carefully before signing it, and if there appear to be loopholes you'd rather see closed, point them out.

Suppose that, somewhere during the process, someone at the firm comments suspiciously that you seem remarkably well briefed on this topic. You might reply along these lines.

> "Yes, I am; this is because I realize that there is only one thing more important to a professional than his or her competence, and that is reputation. Being a person who is attentive to detail and proud of it, I took the time to research this issue thoroughly."

Your demeanor is all-important; if you act like you have something to hide, people will assume that you do. Stay calm, and express your concerns from a position of self-assured professionalism.

So much for the preliminaries. We move now to the question of what to do if you have decided it is in your best interests to take a drug test. If you are, rightly or wrongly, identified as a drug user, there will be three pertinent questions to answer.

- Will word reach your colleagues in the professional community, and if so, when?
- Will word reach your neighborhood, and if so, when?
- If you are branded as a drug abuser, just how long will it take you to get another job?

They aren't pleasant questions to have to answer; my feeling is that you should give yourself every advantage before the test, so that you will reduce your chances of ever having to face these quandaries. I am not saying you should "cheat"; as we have seen, the problem is not so much people cheating on drug tests as drug tests cheating innocent people out of rightful opportunity. You should, in my view, do everything in your power to avoid being placed in a compromising position. Following are suggestions of some things you can do to put the odds in your favor before you take the test.

The moment you learn that you may have to take a test, your objective should be to flush your body out. Drink lots and lots of water; seize every opportunity to void yourself the day of the test. If you can, schedule the test for after work; claim that it is impossible for you to get away in the morning. The most concentrated urine specimens are those generated first thing in the morning; those given later in the afternoon are less potent.

You will want to make use of as many diuretics (items that promote urination) as you can work into your diet. Coffee, tea, and juices are excellent diuretics; so is beer, but you should not drink alcohol prior to an interview, for reasons I have outlined elsewhere in this book.

Jogging or working out makes you sweat, which helps clean out the system. Exercise also improves alertness and physical agility. (Anyone in pursuit of a new job should exercise on a regular basis, anyway.)

Saunas and steam baths will help remove impurities from your system, as well as increase your need to consume liquids. What's more, they are relaxing, rejuvenating, and good for the skin.

Finally, you may want to pick up a bottle of B-complex vitamins and take some for the few days preceding your test date. They are good for you, of course, and will leave all sorts of wholesome stuff in your specimen, but they will also give the little glass jar you pass in a healthy yellow glow that fairly shouts: "This one is no crack addict!" (Well, appearances do count for something.)

□   □   □

Remember, in the early stages, your goal is to generate offers; you want people bidding for your services. Even an offer you don't want can be leveraged into another and better offer elsewhere. Once you know you want to work at a given company, you will have to decide for yourself whether it is worth undergoing the rigors and uncertainties of drug testing to obtain a job there. Many people decide that it is, and for reasons that are perfectly valid for them. I would suggest, though, that you bear in mind that potential employers are on their best behavior when wooing new recruits; if you have to go through all of this prior to the wedding, what sort of marriage is it likely to be?

By the way, if you do decide *against* working for a company that insists on drug testing, you might consider writing the higher-ups in the firm to tell them— politely—the reasons underlying your decision. Many of these executives have no idea how difficult or degrading undergoing a drug test can be. An argument can certainly be made that they should be exposed to the concerns of the people whose lives their decisions affect; too often, company policies are established in an insulated environment that does not take basic human sensibilities into account.

Corporate America is currently wringing its collective hands over the perceived fickleness and lack of loyalty in today's work force; but those in authority really should not be surprised if this is the case. Loyalty is a two-way street; today, employees and potential employees are sometimes so casually assumed to be guilty before proven innocent that they cannot be faulted for seeking to make a contribution elsewhere.

26.
How to Beat the Psychological Tests

In late 1989, Congress banned most private-sector applications of the polygraph test, voice stress analysis, and other electronic screening methods. While many government personnel (for instance, those involved in drug interdiction activities) are still subject to these tests, many private employers have had to change their ways, and are increasingly turning to psychological testing to weed out what they consider to be undesirable job applicants. These tests may be known as aptitude tests, personality profiles, or some other name, but in the end they are all the same thing: the next-best thing to the old, now-illegal methods for finding out whether you show signs of being a "risky" hire.

Actually, although the 1989 legislation has led to new popularity for the psychological tests, they have been around for decades. Psychological exams come in two flavors: One is a face-to-face meeting with a psychologist, and the other (far more common) is a written test, often multiple choice.

In any discussion of this issue, we should bear in mind that psychology is, by the admission of its own practitioners, an inexact science. It cannot yield any definitive litmus test on your potential employability. Yet many companies are pretending that it can, and are grafting the imprecise discipline of psychological testing onto the equally imprecise one of employment selection. The result is an essentially insight-free mess that is, nevertheless, easy to administer, relatively cheap, and increasingly popular. Those seeking employment are often asked to answer "a few routine questions" that end up being anything but routine. The tests, which are (in theory) not to be used as the sole basis for a hiring decision, can nevertheless have a huge effect on people's livelihoods.

The whole concept of psychological testing is fraught with controversy. Some view the tests as an intrusion into private life, and with good reason: They often ask blatantly illegal questions about, say, your religious beliefs. Others request information about your sexuality, and many of these queries are illegal in states that have adopted legislation protecting freedom of sexual preference. Laws or no laws, however, there the questions are, in black and white. If you refuse to take a test that is a "required" part of the selection process, you will almost certainly be denied employment. (Not surprisingly, several court cases have been initiated by disgruntled applicants.)

It isn't surprising that many of the companies using the tests are concerned about the potential honesty of prospective employees. Each year American industry loses an estimated $40 billion from employee theft. But while honesty is often one of the behavioral profiles examined, the tests tend to emphasize the examination of aptitude and suitability. Often, the exams are geared to evaluating the amount of energy a person might bring to the job, how he or she would handle stress, and what attitude toward job, peers, and management would be likely to be prevalent.

Unfortunately, answering a psychological test with complete personal honesty may very well threaten your chance of being offered employment. That's the bad news. Here's the good news: you can beat the tests without having to compromise your personal integrity.

Not long ago I did an in-house employee selection and motivation seminar for a large corporation; I was asked for my opinion on the subject of psychological testing. I replied that the tests were often used inappropriately as a pass/fail criterion for hiring, and that anyone with half a mind could come up with the desired or correct answers. "The question is," I concluded, "how many people who could have served you well will you miss out on because of a test?"

The managers assured me that they had a test in use that was "virtually infallible" in helping to identify strong hires, and certainly not subject to the machinations of the average applicant. They asked if I would be prepared to take it. I not only agreed, but also promised to prove my point. "Let me take the test twice," I said. "The first profile you get will tell you to hire me; the second will say I'm a bad risk."

I took the test twice that day. "Applicant #1" came back with a strong recommendation for hire. "Applicant #2" came back with a warning to exercise caution before considering taking him on.

How was this possible? Well, there is something the tests ignore: None of us is the same person in the workplace as in our personal life. Over a period of time at work, we come to understand the need for different behavioral patterns and different ways of interacting with people.

Sometimes our more considered, analytical, logical approaches pass over from our "professional self" into the personal realm. However, in the world of work, we are not expected to try to override the "corporate way" of doing things with our personal preferences. When this happens, and personal preferences take precedence over existing corporate theories of behavior, we get warnings and terminations. In other words, as professionals we are inculcated with a set of behavioral patterns that are supplied to us over the years to enable us to be successful and productive for our employers.

Did I really "fool" the test? No. I was completely honest both times. The "winning" test was the one in which I viewed myself—and, thus, described myself—as the thoroughly professional white-collar worker in the job for which I was applying. The "losing" test was the one I used to describe myself as the kind of person I see myself in my personal life.

This was not a hoax perpetrated by a smart aleck. I am that person they would have hired, and I possess a strong track record to back up my claim. I learned the behaviors necessary to succeed, adopted them, and made them my own—just as you have undoubtedly done.

Many of the tests simply lack an awareness of the complexity of the human mind. They seem to miss the point when they ask us to speak honestly about our feelings and beliefs. They do not take into account that our learned behaviors in our professional lives are, invariably, quite distinct from the behaviors we accept in our personal lives.

The secret of my success—and of yours, if you must take a psychological test—is really quite simple.

How to Prepare for, Read, and Answer the Tests

Born independently wealthy, very few of us would be doing the jobs we do. But we *are* doing them, and we have learned certain sets of skills and behavioral traits that are critical to our ability to survive and succeed professionally. The first thing you must do, then, is identify and separate the professional you from the personal you.

☐ **Step One: Never consider answering a test from the viewpoint of your innermost beliefs.** Instead, use your learned and developed professional behavior traits and modus operandi. Ask yourself, "How has my experience as a professional _____ taught me to think and respond to this?"

To do this effectively (and to understand ourselves a little better in the process), we need some further insights into the three critical skill sets that every professional relies on to succeed.

- Professional/technical skills (whether you're a secretary or a senior vice president)
- Industry skills (such as—if you happen to be in banking—your overall knowledge of the world of banking: how things work, how things get done, what is accepted within the industry, and so on)
- Professional behavior traits (the traits, discussed in chapter 14 of this book, that all employers look for, and that will get you ahead once you are on the job)

☐ **Step Two: Look at yourself from the employer's point of view.** (Review "The Five Secrets of the Hire," and "The Other Side of the Desk" for some helpful ideas.) Evaluate what traits come into play that enable you to discharge your duties effectively. Examine the typical crises/emergencies that are likely to arise: What supportive behavioral traits are necessary to overcome them? As you do this, you will almost certainly relive some episodes that seemed to put you at a disadvantage for a time. When it was tough to do things the right way, you had to buckle down and see the problem through, even though doing so did not necessarily "come naturally." The fact is, though, you overcame the obstacle. Remember *how* you did so, and keep that in mind as you answer the questions.

Conversely, you will want to look at those instances where a crisis had a less-than-successful outcome. What traits did you swear you would develop and use for next time?

Highlighting such traits simply constitutes your acknowledgment of the supremacy of learned behavior in the workplace. It does *not* constitute lying. (Why do you think so many professionals strive to keep their business lives separate from their personal lives? What is the point of such a separation if the two lives are identical?)

☐ **Step Three: Think of people you've known who have failed on the job.** Why did they fail? What have you learned from their mistakes and made a part of the "professional you"?

☐ **Step Four: Think of people you've known who have succeeded on the job.** Why did they succeed? What have you learned from their success and made a part of the "professional you"?

Once you have completed this exercise in detail, you will have effectively determined how a professional _____ would react in a wide range of circumstances, and identified the ways in which you have, over time, developed a "professional self" to match that profile.

Getting Ready for the Test

Any test can be nerve-wracking, but when it comes to psych tests your livelihood is in the balance. Desperate times, of course, call for desperate measures. Accordingly, you should be sure, as you enter the testing area, that you are armed with the ultimate failsafe. If at all possible, carry with you the one object that will guarantee you the chance to make the best possible impression as you take the test: a cup of coffee. (Yes, I am serious; the reasoning here will become clear very soon.)

The tests instruct you to answer quickly, offering the first response that comes to mind. Don't. Following this path may well cost you a job. Instead, look at the test in terms of the exercises outlined above; provide reasoned responses from the viewpoint of the "professional you."

Time limits are usually not imposed; on the contrary, those administering the test will often begin the proceedings with a soothing "Take your time, there's no pressure." (Except, of course, the minor pressure of knowing a job offer is on the line!)

In a face-to-face meeting with a psychologist, use the same techniques we have discussed throughout *Knock 'em Dead* to qualify the questions before answering them; when you suspect a trap, employ the tricks that will help you clarify things and buy time.

Beware: the written tests may contain "double blinds," where you are asked a question on page one, and then asked a virtually identical one thirty or forty questions later. The technique is based on the belief that most of us can tell a lie, but few of us can remember that lie under stress, and are therefore likely to answer differently later. This is held to show the potential for untruthfulness. The problem isn't that one answer is likely to deny you employment; the questions are asked in patterns to evaluate your behavior and attitudes on different topics.

So: Read the test through before you start answering questions! (There's "plenty of time" and "no pressure," remember?) Review the material at least three times, mentally flagging the questions that seem similar. This way you will be assured of consistency.

Of course, you are likely to encounter ethics questions. "Have you ever stolen anything?" "Have you ever felt guilty?" "Have you ever told a lie?" Avoid the temptation to respond impulsively with something like "Lies? No, I prefer to chop down the damned cherry tree." The truth is we have all done these things in our lives. When you are asked, for instance, whether there is anything you would ever change about yourself, or whether you think everyone is dishonest to some degree, the overwhelming likelihood is that your own honesty is being tested: The best answer is probably yes.

If you must address ethics matters in a face-to-face encounter, you can explain your answer, placing it far in the past where appropriate, and explain what you learned from the experience. If such questions must be answered on paper, the best approach is to follow the dictates of your own conscience and try to bring the issue up after the test. You might say something like this:

> "Gee, that question about lying was a tough one. I guess everyone has told a lie at some time in the past, and I wanted to be truthful, so I said yes. But I'd be lying if I didn't tell you it made me nervous. You know, I saw a show on television recently about these tests. It told the story of someone who lost a job because of answering a question just like that; the profile came back with an untrustworthy rating."

This should reduce the odds of your being denied the job in the same way. If the test does come back with a question about your honesty, you will at least have sown seeds of doubt about the validity of such a rating in the interviewer's mind. That doubt, and your disarming honesty, might just turn the tables in your favor.

Resist any temptation to project an image of yourself as an interesting person by the answers you select. These tests are not designed to reward eccentricity; think sliced white bread. You are happy at work and home. You enjoy being around people. You don't spend all your evenings watching movies (unless your name is Siskel or Ebert). You don't spend your weekends with a computer or pursuing other solitary pastimes (unless you are a programmer or an aspiring Trappist monk). You have beliefs, but not too strong. You respect the beliefs of all others, regardless of their age, sex, race, or religion.

When you finish the test, read through your answers a few times; if you don't like one or two, change them. Don't change too many; if you do, you will risk appearing indecisive. However, if you have a lot of changes, just spill your coffee . over the test (I told you there was a reason to bring that cup in with you). Throw the test in the trash—near the top, of course, where its condition can be verified— and ask for another copy. Since you will likely have some measure of privacy for taking the test, you can take on the new test with the added benefit of having the old one in front of you. (You don't mind retrieving that slightly sodden document for the sake of your career, do you?)

□　　□　　□

All of what I have said here takes for granted that the overriding goal of the employer is to determine whether or not you are suitable for the job. If you can give an accurate affirmative answer to that question, then the approach you take in doing so is—to my way of thinking, anyway—of little consequence. If you have learned and applied what it takes to prosper in your profession, then it is emphatically your right to provide an honest profile of your professional self, in whatever forum you are to be evaluated.

V

In Depth

What if things aren't clicking?

It has happened to more than one job search. A strong start encounters an occasional obstacle, then a somewhat-more-than-occasional obstacle, then a series of increasingly predictable obstacles, and finally a steady rain of obstacles. On some days, it looks like there is considerably more obstacle to your campaign than anything else. Lethargy and discouragement set in. What's more, bills maintain a nagging habit of requiring payment, which can be tiresome even if you are still employed—and downright crushing if you're not. Rejection, pressure, withering self-esteem: You know them better than you'd ever imagined you would. Nobody else on earth seems to have a sense of humor about all this. Why should you?

Similar obstacles, of course, can arise on the job. Careers get stalled, promotions fail to materialize, jobs demand change. While there's nothing particularly amusing about career problems, you should bear in mind that your biggest potential asset and/or liability in the search is the person staring back at you from the bathroom mirror each morning. That person is a walking, talking advertisement—pro or con—of your professionalism. If the face you see is drawn, pale, aggravated, or simply tired, you need to stop and take stock. You may be short-circuiting your own efforts.

In this section of the book, we'll look at a number of different ways to rescue a stalled job hunt, as well as some techniques for making the financial pinch you may be feeling a little more bearable. Finally, we'll examine the best ways to maintain strong career growth and stability once you actually get the position you want.

27.
How to Jump-Start a Stalled Job Search

Okay. You've been out of work for a while. You're low on ideas, and your get-up-and-go gas tank reads "empty." You don't know which way to turn. The things you've done so far just haven't panned out. It's time to take it from the top.

Believe it or not, you can start over again, and you have certain advantages in doing so. At least some of the people who screened you out so many months ago have, in all likelihood, moved on to another place (hopefully a hot and fetid one in the hereafter). Sure, most of the jobs you applied for have been filled, but a whole new batch has now opened up. And if there were ill economic winds blowing through an industry you took a fancy to, perhaps things aren't looking quite so bad anymore for some of the companies that were on your list.

With little adjustments here and there, and a bit more attention to a few key points, this can be a whole new ballgame. Following are some suggestions on how to rescue a faltering job search campaign.

Get a New Resume
White collar or blue collar, executive V.P. or electrician, you should throw out what you've got and start over from scratch. The current version isn't working. Your resume must get your foot in the door, set the tone for the interview, and, after all the shouting, act as your last and most powerful advocate when the final hiring decision is being made. Build one from ground up that does this.

Write at least two new drafts. One should be in chronological format; the other should be in either functional or combination format. Although there is helpful advice on resume writing in this book, at this stage I recommend that you complete the detailed questionnaire in the first part of *Resumes that Knock 'em Dead*, which will help you evaluate exactly what you have to offer potential employers.

Don't pooh-pooh the idea of rewriting your resume by claiming that "getting your foot in the door hasn't been the problem." It is entirely possible that your resume is strong enough to get you in the race, but doesn't pack enough punch to get to over the finish line ahead of the competition.

Rewrite Your Cover Letter

Adhering to a single, bland, "one-size-fits-all" cover letter is a common mistake. Remember, different circumstances require different letters. There are over a dozen different categories of cover and follow-up letters; they are detailed in my book *Cover Letters that Knock 'em Dead*. By following the advice there you will be able to craft a unique, memorable set of professional letters.

I would advise you to make a commitment to send follow-up letters with religious zeal if you are not already doing so. This may seem like a minor detail, but it is one of the most important—and easiest—ways for you to stand out from the competition.

When it comes to cover and follow-up letters, the whole really is greater than the sum of its parts. Employers maintain dossiers on every candidate during the selection process; your coordinated written campaign makes you stand out from the other contenders as someone who pays a little bit more attention to detail, who goes a little further to get the job done. Armed with your improved resume and cover letter, reread chapter 4 ("The Hidden Job Market") and follow its advice to the letter. Don't worry about sending your new resume to companies you've already contacted. A new resume means a new you.

Work as a Temporary

Get hold of a temporary employment directory for your area. (See chapter 4 for details on this resource.) Contact every appropriate temporary-help company listed and offer your services.

There are two benefits to working with a temporary help company. First, while you retain adequate time to pursue a structured job hunt, you get some work and a paycheck—thereby keeping your skills current and, just as important, the wolf from the door. Second, you may be able to upgrade that temp job into a full-time position. (At the very least, you can expand your contact network.)

Today, there are temporary companies that represent professionals at virtually all levels. Some even specialize solely in management people, and high-level ones at that, because companies are increasingly inclined to "test-drive" executives before making a permanent commitment to them. Interim Management Corporation (IMCOR) is typical of this new breed of temporary company; almost 40 percent of their assignments result in full-time employment.

Check Your References and Credit Rating

Do it now. Don't let a mystery problem sabotage an offer at the last moment. You'd be surprised how many otherwise qualified candidates eventually learn that they were taken out of the running by flunking the "tiebreaker" test. Two or more people are under final consideration; management decides to run a credit check and/or call references to help them decide who will get the job. If you have not attended to these areas, you should. Credit problems can undo months of preparatory work on your part; mediocre (or worse) references can be just as problematic.

Chapter 4 covers the topic of references in detail. (And remember, *all* of the references you give must be sterling!) For some ideas on repairing a negative credit report, see chapter 28.

Widen the Scope of Your Job Search

Under what other job titles could you work? Can you commute an extra twenty minutes for the right job? Consider relocation to another city, but bear in mind that for most of us this is an extremely costly proposition, and that you should not depend on a firm's picking up your moving expenses. On the other hand, if you are single and can fit all your earthly possessions in the back seat of your Festiva, some far-flung operation may be worth serious consideration.

Twenty Keys to Success

If you are having trouble at the interview, odds are you have not thoroughly assimilated Chapter 14 of this book, which highlights the twenty key personality traits employers love and shows you how to project them. Reread this chapter.

Smokestack

This used to mean keeping an eye out for smokestacks over the course of the day. Today it more commonly means remembering to incorporate job hunting as part of your daily routine. Stop in and see what firms are in that office building you pass every morning. Perhaps there are opportunities there for you.

Of course, you are not going to get far by simply appearing at the reception desk and demanding an interview. Be a little more circumspect. Ask—politely—about the firm in question. What does it do? Who is in charge of hiring? Are there any circulars, advertisements, or company reports you can take home with you? After your initial visit, you can incorporate this information into a new research file for the company and add the firm to your database of leads.

Body Check

This topic was covered briefly in the earlier section on dressing for interview success, but if you find yourself running into brick walls on the job search front it's a good idea to look at the most important points more thoroughly. Remember, one's personal friends often have trouble bringing up this subject; people in a position to hire simply move on to the next applicant.

If you do not brush and floss regularly, you have bad breath, and this will not aid your candidacy. If you eat a lot of spicy foods (onions, garlic, cilantro), you may be aware of the importance of keeping your breath fresh after a pungent meal, but this is not, alas, your only worry. These foods typically sour your sweat and taint your clothing. Change your diet and have your interview clothes cleaned before every wearing. (But note that polyester and other synthetic fabrics are notorious for retaining body odors even after cleaning—one of many reasons to avoid them.)

Have you put on a few pounds while looking for work? Many people use eating as a response to stress. Turn off the TV once a day and get some exercise; Nick at Nite will still be there after you work out. Couch potatoes don't make good candidates—period. Regular physical activity will improve your appearance *and* your mindset, so don't skip it.

These suggestions may be difficult for you to implement if they run counter to long-established patterns, but being in a permanent job-search mode is, you must admit, a much more daunting prospect. If you need motivation, recall the statistical truth that overweight and malodorous people are always the last to get hired or promoted.

Prepare, Prepare, Prepare

It may seem obvious, but all too often this is the step that people take for granted. When you walk into the interview, you should be ready to answer all the questions you could ever be asked, as well as all the ones you couldn't. Relevant portions of this book, especially part 4, "How to Knock 'em Dead," will be invaluable on this score.

Don't make the mistake of preparing only for the questions you want to hear!

Follow Up

I worked for some years as a headhunter and corporate personnel director. I can't count the number of times managers told me that there was really nothing to distinguish Candidate A (who got the job) from Candidate B (who didn't)—*except that Candidate A showed an unusual level of determination and attention to detail.* The way Candidate A conveyed this, of course, was usually through a dogged follow-up campaign.

After every job interview, review the recommended follow-up procedure in chapter 21 and implement it.

Remember: There Are Dream Jobs and There Is the Dream of a Job

Even though this has been touched on earlier in this book, it bears repeating in this context. If you have been unemployed for a significant period of time, you might find it fiscally prudent to accept that less-than-perfect job. That's okay. By the same token, there is a big difference between settling for less than your dreams and making the wrong job your life's work. If circumstances force you to take a temporary detour from your ultimate career goal, give an honest day's work for an honest day's pay and continue to pursue other opportunities.

Remember: You're the Most Important Part of This

Maintain ongoing motivational input. Reading this book and its two companion books, *Resumes that Knock 'em Dead* and *Cover Letters that Knock 'em Dead* is a good start; you should also keep an eye on the *National Business Employment Weekly* (NBEW), available at newsstands. It is full of help wanted ads and features motivational, how-to, career, and job-hunting articles. NBEW also provides a weekly list of self-help group events. Additionally, you should consider visiting the library to check out motivational tapes and related materials. You're worth it.

You are not a loser; you got blindsided. The trick is to get back in the saddle. If you climb up and grip the reins, tomorrow you'll see all kinds of opportunities you didn't see before.

28.
Keeping the Financial Boat Afloat

For too many of us, it actually takes losing a job in tough times to illustrate how close to the economic edge we usually live. To be sure, we take on financial obligations of our own free will—but the media, the society we live in, and, yes, our erstwhile employers all encourage standards of consumption we quickly learn to take for granted.

If you are reading this in a state of shock because you have recently been terminated, have a seat and take a deep breath. Things are probably not as bad as they seem right about now, but even if they were, you would need to keep your wits about you. Rash decisions, decisions made in desperation, are the ones we end up regretting. Take some time to decompress.

When Still inside the Building . . .
If, on the other hand, you are lucky enough to be reading this before your termination has been finalized, you should be very careful how you approach matters. It goes without saying that you should check your instinct to settle old scores or to lash out at the firm that is letting you go, but there are other important pieces of advice you should follow as well. Most of what follows is meant for those who have fallen victim to staffing cuts, but some of the ideas can be adapted to those who are terminated under less than favorable conditions—especially Rule Number One.

Rule Number One is simple: *Don't sign anything* until you are convinced you have everything the law, ethical considerations, and good old-fashioned guilt can elicit from the employer.

Ask about outplacement services. Outplacement firms are companies that provide you with job-hunting assistance ranging from a one-day seminar to "as-long-as-it-takes" counseling. This type of program is increasingly common; don't feel guilty about asking for it.

Negotiate the best-possible severance package. A week's severance pay for every year of service is the standard, inadequate though it is. Whatever you are offered, try to wheedle a little more. Point out that times are tough; if the unemployment rate is high, say so, and use actual numbers if you can. Remember, guilt works. Those that don't ask, don't get.

Find out what your benefits will be over the next months. Murphy's law, which states that whatever can go wrong will, applies with double force to the unemployed. Under the current insurance laws, you can continue the health plan your employer provided for you at a subsidized rate for up to eighteen months, after which time you can continue on the same plan at a (much higher) personal rate.

Determine the company policy on providing references. Sometimes companies will give no more than salary and dates of employment to those who call asking about your tenure there, regardless of your level of performance; this can adversely affect your job hunt. If you learn that this is the policy in your case, get a written letter to that effect to show to potential employers. If at all possible, you should obtain a written testimonial from your manager before you sign anything or leave the company.

You and I know, of course, that a reference is essentially the same thing as a letter testifying to your character. It is gratifying, however, how many superiors bidding a reluctant adieu to a team member are willing to forget this point. If you run into "company policy" trouble here, you can point out that you are not asking for an official reference, but the supervisor's personal evaluation of you as one professional discussing another. The fact that the personal reference need not appear on company stationery is usually a plus in obtaining the letter.

Request that the employer tell callers that you are unavailable, rather than unemployed, and that you will return all calls. Obviously, you won't be able to make this last forever, but you may be able to maintain at least the appearance of gainful employment. Every little bit helps.

If it isn't part of your outplacement package, try asking for desk space and telephone cost reimbursement for your job hunt. Of course, this is only feasible if you work in an appropriate office environment. Asking for desk space and telephone time in, say, a retail setting will do nothing but brand you as a head case. Assuming the circumstances are favorable for such a request, you may be able to get two or three months worth of help, or perhaps a flat cash payment. You certainly shouldn't rely on this, but it could be worth asking about.

Ask for professional financial counseling. In case the employer hasn't thought of this (a good bet), call an accountant for an estimate of the amount of money involved; the Yellow Pages are a good resource to use if you don't already know of a reputable accountant. Say, "I've just been laid off; I'm married, with two kids and a mortgage. I want to know how much you'd charge to help me create a liveable, pared-down budget." Then go to the employer with the figure. If a number of people are being let go, you may be able to get the employer to spring for a seminar for everyone.

Once You've Left the Building . . .
The time for all of the above has passed. You and the employer have parted company, and you must make some sense of the financial picture before you. If you don't face up to the financial problems of unemployment in a timely fashion, you may end up losing everything except the shopping cart. So face the facts early— and if you didn't do it early, do it now. Immediate action will only help you reach the point where problems are rectified all the sooner. Procrastination can only worsen your situation.

If you have stocks or stock options, you may want to consider cashing them in. However, you should be prepared to pay a capital gains tax on your profits. If you have a vested company-sponsored pension plan, this will merit your close attention, as well. I have heard of employees who had to sue to get monies owed them through these plans, but this problem generally arises only with smaller employers. Check with an accountant or financial advisor for all the details.

You may have the option of having your severance moneys paid out to you on a regular basis, approximating the payment pattern of your wages, or in a lump sum. Arguments run in two directions on this. Some feel that it is to your advantage to have the payments spread out because this realistically defines you as being on the payroll and, therefore, at least technically employed. Others argue, though, that such a ruse is often of marginal aid, and point out that in a time of severe financial stress, you should at least earn some interest on your money.

Your best course is probably to ask to have the money paid out over a period, if you see a realistic prospect of an offer on the horizon, and if that offer will be aided by your being able to claim, legitimately, that you are still on someone's payroll. Otherwise, bank it all. If you do choose to deposit all the money, look at your calendar before the check is cut; for tax reasons, you will almost certainly want to avoid receiving huge sums late in the year.

That lump sum can be dangerous if you're not used to dealing with large amounts of cash; beware of the Payday Millionaire Syndrome. Now is not the time to use "all that money" to refinish your basement or get a new car. Be prudent with your cash. Strike that: Be *miserly* with your cash. Bear in mind that some authorities estimate it will take you, on average, one month of job hunting for every ten thousand dollars of yearly salary in your desired job. Whether or not that is accurate, you should prepare yourself for quite a wait between paychecks!

No matter how bad things get or how tempted you may be, avoid cashing in any IRAs you have—you will pay huge tax penalties. Instead, look into a loan against your IRA or any other tax-deferred annuity.

If you consider refinancing your home mortgage, take into account not only the new interest rates you will pay and your likelihood of moving within five years, but also any closing fees you will encounter. Closing costs on refinanced mortgages typically run between three and six thousand dollars as of this writing. There may also be tax issues to consider, and these could add to the cost of refinancing as well. You may end up pursuing savings that are illusory; check with a qualified financial adviser before refinancing.

Get a handle on your credit card use. *This is a vitally important point.*

It is natural to avoid the unpleasant, and no one enjoys the business of downgrading one's lifestyle expectations. But as bad as the picture may be, it can't be half as depressing as turning a blind eye to your problems. Avoid, at all costs, maintaining a false standard of living by pushing your credit card limits to the upper ionosphere. As will be detailed later in this chapter, your best course for now is simply to cut all existing cards (but one) in half.

Getting into credit difficulties will undermine your confidence, strain your personal relationships, put a big dent in your morale, and, most important of all, *stop you from getting hired*! You will remember from past experience, no doubt, that virtually all professional interviews these days are preceded by an application form with a space for your signature beneath a block of minute type. In that unreadable thicket of words, required by the Fair Credit Reporting Act of 1972, is an authorization for the employer to check your references and your credit history. Employers are usually quite content to process your application if they have your resume, your name, your address, and your signature on the application form. This signature, they will tell you, is simply something they "need for their records."

Uh-huh.

Credit agencies make a business of marketing their files to corporate employers, who use them as tools for evaluation of potential employees. The service is popular because credit information is seen as an indicator of future performance. This, of course, is based on the premise that knowing how a potential employee handles fiscal obligations provides a preview of that person's likelihood of stealing from the company, acting irresponsibly, or otherwise compromising the employer. Whether or not you agree with this idea, you should know that a bad credit rating has the potential to blow your candidacy right out of the water—and that it can do so even if *all* the other variables point to a successful outcome for your job search.

You can find out more about your credit rating by contacting the major national credit rating bureaus.

CSC Credit Services, Inc. (Houston, Texas): 713/878-4840
TransUnion Credit Information (Chicago, Illinois): 312/408- 1050
CBI/Equifax (Atlanta, Georgia): 1-800/685-1111
TRW Consumer Assistance (Cleveland, Ohio): 214/390-9191

The last entry on that list may be the most useful to you. If you write TRW Consumer Assistance (the address is P.O. Box 2350, Chatsworth, California, 91313), you can get a printout of your credit report; this is free for the asking. The only limitation is that you can receive only one free report per year.

Credit bureaus are legally obligated to update reports containing factual errors, so be sure to notify the appropriate companies immediately if you find any mistakes. Even if you do not find outright misstatements on your report, you have some options. Many experts recommend that you send the credit bureau a letter explaining that your late or incomplete payments resulted from the loss of a job—a temporary state of affairs that is a world away from simple fiscal irresponsibility.

Starting Over
If you are in or are getting into debt as a result of losing your job, you should by all means face the problem squarely.

Sit down (with your family, if this is applicable) and review the situation. Air any unresolved issues and thoroughly examine your situation. Then work out your current monthly financial picture with a form something like the one reproduced below.

MONTHLY INCOME

Earnings	_____
Severance	_____
Spouse's salary	_____
Unemployment benefits*	_____
Withdrawal from savings	_____
Dividends	_____
Interest	_____
Gifts	_____
TOTAL INCOME:	_____

MONTHLY OBLIGATIONS/PAYMENTS

Rent/mortgage	_____
Taxes	_____
Groceries	_____
Clothing	_____
Household	_____
Loan repayments	_____
Car expenses	_____
Insurance	_____
Recreation	_____
Charitable contributions/dues/gifts	_____
Medical expenses	_____
Auto-related expenses	_____
Credit card repayments	_____
Job-search-related expenses	_____
Mortgage	_____
Home-equity loan	_____
Miscellaneous	_____
TOTAL OUTGOING:	_____

---

* If you have worked and received unemployment benefits in the same tax year, those unemployment benefits will be regarded as taxable income.

Once you know where you stand, there comes the dreaded task of taking action.

I said a little earlier on that you should, if you find yourself in financial difficulties while conducting your job search, simply cut your credit cards in half—all but one of them, at any rate. The one exception is to allow the member of the family who is conducting the job search to have some flexibility in obtaining stationery supplies, strategically selected interview wear, printing services, and the like. But even this carries with it a warning: Make your plastic job-search purchases prudent ones! This is not the time to update your entire wardrobe on the vague idea that you'll be going on *lots* of interviews and will therefore need *lots* of great clothes.

Treat your remaining credit card with the wary respect you would accord an adversary who has become a temporary ally—that is, someone who still very much bears watching. Bear in mind that it is misuse of credit cards, more than anything else, that is responsible for plunging the professional into hopeless levels of debt.

If your financial situation is giving you cause for concern, you might consider contacting the non-profit National Foundation for Consumer Credit at 301/589-5600. They have been providing free and low-cost counseling to people in financial hot water for over thirty years. With branches throughout the country, they can assist you in creating a workable budget and realistic plans for debt repayment, and they can even contact creditors on your behalf. Another good organization to contact is the National Center for Financial Education, which can be reached by calling 619/232-8811. They can advise you on a wide range of financial issues, including repairing your credit.

If Things Don't Look Good . . .
You might want to consider a debt consolidation loan. This is an arrangement whereby a loan is taken out to pay off all debts, giving you just one simple bill to deal with per month.

Such a loan looks like a great hassle eradicator, but it can cause more problems than it solves if you're not careful. Some people have taken out consolidation loans and gotten everything ship-shape—only to use the new "breathing room" they've won to charge their credit cards back up to the limit and push their home equity lines to dangerous levels. The result is not a reprieve from financial woes, but a doubling of their severity.

Whatever you do, watch out for the "credit repair" companies that offer to "fix" all your credit problems for a substantial but (considering the stakes) seemingly reasonable fee. The Federal Trade Commission has been all over these fly-by-night outfits, and with good reason. The overwhelming majority do nothing but take your money, dazzle you with words, and baffle you with B.S.—and I'm not talking undergraduate degrees here.

If the situation deteriorates to the point where bankruptcy seems to be a realistic prospect, I recommend that you contact creditors to negotiate even smaller payments than the ones you've been making. You may be surprised at their eagerness to work with you. Tell them what you can pay; if it's interest plus something, there is probably a deal to be worked out. Using the legitimate threat of bankruptcy to get creditors to offer you more favorable settlement arrangements is a powerful tool; credit card companies have been known to accept a fraction of what is owed them under these circumstances. The reason is simple: Once you go into bankruptcy, the creditors are likely to get nothing whatsoever from you. (By the way, this maneuver is one you can use but once in a lifetime. Sadly, it cannot be employed as an annual cost-cutting measure.)

For more information on personal bankruptcy, consult your attorney or contact the local bar association, which is listed in your phone directory and can refer you to a bankruptcy specialist in your price range.

On a more positive note, remember that there are many steps you can take to generate some interim cash that will see you through the tough times. You can:

- Rent out a room in your house.
- Get a part-time or temp job.
- Take out an ad in the local penny saver promoting your services as a repairperson (if you've always been good with your hands).
- Sell your professional services as a consultant.
- Turn a hobby into a profitable occupation. (A friend of mine lost her income and, being an artist, started an after-school art program for kids. Now she has three employees, is looking for more space, and is making over $60,000 per year. Very wisely, she contacted SCORE, the Service Corps of Retired Executives, for free counseling on how to start and operate her business. SCORE is sponsored by the Small Business Administration and has offices just about everywhere. For women and minorities, there are numerous low-interest loan programs available through the Small Business Administration. Contact your local office.)

Debt Collectors
If you're seriously considering talking to an attorney about filing for bankruptcy, chances are you are also being dunned by debt collectors, a fearsome species to say the least. People in this profession generally do not attend charm school as part of their training, so don't be surprised if you are addressed in a way that oversteps the *social* niceties. On the other hand, you should know when these people overstep their *legal* bounds.

The Fair Debt Collection Practices Act of 1977 protects you and your loved ones from illegal, rude, unfair, and unreasonable collection practices. Some of the specific limitations under which the debt collection industry must act are listed below.

- Debt collectors are forbidden to ask you for your telephone number, salary, payment dates, or place of employment. (But they may still use their own best efforts to locate you, and they can be depended upon to come after you when you find a new job.)

- Debt collectors can only speak to others about you in the context of determining your whereabouts. They cannot discuss with anyone the nature of their business with you unless you give them permission to do so.
- Debt collectors can contact you in person, by phone, or by letter—but only at times and places convenient to you.
- Debt collectors cannot harass or abuse you or anyone connected with you (such as a spouse or other family member) about the collection of your debt. This means telephone harassment, abusive language, and threats of violence are all out.

In all fairness to debt collectors, they have a job to do and bosses to pacify just like everyone else. Treat them with respect and they will probably return the favor. If you keep the channels of communication open, you probably won't have to worry about any of the above-mentioned horrors. But if you do have problems in any of these areas, don't hesitate to talk to a lawyer.

The Second Time Around
Time passes. (It always does.) Life continues, crises recede. This is a tough stretch, but it won't last forever. Once you make it through to the other side—and you will—take a look around and prepare yourself for a surprise. You will probably be a better person for all of this. The next time you're on a career roll, you will likely find it easier to forget the myriad admonishments we all receive to "live up to our income." The next time, you might be perfectly positioned to live up to your dreams instead.

29.

The Seven Secrets of Long-Term Career Survival

We talk about "job security," but in fact the only long-term career security you have sits between your ears. Even if you land the greatest job in the world, you must live your life in a world in which nothing, ultimately, is guaranteed. In this chapter we will cover some of the important truths that underlie any attempt to endure and prosper in a time of rapid technological and economic change.

Before we get into the specifics, a few words on mindset are in order. You will be happier if you do not view your career as an even tradeoff—your unquestioning loyalty for the employer's promise to require your services always. This unwavering relationship may have been the standard twenty or thirty years ago, but it is not so now. People should certainly have a measure of loyalty to the firms for which they work, but these days lifetime commitment is for altars, not cubicles.

After all, companies only have loyalty to the bottom right-hand corner of the quarterly profit and loss statement. (If they didn't have that loyalty, your paycheck would bounce.) It may seem harsh, but the fact is that you are a plentiful and renewable resource. You are, in a word, expendable.

But if a company has a responsibility to survive, you do too. This fact has not been lost on many of today's career writers and counselors, who have advised the development of a single area of high performance, one that transfers easily from one company (or industry) to another. Slogans such as "Become a specialist" and "Develop an expertise" have been offered as answers to the rapidly changing career picture so many emergent careerists face. Yet these are only partially correct responses to the problem.

Recognition in your "specialty" can actually get you pigeonholed and damage your future employability. The problem is that "specialists" all too often repeat a single year's experience, year in and year out. With the rapid technological changes in our world, the "specialist" may, ten years on, have the marketable equivalent of one year of experience repeated ten times—in an obsolete area of expertise, no less! This is not positioning yourself in a seller's market, not by a long shot.

No matter how stellar your performance, no matter how shrewdly you focus your efforts, you remain open to the risk that economic and technological changes will undermine your career. Of course, the "specialize" crew is right in pointing out that you can no longer expect the modern corporation to guarantee your employment. But there are seven important ways you can protect your *employability* over the long haul, ways you don't usually hear or read about. Here they are.

Secret #1: Join the Inner Circle
I have written in other books about the inner circles that develop in every department and in every company. These are the people whose input is requested on key decisions, and who are likely to have the best sense of *why* a given initiative is being pursued, rather than just *what* steps are being delegated to carry them out.

How do you get the invitation to that inner circle—which carries with it visibility, raises, plum assignments, and, most important for our purposes, the greatest possible relevant experience, stability, and future employability? There is a step-by-step approach you can follow.

During your first few days on the job, sit down with your boss and explain how much you want to make a success of your new position. Add that you are prepared to do whatever it takes to make your goal of becoming a valuable member of the team a reality (and mean it). There isn't a manager in the world who wouldn't like to hear this.

Continue by stressing that you want to maximize your strengths and minimize any weaknesses related to your inexperience by turning them into strengths. With this in mind, ask whether it would be possible for you and your boss to sit down on a regular basis over the first few months to make sure you are on the right track.

It should go without saying that, having begun in such a remarkable fashion, you must follow your plan to the letter and assiduously follow up any suggestions or guidance you receive. (Be forewarned: This plan is not recommended for members of the "4:59-and-I'm-outta-here" club!) Once the first three months have passed, tell your boss that you are so appreciative of the help you've received that you would like to continue the process on an informal basis by sitting down for a few minutes every two or three months to get feedback on your performance.

Several very interesting things happen when you take this approach. If you've been working for any length of time, you've probably noticed that, once a year, you have a formal performance review meeting with your manager—who typically knows little or nothing about the actual quality of your work. If you follow the advice I've just given, that same manager will be meeting with you six times more frequently than with anyone else in your department. You will also be the beneficiary of a great deal of one-on-one attention and positive feedback, not to mention the possibility of exposure to important information that might not otherwise come your way. As you travel down the road, you'll be picking up points and protecting your future at the same time.

Secret #2: Achieve Twenty-first Century Literacy
If you expect to be employable a decade from now, you had better set about achieving basic computer literacy. The bare minimum for anyone aspiring to a professional position will be an ability to execute daily communications at the terminal.

There is simply no excuse now for inability to function with a computer. Note that, by taking the minimal time to learn how to operate, say, a popular word processing program such as Microsoft Word, you will experience the added benefit of having a far more efficient and professional job search the next time you are out of work.

Secret #3: Mend Your Patchwork Quilt

The typical working professional is still clinging to an "updated" version of the same resume created to meet the needs of that first professional job hunt. After five, ten, or fifteen years of carefully adding subsequent jobs, the resulting document is less a resume than a patchwork quilt. Quilts don't win jobs nowadays.

Take the time to update your resume by rewriting it from scratch to reflect the dictates of the current employment environment. You never know when you will need it; don't procrastinate! Prudence dictates that we expect the best in our lives and prepare for the worst. Do it now.

Secret #4: The In Crowd

Have you noticed that all the really top-notch people in a given field seem to know one another—or at least are no more than a handful of phone calls from anyone in the business they have to contact?

How did these people get in the enviable position of being "in with the in crowd"? It's a little far-fetched to delude ourselves that they are all sons and daughters of Fortune 500 executives!

The truth is more prosaic. The top people in every field got that way by concerted long-term effort, and by making a point of communicating with and learning from their peers. These people have done many inspired things, and maintaining membership in at least one professional association is virtually always one of them. The theory is simple: If you can't have the opportunity to get to know everyone within the context of your job, you *can* get to know just about everyone of consequence by working with them at the same association meetings and functions.

When an employment need arises at a company, the first thing management does is scratch its collectively balding head and mutter, "Who do we know?" Then, apart from everyone management has worked with in the past, a mental spotlight shines on those extra special professionals, those folks who go that extra mile, the people who demonstrate their commitment and dedication to the profession with big infusions of time and effort. The people who come to mind are those met at association meetings.

Fortunately for you, finding and joining appropriate associations requires little more than thirty minutes in the local library. There you will examine a big fat book called the Encyclopedia of Associations, which details thousands of national and regional associations with appropriate contact information.

Don't get discouraged by that old saying, "It's not what you know, it's who you know." That only goes halfway. It should really end like this: " . . . it's who you get to know."

Secret #5: Reach Out and Touch Someone

Having amended the saying we discussed in Secret #4, let's do it again: "It's not just what you know, it's who you get to know *and who you stay in touch with.*"

Have you ever had someone call you for career help, someone you've stayed in touch with over the years? Isn't your instinct to try to move heaven and earth to help that person? Now think of someone who calls *just* to ask you for help—that's the only context in which the two of you communicate. If you're like most of us, the assistance you offer in this situation is cursory at best.

The idea here is to make as many professional contacts *for their own sake* as you can over the years. Make it a daily priority. Collect business cards from everyone you meet during the general run of business: at conventions, during sales presentations, at seminars, and so on. Note on those cards, for future reference, the circumstances under which you met the person.

Talk to each of your contacts at least once a year just to stay in touch and see how things are going. The dividend comes down the line when you need help, or when you receive a call from someone who says, "Carol, we're starting a search for a [position], and we wondered whether you could refer us to anyone." Make no mistake; the caller is discreetly asking if you are interested.

Reach out and touch lots of people so they can reach out and help you. It's called safety networking.

Secret #6: Work on the Day of Rest

Every Sunday, remove and file the Help Wanted section of your major metropolitan newspaper. You may not need it today or even this year, but at some point you will be in need of job leads, and this collection of want ads will provide you with an essential roadmap of where the jobs are in your area. A company that needed an accountant a year ago could just be starting a search for another one today.

As discussed in chapter 4, even aged want-ads give you specifics about exactly what kind of experience a particular company looks for. The "hidden job market" should perhaps be renamed the "forgotten job market," since a review of advertising in a national or metropolitan daily will give you the skinny on virtually all types of jobs in your field. For you, however, it won't be a forgotten market at all. It will be nestling safely in your bottom drawer.

Secret #7: Say Hello to Harry the Headhunter

My career began with a long stint as a headhunter, and a couple of things about daily life in that particular salt mine have always amused me. I noticed that entry-level professionals tended to be offended that a headhunter would try to lure them away from a current position for another one with better opportunities and rewards, while more senior people appreciated the opportunity to keep their options open. I also noticed that line managers and human resources professionals would have conniption fits on finding a fox in the chicken coop—but that those same managers would change their feelings entirely when it came to their personal career options.

My advice, then, is that you never blow off a headhunter. Provide assistance to them when it cannot hurt you and when you are confident of the headhunter's professional integrity. After all, you never know when they will have the perfect job for you. Most successful professionals have "a friend in the business." You should, too.

□   □   □

Some call me cynical, but I prefer to think of myself as a practical urban survivalist. Give your employer the very best you can, every day and in every way—and do the same for yourself.

Conclusion:
The Glittering Prizes

All victories have their foundation in careful preparation, and in finishing *Knock 'em Dead*, you are loaded for bear and ready for the hunt.

Your winning attitude is positive and active—dream jobs don't come to those who sit and wait—and you realize that success depends on getting out and generating interviews for yourself. At those interviews, you will maintain the interviewer's interest and attention by carrying your half of the conversation. What you ask will show your interest, demonstrate your analytical abilities, and carry the conversation forward. If in doubt about the meaning of a question, you will ask one of your own to clarify it.

The corporate body recognizes that its most valuable resource is in those employees who understand and contribute toward its goals. These people have something in common: They all recognize their differing jobs as a series of challenges and problems, each to be anticipated, met, and solved. It's that attitude that lands jobs and enhances careers.

People with that attitude advance their careers faster than others, because they possess a critical awareness of universally admired business practices and value systems. They then leverage their careers by projecting the personality traits that most closely complement those practices and values.

As I said at the beginning of this book, your job search can be seen as a ritualized mating dance. The name of that dance is "attitude." Now that you know the steps, you are ready to whirl away with the glittering prizes. There is no more to say except go to your next interview and knock 'em dead.

Appendices

Appendix A
When You See Clouds on the Horizon

Yes, it *can* happen to you.

In today's changing economy, any, repeat *any* employee can be laid off. Anytime. Anywhere. And make no mistake about it, if your number comes up it will in all likelihood be time for you to begin looking for another job somewhere else. Despite any delicate layers of euphemism that may accompany your notice, your employer will almost certainly not, as in the past, be calling you back. And in virtually every sector, the competition for available jobs is stiffer than it was a decade ago. So you have to ask yourself: Where would a layoff leave you?

Ten years ago, businesses absorbed employees hungrily and even created jobs based on incoming talent rather than existing need. By the end of that decade, however, the guillotine began to fall, enacting sweeping cuts worthy of *A Tale of Two Cities*. The American Management Association's annual survey on downsizing found that, over a five-year period, fully two-thirds of its sample had downsized at least once; 43 percent had downsized at least twice; and 24 percent had downsized three times or more. In a recent twelve-month period, the average number of positions eliminated in a layoff was more than double that of the previous survey (317 compared to 133).

In other words, heads have rolled—and not solely as a result of the 1989-1991 recession. Today's business climate and technology have changed forever the nature of our workforce. Today's markets are ultracompetitive, geared toward sudden technological shifts, and, are increasingly, international in nature. For these and other reasons, all companies—even those showing record profits—are streamlining their organizations. When there are mergers and acquisitions, the elimination of duplicate employees is now the first order of business. An infusion of "new blood" is typically accompanied by a decision to purge the "old blood."

As if that weren't disorienting enough, companies have begun rethinking whether much of the work they do should even require employees in the first place. More and more, noncore business functions are being contracted out and completely eliminated from the corporate structure. Areas in the direct line of fire include such former "untouchables" as accounting and finance, information systems, and human resources. There is increasing talk of paring down to an "irreducible core" of permanent employees and supplementing cyclical needs with temporary or contract workers.

Yes. All of this is depressing. But for the companies involved, these changes are often unavoidable. In many cases, keeping the guillotine sharpened is the only alternative to shutting the doors and laying *everyone* off.

Your ability to keep your head—and keep yourself employed—will depend on your ability to accept some facts about today's work world. First, you must accept that the idea that you will work for one employer for the bulk of your career is no longer viable. Check the demographics yourself; employers have shown no hesitation in laying off mid- to senior-level managers short of retirement by a few years, months, or even days. Continued employment no longer depends on company loyalty, but rather on your ability to change with the times.

A Watchful Eye

By continuously assessing the health of your employer, you will be able to make informed decisions about what kind of changes you must make. In some cases, you will find the company so troubled that looking for another job before the axe falls is the best course of action. In other situations, adapting to a new way of doing business may be a sure-fire way to be among those valued employees in the irreducible core. Only you will be able to tell.

While restructuring does not necessarily mean that a company is planning a major layoff, it's a pretty darned good indication. Call it better-than-even odds that the one follows the other. Once you see evidence of unspecified Bug Changes on the Horizon, your diagnosis of the situation—and your ability to adapt to it—should come into play. As corporations flatten their structure to become more efficient, employees are asked to work and think in new ways. Those who are unable to adapt to the new structure, or whose roles are found to be untenable in the new organization, will be the first to go.

Unfortunately, many people (and particularly those with a long history at the company) ignore what is going on right under their noses. Witness the case of the flight engineer who worked for a major airplane manufacturer. He saw his own name on a list of people the organization had determined it could do without—and refused to believe it. When he was handed his pink slip, he was speechless with shock.

As an employee, you probably have as much access to information as you need to make an informed judgement about what's on the horizon. When it comes to your own corner of the organization's universe, you know as much as the C.E.O. and probably a good deal more. An accountant can see that revenues are not meeting expenditures. A salesperson knows when quotas aren't being met. Think carefully about the events that affect your department or position, and (discreetly, of course) investigate them further whenever you can.

On the brink of disaster? Or poised for explosive growth to which you can contribute? You must find out into which category your company falls. But some changes in the company may be difficult to interpret. For instance, your company might use attrition—simply not filling vacated positions—as a way to cut costs. The next step might be to reduce administrative or support staff. You have to determine whether the company is sincerely attempting to improve efficiency and productivity, or whether these actions are leading to deeper staff cuts.

The signs will differ depending on the size of your employer, and you may have to put on your Sherlock Holmes hat to get the type of information you need. Then again, learning more about your company, your industry, and your market will also make you a better and more valuable employee. More important, it will enhance your career buoyancy.

Let's say you work for a publicly held corporation. By watching the price of your employer's stock over a specific period, you should be able to get an idea of the firm's performance and standing in the marketplace. It's simple enough to check the price of your company's stock (and, for comparison, that of its competitors) in a daily newspaper. Your firm's annual report may have similarly useful information, such as long-term plans and recent successes and failures. Has the company consolidated any of its operations? This may be a clue to future downsizing plans.

Many public libraries have CD-ROM services that allow you to access a massive volume of published material in a very short period of time; you can use this resource to scan articles about your company. Are the pieces positive or negative in tone? Do they relate, directly or indirectly, to your work? Read about your employers' competitors as well; you'll be in a better position to understand your company's moves. Trade and business publications are excellent sources of information about your company and its competitors; they will also give you an indication of the overall condition of the market.

During the middle eighties, one professional woman in the petroleum industry saw the bid rates for consulting work drop dramatically due to an overabundance of workers. Virtually every company in the industry, it seemed, was either laying off employees or going out of business. By understanding the market, she was able to begin her job hunt long before the bottom fell out of the industry in the late eighties. She's now happily employed in another field.

Knowing the strategic advantages your company holds in the market can also be helpful. If you see these advantages disappearing (either because of new technology or other unexpected developments, such as sudden demographic changes or a natural disaster), collapse may be inevitable. If this is the case, you are well advised to start looking for another job *now*. Don't talk yourself into believing that things will eventually get better; they almost certainly won't.

Unfortunately, the downward spiral of a large corporation may be slow and subtle. In many cases, you may have to do more than simply read the trade papers. By successfully building a network of contacts throughout the organization, you may be able to find out exactly what is going on in departments far removed from your own. Developing a strong ally or two in the Human Resources department is often a good first step; people in this area will know in advance about any workforce changes. By knowing and understanding what the company's plans are for the next one to five years, you will be better able to judge your employer's stability.

If you work for a large corporation, and you find that the firm is planning for next year, next quarter, or next month—but has no idea where it is going in five years, a red flag should go up immediately. There's a problem somewhere. Either management is simply inept, flying by the seat of its collective pants, or it is in a firefighting mode, living from one day's crisis to the next. You will have to make your own judgment as to whether or not the people at the top will be able to get their act together.

What about a smaller or mid-sized organization? Some clues are bound to be more obvious in a close-knit environment, where people often wear several hats. Look for bills that don't get paid, new work that doesn't come in, and old contracts that end without renewals or new work to take their place. You should also keep an eye on your workload and that of your fellow employees. If the company is shuffling people around more than usual, or if job responsibilities are changing significantly or frequently in a short period of time, there may be trouble ahead.

With work wrapping up on the two key projects in which he was involved, a highway engineer found himself shuffled between southern California, Milwaukee, and his home office in Phoenix several times in one year. He knew that, when things were going well, he rarely traveled, because he had enough work to keep him in the office. From these clues, he deduced that his number was up. Not long after the new travel pattern emerged, his employer asked him to take early retirement.

Dramatically increased or decreased travel can be one sign that new initiatives affecting you may be on the way; there are others. A sudden change in your performance evaluations may indicate some behind-the-scenes politicking—or a more straightforward attempt to discredit you and justify your dismissal.

Similarly, any indication that your boss's position is shaky may mean that your job is at risk as well. Changes in top leadership often mean a shakeup of philosophies, standard operating procedures, and staffing levels. Your value to members of the "old guard" may prove to be of little consequence to the incoming "new guard." However, proving yourself valuable to the organization in general may help stall your demise—and buy you the time you need to look for another job. (It may also provide you with better referrals, or a chance to be redeployed elsewhere in the company.)

The Hammer Falls

Some layoffs are completely unavoidable. Perhaps the company is no longer involved in the part of the business in which you have worked, or it cannot support more than the most elementary operations.

If you are asked to leave, it's in your best interest to keep your cool. Resist the temptation to blow up at your employer. Sure, it's unlikely you'll ever be asked back to your job, but there is that saying about burning bridges, remember? Concentrate on getting the best severance package (and future references) you can.

Ready for a surprise? You might be in a good negotiating position when it comes to that severance package. There are a number of reasons for this. First, it's likely that the employer is feeling guilty about the layoff. Second, other employees will watch how you're treated when you leave. It's bad for company morale if you're treated unfairly at this stage, and the employer knows it. Finally, there are pragmatic reasons to be fair. Who knows where you'll find yourself after you leave the company? Someday, when you make it to the top, your former boss may even approach *you* for a job!

When a severance package is presented to you, listen calmly. Once the details have been laid out, you will probably want to ask for more. Unless the company's employee handbook clearly details the benefits you are entitled to, it is almost certainly to your advantage to attempt to negotiate a higher severance figure. But how and when you ask are key.

You may want to take more time to think about a severance package before signing anything. By then, you will have had time to think clearly, assess your situation, and figure out your financial needs. (See chapter 28, "Keeping the Financial Boat Afloat," for more details on this.) Taking a little extra time also allows you a "chill-out" period, which will reduce the likelihood that you will come across as angry and irrational when you present your arguments.

Whether or not you decide to ask for time to think about the severance offer, you should approach any attempt to increase the severance package in a non-threatening manner. Be sure to begin by saying, "I'm certain that you're making every effort to be fair." Then summarize your contribution to the company so the employer knows exactly why you deserve the increased consideration.

Try for benefits that are already in the company's budget, such as magazine and newspaper subscriptions or professional association membership renewals. You might even be able to talk your former employee into continued use of a company car for a time.

As helpful as it may have been in helping you forecast the rough weather you are now negotiating, the Human Resources department, with its rulebooks and set policies, is unlikely to be your greatest ally in this cause. You should try to avoid negotiating your severance package solely through this office. Instead, co-opt your former supervisor, who is likely to feel much more guilt. Granted, the meeting may not be one you look forward to with great enthusiasm, but then again, this is not about getting mad or becoming vindictive; this is about survival. The best recipe calls for generous amounts of calm objectivity and carefully measured doses of despair.

The Emotional Costs

Take time to mourn the loss of your job, as you would any other loss. Don't tough it out. Admit that this hurts. The degree to which you effectively work through the shock will determine how quickly you can get back on your feet and mount a successful job search.

The aftereffects of job loss are similar to the stages of grieving that follow divorce or the death of a loved one: denial, bargaining, anger, depression, and acceptance. Dealing with these can be difficult, and may require more time than you would think.

Finding support is crucial to your success in landing another job. Consider joining community job search clubs or meeting with an ad hoc group of other people in your situation. (Perhaps there are others who were laid off at the same time you were at your old firm.) By following these steps, you will expand your opportunities and maintain some perspective on the situation.

When you're ready, turn this horrible experience into a growth opportunity.

Assess the experience and be honest with yourself. Did you inadvertently contribute to the situation? Was there anything you might have done differently? Did you learn anything that you can apply in your next job?

Appendix B
What Disabled Job Seekers
Should Know

Discrimination—in the workplace and in practically every other aspect of everyday life—has been no stranger to the estimated forty-three million disabled Americans. Unemployment among people with disabilities, in fact, is higher than that in any other demographic group.

Many talented people with disabilities, denied employment and a chance at independence, find themselves forced to live as second-class citizens, ignored by society and forced to depend on the financial support of friends and relatives. Until recently, there was no national civil rights law that addressed the problems of the disabled in (or out) of the workplace.

Exactly why this lapse went unremedied for so long remains something of a mystery. Any able-bodied person, of course, could join the ranks of those with substantial physical or mental impairment at any time and with no warning. A traffic accident on the way home from work can rob a sighted person of eyesight or mobility. The sudden onset of a long-undiagnosed illness such as multiple sclerosis can leave the accountant who moaned about the expense of the company's wheelchair-access program with a different state of mind entirely.

Of course, no one chooses to be disabled. Similarly, no one wants to be unemployed. Today, however, if you are both disabled and out of work, that doesn't mean you are out of luck.

The New Rules

In 1990, the Americans with Disabilities Act (ADA), which bans most employment discrimination against disabled people, became the law of the land. (Previously only companies that did more that $2,500 worth of business per year with the federal government were prohibited from discrimination against disabled job applicants and employees.)

Title I of ADA (the part of the statute that deals with disabled job hunters) takes an across-the-board approach to weeding out discriminatory practices. It states that private employers, state and local governments, employment agencies, and labor organizations may not discriminate against job seekers because of their disabilities. It requires nondiscrimination in job application procedures, hiring, advancement, pay, job training, assignments, benefits, and other privileges of employment. And ADA makes it illegal to retaliate against any applicant or employee who asserts his or her rights under the Act.

Employers with twenty-five or more workers were required to comply with the provisions of ADA as of July, 1992, and employers of fifteen or more must comply beginning as of July, 1994. Private membership clubs (except labor unions) are exempted.

ADA guarantees you equal rights in the workplace if you are disabled—that is, if you have a substantial physical or mental impairment that limits a major life activity (hearing, seeing, speaking, walking and so on) in the long term. It also protects you if you have a history of a disability, if an employer believes you are disabled (regardless of whether or not you are), and if you're married or have a relationship with someone who is disabled.

A few words are in order on that last issue. Specifically, the ADA forbids discrimination based on "relationship or association." That means an employer cannot refuse to hire you because he or she feels that your relationship with a person who has a disability would affect your job performance. So, if your spouse is disabled, you cannot be denied a job because the interviewer believes that you would require excessive amounts of sick time to care for him or her. By the same token, you can't be discriminated against because you do volunteer work for people who have disabilities, such as AIDS.

In addition, ADA protects people with AIDS and those who are HIV-positive. It also applies to alcoholics. While it does not protect current illegal drug users, ADA does extend protection to recovering drug users and those who are participating in supervised drug-rehabilitation programs and no longer using controlled substances.

ADA also deals with non-workplace issues. It prohibits discrimination against the disabled in public accommodations, including hotels, restaurants, stores, theaters, museums, and public transportation. The Act also bans discrimination in any activity or service either operated or funded by federal, state, or local government and requires some businesses to adjust their operations to meet the needs of the disabled. Telephone companies, for instance, must provide relay services for people who use keyboard devices, enabling people with speech or hearing impairments to communicate with people and businesses that use conventional voice phones.

It should be noted here that ADA does not *mandate the hiring* of any individuals who fall into one of the protected categories; rather, it forbids discrimination by employers in cases where the disability would not affect the employee's job performance, or where the disability could be accommodated to enable the employee to perform the essential functions of the job. We'll look at this theme throughout this section.

ADA also does not extend protection to individuals with short-term disabilities, such as a broken arm. In a case such as this, although there is a physical impairment, it is not one that will interfere with a major life activity in the long term. The Act does, however, protect diabetics. Even though the condition of diabetes can be controlled through medication and, in most cases, does not adversely affect one's performance in any noticeable way, it is still viewed as a disability that substantially limits a major life activity.

Persons with infectious diseases *can* be refused positions that involve handling food. Who, you might well ask, falls into this category? Well, anyone with a disease that appears on the list maintained by the Department of Health and Human Services. A person with tuberculosis would qualify as having a communicable disease; a person with AIDS, or one who is HIV-positive, would not.

If this all sounds a bit confusing, that's because it is. Many provisions of ADA are ambiguous, and parts of the law are currently being wrangled over in the courts. It may be many years (and lawsuits) before the final ramifications of the Act are clear. In the meantime, if you need clarification on a particular point, see the *Resources* section that follows this one. There you'll find many agencies and organizations that will be able to help answer your questions.

Other Laws that May Affect You

Other federal laws, such as those associated with the Occupational Safety and Health Administration, may have requirements that affect the disabled. Employers must still conform to these laws; ADA does not override them.

If there are state or local safety laws that conflict with ADA requirements, the ADA *may* override them. For example, if a state or local law excludes a disabled person from a job because of a perceived safety risk, the employer must still abide by the ADA and determine whether an actual and serious risk exists, and whether the risk can be reduced to an acceptable level or eliminated with a reasonable accommodation.

As a general rule, it is against the law for an employer to ask you specifically whether you are disabled or inquire into the nature of your disability. However, federal contractors and subcontractors who are affected by the affirmative action requirements of section 503 of the Rehabilitation Act of 1973 may ask applicants to identify themselves on job application forms or during an interview. (Other federal laws or regulations, such as those that apply to disabled veterans, might necessitate preemployment inquiries about disabilities.)

Are You Protected by ADA? If So, How?

To be protected under Title I of ADA, you must be qualified to do the job in question. This means that you must possess whatever education, experiences, skills, or licenses would be required of any other applicant. You must also be able to perform the responsibilities of the job you're seeking. ADA does not protect the person with no legs who would like to be a firefighter—as a result of the disability, that person would be incapable of executing essential firefighting tasks. Nor does it help the blind person who wants to be a bus driver, even though that person may have driven a bus before his or her disability.

Gather as much information as you can about the requirements of the job before the interview; you can do this with intelligent questions during the telephone interview, if there is one. Employers are not required by law to develop and maintain written job descriptions, but many do. An applicant may use a written job description—if one exists—as evidence in a later discrimination claim.

You should understand that, while ADA is a comprehensive civil rights act, it is not in any way an "affirmative action" program. ADA will entitle you to get to the interview, and will protect you from discrimination due to your disability once you get there, but it will not hand you the job on a platter. You'll still have to earn it. If more than one qualified person applies for the job, an employer isn't under any obligation to hire the candidate who is disabled. The employer is entitled to hire whichever applicant he or she prefers.

If you are hired, you can be held to the same standards of productivity and performance as similarly employed individuals without disabilities. However, this only applies to areas that are considered essential to the job. For instance, a deaf delivery person who works for a bottling company would not be required to perform marginal functions associated with the position (such as telephone work). Job restructuring may be an appropriate accommodation in some cases to ensure that disabled workers are not penalized if they are unable to perform extraneous duties.

If your disability requires reasonable accommodation—such as equipment, interpreters, or readers—the employer is required to provide them. *That goes for the period of time that you are applying for the job, as well as after you are hired.* Reasonable accommodations might also include making facilities accessible to persons with disabilities, incorporating part-time or adaptable work schedules, making reassignments to vacant positions, and modifying training materials and policies.

An employer may also be required to adapt an existing applicant or employee examination so that it measures a person's ability to perform the job—and *not* the limitations caused by a disability. The format of the tests should not require the use of skills that may be impaired (sensory, speaking, or manual ability, for instance) to demonstrate competence in an essential area of the position that does not require those skills. Put more simply, if the job does not require, say, the applicant's sight as far as essential functions are concerned, the employer should be prepared to adapt a written test designed for sighted people (by, perhaps, changing it to an oral test).

An employer may also need to make reasonable accommodations in nonwork areas, including cafeterias, lounges, or transportation that the employer provides. It is against the law for the employer to penalize you as a result of these changes. The ADA forbids the employer from lowering your salary or paying you less than other employees who do the same job because you need an accommodation.

There are limits to an employer's responsibility to provide accommodations; reasons such as prohibitive expense or undue hardship may waive some obligations. These claims are weighed against such issues as the actual cost of the accommodation, the size of the business, its financial resources, the number of facilities, and the workforce structure. Generally speaking, though, an employer must have a very good reason to deny a job applicant's or employee's request for an accommodation.

If the employer makes a legitimate claim that it is impossible to provide the accommodation you need, you have the option of providing the accommodation yourself or paying for part of it. But there is less reason to plead poverty when it comes to making accommodations than many employers might think. Financial assistance and a special tax credit may be available to help employers make accommodations to comply with ADA. (If anyone asks you about this, you can refer him or her to the local IRS office, or the Job Accommodation Network, whose phone number is 1-800-526-7234.) The smart disabled job hunter will have verified his own eligibility with these resources prior to the job hunt. When this is done, questions of cost, financial assistance, or tax credit can be raised in a follow-up letter or interview as circumstances dictate.

Obviously, the specifics of accommodations will vary. Each person's situations and needs are unique. If you need an accommodation for your disability, it is your responsibility to bring that need to the attention of your employer or potential employer. You may be in the best position to suggest an appropriate accommodation, but the process of identifying and implementing an accommodation is ideally an interactive one, with both you and your employer participating in a dialogue. If you have more questions on this score, contact your local Equal Opportunity Employment Commission or local vocational rehabilitation agencies; you'll find contact information in your phone directory. Another good bet is the aforementioned Job Accommodation Network.

Should You Bring up the Subject of Your Disability?

You may or may not want to bring up the subject of your disability before you are hired. That's a matter of personal preference. However, since employers are required only to accommodate "known" disabilities, many employers do recommend that you "self-identify" during the interview. Richard Torockio, General Manager of the Host Travel Plaza Division of the Marriott Corporation, says, "If the applicant tells us what special accommodations he or she will need, it's a big plus. We like to know what changes will need to be made in advance."

Of course, you must find an appropriate time to bring up the topic of accommodations. Paul L. Scher, CRC, a partner at Jordon & Scher Associates, suggests you take the following approach: "When the interviewer asks whether you did this kind of work at your last job, take the opportunity to explain how well you performed and which special accommodations have helped you in the past." In other words, apply the *Knock 'em Dead* philosophy!

We saw earlier that, as a result of the specific requirements of certain preexisting federal laws and regulations, very few employers may legally ask you questions during the application process concerning your disability. Under most circumstances, an interviewer may not ask whether you are disabled or question you about the severity of your disability during a job interview. However, the employer can (and probably will) ask you whether or not you can perform the essential responsibilities of the job. And he or she can also ask you to describe or demonstrate how you can perform those duties.

Your Interview

It is important that you give positive answers with illustrations and examples. Simple "yes/no" answers are guaranteed to keep you from leading the field. The idea is not to hide behind the law and your rights, but rather to use it as foundation for open communication. Don't allow a disability to give you a blind spot when it comes to an employer's real needs. See chapter 13, "The Five Secrets of the Hire."

You must win this job on your own merits, not as a result of your status as a disabled person! But you do face certain special challenges. Along with knowing how to answer all the questions put to you and how to hold up under pressure, you will have to take care to put the interviewer at ease.

Your potential employer may feel awkward because of your disability, or even feel unnerved by the implications of ADA. What can you do about it? Do the unexpected! Take your interviewer by surprise and make light of your disability. Show that you have a sense of humor. A blind friend of mine was interviewed for a job over lunch at an Indian restaurant—but soon sensed that his companion was having second thoughts about this choice, given the complex plate arrangements and exotic presentations of some of the menu items the waiter recited. To put the interviewer at ease, my friend quipped, "Would it be okay with you if I just ordered a rice dish?" Later, when his potential employer asked what his greatest weakness was, he confessed, "Well, I suppose it may not be a good idea for me to pour everyone's morning coffee!"

Use whatever positive personality traits you have developed the most highly. Drive, motivation, communication skills, energy, confidence . . . find the most flattering aspect of your work identity and showcase it to the fullest. It is likely that you have more than your share of determination. Now is the time to use it to your advantage.

Stress your similarities with the interviewer rather than your differences. One deaf woman who has been through the process suggests, "Instead of saying, 'I'm the same as you,' show it. Simply express your professional opinions and attitudes, and let the interviewer see how 'normal' your are."

Do feel free to be diplomatically pushy when necessary. It's okay to refuse to take no for an answer. Help the interviewer see ADA as an opportunity to find a way to let you, a potentially valuable employee, perform for his or her company.

One more important note on interview preparation. Don't be afraid to ask for help with your personal appearance before you head out to meet the prospective employer. When you dress for an interview, always look (and smell) your best. Charles Rich, a paraplegic writer and broadcaster, suggests that you consider each interview you go on as a date: "You didn't get used to your disability in the first fifteen minutes. You can't expect your interviewer—your 'date'—to either." Take the time you need to get ready. Look your best, and give the employer the time and opportunity to see the real you; ADA has at last provided him or her with the motivation to do so.

Success Stories
Here are a few true stories of disabled job applicants who were able to showcase their talents to prospective employers and land the jobs they wanted.

- One newspaper columnist went out and made an opportunity for himself. He told a managing editor that it was about time the paper had a column about people with disabilities. As a deaf person, he naturally felt that he was uniquely qualified to do the job. And he got it!

- A young man with Crohn's disease who has arthritis of the hips and back was homebound for two and a half years. Here's how he reentered the workforce: "I prepared a great resume and got a letter of reference from my physician. Then I simply convinced my employer that I was very creative and a hard worker."

- Another disabled applicant wrote a short story about his determination to succeed, detailing the steps he took to triumph over adversity. The piece got him hired.

- In 1989, a manufacturing firm hired a woman who was deaf and blind. She had previously been evaluated by a rehabilitation service organization professional as being incapable of any competitive employment. Since joining the company, she has been cross-trained to perform more jobs than anyone else in the organization. "We've *had* to cross-train her in so many jobs just to keep work in front of her," her manager confesses. "It's because she's so quick. In fact, she can outwork me!"

- Before he became a quadriplegic, Tony was a shoe buyer. Now he's a full-time market research analyst; he uses special software that allows him to operate a computer without using a keyboard. He's been so successful that his former boss recently asked whether he'd consider moving back to his old position.

Bear in mind that most employers view all job seekers, disabled or otherwise, in the same way. The big question is: What can you do for our company? Your past performance, skills, and ability to do the job are what will make the most bottom-line difference to the interviewer, not your limitations.

"We have the same success rate in hiring disabled people that we have with the general population," says Marriott's Richard Torockio. "Some people work out, some don't. We don't want to hear 'I'm good because I'm disabled.' We like to hear, 'I'm good because I'm me.'"

Carole Rogers, Director of Employment Activities at McDonald's, agrees. "We look for the ability and skills needed to do the job," she notes, "and the experience that relates to what we're trying to accomplish. We look for the same things in people with disabilities that we look for in people without disabilities."

Remain upbeat and friendly throughout the interview. As Susan Brake, Director of Human Resources as Pizza Hut, puts it, "We look for a good attitude and flexibility—someone who's excited about working for us."

The Insurance Question

Health insurance is a topic that is on the minds of many Americans these days, and it's a safe bet that it is also on the minds of many disabled job applicants as they head into the interview room.

ADA, unfortunately, is not a cure for health insurance problems. The Act does require that employers allow all employees access to health insurance. But employers *are* entitled to offer only health insurance policies that feature clauses excluding pre-exisiting conditions. Obviously, such clauses affect the disabled more than any other employees.

By the time you read this, the picture may well have changed significantly— but not as a result of ADA. As this book goes to press, published reports indicate that the Clinton Administration will include as part of its proposed health care reform plan new regulations forbidding insurers from withholding coverage for persons with preexisting medical conditions.

Physical Exams and Questions about Your History

Can the employer ask you to take a physical exam? Only if he or she is willing to give you the job first! An employer may not require a medical exam until *after* a job offer has been made, and then only if the company requires physicals of all employees who are starting similar jobs. (Note, however, that ADA does permit tests for illegal drug use administered in accordance with existing laws. Drug tests are not considered medical examinations under the Act, and an employer may legally conduct drug tests and make hiring decisions based on the results.)

An employer may not rescind your job offer because of information revealed by a physical exam unless the reasons for the rejection are strictly job-related. Thus, the employer would have to show, for example, that the physical exam revealed that you would be unable to perform the essential functions of the job even with a reasonable accommodation, or that no accommodation exists that would enable you to perform the job. Another example is medical evidence showing that, by virtue of your disability, you would pose a direct threat to the health and safety of yourself or others in the workplace. The direct threat must be actual, current and serious, rather than based on stereotype, fear, or prejudice. Moreover, the employer must demonstrate that the threat could not be reduced to an acceptable level or eliminated by a reasonable accommodation.

Any information resulting from your physical exam must be kept confidential, in a file separate from personnel records. These files should be available only under extremely limited conditions. An employer may, however, submit medical information to state workers' compensation offices without violating ADA confidentiality requirements.

What does all this boil down to? Your medical records are your business, that's what. You cannot be refused a job (or fired) simply because an employer suspects that your disability may cause increased workers' compensation costs. But beware! An employer *can* terminate consideration of your employment or fire you if you lie in answer to a legal question about your condition or workers' compensation history.

How, you may ask, can an employer legally pose such questions? Well, the key fact to bear in mind here is that a person who is receiving workers' compensation, or is receiving benefits under another disability law, is *not necessarily also considered disabled under ADA*. Work-related injuries do not always "significantly limit" a major life activity. Many on-the-job injuries are temporary, and do not cause severe long-term mental or physical impairment. If yours is one of them, you should be prepared to answer questions about your past medical history if they come up.

And remember, it's not at all in your interests to sign on or continue with a job for which you are not suited. Even if it means considering a lifestyle or career change, you should make an honest assessment of your abilities. Janet is a fire-fighter who was recently diagnosed with multiple sclerosis, an illness that could potentially cause risk to herself and others if she were to attempt to continue as before in her career. She decided that it was absolutely necessary to tell her superiors about the condition on her own initiative. "The most important thing I did," she says, "was provide education about the disease, and let my reputation as an honest, open person stand for itself. My peers know that I will not do anything that will jeopardize anyone." She was eventually transferred to a position with which both she and her supervisors felt comfortable.

The Long View

You don't have to give up your life's ambitions simply because of a disability. With modern technology—which includes such devices as robotic arms, braille printers, word-prediction software programs, voice-recognition systems, optical readers, and telecommunications devices—more disabled people than ever before are succeeding in the workplace. And more employers than ever before are benefiting from their success.*

You can make success *your* reality, as well. Stay active in churches, professional organizations, commuinty organizations, and groups for the disabled. Not only is every person you meet a potential job contact, but some employers are more receptive to hiring disabled people who are backed by an organization. This is especially true if the group is one that offers job coaching for the first few weeks of work, when intensive training may be needed. And, of course, there are some important morale considerations related to keeping active in this way.

You are a valuable, empowered person. Never sell yourself short. (If all else fails, remind yourself that job discrimination is illegal, and that the suits are currently being settled at a three-to-one rate in favor of the disabled applicant.)

If you do need an extra shot of self-confidence, consider the observation of Brent Stull, Plant Manager at Kreonite Corporation. "In integrated workforces," Stull observes, "I find that turnover rates decrease, attendance rates go up, and re-work rates decrease." Managers pay attention to things like that. Although you may have been denied the chance to work in the past, you have a chance now to make a real difference—not only in your own life, but in the workplace as well.

Don't spend time poking holes in your own self-esteem if you get turned down

---

* Let the record show I speak not in the abstract, but from experience. As a result of recent hires related to the research required for this section, *half* of my own team here at Peregrine McCoy is now disabled. I'm ecstatic with the results and I'm sure the experience is being replicated throughout the business world. When it comes to productivity, loyalty and extra effort, I've been simply blown away. Give me a team of so-called "challenged" people with a sense of humor and I'll conquer the world. You can quote me on this!

for jobs a few times. It happens to everyone! Remember, the more interviews and prospects you initiate, the more opportunities you'll have. Follow a plan as its outlined here and remain optimistic.

When you do land the right job, remember that you don't have to work twice as hard as the person next to you just because you're disabled. As writer/broadcaster Charles Rich says, "You are as entitled as any other employee to look tired every now and then. You can even be out sick once in a while. You don't have to prove yourself every hour of every day."

If You Have to Use ADA to Obtain a Legal Remedy...

ADA has made job discrimination against disabled persons illegal—but it has not abolished that discrimination. If you feel you have been discriminated against as the result of a disability, you can fight back. If you decide to do so, you will have the power of the federal government behind you.

Contact the Equal Employment Opportunity Commission (see the *Resources* section that follows for contact information) within 180 days of the incident you feel was discriminatory. Under some state and local laws, you may have a bit more time to file a charge: up to three hundred days. Call for details. The number is 1-800-669-EEOC (voice) or 1-800-800-3302 (TDD).

The EEOC will investigate and attempt to resolve the charge through conciliation. The same procedures used to handle charges of discrimination filed under Title VII of the Civil Rights Act of 1964—the law that covers race, color, sex, national origin, and religious discrimination—apply. (Note: the EEOC is responsible for handling discrimination charges for actions that took place on or after July 26, 1992. If the incident took place before that date, you should still contact the Commission for information on what agencies to get in touch with next.)

If it is found that you have in fact been discriminated against on account of your disability and in violation of the ADA, you will be entitled to a remedy that may include: hiring, promotion, reinstatement, back pay, or a reasonable accommodation (such as reassignment). You may also be entitled to attorney's fees.

The EEOC can provide you with more detailed summaries of the ADA and other federal requirements for nondiscrimination. Call them at the numbers provided above for additional information if you need it.

Resources

ADA Regional Disability and Business Technical Assistance Centers

Connecticut, Maine, Massachusetts, New Hampshire, Rhode Island, and Vermont:
New England Disability and Business Technical Assistance Center, 145 Newbury Street, Portland ME 04101. 207/874-6535 (voice/TDD).

New Jersey, New York, Puerto Rico, and Virgin Islands:
Northeast Disability and Business Technical Assistance Center, 354 South Broad Street, Trenton NJ 08608. 609/392-4004 (voice), 609/392-7044 (TDD).

Delaware, District of Columbia, Maryland, Pennsylvania, Virginia, and West Virginia:
Mid-Atlantic Disability and Business Technical Assistance Center, 2111 Wilson Boulevard, Suite 400, Arlington VA 22201. 703/525-3268 (voice/TDD).

Alabama, Florida, Georgia, Kentucky, Mississippi, North Carolina, South Carolina, and Tennessee:
Southeast Disability and Business Technical Assistance Center, 1776 Peachtree Street, Suite 310 North, Atlanta GA 30309. 404/888-0022 (voice), 404/888-9007 (TDD).

Illinois, Indiana, Michigan, Minnesota, Ohio, and Wisconsin:
Great Lakes Disability and Business Technical Assistance Center, 1640 West Roosevelt Road (M/C 627), Chicago IL 60608. 312/413-1407 (voice), 312/413-0453 (TDD).

Arkansas, Louisiana, New Mexico, Oklahoma, and Texas:
Southwest Disability and Business Technical Assistance Center, 2323 South Shepherd Boulevard, Suite 1000, Houston TX 77019. 713/520-0232 (voice), 713/520-5136 (TDD).

Iowa, Kansas, Nebraska, and Missouri:
Great Plains Disability and Business Technical Assistance Center, 4816 Santana Drive, Columbia MO 65203, 314/882-3600 (voice/TDD).

Colorado, Montana, North Dakota, South Dakota, Utah, and Wyoming:
Rocky Mountain Disability and Business Technical Assistance Center, 3630 Sinton Road, Suite 103, Colorado Springs CO 80907-5072. 719/444-0252 (voice), 719/444-0268 (TDD).

Arizona, California, Hawaii, and Nevada:
Pacific Coast Disability and Business Technical Assistance Center, 440 Grand Avenue, Suite 500, Oakland CA 94610. 510/465-7884 (voice), 510/465-3172 (TDD).

Alaska, Idaho, Oregon, and Washington:
Northwest Disability and Business Technical Assistance Center, 605 Woodview Drive, Lacey WA 98503. 206/438-3168 (voice), 206/438-3167 (TDD).

Other Resources

Job Accommodation Network, P.O. Box 6123, 809 Allen Hall, Morgantown WV 26505-6123. 800/526-7234 (voice/TDD).

The President's Committee on Employment of People with Disabilities, 1331 F Street NW, Washington DC 20004. 202/376-6200 (voice), 202/376-6205 (TDD).

U.S. Department of Justice, Civil Rights Division, Office on the Americans with Disabilities Act, P.O. Box 66118, Washington DC 20035-6118. 202/514-0301 (voice), 202/514-0381 (TDD).

Appendix C
Electronic Job Hunting Resources

To use an on-line service for your job search, you can subscribe directly to one or visit your local library. There are many public and university libraries that provide walk-in uses of on-line services; some will conduct the search for you at a nominal cost. Some fee-based services offer same-day turnaround for customized research, or even one-hour rush service. An invaluable resource guide called *The Directory of Fee-Based Information Services* lists more than four hundred U.S. and Canadian library systems that provide fee-based search services. The price of the directory is $65.00. For more information, call the American Library Association at 800/545-2433.

In the first part of this section of *Knock 'em Dead*, the Electronic Database Public Access Directory, you will find information on universities or public libraries that offer complete research and document delivery services, from in-library research to on-line services with hard-copy delivery. We have provided regional listings, and only a handful in most major metropolitan areas. You can also find out the facility closest to you by calling your public library (or one of the full service libraries listed here) and asking for information on the nearest library that offers "on-line information services and a public-access computer center." (Use that wording exactly; it will save you some time.)

The next series of listings is the Electronic Record Database Directory, which lists on-line databases in most major U.S. cities. Some are quite specialized; others offer services of interest to most job hunters. Typically, these services will charge subscription dues, password fees, access charges, or a combination of these. Phone costs are extra.

□　□　□

Whether you own your own personal computer, would use a library's computer, or plan on having a search done for you, the resources are waiting for you. Even if you are intimidated by computers, you should consider calling some of the organizations listed in this part of the book. Many of these facilities will allow you to take advantage of all the benefits of cutting-edge technology without ever touching a keyboard.

Important Note: Before you dive headlong into the world of electronic information, a word of caution is in order. Electronic job hunting (EJH) can be very effective, but it can also be very expensive. In EJH, time is money. The more information you gather, the longer it will take to print out or fax to you; the more time you spend on the line, the more you will pay in telephone and access charges. EJH can be more comprehensive and faster than regular hard-copy methods of finding leads, but as of this writing it is best viewed as a judiciously used supplement to standard research methods.

Electronic Database Public Access Directory

An asterisk (*) by a listing indicates that the library in question specializes in business research.

If a university or public library in your area isn't listed, call your local library and ask about "on-line computer services available to the general public" in your area. The services you come up with may not be equipped to run the search for you, but they will probably have computers and several on-line resources available for your use.

Arizona State University*
602/965-3415

Boston University Metropolitan College Corporate Education Center
(CD-ROM or customized research only)
508/649-9731

Broward County Library (Ft. Lauderdale, FL)
305/357-7444

Buffalo and Erie County Public Library (Buffalo, NY)
716/858-8900

Carnegie-Mellon University
412/268-6365

Cleveland Public Library
216/623-2999

County of Los Angeles Public Library*
310/868-4003

Data Center Search Service (Oakland, CA)
510/835-4692

Denver Public Library
303/640-8846

Fairfax County (VA) Public Library
703/222-3155

Fairleigh Dickinson University*
201/460-5468

George Washington University*
202/994-6973

Georgia Institute of Technology*
404-894-4511

Highsmith Co., Inc. (Fort Atkinson, WI)*
414/563-9571

James T. Hill Reference Library* **(Ames, IA)**
612/227-9531

ICFAR-ARAC (Indianapolis, IN)
(NASA's Industrial Engineering Center)
317/262-5003

Industrial Technology Institute (Ann Arbor, MI)*
313/769-4286

Lewis & Clark Law School
503/245-7878

Los Angeles Public Library*
213/612-3200

Louisville Free Public Library
502/574-1600

National Water Well Association
(Customized environmental research on all groundwater-related topics.)
614/761-1711

New Jersey State Library
609/292-6220

New York Academy of Medicine
Library
212/876-8200

New York Public Library
212/930-0724

North Dakota State University
701/237-8900

North York Public Library (Ontario,
Canada)
416/395-5579

Ohio State University
(Medical and health information)
614/292-9810

Ohio University
614/593-2931
614/695-1720

Purdue University
317/494-2808

Rice University*
713/528-3553

Seltzer Daley Companies, Inc.
(Princeton, NJ)
(Customized research for hospitals,
healthcare systems, and health-related
businesses.)
609/924-2420

South Dakota State Library*
605/773-3131

Temple University/Paley Library
215/787-3836

Texas Tech University
806/743-2200

Tulsa City (OK) County Library
918/596-7991

University of Alberta (Canada)
403/492-2728

University of California at Irvine
714/856-6654

University of California at Riverside
909/787-3221

University of Central Florida
407/823-2562

University of Florida*
800/225-0308

University of Georgia
706/546-2477

University of Illinois at
Urbana-Champaign*
217/333-6202

University of Michigan at Ann Arbor
313/763-5060

University of Minnesota: BASIS
Service
612/624-3793

University of Minnesota Biomedical
Information Center
612/626-3730

University of Minnesota: ESTIS
Service
612/624-2356

University of New Mexico
505/277-7135

University of Oklahoma Health
Science Library
405/271-2343

University of Oregon at Eugene
503/346-2368

University of Pittsburgh
412/648-7000

University of Richmond
804/289-8666

University of South Florida*
813/974-4880

University of Southern California*
(NASA's Industrial Applications Center,
with access to over 500 databases)
213/743-6132

University of Texas at Dallas
214/690-2999

University of Wisconsin at Madison
608/262-5913

Electronic Record Database Directory

Accessing any one of the following databases for the first time will probably make you feel as though you're walking into the biggest library in the world. The specialties and fee structures of the various services vary widely, however, and we cannot do full justice to any of them in our allotted space. For additional information, call the numbers listed. (Many are toll-free.)

ADP
ADP Network Services
175 Jackson Plaza
Ann Arbor MI 48106
313/769-6800

BRS
BRS Information Technologies
8000 Westpark Drive
McLean VA 22102
703/442-0900
800/289-4277, 800/955-0906
Fax: 703/893-4632

CompuServe
CompuServe Information Service
5000 Arlington Centre Boulevard
P.O. Box 20212
Columbus OH 43220
614/457-8600
800/848-8990

Corporate Jobs Outlook!
Corporate Jobs Outlook, Inc.
P.O. Drawer 100
Boerne TX 78006
210/755-8810
Fax: 512/755-2410

Datatimes
Datatimes, Inc.
Suite 450
14000 Quail Springs Parkway
Oklahoma City OK 73134
405/751-6400

Dialog Information Services
Dialog Information Services, Inc.
3460 Hillview Avenue
Palo Alto CA 94304
415/858-3785
800/334-2564
Fax: 415/858-7069
In Canada: 800/387-2689

Dun's Electronic Business Directory
Dun & Bradstreet
Three Sylvan Way
Parsippany NJ 07950
201/605-6000
800/223-1026
Fax: 201/605-6921

G.E. Information Services
Client Services
401 North Washington Street
Rockville MD 20850
301/340-4572
800/638-9636

Human Resources Information Network
Executive Telecom System
1200 Quince Orchard Boulevard
Gaithersburg, MD 20870
301/590-2300

Medline
U.S. National Library of Medicine
8600 Rockville Pike
Bethesda MD 20894
301/496-6193
800/638-8480

NewsNet
NewsNet, Inc.
945 Haverford Road
Bryn Mawr PA 19010
215/527-8030
800/345-1301
Fax: 215/527-0338

Nexis/Lexis
Mead Data Central
9443 Springboro Pike, P.O. Box 933
Dayton OH 45401-9964
513/865-6800
800/227-4908
Fax: 513/865-6909

Orbit
Info-pro Technologies
8000 Westpark Drive
McLean VA 22102
703/442-0900
800/456-7248
Fax: 703/893-4632

Prodigy
Prodigy Services Company
445 Hamilton Avenue
White Plains NY 10601
914/993-8000

Reuters Accountline
Reuters Information Services
1333 H Street NW, Suite 410
Washington DC 20005
202/898-8300

Standard & Poor's On-Line Services
Standard & Poor's Corporation
25 Broadway
New York NY 10004
212/208-8300
Fax: 212/412-0498

***Technical Employment News* Job Listings**
Publication and Communications, Inc.
12416 Hymeadow Drive
Austin TX 78750
512/250-8127
800/678-9724
Fax: 512/331-6779

Vu/Text
Knight-Ridder Corporation
75 Wall Street, 22nd Floor
New York NY 10005
212/269-1110
800/433-8930

Wilsonline
H.W. Wilson Company
950 University Avenue
Bronx NY 10452
718/588-8400
800/367-6770
Fax: 212/590-1617

Appendix D
Printed Job Hunting Resources

The Adams Jobs Almanac
Bob Adams, Inc., Holbrook, MA.
Detailed information on over ten thousand major employers, including, for most companies, jobs commonly filled, experience required, and even benefits packages offered.

The Almanac of American Employers
Corporate Jobs Outlook, Boerne, TX.
Lists five hundred of the country's most successful large companies; profiles salary ranges, benefits, financial stability, and advancement opportunities.

American College of Healthcare Executives Directory
American Association of Healthcare, Chicago, IL.
Lists over sixteen thousand health care executives in public and private organizations. Published every other year.

The Capitol Source
National Journal, Inc., Washington, DC.
Includes names, addresses, and phone numbers for key figures in the District of Columbia; also features information about corporations, interest groups, think tanks, labor unions, real estate organizations, financial institutions, trade and professional groups, law firms, political consultants, advertising and public relations firms, private clubs, and the media. Published twice a year.

Congressional Yellow Book
Monitor Publishing Co., New York, NY.
Gives detailed information on congressional staff positions, committees and subcommittees, and top staff in congressional support agencies. Published annually.

Corporate Jobs Outlook
Corporate Jobs Outlook, Inc., Boerne, TX.
Each issue reviews fifteen to twenty major (five thousand employees or more)

firms. The report rates the firms and provides information on: salaries and benefits, current and projected development, where to apply for jobs, potential layoffs, benefit plans, the company's record for promoting women or minorities to executive positions, and college reimbursement packages. Also includes personnel contact information for each firm. Published bimonthly; a yearly subscription is $159.99. Call 210/755-8810.

Note: This resource is also available on-line through NewsNet (800-345-1301) or the Human Resources Information Network (800-638-8094). Call for more details.

Corporate Technology Directory
CorpTech, Woburn, MA.
Lists over 35,000 businesses and 110,000 executives. Describes products and services in such fields as automation, biotechnology, chemicals, computers and software, defense, energy, environment, manufacturing equipment, advanced materials, medical, pharmaceuticals, photonics, subassemblies and components, testing and measurements, telecommunications, transportation, and holding companies. Published annually.

CorpTech Fast 5,000 Company Locator
CorpTech, Woburn, MA.
Lists over five thousand of the fastest-growing companies listed in the Corporate Technology Directory, but includes addresses and phone numbers, number of employees, sales, and industries by state. Published annually.

COSLA Directory
The Council of State Governments, Lexington, KY.
Provides information on state library agencies, consultant and administrative staff, plus ALANET numbers, electronic mail letters, and FAX numbers. Published annually.

Directory of Corporate Affiliations
Reed Reference Publishing Company, Wilmette, IL.
Lists key personnel in 4,700 parent companies and 40,000 divisions, subsidiaries, and affiliates. Includes addresses and phone numbers of key executives and decision makers. Published five times a year. For more information, call 800/323-6772.

Directory of Environmental Information
Government Institutes, Rockville, MD.
Lists federal and state government resources, trade organizations, and professional and scientific newsletters, magazines, and databases. Published every other year.

Directory of Federal Libraries
Includes library's administrator and selected staff for three thousand special and general, presidential, and national libraries, as well as library facilities in technical centers, hospitals, and penal institutions.

Directory of Legal Aid and Defender Offices in the U.S. and Territories
National Legal Aid and Defender Association, Washington, DC.
Lists legal aid and defender offices across the U.S. Published annually.

Directory of Leading Private Companies
National Register Publishing Company, Wilmette, IL.
Profiles over seven thousand U.S. private companies in the service, manufacturing, distribution, retail, and construction fields. Includes companies in such areas as healthcare, high technology, entertainment, fast-food franchises, leasing, publishing, and communications. Published annually.

Encyclopedia of Associations
Gale Research, Inc., Detroit, MI.
Published in three volumes. Volume 1 lists national organizations in the U.S. and includes over twenty-two thousand associations, including hundreds for government professions. Volume 2 provides geographic and executive indexes. Volume 3 features full entries on associations that are not listed in Volume 1.

Note: This resource is also available on-line through Dialog Information Services (800/334-2564). Call for more information.

Environmental Telephone Directory
Governmental Institutes, Rockville, MD.
Lists detailed information on governmental agencies that deal with the environment. The directory also identifies the environmental aides of U.S. senators and representatives. Published every other year.

Federal Careers for Attorneys
Federal Reports, Inc., Washington, DC.
A guide to legal careers with over three hundred U.S. government general counsel and other legal offices in the U.S. Explains where to apply, the types of legal work common to each field, and information on special recruitment programs.

Federal Executive Directory
Carroll Publishing Co., Washington, DC.
Profiles a broad range of agencies both executive and legislative, including cabinet departments, federal administrative agencies, and congressional committee members and staff. The directory also outlines areas of responsibility for legal and administrative assistants. Published six times a year; an annual subscription is $198.00. Call 202/333-8620 for more information.

Federal Organization Service: Military
Carroll Publishing Co., Washington, DC.
Lists direct-dial phone numbers for 11,500 key individuals in 1,500 military departments and offices. Updated every six weeks; an annual subscription is $625. Call 202-333-8620 for more information.

Hospital Phone Book
U.S. Directory Service, Miami, FL.
Provides information on over 7,940 government and private hospitals in the U.S.

International Directory of Corporate Affiliations
National Register Publishing Company, Wilmette, IL.
Lists over 1,400 major foreign companies and their 30,000 U.S. and foreign holdings. Published annually.

The JobBank Guide to Employment Services
Bob Adams, Inc., Holbrook, MA.
Profiles over six thousand employment agencies, temporary help firms, executive recruiters, and other counseling services.

The JobBank Series
A top-notch series of paperback local-employment guides. The 1993 editions list virtually every local company with over fifty employees in a given metro area. Company listings are arranged by industry for easy use; also included is a section on the region's economic outlook and contact information for local professional associations, executive search firms, and job placement agencies. The series covers twenty major metropolitan areas: Atlanta, Boston, the Carolinas, Chicago, Dallas/Ft. Worth, Denver, Detroit, Florida, Houston, Los Angeles, Minneapolis/St.Paul, New York, Ohio, Philadelphia, Phoenix, St. Louis, San Francisco, Seattle, Tennessee, and Washington, D.C. Available at most bookstores. Updated yearly.

Judicial Staff Directory
Staff Directories, Ltd. Mt. Vernon VA.
Lists over 11,000 individuals employed in the 207 federal courts, as well as 13,000 cities and their courts. The book also has information on court administration, U.S. marshalls, U.S. attorneys, and the U.S. Department of Justice. Includes 1,800 biographies.

National Association of County Health Officials Sustaining Membership Directory
National Association of County Health Officials, Washington, DC.
Lists national health officials for almost every county in the U.S. Published annually. Free. Call 202-783-5550 for more information.

The National JobBank
Bob Adams, Inc., Holbrook, MA.
The 1993 edition includes over sixteen thousand employer listings; future editions are slated to profile even more. Many listings feature common positions hired for and benefits information. Updated annually.

National Trade and Professional Associations of the United States
Columbia Books, Washington, DC.
Lists information on over 6,500 trade and professional associations. Published annually.

Nationwide Jobs in Dietetics
Jobs in Dietetics, Santa Monica, CA.
Lists jobs nationwide in the field of dietetics. Published monthly; an annual subscription is $84.00. Call 310/453-5375 for more information.

NDAA Membership Directory
National District Attorneys Association, Alexandria, VA.
Lists all district attorneys' offices across the U.S. $15.00 for nonmembers, $10.00 for members. Call 703/549-9222 for more information.

Paralegal's Guide to Government Jobs
Federal Reports, Inc. Washington, DC.
Explains federal hiring procedures for both entry-level and experienced paralegals. The volume describes seventy law-related careers for which paralegals qualify and lists over one thousand federal agency personnel offices that hire the most paralegal talent. Also profiles special hiring programs.

Technology Research Guide
CorpTech, Woburn, MA.
Covers over three thousand company profiles and twelve thousand executive contacts. Includes specific details on each company's products and services. Published quarterly; a yearly subscription is $185. Call 617-932-3939 for more information.

Transportation Officials and Engineers Directory
American Road and Transportation Builders Association, Washington, DC.
Lists over four thousand state transportation officials and engineers at local, state, and federal levels. Published annually.

U.S. Medical Directory
U.S. Directory Service, Miami, FL.
Over one thousand pages of information on doctors, hospitals, nursing facilities, medical laboratories, and medical libraries.

Washington Information Directory
Congressional Quarterly Inc., Washington, DC.
Provides important information on the federal government as a whole, and on each federal department and agency. The volume also provides details on regional federal information sources, nongovernmental organizations in the Washington area, and congressional committees and subcommittees. Published annually.

Washington '92
Columbia Books, New York, NY.
Contains addresses, phone numbers, and profiles of key institutions in the city. Includes chapters on the federal government, the media, business, national associations, labor unions, law firms, medicine and health, foundations and philanthropic

organizations, science and policy research groups, and educational, religious, and cultural institutions. Published annually.

Who's Who in Special Libraries and Information Centers
Gale Research Inc., Detroit, MI.
Lists special libraries alphabetically and geographically. Published annually.

Appendix E
Index to the Questions

How many other jobs have you applied for? See page 147.

How much are you looking for? See page 85, 214.

How much are you making? See page 85, 214.

How much do you need to support your family? See page 214.

How much do you want? See page 85, 214.

How much experience do you have? See page 87, 136.

How much will it take to get you? See page 214.

How old are you? See page 183.

How well do you feel your boss rated your job performance? See page 152.

How will you be able to cope with a change in environment? See page 173.

How would you define a conducive work atmosphere? See page 153.

How would you define your profession? See page 173.

How would you evaluate me as an interviewer? See page 179.

I'd be interested to hear about some things you learned in school that could be used on the job. See page 193.

[Illegal interview questions] See pages 181-183.

I'm not sure you're suitable for the job. See page 180.

In hindsight, what have you done that was a little harebrained? See page 157.

In what areas do you feel your supervisor could have done a better job? See page 152.

In what ways has your job changed since you originally joined the company? See page 146.

In what ways has your job prepared you to take on greater responsibility? See page 146.

In your last job, how did you plan to interview? See page 162.

In your last job, what were some of the things you spent most of your time on, and why? See page 146.

People from your school/major never work out here. What makes you different? See page 193.

Rate yourself on a scale of one to ten. See page 150.

See this pen I'm holding? Sell it to me. See page 172.

Tell me about a time when you experienced pressure on the job. See page 168.

Tell me about a time when you put your foot in your mouth. See page 176.

Tell me about an event that really challenged you. See page 161.

Tell me about the last time you felt anger on the job. See page 151.

Tell me about the problems you have living within your means. See page 171.

Tell me about yourself. See page 150.

Tell me a story. See page 156.

Tell me how you moved up through the organization. See page 140.

Tell me why you have been with one company so long without any appreciable increase in rank or salary. See page 171.

Were you ever dismissed from your job for a reason that seemed unjustified? See page 146.

What area of your skills/development do you want to improve at this time? See page 171.

What are some of the problems you encounter in doing your job? See page 177.

What are some of the things about which you and your supervisor disagreed? See page 152.

What are some of the things that bother you? See page 151.

What are some of the things you find difficult to do? See page 178.

What are some of the things your supervisor did that you disliked? See page 152.

What are the broad responsibilities of a _____? See page 136.

What are the reasons for your success in this profession? See page 135.

What are you looking for in your next job? See page 141.

What are you making now? See page 213.

What are your biggest accomplishments? See page 140.

What are your future vocational plans? See page 191.

What are your outstanding qualities? See page 141.

What are your pet hates? See page 151.

What are your qualifications? See page 139.

What are your salary requirements? See page 214.

What aspects of your job do you consider most crucial? See page 137.

What can you do for us that someone else cannot do? See page 142.

What college did you attend, and why did you choose it? See page 192.

What did you dislike about your last job? See page 137.

What did you like about your last job? See page 137.

What difficulties do you have tolerating people with different backgrounds and interests than yours? See page 157.

What do you feel is a satisfactory attendance record? See page 177.

What do you hope to be earning two to five years from now? See page 216.

What do you know about our company? See page 195.

What do you think determines progress in a good company? See page 195.

What do you think of your current/last boss? See page 149.

What have you done that shows initiative and willingness to work? See page 193.

What have you done that shows initiative? See page 151.

What have you learned from jobs you have held? See page 138.

What have your other jobs taught you? See page 156.

What interests you least about this job? See page 176.

What interests you most about this job? See page 141.

What is an adequate reward for your efforts? See page 212.

What is the least relevant job you have held? See page 138.

What is the most difficult situation you have faced? See page 151.

What is the worst thing you have heard about our company? See page 173.

What is your current salary? See page 213.

What is your energy level like? Describe a typical day. See page 135.

What is your general impression of your last company? See page 177.

What is your greatest strength? See page 141.

What is your greatest weakness? See page 170.

What is your salary history? See page 212.

What kinds of decisions are most difficult for you? See page 171.

What kind of experience do you have for this job? See page 136.

What kinds of people do you find it difficult to work with? See page 179.

What kinds of people do you like to work with? See page 178.

What kind of salary are you worth? See page 215.

What kinds of things do you worry about? See page 150.

What levels are you most comfortable with? See page 160.

What makes this job different from your current/last one? See page 147.

What personal characteristics are necessary for success in your field? See page 153.

What qualifications do you have that will make you successful in this field? See page 194.

What religion do you practice? See page 183.

What type of decisions did you make on your last job? See page 143.

What type of position are you interested in? See page 194.

What was the last book you read? How did it affect you? See page 144.

What was the last movie you saw? How did it affect you? See page 144.

What was there about your last company that you didn't particularly like or agree with? See page 177.

What was your salary progress on your last job? See page 212.

What were some of the minuses on your last job? See page 178.

What were you making on your last job? See page 213.

What would you do when you have a decision to make and no procedure exists? See page 162, 163.

What would you like to be doing five years from now? See page 139.

What would you say about a supervisor who was unfair or difficult to work with? See page 154.

What would you say if I told you your presentation was lousy? See page 181.

What would your references say? See page 143.

What's your idea of how industry works? See page 195.

When do you expect a promotion? See page 156.

When you joined your last company and met the group for the first time, how did you feel? See page 162.

Which of the jobs you have held have you liked least? See page 191.

Who else have you applied to? See page 147.

Why aren't you earning more at your age? See page 173.

Why did you leave your last job? See page 176.

Why do you feel you are a better _____ than some of your co-workers? See page 155.

Why do you think you would like this type of work? See page 194.

Why do you want to leave your current job? See page 176.

Why do you want to work here? See page 135.

Why have you changed jobs so frequently? See page 175.

Why should I hire an outsider when I could fill the job with someone inside the company? See page 174.

Why should I hire you? See page 142.

Why were you fired? See page 145.

Why were you out of work for so long? See page 175.

With hindsight, how could you have improved your progress? See page 170.

Would you be willing to take a drug test as a condition of employment? See page 228.

Would you like to have your boss' job? See page 149.

Wouldn't you feel better off with another firm? See page 180.

You have a doctor's appointment that conflicts with an emergency meeting. What do you do? See page 155.

You have been given a project that requires you to interact with different levels within the company. How do you do this? See page 160.

Index

National Job Campaigning Resource Center, 50
National Water Well Association, 282
Neckwear, men's, selection of, 102-103
Neckwear, women's, selection of, 106
Negotiating salary and benefits packages,
    209-225
Networking, 56-58, 69, 258, 259
New Jersey State Library, 282
New York Academy of Medicine Library, 283
New York Public Library, 283
NewsNet, 284
Newspapers, as research method, 41-45, 259
Nexis Express, 63-64
Nexis/Lexis, 63, 284
North Dakota State University, 283
New York Public Library, 283
Notes, importance of during telephone
    interview, 96

Objections, dealing with, 88-91
Objectives, career, use of on resume, 29
Ohio State University, 283
Ohio University, 283
Orbit, 285
Overcoats, men's, selection of, 104

Permanent vs. temporary job issues, 192
Personal hygiene, 108, 246
Phone *see* Telephone
Polygraph testing, 234
Post-interview steps, 203
Posture, 115-116, 117
Preparation for interview, final, 119-121
Pressuring interviewer for decision, dangers of,
    196
Pride, importance of, 133
Problem-solving abilities, importance of
    highlighting, 25-33, 129-131
Problems in job search, addressing, 244-247
Procedure-orientation, importance of, 134
Prodigy, 285
Professional associations, 53-54
Professionalism, importance of, 129
Profit-orientation, company's, 23
Profit-orientation, importance of, 23-24, 134
Promotions, 156
Prospective employers, targeting, 25-33, 38-73
Psychological tests, 234-239
Purdue University, 283

Questions, common interview questions,
    135-157, 160-163
    See also: separate index to questions

References, 143
Rejection, turning around, 92-94, 205-208
Reliability, importance of, 133
Relocation, 137
Research, strategy for library, 25-33, 38-40
Research, importance of, 69
Resignations, 146, 225
    See also Termination
Restaurant interviews, 186-189
Resume
    construction of, 25-33
    databases featuring, 64
    drawbacks of general, 34
    length of, 29
    purpose of, 25
    rewriting, 244, 258
    samples of main types, 30-33
    types of, 28-33
    use of at job fairs, 54
    use of during interview, 119
Reuters Accountline, 285
Rice University, 283

Salary, current, whether to mention on resume,
    29
Salary issues, discussing with employer, 196,
    209-255
Salary negotiations, 209-225
Salary questions during interview, 85-86, 173,
    209-225
Scarves, women's, selection of, 106
Secretaries and receptionists, dealing with,
    81-82
Seller's markets, 24
Seltzer Daley Companies, 283
Shirts, men's, selection of, 102
Shoes, men's selection of, 103
Shoes, women's, selection of, 106-107
Skills, two major categories of, 69
Smoking, 121, 187
Socks, men's, selection of, 103-104
South Dakota State Library, 283
Standard and Poor's Research
    Reports/On-Line Services, 64, 285
State employment agencies, 45
Stockings, women's, selection of, 107
Stress interviews, 167-180
Suits, men's, selection of, 101-102
Suits, women's, selection of, 105-106
Superfluous information, danger of providing
    during interview, 126
Supervisor, relationship with, 149, 152,
    267-268

Your Two Cents' Worth

Comments, questions, or suggestions? Please complete this questionnaire and mail it to me:

Martin Yate
c/o Bob Adams, Inc.
260 Center Street
Holbrook, MA 02343

Hey Martin,

Here's how I used *Knock 'em Dead*:

By the way, I'm thinking of changing my will and naming you as my major beneficiary if you . . .

1. Give me some additional information about the following issue.

    _____

2. Tell me how to find the resource described below, since I drew a blank. (Circle one: This is something I came up with. / You mentioned it on page _____.)

    _____

3. Add a chapter on the following topic, since it would really be helpful to people like me.

    _____

I guess that's it. No, wait—please SEND ME/DO NOT SEND ME some information on your *Career Survivalist* newsletter.

And, oh yeah, stick my name in the hat when you're done reading this. I deserve a shot at a free dinner for two at the restaurant of my choice as much as anyone else who fills this out.

Name: _____

Address: _____

_____

Daytime phone: _____

Evening phone: _____

Occupation: _____

RELATED TITLES
OF INTEREST

Resumes that Knock 'em Dead

Martin Yate reviews the marks of a great resume: what type of resume is right for each applicant, what always goes in, what always stays out, and why. Every single resume in *Resumes that Knock 'em Dead* was actually used by a job hunter to successfully obtain a job. No other book provides the hard facts for producing an exemplary resume. $8\frac{1}{2}$ x 11 inches, 216 pages, $7.95.

Cover Letters that Knock 'em Dead

The final word on not just how to write a "correct" cover letter, but how to write a cover letter that offers a powerful competitive advantage in today's tough job market. *Cover Letters that Knock 'em Dead* gives the essential information on composing a cover letter that wins attention, interest, and job offers. $8\frac{1}{2}$ x 11 inches, 184 pages, $7.95.

ALSO OF INTEREST...

The JobBank Series

There are now 20 *JobBank* books, each providing extensive, up-to-date employment information on hundreds of the largest employers in each job market. Recommended as an excellent place to begin your job search by *The New York Times, The Los Angeles Times, The Boston Globe, The Chicago Tribune,* and many other publications, *JobBank* books have been used by hundreds of thousands of people to find jobs.

   Books available: *The Atlanta JobBank—The Boston JobBank—The Carolina JobBank—The Chicago JobBank—The Dallas-Ft. Worth JobBank—The Denver JobBank—The Detroit JobBank—The Florida JobBank—The Houston JobBank—The Los Angeles JobBank—The Minneapolis JobBank—The New York JobBank—The Ohio JobBank—The Philadelphia JobBank—The Phoenix JobBank—The St. Louis JobBank—The San Francisco JobBank—The Seattle JobBank—The Tennessee JobBank—The Washington DC JobBank.* Each book is 6 x 9 inches, over 300 pages, paperback, $15.95.

If you cannot find a book at your local bookstore, order it directly from the publisher. Please send payment including $3.75 for shipping and handling (for the entire order) to: Bob Adams, Inc., 260 Center Street, Holbrook, MA 02343. Credit card holders may call 1-800-USA-JOBS (in Massachusetts, 617-767-8100). Please first check at your local bookstore.

Her
N

Also by Kimberla Lawson Roby

The Reverend Curtis Black Series

Better Late Than Never
Sin of a Woman
A Sinful Calling
The Ultimate Betrayal
The Prodigal Son
A House Divided
The Reverend's Wife
Love, Honor, and Betray
Be Careful What You Pray For
The Best of Everything
Sin No More
Love & Lies
The Best-Kept Secret
Too Much of a Good Thing
Casting the First Stone

Standalone Titles

Copycat
Best Friends Forever
A Christmas Prayer
The Perfect Marriage
Secret Obsession
A Deep Dark Secret
One in a Million
Changing Faces
A Taste of Reality
It's a Thin Line
Here and Now
Behind Closed Doors

Here *and* Now

KIMBERLA LAWSON ROBY

KENSINGTON PUBLISHING CORP.
www.kensingtonbooks.com

First Kensington Hardcover Printing: February 1999
First Trade Paperback Printing: January 2000

ISBN-13: 978-1-4967-2513-4
ISBN-10: 1-4967-2513-1

20 19 18 17 16 15 14 13 12 11 10

Printed in the United States of America

In loving memory of
Erick Haley, Ben Tennin, Jr., Derrick Horton,
and Derrick Jones

Acknowledgments
(Spring 1998)

I am thankful to God for blessing me over and over, time and time again.

To my husband Will for eight wonderful years of marriage and for encouraging me to self-publish my first novel, BEHIND CLOSED DOORS. I love you from the bottom of my soul.

To my mother, Arletha Stapleton, for always being there when I need her to be and for having total confidence in everything I do. But most of all, Mom, thanks for just being you.

To my brothers, Willie Jr., and Michael Stapleton for their unconditional love and support.

To Peggy and Steven Hicks, Kelli Tunson Bullard, Aileen Blacknell, Keith and Shari Grace, Tammy Roby, Janell Green, Mary Carthell, and Ace Fehr for giving me their opinions, praises, and constructive criticism after reading HERE AND NOW.

To Dr. Ronald E. Burmeister, M.D. from the Department of Reproductive Medicine at Rockford Health System for taking the time to answer every infertility question I could think of.

To Evelyn Barmore of Evelyn's Hair Studio and Susan Saylor at Very Vogue for accomodating my sporadic traveling schedule. And to Pamela Sims of Braider One in Chicago for her braiding talent and amazing spirituality.

To Lori Whitaker Thurman, Veronda Johnson, Martha Moore,

Vicky Pruitt, and Patricia Brown for calling me from time to time to see how everything was going.

To my incredible editor at Kensington, Karen Thomas, who is clearly one of the most pleasant persons I've ever worked with. You are simply wonderful.

To Christy Fletcher for introducing this novel to Monica Harris. And to Monica for believing in my idea from the very beginning.

And finally, to all of my readers everywhere, I thank you.

Chapter 1

JANUARY 1993

A wave of depression settled over Marcella as she drove her beat-up Cutlass into the low-income housing complex. Pierce Commons had been her permanent residence for almost five years, but today the place looked different. It looked worse than ever before. Beer cans and liquor bottles thrown across the parking lot; trash spread over the sidewalks; and graffiti plastered across the once white, but now dirty-colored building. She couldn't help but wonder how she'd been so silly as to get herself caught up in this poverty-stricken situation. And Lord knows she was worn out from struggling to make ends meet by way of a seven-dollar-an-hour job, not to mention the child support Tyrone paid only when he felt like it. This wasn't at all how she'd hoped things would turn out for them. And never in her wildest dreams had she thought Tyrone, the so-called love of her life, would end up her worst nightmare. She regretted the day she'd ever laid eyes on him, let alone started dating him. And just thinking about how he treated her, and how he neglected Ashley and Nicholas, made her sick to her stomach.

She parked directly in front of her building, turned the ignition to the off position, and stepped out of the car. As she shut the door, she saw the children making their way off the school bus. She frowned when she spotted Ashley's bare head and Nicholas's pile-lined coat flagging wide open. No matter how often she lectured them about bundling up in the wintertime, it always seemed to ease through one ear and right out the other. Why did they always have to be so hardheaded? Didn't they know she couldn't afford to take off work when one of them got sick? If their sickness couldn't be helped, that was one thing, but if it was primarily because they were being careless and absentminded, that was another. Of course, Nicholas was like most boys and just didn't have time to zip up his coat and put on his hood, but Ashley, on the other hand, was simply trying to be cute, and didn't want some knit hat messing up her little hairdo.

Marcella started fussing as soon as they approached her.

"Nicholas, haven't I told you a thousand times about walking around in zero-degree weather with that coat wide open? And Ashley, you know you're old enough to know better." The children just looked at her in silence. And it was obvious that they didn't have the slightest idea why she was so upset. She could see it in their faces, and that irked her even more. Marcella couldn't remember ever being that forgetful when she was a child, and couldn't understand at all where this particular generation had come from.

She shook her head and decided that maybe she was overreacting, which was possible since she'd had such a horrendous day at work. Right now anything would have stirred her nerves, and it wasn't fair to take her frustrations out on the children. Especially, since for the most part, Ashley and Nicholas were exceptional. They were obedient, intelligent, and had wonderful personalities. She loved her children, and most of all, she was proud of them. Proud because, even though they hadn't been born with silver spoons in their mouths or with the stability of a two-parent household, they were better mannered than some children who'd been blessed with all the financial advantages.

Marcella slid the key in the front door and opened it. They all walked in one by one; Ashley shut the door behind them, and they each kicked off their boots so they could dry. Marcella opened the hall closet, hung up her black wool scarf and charcoal-gray winter coat, and then reached for Nicholas's and Ashley's outer garments.

"You two have any homework to do?" Marcella asked, closing the closet door.

"I don't, Mom," Nicholas quickly offered, with a huge smile on his face.

"Good, then that means you can go work on those spelling words so you'll be ready for your test on Friday," Marcella responded back to him.

"Aw, Mom," Nicholas said, replacing his smile with a pout.

"Go on. I'll be in there to test you in a bit." Marcella knew if he didn't have anything constructive to do, he'd spend the rest of the evening glued to the Nickelodeon channel. Too much TV wasn't good for anyone, and it especially wasn't good for an eight-year-old little boy.

"What about you, Ashley?" Marcella asked.

"I have some math homework to do, but I finished everything else in class," Ashley answered and headed toward her bedroom.

Marcella smiled to herself, because at that moment she saw something in her daughter that she hadn't seen before. A ten-year-old version of herself. She'd been the very same way when she was growing up. She'd loved school from her very first day in kindergarten, and all the way through her graduation from high school. Ashley was a straight-A student, and was clearly following in her mother's footsteps academically. Which was fine. But when it came to falling hopelessly in love with some little boy—Marcella prayed that Ashley would find her own path to follow. Because the last thing Marcella wanted was for Ashley to end up pregnant, the way she had during the last month of her senior year in high school. It wasn't that she didn't love her daughter. Or both of her children, for that matter, because she did. But she could kick herself a thousand times for not being more careful when she started having sex with Tyrone. She'd loved him from the very first moment she laid eyes on him during their sophomore year. He, the school's top football star, and she, the girl voted most likely to succeed. The world had been theirs for the taking, but without even having the sense to know it, they'd ruined everything. Marcella had received acceptance letters from colleges and universities all across the country, but she'd had no choice except to decline each and every one of them. She'd tried hopelessly to overcome this irreversible mistake, but now that almost eleven years had passed and she was twenty-eight, her efforts to do so still didn't seem to be working.

Marcella dropped down on the leatherlike beige sofa, and leaned her head back. She closed her eyes and rested them for a moment. When she opened them, she gazed around her apartment. The desperately discounted furniture, dull-looking mini-blinds, and second-hand wall portraits were disgusting, and now she was even more depressed than she had been earlier. No matter how hard she tried, she was still barely making ends meet. Her salary alone just wasn't enough, and the few food stamps she received each month never seemed to last more than two weeks. And the only reason they lasted that long, was because of how conservative she was when it came to buying meat. If it hadn't been for her mother and sister, she wasn't sure what she would have done. They helped her out financially whenever she needed them and they went out of their way to show Ashley and Nicholas how much they loved them.

Marcella could ring Tyrone's neck. Sure, she'd been just as much at fault for not using the diaphragm, IUD, the pill or something, but he'd never made any attempts to use any form of protection, either. She could still hear him now: "Baby, I won't do it inside of you. I promise." *Hmmph,* some promise. Because the only thing that had resulted from his promise was her realization that the withdrawal method just didn't work. Somehow, though, she hadn't been the slightest bit upset when she'd first found out she was pregnant. If anything, she was thrilled. She loved Tyrone; he loved her; and they were going to have a beautiful baby girl that belonged to both of them. It was perfect. He'd go off to college on his football scholarship, marry her immediately after he graduated, allow her to work toward an accounting degree, and then she, Tyrone, and the baby would live happily ever after. And things just might have turned out that way, if he hadn't injured his knee two weeks before the start of his freshman year. Marcella could still remember that day the sports medicine specialist informed him that his football career was over; that he would never play any sport on a professional or continuous basis ever again. Tyrone had cried like a baby, and for a while she'd been worried that he was going to experience a nervous breakdown. Because not once had he ever imagined life without playing football. The boy ate, drank, and slept it. It was his sole reason for existing.

Eventually his depression passed, but everything changed for the worst when he slipped into a horrible and unbearable mode of bitterness. He snapped at Marcella for just about everything, and was angry at the world. Her wonderful pregnancy had become a total nightmare, and she regretted the day she conceived his baby. By the end of her third trimester, he was barely speaking to her, and rumor had it that he was messing around with a girl she'd been friends with since third grade. At one point Marcella hadn't known whether she was coming or going. Her parents were completely put out by the fact that she'd gone to such extremes to disappoint them, and they proved it by not offering her one ounce of moral support. Partly because they spent the majority of their time arguing, but mostly because they each worked tons of overtime trying hard to make ends meet. All they saw when they looked at Marcella was an extra mouth they were going to have to feed, and they weren't at all happy about it. Which is exactly how it had turned out, too. They'd been stuck with a $2,000 hospital bill, and the responsibility of purchasing Pampers and formula for a baby they hadn't asked for.

Her sister, Racquel, had been wonderful throughout the entire pregnancy. She'd been away at school during most of it, but she always called to talk with her. And when she came home on weekends, she spent the majority of her time with Marcella. Racquel had thought having a baby was the most joyous and precious gift there was, and at the time Marcella had agreed with her. But now, she felt like a failure. Here, at the age of eighteen she'd had a child, and then gone on to have another child out of wedlock by the same man, who hadn't shown any interest in taking care of the first one. Things could have been so different had she gone to college, gotten married, and then took the time to plan for children. Children didn't ask to come here, and the very least a parent could do was make sure they could take care of them and give them the best possible life available.

A sadness engrossed Marcella, and she could feel the tears building as fast as the thoughts were twirling through her mind. She'd been sure that the children would bring her and Tyrone closer together. How could she have been so selfish? And so stupid? She'd had no right bringing Nicholas and Ashley into such a cruel world without the means to support herself, let alone the resources to provide for them. If only Tyrone would pay his child support, things would be so much easier. Their lives could be so much happier. If only he would spend more time with them. Didn't he know that little boys needed their fathers? Didn't he know that Nicholas needed him? How could someone simply walk away from the innocent little faces of his own children, and pretend they didn't even exist?

Marcella tried to blink back the tears, but she was unsuccessful at doing it. She placed her hands on each side of her head and looked down. "How could I have screwed things up like this?" she whispered softly.

"Mom, what's the matter?" Nicholas asked, walking toward her with a confused look on his face.

Marcella wiped the wetness from her face as best she could, looked up at him, and tried to smile. "Nothing, baby. Mom just had a hard day at work. That's all."

"Don't worry, Mom. Everything's gonna be okay. And things will be better when you go to work tomorrow because that's what you always tell me and Ashley when we have a bad day at school."

Marcella smiled, but the tears were still rolling. Nicholas was so considerate and so loving where she was concerned. Both of the children were. Especially, if they thought something was bothering her. Which was even more the reason why they deserved so much more than she was giving them.

She noticed a piece of notebook paper in his hand. "Is that your spelling list?"

"Uh-huh. You said you were going to test me on it, and I'm ready."

Marcella smiled, pulled him closer, hugged him as tight as she could, and then let him go.

"What was that for, Mom?" he asked, frowning like boys his age do when they think they're too old to be hugged by their mothers.

"It's because I love you."

Ashley had been listening from her bedroom and decided to come out to see what was going on.

"I love both of you so much. And don't either of you ever forget it," she said, reaching her hand out to Ashley.

Ashley looked at her, still trying to figure out why her mother was acting so strangely.

"We know that, Mom. We love you, too," Ashley said, leaning down to hug her mother.

"Come on, Mom, test me on my spelling words, so me and Ashley can watch Nick at Nite after dinner."

"Ashley and I," Marcella corrected Nicholas.

"Boy, I'm not even finished with my math homework yet," Ashley said to Nicholas and frowned.

"So what. You will be by the time Nick at Nite comes on."

"But that doesn't mean I want to watch TV with you."

"You just want to get on that phone with your friends. Mom, make her watch it with me."

"Okay, you two. That's enough. Ashley, you go finish your homework. And Mr. Nicholas, we'll see how many of these words you can spell before we discuss watching any television."

"I know them all, Mom. I promise."

"We'll see. You keep studying while I go change out of my work clothes, and I'll be back in a few minutes to start warming up dinner," Marcella said, rising from the sofa.

"Okay, Mom, but I'm telling you, I already know them all."

Marcella shook her head and smiled at him.

When she arrived inside of her bedroom, she shut the door behind her. It was so amazing how the children always managed to eliminate her depression. They were such a joy, and they were so special. All children were special to their mothers, she guessed, but hers were special because they were surviving a way of life that was barely one step up from living on welfare. They didn't live in the projects, but still, there were roaches, drug dealers, and gangs to contend with just the same. So, as far as she was concerned, it was the next best thing to being there.

Marcella pulled her black sweater dress over her head, hung it in the closet and walked toward the dreadful-looking wooden dresser. Then she slid off her black tights, stuffed them into the top right drawer, and slipped on the royal-blue jersey sweat suit she'd left scattered across the bed earlier that morning. She never liked leaving her clothing all over the place, but after pressing the snooze button on the alarm clock twice, she hadn't had any time to hang them up. Tomorrow, though, she was going to make time because she despised keeping a messy apartment. She hadn't been raised that way, and she made sure Nicholas and Ashley weren't, either. And even though the three of them didn't have any luxuries worth writing home about, they went out of their way to take care of what they did have. Ashley understood that no dinner dishes were to ever be left in the sink overnight, and Nicholas automatically took the garbage out without being told.

That's how it had been for her and Racquel when they were growing up. And she was glad her mother had taught them as well as she had. Her father had been the only messy one in the household. Walking across their off-white kitchen floor and their light-tan carpet with his filthy work boots had just about run her mother insane. But no matter how much she complained, he never stopped doing it. If they hadn't gotten divorced, she supposed he would still be tracking dirt. It was almost as if he did it just to get under her mother's skin. Her parents were at each other's throats constantly, and the only time there had been at least some peace in their household was when one or both of them were gone. They had had the perfect marriage, until she and Racquel became teenagers. Her parents seemed perfect for each other, and everyone said so. But, somewhere along the line, their father started staying out until midnight. And it wasn't long before midnight became one, two and even three in the morning. And finally when that wasn't good enough, the wee hours of the morning had become the next day's afternoon. It was obvious that he'd found someone else, but hadn't had the guts to leave. Then one Friday night, when her mother decided that enough was enough, and that she wasn't in her own words "putting up with his sleeping around any longer," she dragged every piece of anything that belonged to him out to the street, called the locksmith to change the locks, and flipped through the Yellow Pages until she found a reputable divorce attorney, whom she hadn't hesitated to call first thing that Monday morning.

Marcella could still see the look on her father's face when he'd finally arrived home that Saturday morning. She and Racquel had stared at him through the window from the moment he'd pulled up until the second he'd thrown the last of his things in the car and sped off. They'd wanted to help him, but their mother had promised each of them two weeks on punishment if they did. And they had no choice but to obey her.

As the weeks continued, their parents started seeing each other again, and it wasn't long before their father moved back into the house. Their mother stopped the divorce proceedings, and for the most part, they seemed to be enjoying each other's company. It was almost as if they couldn't keep their hands off of each other.

That lasted for two years, but then suddenly Daddy had started staying out during all hours of the night again. Their mother had wanted to kick him out for good this time, but her financial situation hadn't allowed it. She needed help with paying the household bills, Racquel's college tuition, and yes, supporting Marcella and her new baby. But it wasn't long before she realized that she couldn't take it anymore, and that it wasn't worth living with a man who spent all of his time with some other woman. So, again, their father moved out; and this time when their mother filed for a divorce, she went through with it.

Marcella shook her head as she reminisced about her past. Her unnecessary mistakes had caused financial problems not only for her, but for everyone involved. And the more she thought about it, the more convinced she was that her situation had to change. She was born, raised, and still lived in Covington Park, a working-class suburb just south of Chicago, but her dream had always been to work for a prestigious accounting firm somewhere downtown in the Loop. Actually, part of the dream had come true, because she did work for an accounting firm, but not as a CPA, like she'd planned. Instead, she'd been hired as a glorified administrative assistant who spent the entire day greeting uppity clients and answering umpteen phone lines. She was capable of so much more, and each of the partners at the firm knew it. And they would have loved nothing more than to promote Marcella, but since she didn't have a four-year degree, their hands were tied, and there really wasn't much they could do to help her.

Marcella stepped in front of the mirror attached to the back of her bedroom door, pulled back her shoulder-length jet-black hair, and wrapped a beige rubber band around it. As she scanned her face, she noticed a pimple just under her right cheekbone. It took everything she had in her not to squeeze it. She hadn't had any problems with acne since adolescence, but this past year facial breakouts had become common. Of course, her medium-chocolate skin had never been babylike smooth, but at least it had always been above average. Maybe it was stress, but more than likely, it was because of her terrible eating habits. She was average height, but had lost close to fifteen pounds over the last six months. Which wasn't good, given the fact that most everyone she knew had always thought she was way too thin in the first place. She tried to make a conscious effort toward eating more regularly, but most of the time her stomach felt nervous. And it was obvious that it was because of all the worrying she'd been doing about bills. Why were there so many bills? And how was she going to pay them?

Plus, she worried about everything else she could think of, too. Like, why she'd gotten pregnant at such a young age? And why on earth had she been crazy enough to make the same mistake twice? Why couldn't she have been blessed with a wonderful husband, like her sister, Racquel? Or even better, why couldn't she have married someone who earned a decent living? And most of all, why couldn't she have had the sense enough to go to college? Her sister had been blessed with everything any woman could ever hope for, and although Marcella loved her children more than life itself, she'd trade places with Racquel in a second. Marcella knew the grass usually appeared a lot greener than it actually was, but compared to her lifestyle, anything would be an improvement.

But she knew all this wishful thinking was nothing more than some far-fetched fantasy, and that no miracle was going to just happen. And that in order for her life to become better, she was going to have to take matters into her own hands. Make some very drastic changes in the way she viewed life in general, and the way she dealt with Tyrone James. No more feeling sorry for herself, and no more complaining. Her decision was made. She was going to give her children the decent life that they deserved. If it was the last thing she did.

Chapter 2

Racquel placed the phone receiver on its hook and slowly sat down on the side of the king-sized brass bed. She'd promised herself that she wouldn't cry this time, but as usual she just couldn't control it. She'd heard the nurse at her doctor's office announce enough negative pregnancy results to last a lifetime, but still, she wasn't able to handle it.

Tears rolled down her cheeks slowly at first, but it wasn't long before they began falling much more rapidly and in an uncontrollable manner. Her body shook, and her stomach raised up and down continuously. She locked her arms together in front of her and leaned her body toward her lap, rocking back and forth. She felt like the entire world was coming to an end.

One hour had passed when Racquel woke up and realized that she'd somehow fallen off to sleep. She lay there replaying what the nurse had said to her, "I'm sorry, Racquel, but your pregnancy test came back negative." It just wasn't fair, and for the life of her, she couldn't understand why God kept punishing her over and over again. She was a good person, and none of what was happening to her made any sense. The emotional pain she was feeling was worse than anything she'd ever felt, and she wasn't sure how much more of it she could take without cracking up. All she'd ever wanted was to have two beautiful, healthy children, and she couldn't understand why she was being cheated out of what rightfully should have been hers. If she'd done anything to deserve punishment, she wished He'd choose something else. Anything but deny her the right to have children. Because as far as she was concerned, nothing else was more important.

She'd fantasized about having children ever since the day Marcella had given birth to Ashley, and from that point on, she'd made the idea of getting pregnant her reason for living. She'd planned everything out so well. Graduated from college with a teaching degree, married a loving, intelligent husband, saved money for the future, bought a house. She and Kevin had done all the right things, and there was no doubt that they had all the love and financial resources it took to give any child a wonderful life.

Here, thousands of girls were running around having babies and then dumping them off on their parents because they had no way of taking care of them. And the ones who kept their own children were raising them irresponsibly on welfare. Not to mention, all the women who took their welfare checks and spent the money on some outfit, or even worse, gave it to the deadbeat father or some new lowlife they were trying to latch onto.

The thought of all this was enough to make Racquel sick. Even her own sister had gotten pregnant twice out of wedlock, still wasn't married, and struggled daily trying to take care of her children. And she didn't even want to think about that jerk Ashley and Nicholas called their father. Tyrone had to be the poorest excuse for being a father that she'd ever come in contact with, and she couldn't stand him.

She loved Marcella dearly, and there was nothing she wouldn't have done for her and the children, but it just wasn't fair that Marcella had been blessed with two adorable children, while she'd been blessed with nothing. She'd been raised with the understanding that she was never to question God and His actions, but this not-getting-pregnant business was going too far. In fact, it was becoming ridiculous, and her sadness and feeling of inadequacy were slowly turning to anger.

Racquel sat up on the side of the bed for a few seconds and then stood up. She dragged herself into the master bathroom and looked into the mirror above the double sinks. But to her surprise, she didn't see the attractive woman that everyone said she was.

Her bobbed blackish-brown hair needed a serious trim, her deep-mocha skin had an ashy look to it, and her light-brown eyes looked depressingly dim. Her eyes were bloodshot red and severely swollen. She pulled a plush face towel from the rack, ran some cold water on it, squeezed it tight, and rubbed it across her face. When she was finished, she rehung the towel and headed back out to the bedroom. She felt like she was losing her mind. Like she didn't know Sunday from Monday. Like her whole life wasn't reality, but merely a bad dream.

She heard the front door shut and realized Kevin was home from work.

After removing his gloves, winter jacket, and boots, he headed up the stairs—the way he always did to greet his wife—and walked into the bedroom.

"How's my baby doing?" he asked, dropping his blazer on the bed and moving closer to Racquel, who was now staring through the window.

Racquel opened her mouth to respond, but instead burst into tears and then fell into his arms.

"Hey, hey. What's this all about? Baby, what's wrong?"

Racquel still wasn't able to answer him.

"Baby . . . ," Kevin started to ask her again, but then paused when it dawned on him that she must have received the results from the pregnancy test she'd taken earlier that morning. How he could have allowed that to slip his mind for even a moment was beyond his understanding. Whenever Racquel thought she was pregnant, it was all she talked about. This morning he had begged and pleaded with her not to get her hopes up, but like always, she completely ignored what he was saying. He'd gone through this so many times with Racquel that he wasn't even sure what to say anymore. And although he loved his wife, he was starting to get fed up with this whole pregnancy obsession.

"Baby, I'm so sorry," he said, hugging and caressing her.

She hugged him back, but didn't say anything.

Kevin took a deep breath. "Baby, maybe it's time for us to accept the fact that you can't get pregnant."

Racquel released her arms from around him and stepped a couple of feet back. "What do you mean, I can't get pregnant?" she said defensively. "You make it sound as though it's all my fault. For all we know, it's you who's causing the problem. It's not like either of us have gone through any physical exams to find out one way or the other."

"What are you talking about?" Kevin asked in a state of confusion. "I wasn't blaming you for anything. But since you brought it up, you were the one who didn't want us to get evaluated. I wanted to be tested a long time ago. And why are you so pissed off at me, anyway?"

"Look, I'm sorry, okay? It's just that I'm so frustrated with all of this, and I'm having a hard time accepting any of it."

"I realize that, baby, but maybe we're at a point where we need to get on with our lives. We can always adopt a child. It's not the act of having a child that makes someone a parent, it's the love and commitment that make all the difference."

"Why are you still pressing me about adoption? I told you that I want to have my own baby. Our own flesh and blood. It just won't be the same raising a baby who belongs to someone else. And I'm not about to spend the rest of my life wondering when the biological parents are going to show up wanting to take their child back."

"Well, answer me this. How long are you going to keep this up? I mean, Racquel, come on. Our lives haven't been the same since you had that miscarriage last year."

"I'm going to keep it up for as long as it takes. If only you could find a little more faith and patience, I know this can happen for us."

"As long as it takes? That could be forever. Look, I'm not going to keep arguing with you about the same thing over and over again. I've told you numerous times how much I love you, and whether you have a baby or not, my feelings for you won't ever change."

"I love you, too, honey, but if you could just hold on a little while longer, everything will work out. We just have to try harder is all."

"Racquel. We have sex almost every day of the week, and it's not even that great any . . . ," Kevin said, and then closed his eyes and sighed deeply. "Baby, I didn't mean that."

"Of course you meant it. Words like that don't just slip out, unless you've been saying them to someone else, or thinking about it awfully hard. I didn't realize making love to me had become so horrible."

"I didn't say that, but the fact of the matter is, we don't make love anymore. The whole idea of having sex has become more of a routine. Like some daily chore. It's not supposed to be like that, but you've become so obsessed with getting pregnant, that you don't seem to care about anything else. Much less about how I feel, or what's happening to our marriage."

"I do care about you and our marriage, but can't you see what I'm going through? I mean, Kevin, we're thirty years old, and we're definitely not getting any younger. We have to try as hard as we can now, before it's too late."

Kevin just looked at her and shook his head in disagreement. "I'm going to the 'Y' to work out. Do you need anything while I'm out?"

It was just like him to go running out to the "Y" when they were having an argument, and it really pissed her off. But at the same time, she knew if he didn't work out so diligently, there was a chance he wouldn't have such a tall, gorgeous-looking, muscular body. The same body she'd been attracted to when she first met him three years ago. Not to mention his thin, yet manly looking mustache and cocoa-colored complexion.

"So, just like that, you're going to leave?" Racquel asked, folding her arms against her body.

"You're not listening to any of what I'm saying, anyway."

"I *am* listening to you, Kevin. But you know how strongly I feel about this."

Kevin didn't even bother commenting. He pulled off his suit pants, shirt, and tie. After hanging them up, he removed his dress socks and slipped on an athletic-gray sweatshirt and a pair of matching sweatpants. After he'd pulled on his thick white socks and tied his Nikes, he stood up. Racquel was staring out of the window again, crying.

He walked over to her and hugged her from behind. "I'm sorry that we don't see eye to eye about this situation, but I know we can work through this, okay?"

She nodded her head yes.

"You try to relax, and I'll be back in a couple of hours," Kevin said, kissing her on the side of her face.

Racquel never even turned around to face him, and as he left the room, she started to feel numb. She felt like that a lot lately; especially on days like today. She pulled the winter-white lamb's-wool sweater over her head and slid off matching pure wool pants and hung them inside the walk-in closet. She pulled her terrycloth robe from the rack, wrapped it around her, tied the belt, and headed downstairs. Once she was in the kitchen, she opened the refrigerator, removed a can of pop, pulled the tab, and sat down at the glass table. She took a few sips from her soft drink and reached over to the chair next to where she was sitting and picked up her briefcase. She wasn't at all in the mood, but she'd promised her second-grade class that she would correct their math quizzes and return them the next day. And whenever she gave them her word on something, she followed through on it. The children trusted and depended on her, and she had a close relationship with all of them.

She'd worked at Covington Park Elementary for the entire eight years she'd been teaching, and she couldn't have been happier. It was one of the few careers that allowed a person to build a personal relationship with small children. In a sense, they were like her own, and she went out of her way to do special things for them. One month ago, just before Christmas, she asked Kevin to visit the class so he could tell them about Whitlock Aerospace, the company he worked for. He'd brought photos of the airplanes that the company manufactured parts for, and the children had been so impressed. As a matter of fact, two of the boys in the class said they wanted to be aerospace engineers, just like Kevin.

As Racquel pulled out the math quizzes, the phone rang. She reached up and pulled the cordless receiver from the wall. "Hello?"

"Hi, how are you?" the voice on the other end said.

"I'm fine, Mom. How are you?" Racquel said, crossing her legs.

"Pretty good."

"You must be on your break?"

"Uh-huh. I just thought I'd call you for a couple of minutes to see how you and Kevin were doing."

Racquel smiled. Corrine had been a second-shift mule driver at a local factory for almost thirty years, and still, she insisted on using her nightly breaks to call and check on her daughters. The same as she had when they were children.

"Not too well. We just had a huge blowup about me trying to get pregnant, and he left a little while ago to go work out. I got another negative test result, and he thinks we need to stop trying."

Corrine was silent on the phone because she was beginning to think the same thing herself. She'd seen Racquel's obsession growing deeper and deeper, and she was starting to get worried about her. "Well, honey, maybe it is time to accept things the way they are. And I know you aren't interested in adoption, but maybe you need to rethink how you feel about it. There are thousands of children that need a good home and the kind of love you and Kevin could give."

Racquel was already becoming pissed off. The last thing she wanted to do was disrespect her mother, but right now she was only an inch away from doing just that. "Not you, too? Sometimes it takes a little longer for some people to get pregnant than others. And it's not like I haven't been pregnant before. I was at the end of my first trimester when I lost the baby last year, but I know it will be different next time."

"But you've already been trying for three years, and I just don't want to see you and Kevin break up over something like this."

Racquel could no longer tolerate any more of these negative comments, and decided that it was time to end the conversation. "Mom, not every man is like Daddy. I mean, some men do stick by their wives until the end."

Corrine was silent at first, and it was obvious that her feelings were hurt. "Well. Maybe it will happen sometime soon," she said softly.

"I know it will, Mom," Racquel said, feeling bad about the way she'd spoken to her mother. "All Kevin and I have to do is have a little faith."

"Well, I'd better get off of here, so I can check on Marcella and the children before my break is over. You take care of yourself. And try to work things out with Kevin when he gets in."

"I will. And Mom, have a good evening at work, okay?"

"Talk to you tomorrow."

"Bye," Racquel said and hung up the phone.

She couldn't believe it. Even her own mother didn't have any faith in her. And come to think of it, Marcella had made some of those same pessimistic remarks. Racquel was becoming fed up with all of them, and it was times like this that she needed her father. She hated him for messing around on her mother, for marrying that overbearing, facially challenged woman he called his wife, and for running off to Texas like some schoolboy ten years ago. But at least he believed in her and never doubted that she could do anything she set her mind to. If only she could lie in his arms the way she used to when she was still Daddy's little girl. She could still remember how safe she felt. As a matter of fact, she hadn't felt such a total sense of security ever since. Didn't he realize that his walking out was going to affect her for the rest of her life? Didn't he know that his leaving had forced her to live an unthinkable and totally unacceptable lifestyle during her college years? The kind of lifestyle that she'd never even told Marcella about, let alone anyone else like Kevin or her mother. And what if those mistakes were the real reason why she couldn't get pregnant? She'd wondered about this very thing off and on for some time now, but she kept telling herself that it just couldn't be. That there was no obvious connection between what happened then and what was going on now.

If only everyone would stop saying that she wasn't going to get pregnant. Because what did they know anyway? It wasn't like they were doctors or anything like that. But then, what the rest of them thought really didn't matter, because she was going to show all of them just how wrong they were. And it was only a matter of time before she did exactly that.

Chapter 3

Marcella blew out a sigh of frustration and shook her head when she realized the baby shower was less than three hours away, and still, she hadn't gone out to buy a gift yet. She and Racquel had known about Michelle's baby shower for over a month, but it hadn't been until this particular pay period that she'd managed to scrounge up the money. It seemed like somebody was always having a baby, getting married, or celebrating a birthday, and she hated it. Not because she didn't want to be a part of these special occasions, but because she simply just couldn't afford it. Racquel had offered to add Marcella's name to the gift she'd purchased, but Marcella had gone that route so many times before that she didn't feel comfortable doing it again. Not to mention the fact that they'd lived next door to Michelle since she and Racquel were five and seven. Michelle had been almost like a sister to them, so Marcella felt a certain obligation toward giving her a gift.

Marcella walked into the bathroom, plugged the bathtub drain, and turned on the water. As the water covered the bottom of the tub, she ran her right hand through it to check the temperature. It was hotter than she liked, so she turned the knob just a tad more clockwise to cool it down a bit. She checked the temperature again, and this time it was perfect. She stepped back out into the hallway, into her bedroom, and began browsing through her closet for something to wear. When she thumbed past the black pantsuit, she shook her head in disgust. She'd worn this thing to every "dressy-casual" event she'd gone to over the last twelve months, and she knew everyone was sick of seeing her in it. In all honesty, *she* was sick of seeing it herself. Just once, she wished she could buy something nice for herself. Whenever there was extra money, which was rare, she used it on the children. She didn't regret doing that, though, because she'd give her life for them if she had to. But she was human, like anyone else, and sometimes wanted to fulfill her own wants and needs.

She pulled the pantsuit out and held it away from her to check for closet wrinkles. She spotted a couple on each piece and laid the entire outfit across the bed. As she stepped into the hallway, where the iron was located, she heard someone knocking at the front door. It was always like this on Saturday mornings. Winter, spring, summer, or fall. It was almost as if each of the other mothers in the complex had voted her weekend baby-sitter. They didn't seem to care where their children went, so long as they weren't in their hair, and it was really a crying shame. It was obvious that most of the children didn't know where their mothers were, and that was one of the main reasons Marcella usually let them stay. Unless of course, Ashley and Nicholas had homework to complete, chores to take care of, or like today, weren't at home. Corrine had picked them up early that morning, so they could go grocery shopping with her and planned to keep them until Sunday afternoon when they got out of church.

Marcella strutted to the door. "Who is it?"

"Tyrone."

Marcella rolled her eyes as far back in her head as they would go and frowned. What did he want? Unless he was about to pay this week's, last week's, and all of the other missed child-support payments, she didn't want to be bothered with his no-good behind. But she went ahead and opened the door reluctantly.

"Hey, how's it going?" Tyrone asked as he crossed the threshold, and stepped inside the apartment without being asked.

How in the world did he *think* she was doing? Here this fool had just arrived a couple of seconds ago, and he was already sounding stupid. She felt like killing herself a thousand times over for ever getting mixed up with him. And the fact that he was dressed in an expensive pair of black jeans and an extremely costly-looking sweater wasn't helping the situation. And she hated him for still having that same smooth-looking dark-chocolate skin that she'd been so attracted to in the very beginning. "Ashley and Nicholas aren't here," she said, ignoring his question and heading toward the bathroom to turn off her bathwater.

"I see you still got that jacked-up attitude," he said, plopping down in the chair adjacent to the sofa.

Marcella stopped solidly in her tracks and turned around. "Tyrone, how do you expect my attitude to be? You only pay child support whenever you feel like it, and then you show up to play Daddy whenever it's convenient. I'm sick of *it,* and I'm sick of *you.*"

"Look, girl, I didn't come over here for this," Tyrone said in a hostile tone of voice and stood up. "All I want to know is where my kids are, and when they're going to be back home?"

What nerve. Marcella rolled her eyes at him and headed toward the bathroom. When she arrived, she reached to turn the water off, which had filled just short of two inches from the rim of the tub. She'd almost flooded her whole apartment by messing around with Tyrone. Her blood was starting to boil, and she'd had just about all she could take of him for one day. She went back out to the living room.

"You know, Tyrone, you are such a joke. While you're asking all these ignorant questions, where is my child support?"

"I don't have it," he said in a cocky tone of voice, staring her straight in her face. "My car payment is due, and my mom needs some help with the utilities."

"So what. Ashley and Nicholas still have to eat regardless of what you have going on. Whether you realize it or not, they are your first priority. Everything else is second. Your car payment wasn't due last week, so what happened then?"

"Marcella, I don't owe you any explanations on how I spend my money. I'm not married to you. I'll see what I can do next week, and that's that."

"What do you mean, you'll see what you can do? You're already two weeks behind, and I know you don't want me to talk about all the payments you missed this past year. How do you expect for us to make it, Tyrone? I mean, don't you care about what happens to your own children? And it's not like you don't make a lot of money at that electric company, because I know you do."

"From what I can see, Ashley and Nicholas are doing just fine.

You always make it seem like they don't have food to eat or clothes to put on their backs, but I know better than that. I get so sick of you exaggerating about how you're barely making it. You get food stamps to feed them, the housing authority allows you to stay here practically rent-free, and your mother and sister are always buying something for them. So, don't even waste your time trying to make me feel guilty, because it's not going to work."

"You know, Tyrone, I'm doing the best that I can. You can criticize me and make all the excuses that you want, but it still doesn't dismiss the fact that you don't take care of your children the way you should. In fact, you don't even spend time with them. I didn't have them by myself, but for some reason you always act like I did. You should be ashamed to even say your children receive food stamps. Especially when they have a father who works full-time as an electrician. And worse than that, you still live at home with your mother. And as far as my mother and sister go, they aren't obligated to do anything for Ashley and Nicholas. They do it because they love them, but it's your responsibility."

Tyrone stood up. "Look. I'm not about to waste the rest of my Saturday afternoon listening to all this madness. Can you just have Ashley or Nick call me when they get home? Geez. It always has to be such an ordeal every time I see you."

Marcella laughed. "If you want to talk to them, I suggest you keep calling until you get in touch with them yourself, because I'm not going to have my babies runnin' behind you. As soon as Nicholas hears your voice, all he's going to do is beg you to come pick him up, and then all you're going to do is give him some sorry excuse as to why you can't. I'm sick of you disappointing them. And I'll tell you another thing. If you don't start paying my child support on time, I'm taking your deadbeat behind to court so I can get it directly from your paycheck."

Tyrone looked at her in total amazement. "Are you threatening me?"

"Take it however you want to," she said with her arms folded. She knew Tyrone would start to think twice, because they'd had this conversation before. He was well aware that if she took him to court, she'd get twenty-five percent for two children, which would end up being far more than that measly sixty dollars a week they'd agreed on eight years ago when Nicholas was born.

"You know what, Marcella? I hate the day I ever laid eyes on you, and I wish I had never allowed you to trap me the way you did. You'll get your child support. Don't even worry about it," Tyrone said, walking toward the front door.

"Good. Because that's all I want from you. And just for the record, a man can't be trapped when he knows what he's doing. When you were getting what you wanted, and I know you know what I'm talking about, you had a big smile on your face. But now that it's time to take responsibility for your actions, you have a problem with it."

"Whatever, Marcella," Tyrone said and slammed the door.

Marcella cringed. Why was he doing this? She'd thought she was making things easier for both of them when they'd made that verbal agreement concerning the child support. He'd pay sixty dollars a week and would help out with extras, like lunch money, birthdays, Christmas, and medical bills. And although she knew it was wrong, she'd be able to get a few food stamps to help out with their groceries, as long as the welfare agency never found out that she did in fact know where Tyrone was.

Before she'd found a full-time job, she'd been solely dependent on Aid to Families with Dependent Children. And while she wasn't proud of it, she'd told her caseworker that she didn't know where the father was, and that she hadn't seen him since the birth of her second child. When she'd given birth to Ashley, her mother had supported them, and she'd had no reason to apply for welfare, but after Nicholas was born, her parents had told her she didn't have a choice. If she told the agency about the sixty dollars a week, they would cut her food stamps off completely. But on the other hand, if she told them where Tyrone was, they would order him to pay child support through payroll deduction, and he'd be forced to give her at least one hundred twenty dollars a week. If she could get what was rightfully hers, though, she wouldn't need the food stamps to make ends meet.

The thought of going to court made her feel uncomfortable. But if Tyrone didn't start doing what he was supposed to, she didn't see where there was going to be any other choice. She owed it to her children, and that's just the way it was. She'd warned him, and now the ball was in his court. She was going to give him one more chance to improve his payment patterns, but if he was so much as one day late with the next or any future payments, she was going to take legal action.

After bathing, lotioning her body, and slipping on her underwear, Marcella stood in front of the bathroom mirror putting on her makeup. She plugged in her goldtone curling iron so that it would be nice and hot by the time she was ready to curl her hair. This particular brand didn't take as long to heat up like some of the others she'd owned, and they seemed much more equipped to handle the kind of coarse hair that most Black people had been blessed with.

When she finished, she unplugged the curling iron and stepped back into the bedroom. She pulled on her pants and slid on the matching jacket. As she sat down on the side of the bed and reached for her shoes, she glanced at her watch and noticed that it was two o'clock. Michelle's shower started at four, and she still needed to stop to pick up a gift. She was starting to think that maybe it was a better idea to buy a money holder and place twenty-five dollars in it. That way she wouldn't have to rush, and she'd also have a little time to stop by and see the children at her mother's.

She lifted the phone from the receiver next to her bed and dialed Racquel.

"Hello?" Kevin answered.

"Hey, Kevin. It's Marcella."

"What's up, sister-in-law. How are you?"

"Good, now that Tyrone is gone."

"What did *he* want?"

"He came by looking for Ashley and Nicholas, but they're over at Mom's. But, of course, we got into it because he's two weeks behind with his child support."

"I can't believe that deadbeat is still playing games. He should be ashamed of himself. What you need to do is take his butt to court, so you can get everything he owes you."

"I know. And that's why I'm only giving him one more chance, but if he's late again, that's it."

"I hate to tell you this, but once a deadbeat, always a deadbeat. He'll pay you on time until he thinks you're happy, but you can bet he'll start messing up again. You might as well get ready for it."

"Well, all I know is that I'm not playing with him anymore. So, if he wants to hang himself, that's fine with me."

"Might as well get ready for what?" Racquel asked in the background. She'd obviously walked in on the tail end of what Kevin had just said.

"Well, Marcella, since your sister is dying to get into our conversation, I'll let you speak to her," Kevin said and laughed. "I'll probably see you later this evening, though, when you guys get back from the baby shower."

"Talk to you later, Kevin." Marcella waited for Racquel to take the phone.

"Girl, what were you and Kevin talking about?" Racquel asked.

"That good-for-nothing Tyrone. Who else?"

"Please. What did he do this time?"

"You mean, what *didn't* he do."

"I can't believe him. He's still trying to slide by without taking care of his responsibility, huh?"

"Some things never change, but it's like I just told Kevin, he's got one more chance. If he messes that up, I'm taking him to court."

"Good for you, girl. You should have done that a long time ago, if you ask me."

"Yeah, I know. So, do you want to pick me up on the way to the shower, or what? I'm going by Mom's to check on Ashley and Nicholas, so if you want, you can pick me up over there."

"That sounds good. Kevin and I just finished eating a late lunch, but I already took my shower, so I should be ready in about an hour. I'll come by Mom's around three-fifteen."

"Don't even talk about food. I'm starved. What did you guys have?"

"Kevin made some spaghetti with ground beef, and of course I ate too much."

"Girl, you should be thanking God daily for giving you such a wonderful husband. You are so blessed."

"Oh, I'm thankful, but still, you're the lucky one."

"Please. How am *I* lucky?" Marcella asked, trying to figure out what Racquel could have possibly been talking about.

"Those two beautiful children. You have everything, and don't even realize it."

"I do thank God, but I'm far from having everything. It's hard raising two children all alone on seven dollars an hour. And even if

Tyrone paid his child support like he should, it still wouldn't be the same as having a good husband by my side. Especially one who earns a decent income."

"I'm telling you, Marcella, having children is a blessing. And finding a good man is the easy part. I mean, look at you. You're beautiful. You're intelligent. And you're a good person. Any man would be lucky to find you."

"Not every man is looking to date, let alone marry, a woman with two children. And that's a fact."

"But at the same time there are a lot of men who don't have a problem with that. Especially when the children are as well-mannered as Ash and Nick."

By now, Marcella was starting to become slightly annoyed. She and Racquel were always going around and about when it came to who was lucky, blessed, and had everything they could hope for. It was definitely time to end the conversation before it stretched too far out of hand. "Hey, I'd better get off of here, so I can pick up a money holder at the drugstore."

"Okay, then. Well, I'll see you when I get to Mom's."

"See ya," Marcella said and hung up the phone. She took a deep breath. Partly because Racquel didn't have the sense enough to appreciate the life she'd been given, but mostly because her sister never seemed to understand where she was coming from. Whether she wanted to see it or not, Racquel was the one who had everything: Kevin. A career that she loved. A semi-brick, two-story home. The girl needed to count her blessings and be thankful for what she had, and that was that. But Marcella knew that having children was the most important thing to her sister, and that she would have done just about anything to make it happen. But for the life of her, Marcella never saw what the big deal was, since she had the option of adopting as many children as she wanted at any time. Newborn babies—that is, Black newborn babies were being put up for adoption on a daily basis. Even White people were starting to adopt biracial babies, as soon as they realized they'd be waiting for all eternity to adopt a White one.

Marcella just couldn't understand it, and the more she thought about it, the more she hoped Racquel wasn't going to ruin their afternoon at the baby shower by becoming depressed. They'd gone to their cousin's baby shower last year, which had been a major mistake. Racquel had been fine until she entered the house and laid eyes on little Nathan. She'd stared at him on and off, but under no circumstances would she agree to hold him. As a matter of fact, when Marcella had brought the baby over to where Racquel was sitting, she'd gotten up and walked into the kitchen, totally ignoring him. But then, maybe today would be different, since Michelle's baby hadn't been born yet, and Racquel wouldn't have to physically see it. At least that's what Marcella was praying for.

After running into her best friend, Sharon, at the drugstore, Marcella hadn't arrived at her mother's until three o'clock. After locking her car doors, she walked around to the back door and knocked. After a few seconds, she knocked again, and her mother finally opened the door. Marcella opened her mouth to say hello but paused when she noticed that her mother had been crying.

"Mom, what's wrong?" Marcella asked in a very concerned manner.

"That Tyrone has only got one more time to come in my house disrespecting me the way he did today."

A look of horror covered Marcella's face as she walked up the back steps into the kitchen. "Tyrone? What was he doing over here?"

Corrine wiped the last of her tears and swallowed hard. "I guess he figured out that the children were with me, so he decided to come by to see them. He wanted to take them to his house, and you know I don't mind that, because that's their father. But first I wanted them to finish their lunch, because they hadn't eaten since this morning. But when I asked him to have a seat until they did, out of nowhere, he started rantin' and ravin'. Saying that he didn't have time to wait. That he'd already been by your house looking for them and wasn't going to wait any longer. He told Ashley to go get their coats, and when I asked him why he was acting the way he was, he told me that I needed to mind my own business. That if I wanted to worry about somebody and what they were doing, I should have done that with you. He even had the nerve to say, that if I had raised you better, *he* wouldn't be in this situation. And that's when I'd had enough. I told him that if he didn't get out of my house right then, I was calling the police."

Marcella was speechless. She couldn't believe what she was hearing, because for as long as she could remember, Tyrone had always gotten along with her mother. Regardless of how she felt about him, he and her mother had never had any conflicts with each other. "Mom, I'm so sorry. I don't know what to say."

"Marcella, I don't know if Tyrone was having a bad day or what, but what hurt me the most was when he said I should have raised you better. Lord knows, I did the best that I could with what I had, when it came to taking care of you and your sister."

"Mom, don't pay Tyrone any attention. He's crazy. Just plain crazy," Marcella said, starting to get angry.

"Crazy or not, he still disrespected me in my own house and got away with it. And I won't ever forget that. Even though he never does anything for my grandbabies, and he's treated you like nothin' since you first got pregnant, I still gave him his respect. This doesn't make any sense at all, and it was uncalled for."

"When is he bringing them back?"

"I don't know. He stormed out of here so fast, I didn't even think to ask him. Plus, I was too upset anyhow."

As Marcella started toward the phone in the kitchen, someone knocked at the back door. Corrine went down the steps, peeped through the mini-blind, saw that it was Racquel, and opened the door. Corrine started back up the steps, and Racquel followed behind.

"Hey, Mom," Racquel said.

"Hi, honey." Corrine responded in a soft tone of voice.

Racquel looked around the corner and saw Marcella on the phone and waved at her.

"Tyrone, what is your problem?" Marcella screamed through the phone as soon as she heard him say hello. She wanted to say a whole lot more, and he had better thank his God that her mother was standing there listening to her.

Tyrone hung up the phone, and she could tell by the way it sounded that he'd slammed it down as hard as he could.

Racquel frowned and set her purse down on the counter. "Marcella, what's going on?"

"Tyrone came over here disrespecting Mom and then took the children."

"What?" Racquel screamed. "I just know he didn't. What's his phone number?" Racquel said, reaching for the phone.

"Racquel, don't even bother with him," Corrine said, sitting down at the breakfast table. "You know I didn't teach you girls to act this way. And just because he's acting ignorant doesn't mean the two of you have to stoop down to his level. I'm okay, and Tyrone will get what's coming to him one way or the other. We all have to reap what we sow, and there's definitely no way of getting around it. So it's best to just leave it alone."

"Mom, I promise you, this won't happen again. From now on, I'll make sure he comes to see the children at my house, and my house only. But I still can't understand why he did this. He and I had some words earlier, like we always do, but he had no right taking it out on you. I mean, this is so ridiculous."

Racquel didn't say anything because she didn't want to upset her mother any more than she already was, but she couldn't wait until she saw that Tyrone. She was going to give him more than a piece of her mind. She was sick of how he treated her sister anyway, and a much-awaited confrontation with him was long overdue. Marcella had been playing games with him far too long, and it was time someone put him in his own pathetic little place. And if it had to be her, that was fine, too.

"That was a really nice shower, wasn't it," Racquel said to Marcella as she drove away from Michelle's northwest-suburban home, which was located about twenty minutes away from Chicago's city limits. "As a matter of fact, it was one of the nicest ones I've ever been to."

Marcella couldn't believe what she was hearing, and she was even more surprised at how pleasant Racquel's attitude had been throughout the entire afternoon. She'd participated in all the games, and she'd even went as far as holding Michelle's three-month-old nephew, little Joshua. Marcella didn't know what had come over her sister, but she was happy about it just the same. "Yeah, it *was* really nice, and she got a ton of nice gifts, too."

"And that little Joshua was about the most precious thing I've ever seen. Almost as precious as Nicholas and Ashley were when you had them."

"He's definitely a little cutey, and he's such a happy baby, too,"

Marcella said, gazing out the window at all the gorgeous homes they were passing. "My God. Wouldn't you just love living in this neighborhood?"

"Wouldn't we all? Michelle and her husband have definitely done well for themselves. That's for sure. And in a few months they're going to have a baby to complete the package," Racquel said, and then slowed down when she saw the green traffic light switch to yellow.

Marcella didn't comment.

"Some people have all the luck. I mean, why can't Kevin and I have a baby, so we can live happily ever after like everybody else? I know it's not right to envy what someone else has, but I just can't seem to help it. As a matter of fact, sometimes I hate myself for feeling the way I do, because I know how wrong it is. Sometimes I think I'm going crazy. And sometimes I can't help but wonder why having a baby is so important to me."

"Everybody has something that they want more than anything else. That's just the way life is. But instead of dwelling on our own self-defined misfortunes, what we need to do is spend more time trying to find satisfaction in what we *do* have. I know I've probably said all this before, but that's because it's the truth."

"I know, but no matter how hard I try to push the idea of getting pregnant out of my mind, it seems to haunt me more and more. It's almost like I'm on a mission to fill some kind of void in my life."

"What kind of void?" Marcella asked, obviously confused about Racquel's statement.

"I know it sounds crazy, but I've never gotten over the fact that Daddy started messing around on Mom the way he did. And even though he was still living in the house the whole time I was in high school, you know he was hardly ever there. Sometimes, it felt like we didn't even have a father. And even though I know Mom loved us more than anything in this world, it still wasn't the same as having both of them love us that way."

"Girl, what are you talking about? As far as I can tell, Daddy loved both of us just as much as Mom did. He may not have shown it very well, but I know for a fact that he loved us."

"Well, all I know is that my life, and yours, too, for that matter, might have turned out totally different if he hadn't started all that hangin'-out-with-other-women business. Sometimes I miss him so much, but at other times I despise everything that he stands for."

Marcella gazed at Racquel in amazement. She couldn't believe they were even having this particular conversation. Yes, her father had made some serious mistakes, and yes, he had remarried and moved almost a thousand miles away from them in the process, but that didn't mean he no longer loved them. And why was Racquel bringing all this up in the first place? She never had before, and Marcella couldn't help but wonder why she was so adamant on discussing it now. "Why are you all of a sudden blaming Daddy for the way our lives turned out?"

"I'm not blaming him. At least not totally, anyway. But I do think that if he had been a better husband and hadn't caused Mom so much pain, she could have spent way more time concentrating on our emotional needs, and not just what we needed to survive physically. Food, clothing, and a home are fine, but what good is any of that if a child still feels emotionally bankrupt? And don't get me wrong, I'm thankful for everything they did in that respect, but I still always felt like something was missing. It wasn't so bad when we were little, but by the time I went to the ninth grade, things were pretty bad between them. And I don't know how many nights I cried myself to sleep after listening to all their yelling and screaming at each other," Racquel said in a trembling voice.

Marcella looked at her sister and saw tears building in her eyes. She wasn't sure what to say, because she had no idea that Racquel felt this way, or that their parents' breakup had caused her so much pain. But she knew she had to console her somehow. "Girl, that's all in the past, but if it's bothering you this much, maybe you should talk to Mom and Daddy about the way you feel."

Racquel pulled into a CITGO parking lot, pushed the gear in park, and then searched through her purse for something to wipe her tears. Marcella turned her body toward her and caressed the side of her arm, trying her best to comfort her sister. After Racquel dried her face, she took a deep breath. "Girl, I am so sorry for taking you through all these changes, but sometimes just thinking about their divorce really takes a toll on me. And I guess I keep telling myself that if I have my own child, I'm going to do everything I can to make up for what I didn't have. And I'll finally have someone in my life who won't simply just walk out on me just because they feel like it. I want my child to know what it's like to have a loving, stable, two-parent household. It might sound silly, but that's honestly how I feel."

Marcella wanted to tell her that there were no guarantees with any marriage, that no one knew what tomorrow was going to bring, and that her relationship with Kevin was no exception to the rule. But she decided instead that it was best not to say anything.

"Sometimes I get so angry at him for leaving us the way he did, and I get even angrier when I think about how much I still love him."

"It bothered me, too, when they got divorced," Marcella finally said. "But, based on my experience with Tyrone, I realize that not every relationship can work. And I'll tell you another thing, just because two people get divorced doesn't mean that they don't love their children."

"Then, why did he have to move so far away?" Racquel asked, looking directly at Marcella. "And why did he hardly call us? And why didn't he ask us to come visit him during the summer and on holidays? The man had a responsibility to us, and he acted like he didn't even care."

Marcella didn't like what Racquel was saying, but at the same time she knew her sister had a point. And a very good point, for that matter. He hadn't communicated with them nearly as often as he should have, and there wasn't any legitimate reason for his actions that she could think of. "To tell you the truth, I don't know why he didn't keep in contact with us."

"And he still doesn't now, either. And even worse, he's barely even seen Ash and Nick more than once, and they're the only two grandchildren that he has."

"Well, it's his loss, not mine. And to be honest, I really don't care, so long as my babies get to spend as much time as they want with their grandmother. Mom is there for them whenever they need her, and I'm just thankful for that."

"I know, Marcella, but it's still not right for him to just pretend like we don't even exist," Racquel said, pulling the gear down to drive and heading back out onto the street.

Marcella sighed deeply. She'd heard her grandmother say that a person's childhood could affect her for the rest of her life, and now she realized just how true that statement had been. She wished there were something she could say, or something she could do, to make Racquel feel better about this whole situation, but for the life of her, she had no idea what that something was. Sugarcoating her father's actions wasn't going to make things any better, and criticizing him the way Racquel wanted her to wasn't going to do a bit of good, either. But on top of all that, she wondered why their parents' divorce had affected Racquel so much more severely than it had her. Especially since Racquel was the oldest and always seemed to have everything in her life so nicely put together. Marcella had some other questions, too, but instead of adding more fuel to the fire, she decided to change this whole depressing conversation. "So, what are you and Kevin doing tonight?"

"As far as I know, watching some videos. What about you?"

"Girl, please. With Ashley and Nicholas spending the night with Mom, probably nothing at all. Which reminds me. Let me call Mom to see if this nut has brought the kids back or not," Marcella said, picking up Racquel's car phone. She dialed the number and waited.

"Hello," Corrine answered.

"Hey, Mom. Did Tyrone bring Ashley and Nicholas back yet?"

"He just dropped them off a few minutes ago."

"Did he say anything to you?"

"He walked them around to the back door, and when I opened it, he said he was sorry for acting the way he had earlier, and that he was having a bad day."

"Yeah, right," Marcella said, pursing her lips together in disbelief.

"Well, whether he's sincere about being sorry or not, you know I'm not going to waste my time holding any grudges. Because like I said before, if Tyrone keeps treating people the way he does, he'll get what's coming to him. And I definitely don't want to keep a bunch of mess going on in front of these children."

"I know, Mom, but it's just that I feel so bad about him talking to you the way he did."

"It's over now, so don't worry about it. And anyway, how was Michelle's shower?"

"It was wonderful, and we had a good time."

"How did Racquel do?" Corrine whispered, and it was obvious that she thought Racquel might hear what she was asking Marcella.

"Fine," Marcella answered, hoping Racquel wouldn't pick up on the conversation.

"Good," Corrine said, and was clearly relieved.

"I'll probably come in for a while when Racquel drops me off to pick up my car."

"Okay, and tell Racquel I'll talk to her in the morning."

"I will. Bye, Mom," Marcella said, and placed the phone on its base.

"Why don't you come watch videos with us?" Racquel asked.

"Girl, the last thing you and Kevin need is a third wheel."

"Kevin will be offended if you don't show. You know how he likes to have people over when we're watching videos."

"I don't know. Maybe I will."

"There's no maybe to it. You're going to my house now, and you can pick your car up later. Shoot, you can spend the night if you want to."

Marcella smiled. And was glad that she had a sister like Racquel.

Chapter 4

"**B**aby, I've got a good feeling about it this time," Racquel said, stretching both her arms up toward the brass headboard, with a confident smile on her face. It was spring break, and since she had the entire week off, Kevin had decided to take two vacation days.

"You think so, huh?" he said with an even bigger smile than hers. He'd just awakened, but his mind was already replaying every bit of what had gone on last night after they arrived home from dinner. They'd made love like they never had before. And for the first time in what seemed like years, it didn't feel like some job assignment. It was spontaneous, and Racquel had wanted him solely because of the pleasure he brought to her, and not simply because she wanted to conceive a baby. This is how it was supposed to be, and he was glad that the woman he married in the first place had come back. He had missed her more than he thought, and he'd been worried about what was going to happen to their marriage if she didn't start treating him like her husband again. But now things were finally starting to look up.

"I'm telling you, after we drop the urine off this morning, we may as well spend the rest of the day planning for the baby."

Kevin just lay there with his eyes closed, nodding his head in agreement. But he didn't say anything. He'd learned his lesson about showing any signs of negativity when it came to the subject of Racquel getting pregnant. He hated it when she got her hopes up so high, because whenever she did, she was never able to handle the disappointment. He hoped for her sake, though, that she was right this time. That it would be different from last month, and all the others previous. They needed some good news. And more than that, he wasn't sure how much more stress their marriage could actually survive.

"Kevin," she said. "Are you listening to me?"

"Yes, baby. I'm listening."

"Well, say something. I mean, since my period is at least five days late, I know this could really be it."

"I pray that it is. I really do," he said, pulling her closer to him. "I know you don't think I care about this as much as you, but I do. I want to have a child with you more than anything, because you mean everything to me. I didn't think it was possible to love another human being the way that I love you. Sometimes when I as much as think of you and the love that we have, my heart hurts, I mean it physically hurts."

"I love you, too, Kevin, and that's why I want to give you a child. I want to give you something that is a part of both of us. Something that can't be bought and paid for. Bringing a child into this world is the most beautiful thing. And it's so miraculous," she said, hugging him tight.

He hugged her back, and one thing led to another. The same way it used to when they'd first met.

After Racquel and Kevin had dropped her urine sample off at the clinic, they'd eaten breakfast at the nearby pancake house, and decided to ride downtown to do some shopping at Water Tower Place. This was Racquel's favorite mall, and if it had been left up to her, she would have shopped in Lord & Taylor's baby department until closing time. Three years ago, when they'd married, she looked forward to shopping for Kevin and herself, but over the last two years she seemed to spend the majority of her time shopping for the baby she was sure she was going to have. In the beginning she bought things that would have worked fine for a boy or girl. But when she realized that there were only so many diapers, bottles, receiving blankets, and bibs a person could buy, it wasn't long before she began purchasing anything that was cute. Dresses—just in case it was a girl, and little pants outfits—if it was a boy. She knew it was a waste of money, but she couldn't help herself. She wanted everything to be perfect because sooner or later the baby *was* going to arrive. And regardless of how many negative results there had been, she still believed it was all just a matter of time.

When they stepped up to the checkout counter, Racquel had each of her arms loaded with merchandise. Kevin wanted to tell her to put some of it back. To wait until they got home and found out the test results. But they'd been having such a wonderful time together, it wasn't worth breaking the mood. It almost felt like they'd fallen in love all over again. She hadn't overcome the pregnancy obsession, but at least she was making love with him again, and not just giving him sex. And she was happy. No, the last thing he wanted to do was piss her off and take the chance of her not wanting him tonight, so he decided to keep his mouth shut. He wasn't a wimp or anything like that, but he wasn't stupid, either.

"Aren't these cute?" Racquel asked Kevin, placing the three infant-sized dresses across the counter before the saleslady.

"Yeah, they are, but you better hope it's a girl, otherwise you're going to be returning an awful lot of stuff."

"I know, but it's better to have enough of both until we know for sure."

The saleslady, who was pushing middle fifties in age, looked at both of them like they were crazy. Like they needed psychiatric help.

Racquel never even noticed and continued to pass the rest of the items to her to ring up. After she'd handed over the last piece, she was shocked at all the things she had gathered up throughout the store.

"Your total is two hundred ninety-four dollars and ninety cents. Will this be on your Lord and Taylor charge?" the cashier asked, waiting for a response.

"No," Racquel said, pulling out her Visa card instead.

Kevin wanted to scream. This keeping-his-mouth-shut business was about to wear out, and fast. He couldn't believe she'd spent almost three hundred dollars on a baby she wasn't even sure she was going to have. And if she *was* pregnant, she didn't even know what sex it was going to be. He wanted to let her have it right there, but decided that this wasn't the place or the time; especially in front of someone they didn't even know. This was so unlike Racquel. She had always been so good with their finances. She was one of the most sensible women he'd ever met when it came to spending and saving money. But now she didn't even bat an eye when it came to blowing money on an infant they didn't have, or even worse, one they might not ever get.

"Baby, I'm going outside to get some fresh air. I'll be directly in front of the mall at the Michigan Avenue entrance," he said, and walked away without as much as glancing at her.

She watched him as he left the children's department until he was out of sight. He was pissed off at her, and she didn't know how she was going to change the way he was feeling. When the cashier passed her the receipt, she signed it, waited for her to place her copy in one of the two shopping bags, and proceeded toward the store entrance. As she stepped outside of the store and took a breath of fresh air, she suddenly felt better about the whole situation. She decided that there really wasn't anything to worry about at all. They'd be home in less than an hour, the nurse at the clinic would confirm that she was in fact pregnant, and Kevin would immediately forget about all the money she'd spent. She smiled when she realized everything was going to work out fine.

They'd argued almost the entire way to the interstate, but once they drove onto it, they'd rode the rest of the way in complete silence. Kevin was angrier than he had been in a long time, and Racquel's feelings were hurt. If only she could have gotten the test result before she purchased the clothing, maybe then he wouldn't have gotten so uptight about it.

As they drove into the subdivision, she turned to look at him, but he continued to look straight ahead, ignoring her. He was being stubborn, and she hated when he did that. It was almost like he was dismissing her and all that she believed in. All that she dreamed and hoped for. He was her husband, and it was his duty to stand by her through the good times and the bad. And he was going to feel like a complete fool, once she made the phone call to the clinic.

Once they were inside the house, Racquel headed toward the off-white and black living room, dropped both shopping bags and her shoulder purse onto the carpet, and then backtracked toward the kitchen to pick up the cordless phone. Kevin proceeded up the stairs to their bedroom. She dialed seven digits and waited for the obstetrics and gynecology receptionist to answer.

"Obstetrics and Gynecology, how may I help you?"

"Yes, could you ring Dr. Mallard's nurse, please?" Racquel said, sitting down at the kitchen table. She could feel her nerves racing faster and faster by the second.

She never liked being placed on hold, but it was even worse when they played that irritating music. She'd only been waiting one minute, but it felt like ten. She was anxious, and she wished the nurse would hurry.

"This is Charmaine," the nurse said.

Finally. "Hi, Charmaine. This is Racquel Wilson, and I'm calling to check on my pregnancy test."

"Hi, Racquel. I just received the results from the group of tests I sent out this morning, but I haven't had a chance to review them yet. If you can wait, I'll pull yours right now."

"Fine." If she could wait? What kind of question was that? She and Charmaine had been on a first-name basis for over two years, and if there was anyone at all who knew how desperately she wanted to have a baby, it was Charmaine. She'd dropped off so many urine samples, that almost everyone in the department knew who she was, and most of them knew her personally. She could have easily taken home pregnancy tests, which she did occasionally on weekends when the clinic was closed, but it didn't make a lot of sense to spend that kind of money over and over when Kevin's insurance plan covered it.

"Racquel. I'm sorry, but your test came back negative."

Racquel didn't move and was speechless. She couldn't believe what she was hearing. How could this be happening again? She'd been so sure this time.

"Racquel? Are you there?"

"Yes, I'm here. Are you sure?"

"Yes. Again, I'm really sorry. Maybe you'll have better luck next time."

Racquel hung up the phone by reflex because her thoughts were too deep to realize any of what she was doing. How was she going to face Kevin? He'd doubted her all morning. And to think how stupid she was spending all that money at the department store. She must have been out of her eternal mind to even consider doing something like that. She closed her eyes, clasped her hands together, and prayed that Kevin would be more understanding this time than he had in the past. The last thing she needed to hear was his ideas on giving up and getting on with their lives. Because as far as she was concerned, there was no life for either of them without children.

A few minutes passed, and Kevin finally came back down to the main floor. As he entered the kitchen and saw Racquel, it was obvious to him that she'd gotten the news about her test. He was still upset with her for making all those charges on the credit card, but he felt sorry for her, as well. He walked over to where she was sitting and pulled her up from the light-tan wooden chair. He held her in silence. She laid the side of her head against his chest, and it was obvious that neither of them knew what to say. They were all talked out, and for the first time Racquel wasn't shedding any tears.

They held each other for a few more minutes, and finally Kevin broke the ice. "Baby, I know this isn't what you expected, but it's not the end of the world. We'll get through this. We always have, and this time won't be any different."

"I just can't understand what's wrong with me. I got pregnant last year, so I know it's not impossible. Maybe it's time we started thinking about some other options."

Wait. Was he hearing her right? After all this time, was she finally coming to the realization that maybe it wasn't meant for her to physically have a child? He'd been wanting to adopt, ever since she had that miscarriage last year, and it was about time she realized that it wasn't such a bad thing, after all. "Well, you know how I feel because I've been trying to convince you of that all along."

"I'll call Dr. Mallard's office first thing tomorrow morning, so he can refer us to an infertility specialist. I'm sure the insurance will cover it. At least some of it, anyway."

Man. After all that had happened, he couldn't believe she still planned to continue this pregnancy crusade. And from what he could tell, this new bright idea was going to be worse. Infertility drugs and the like were going to cost them a ton of money, and he wasn't at all sure that this was the right thing to do. "Do you have any idea how much this is going to cost us? We'll go broke trying to make something happen, something that obviously isn't meant to be in the first place."

"Why are you always so negative about everything?" she asked, releasing her arms from his waist and stepping away from him. It really got under her skin when he made comments like that.

"I'm not negative about everything, but after three years of trying to have a baby, I've learned to accept things the way they are."

"Well, that's not good enough for me. For all we know, an infertility specialist could be the answer. So, the least you can do is go with me to find out."

"Are you ever going to give this a rest?"

"With the help of a specialist and all the new technology, the success rate of getting pregnant is a lot higher than it used to be. So, please, sweetheart. I'm begging you to do this one last thing. Not just for me, but for both of us."

"Fine, Racquel. I'll go. But only under one condition."

"What condition?" she said, scrunching her face together. She never liked ultimatums, but he'd sure been giving her a lot of those lately. And she could tell he was about to issue another one at this very moment.

"That if none of the treatments work after the period of time that they should be working, you'll give this up once and for all. We have the rest of our lives ahead of us, and I'm ready to get on with it."

"I promise you, baby, if this doesn't work, I'm through with it," she said, hugging him tight and smiling.

"I'm serious, Racquel," he said, hugging her back. "This is it."

He was right. This *was* it. She could feel it. Now she wished they'd gotten tested when Kevin had wanted them to. But she'd been so afraid that there was something wrong with her, that she decided against it. The last thing she wanted was to feel less than a woman. And if there was something wrong with Kevin, she didn't want to know that, either, because she didn't want to end up resenting him for something he couldn't help. But now, push was coming to shove, and she didn't have much choice. She still believed that with time, she'd get pregnant without drugs, artificial insemination, or whatever else medical researchers had come up with, but at least consulting with an infertility specialist would buy her more time. The kind of time Kevin wasn't willing to wait on.

Right now she felt more confident than she ever had before, and like always, she knew it was just a matter of time.

Chapter 5

No sooner than Marcella had sat down at her desk, the phone rang. It wasn't even eight yet, ten minutes until to be exact, and clients were already calling in. It was always like that on Monday mornings, and even worse when their business clients were preparing to pay their quarterly tax bills. Their firm dealt mostly with sole proprietorships and partnerships, but right now they were being flooded with calls and visits from individuals who were trying desperately to beat the April 15 deadline, which was only two weeks away. She never understood why people waited until the last minute to file. Employers were required to get W-2's and 1099's out to employees and independent contractors by January 31 of every year, so Marcella didn't know what the problem was. This annual rat race was stressful, and she avoided it like it was a deadly virus.

Come to think of it, Covington Park residents weren't much better when it came time to renew their vehicle stickers, either. And the ones who waited until the expiration date to make their purchases were the same ones who complained about how long they had to stand in line. This was total nonsense, and the reason why Marcella had completed and mailed her taxes by the first week in February. But then, maybe she was in more of a hurry than most people, since she was getting back a refund. Just about every dime she paid in, too, thanks to the government's earned-income credit. Which was the least they could do for a struggling mother who was raising her children all by her lonesome.

Finally at 8:01 A.M., she answered what she considered to be the first legitimate phone call of the day. "Good morning, Nicosia and Associates. How may I help you?" she said in a crisp, professional voice.

"Boy, don't we sound chipper for a Monday morning," Sharon said, laughing.

"Girl, please. It pays the bills."

"I know that's right. So what do you have up for lunch today?"

"Oh, didn't I tell you? I've got a hot date with this gorgeous guy I met over the weekend. I can't believe I didn't tell you yesterday."

"I can't believe you didn't tell me, either. I could just kill you. What's his name? Where did you meet him? What kind of car does he drive? And most of all, where does he work?"

Another phone line rang. "You are such a trip, Sharon. Hold on for a second," Marcella said and placed her best friend on hold.

"Good morning, Nicosia and Associates. How may I help you?"

"Good morning. Could you ring the auditing department, please," a female voice on the other end of the phone requested.

"Sure. One moment," Marcella responded, transferred the call, and then pressed the line that Sharon was waiting on.

"You still there?"

"Now, Marcella. Do you actually think I was going to hang up before you gave me the four-one-one on this guy you met? Please."

Marcella cracked up, but didn't say anything.

"Girl, why are you keeping me in all this suspense? I can hardly stand it."

"Gosh, you're really taking this seriously, aren't you?"

"Marcella," Sharon demanded.

"Girl, I was just messing with you. I didn't meet anybody. I don't go anywhere *to* meet anybody."

"I don't believe you. You got me all worked up, and now you don't have anything to tell? You know that's not right," Sharon said, sounding disappointed.

"I know. I'm sorry," Marcella said, still laughing. "So, what are you *really* doing for lunch then?"

"Nothing that I know of. Why? You wanna meet somewhere?"

"We should. What about that rib place by your office?"

"You must be working at the Covington Park location today?" Marcella asked, holding the phone with her chin so she could sort through some filing while she conversed.

"I am, but I'll be going back to the main office downtown after lunch."

"Well, the rib place is fine with me," Marcella said, then noticed two phone lines blinking. "I've got to answer these calls, so I'll see you then."

"See ya," Sharon said and hung up.

Marcella answered ten more calls, and greeted seven visitors before things finally started to calm down. This was going to be one of those days, and she couldn't wait for noontime.

As she stacked some of the tax files that needed reviewing, Thomas walked by and spoke to her. He had to have been the finest man she'd ever imagined. And he was as intelligent as they came. The man had a master's degree in accounting, and practically aced the CPA exam without the tiniest bit of difficulty. The partners at the firm had snatched him up without as much as even a second thought.

And he was smooth. Which was unusual, because most men graduating in the top five percent of any master's degree program from a school comparable to Northwestern University were dorks. She wasn't sure why, but they just were. Except Thomas wasn't like that. Now, why couldn't she ever meet men like him? The type of man who had it all? He was facially fine, intelligent, responsible, and well-dressed. And surprisingly enough, he was both book smart and street smart. Her grandmother used to say that when a person had too much book sense, they usually didn't have any common sense. But Thomas had loads of it. So, what more could a woman ask for? But then there was one downfall. He was married. The good ones were always married. That was the problem, and the reason why she only seemed to meet guys who wanted nothing more than to toss her into bed. The thought of it all was sickening. After Tyrone she'd learned her lesson and refused to be used by any man. She didn't have much, but at least she had her pride. And what if she did find a good man? He probably wouldn't be too happy about taking on a readymade family, anyhow. Which is exactly how it would have to be if he wanted a relationship with her.

She wasn't like a lot of these women who dumped their children wherever they pleased, whenever they felt like it, just so they could lie up with some man who couldn't care less about them. Every mother needed a break sometimes, but *all* the time was totally unacceptable. No, she, Ashley, and Nicholas were a package deal, and any man who couldn't accept those terms was better off moving on to his next victim.

Marcella had buried herself so deep in thought, she'd forgotten where she was. Five phone lines were blinking simultaneously. She hurried to answer each as fast as she could, but in the same professional manner as she always did. Two of the callers sounded irritated, but there was nothing she could do about that now. She transferred each of them accordingly.

It was only five minutes before lunchtime, so she grabbed her purse from her lower right-hand desk drawer. Most everyone had already left, so she decided to pull out her pressed-face-powder compact. She ran the sponge across the powder, and then across her face to remove the shine that had accumulated over the last four hours. Then she touched up her lip liner and Deep Raspberry lipstick. She liked this color a lot, but the name brand was already worn off the container. If it had been one of the better cosmetic lines like Fashion Fair, Flori Roberts, or Mary Kay, she would have recognized it by the packaging alone, but she'd purchased this from one of the many drugstores she frequented. And there was no telling which one she'd gotten it from.

Marcella drove three blocks from the accounting firm, pulled into the parking lot of The Rib House, parked near the entrance, and waited for Sharon to arrive. After about two minutes Sharon pulled her white BMW convertible into the stall next to Marcella. Which was a surprise, because usually the lot was so crowded by now that customers were forced to park on the street. But then again, Mondays always seemed to be much slower than the rest of the days in the week.

"How long have you been waiting?" Sharon asked, shutting her car door. She was dressed in a navy-blue all-weather coat, a navy-blue business suit, and matching heels. Her hair was pulled back in a French twist. Her body was long and lean, but her behind stuck out just far enough to give her the perfect shape. That is, the kind of shape that was required by most Black men.

Marcella had on a two-piece, short-sleeved purple suit and a pair of off-white sling-backs.

"Just a couple of minutes," Marcella answered, strutting toward the entrance of the restaurant.

Once they were inside, Marcella ordered a barbeque shoulder sandwich, steak fries, and a large lemonade.

"Will this be on one ticket?" the cashier asked. "Yes, and I'll have the same as her," Sharon said, removing a twenty-dollar bill from her navy Coach shoulder bag.

"You didn't have to do that," Marcella said, feeling semiembarrassed.

"Please. I asked *you* to go to lunch. Remember?"

Marcella smiled because Sharon was always making financial gestures, such as this one. She was the best friend she ever had, and she was thankful just to know her. Money was never an object to Sharon, but then why should it be? She earned over sixty thousand dollars a year working as a software engineer, and the girl was clearly living comfortably. Especially for a Black twenty-eight-year-old female.

They'd graduated high school side by side, and they'd had every intention of being roommates in college. But when Marcella ended up pregnant, Sharon went to Spelman on her own. And when she finished her master's degree, she began working for a computer-information company downtown, and it wasn't long before she'd moved steadily up the engineering ladder. At least, one of them had made it to where they wanted to be, and Marcella was proud of her.

"So what did you end up doing yesterday evening after we talked?" Marcella asked, taking a seat at the table near the back of the restaurant. Sharon sat down in front of her.

"Marcus came by with some videos, and we sat around for the rest of the evening. That was about it."

"So, is he still pressing you about getting engaged?"

"Of course. And it's becoming harder and harder to say no. I mean, even though I love Marcus, I'm really not quite ready to get married yet. But on the other hand, all I have is my career, and sometimes it's hard being alone in this crazy world we live in."

"You're *not* alone. You know you have me. I'll always be here for you. You're just like my sister, and you know how Mom feels about you."

"I know, Marcella, and I appreciate that, but it's just not the same as having blood relatives. I feel like I don't have any roots. Every time I think about my mother dying while giving birth to me, it tears me apart. And who knows where my father is. No one ever knew for sure who he was, anyway."

"I know, but at least you knew your grandparents. They treated you as if you were their own, and nothing can ever replace that type of love."

"Yeah, but now they're gone. I guess I should be thankful that they were able to see me graduate from college, but still they're gone."

A heavyset almond-colored lady with a beautiful smile brought out their food and set it on the table. "Can I get you ladies anything else this afternoon?" she asked.

"No," Sharon said. "Everything is fine. Thank you."

"If you need anything else, just holler. Otherwise, enjoy your meal," the waitress said and strutted away.

Marcella couldn't understand why Sharon was so sad. She'd seemed so happy when they'd spoken earlier, but now she was sounding like her whole life was falling apart. "Well, all I can say is, you are blessed whether you believe it or not. I mean, you've only been out of college for four years, and look how much money you make. Most people don't even make that kind of money when they're in their thirties and forties," Marcella said, picking up her shoulder sandwich.

"Honey, let me tell you," Sharon said, dousing her fries with ketchup. "I'd give it up in a second, if I could bring my mother and my grandparents back. Having a family to love and to spend time with is the real blessing. You have a mother, father, sister, and two children. Not to mention your aunts, uncles, and cousins. My mother was an only child, so I don't even have that. Now tell me, what are the chances of that happening to a person?"

"Well, if you want my opinion, I think you should seriously consider marrying Marcus. He's a good man, and he practically worships the ground that you walk on," Marcella said, taking another bite from her sandwich.

"I don't know what my problem is, because I do love him.

Maybe I'm just afraid of being hurt. I've always stood my own ground and taken care of myself. And I haven't depended on any-one for anything since my grandparents passed away."

"Marcus will still let you be yourself, and you know it. He's not the controlling type, and from what I can tell, he's the type of man that sort-of goes along with the program, not wanting to change the channel unless you say something better is on."

Sharon laughed for the first time since they'd taken their seats. "He's not that easy. Believe me, he can get an attitude just as quick as the rest of us, if you cross him."

"But that's normal. Everybody gets angry or irritated every once in a while, but overall, you know I'm right about him."

"Well, there is one thing, and you know I've mentioned it be-fore. The sex isn't that great. I mean, it's not terrible, but still it's not anything to jump up and down about, either."

"I'm sorry, but, girl, that is so hard for me to believe. Especially about a man that gorgeous," Marcella said, shaking her head.

"Well, believe it or not, it's true. And sometimes I feel so guilty for feeling that way because there's definitely more to a relation-ship than just sex."

"I don't know, Sharon," Marcella said, raising her eyebrows. "With a man like Marcus, I think I'd have to overlook that one lit-tle flaw."

"I keep trying to, but it's hard. But, enough about me. What's going on with you?" Sharon asked, taking a sip of her lemonade.

"Not much. I haven't spoken with Tyrone more than once since he clowned my mother a few weeks ago, but he has been paying his child support on time. And to tell you the truth, that's all I want from him."

"You know, I really hate that things turned out the way they did for the two of you. I can't help but remember how in love you guys were when we were in high school. Every girl that went to school with us envied you. Tyrone was the man back in the day," Sharon said, laughing.

"Maybe so, but now he's nothing but a low-down, conniv-ing dog."

"I know what you're saying. I despise any man who tries to dodge his responsibility to his children."

"He's been working for the electric company as an electrician ever since he finished that apprenticeship program at the community college, so I know he's making decent money. But he still has the nerve to come up with every excuse in the book as to why he can't take care of his children. And the only reason he's doing it now, is because I threatened to take him back to court," Marcella said and bit into two fries at the same time.

"I don't blame you. That fool should be paying more than sixty dollars a week for two kids anyway. Plain old highway robbery is what that is."

"I know, but if he messes up one more time, and I do mean one more time, we're going to court."

"I know you would rather not go to court, but for Ashley and Nick's sake, I hope he does mess up, so you can finally get what's rightfully yours."

"Girl, what I really need is someone to hold me at night. You say you get lonely, but you don't know what being lonely is until you've had to sleep alone every single night for the last . . . I don't even know how many years it's been," Marcella said, laughing slightly. "And even though Ashley and Nicholas mean everything in this world to me, sometimes my life feels empty. Plus, I wish I could give them so much more."

"You'll find someone to fall in love with, you just have to be patient. But in the meantime, what you need to do is go back to school. Go get your degree, girl. You're too smart not to."

"I don't know if I can handle cutting my hours to part-time, because who knows when Tyrone will start acting scrappy with his payments again. And between working, going to class, and doing homework, I would hardly see my babies at all during the weekdays."

"I understand your point, but if you want to give them a better life, you might have to sacrifice some of your time. In the long run, you'll be glad you did. Maybe Tyrone will keep them in the evenings at his house. And you know his mother will do whatever she can to help you out."

"Tyrone? Are you kidding? He'll refuse to do it, just to spite me."

"Well, you do have your mother and Racquel. And don't forget me," Sharon said, smiling.

"I know. It's definitely something to think about, because Lord knows, I'm not getting any younger. And on top of that, I've got to find some way to make more money, so I can start saving for Ashley's and Nicholas's college educations. Because the last thing I want is for them to end up with some low-paying job."

"I'm telling you, Marcella, call and make an appointment with an admissions counselor at CU. At least, then, you can see what your options are and what they have to offer."

"Maybe I will. If I get a chance, I'll call this afternoon," Marcella said, leaning back in the chair.

They chatted a while longer and finally Marcella glanced at her watch. It was almost ten minutes to one. "Shoot, I'd better start heading back. Those phones will be ringing off the hook, if I don't," she said, pushing her chair away from the table.

"Yeah, I need to head downtown myself," Sharon said, standing up. Since she was between offices, though, she really didn't have a particular time to be back.

"I'll talk to you later on. I might stop by this evening to see what you found out from the university."

"Okay, I'll see you then. Oh, and thanks again for lunch."

"No problem," Sharon said, getting into her car.

Marcella turned her ignition, but nothing happened. She turned it again and again, and still, nothing happened. She groaned. "Come on. Not today. I need to get back to work." She calmed herself down, turned the ignition again, and breathed a sigh of relief when it started. Sharon was still waiting to make sure it did. Marcella waved at her and left the parking lot.

"That was a close call," Marcella thought as she drove down the street. If something went wrong with her car, where was she going to get the money to fix it? Money, money, money. Maybe Sharon was right after all. Maybe what she needed *was* a four-year degree, and she decided that this day would not end without her checking into it.

Chapter 6

The mere sight of Covington Park University's campus gave
Marcella a warm feeling, and she could tell she'd made the
right decision in scheduling a counseling session for possible admission. It was already the end of April, but if everything went okay
with the application process, she'd be starting classes in less than
four months.

She entered the building where the office of admissions was located, climbed two flights of stairs, and walked down the hallway,
searching for Room 300. Once she found it, she walked in. A
blond-haired girl, who looked to be in her mid-twenties, was sitting
behind the desk. Marcella assumed she was the receptionist and
walked over to her.

"Hi, my name is Marcella Jones, and I'm here for a two o'clock
appointment with Mrs. Harrison."

The receptionist searched through the appointment book, and
Marcella looked on as she crossed through her name with a black-
ink pen. "If you'll have a seat, she'll be with you shortly."

"Thank you," Marcella said, smiling.

After sitting down, she gazed around the room and noticed that
three other women were already seated. If that's what you could
call them. They didn't look to be much older than high-school seniors. Suddenly she felt uneasy. Almost embarrassed. Here she

was, barely two weeks away from turning twenty-nine, and had the nerve to be sitting here with these young teenaged girls, who had their whole lives ahead of them. Just the sight of them made her feel like an old woman, and she didn't like it one bit. What was she doing here, anyway? She wished she'd had better sense than to let Sharon talk her into this, but four weeks ago it hadn't seemed like such a bad idea.

"Kayla Johnson?" a short, partially bald gentleman said, eye-searching the waiting area. The tall Black girl dropped what looked to be an old issue of *Seventeen* down on the table, stood up, and walked toward him. He introduced himself, shook the girl's hand, and they both proceeded toward his office.

Marcella looked at her watch and noticed that it was five minutes past her appointment time. She'd barely gotten there on time herself, but she resented with a passion the idea of waiting. She was already getting restless, and she wished this Mrs. Harrison would get a move on. What was the point of scheduling an appointment if the session wasn't going to start on time? If it hadn't been for all the White employees running around the department, she'd have easily blamed it on CP time. She sighed deeply with frustration.

After another ten minutes had passed, the second and third girls were called in by two additional counselors, but Marcella remained waiting. This was ridiculous. Here it was 2:30 P.M., and still, she hadn't been called in. Had she known this, she'd have worked another half hour. Her nerves were already twirling every which way, and all this waiting was making things worse. When she finally couldn't take it any longer, she strutted over to the reception desk. "I've been waiting for almost thirty minutes now. Can you tell me how much longer Mrs. Harrison is going to be?" Marcella asked with no smile on her face.

"Let me check," the receptionist said reluctantly.

As she dialed the first two digits of Mrs. Harrison's extension, Marcella noticed a middle-aged, professionally dressed Black woman approach the waiting area.

"Marcella Jones?"

Well, it was about time. "Hi," Marcella said, forcing a smile on her face.

"I'm Mrs. Harrison," the counselor said, extending her hand to Marcella.

"Nice to meet you," Marcella said.

"My office is through this door, so if you'll follow me, we can get started."

Marcella followed Mrs. Harrison's lead, but something didn't feel right. This woman didn't seem too friendly, and she hoped this didn't mean trouble.

They walked until they reached the last office on the left side of the hallway. The office had a desk and chair that looked to be fifteen to twenty years old, and the carpet didn't appear to be much newer. Marcella had never been inside any university office, but she had expected a lot more glamour. But then, this was a state-funded university, and she was sure their tax dollars only went so far.

"So, Marcella Jones, you're interested in enrolling at the university this fall?"

"Yes, I am," Marcella answered, repositioning her body from the left side of the chair to the right.

"Well, what I'd like to do first is find out a little more about you, review your entrance exam with you, and explain the entire application process. So, why don't you tell me a little about yourself."

Marcella didn't know what else she could tell her that wasn't on her application, but she decided to give her the basic intro. "I graduated from Eisenhower High almost eleven years ago in the top ten percent of my class, and I've been employed with Nicosia and Associates for the past two years as a receptionist."

"Are you married?"

What difference did that make? Those sort of questions were illegal when it came to job interviews, and she couldn't see where it should be any different with this. "No, I'm not."

"Any children?" the counselor asked, leaning back in her chair and slightly rocking.

This woman was crazy. Who did she think she was anyway, sitting there with her nose all stuck up in the air like she was God's gift to the world? Marcella wanted to ask her what her problem was, but her better judgment led her to respond differently. "Yes, two," she answered with no excitement in her voice.

"Well, the reason I'm asking you all of these questions is because I want you to be aware of how time consuming it will be going to classes and completing your assignments. And it will take even more determination for you than most because you've been away from school for so long and you have two children to take care of."

What did she think she was, stupid? This woman was really pushing it. "I'm aware of what it'll take, but this is still what I want to do. My employers have agreed to let me work part-time in the afternoons, and since my children are eight and ten, they're both in school all day."

The counselor looked at her doubtfully. "Your test scores were higher than most of the high-school seniors who take this exam," she said, skimming over Marcella's test scores.

Marcella had forgotten all about the entrance exam. At first she'd been nervous about it, but when she'd finished, she'd felt good about it. As a matter of fact, it had come pretty easy to her. "Thank you."

"That's unusual. I mean, you've been out of school since, what? 1982?"

"Yes," Marcella answered, trying to figure out what Mrs. Harrison was trying to get at. She hoped she wasn't insinuating that she'd cheated.

"And it says here that you want to complete a degree in accounting."

"That's right. I've wanted to be an accountant for as long as I can remember, and even more so after I began working for an accounting firm."

"Those are some pretty tough courses. They require lots of analytical thinking and strong perseverance. Have you had any accounting courses in the past?"

If she had, would she be sitting here going back and forth with *her* pompous behind? Why was this woman trying so hard to intimidate her? And she was a sister, too. She'd thought this whole meeting was supposed to be informative and encouraging, but instead it was turning out to be nothing less than total humiliation.

"No, I've never had any accounting courses, but I'm very good with numbers, and the partners that I work for think I would be good at accounting based on what I've learned on the job. Sometimes they give me some of the smaller projects when their junior accountants get overloaded with work."

"Going to class and taking exams are a lot different from on-the-job assignments."

"I'm aware of that," Marcella said, starting to lose her temper. "And I'm also aware that getting a degree doesn't mean anything, if you can't perform a job in the real world. I work at one of the most prestigious accounting firms in the area, and the guys that I work for think I'm the perfect candidate to pursue an accounting degree. And I tend to listen to them, because they're not just outsiders looking in. They're certified public accountants who have been in business for years and obviously have plenty of experience in the field," Marcella said and felt good afterward.

"Well, have you thought about the cost of tuition and books? College is expensive, and I suspect that over the next four years, the cost will climb even higher than where it is now."

"I earn seven dollars an hour, and I have two children. And from what I've researched so far, I should be more than eligible for some sort of financial aid. Grants, and even loans if necessary. I'll do whatever I have to. If the government is good enough to loan me the money while I'm going to school, I figure I'll be more than able to pay them back once I'm a CPA," Marcella said confidently.

The counselor didn't comment, and it was obvious that she was irritated.

Marcella continued. "Now that you have my application for admission and the results from my entrance exam, what else do I need to complete the admission process?"

"You still have to take the ACT exam, which should be coming up in a few weeks. Hopefully, there's still time for you to get your registration form and fees in before the deadline."

"Do you have any of the registration forms here?"

The counselor hesitated, and Marcella dared her to say she didn't have any. She pulled out the form from her left-hand drawer and passed it to Marcella without even looking at her. Without even the slightest comment. But Marcella didn't care, just so long as she'd given it to her.

"So, is that it?" Marcella said sternly.

"For now. However, *if* you pass the ACT exam, you'll need to come back so we can put together your first-semester schedule."

Hmmph. I'll be back, but I won't be meeting with you, Marcella thought.

"Well, thank you so much for your time," Marcella said, standing up.

"Thank you for coming in," Mrs. Harrison said, gazing down at her desk.

Marcella couldn't believe what had just happened. This woman had turned her first college experience into a total nightmare. She'd done and said everything she could to discourage her from enrolling at the university, and Marcella couldn't understand why. This sort of thing happened all the time when a young Black woman was trying to get ahead in White corporate America, but this was a Black woman she'd been talking with. She had a lot of nerve, and she'd obviously forgotten who she was. That expensive suit and classy hairdo didn't mean jack. And regardless of how educated she was and how much money she made, she was still Black, and nothing was going to change that. Instead of trying to intimidate Marcella, she should have been doing everything she could to help her, and then some.

As Marcella left the main entrance of the counseling department, heading down the main corridor, she realized that she'd forgotten to ask for a college catalog. So, she turned around and went back into the waiting area. "I forgot to get a college catalog from Mrs. Harrison. Do you think I could run back to her office to get one?" she asked the receptionist.

"Sure, go ahead," the receptionist said, picking up the phone to answer a call.

As Marcella walked closer to Mrs. Harrison's office, she noticed that the door was closed halfway. She raised her fist and was about to knock, until she heard her talking on the phone.

"It really pisses me off when I see these welfare women getting over the way they do. I just met with one who thinks she's going to conquer the world. She claims to be working at some accounting firm, but I know she's lying. She's just like all the rest, laid up on welfare, collecting money and medical benefits that people like you and I are paying for. Now she's going to take it even further by using government grants to go to school scot-free. Nobody gave us any breaks like that. I worked my behind off while I was going to school, and it hasn't been that long since I paid all my student loans off."

Marcella bucked her eyes wide, shaking her head in disagreement and covered her mouth with her hand.

Mrs. Harrison continued. "And you should see the score she got on this entrance exam that we require all students to take. It was so high, that it doesn't take a rocket scientist to figure out that she cheated. No Black girl that I can think of, living on Covington Park's west side, could possibly be that smart. Especially if she was stupid enough to get pregnant in the first place. And you know she can't be too bright, if she made the same stupid mistake twice."

The deeper Marcella fell in thought, the more Mrs. Harrison's voice faded. Marcella's heart dropped to her stomach, and her eyes filled with tears, which couldn't be controlled. Why was this woman criticizing her the way that she was? And why was she so bitter? Yes, she'd been on welfare a long time ago, and yes, she still received a small allotment of food stamps from time to time, but she worked forty hours a week like everyone else did. She didn't earn a lot, but it was honest work and the best she could do, considering the fact that she didn't have any education past high school. Which was the sole reason why she'd come here in the first place.

"Miss?" the short, bald gentleman she'd seen earlier said, standing behind her.

Marcella jumped and turned to face him.

"Are you okay? Is there something I can help you with?"

"Um. No. I mean, yes, I forgot to ask Mrs. Harrison for a college catalog, but now she's on the phone."

"Oh, I can get that for you from my office. Wait here," the man said, looking at her strangely.

Marcella pulled a tissue from her black shoulder purse and wiped her face during his absence.

When he returned to the hallway, he passed her the current catalog and a copy of the fall-semester course schedule. "Here you go."

"Thank you so much, Mr. . . . ."

"I'm Mr. Dahl, another one of the counselors here. Are you sure you're okay? You seem to be upset about something," he said in a concerned and caring manner.

She didn't know whether to blow the whistle on this witch or pretend that she hadn't heard anything. And who was going to believe that one Black woman was trying to discriminate against another, anyway? "Mr. Dahl, could I have one of your business cards, just in case I have questions or need more information?"

"Didn't Mrs. Harrison give you one?"

"No. And to be honest, I'd prefer she didn't."

Mr. Dahl gazed at her, but then pulled a business card holder from his shirt pocket and gave her one of his cards.

"Thank you," she said, sniffling as she prepared to walk away.

Marcella turned and headed toward the main entrance again, and this time continued all the way out of the building. She wasn't sure how a person could feel happy about attending college, excited about pursuing an accounting degree, pissed off at some snotty counselor, and sad about her low-income situation all at the same time, but she did know two things for sure. She'd be attending Covington Park University in the fall, and graduating with an accounting degree four years from now. And no one, absolutely no one, was going to prevent her from doing just that.

Marcella removed three, plump hot dogs from the portable electric grill, placed one each on her and the children's plates, and removed three hot-dog buns from a plastic bag. This wasn't at all what she wanted for dinner, but since the children had practically begged her to cook them, she decided to go along with their request. Plus, with everything that had gone on at the university, she wasn't in the mood for fixing anything else. A few hours had passed since the incident had taken place, but her feelings were still pretty hurt. She couldn't wait to tell Sharon about it, and she was going to call her as soon as she finished her meal.

When they'd all finished eating, Ashley placed the dishes in the sink and started running the dish water, while Nicholas went to his room to begin his homework. Marcella went in her bedroom to call Sharon.

"Hello?" Sharon answered on the second ring.

"Hey, girl," Marcella said, sitting down on the edge of her bed.

"Hey. We must have been thinking on the same wavelength, because I was just about to call you as soon as I finished heating up Marcus and me some leftovers."

"Oh, I didn't know you had company. Tell Marcus I said hey. And you can call me back later, if you want to."

"Girl, you know Marcus doesn't mind. And you know I'm dying to know how things went at the university today, anyway."

"Well, to make a long story short, it went horrible."

"What do you mean?" Sharon asked, sounding serious.

"First of all, the counselor I met with gave me the third degree about my personal life, and pretty much did everything she could to try and discourage me from enrolling into the accounting program. Then after I left her office, I realized I didn't get a school catalog, so I went back. And when I stepped in front of her office door, which was cracked, I heard her talking to someone on the phone. And, girl, she was practically tearing me apart."

"Wait a minute. Did you know this woman?"

"No, but she was going on and on about how I must've cheated on the entrance exam because no one like me could have scored so high otherwise. And that she was sick of paying for welfare women like me who basically get everything scot-free."

"Pah-leeze! Why was she saying you were on welfare?" Sharon asked, totally appalled at what she was hearing.

"Because she said she knew I was lying about working for some accounting firm. And this is the best part. This witch has the nerve to be Black. Can you believe that?"

"You have got to be kidding, Marcella."

"No, she's just as Black as you and I, but you'd never know it, with the way she was acting toward me."

"So, did you confront her or what?"

"No, because the whole thing really caught me completely off guard, and before I knew it, I was in tears. But, of course, now I wish I had said something."

"Well, it's not too late, if you ask me. And to tell you the truth, if it were me, I would report her butt to the department head, university president, or somebody. Because there's no telling how many other times she's gotten away with treating people like this. What she needs is to be put in her little place."

"I know. My feelings are still hurt over this whole mess."

"Girl, I wouldn't pay her a bit of attention. You're the last person to try and get over on somebody. I mean, you're a decent person, you always try to do the right thing, and you treat other people the way you want to be treated, so what does that woman know, anyway?"

"Nothing. But with the way she was talking, you'd have thought she knew everything about everybody."

"Well, I hope she hasn't changed your mind about going back to school in the fall, because I know if you go, you'll do well."

"Oh, don't get me wrong. My feelings may be a little hurt, but

I'm not about to let her or anyone else keep me from getting an education. I made that decision before I even left the campus."

"Good, because I'm telling you, this will be the best thing for you. Just wait and see."

"I know, and I can't thank you enough for being so supportive because it really means a lot to me."

"I'm behind you one hundred percent, and I'm here for you whenever you need something. Regardless of what it is."

"I know, but hey, I'm gonna let you get back to Marcus, okay?" Marcella said, standing up.

"Alright, but call me if you need to talk, okay?"

"I will."

"I'm serious, Marcella."

"I know you are, and you know I'll call if I need to."

"Okay, then, I'll talk to you tomorrow."

"See ya," Marcella said and hung up the phone. She felt better already.

Chapter 7

Racquel pulled the seat belt across her stomach, snapped it down near her waist on her right side, and turned the ignition of the pure-white, gold-packaged Camry. As she headed out of the school parking lot, a feeling of nervousness took control of her. She'd been on pins and needles ever since she'd made the appointment with the infertility specialist one month ago, but now she wasn't so sure she wanted to go through with it. She still wanted a baby more than anything, but she couldn't help but wonder how she was going to feel if the doctor determined that she was unable to carry a fetus to full term. And as much as she hated herself for thinking it, a part of her wished that it was Kevin who had the problem. It wouldn't make things any better, but at least she wouldn't feel so much like a failure. But in reality, she knew it couldn't be him, because if it had been, she never would have gotten pregnant the first time.

She continued cruising down the street until she came to the first stoplight. As she sat there, an old woman pushing a cart crossed the street staring at her. It was the end of April, and while there was still a slight chill in the air, it wasn't cold enough for all that the lady had on. A pair of corduroy pants, which was clearly two sizes too large, a dingy-looking sweatshirt, and a plaid wool coat trimmed with fake fur around the collar and the end of the sleeves. The cart was filled with everything from empty milk jugs to worn-out dresses. Racquel felt sorry for her and wanted to help her. It was so sad how some people were burdened with the worst situations, while others seemed to practically walk on water. A person could be homeless or living comfortable in a mansion, struggling on welfare or employed as a CEO of some corporation, blessed with a house full of children or not able to have any at all.

She exhaled deeply. Why did everything always have to point back to her own situation? Why couldn't she just leave well enough alone and be happy with what she had? It seemed easy enough when she offered that advice to her sister and everyone else. But no matter how she weighed it, there could never be any real happiness for her without children.

As she drove into the parking lot of the infertility clinic, she spotted Kevin waiting patiently in their Ford Explorer. He was such a good husband. She didn't know how she would have gotten through the miscarriage and all the unsuccessful trying without him. All he seemed to care about was her, and she loved him for it, but their marriage alone just wasn't enough for her. She wished to God that it was, but it wasn't. She simply could not be content with the way things were. No matter how much she loved and trusted him, she always felt like something was missing. But maybe, things would start to look up after today. Maybe the specialist would have the answer to all her prayers.

"How long have you been here?" she asked, shutting the car door.

"About five minutes or so, not too long," he said, walking toward her.

He pulled the glass door open, waited for Racquel to step inside, and followed behind her. Racquel stepped up to the sliding glass window, wrote her name on the registration sheet, and sat down next to Kevin. Racquel was shocked when she noticed that no other patients were waiting in the reception area. She knew it wasn't because she and Kevin were the only ones having trouble with getting pregnant; she'd seen and read too many articles about it. Not to mention the women she heard talking about it from time to time. So, maybe this was just a slow day.

"Mrs. Wilson, since this is your first time, I need you to complete a medical-history form for us, and then, I'll need to get a Xerox copy of your insurance card," the young secretary said, looking in Racquel's direction.

Racquel walked back up to the window, reached for the clipboard, which had the medical-history form attached to it, and returned to her seat to fill it out.

On the first page were basic questions like what her name was, where she lived, what her phone number was, and who to contact in case of an emergency. When she came to the second, there were loads of questions asking about not just what she'd had as far as infections, diseases, and surgeries, but what her immediate family members had had or did have, as well. She checked yes or no to each of the ones she was sure of, and left the others blank. When she finished, she pulled her insurance card from her wallet, proceeded back up to the window, and passed everything to the secretary.

The secretary made a copy of the insurance card and returned it to Racquel. "The doctor will be with you shortly."

"Thank you," Racquel said and sat back down next to Kevin, who was thumbing through *Prevention* magazine.

"They've got some pretty interesting articles in here. I wouldn't mind getting this on a regular basis."

"Yeah, I've heard they have excellent information on health," Racquel said hesitantly. She didn't want to encourage him too much, because the last thing they needed was another magazine subscription. They already received more than they ever had time to read through: *Essence, Ebony, Ebony Man, Jet, Black Enterprise, Body & Soul, Better Homes and Gardens.* Not to mention every baby magazine available to mankind. Some of these she'd subscribed to herself, but most of them had been ordered by Kevin from the various sweepstakes organizations. He wholeheartedly believed that there was a much better chance at winning the grand prize if you purchased the magazines they offered than if you simply returned the entry blank all by itself. Especially since one of the sweepstakes he'd entered last year came with two separate return envelopes. One addressed to Georgia if you weren't purchasing any magazines, and the other to some location in Florida if you were. And of course, ever since that day, he'd been convinced of his theory.

When Racquel noticed the words "Blessings Come In All Sizes" printed across an old issue of *Working Mother,* she picked it up and turned straight to the index to see what page the article was on. She scanned down the page with her forefinger until she found it and turned to page 52. The article had been written by a thirty-seven-year-old woman who'd experienced a miscarriage about a year ago, and had finally come to the conclusion that instead of dwelling on what she didn't have, it was much healthier to pour all of her energy into what she did have, before she lost that. A beautiful three-year-old son, and a husband who loved both of them.

The story ended with the woman stressing how months and months of therapy had changed her way of life and thinking in general. She was finally at a point in her life where she no longer worried about what she didn't have, but instead showed thanks and appreciation for what she did.

Racquel closed the article with disappointment. Partly because she'd thought the article was something completely different from what it was, but mostly because this woman made it sound like there was no hope. That you simply had to give up and accept things the way they were.

But, Racquel wasn't buying into that. She'd come too far and tried too hard to even think on those terms, and she wasn't going to. Regardless of what Kevin, Marcella, and her mother thought, she wasn't obsessed. She just knew what she wanted and had more determination than most people when it came to getting it.

"Mr. and Mrs. Wilson," an attractive-looking caramel-complexioned nurse called out. Kevin and Racquel rose from their seats and walked through the door behind her.

"I'm Dr. Reed's nurse, Vivian."

"Nice to meet you," Racquel said, smiling.

"Is it okay if I call you Racquel?" the nurse asked. "We like being on a first-name basis with our patients because it usually makes them feel a lot more comfortable."

"That's fine."

"The first thing I need to do is get your weight," the nurse asked, pointing toward the scale. Racquel set her purse down on the carpet, removed her brown leather pumps, and stepped up onto the black rubbery platform. She didn't know why she always took off her shoes because if a person was overweight, shoes weren't going to make that much of a difference anyhow.

"One forty-one," the nurse said, jotting it down inside Racquel's newly created chart. "You can have a seat in the second room on the right, and I'll be in to review your medical-history form and to get some additional information."

Once they arrived in the room, Racquel hopped up on the tan table, which had shiny white paper running down the center of it. Kevin sat down in the orange plastic chair. They looked at each other, smiling, but didn't speak.

"Okay," the nurse said, entering the examination room. "You're here for an infertility consultation, right?"

"Yes," Racquel said, sounding nervous.

"Actually, if you like, you can take a seat in the chair next to your husband, because we won't be examining you until after the consultation with Dr. Reed," the nurse said, skimming through the form.

Racquel took a seat next to Kevin, and the nurse leaned against the table facing them.

"Are you currently on any medications?"

"No," Racquel said, realizing she must have missed that question by mistake.

"Is there any history of endometriosis in your family?"

"No. Not that I'm aware of."

"Have there been any miscarriages?"

"Yes. Last year."

"How far along were you?" the nurse asked, looking at Racquel.

"Almost at the end of my first trimester."

"As far as you know, has anyone else in your family had problems with infertility?"

No, she thought. Just me. I'm the only one with this stupid problem. "No. My mother had two children, and so did my sister, but there were no problems that I know of."

"Okay. I think that covers just about everything," the nurse said, quickly scanning the form a second time. "If you'll follow me, I'll show you to Dr. Reed's office."

Once they were seated, Racquel's eye wandered around the entire office. It was simply gorgeous. It was more like a study, office, living room, and family room combined with all the books, office equipment, furniture, and exercise equipment. Dr. Reed's office wasn't much different from being at home. And it must have cost a fortune to furnish something so elaborate. But then, he was an infertility specialist who performed services that sometimes escalated into the thousands per patient. So, it was obvious that he could afford it.

Kevin sat in the chair looking straight ahead waiting for the good doctor to enter. He didn't seem the least bit excited, and Racquel wanted to ask him why he was so quiet. This could be the best day of their lives, and here he was acting as if it was some normal workday. She couldn't understand him at all. Especially after all they'd gone through. They were finally going to reap their reward. She was sure his attitude would be a lot different, though, once he heard everything the doctor had to say.

"Good afternoon. I'm Dr. Reed," he said, extending his hand first to Kevin and then Racquel. "Kevin and Racquel Wilson, correct?"

"That's us," Racquel said, smiling.

They both shook the doctor's hand one after the other. Then Dr. Reed, who was tall, broad-shouldered, and had salt-and-pepper hair, walked around his desk and took a seat in the burgundy leather high-back chair.

"I just reviewed your chart, and I think the first thing we need to do is schedule some testing to make sure there isn't some special reason why you haven't been able to conceive, or in your case, carry a child to full term." Dr. Reed looked at Racquel and Kevin, his eyes moving from one to the other. "Do you have any specific questions before we discuss some of the procedures you might be a candidate for?"

Racquel looked at Kevin. "Is there anything you'd like to know more about?"

"No. Not really, except how much all of this is going to cost," Kevin said with his eyes gazing in the direction of the doctor.

Racquel could just kill him. Who cared how much money this was all going to cost? She knew she didn't. And why did he always have to be so straightforward? Just couldn't beat around the bush or show some discretion like most people. And she didn't know what was wrong with him now anyway. He'd seemed perfectly fine this morning, and even appeared okay with all of this when they'd first arrived at the clinic. But now he was acting as if he didn't want to be there. She decided though, that Kevin Wilson was not going to rain on her much-awaited parade, and it was better just to ignore him.

"Well," Racquel said, pausing. "I'd like to know how long it will take before the test results are back?"

"It shouldn't take much longer than six weeks. That is, after we've run them all."

"What sort of tests will you be conducting?" Racquel asked.

"First, we'll do your initial examination, which will include a pelvic exam, and after that, we'll do a hysterosalpingogram, which is an X-ray of the uterus and the fallopian tubes. We'll also be doing some blood work to check for pelvic infections and to measure the levels of your thyroid, pituitary, and ovarian hormones. And if necessary, we'll do a vaginal ultrasound to check for proper ovulation and to make sure there are no fibroids or cysts. There are a number of tests we can do because there are a number of reasons why women have problems with getting pregnant. But at the same time you might fall into the category of women who have what we call 'unexplained infertility.' There's only a five to eight percent factor, but it's still a possibility," the doctor said, leaning back in his chair with his hands locked together, pivoting his chair from side to side.

Racquel felt comfortable with Dr. Reed. He was definitely knowledgeable in his area of expertise and seemed to be very caring. She'd just met him, but she already sensed that she could trust him. Which was important, because she'd always felt that a doctor should be just as personable and caring as he was competent.

"How soon do you think we can schedule the testing?" Racquel asked.

"Probably as early as next week, but Vivian will check the calendar and let you know before you leave today."

Dr. Reed glanced over at Kevin, who was still sitting in complete silence. He'd nodded his head a few times to acknowledge what the doctor was saying, but that was about it.

"And to answer your question about cost," Dr. Reed said to Kevin. "It really depends on what sort of infertility treatments and procedures we're talking about, because there's a variety of options. Using infertility drugs is the least expensive, but if we consider something like 'in vitro fertilization,' the cost can be as much as ten thousand dollars. And you might want to check with your health-insurance carrier because the State of Illinois has a mandate that requires all group insurances and HMO's to provide infertility coverage to patients who work for companies or organizations that employ twenty-five or more employees. You may have to fight hard to prove that this particular procedure is what *they* consider medically necessary, and that it's not a preexisting condition, but it's worth it."

Kevin nodded in acknowledgment and continued listening.

"It's hard to say until we know what we're dealing with."

"But there is a chance that the infertility drugs might do the trick?" Racquel asked hopefully.

"Yes, many of my patients have had success by using them, but then there's the chance of multiple births," Dr. Reed said.

"After struggling this hard, I don't think that will be a problem. But if it did happen, we'd still be just as happy," she said.

Kevin just smiled again, and he was making Racquel sick. As a matter of fact, she was downright embarrassed at the way he was acting. If she had known he was going to have such a messed-up attitude, she never would have asked him to come in the first place. And if he didn't cut it out real soon, she was going to let him have it as soon as they made their way back out to the parking lot.

"Also," Dr. Reed said to Kevin, "we'll need to do a semen analysis on you to check for sperm motility, which is the sperm's ability to swim; sperm count, which is the number of sperm per cubic centimeter of semen; and the sperm shape, to make sure the sperm has an oval head and a long tail, which is necessary to properly penetrate an egg."

Kevin did his usual nod and forced another fake smile.

"So, if that's it, we'll step outside the office so Vivian can get you scheduled. I usually like to do an initial exam, but I think we can just wait and do everything next week."

They all walked outside the doctor's office and waited for the nurse to check his schedule.

"We have an opening next Tuesday morning at eight A.M."

"Let's see," Racquel said, thinking if that date and time were okay. "Do you know how long I'll be here?"

"I'd say at least two hours or so. Give or take."

"That should be fine. I just need to make sure the school finds a substitute for my class during the morning."

"Our lab will be doing some blood work, so you'll need to fast at least twelve hours before the appointment."

Racquel didn't like the sound of that. She always had breakfast no matter what the situation was. Just didn't feel right throughout the day if she didn't. But then, she would have starved herself a whole week, if they'd asked her to. To tell the truth, she'd have done just about anything, if it meant they could help her with getting pregnant. "Sounds good," Racquel said.

As soon as they stepped outside to the parking lot, Racquel went off. "What was that all about?" she asked in an elevated, salty tone of voice.

"What was *what* all about?" Kevin asked, like he had no idea what she was talking about.

"You know what I mean. That attitude of yours. And that comment you made about the cost."

"He asked if we had any questions, and I told him what it was."

"But you acted as though you'd been forced here against your own will, and that made me look stupid."

"I told you I would come, and I did. I'm just not going to get my hopes up until I see something more concrete."

"How can anything positive happen with this, if your attitude stays like that? I don't believe you, because just a few weeks ago you said you were willing to try this, but now you're acting as if you couldn't care less."

"I haven't changed my mind, but I want you to understand that this is it."

"What do you mean, 'this is it'?" Racquel asked, squinting her eyes.

"If the infertility drugs don't work, we have to end all of this," Kevin said, noticing that the young couple who'd just stepped out of their car was staring, and he was slightly embarrassed.

Racquel felt total humiliation when she spotted the couple passing by them. This was ridiculous.

"This isn't the place for this, Kevin, so I'll see you at home," she said, walking toward her car without waiting for any response that he might have. Once she was in the car, she drove off without as much as even glancing back at him.

She hadn't gotten this angry since last year when she'd had the miscarriage, and Kevin kept insisting that everything happens for a reason, and that God didn't make mistakes. She'd heard it a zillion times from all their church members and most of her relatives. So by the time Kevin decided to bring those same two theories to her attention again, she'd had it up to here.

It wasn't that she didn't believe in God or that she was losing her faith in Him, but she just couldn't help but question why He allowed things to happen the way He did. And it wasn't just about her not being able to have children, either. What she wanted to know was why innocent people, especially children, were murdered for no reason at all. Why there was even such a thing as cancer, leukemia, and AIDS. And why on earth there were thousands of children starving and dying in almost every Third World country she could think of. It just didn't make sense. She knew it wasn't right, but she was angry at God. And anyway, who else could she blame all of her problems and shortcomings on?

As soon as that last thought passed through her mind, she regretted it. She wasn't by far Little-Miss-HolierThan-Thou, and didn't go to church every time the church doors swung open, but she'd been raised to fear God and everything He stood for. She could still remember all the times it stormed, when she, Marcella, and their mother unplugged every appliance and anything that looked to be electric from its outlet. Just in case the lightning struck it. And after they'd all rushed through the house trying to take care of that, they would all huddle together in one room, sitting quietly until it was all over. Racquel and Marcella had thought it was silly, but Corrine had stressed on more than one occasion that it was their duty to remain still until God finished His work.

Racquel pulled into the driveway, pressed the garage door opener, and continued into the garage to park. When she slid her key into the door leading to the kitchen, she heard the phone ringing.

"Hello?" Racquel answered in a rushed voice, with her purse still hanging from her shoulder.

"Racquel? This is Vivian, Dr. Reed's nurse."

"Oh, hi, Vivian."

"I'm sorry to bother you, but there was another question that you missed on the medical-history form. But I didn't want to ask you in front of your husband. So, if he's there, you can just answer yes or no, and we'll discuss the details when you come in next week."

Racquel felt like dropping the phone. And it took everything she had not to fall to the floor. For years she'd tried to forget that horrible day in December, just two months before her seventeenth birthday, but now it was being brought to the forefront, and there wasn't a thing she could do about it.

The nurse continued. "Have you ever had any induced abortions?"

Racquel's first instinct was to lie. Especially, since she was sure that having an abortion had nothing to do with her not getting pregnant. She'd proven that last year. But she knew if these people were going to help her, she had to be honest with them. Completely honest.

"Yes, I had one about thirteen years ago when I was seventeen."

"Was that the only one?"

Racquel sighed. What difference did that make? An abortion was an abortion, regardless of how many a person had had. "No. I had another one three years later when I was in college."

The nurse was silent at first, and then spoke. "Okay. That's what I needed to know. You take care, and we'll see you on Tuesday."

Racquel hung up the phone as best she could, but her hand was shaking like a leaf on a tree. What was going to happen if Kevin found out? He'd surely think the worst of her if he did, and their marriage would be over. She'd heard him on more than one occasion stress his opinion of women who killed babies. And he'd be convinced that this was the reason she wasn't able to have a baby.

She'd been young and dumb each time it happened, but she'd learned from her mistakes and paid for them. She'd thought.

She took a deep breath, stroked her hair from front to back with both of her hands, and rethought the whole situation. Maybe her secret was still intact, because from the sounds of what the nurse had said, this was strictly confidential. Something between her and them only. And since they weren't going to inform Kevin of anything, there really wasn't anything to worry about. Marcella knew about the first one, but she'd never even consider squealing on her own sister. Maybe she'd gotten herself all bent out of shape for nothing. In a few weeks, they'd find out what the problem was and would figure out how to help or correct it. But then, what if the abortions *were* the problem. And what if Kevin found out how she'd gotten pregnant the second time around. If he did, she'd never be able to face him. As a matter of fact, she'd never be able to face anyone ever again. No. What she had to do was keep her cool and pretend that this subject was nonexistent. Because if she didn't, everything was going to be ruined.

Chapter 8

For as long as Racquel could remember, her family had always gotten together for a huge cookout on the Fourth of July, and today the tradition was continuing. Years ago it had always taken place at her mother's house, but ever since she and Kevin had gotten married, they became the ones who hosted it. Thanks to Marcella and Corrine, who literally fell in love with their patio the very first time they laid eyes on it. "There's so much more room at your house," Corrine would say. "Girl, just think how much more space we could have if we do it at yours and Kevin's," Marcella would add in. But really, Racquel didn't mind, because she loved entertaining in the summertime. There was nothing better than grilled brats, chicken, and steak. And sitting outside breathing in all the fresh air was so exhilarating. As far as she was concerned, summertime could have lasted twelve months out of the year, and she would have been just fine with it. But she knew that was wishful thinking for any city within a hundred-mile radius of Chicago. This wasn't Florida, and she had long since learned to live with it.

She opened the white plastic Wal-Mart bag sitting on the table, pulled out the red, white, and blue napkins, matching cups, plates, and silverware, and lined them across the light-beige cabinet. She knew her mother was going to die when she saw all of the colored eating utensils and decorations Racquel had picked up the day before. Corrine didn't see a reason to spend all that money for one day out of the year, and the white paper and plastic products suited her just fine. She'd said that every year since they'd started having the Fourth of July cookout, and Racquel knew this year wasn't going to be any different. And maybe it *was* ridiculously expensive, but all of the colors seemed to make the atmosphere so much more interesting, and Racquel liked that.

She pulled open the refrigerator and scanned through it to make sure she hadn't forgotten anything. The potato salad was there, and so were the macaroni, fruit, and pasta salads. Corrine was bringing all of the beverages, breads, and condiments, and Marcella was cooking macaroni and cheese, and barbequed baked beans. Kevin had purchased the meat yesterday evening, and was just about finished grilling all of it.

As she closed the refrigerator door, she noticed a small card attached by a magnet bearing their auto insurance company's name. It was an appointment reminder for this coming Wednesday with her infertility specialist. A sadness engrossed her. Here she'd been taking this medication called Clomid for two months, and still wasn't the slightest bit pregnant. It was starting to seem like a waste of time, and a lot of unnecessary money. Dr. Reed kept insisting that it sometimes took a little longer for some patients than others, but she was sick of all this waiting, and her patience was starting to wear extremely thin. And of course, Kevin wouldn't even discuss any of the other methods like artificial insemination or in vitro fertilization because he said they were too costly. She agreed with him one hundred percent, and that was the reason why she suggested they take out a second mortgage, instead of spending their life savings, but he was still dead set against it. And it wasn't like she would forge his name or anything, so her hands were tied. If only their HMO would stop being so difficult. They'd approved payment for the medication, but when Dr. Reed had attempted to secure pre-approval for the other procedures, they'd flat out denied them. She and Kevin had filed an appeal, but so far, nothing had resulted from it. And she was afraid nothing was going to.

Racquel's emotions were high-strung. Sometimes she loved Kevin, but most of the time she hated the ground that he walked on. And she never knew when those feelings were going to come about. It simply depended on what day it was, and how she felt when she woke up in the morning.

She'd thought the medication would make a world of difference, since all of her test results had come back conclusive: There wasn't anything wrong with her, and there was no reason at all why she shouldn't eventually get pregnant.

And while it had only taken seven weeks to obtain the results, it had seemed like a whole year. For years she'd been in denial about the possibility of those two abortions being the problem, but it wasn't long before she convinced herself that maybe they *had* damaged her entire reproduction system. But when Dr. Reed confirmed that everything was kosher with both her and Kevin, she'd been happier than she had been in a long time.

But, she wasn't going to think about any of this today, and she was going to keep things as cordial as possible with Kevin. Holidays were supposed to be a happy time, and it wouldn't be fair to spoil the day for everyone else. Especially since it seemed like they were having more people this year than they'd ever had before. Her mother, Marcella, Ashley, and Nicholas. One of the new engineers that Kevin worked with and his wife. Marcella's best friend Sharon and her boyfriend, Marcus. And her mother's only and older sister, Clara, and her husband, Leroy.

Including her and Kevin, that made twelve people, not to mention the few drop-ins who claimed they didn't want anything but ended up eating more than the people who'd actually been invited. But Racquel never minded, because the more people that were there, the better time everyone seemed to have.

Kevin slid open the glass patio door, walked through it, placed some of the meat he'd cooked on top of the stove, pulled Racquel into his arms, and kissed her on her forehead.

Racquel was surprised. They'd had another falling out this morning when she'd brought up the artificialinsemination subject again, and they hadn't spoken a single word to each other since. But she was glad he was making the first move, because that meant he wasn't nearly as pissed off as she thought.

"What was that for? " she asked, glaring straight into his light-brown eyes.

"Baby, you know I hate it when we argue like this. And I feel even worse when we're not speaking to each other."

"I don't like it, either, but it seems like we've been doing it a lot lately."

"We've got to work this out, but today isn't the day for it."

She'd just decided the same thing herself and was glad to know that they agreed on at least something. "No. It's not."

"Baby, regardless of what you think, I do still love you," he said, hugging her firmly.

In all honesty, she wasn't sure if he did or not, but there was no sense in making any unnecessary waves. "I know you do, and I love you just the same," she said, laying her head against his chest.

He placed his finger under her chin, tilted her head up, and kissed her rough—the way she liked it. She kissed him back, and her heart became heavy. His beat so rapidly, that he was sure he was going to have a heart attack. They hadn't made love in over a week, and he wanted her right then and there. She wanted him just as badly. They kissed passionately, and cold chills ran through Racquel's entire body. Wild pulsations took control of his.

When he couldn't take it anymore, he tore off her white rayon shirt. See-through buttons flew all over the place, but neither of them paid any attention to it. He reached to pull his T-shirt off, and she quickly assisted him. Then he unzipped her black jean shorts and pushed them down her legs until they touched the floor. She stepped out of them. Now it was her turn. First she released the button of his pants, then pulled the zipper down as far as it would go. He slipped out of them without taking his eyes off her, pulled her toward him, and kissed her more passionately than he had the first time. She responded willingly.

He led her up the stairs to the master bedroom and turned the covers back on the bed. She sprawled across it, and he lay on top of her. They each moved back and forth, but in opposite directions, until they were both satisfied.

Tears flowed down each side of Racquel's face, and Kevin smiled at her, wiping them away. She'd thought for sure the passion between them was gone forever, and he basically felt the same. As of late, they'd only been going through the motions. Not because they longed for each other, but primarily because they needed to make a baby. And not only was there never any high-powered foreplay, like the kind they'd just given each other a short while ago, but it had gotten to the point where there was no foreplay at all. And they didn't hold each other the way they used to afterward, either. As a matter of fact, Kevin had become totally disgusted with Racquel lying on her back and pushing her butt upward, with her legs straight in the air, trying to help his semen make it all the way through to wherever it needed to be to get her pregnant. It had all become monotonous, and he'd become bored with it.

"Now, this is how it's supposed to be," Kevin said, still lying on top of her with his head lying to the side of hers.

"It was so wonderful, Kevin. We haven't made love like that since . . . Gosh, I can't even remember when," she said, kissing him on his shoulder.

They lay there for a few minutes in silence trying to recover from all the excitement. Kevin was exhausted, but he finally rolled over to his side, looked at Racquel, and shook his head. "Girl, I don't know what you've got down there, but I feel like falling into a coma."

"Please. It's no different than it's always been."

"Then, maybe I'm just getting old, because you've worn me completely out."

"At thirty years old? I don't think so," she said, laughing slightly.

"You might as well say I'm thirty-one. You know my birthday's next month. And come to think of it, so is yours."

"Don't remind me. You know how I feel about that subject."

Racquel glanced over at the digital clock on Kevin's side of the bed and saw that it was 12:15 P.M. "Oh, my God, everyone is supposed to be here at one," she said, jumping up from the bed.

"All we have to do is take a shower. We've got plenty of time," he said, closing his eyes, obviously not wanting to get up.

"Did you finish all the meat?"

As soon as he heard the question, he bucked his eyes wide open. He'd left an entire package of bratwurst on the grill before he'd come into the house. "Oh, shoot. I forgot about those brats," he said, pulling his robe from the chair, where he'd left it that morning. He slipped it on, and raced down the stairs as fast as he could.

When he opened the lid to the triple-rack gas grill, an enormous cloud of smoke forced its way out right into his face. He coughed uncontrollably for a few seconds and then looked down to see if the meat had been ruined. And it had. He turned each of the two flame controls off, and forked the brats into the pan lined with aluminum foil. Then he turned the knob on top of the gas-filled tank until it was completely closed.

They had more than enough meat to go around, so he wasn't

going to worry about it. He walked into the kitchen, dumped the brats into the garbage container, picked up his and Racquel's clothing, and headed back upstairs to take his shower.

As soon as Racquel slipped on her full-length, sleeveless red dress, she went back down to the kitchen. When she arrived, the doorbell rang. "Goodness. We just barely made it," she said out loud to herself, walking to the front door.

"Hey, girl," Marcella said, walking through the door with a long, white baking dish covered with clear plastic wrapping. She was dressed in a rayon white summer jumpsuit.

"Hey, sis," Racquel said, already turning her attention to her niece and nephew. "How're my babies doing?" she asked.

"I'm good, Aunt Racquel. How are you?" Ashley said, following her mother with a medium-sized clear baking dish filled with macaroni and cheese.

"Fine," Nicholas said in a low tone, with a pout on his face.

"What's the matter with you, sweetheart?" Racquel asked, placing her arm around him. They walked side by side into the kitchen.

"Nothing," he lied.

"Marcella, what's wrong with Nicholas?" Racquel asked.

"I don't know, but if he doesn't get rid of that little attitude, there really will be something wrong with him."

"He's just mad because Mom wouldn't let him get a candy bar when we stopped at the store," Ashley said, laughing.

"Shut up, Ashley!" Nicholas yelled.

"Look," Marcella said, pointing her finger at him. "I'm not going to have this today, Nicholas. I told you, your aunt Sharon is bringing over two different desserts, and you can have some of that after you eat dinner. And that's that."

Nicholas changed his whole tune as soon as he saw the I'm-not-playing-with-you look on his mother's face.

"Now, you apologize to your aunt Racquel for acting like this," Marcella told him.

"I'm sorry, Aunt Racquel," he said.

"That's okay, sweetheart," Racquel said to Nicholas, and then turned her attention to Marcella. "Girl, he doesn't have to apologize for something like that."

See, it was exactly this kind of thing that pissed Marcella off.

Racquel brushed off everything the children did, regardless of how serious it was. If it had been left up to her, the children would have never been disciplined at all. But instead of telling her to mind her own business, she decided to look over her. It just wasn't worth going into it.

"So, did you talk to Mom this morning?" Marcella asked.

"Actually, I spoke with her twice. She said she was going to be here by one, but maybe she decided to wait for Aunt Clara and Uncle Leroy, and you know they're never on time for anything," Racquel said.

"That's for sure," Marcella said, laughing. "Uncle Leroy is always saying how he's not about to rush his life away like the rest of us. And he doesn't."

"But it's kind of irritating when you're trying to keep the food warm. It's not so bad with the meat, because we eat that at room temperature anyway, but for the macaroni and cheese and baked beans, you have to keep reheating it."

"Aunt Racquel, how come all these buttons are on the floor?" Nicholas interrupted, picking them up one by one.

Racquel couldn't believe she'd forgotten about the buttons, and she should have known Kevin hadn't thought twice about them, either. She had to come up with something quick, but she had no idea what. Maybe she could pretend she hadn't heard him. "So what kind of dessert is Sharon bringing?" Racquel asked Marcella.

"Buttons?" Marcella said in a confused tone of voice. "Let me see," she said, reaching her hand out to Nicholas.

"See," he said, showing his mother.

"Aunt Racquel, where did they come from?" Nicholas said, figuring that even though his mother *had* heard him, maybe his aunt Racquel *hadn't*.

"Oh, from my sewing box. I dropped it earlier, and a bunch of buttons fell out. I guess I missed a few," Racquel answered in a squirrelly tone of voice.

Marcella looked at her suspiciously, because these definitely weren't stray buttons, or the extras you got when you purchased something new from a clothing store. They were all alike. Something was wrong with Racquel's story, but at the same time she couldn't tell what the truth was, either.

"Ooooh," Ashley said, cracking up with laughter. "Look at all those brats Uncle Kevin burned up," she said, pointing at the plastic garbage container.

Racquel felt like running for her life. She loved her niece and nephew, but why did they have to be so nosey? Of course, they had no idea what was going on, but it was just a matter of time before Marcella put two and two together and figured out exactly what had really happened. "Yeah, he sure did," Racquel responded, laughing innocently.

Marcella could barely keep a straight face as it was, but when Kevin entered the room, she burst out laughing. "What's up, Kevin?"

"Hey, sister-in-law," he said, wondering what was so funny.

"Hey, Uncle Kevin," Nicholas said, hugging him.

"Hey, little man, what's goin' on?" Kevin said, grabbing Nicholas playfully in a headlock.

"Hi, Uncle Kevin," Ashley said, still laughing.

"Hey, Little Miss Giggles," Kevin said, hugging Ashley. "And what's so funny, anyway?"

"You burned up all that meat," Ashley said, looking at Nicholas, who started laughing right along with her.

"Oh, so you two are making fun of my cooking, huh?"

"Yep," the two children answered in unison.

Marcella looked at Kevin and thought, Yeah, right. She couldn't believe him and Racquel. Two grown people tearing their clothes off in the middle of the day like wild savages. Acting like they'd just met two weeks ago.

"Ashley and Nicholas. You two go outside and wait for Granny, so you can help her bring the pops in," Marcella said.

"Okay, Mom," Nicholas said, placing the buttons on the counter. "I think I got all of them, Aunt Racquel," he said, making a beeline toward the front door. Being outside was his most favorite place to be, so he didn't have any problem at all with waiting for his grandmother. Ashley followed behind him reluctantly. Unlike Nicholas, she wanted to stay and listen to what the grown-ups had to say.

"Don't even say it," Racquel said to Marcella as soon as she saw her opening her mouth.

"What? It's not my fault that you and Kevin got buttnaked in the center of the kitchen. And Kevin, did you have to tear all of my sister's buttons off in the process?" she said, smirking.

Kevin gazed at her in horror. And he felt like crawling under the table. He'd wondered where those buttons had come from when he saw Nicholas picking them up, but hadn't really given it much thought. He'd been so heated up, that he hadn't paid the slightest bit of attention to Racquel's buttons or anything else. But now, Marcella was calling him on it, and he could barely look her in her face. So, instead of acknowledging what she'd just said, he strolled out to the patio.

"Girl, why did you have to embarrass him like that," Racquel said, smiling.

"I didn't mean to. But you know it's funny. If it was the other way around, you would *never* let me live it down."

Racquel laughed. "I know, but you know how Kevin is."

"I'll apologize to him later, but not with a straight face."

"You're sick," Racquel said, shaking her head.

"Hey, where is everybody?" Marcella asked, glancing at her watch.

"Where else? On CP time, of course."

"Well, I'm going to warm the macaroni and cheese, and the baked beans now, and if they don't get here soon, they'll have to eat it the way it is," Marcella said, turning on the oven. "Sharon said she had to go into work for a couple of hours, and that she might be a little late, but the rest of them don't have an excuse."

"I wonder what happened to Kevin's friend from work. He and his wife should have been here by now, too," Racquel said curiously.

Marcella sucked her teeth. "Are they Black or White?"

"If they're late, what do you think?" Racquel said, laughing.

"Should've known," Marcella said.

Shortly after 1:30 P.M. all the other guests finally arrived. And now they were all laid back on the patio chairs with their stomachs poked out. Racquel had always known that Aunt Clara and Uncle Leroy were big eaters, but they'd really shown out today. They'd each piled food on, not one but two plates on the first go-around, and then went back for what they called "seconds" when all of that was gone. They were both fairly large, but Racquel still couldn't figure out where they found the room to hold so much food. Steaks, brats, chicken, side dishes. You name it, they had it, and were already looking forward to dessert. It really didn't matter to her that they were overweight because she loved both of them like they were her second parents. However, Uncle Leroy had already had a slight heart attack last year, and Aunt Clara's "pressure" was sky-high every time you spoke with her. If they didn't start watching what they ate, both of them were going to be buried six feet under.

"So, can I get anybody anything?" Racquel asked.

"Noooo, honey. But we'll take a couple of plates home with us for this evening," Aunt Clara said.

Racquel wanted to say something. Anything. But she knew better. Plus, they'd never understand any advice like that, anyhow. Instead, their feelings would be hurt, and she didn't want that. "Take whatever you want. I'm hoping all of you will, because if all this food stays around here, I'll be tempted to eat it myself."

"That's what's wrong with you little folks," Uncle Leroy said. "You just don't know how to eat."

"Ain't that the truth," Aunt Clara said, chuckling.

Everyone laughed. Especially, Sharon and Marcus, who thought Aunt Clara and Uncle Leroy were hilarious. The rest of the family was used to it, and that was none of the main reasons they all looked forward to sharing the holidays with them.

"I do eat right, and sometimes too much," Racquel said, patting her stomach.

"Girl, get on away from here," Uncle Leroy said, fanning his hand to the side in disbelief.

"And this one over here *really* needs to put some meat on those bones right there," Uncle Leroy said, pointing to Marcella.

Oh, shoot. Everything was funny to Marcella as long as he wasn't talking about her, and this meat-on-the-bones comment wasn't making her too happy. Especially since she hated the fact that she'd lost so much weight without even trying. But she played the comment off by laughing right along with everyone else.

"And look at your friend," Uncle Leroy said, looking at Sharon. "She's in the same boat," he said, and cracked up at his own joke.

"Birds of a feather," Aunt Clara agreed, and then fell out laughing right with him.

Sharon laughed harder than ever before, and it was obvious that she wasn't offended in the least little bit. Which was fine, because everyone knew Uncle Leroy was a big jokester and didn't mean any harm. It was just that Marcella hated being reminded of what she already knew.

"Sharon, don't you mind my sister and brother-in-law," Corrine said, laughing. "They mess with everybody."

"I know, Mom," Sharon said. Since Sharon had never had the opportunity of knowing her own mother, she asked Corrine a few years ago if she could call her Mom. And of course, Corrine was honored, because she loved Sharon like she was her own.

"When are you two going to tie that knot?" Uncle Leroy said to Marcus.

"I'm ready right now," Marcus said to Uncle Leroy, and then smiled at Sharon.

"It must be you who's not ready," Uncle Leroy said to Sharon.

"Marriage is a big step," Sharon finally said.

"He seems like an awfully nice young man," Aunt Clara interrupted. "And handsome, too."

"You one of them career women, huh?" Uncle Leroy said, laughing.

"Yes," Sharon said, blushing. "But that doesn't have anything to do with it."

"You make some nice money, too, don't you?" Uncle Leroy continued.

Sharon laughed. "I do okay."

"See. I knew it. Career women don't need a man."

"That's not true, Uncle Leroy," Sharon said. "We need a man just like any other woman."

"Yeah, I bet," Uncle Leroy said, still snickering. "Tell me anything."

Everyone shook their heads and laughed again.

"Kevin, since your friend from work wasn't feeling too well, maybe you can take some of this food over to their house," Racquel said.

"I'll give him a call to see," Kevin said, and stretched out on the chaise.

"Where did Ashley and Nicholas sneak off to," Marcella said, realizing that they'd disappeared.

"Oh, they're probably upstairs playing that Nintendo," Racquel said.

"Did they ask you or Kevin?" Marcella asked.

"I don't think so, but I've told them before that they don't have to. Part of the reason why we bought it was so they'd have something to do when they stay over here, anyway."

Marcella had had just about enough of Racquel telling her what the children should and shouldn't have to do. Enough was enough, and she wasn't having any more of this backseat parenting. "Racquel, you know I don't like it when they do things without asking. It's not respectful, and I won't have it."

"Girl, leave those children alone. They're not bothering anybody."

"I didn't say they *were* bothering anybody, but when I tell them to do something, I expect them to do it. And they usually do, until they come around you," Marcella said angrily.

"And what is that supposed to mean?" Racquel said, becoming just as irritated.

"Exactly what I said. You let them get away with murder, and then they come home thinking I'm some sort of prison guard. And I'm sick of it. You know all the rules I've laid down for them, and it's your responsibility to enforce them, whether I'm around or not."

"No, my responsibility is to do whatever I feel like doing. Especially when it comes to anything going on in my own house," Racquel said, staring at Marcella.

"You know," Marcella said, laughing sarcastically and then standing up, "you're right. This is your house." Marcella gathered up her plate and cup.

"Marcella!" Corrine said. "I know you're not going to leave over something like this. You girls need to quit all of this arguing."

Racquel just looked at Marcella and rolled her eyes.

"No, Mom," Marcella said. "I'm sick of this. Those are *my* children, and I know what's best for them."

"I can tell you one thing, if they were mine, I'd raise them a lot differently than the way you are," Racquel said nonchalantly.

"But they're not yours, Racquel. And from the way things look to me, you won't ever get the chance to raise your *own* children, anyway," Marcella said, walking toward the patio door.

"Marcella, that's enough," Corrine said, standing up. "You and Racquel are sisters, and you know this doesn't make any sense at all."

Racquel felt as though a bolt of lightning had struck her. How could Marcella have been so cruel? And in front of all these people. Everyone already knew the situation, so why did she have to put her down like that? This had gone too far, and Racquel wasn't about to let her humiliate her like that and get away with it. Sister or not. "At least I wasn't stupid enough to sit up there and have two babies by some no-good fool like Tyrone. Even the most ignorant person would have had better sense than that."

"You're just jealous. Always have been and always will be. Face it, Racquel. You're never going to have any children, and trying to criticize me isn't going to change that. And I'll tell you something else, you don't ever have to worry about Ashley and Nicholas coming over here anymore, either, because I'm through with you for good," Marcella said and stepped into the house.

Everyone looked on in amazement, but didn't say anything. Sharon finally stood up and went in behind Marcella, and Kevin pulled Racquel down on his lap, not knowing what to say, either.

"Lord, have mercy on these children," Aunt Clara said.

"Mm, mm, mm," Uncle Leroy said, shaking his head, obviously not believing what he was hearing. "I'm tellin' you the truth."

"Let me go in here and talk to Marcella," Corrine said, and walked into the house.

"Racquel, maybe you ought to go and talk to your sister, too," Aunt Clara said. "You girls know you weren't raised like that."

"I'm not apologizing for something I didn't do, Aunt Clara. She's the one that got upset about nothing."

"Baby, two wrongs don't make a right," Aunt Clara continued. "And I know you're not going to let something like this come between you."

Racquel didn't respond because she knew if she kept going back and forth with her aunt, it wasn't going to be long before she said something disrespectful. She loved her aunt, but she wanted her to mind her own business just as well.

Sharon's boyfriend, Marcus, was the only one left on the patio who wasn't a relative, and from the look on his face, it was obvious that he felt uncomfortable with all that had gone on. Racquel felt bad for him, and decided that she at least owed *him* an apology, if not anyone else. "Marcus, I hope you will accept my apology for what just happened."

"Oh, no, that's okay," he said, partially smiling.

"No," Racquel said. "It's not okay. You are a guest at our house, and you shouldn't have had to witness any of this confusion."

Marcus nodded his head, acknowledging what Racquel said.

When Marcella had finished scraping out her baking dishes, she went back out to the patio, said goodbye to everyone except Racquel, and then she and the children left. Sharon and Marcus followed right behind them. Then, Aunt Clara and Uncle Leroy fixed up their take-home plates, and went on their way an hour later. And when Corrine finished helping Racquel and Kevin with the dishes, she decided she'd better get home as well.

Kevin took a couple of plates over to his friend's house, and Racquel lay down on the chaise on the patio. Her whole body felt numb. Marcella had always meant everything in the world to her. She didn't know what she was going to do if Marcella was serious about keeping Ashley and Nicholas away from her. She loved them no differently than if they were her own. The cookout had started so perfectly and then ended in such turmoil. What she regretted the most was calling her sister stupid. And she never would have, if Marcella hadn't kept forcing that never-going-to-have-any-children business down her throat.

She breathed deeply, closed her eyes, and prayed—like she never had before—that all of this was nothing more than a very bad dream.

Chapter 9

Marcella was more excited than she'd ever been in her entire life, but at the same time she couldn't wait to find Messner Hall, the building her college algebra course was located in. This was her first day at Covington Park University, and without a doubt, the hottest day of the year. When she'd watched the six A.M. weather report on television this morning, the temperature had already reached eighty-six, but now it had to be right around a hundred degrees. She'd worn her brown skort set, which had a sleeveless shirt, and still she was burning up. It felt like her whole body was on fire, and the humidity was so high that she felt like she was going to suffocate. And the reason why she couldn't wait for the month of August to be over with.

She strolled up the sidewalk slowly, skimming through the campus map that the admissions office had mailed to her two weeks ago, trying anxiously to figure out where she was. It would have been just as easy to ask one of the hundreds of students walking around from building to building, but she didn't want to sound like she was new. She was self-conscious as it was about being twenty-nine and just starting college for the first time and didn't feel comfortable asking some eighteen- or nineteen-year-old where her class was. She knew it was silly to think that way, but she just couldn't do it.

She stopped when she realized she was in a familiar area and looked up at the building she was standing in front of. No wonder. It was the building she'd gone to four months ago for that counseling session with that witch-of-a-counselor, Mrs. Harrison. Just the thought of the woman pissed her off, and she was glad she'd finally gotten the chance to put her in her place.

When Marcella's ACT scores had arrived at the university, Mrs. Harrison had scheduled another appointment for her to come in and discuss her course load for the fall semester. Marcella's first thought was to tell her where she could go, and then reschedule with Mr. Dahl, the counselor who had given her the school catalog. But since she'd ranked well above the national testscore average, she decided instead to go and rub Miss High-and-Mighty's nose in it.

She could still remember that day so vividly. She'd gone into Mrs. Harrison's office, took a seat, and waited for her to start the conversation.

The woman had done just about everything imaginable to avoid any conversation relating to Marcella's test scores, and it was obvious that she would have rather died than compliment Marcella on her accomplishments. Finally, though, she didn't have a choice.

"I assume you received your letter of acceptance from the university," Mrs. Harrison said, keeping her eyes on some irrelevant piece of paperwork on her desk.

"Yes, I did," Marcella said in an overly polite manner.

"So what we need to do now, is plan your schedule for the fall semester. You'll be taking mostly general studies, but those will also include a couple of the prerequisites that you'll need to enter the Business School."

Ha! Marcella had big news for this heifer. She'd already reviewed the requirements of the accounting program and had determined on her own which classes she'd be taking. "I've already figured all of that out, so that won't be necessary," Marcella said, feeling more tickled than she had in a long time.

"You do know that your financial-aid forms will have to be filed right away, since classes begin in less than two months," Mrs. Harrison said. And from the sarcastic look on her face, it was obvious that she thought she was telling Marcella something she didn't know. But Marcella had a surprise for her, the kind of surprise that was going to make her hair stand up on ends.

"Oh, didn't you know?" Marcella said, knowing good and well

she didn't. "The partners of the accounting firm that I work for have decided to include part-time employees in their educational reimbursement program, which means they'll be paying-fifty percent of my tuition. And I've already applied and received approval from my bank for a student loan to cover the rest of my expenses," Marcella said with her head held high.

"Well, it looks to me like you wasted both my time and yours by coming in here," Mrs. Harrison said, rolling her eyes away from Marcella with an attitude.

Marcella had been waiting for the perfect opportunity to tell this wannabe witch about herself, and the time was finally here. "To tell you the truth, I really couldn't care less about you or your precious little time. And the next time you decide to talk about someone behind their back, you might want to close your door. Not halfway, like the first day I was in here, but all the way. I know you thought I was gone, but I wasn't. 'It really pisses me off when I see these welfare women getting over the way they do,' " Marcella said, mocking Mrs. Harrison's voice.

Mrs. Harrison gazed at her in total shock, and didn't open her mouth.

"Oh, yes, I heard every word you said. And what was that other comment you made about me thinking I was going to conquer the world? Well, I may not conquer the world, but I *will* graduate from this university with a four-year degree, pass the CPA exam, and become one of the best accountants Nicosia and Associates has ever had," she said, standing up from the chair. "Regardless of what you or anyone else has to say about it."

Mrs. Harrison continued looking at her with a wow-I'm-busted expression on her face, without speaking.

"What you need to do is learn some professionalism," Marcella continued. "And more than anything, you need to take a long look in the mirror, because somehow, someway, you seem to have gotten the idea that you're better than I am. And whether you want to accept it or not, *your* face is just as black as *mine*. And nothing is going to change that one bit. Not your little uppity attitude or that little desk you're sitting so proudly behind," Marcella said, pointing her finger at Mrs. Harrison.

"I refuse to be talked to in this manner, and I'd appreciate it if you would leave my office," Mrs. Harrison said, sounding nervous.

"What I should do, is report you to the president of this university," Marcella said, ignoring Mrs. Harrison's request for her to leave. "As a matter of fact, that's exactly what I'm going to do."

Mrs. Harrison looked at her with a scared-to-death look on her face.

Marcella wanted to burst out laughing. Especially, since she had no intention of reporting anything to anybody. But she still had to show this woman just who was running things when it came to her education. Had to let her know that she wasn't the naive little welfare girl she'd made her out to be. She was just as intelligent and professional as she was, and she wanted her to know it. Marcella stood up. "Well, it's been nice talking with you, Mrs. Harrison," she said with a smirk on her face. "You take care of yourself, okay?" she said sarcastically and left the office.

Marcella had conjured up at least a dozen more choice words for Mrs. Harrison, but like every other time she told someone off, she never thought of them until after the commotion was already over.

"Hey, can I help you find something?" a gentleman, standing to the right of her, asked.

Marcella jumped. She didn't realize she'd been standing there long enough for someone to recognize it. "Is it that obvious?" she asked, looking up from the map and feeling sort of awkward.

"Well, you've been standing in that same spot for almost five minutes, like you were in deep thought. And when someone does that on the first day of classes, it usually means they're lost," he said.

"Actually, I was kind of daydreaming, but I'm also having trouble finding Messner Hall," she said, slightly embarrassed.

"That's just two buildings down," he said, pointing.

She glanced in the direction of the building, and then back at him. She couldn't believe how handsome he was. Medium-brown complexion, wavy coal-black hair, beautiful dark-brown eyes, and lips to die for. The man was fine. "This is so embarrassing," she said, smiling. "Here I am searching for my class, and the building is practically sitting right in front of me."

"There's no reason to be embarrassed. This is a pretty large campus, and it's easy to get lost, until you learn your way around. But you'll know it like the back of your hand in a few weeks."

"I sure hope so."

"By the way, I'm Keith Howard," he said, extending his right hand to shake hers.

"Nice to meet you. I'm Marcella Jones."

"Nice to meet you, too. So, did you transfer here?"

She wished. She knew it was just a matter of time before she'd have to explain to someone that she was twenty-nine and just starting college for the first time. It was so humiliating. But then, the more she gazed at him, the more she realized he didn't look to be a day younger than twenty-six or twenty-seven himself. Maybe he'd started later than usual, as well. "No. As a matter of fact, this is my first time ever attending college. I worked full-time, but now I'm going to school full-time and working part-time until I graduate."

"What degree are you working toward?"

"Accounting. What about you?"

"This is my last year of law school. I started working right after I finished my bachelor's degree, but then I decided to apply to law school. I was twenty-eight when I finally enrolled."

Not only was the man fine, but he was intelligent, as well. Not to mention the fact that he wasn't as young as she thought, and had to be at least thirty. "That's wonderful."

"Well, I'd better let you get to class," he said, smiling at her.

"Okay. And thanks for pointing out my classroom building."

"No problem. Hey, maybe we can get together sometime, if you're not seeing anyone."

She couldn't believe what she was hearing, and she felt like grinning from ear to ear. "Maybe we can," she said in the voice of a schoolgirl.

"Why don't you write your number down, and I'll give you a call this evening."

She felt like screaming. No decent guy had shown any real interest in her in years, and she couldn't believe someone as well-educated and good-looking as Keith was asking for her phone number, let alone wanting to go out with her. She wrote her name and phone number down on one of her notebook pages, tore it out, and passed it to him.

"So, is there any special time I should call?" he asked, sliding the piece of paper inside his black leather book bag.

"Well, once I pick up my son and daughter from the baby-sitter, and get them dinner, I should be home around six." Usually she wouldn't be home until after nine, but this week she was only working from two to four in the afternoon.

As soon as she finished her sentence, the happy expression on his face went blank. "Oh, I didn't realize you had children. You don't look like the type."

Then what type did she look like? He'd seemed so interested, and now he was staring at her like he'd just seen a ghost. This was so typical. Guys were always doing this. They seemed so interested at first, but once she mentioned the fact that she had children, their whole attitude seemed to change. It was so amazing how quickly they could be turned on and off, without it even fazing them. She wasn't sure how to respond. A part of her wanted to set him straight, but another part of her was hoping that he didn't care that she had children, and that he was still going to call her. "Well, believe it or not, I have an eight and an eleven-year-old. My youngest will be turning nine next month."

"Well, I'll give you a call around seven, if that's okay."

"That's fine," she said, glancing at her watch. "I'd better get to class."

"See ya later," he said, turning to walk in the opposite direction of where she was heading.

Whether he was going to call or not was a thousand-dollar question, and while she was hoping that he did, she didn't have any time right now to dwell on it, or be depressed about it. She walked inside the building and searched for her math class.

After picking up the children and stopping at McDonald's for dinner, Marcella was glad to make it home. She'd been running around ever since six o'clock that morning, and couldn't wait to undress so she could totally unwind. The children would be starting school again in a couple of weeks, which meant she'd have to rise no later than five A.M. to make sure they were dressed and had eaten before their school bus came to pick them up at seven-thirty. The summer wasn't so bad because she didn't have to iron their school clothes, or mess around with Ashley's hair. But during the school year, she had to monitor what they were putting on, making sure Ashley wasn't trying to dress too old for her age, and that Nicholas wasn't going out of the house mismatching. And although Nicholas always whined and sometimes cried when she told him to go to bed at night, he literally hated it when she woke him up in the morning. She had to call him two or three different times, and sometimes had to get downright upset with him before he finally started getting dressed. And that was the main reason she'd changed his bedtime from nine to eight-thirty. A half hour didn't seem like much as far as time was concerned, but it did make a world of difference when it came to waking Nicholas up. Ashley was more of a morning person, so Marcella never had too much of a problem with her. Plus, she was older, and it was only fair that she got to stay up at least a little later than her brother, anyway.

Marcella started toward her bedroom, and then turned when she noticed an argument heating up between Ashley and Nicholas. As usual, they'd drummed up another dispute over what they were going to watch on TV.

"I always watch the Cosby reruns, Nicholas, and you know it," Ashley said, jerking the remote control from her brother.

"Stop it, Ashley. I was the one who turned the TV on first," he said with tears welling up in his eyes.

"Look, you two. I'm not going to put up with this tonight. I've had a long day, and both of you are going to have to cut all of this out. Now, whose turn is it?" Marcella asked with irritation in her voice.

"It's Nicholas's, but they're going to celebrate their grandparents' anniversary tonight, and I want to see it. I told him I'd let him watch his little cartoon two nights in a row," Ashley said, rolling her eyes at him.

"If this is his night, you know what the rules are, Ashley," Marcella said, staring at her.

"Dog. That's why I wish we had another TV set. Everybody else does," Ashley said, throwing the remote control down on the sofa. She stood up and started to walk away, until Marcella stopped her.

"Go back and pick that remote control up and hand it to your brother," Marcella said angrily.

Ashley frowned, but obeyed her mother's orders.

"And I don't want to hear anything else from you about what we don't have. Your grandmother was nice enough to buy us that TV for Christmas, and you ought to be thankful, instead of complaining about it. I'm doing the best I can, and now I'm struggling to work, go to school, and take care of both of you, just so I can try to make things easier for all of us."

"But now you're only working part-time, so how are things going to be better?" Ashley asked, looking at her mother.

Marcella was stunned. This couldn't possibly be her daughter standing in front of her, because *her* daughter would have never spoken that way to her, or disrespected any adult in that manner. Especially when the adult was her own mother. "What did you say?" Marcella asked, squinting her eyes.

"Nothing," Ashley said, with her arms folded.

"Listen, Ashley. I don't know what's gotten into you, or where you got that little attitude from, but you'd better get rid of it. You're the child, and I'm the adult in this house. I don't owe you any explanations. And since your mouth is so smart, I don't want to see that phone up to your ear for the next seven days."

"But, Mom," Ashley begged.

"I mean what I said, Ashley."

"You already took Aunt Racquel away from us, so what difference does it make if you take the phone away, too," Ashley said boldly, without the slightest fear.

Ashley stormed into her room, and it was all Marcella could do not to snatch her up. For the first time since she'd been raising her children, she had to catch herself. Because if she didn't, someone was going to have to bail her out of jail tonight. Who did Ashley think she was talking to, anyway? If Marcella or Racquel had even thought about talking back to Corrine or their father that way, they would have found themselves getting up off the floor. And she knew her grandmother had never taken mess like that from her children, either, because Corrine and Aunt Clara had told them stories about it on more than one occasion. She just couldn't figure out what had gotten into Ashley. It wasn't like her at all, and something was wrong. She'd been warned over and over of what it was going to be like once Ashley turned eleven or twelve, and since she was turning eleven next month, Marcella was starting to see exactly what every other mother was talking about.

Nicholas gazed at her in silence, and it was obvious that he was just as shocked as his mother about the way Ashley had just shown out. Marcella turned and walked into her bedroom, shutting the door behind her.

She knew she had to nip this in the bud immediately, before it got too far out of hand. Marcella knew her mother was working, and usually when something as serious as this happened, she called Racquel. But since they still weren't speaking, she couldn't. She'd thought for sure this little spat between them would have blown over by now, but it hadn't. She'd never gone without talking to her sister more than two days before, and now it had been over five weeks. The thought of not having her sister to lean on made her feel sick. It was almost as if a part of her was missing, and she didn't know what to do about it. They'd had arguments before, but never to the extent of the one that had erupted on the Fourth of July. Marcella wished to God she could take back everything she'd said, because she knew how sensitive her sister was when it came to having a baby, and how seriously she took it. But, then, Racquel had said some nasty things to her, as well. As a matter of fact, she didn't know if she was ever going to forget what Racquel had said about her being ignorant enough to have two children by some fool like Tyrone. But still, they were sisters, and if they didn't have anyone else, they did have each other.

Corrine had been begging both of them to make the first move, but neither of them was willing to do it. She needed desperately to talk to someone. Anyone. It was times like these that she wished she had a husband, or at least a significant other who loved and cared about what happened to her. Someone to comfort her when she was feeling down, or going through trying times like she was now.

As she lay back across the bed, the phone rang. She looked at it and smiled when she realized it had to be Keith. He'd said he was going to call, but she'd thought for sure that her mention of two children had changed his mind completely.

She answered the phone. "Hello?" Marcella said, trying to sound as if she wasn't expecting anyone in particular.

"Marcella? It's me, Racquel."

"Hey," Marcella said, trying to disguise the fact that she was shocked that her sister was actually calling her, and disappointed that it wasn't Keith. But she knew she'd been fooling herself. She'd known the minute that funny expression crossed his face, but a part of her had still hoped he was going to call just the same.

"Don't you think this has gone far enough?" Racquel asked.

"It never should have happened in the first place, if you ask me," Marcella said, sitting up in the center of the bed.

"I said some things I didn't mean, and I'm sorry."

"We both said things we didn't mean, and I'm sorry, too. I've missed talking to you and seeing you so much, that it hurts."

"Girl, I've shed so many tears over all of this, till I don't know what to do, and I don't ever want to go through this with you ever again. It's silly."

"You're right. It is silly. We've both been going through some hard situations, and I think we, for whatever reason, took it out on each other."

"I'll tell you what," Racquel said, sniffling her nose, obviously crying. "I'm not going another day without seeing you, Ashley, or Nicholas. I'll see you in a little bit. Okay?" Racquel said.

"I'll see you, then," Marcella said and hung up the phone.

Marcella hated when Racquel cried, because it made her want to do the same thing. Except now she was feeling so many emotions that, instead of crying, she felt like screaming. Maybe changing her work schedule to part-time and going to school was a mistake. There was no doubt that they were going to have less household money, and starting next week, she'd be going to class full-time during the day, working four hours in the evening four nights a week, and then studying whenever she could in between. The partners at the firm had hired a new receptionist, and then more or less created a clerical position for her, so she could go to school and continue working for them simultaneously. And they'd already offered her a permanent position with them as an accountant as soon as she completed her degree. And while all that sounded good, it meant she would be spending hardly any time at all with the children. After begging and pleading with Tyrone, she'd finally talked him into picking Ashley and Nicholas up from the bus stop and then keeping them until she got off work. But with the way Ashley was acting, she was starting to wonder if this was the right time to be spending all of these hours away from her.

Marcella's head started to pound harder and harder as thoughts zipped through her mind, one right after another. If only she could make it through these next four years, everything would be perfect. She'd be able to give Ashley and Nicholas the lives they deserved, and she'd be the career woman she'd always dreamed of being. No, the more she thought about it, the more she realized she couldn't back out now. She had to make this work. And most importantly, what she had to do was double her determination.

Chapter 10

"Why are you doing this, Tyrone?" Marcella said with tears flowing down her face.

"Because I'm sick of you neglecting your children, that's why," he said, yelling at her. "And if you want to keep going to that little university, I suggest you find another baby-sitter."

Another baby-sitter? How on earth could Ashley and Nicholas's own father call himself their baby-sitter? Marcella had known all along that this agreement with Tyrone wasn't going to work, but she'd been praying hard all last semester that he would, for whatever reason, do right by her just this once. He never had before, but she'd hoped things would be different this time.

He watched the children faithfully from August to December, but now that it was the end of January, and she was two weeks into her second semester, he was backing out of the deal that they'd agreed upon. Her whole world was tumbling down around her, and she had no idea where to turn to next.

"Tyrone, you know I can't continue to both go to school and work if somebody doesn't watch Ashley and Nicholas," she said, sounding as if her life was coming to an end.

"It's your responsibility to watch your own children, and I'm not doing it anymore. Here it is Saturday, and you've got my kids stuck up over at your mother's house. What kind of mother does some crap like that?"

"They're *your* children, too. And you have just as much responsibility when it comes to taking care of them as I do."

"You were the one who got pregnant," he said, pointing at her.

Marcella just stared at him. If she had a dollar for every time he'd made some stupid remark like that, she'd be filthy rich. This man was insane. Had to be, if he honestly believed she had spontaneously gotten pregnant two times without any help from him. He was trying to tear down everything she'd been trying to build up, and he made her sick. And for the first time, she wished she had a gun to blow his brains out. She hadn't felt pressure like this for as long as she could remember. Here she was trying to make something of herself so she could give her children a better life, and Tyrone was doing everything he could to sabotage all of her efforts.

"Can't you at least watch them until the end of the semester? Then I'll try to find someone else for this fall."

"I already told you. I'm not doing it. Not the rest of the semester. Not even next week. *I* don't have the privilege of going to school full-time, so why should you? I have to work myself to death every day, so I can pay that child support you keep whining about."

"Tyrone, please. You go to work for one reason, and one reason only: to wine that dizzy broad you call yourself messing around with. Yeah, I know all about her," Marcella said. Her tears were drying up, and she was starting to get pissed off.

"You don't know anything," he said, getting loud again.

"I don't know why you're trying to hide her from me, because you know I don't care in the least about who you sleep with, anyway."

Tyrone laughed. "Yeah, right, Marcella. If you don't care, then why are you bringing my personal life up in the first place? Huh? Why is that?"

"As long as you're paying my child support, you can sleep with a different woman every night, if you want."

"Whatever, Marcella," he said, moving closer to the front door.

"So, you're not going to keep them?" she asked for the last time.

"I'll tell you what. If you reduce the child support to thirty dollars a week, maybe I'll think about it."

Was Tyrone really that crazy? Or just plain brainless? She felt her blood pressure rising fast and furious, and she wasn't two steps from tearing into him. Physically. "Tyrone, just get out! Now!" she said, walking toward him.

"That little university has turned you into a fool. But you'd better learn some sense when you're around me, because I'm not playing with you. Tryin' to put somebody out. Girl, you'd better wake up before I turn that dreamworld of yours into a nightmare."

"Fine. You just stay right where you are," she said calmly, and then walked as quickly as she could toward Nicholas's bedroom. She slid open his closet door and searched madly for his baseball bat until she found it. Tyrone had practically gotten away with disrespecting her mother one year ago, but now it was high time he paid for that, and all the other cruel things he'd done and said to her, as well.

She reentered the living room. "Now, what was that you were saying?"

"You crazy trick," Tyrone said, struggling to open the door without taking his eyes off of her.

"Yeah, I am crazy, thanks to your no-good behind," she said, moving closer to where he was trying desperately to exit the apartment. He finally succeeded.

Marcella stood in front of the door in a daze, and she felt like she couldn't breathe. When was this situation with Tyrone going to end? Day after day, week after week, year after year, she'd been having to put up with this idiotic mess, and her patience was wearing thinner as time went on. She wasn't sure how much more she could take from him.

When she realized she was holding Nicholas's bat in her hand, she dropped it to the floor. She couldn't believe what she'd just done. She'd actually planned to strike Tyrone across his head. She'd even imagined how the blood would gush out all over her floor. This wasn't like her, and the whole idea of it all frightened her to no end. He brought out the worst in her, and now she was resorting to violence. Something had to be done before she ended up killing him.

And as much as she hated to admit it, she despised the fact that he was dating someone. Usually, it never mattered to her, because most of his women were in one day, and out the other. But this Priscilla had been hanging around for over four months, according to Nicholas and Ashley. Marcella didn't want Tyrone, but she couldn't help but wish she had someone to love her just the same. Someone who wanted to be with her *for her.* Someone who didn't have the slightest problem with the fact that she had two kids. It wasn't fair that Tyrone could get dressed and go out with whomever he wanted, whenever he wanted, while she had to stay home like some ninety-year-old woman, who was waiting patiently to perish. Why did it always have to be this way, when a woman had children by a man she'd divorced or had never been married to? She'd met four different guys since she started the university, beginning with that Keith on the first day of classes, and while they all seemed interested at first, their whole attitude changed when they found out she had two children. It was almost like they saw them as excess baggage. Which was strange because most women didn't seem to care in the least when they found out a guy had children by some other woman. But then, it was probably because they knew there would only be a few select times when they would actually have to have contact with them. Especially, since most men didn't have custody of their children, and didn't want it. It was sick. She knew all men weren't like that, but Tyrone had given her the lesson of a lifetime. And while she hated herself for thinking it, she couldn't help but wonder how her life would have turned out, if she hadn't had Ashley and Nicholas at all. She'd probably have a master's degree by now, and there was a good chance she'd be living in the same neighborhood as Sharon. The mere thought of it all was depressing.

What in the world was she going to do about the children? Her classes stretched daily from eight to noon, and she needed to study and complete her homework in the afternoon. And quitting her job wasn't even an option, because she needed the money so desperately. Not to mention the fact that they were paying a big portion of her tuition. If she had to drop out of school, it was going to kill her, but right now she didn't see where she had any other choice.

Marcella picked up the bat and carried it back to Nicholas's closet, where she'd found it, and went into her bedroom. A pastel-blue fitted sheet was covering the two ends of the mattress at the head of the bed, the way she'd left them when she'd heard Tyrone knocking at the door. She pulled the rest of the sheet across the bed, spread the top sheet across it, and tucked it under at the foot of the bed. She pulled on the pillowcases and then placed the burgundy comforter on top.

After vacuuming her carpet and dusting her dresser, she made her way into Ashley's room. When she arrived, she shook her head in disgust. She'd told that girl to clean her room before going over to her Granny's, but from the looks of it, she'd totally ignored her. Her bed was half straightened, the pair of jeans and T-shirt she'd worn the day before were lying on the floor, and her dresser looked like a hurricane had swooped right through it. Ashley knew better than this, and even when she was just a little thing, Marcella had never had a problem with her cleaning up like she was told. And most of the time, she didn't even need telling. Ashley simply did it on her own.

But now she'd become mouthy, irritable, and hardheaded. Marcella couldn't believe her grades were still intact. Ashley was still the same straight-A student she'd always been. But it was just that little attitude of hers. And she was so withdrawn. She spent most of her time closed up in her bedroom, and when she did decide to come out to the living room to watch TV, she was silent; acting as if no one was in the room except her. Marcella had tried being patient with her, but it wasn't going to be long before she put her foot down. All the way down. Ashley needed to be reminded who was boss, who was paying the bills, and more than anything else, who was still young enough to get her little behind whipped.

Marcella picked up Ashley's clothing and threw them in the hallway, so she could take them to the Laundromat later in the afternoon. She pulled Ashley's bedcovers until there were no wrinkles showing, and walked over to her white mirrored dresser. The more she gazed at the mess, the more disgusted she became. She had a mind to toss it all in the garbage, but figured that might be going too far. She pulled open the top right drawer and shook her head in disagreement again. This was junkier than the top of the dresser, and was filthier than anything she'd ever seen. She rustled through it to see what all the different papers were, and saw that most of it was old homework assignments that had been graded, and a few young-adult paperback books. As she continued rummaging through the drawer, she saw a loose sanitary napkin, and wondered where the box was. Now, what was she going to do with this? It was too dusty to use, so what was the point in keeping it? The whole idea of her starting her menstrual cycle at the ripe old age of eleven still gave Marcella the creeps. She'd started hers at twelve, but it still didn't seem right knowing her baby was actually having a period.

She shut the top drawer, and pulled open the one just below it. Marcella couldn't believe it, her underwear was actually folded. She'd been meaning to check and see if she needed to buy Ashley a few more pairs of panties, so she counted them. When she came to the bottom of the pile, she noticed a fuchsia notebook and pulled it out. There was no label on it, but from the looks of it, it was one of the ones she'd bought for school. When she opened the inside cover, she saw the words "My Diary, 1994" written in blue ink. Marcella lowered her eyebrows in total confusion. Ashley didn't seem like the type of girl who wrote her thoughts down on paper, but maybe that's why she no longer confided in Marcella the way she used to. This diary thing was a huge surprise, and Marcella couldn't help but wonder what was in it. She knew it was wrong, but since she'd come across it, she couldn't resist taking at least a small peek. She turned to the first page, and saw that it was dated January 1, which meant she'd just started writing in it three weeks ago.

Marcella skimmed through the first couple of weeks and laughed at most of it, because some of the things she'd written were so cute. But when she finished reading the entry for the fifteenth, which took up three whole pages, she covered her mouth with her right hand and sat down on the edge of the bed. There had to be some mistake. She read the entry again:

Today is Saturday, and as usual, Mom made us clean up again. I'm so sick of her telling me what to do. She can't even take care of her own life, and still she controls everything I do. That's why when she went to the grocery store this morning, I let Jason in. Mom can't stand him, but as soon as she left, he knocked on the door and I let him in. Nicholas said he was going to tell, but I know he won't, because I promised him he could have control of the TV for a whole week. So, when Jason came in, Nicholas was fine with it. Jason has been wanting to come over for a long time, but of course, with Mom breathing down my neck all the time, he couldn't. But lately she's been leaving us alone for a couple of hours to go to the grocery store on Saturday, so I told Jason yesterday to watch out of his window around ten, because I knew she'd be leaving around that time, and that's what he did. It was so much fun when he got here. He said he really liked me a lot, but that he would fall in love with me if I did something for him. At first he just kept smiling, and then he finally said, it's something that will make him feel good. He said that boys his age (he's 13) had special needs. And that he was almost a grown man. He said that he'd been liking me since last summer, but he thought I was just a little girl. But he said if I did this one thing for him, then he would know I wasn't a little girl at all. He'd know for sure I was a real woman. Finally, he pulled his pants down and told me to get on my knees in front of him. At first I was scared, but he kept saying how fine I was, and he kept smiling at me. I'm in love with him, I just know it. Finally, he told me that he wasn't like most guys who went around making girls do stuff that would get them pregnant. He said he cared about me too much to do that. He told me to close my eyes and open my mouth, and then he put his thing inside of it. I didn't know what to do, so I just closed my lips around it. He told me to suck it, so I did. But then this yucky white stuff came out, and he made these really funny noises. I almost choked on it, and I spit most of it out on the floor. I hope he didn't think I was acting childish. But I must have done it right, because he asked me to go with him, and I said yes. I can't wait to see him again.

Marcella quickly turned to the next Saturday, to see what else Little-Miss-Fast-Butt had written, but that was today's date. "Wait a minute," Marcella thought. "That means this just happened one week ago." A feeling of anger seized her every emotion, and she couldn't wait until that little Ashley got home. Better yet, she was going over to Corrine's to get her little butt, right now. She'd leave Nicholas and bring Ashley back home with her. And she was going to kill that little mannish-tail Jason. And as much as she despised Tyrone, she knew he'd kill that boy, too, if he found out about it. But then he'd also blame her for letting it happen.

Marcella dropped the notebook down on Ashley's bed, stormed out of the bedroom, threw on her coat, gloves, and boots, and headed out the front floor. She had to take care of this Jason business right now.

* * *

"Mom, why did Nicholas get to stay at Granny's?" Ashley asked as Marcella pulled out of Corrine's driveway.

Marcella didn't say anything.

"Mom," Ashley called out, trying terribly to get her mother's attention.

Marcella continued driving without turning to look at her even once, because she was afraid of what might happen if she did. The last thing she wanted to do was slap the crap out of her own daughter. She'd tried to calm herself down on the way over, so her mother wouldn't figure out that something was wrong. But now that it was just the two of them in the car, her anger was slowly starting to escalate all over again. She wasn't two inches from exploding.

"Mom, what's wrong with you?" Ashley asked.

Marcella glanced at her and then looked back at the road.

Ashley saw a look on her mother's face, like she'd never seen before, and decided that it was time for her to keep her mouth shut.

Marcella parked the car, opened the car door, stepped out of it, and then slammed it as hard as she could. Ashley stepped out on the passenger side in slow motion. As soon as they were in the house, Marcella removed her outer garments, and Ashley did the same. When Marcella saw that Ashley had taken off the last boot, she grabbed her by her wrist and dragged her into her bedroom.

"Explain this, Ashley," Marcella said, forcing the notebook into her daughter's hand.

"What?" Ashley said, looking down at the notebook.

"Girl, don't play dumb with me," Marcella said, yelling.

"It's just some notes, Mom, that's all," Ashley said in a shaky voice.

More than anything, Marcella hated to be lied to. This girl thought she was playing games, and she had to let her know how serious she was. "Notes? You call sticking your head between some little boy's legs, just some notes? Ashley, do you think I'm stupid?"

Ashley stared at her, scared to death, wondering if she should answer her, make a comment, or say something. But she decided to keep quiet.

"Did you let that little boy in here last week when I was gone, or not?"

Ashley wanted to lie. And bad. But she knew she was going to get the whipping and punishment of a lifetime if she did. She was going to get both of those anyway, but somehow if she lied, she hated to even think what would happen then. "Yes, Mom," she said, already crying her eyes out. "I'm sorry, Mom." She reached out to her mother to hug her.

"Don't touch me, Ashley," Marcella said, moving away from her. "You mean to tell me that you let that little ghetto boy in here, after I told you specifically not to open the door for anyone when I'm gone? And then you took him into your bedroom, left Nicholas all by himself, and then let him sweet-talk you into puttin' your mouth between his legs? Is that what you're telling me?"

"Mom, I didn't mean it."

"How could you *not* have meant it? You wrote right in there about how you'd told him the day before to be on the lookout around ten o'clock? Oh, yeah, you meant to do what you did. What you didn't mean was to get caught," Marcella said, making gestures with her right hand.

Ashley's face was flooded with water, and she was scared to move out of her tracks. With the rage on her mother's face, she didn't dare say anything.

Marcella took a deep breath and tried to get control of the situation. She was too angry to take a belt to Ashley, and decided against it. Like her grandmother used to say, she was "putting this one up on the shelf for later" because little Miss Thing wasn't getting away with this.

"I don't want you to even answer or use that phone until school is out in June. And as far as any sleep-overs at your aunt Racquel and uncle Kevin's go, you can forget that, too. For the next four and a half months, I want you to go to school, come home, do your homework, and go to bed. Do you hear me?"

"But Mom, I didn't mean it," Ashley said with her chest elevating up and down, crying harder and harder.

"I've said what I have to say, and I don't want to hear another word about it," Marcella said, walking toward Ashley's bedroom door.

Ashley fell on her bed, screaming and boo-hooing as loud as she could, and Marcella was starting to become annoyed.

"Look, Ashley. I want you to cut out all that noise, and I mean cut it out right now, before I give you something to cry about," Marcella said.

The crying stopped instantly.

"I can't believe you, Ashley. For as long as I can remember, you've never given me any reason to be anything except proud of you. So what's wrong with you now? Why are you acting like this? You've been talking back, strolling around here with an attitude practically every day, and now this thing with that Jason. What's wrong with you? I've always been so proud of both you and Nicholas."

Ashley sat up on the side of the bed, and walked toward her mother. "I'm so . . . sorry . . . Mom," she said with her voice trembling. They hugged, and now tears were falling down Marcella's face.

"Baby, I know Mom hasn't been able to spend a lot of time with you since I started school, but I promise you, things will get better. I have to go to school, so I can get a better job. And when I get a better job, I'll be able to take care of you and your brother a lot better than I have been. And I have to work now, because we need to pay bills and buy food. Don't you understand that, honey? I know it's hard, but we can get through this. You're a big girl now, and sometimes I'm going to need you to look out for Nicholas. And when I ask you to do that for a couple of hours, I need to know that I can trust you. Okay?"

Ashley shook her head yes, without moving it away from her mother's chest.

"You really hurt me, Ashley, and I don't want you doing anything like that ever again. Regardless of what that boy says, all he wants to do is use you. When you're old enough to date, you'll find someone who really cares about you, but right now, you're too young to even be thinking about being with some boy. The next thing he'll be doing is trying to get you to go all the way," Marcella said, lifting her daughter's chin. "Remember what we talked about the day you started your period? You have your whole life ahead of you, and the last thing you want is to end up pregnant. You're still a baby yourself. And with AIDS spreading around like it is, you have to be even more careful. And you can still get it by doing what you did to Jason. Oral sex is just as dangerous as regular sex."

Marcella hugged Ashley tight. "What I want you to do now is think about what you did, and then I want you to straighten up this room. Then when I'm finished with cleaning up the rest of the apartment, we'll go back over to your granny's for dinner."

Marcella closed Ashley's bedroom door, and closed her eyes. This was all her fault. If she hadn't subjected Ashley to this run-down, low income, thug infested apartment complex, she never would have come in contact with Jason or anyone like him. And while Ashley was wrong for disobeying her in the first place, she was young, dumb, and naive like most girls her age. Wanting to feel like she belonged to the "in" crowd. Wanting to know what it felt like to be liked by some little boy. Marcella didn't know what she was going to do. This boy's mother seemed like the type who didn't care about anything or anybody, and if she went over there to confront her about her son, she'd probably cuss Marcella out like some sailor. If she told Tyrone, he'd rush right over to take care of the situation, but he'd probably take the whole thing too far, and would end up in jail instead. If she told her mother, she'd be worried sick, and would definitely tell Racquel and Kevin. And Marcella couldn't have that. Racquel was already convinced that she wasn't raising her children the way she should, and this disaster right here would be all the proof she needed. She had to talk to someone, though. And, like when every other major tragedy took place, that someone was Sharon.

Chapter 11

Marcella pulled on the jet-black pantyhose as carefully as she could, praying that she wouldn't tear a run in these, like she had with the previous pair just a few minutes ago. This was the last pair she had, and she had to make them work. It was already 9:30 A.M., and Sharon had phoned earlier saying she'd be by to pick them up around ten o'clock. Church services started at 10:45, and they needed at least fifteen minutes of driving time.

She slipped on a black knit ankle-length dress and then doubled back both of her arms to zip it. Then she slipped on her black pumps and put on her gold-toned hoop earrings. She wondered how far Ashley and Nicholas had gotten, and decided to check on them.

Ashley was completely dressed and was sitting in the living room flipping through the TV channels when Marcella came out of her bedroom. The TV was one of the few forms of entertainment that hadn't been included in her punishment, and she looked to be enjoying it. Nicholas was as slow as a hundred-year-old man whenever he did anything, so Marcella always had to help him along.

She walked into his room and saw him sitting on his bed with nothing except his dress pants on. He was flipping the pages of some *Star Trek* book Sharon had purchased for him a couple of weeks ago. It was filled mostly with pictures, and even though he'd already thumbed through the pages at least twenty times, he still looked just as interested as the first time. Sharon was always buying him and Ashley things like that. Between Corrine, Racquel, and Sharon, the children were spoiled rotten.

"Nicholas, why aren't you dressed yet?" Marcella said, picking up his navy-blue turtleneck sweater. "Your aunt Sharon is going to be here any minute."

"Okay, Mom," he said, still turning the pages of his book.

"Nicholas," she said with more authority than before.

He dropped the book down, stood at attention, and smiled at her. He knew she wasn't playing, but it was still funny to him.

She couldn't help but smile back at him. "Boy, you'd better get this shirt on, and put on your dress shoes."

"I wanna wear my boots," he said in a semi-begging voice.

"Not today. There's not that much snow out there, and the sidewalks and the streets are clear."

"Aw, Mom. I wore them yesterday, and you didn't mind."

"That was yesterday, and this is today. Now put them on," she said, pulling his navy-blue blazer from his closet.

He obeyed her, but he wasn't happy about it.

After Marcella handed him the blazer, he pulled it on, and went out to the living room to sit with Ashley. Marcella knew there was going to be an argument about the television, so she intervened before it even got started.

"I don't want to hear anything about who's watching what on that television. Ashley was watching it first, Nicholas, so don't start with her."

"But, Mom, Ashley said I could have control of the TV for a whole week, if I didn't . . . ," he said and then cut the rest of his sentence off. He looked at his big sister timidly.

Ashley stared at him with anger. Even though her mother had already found out about her deep, dark secret, it was obvious that Ashley still didn't want him bringing it up.

He kept his mouth shut and looked straight ahead at the TV.

Marcella had forgotten all about the deal Ashley had made with Nicholas, if he didn't tell, but now that she'd been reminded of it, she was going to make her stick to it. She should have never put her little brother in that kind of situation anyway.

"Ashley, if you made some deal with Nicholas, then give him the remote control."

Ashley looked at her mother and then at Nicholas. "Here," she said, frowning at him.

Nicholas licked his tongue out and smiled at her. Normally, Marcella would have scolded him about that sort of gesture, but Ashley deserved what she was getting.

Yesterday she had cried herself to sleep and stayed in her room for the rest of the evening. It was obvious that she felt terrible about what she'd done, but she seemed more embarrassed than anything else. Instead of the two of them going back over to Corrine's for dinner, Corrine picked up a pizza, and then she and Nicholas came back to the apartment. Ashley finally dragged out to the kitchen after about an hour, but she couldn't look her grandmother in the face. Corrine knew something had gone on, but never said anything. Marcella knew it was just a matter of time before she started asking questions, though, and she'd either have to tell the truth or have some well-concocted lie ready. She didn't like lying to her mother, but she just didn't see how she could confide in her about what Ashley had done. She just couldn't. She'd played it in her head over and over and over again all last night, and she didn't see how anyone was going to understand any of this. Although, when she'd phoned Sharon and told her the situation, she'd understood, and had given her nothing except moral support. But she was different from the rest of them. Somehow, someway, they'd find a way to blame her for what happened, and she just couldn't take that chance.

As Marcella finger-positioned her curls, which were hanging loosely down the sides of her face, she heard a knock at the door. "Ashley, that's probably your aunt Sharon, but ask who it is first," Marcella yelled out to the living room.

She heard Ashley ask who it was, and then open the door.

Marcella walked out to greet Sharon. "Hey, girl. You're looking awfully nice this Sunday morning."

"So do you," Sharon said, dropping her purse down in the chair next to the sofa.

It was nice to know that Sharon always tried to make her feel good.

"So, how are my favorite niece and nephew doing?" Sharon asked the children.

"Fine," Ashley said with a look of embarrassment on her face.

Nicholas was so glued to the television set, that he hadn't even heard the question.

"Boy, didn't you hear Aunt Sharon ask you how you were doing?" Ashley said, pushing him on the shoulder. "You are so rude."

"What?" he said, coming out of a daze trying to figure out what he had missed.

Sharon laughed. "How are you, Mr. Nicholas?"

"I'm fine," he said, smiling, and then switched his attention back to the cartoon.

Sharon loved Ashley and Nicholas like they really were her niece and nephew, because Marcella's family was the closest thing she had to blood relatives. And that was the reason she helped Marcella out as much as she could, whenever she could.

"Girl, we've still got another twenty to thirty minutes, so come on in my room for a few minutes."

Sharon turned and strutted into the bedroom.

Marcella shut the door behind her and sat down on the bed. Sharon sat down on the other side facing her.

"So, how have things been with Ashley since I talked to you last night?"

"She's been pretty quiet, and she was scared to death that I was going to tell her granny."

"I'm not surprised, because she had a funny look on her face when I spoke to her a few minutes ago. She'll get through this, and I doubt that she'll even think about doing anything like that again."

"Girl, I hope so, because I can't have this. I mean, she's only eleven years old. And I don't know what that little no-good boy was thinking."

"Have you thought any more about talking to his mother?"

"Not really. It was like I told you last night, they're a rough-natured family, and I don't know if I even want to confront them about any of this."

"Yeah, you do have to be careful. You never know about these thirteen-year-old boys from this generation. When we were growing up, everybody's parents in the neighborhood were your parents, but now little thugs like him are liable to blow your head off, just for telling on him. You just don't know anymore," Sharon said, crossing her legs.

"That's what I'm talking about. I am going to tell him to stay away from Ashley, though. And we just have to hope and pray that he listens," Marcella said, folding her arms into her stomach.

"Girl, what about Tyrone? Have you told him?"

"There's no way in the world I would tell him anything about this. First, he'd jump all over me and tell me how terrible of a mother I am, and then he'd be after that boy. It's just not worth it. I mean, if it gets out of hand, and I can't stop Jason from bothering Ashley, then I won't have a choice but to tell him. But other than that, I'm not saying anything to him."

"I guess I can understand that. So, has he been staying on time with his child support?"

"For some strange reason, he has. But get this," Marcella said, anxious to fill Sharon in. "We had one of our usual fallings out yesterday, and he had the audacity to say he's not baby-sitting the children anymore in the evenings, but that he might reconsider it, if I let him reduce the child support to thirty dollars a week. Can you believe that?"

"I know he didn't!" Sharon said in amazement.

"Oh, yes, he did."

"Thirty dollars? He's only paying sixty now, isn't he?"

"Yeah, and he's barely doing that. He's really starting to get on my nerves, and I mean bad. I almost cracked his head with a baseball bat yesterday."

"You what?" Sharon said, laughing. "It's not funny, but I can't help it. And I can't believe you didn't tell me about that last night."

Marcella laughed with her. "Girl, I was so wound up about this thing with Ashley, that I didn't even think about it. And to tell you the truth, I still can't believe I did that."

"You used to be the scariest person I knew when we were in high school."

"Girl, I know, but my whole attitude is changing. I'm under so much pressure, that sometimes I feel like I'm going to explode. It's a wonder I haven't cracked up or something."

"What did he do to get you so upset?" Sharon said, stroking the back of her hair.

"I told him to get out after he made that comment about the child support, and he started talkin' some crap about the university turning me into a fool, and that he wasn't playing with me. So, I politely went into Nicholas's room and found his baseball bat."

"Did he leave?"

"What do you think? Girl, you should have seen him struggling to get out the door. I don't think he thought I had it in me. And to be quite honest, I didn't, either."

Sharon cracked up laughing again, and so did Marcella.

"I know I'm laughing, but I'm telling you," Sharon said on a more serious note. "Tyrone isn't worth it. And you need to keep your distance from that fool."

"How can I do that, when he's the father of my two children? There's just no way of getting around it. And I don't know what I'm going to do next week for a babysitter."

"Well, what time does your mother get off work?"

"She works second shift."

"Oh, yeah. That's right," Sharon said in disappointment. "Well, I can watch them for you a couple nights a week, and I know Racquel will, too. So, all we have to do is find someone to keep them from the time they get out of school to when we get off work."

"I think their school has an aftercare program, but even if they do, I can't afford to add another bill to our budget. It's stretched to the limit as it is."

"Don't worry about it, we'll work this out, even if it means that I have to pay for it myself. So, if you've been thinking about quitting school, you can just forget that," Sharon said, raising her eyebrows.

"You can't be doing that. You have your own bills and your own life to live," Marcella said, feeling like a failure.

"Like I said, we'll work this out," Sharon said, ignoring her. "We'll all get together after church, so we can figure out what to do."

Marcella gazed at her in silence because she knew if she spoke one word, or so much as blinked, tears would fall down her face.

Sharon took notice, moved closer to her and hugged her. "Don't worry about it. Everything will work out fine. I promise."

"I don't know what I would do without you. Sometimes you understand me better than my own family does," Marcella said, wiping her face with her hands.

"I don't know about that, but I do know that I would rather die than see you and those little ones in there suffering unnecessarily. It's not like I'm rich or anything, but I can afford to help you from time to time when you need me to."

"But it seems like you're always doing things for me, even though I'm never in a position to do anything for you."

"Marcella. You're my best friend, you love me like a sister, and that's all the payback I need from you."

Marcella sighed deeply. "Well, all I know is that these next three-and-a-half years are going to be rough, and I'm going to need you more than ever when it comes to emotional support, if nothing else."

"My grandmother used to say that anything worth having, takes a lot of hard work and then some. And she was right. When this is all over, you'll look back on it and laugh. Just wait and see."

Marcella stood up and walked in front of the mirror. "My face is a mess."

"Better fix it," Sharon said, laughing. "You never know who you might meet at church."

"I doubt that very seriously," Marcella said, walking out of the room and into the bathroom. "I really doubt it."

"Hey, Ashley," Racquel said, stepping inside the church door. "Hey, Nick."

"Aunt Racquel," Nicholas said, turning toward his aunt and hugging her. "Hey, Uncle Kevin," he said, hugging him, as well.

"Hi," Ashley said, barely looking at Kevin or Racquel.

Kevin spoke back to her, while Racquel was trying to figure out what was wrong with her.

"What's with that gloomy look on your face, sweetheart?" Racquel asked Ashley.

"Nothing," she said, lying.

"Well, then, put a smile on that pretty face," Racquel said, rubbing her finger softly under Ashley's chin. Racquel knew something wasn't quite right, though, and she couldn't wait to find out from Marcella what the problem was.

Corrine entered the church shortly after Racquel and Kevin, and all of the adults hugged each other and then proceeded toward the church vestibule, where two ushers were passing out the weekly church bulletins and envelopes for tithes and offerings. They each took the appropriate envelope, walked single file into the church, and sat down in the fifth row on the left-hand side of the church. Corrine, Marcella, Sharon, Racquel, Ashley, Nicholas, and Kevin. In that order. There were so many of them, they almost took up the entire pew.

Westside Missionary Baptist Church wasn't the largest church in the Chicago area, but it held about five hundred members if you included the balcony and the choir stand. And since they'd added on the educational center last year, the church looked a lot bigger and much more contemporary than it used to.

When Deacon James stood up to call the church to worship, Racquel looked at her watch, and saw that it was 10:45. Good, she thought. They were actually starting on time for a change. Before Deacon Thurgood passed away, he started devotion like clockwork, but ever since Deacon James had taken charge, they'd been starting anywhere between ten and fifteen minutes late. Which didn't make any sense to Racquel, but who was she to complain.

After the mass choir walked in two by two and spread throughout the choir stand, Deacon James and four other deacons stood up and faced the congregation.

"I love the Lord, He heard my cry," Deacon James sang as loud as he could without the use of a microphone, and it was sort of like follow the leader. Deacon James sang the words of each verse at normal speed, but when the congregation joined in, they sang the words in sort of a dragged-out way. When the hymn was finished, the second deacon read a scripture from St. John; the third spoke a meditational thought; and the fourth led the congregation in prayer.

By the time they'd finished the Lord's Prayer, morning hymn, and responsive reading, Nicholas was fidgeting back and forth in his seat, and Ashley's head started bobbing up and down like she was about to fall asleep. Marcella took notice to it, and gave both of them "the look," and they immediately turned their undivided attention toward the choir members, who were preparing to sing their first selection of the morning.

"If anybody asks you . . . where I am going . . . where I am going . . . soon. I'm going up a yonder . . . I'm going up a yonder . . . I'm going up a yonder . . . to be with my Lord," the choir sang, swaying from side to side and clapping in sync with the rhythm of the music, which was a lot more contemporary than when the youth choir used to sing it fifteen years ago.

When the song ended, the announcement clerk stood and walked into the pulpit to the right of the minister's podium, and asked all visitors to stand, to state their name and what church they were from, and then took up ten more minutes reading every announcement under the sun. By now, Racquel was starting to get a little restless herself. She'd been born and raised Baptist, and still Racquel never understood why the service always had to be prolonged. Some of the information was important, but a lot of it was unnecessary. They were going to have to sit for another ten minutes listening to Pastor Morgan put on the guilt trip for church members who didn't pay their tithes. "You're robbing God, when you don't pay your tithes," he would say. "The Bible says ten percent, and it don't mean take-home pay, either. God wants his off the top, before Uncle Sam or anyone else gets their hands on it."

Racquel had heard him beg the congregation so many times, until she didn't pay much attention to it anymore. And whether it was right or wrong, she just hadn't been moved enough to pay out ten percent of her gross earnings. And she felt even more strongly about it whenever she saw Pastor Morgan cruising around town in that brand-new Lexus. And those flashy rings he had on every finger didn't help much, either. And his wife, "the first lady," made it clear early on that she wasn't about to step inside of Westside Missionary Baptist Church, unless her suit, hat, purse, and shoes were all classily color coordinated.

Racquel just couldn't see it, but her mother thought differently about the subject. She paid her tithes every Sunday, and even made up for the Sundays that she missed if she couldn't attend service for some reason or another. Her mother was convinced that people were blessed tenfold whenever they gave from their hearts. And maybe Racquel would have felt that way, too, if she thought tithing would give her the baby she'd been trying so hard to have. And maybe someday she *would* change her whole way of thinking, but from the way things were going, it definitely wasn't going to be today.

Racquel scanned the congregation as she walked to the front of the church and placed her offering in one of the collection plates. There must have been at least ten women to every man. For the life of her, she couldn't figure out why more men didn't come to church. Maybe they were afraid to, or thought it might lessen their manhood somehow. Racquel didn't know, but she couldn't help but wonder about it.

After Pastor Morgan took his text, preached the first part of his sermon, and asked for a couple of Amens, he changed gears, and the organist played the music the same as he did for the choir when they were singing. Pastor Morgan took the microphone and strutted down the aisle. Then he went back toward the pulpit, but before he stepped up to it, he leaped up on the front pew, preaching as hard as he could.

Ashley and Nicholas jumped and looked around when the woman behind them leaped out of her seat and started shouting and dancing in place. They'd seen this time after time, but they still seemed just as frightened as they did the first time they'd witnessed someone being filled with the Holy Ghost. It was just too intense and too complex for them to understand, Racquel guessed.

When Pastor Morgan finished the benediction, Corrine, Kevin, Ashley, and Nicholas went to shake his hand. Racquel, Sharon, and Marcella stood in the middle aisle, close to where they'd been sitting, and discussed where they were all going to eat for dinner.

Marcella looked toward the back of the church and noticed an extremely handsome-looking man staring at her. And he was smiling. She turned her head back toward Racquel and Sharon, pretending to take part in their conversation, but it wasn't long before she looked again to see if Mr. Fine was still standing there. But he wasn't. Instead, he was making his way up the aisle.

"Marcella, right?" he said, stopping in front of her.

"Yes. Do I know you?" she asked, trying to determine how he knew her name.

"No, but I play ball at the 'Y' with your brother-in-law, Kevin, from time to time, plus I've seen you a few times here at church. I'm Darryl Johnson."

Marcella couldn't believe Kevin had put her on the spot like this without warning her, and she was going to kill Racquel if she'd been aware of this surprise meeting all along and had purposely kept it from her. If she had known she was meeting someone as gorgeous as this man, she'd have borrowed one of Sharon's professional-looking suits. She hoped she looked okay. "Oh," she said, not knowing what else to say.

Racquel and Sharon looked at each other and eased away from where Marcella and Darryl were standing. Marcella was going to murder both of them when this was all over.

"I hope this isn't making you uncomfortable. I told Kevin he should say something to you, so you wouldn't be caught off guard, but he said you wouldn't be offended by me introducing myself."

"Uh . . . no. I'm not offended," she said, eyeing Kevin as he walked down one of the outer aisles of the church. He was smiling, and Marcella wanted to hold up her fist to him. She'd take care of him later, though. The children and Corrine were walking behind him. Marcella saw Nicholas trying to slip through the pew, obviously wanting to come over to where she was at, but Corrine steered him down the aisle toward the back of the church.

Darryl noticed the same thing. "It looks like your son is getting anxious," he said, smiling.

"Yeah, he gets like that sometimes. He just wants to be nosey," Marcella said, wondering how he knew she had a son. Kevin must have told him, which was good because that meant he didn't have a problem with the fact that she had children.

"Well, I'll tell you what. Here's my business card, and my home phone number is written on the back. You can call me if you want, or you can give me your number and I'll call you."

Marcella wanted him to call her. At least when the man made the first move, it felt like he was the one pursuing the relationship. He'd already shown his interest by coming up to her right now, but still, she wanted him to dial her phone number first.

"I think I have a notepad in here somewhere," she said, fumbling through her purse.

"Here," he said, passing her another one of his cards. "Write it on the back of this."

"Thanks," she said, writing her name and number down.

"If you're not doing anything tonight, I'll call you then."

"That'll be fine," Marcella said, smiling at him as they walked out to the vestibule, where the rest of her family was waiting.

When he left, Racquel, Sharon, and Corrine started laughing.

"You guys think you're slick, but you're not," Marcella said, rolling her eyes playfully. "And you know I'm going to pay you back, Kevin," she said.

"I told you," Sharon said, cracking up. "You never know who you might meet at church."

Chapter 12

For the past four months, Marcella had been living in pure heaven, and life was better than ever. She still had to pinch herself whenever she thought about Darryl being a medical resident at Covington Park Memorial. A doctor. The man was actually a doctor. And he was interested in *her*. It was all so hard for her to believe, and no matter how many times he called, came to visit, or took her out, she still couldn't understand it. It was almost like she was living in some sort of fantasy world, waiting to be thrown back to reality. And he adored Ashley and Nicholas. The idea of her having two children didn't bother him at all, and sometimes he even planned outings that included all four of them. He was everything she could have possibly ever hoped for, and she prayed daily that this would never end. Intelligent, decent, caring, and while looks weren't the most important characteristic, he was fine.

He had features similar to that Keith-guy she'd met a year ago on campus. Medium complexion, wavy jetblack hair. The only difference was, he was much taller. At least six-three. And whenever she looked up at him, she felt like melting.

Yes, life was good. And even Racquel seemed happier than usual, and she wasn't nearly as obsessed with getting pregnant. She'd taken that infertility drug for more than six months, and then finally stopped when she began experiencing some weird side effect. She hadn't gotten pregnant, but she didn't seem to be depressed about it the way she used to be. Maybe the fact that she'd been keeping Ashley and Nicholas every evening while Marcella worked was making a difference. Sometimes the children even spent the night when Marcella had tons of studying or needed time to work on some paper she had due. Racquel was finally getting the opportunity to do what she loved most. Taking care of two children on a daily basis. And while Marcella was thankful for all that Racquel and Kevin had done to help her this past semester, it was now summer break, and the children wouldn't be spending nearly as much time with them. Racquel was on summer break from teaching and had offered to keep the children during the day while Marcella worked, but Marcella had found an all-day summer program designed for low-income families instead. It offered all sorts of educational activities, field trips, and other recreational activities, and it was only costing her ten dollars a week per child. She hoped the absence of the children wasn't going to cause Racquel to slip back into a severe state of depression, but Ashley and Nicholas needed to be in an educational atmosphere, because it was better for them. Maybe Kevin would reconsider the option of artificial insemination. He'd always said that it wasn't an option because of how expensive it was, but maybe if Racquel kept working on him in the right way, he might just change his mind.

Marcella washed the last of this morning's breakfast dishes and then waited for Darryl to arrive at her apartment. Her mother had taken a week of vacation and wanted her grandchildren to spend the night with her. Corrine had picked them up from the center, brought them by the apartment to get a change of clothing for the next day, and then took them to the park to watch her company's baseball game.

With school being out, she'd been spending as much time as possible with Ashley and Nicholas and hadn't spent much time alone with Darryl. He didn't seem to mind, but she knew it was important for them to spend some quality time together when it was just the two of them.

It was 6:30 P.M., and since Darryl wasn't scheduled to pick her up for dinner until 7, she picked up the latest issue of *Essence* that Racquel had given her and read through the various articles. When she finished it, she reached to pick up the previous month's issue, and heard a knock at the door. She stood up, strutted over to the door, patted her hair to make sure no strands were out of place, and opened it.

"Hey, sweetheart," he said, pulling her into his arms and kissing her.

"How's it going?" she said as they released each other.

"Tired. The hospital was a madhouse today."

"Did you just get off?"

"Yep. I worked a twelve-hour shift today, but I'm off tomorrow," he said, dropping down on the sofa.

"Then, you probably don't feel like going out to dinner."

"Not really, but we can if you really want to."

"It doesn't matter to me. We can order a pizza or something instead, if you want."

"That sounds good," he said, leaning back on the sofa with his eyes closed.

"You wanna pick it up on the way to your apartment or have it delivered?" she asked, walking toward the phone in the kitchen.

"We might as well pick it up, since it's on the way."

Marcella looked up the number in the phone book and dialed it. "Hi. I'd like to order a medium pizza with sausage, mushrooms, and double cheese," Marcella requested and then paused, waiting for the waitress to tell her how long it would be. Carl's was the busiest and best-tasting pizza place in the area, and it usually took thirty to forty minutes for them to prepare each order. And since today was Friday, it was probably going to take even longer.

"Thank you," she said and hung up the phone.

"How long?" Darryl asked.

"Forty-five minutes," she said, sitting down on the sofa next to him. "We might as well watch TV or something until then," she said, realizing that the pizza place was only about ten minutes away from her apartment.

"I promise you, things will be different when my residency is completed next year. No more long hours, and I'll finally have the money to take you out to nice restaurants for a change," he said, as if he felt bad because they were having pizza. They did have it a lot, but Marcella didn't mind at all. She was just happy to be with him.

"Don't worry about it. I'm happy just the way things are."

Darryl leaned his head into Marcella's chest and placed his arms around her waist, while she caressed the back of his head. It felt good to have him so close to her. So close to her heart. She'd been trying to contain her feelings for him for months now, but it was becoming more and more difficult to keep it up. She was in love with him and wanted to tell him. Something told her that he was in love with her, too, but he'd never actually said the words, and the last thing she wanted was to take the risk of telling him how she felt and then getting her feelings hurt. Being with him was almost unrealistic, and she had to take some precautions. She didn't want to end up getting hurt the way she had with Tyrone. But then, Darryl wasn't at all like Tyrone because the two of them were as different as Black-folks dressing and store-bought stuffing. To put it plainly, they were different in every aspect.

She smiled when she heard Darryl breathing deeply. He was so cute when he slept, and she could have sat there holding him forever. She flipped through the channels on the TV set and didn't see anything interesting. She wasn't a frequent TV watcher, but on days like today she wished she had at least one of those overpriced pay channels. But, of course, that wasn't even an option, since she could barely pay the monthly basic-cable rate as it was. And the only reason she had that, was because her mother had paid to have it installed for the children. And she helped out with the bill, as well, when times were rougher than usual for Marcella.

When she finally settled on CNN, she heard a couple of knocks at the door and frowned. It was probably some of those kids looking for Ashley or Nicholas, and since they weren't home, she decided to ignore it. But it wasn't long before there were more knocks, and this time they sounded a lot harder, like someone was pounding a fist against the door. The sound was so loud that Darryl sat straight up.

"What was that?" he asked with his eyes still half closed.

Marcella felt nervous, because she knew there was only one person crazy enough to beat on her door in that manner. "Someone's knocking," she said, standing up. She walked over to the door and opened it.

"What took you so long to answer the door?" Tyrone asked, brushing past her.

Now, who did he think he was bulldozing his way into *her* apartment?

"I should have known you had somebody up in here," Tyrone said, casting his eye at Darryl.

"Hey, man, what's up?" Darryl said, speaking to him cordially.

Tyrone ignored him. "Where's my kids?" he asked Marcella.

"They're with my mom," she responded.

"Wow. Just wow. Do you *ever* keep your own kids? You go to school nine months out of the year, and now that you're out for the summer, you mean to tell me, you're still throwing them off on your mother?"

"This is not the time for this, Tyrone. I told you where they are, and if you want to see them, you know where my mother lives."

"You barred me from going over there. Remember?" he said, laughing sarcastically.

He'd only been there for a few minutes, but Marcella had already taken as much of him as she could stand. "Please leave, Tyrone," she said, trying to see what expression Darryl had on his face. She was so embarrassed.

"Oh, now you want to be nice in front of your little company, when just a few months ago you told me to get out and threatened me with physical harm. Remember that? So don't be trying to put on that Little Miss Innocent act now."

Where was that baseball bat when she needed it? Darryl had never heard her use words like that, and she felt like crawling under a table or into a closet. Anywhere. Anywhere at all. Why was this fool doing this? He was supposedly so in love with that Priscilla, so it couldn't have been jealousy causing him to act so stupid. She had to get rid of him. "Tyrone, I'm asking you again. Please leave," she said as calmly as she could.

"I'll tell you one thing, you better not be laying up with this punk when my kids are here," Tyrone said.

What? She'd known from the very beginning that it was a mistake in opening the door to let him in. And worse than that, she knew it was just a matter of time before Darryl broke his silence.

"Man, I think you'd better leave," Darryl said, standing up.

"I'll leave when I feel like leaving," Tyrone said, scanning Darryl from head to toe. "And if you ever try to put your hands on Ashley or Nick, you'll be dealing with me. Nicholas told me how you be hanging around over here all the time, but if you think you're about to play Daddy with my kids, you can forget that."

"If you spent more time with them, you wouldn't have to worry about it. Now would you?" Darryl said, just as pissed off as Tyrone.

"Don't let that little medical degree get your tail kicked," Tyrone said. "You might think you're this and that, but you don't mean jack to me."

"Tyrone, stop it!" Marcella screamed. Things were escalating at top speed, and it was time to end all of this before it got physical.

"If you don't leave, Tyrone, I'm calling the police," Marcella said, opening the front door.

"Crazy trick. This isn't the end of this. I promise you that," Tyrone said, storming out the door.

Marcella closed the door behind him and dreaded turning around to look in Darryl's face. How was she going to explain all of this? Tyrone had known all along that she was seeing someone because Nicholas had told him about it shortly after they'd gone out on their first date. He hadn't acted like he had any problem with it then, so she couldn't understand at all what the problem was now. He'd been slacking on his child support again and was spending less and less time with the children, but she hadn't made one complaint about it. She never messed with him about anything anymore because she didn't care. For the first time in her life, she was happy and didn't have time to be worrying about what Tyrone was or wasn't doing. She'd made it without his help the first year, and now that she was starting her sophomore year in the fall, she figured she could make it through that one just as well.

"I am so sorry about this," Marcella said, looking at Darryl.

"He's got a lot of nerve coming in here acting like he owns the place," Darryl said in an angry tone.

"I don't know what's wrong with him. He knows I spend as much time as I can with Ashley and Nicholas, so I don't know why he's trying to make it seem like I don't. This is the first night since the semester ended that Ashley and Nicholas have spent the night anywhere else. And the only reason they spent a few nights here and there with Racquel and Kevin was because I had to study or do research for one of my papers. And it definitely wasn't because I was out having the time of my life."

"Well, he's got one more time to approach me the way he did tonight. And I don't know who he thinks I am, but I grew up in the same neighborhood that he did."

"Darryl, look. You're a doctor, and I know you're not going to stoop to Tyrone's level. He's not worth it."

"I know he's not worth it, but I'm not about to let him walk over me like I'm some child, either. And I definitely don't appreciate the way he talks to you. If anything, you should be the one complaining. He doesn't do anything for Ashley and Nicholas. I do more for them than he does, and I'm not even their father."

"I know you do, baby, and I love you for it," she said, immediately wishing she could take every word back. This was the last thing she wanted, and now that he knew how she felt, it was probably just a matter of time before his calls and visits started to lessen, and then eventually ended permanently. She looked the other way.

"Hey," he said, turning her face toward him delicately with his hand. "What did you say?"

"Nothing," she replied, walking away from him. Her emotions were running wild, and she couldn't think straight.

"Well, unless something's wrong with my hearing, I could have sworn you said you loved me," he said, smiling.

"We have to pick up the pizza," she said, grabbing her purse. "Are you ready?" she asked, ignoring his last comment.

"Not until you tell me what you just said," he said, folding his arms, still smiling.

"I love you, okay. Now, are you satisfied?" she said, pretending to be mad at him.

"Oh, I'm very satisfied," he said, hugging her and laughing slightly.

Why wasn't he saying it back, she thought. That's what she got for getting herself all wrapped up in someone so sophisticated and as intelligent as him. She'd been fooling herself for months now, and it was finally coming to a head. What she should have done was leave well enough alone. In fact, she was starting to get a little upset at him because it was almost as if he was gloating about it. She pulled away from him. "By the time we get to the restaurant, the pizza is going to be cold," she said, walking toward the door.

"So what. That's what microwaves are for."

"I know you think you're funny, but you're not," she said, without any sign of a smile on her face.

Darryl must have picked up on it. "Come here," he said, reaching out to her.

"No. I'm ready to go," she said, opening the door.

"Marcella, close the door, and come here. Please," he said, sounding serious.

"What?" she said, closing the door.

He pulled her against his body again, and then gazed down at her. "I'm in love with you, too, Marcella, and I have been for a long time now."

She felt paralyzed. These were the words she'd been waiting for, and now that she was actually hearing them, she wasn't sure how she should react.

When she didn't say anything, he continued. "For weeks, I've wanted to tell you, but I wasn't sure if you felt the same way or not, and the last thing I wanted was to end up hurt like I did just before I started dating you."

Just before? He'd never mentioned anything like this, and she didn't like the sound of it. For all she knew, he'd started seeing her on the rebound from some other relationship gone bad. Maybe he just *thought* he was in love with her. Maybe he just needed someone to ease his pain. Someone to keep him from being alone. And what was going to happen if this ex-lover came back into the picture and decided that she wanted to get back with him after all. Marcella had told herself from the beginning that this whole situation was too good to be true.

"I didn't realize you were just getting out of a relationship when we met," she said, trying to sound like she wasn't bothered by what he'd just told her.

"It was a terrible situation, and as far as I'm concerned, it's in the past. You're all that I care about now, so none of that matters."

She prayed that he was being honest with her. Some men had a problem when it came to honesty, and she hoped he wasn't one of them. "We'd better go," she said, glancing at her watch.

Once Marcella was securely seated inside the Volkswagen, Darryl closed her door and walked around to get in on the driver's side. He pulled his seat belt on, placed the car in reverse, and drove out of the parking lot.

*   *   *

After eating a few slices of pizza, Marcella and Darryl had ended up making love, and now they were in bed snuggling close to each other.

"Baby, I love you so much," Darryl said, stroking Marcella's hair.

"I love you, too," she said with her face leaning against his chest, and her eyes closed.

"And you make me feel so good when we make love," he continued.

"I'm glad," she said, wishing she could return the same compliment back to him. It wasn't that he made her feel horrible, but at the same time, she really wasn't all that impressed with his performance in bed. She'd been hoping that it would get better as time went on, but so far it hadn't. And she was pretty sure that this mediocre lovemaking had a whole lot to do with the fact that he wasn't all that big. Sharon had complained about this very thing when it came to Marcus, and now Marcella knew exactly what she meant. But she still didn't see sex as being a good enough reason not to marry someone. As a matter of fact, she'd marry Darryl in a heartbeat if he asked her to, because there were far too many good things that more than outweighed this one deficiency. And anyway, nobody was perfect.

"So, what about you?"

"What do you mean?" she asked, opening her eyes but was glad he couldn't see the guilty expression on her face.

"You know. How do you feel when we make love? I mean, do I satisfy you?"

There was no way she was going to tell him the truth about this. She wished that she could, but she just couldn't. "I feel wonderful, and yes, you do satisfy me," she said, trying to sound as sincere as possible.

"Good, because your satisfaction is important to me."

Marcella didn't know what to say, so she said nothing.

"And if you have a certain desire, I hope you'll tell me, because otherwise, there's no way I'll know."

There *was* something he could do, but she was a coward and didn't have the nerve to ask him. Tyrone had done it all the time, and never thought twice about it, but some men had a problem when it came to going down on a woman, and she didn't want to push it. "No. I'm fine with the way things are between us. I'm fine with the sex and our relationship overall."

"You're sure?" he asked, holding her tight.

"Yes. I'm sure," she said, kissing him on his chest and wondering why he was asking her all these questions. She hoped he hadn't sensed her dissatisfaction, because the last thing she wanted was to hurt his feelings. And more than anything, she didn't want something like this to come between them.

They lay there for a while, enjoying the moment, and then Darryl finally spoke. "I still can't believe Tyrone tripped out the way he did earlier."

"Yeah, I know," Marcella said and wished Darryl would drop the Tyrone subject.

"I mean, how long is it going to take for him to realize that you and he are living totally separate lives, and that what you do with your life is your business?"

"Tyrone knows that what I do is my business, and all he's trying to do is mess up what you and I have with each other."

"Well, he needs to get over it, because you and I are going to be together whether he likes it or not."

"Look, let's forget about Tyrone," she said, looking up at him. "Because all that matters to me is you."

Darryl smiled and then kissed her passionately. Marcella knew he was preparing for round two, and she hoped that through some miracle, it was going to be much better this time. But then, even if it wasn't, she was still going to love him as much as always.

Chapter 13

"We mortgaged our house for this, Racquel. Have you forgotten that?" Kevin screamed at the top of his lungs.

Racquel shivered. She couldn't remember Kevin ever being this angry, and he was scaring her. "Sometimes it takes more than one try," she said, changing her position on the side of the bed.

"More than one try? We did that artificial insemination thing six months in a row, paid almost ten thousand dollars for that in vitro whatever you call it, and now you think I'm going to agree to try it again? You must be crazier than I thought," he said, leaning against the wooden armoire.

"But Kevin . . . ," she cried.

"Do you realize how long this has gone on?" he asked, ignoring whatever she was going to say. "Ever since the day we got married, I've had to hear you go on and on about getting pregnant, but I still stood by you. Then you started buying all that unnecessary crap from I don't know how many different department stores for a baby we still don't have. Then instead of making love, we started having sex just to try and make a baby. Then you insisted that we go to an infertility specialist. And I did. Then you practically killed yourself trying to take that infertility medication, and when you found out that that wasn't going to work, you started hounding me again about all these other overpriced procedures. And for whatever ridiculous reason, I agreed to those, too. And now that we've spent all this money for nothing, you've got the audacity to ask me to take out another mortgage against the house? What's wrong with you?" he said, staring at her. "Huh? What's wrong with you, Racquel?"

She cried hysterically and didn't say anything.

And it was obvious that he didn't feel sorry for her one bit, because he kept on screaming at her. "How much more of this do you think I can take? We've been married for almost four years, and I've had enough of this. You said that if I went to the infertility specialist with you, and none of the options worked out, you would put this whole baby business behind you. That's what you told me, and I believed you. But now you're starting this all up again. Not to mention the fact that you were in so big of a hurry that you couldn't even wait for the insurance company to review our appeal. It's just not meant to be, Racquel. So why can't you just accept that?"

Why was he torturing her like this? And no matter what he said, it *was* meant to be. She'd read about women who went years without having a child and then ended up pregnant. And their babies were born healthy, too. He just didn't understand, and she couldn't believe he was blowing up at her like this. She was lost for words, but she wanted to say something. Anything. "One more try isn't going to hurt anything, Kevin. The success rate is a lot higher with the in-vitro-fertilization method. So, maybe all we need is a second try at it. I'll get a parttime job to help pay for it, if I have to. Just one more try, and I promise I'll never mention the idea of trying to have a baby ever again. I promise," she said, rising from the bed and walking toward him. She reached out to touch him.

"What are you? Deaf or something?" he said, pushing her hand away from him. "You haven't been listening to a word I've said, have you? Everything is always about what you want, and I'm sick of it. I've been as patient with you as I can, but things are getting worse instead of better. I used to think that our love for each other would outweigh all of our problems, but I was wrong. Love doesn't seem to mean anything to you anymore, and I'm starting to feel the same way. I'm too young to spend the rest of my life chasing some fantasy, and I'm not doing it anymore."

"So what are you saying?" she asked pitifully, with tears still rolling down her face.

"Exactly what I said, Racquel. I'm not doing this anymore. Either you give this up, or I'm filing for a divorce."

Her heart did a cartwheel, and her stomach turned in the same manner. "Honey, you don't mean that," she said, almost begging.

"I love you more than anything, Racquel, but I'm telling you, if you don't stop this obsession of yours, I'm moving out, and I'm divorcing you."

"How can you say you love me in one breath, and then threaten me with divorce in another? How can you do that?"

"First of all, it's not a threat. I'm telling you honestly what's going to happen if you don't stop this. It's as simple as that. And no matter what you think, I do love you. If I didn't, do you think I would have spent these last four years arguing with you, putting up with your depressed moods, and paying all this money to some infertility clinic? And to think I let you talk me into taking out a second mortgage on this house—knowing good and well I didn't want to. Only a fool or somebody in love would do any of that. Especially, when you don't show any appreciation for any of it. So now I'm giving you a choice."

"How can you expect me to just give up? You know how badly I want a baby, and I can't believe you're doing this."

"I'm not going to spend the rest of the day arguing with you. I took the afternoon off so we could spend some time together, but if I had known you were going to ask me to spend more money on this infertility obsession, I would have stayed at work. It's getting to the point where I hate being here."

"Well, then leave," Racquel said, raising her voice for the first time since the conversation started.

"So, are you saying that you're not going to give this up?" he asked, waiting for an answer.

"What I'm saying is, if you don't want to be here, then leave," she said, calling his bluff. The last thing she wanted was to be without Kevin, but she wasn't going to keep begging him, either.

"What a waste," he said, and stormed out of the bedroom.

Racquel stood in the middle of the floor crying silently, yet uncontrollably. She wiped her tears with her hand and then held them across her face leaning her head back. She felt like dying. Like her whole world was over. This was all wrong, and she didn't have the slightest idea as to how she could fix it. She'd drawn a picture of how her life was going to be before she'd even met Kevin. She would graduate from college with a degree, find a job teaching small children, get married to the perfect husband, have lots of healthy, beautiful babies, and live happily ever after. But now, everything was going in the wrong direction. Kevin was actually threatening her with a divorce. What nerve. She'd been the best wife she could be, and then some. At least she thought she had. She was faithful to him, and she loved him. What more did he want? As far as she was concerned, he was getting everything he wanted, and it was she who had always gone lacking. All she wanted was this one thing, and she couldn't have it. And even worse, Kevin wasn't willing to go the extra mile to make sure it happened. Yes, they had paid a ton of money to the clinic, but it was worth it. They'd spent more money on each of the cars they drove than what they had on that. It was only money, and something as miraculous as having a child was far more important. Kevin just didn't get it, and she wasn't sure how she could make him see it. He was carrying on like she was some crazed maniac, and he kept saying she was obsessed, but she wasn't. She would have loved nothing more than to see him move out, so she wouldn't have to hear his complaints and ultimatums anymore. But she knew she was fooling herself. She loved him too much for that, and she needed him for more reasons than she cared to think about.

She pulled a tissue from the Kleenex box, wiped her face, and blew her nose. Before this argument had erupted between her and Kevin, they'd planned on going out for a late lunch, but now she didn't have an appetite. She never knew what to do with herself when they got into it like this. At least when school was in session, she could tune all of her problems out by concentrating on the children in her class, but now that school was out, she didn't even have that to turn to. Maybe Kevin would come to his senses and everything would be fine. But, based on how enraged he was, she knew that was doubtful.

When she looked out the bedroom window and noticed that Kevin's truck was gone, she did what she always did after they argued: lay across the bed and fell asleep. After about an hour and a half, the phone rang and woke her up.

"Hello?" Racquel said in a muzzled voice with her eyes closed.

"Hey, girl. What's up?" Marcella asked.

Racquel cleared her throat. "Not too much. I must've dropped off to sleep for a minute."

"What are you doing sleeping in the middle of the afternoon?" Marcella said, sounding surprised.

"Kevin and I were at it again, and like always, he left."

"At it about what?"

Racquel hated even going into this with Marcella because she knew Marcella was going to have the same attitude as Kevin. What she needed now was some encouragement. What she needed was a vast amount of moral support. But there was no sense in trying to disguise the situation because chances were, Marcella already had a pretty good idea of what was going on anyway.

"I want to try that in-vitro-fertilization procedure one more time, but Kevin is totally against it."

Marcella paused for a moment to choose the right words. The last thing she wanted was to piss Racquel off or hurt her feelings. "I don't know what to say, except that, you did say you were through with trying if this last attempt didn't work."

"I know, but I just want to try this one last time. That's all. But all Kevin can see is how much money it's going to cost."

Marcella was lost for words and felt like her hands were tied. If she told Racquel that she agreed with Kevin, which she did, Racquel would probably hang up on her. But she didn't see where she had much of a choice. "Look, Racquel, don't take this the wrong way, but doesn't this in vitro fertilization cost close to ten thousand dollars? Maybe that's why Kevin is so concerned about it."

"I know it's a lot of money, but it won't hurt to take out another mortgage. And if it came down to it, we wouldn't even have to do that, because we already have enough to cover it in our savings account."

"Yeah, but do you think it's a good idea to spend your life savings on something you're not sure of?" Marcella asked. She'd tried not to side with Kevin, but Racquel was making it hard for her not to.

"But that's just it. I *am* sure it will happen. And I don't know how Kevin can put a price tag on the life of a child anyway."

"Well, I don't know," Marcella said, doing everything she could not to make any more negative comments.

"I don't either. And even worse, he threatened to divorce me. He's never done that before, so I don't know if he was serious or not," Racquel said and switched the phone from her left ear to her right.

"Divorce?" Marcella said in an upset tone of voice. "He actually said that?"

"Yes. He did. And I'm telling you, Marcella, I'm scared."

"Maybe he was just upset. We all say things we don't mean when we're upset."

"I don't know, but he sounded awfully serious to me."

"Girl, I know you don't want to hear what I'm about to say, but this isn't worth losing Kevin over. He loves you, and he practically worships the ground you walk on. And he's such a good husband. You've got to give this up, so the two of you can get on with your lives," Marcella said, and waited for Racquel to start yelling at her.

But she didn't.

"I know, but I want to have a baby so bad, and I'll never be able to forgive myself if I don't."

"Forgive yourself for what?"

"You remember that abortion I had when I was in high school."

"Racquel, you can't look back on that. You've asked God for forgiveness, and that's all you can do. You made a mistake, and you learned from it."

"But it was the biggest mistake of my life. And, God, Marcella," Racquel said, covering the mouthpiece of the phone and leaning her head back trying to fight back the tears. "I had another one when I was in college."

"You what? By who?"

"You wouldn't believe it if I told you."

"Wouldn't believe what?" Kevin asked, leaning inside the doorway of the bedroom.

Racquel jerked her head and looked at him in total shock. She shook her head slowly from side to side. She'd thought for sure he was gone. She had checked out the window before she laid down, and had only fallen asleep for a few minutes. At least, she'd thought it was just a few minutes. How was she going to explain this to a man who was talking about divorcing her? And even worse, she wondered how long he'd been standing there. Eavesdropping. She was speechless.

"Won't believe what?" Marcella asked.

"Hey, let me call you back. Okay?" Racquel said softly.

"Why can't you tell me now?" Marcella asked anxiously.

"I have to call you back. Okay?" Racquel repeated and hung up the phone.

"Answer me, Racquel," Kevin said with anger flowing through his voice.

"Baby, it's not what you think," she said nervously.

"Just stop it, Racquel," he said sternly. "How long do you think I've been standing here listening to your conversation? I'll tell you how long. Long enough to know that you've had two abortions, and that you never told me about them. We've even discussed this before, and you flat out lied to me. How could you do that?"

"I didn't know how to tell you," she said desperately.

"But you lied. And you've been lying all along. What *else* have you been lying about?" he asked.

"Nothing, Kevin. I swear."

"Really? Because I just heard you telling your sister that she wouldn't believe something. So what was that all about?"

Racquel was caught and felt like crawling under the bed. She'd never told anyone about the life she led while she was in college, and she just couldn't bring herself to tell Kevin now. If she did, he really would divorce her, and wouldn't think twice after doing it. But if she continued to lie to him, he would hate her even more, and she couldn't bear that, either. She felt like the walls were closing in on her.

"Tell me, Racquel!" he screamed when she didn't respond.

"Stop yelling at me, Kevin!" she said, screaming back at him.

"Well, then, you'd better start explaining," he said with no sympathy for her.

She stared at him, but didn't respond.

"Tell me!" he said, screaming at her again. "Now!"

"I got pregnant by a married White guy," she yelled. "Are you satisfied now?"

Kevin paused and then backed away from her slowly. He shook his head in denial. "No, you're kidding. Right? You've got to be?"

"I'm telling you the truth. I got pregnant by someone else's husband," she said with humiliation.

"So what you're telling me," he said, pausing, "is that I'm married to a tramp who kills babies."

Racquel just looked at him and figured it wasn't worth saying anything. And what could she say, anyway?

"Wow. If I hadn't interrupted your phone conversation, there's no telling what else I would have heard, is there?"

Racquel remained silent but didn't take her eyes off of him.

"This is too much for me. I'm outta here," he said, walking out of the bedroom.

She wanted to call him, beg him, plead with him. She wanted to do something to make him come back. Maybe if she explained it better, he would understand. But realistically, she knew he never would. This was the last straw. And while she feared even thinking about the future, she knew her marriage was over.

Marcella waited by the phone for a whole hour, expecting Racquel to call her back, but she didn't. She wanted to know what Racquel was trying to tell her, and why she had to end their conversation so suddenly. None of this was adding up, and she couldn't wait any longer to find out what was going on. She picked up the receiver and dialed her sister's number.

"Hello?" Racquel answered.

"Why didn't you call me back?" Marcella asked impatiently.

"I was going to, but the longer I sat here, the more I didn't feel like talking to anyone."

"What's going on over there?"

"I thought Kevin was still out when you called, but he wasn't. I fell asleep for almost two hours and didn't realize how much time had gone by. So I didn't hear him when he came back in the house."

"So what does that have to do with anything?"

"Everything. He heard every word I said about the abortions, so I didn't have a choice except to tell him how I got pregnant that second time."

Marcella wanted to know the same thing. And even more, she wanted to know why Racquel had kept this from her in the first place. "Well, how did you?"

"This is so embarrassing," Racquel said, taking a deep breath. "Remember when Daddy moved out for good?"

"Yeah."

"And when Mom thought I was going to have to drop out of school because Daddy was acting iffy about paying my tuition?"

"Mmm-hmm."

"Well, I ended up meeting this White guy, who just so happened to be CEO of Trasco, Inc."

"Not Trasco, the huge electronics corporation?"

"Yeah. *That* Trasco."

"How did you meet him?"

"My roommate and I used to go to this elite bar and grill that a lot of businessmen went to after work. And of course, I ended up meeting all sorts of people."

"A White guy, Racquel?" Marcella asked, like maybe she'd misunderstood her.

"Yes, and on top of that, he was married and had three children."

"Married with three children?" Marcella said in total shock. "How come you never told me about this?"

"I couldn't tell anybody, and I've regretted it ever since."

"How long did this go on?"

"Right up until I graduated. He paid practically all of my tuition during my junior and senior years, and how do you think I got that apartment off campus?"

Marcella was flabbergasted. This couldn't have possibly been the same woman who was supposed to be her sister. And how could Racquel have been carrying on like this without her finding out about it. They knew each other like the back of their hands. At least, she'd always thought they had. "Girl, this is unreal."

"Don't get me wrong. I'm not proud of what I did in the least, but it happened just the same. I made a lot of mistakes back then, and I knew one day they were going to come to the forefront. Everything always comes back to you. Good or bad. And now I've probably lost Kevin because of it."

"Where is he now?"

"He left again, but I don't know where he went. He was pretty mad."

"Well, it's not like this happened while you were married to Kevin. As a matter of fact, you didn't even know him back then."

"It's the fact that I had two abortions, and messed around with someone else's husband. When it comes to family, Kevin has high standards. That's one of the main reasons why I was so attracted to him in the first place, and you know how much he despises any woman who messes around, including his own mother. He never forgave her for running off and leaving his father for another man, and he's never going to forgive me for this, either. Plus, I know he feels like I deceived him. And as much as I hate to admit it, I did lie to him when he asked me if I had ever had an abortion."

"Girl, you've got to talk to him as soon as he walks through that door."

"Hmmph. I don't even know if I can face him, let alone talk to him."

"You don't have a choice."

They were both silent for a few seconds.

"I'd better get off of here, so I can fix dinner for Ashley and Nicholas. But you call me if you need me, okay?" Marcella said.

"I will," Racquel said, grabbing the phone from her shoulder.

"And try not to worry. Everything will work out fine."

"Oh, and Marcella. Whatever you do, please don't say anything to Mom about this. I just couldn't take that."

"You know better than that. I would never tell her something like this."

"Then, I'll talk to you later," Racquel said.

Marcella hung up the phone without moving the rest of her body. Racquel had actually messed around with a married man. And not just any married man, but a wealthy White one who was probably old enough to be her father. What could she possibly have been thinking? And why couldn't she have taken out a student loan like everyone else did when they needed money for school? It just didn't add up. And it was so unlike Racquel. And even worse, she dreaded even thinking about what was going to happen to her sister's wonderful marriage.

Chapter 14

Washing, blow-drying, and curling her hair had taken Marcella longer than she'd planned. Darryl had phoned earlier to say he'd be picking them up at five o'clock sharp, so they could make the 5:45 P.M. showing of some Disney remake, because if they went after six o'clock, they'd have to pay full price.

Nicholas had been begging Tyrone to take him for the longest, but as usual he never had the time to do it, and now that he was finally going, he couldn't wait. Ashley, on the other hand, didn't see what the big deal was. As far as she was concerned, she didn't want to see this "baby" movie anyway.

"Are you guys ready?" Marcella yelled, pulling on her black jeans and sweatshirt. She wanted to wear the black sleeveless mock turtleneck that Sharon had given her last month, but the weather was just a little too nippy for it. Which was sort of strange, she thought, since it was only the first week in September.

"I'm ready," Nicholas said proudly.

Ashley didn't respond.

"What about you, Ashley?"

"I'm ready," she said with no enthusiasm.

Marcella didn't say anything back to her, but if she didn't lose that funky attitude by the time they made it to the movie theater, she was going to wish she had. She didn't know what was wrong with that girl. She was so moody. Not to the extent that she had been at the beginning of the year, but she was still pretty bad with it. Everyone kept saying it was just a phase she was going through, but Marcella couldn't wait for it to end. She'd thought for sure that her worries were over the day Children and Family Services had taken that Jason and his little brothers away from their mother, but Ashley was still walking around acting like she was mad at the world and didn't want to be bothered with anyone except herself. But at least she was keeping her grades up in school. They'd only been in school for a couple of weeks, and already she was getting A's on all of her homework assignments.

Darryl picked them up a few minutes early, and they headed for the theater. When they arrived, Darryl stepped out of the car, and Nicholas pushed the front seat forward and then jumped out of the car filled with excitement.

"You wanted to see this movie bad, didn't you," Darryl said, shutting the door.

"Yep," Nicholas said.

"He likes to see any movie," Marcella said, holding the seat so Ashley could get out on her side. "Especially when it's at the movie theater."

They all walked toward the entrance, which had a long line winding from the ticket window all the way around the building. It was so funny how everyone always tried to beat the six o'clock cutoff, Marcella thought. It was still early, but maybe they hadn't gotten there early enough.

They walked to the end of the line and took their. places in it.

"Mom. Isn't that Daddy's car?" Ashley asked, pointing toward the parking lot.

Marcella watched as Tyrone drove through the parking lot searching for a park. Oh no, she thought. Not today. The last thing in the world that she needed was a confrontation with him. And from the looks of it, he had that Priscilla in the car with him, as well. What luck.

"Yeah, I think it is," Marcella finally answered.

"Who are those kids with him?" Nicholas asked, stretching his neck to see who was walking through the aisle holding his dad's hand.

Marcella and Darryl looked at each other but didn't say anything because they knew what Nicholas was thinking. Tyrone was always saying he didn't have time to take Nicholas and Ashley anywhere, but here he was big as day bringing somebody else's children to the movies.

As Tyrone and his posse walked closer to the line, he recognized Ashley and Nicholas.

"Hey, Ashley and Nick," Tyrone said, pretending he didn't see Marcella or Darryl.

"Hi, Daddy," Ashley said with a quick wave.

"Hey, Dad," Nicholas said with an almost-sad look on his face, and kept staring at the little boy and girl.

Marcella was getting more pissed off as the seconds passed by. It was one thing for him to clown with her, but it was another when he did something to hurt her children. She hated to act ugly out in public or in front of Darryl, but if Tyrone said anything else out of the way, she was going off.

"So what are you here to see?" Tyrone said, patting Nicholas's head.

"He's here to see the same movie he's been begging you to take him to see for the last three weeks," Marcella said and wasn't whispering. "You know. The movie you didn't have time to take him to."

"I'm telling you now, Marcella. Don't start this stuff with me, because I'm not in the mood for it."

"I don't care what you're in the mood for. And you're not going to keep treating my babies like this and getting away with it," Marcella said and looked around when she noticed an immediate silence. All the people in line were now giving her their undivided attention, and she felt so ashamed.

Priscilla looked at Marcella like she was crazy, but didn't dare say anything.

"Why are you trippin' like this?" Tyrone asked Marcella with a frown on his face.

"Baby, it's not even worth this," Priscilla interrupted. "We can go somewhere else if you want to."

Marcella wanted to slap this synthetic-weave-wearing heifer more than anything, but she knew she didn't have a reason, because this woman hadn't done one thing to her. She hated Tyrone and everything he stood for, and she wished he would drop dead. Things would be so much easier without him.

By now, Nicholas was crying, but Ashley pretended like none of this was bothering her in the least.

"Hey," Tyrone said, squatting down next to Nicholas. "I'll come by and pick you and Ashley up tomorrow. Okay? And I'll take you anywhere you want to go," he said, hugging him.

Nicholas nodded his head yes, but Ashley just stared at him with no response and no expression on her face; obviously tired of his lies and unkept promises.

Tyrone and his extended family left the line, strolled over to his car, got in, and drove off.

Marcella placed her arm around Nicholas to comfort him and looked at Darryl for the first time since this whole fiasco had started, but he continued looking straight in front of him.

"Can you believe him?" Marcella asked Darryl.

He turned to look at her, and then turned his head away again without answering her. He was angry, and now Marcella wished she hadn't said anything to Tyrone. She didn't know what had come over her, but she just couldn't help herself. She knew she had embarrassed all of them, but when she saw the looks of disappointment on her children's faces, she didn't care about anything else. She was tired of Tyrone getting away with murder. Tired of him acting as if Priscilla's children were more important than his own. To be honest, she wasn't even aware that this woman had any children, and based on how Nicholas was acting, he and Ashley couldn't have known about them, either.

"What's the matter, Darryl? Why aren't you saying anything?" Marcella asked in a more soft-spoken tone.

"There's nothing to say," he said, still looking straight ahead.

Marcella felt nervous. Darryl had never been this upset with her before, and she could tell he was fed up with this Tyrone situation. Why couldn't she have kept her mouth shut? She had wanted to, but when she saw Tyrone entertaining his little girlfriend and her children, she'd lost it. But she had to make Darryl see that she didn't mean to cause any embarrassment or humiliation for him, and that she wasn't going to ever have another confrontation like that with Tyrone ever again. She couldn't lose him over something as petty as this. She just couldn't.

* * *

Racquel backed the Camry out of the driveway and drove out of the subdivision. After sitting in the house all afternoon, wondering where Kevin was, she'd finally decided to pay her mother a visit. She would have loved nothing more than to spend some time with her niece and nephew, but since they were going to the movies, that was out of the question.

She headed down Baxter Avenue, Covington Park's main strip, and debated as to whether she should stop at some carryout joint to get something for dinner. She'd wanted to spend the evening with Kevin at some nice restaurant, but he still wasn't speaking to her. She'd prayed all week that he would forgive her, but he hadn't. She'd thought for sure this whole situation would blow over in a matter of days, but now it was plowing into its second week.

She was so miserable, and while she knew Kevin realized it, he didn't seem to care. She'd seen him angry many times before, and they argued from time to time the same as any other married couple did, but eventually they always made up. As a matter of fact, they never even went to sleep without making up. They had always loved each other too much for that. But now their relationship was at its worst, and she didn't have the slightest idea as to what she should do about it. She tried to explain everything to him that night he'd overheard her talking to Marcella, but he had ignored her completely. Wouldn't even look at her for that matter. And he'd even had the audacity to move into the guest bedroom. Something he'd never done the whole time they'd been married. She'd thought they could work all of this out, but the odds were slowly piling heavily against it.

She continued down Baxter scanning each side of the street searching for a restaurant, but none of them sounded good. Then it dawned on her. Her mother usually fried fresh catfish every Saturday, and always had way too much left over when she finished. She was the only one in her household, but she always cooked a lot, just in case Racquel, Marcella, or some of her other relatives dropped by for dinner.

As she drove closer to her mother's house, she saw Kevin's truck parked in the driveway, so she parked on the street. A warm feeling came over her. Maybe he had come to his senses. Because if he hadn't, the last place he would want to be was at her mother's house. But then again, Kevin was the sort of man who didn't believe in falling out with the rest of the family, simply because he wasn't speaking to her. And he loved catfish more than Racquel did. Maybe he hadn't come to his senses at all and had only stopped by there to eat dinner. When Racquel had spoken with her mother earlier, she'd asked about Kevin, but Racquel had played it off, like he was out running some errands. Corrine had asked about him earlier in the week, as well, but Racquel had made up some excuse for his absence that time, too.

She stepped outside her car, shut the door, headed up the driveway, and heard the back door slam shut. She felt nervous when she realized it was probably Kevin on his way out. She continued walking toward the back of the house, until she saw Kevin walking toward her. A part of her wanted to reach out and grab him, so she could hug him as closely as she could. It was near dusk, but she could already see the anger and the leave-me-alone attitude covering his face. When he was no more than three feet away from her, she opened her mouth to speak to him, but he walked past her without so much as glancing at her. She turned around with her mouth still wide open and watched him as he opened the door of his truck. He looked at her, shook his head, and stepped inside of the vehicle. This was no different than a nightmare. And how could he simply ignore her like that? She continued staring at him, until he turned the key in the ignition. After he backed out of the driveway, he pressed the accelerator to the floor as far as it would go.

Racquel felt like crying her eyes out, but she knew she couldn't. Because if she did, she'd have to explain this whole mess to her mother. And the more she thought about that, the more frightened she became. What if Kevin had told her mother everything? Maybe it wasn't dinner at all that he'd been looking for. Maybe he had come to tell Corrine how terrible her oldest daughter was. And what was she going to do if he had? She'd never be able to face her mother, or anyone else, if they found out what she'd done. Maybe it was a bad idea to visit her mother, after all. But, then, on the other hand, Kevin would never say anything to hurt his mother-in-law. He cared about her too much, and plus, he just wasn't like that. And on top of that, he had no business telling her mother anything that Racquel didn't want her to know. She'd made that clear since the day they got married.

Racquel felt better now that she'd thought this whole situation through. She walked up to the back door and knocked.

Corrine opened the door without delay and walked back up to the kitchen without looking at Racquel.

"Hey, Mom," Racquel said, shutting the door and walking up to where her mother was standing.

"Racquel, tell me it's not true," Corrine said without hesitation.

Racquel could tell that her mother knew everything, and she felt like dying. While she wanted to turn and walk back out the door, she knew it was better to confess so this could all be over with.

"It's true. Everything that Kevin told you is true."

"After all this time, I can't believe this is happening."

"Mom, what was I supposed to do?"

"I don't know, but you should have done everything in your power to hold your marriage together. I told you a long time ago that if you didn't get rid of this obsession about having babies, something bad was going to happen. But I didn't have any idea it was going to come to all of this."

Racquel couldn't believe Kevin had the audacity to tell Corrine about her abortions. It wasn't his place, and he knew it. This was *her* mother, not his. But now that the beans were spilled, she figured she might as well tell her mother all of it. From beginning to end.

"Mom, sit down," Racquel said, pulling a chair out from the kitchen table. Corrine sat down directly in front of her. "I know it was wrong to have two abortions the way I did, but I was young, dumb, and didn't know any better. And I couldn't bear the thought of dropping out of college . . ."

"What are you talking about?" Corrine interrupted with a worried look on her face. Racquel knew this was hard on her, but she had to tell her the truth.

"Mom, please. Just let me finish," Racquel continued. "I don't know what was going through my mind when I started messing around with Tom, but I know part of it was money. He took care of all my college expenses, and paid the rent for my apartment. I needed money so bad back then, and as time went on, it didn't seem to matter that he had a wife and three kids, or that he was White. I know it was wrong, but it just didn't matter," Racquel said, and it was all she could do not to run out of her mother's house.

"What abortions? And in God's name, who is Tom?" Corrine said, raising her voice.

Why was her mother acting as if she didn't know what she was talking about? Kevin had already told her everything, so why was she in denial about all of this? It didn't make any sense. "Mom, I know you don't want to believe what Kevin told you, but it's all true."

"All Kevin told me was that you guys haven't been getting along, and that you might be getting a divorce. So what are *you* talking about?" Corrine asked fearfully.

Divorce? Racquel stared at her mother in disbelief, and felt as though a dark shadow was surrounding her entire body. From the way her mother had been acting, she'd thought for sure that Kevin had told everything. But apparently he hadn't. And because of her assumption, she'd told on herself for no good reason. Why couldn't she have kept her mouth shut, until her mother had given her a better indication of what she knew. It was just like her to jump to conclusions, or become overly obsessed about everything, the same as she had been when it came to getting pregnant. She'd already ruined her marriage to Kevin, and now she'd ruined her mother's whole way of thinking. Her mother had always been so proud of her and her accomplishments, but now she knew the rest of the story. The part of the story that Racquel would have rather kept a secret.

Corrine stood up from the table. "Where did I go wrong in raising you girls?" she asked. "First, Marcella went and got pregnant during her last month of high school, and now you're telling me you needed money so bad, that you had to sleep with some married White man?"

Racquel remained silent.

"Why didn't you tell me that you needed money? And what about the financial aid you told me you were getting?"

"I did get some grants, but it wasn't enough to cover everything. And right after I applied for a student loan, I met Tom."

"What were you thinking? This is such a disgrace. No wonder Kevin wants to file for a divorce. Who could blame him?"

At first, Racquel felt bad about her mother finding out the truth, but now she was starting to become irritated with all these insults. Her mother was making it sound like she was stupid. Maybe if she'd been more concerned with raising her daughters instead of trying to keep their father from messing around with other women, her and Marcella's lives might have turned out a lot different. But Racquel decided not to point any fingers. Especially at her own mother. "Mom, I'm sorry for what happened, but there's nothing I can do to change it. I apologized to Kevin, and that's all I can do."

"I told you to stop pressing him about this infertility thing, but you just wouldn't listen. And now that he knows about you having two abortions, that's even worse."

"I know I made some terrible mistakes, but there's nothing I can do to change them now. I regret everything I did, and I'm sorry, but if Kevin can't forgive me, then that's just the way it is."

"How can you say that? You should be at home begging him to forgive you. He's stood by you all these years, only to find out that you're not the person he thought you were. He was so devastated when he was here, but I had no idea, he knew about all of *this*."

"I'm still the same person I was when I met Kevin. Plus, all of this happened before I met him. What's in the past is in the past, and this is now. And I'm not about to beg him or anybody else for anything, let alone forgiveness. We married each other for better or worse, but it seems like he's forgotten about that. And anyway, why are you taking sides with Kevin?" Racquel asked, getting angrier by the minute.

"I'm not taking sides with him. I'm just trying to get you to see how good of a husband you have, and how you need to do everything you can to keep him."

"I'm not like you, Mom. I'm not going to beg Kevin to stay with me simply because he's my husband," Racquel said, instantly wishing she could do some sort of disappearing act. She hadn't meant to say anything that would hurt her mother's feelings, but Corrine had pushed her too far.

Corrine gazed at her painfully.

"Mom, I didn't mean that, and I'm sorry."

"I didn't beg your father to be with me for my sake. I did it for yours and Marcella's," Corrine said, pointing at Racquel. "The only thing I ever wanted was for you girls to grow up in a two-parent household. I stopped loving your father a long time before I finally put him out that last time. So don't ever think I was some hopelessly-in-love wife who was willing to put up with anything just to keep a man, because I wasn't. And if I'd known you were going to resort to messing around with some wealthy married man for money, I would have never put your father out until after you finished college."

Racquel felt like crap, and didn't know what to say. This was the second time she'd disrespected her mother like this, and she wasn't sure how to make up for it. But she had to say something. "Mom, I know I've said this a lot tonight, but I'm sorry. I'm sorry that you had to find out about all of this, and I'm sorry for talking to you the way I just did. I know you did everything you could for Marcella and me, and I love you for it," she said, standing up from the table and walking toward her mother. She reached out to Corrine and hugged her.

"All I want is the best for you and Marcella, and right now, I think the best thing for you to do is go talk to your husband. It's hard to find a man like Kevin, and I just don't want to see you guys busted up over something that can be worked out."

"I know, Mom. I promise, I'll try to talk to him again tonight, when I get home."

"Everything will be fine," Corrine said, forcing a smile on her face. "Everything will be just fine."

Chapter 15

Marcella was happier than she had been in a long time. School was going well, Ashley had finally gotten her attitude back on track, and things couldn't have been better between her and Darryl. He'd been upset about the incident at the movies, but he eventually came around after a couple days had passed. She'd thought for sure that their relationship was going to end, but it hadn't, and she was glad. She loved him so much, and it was getting to the point where she didn't know what she would do without him. Ashley and Nicholas seemed to like him a lot, as well, and it was almost like they were attached to him. He was clearly the father that they wished they had, and she was glad that Darryl treated them as well as he did.

Tyrone had come by yesterday to drop off his child support payment, and although it was the first payment he'd made in three weeks, Marcella had decided not to make any waves. Especially since she knew Darryl wanted her to avoid any conflicts or confrontations with Tyrone as much as she could. Darryl couldn't stand Tyrone, and Tyrone couldn't stand Darryl. She wished things could be better between the two of them, but she knew that was never going to happen. She loved Darryl, but Tyrone was her children's father, and there was nothing she could do to change that. And it was simply a fact that, from time to time, she was going to have to deal with him. Plus, things hadn't been so bad as of late because he seemed so wound up with that Priscilla. Which was a blessing, as far as Marcella was concerned, because that meant he didn't have as much time and energy to mess with her. He still didn't spend as much time as he should have with the kids, but Darryl took Ashley and Nicholas lots of places, and that made a world of difference. She never thought the day would come when she didn't have to argue with Tyrone, but now it actually had.

Ashley and Nicholas were on the sofa watching a long, lost episode of *Lassie,* so she sat down at the kitchen table to write out checks for this week's bills. This was the one thing she hated about Saturday mornings, but she knew there was no sense in complaining. She searched through the envelopes stacked on the table and smiled when she realized that this was her "easy week" because the only bills she had to pay were the ones from the electric and phone companies. This meant she'd have a little left over for buying Christmas gifts. It was only October, but the children had already picked out everything they wanted in the Christmas catalog. Sharon had already assured her that she would take care of everything on their list, but still, Marcella wanted to contribute at least a portion of it. It was her responsibility, and she wasn't going to feel right if she didn't.

After she finished writing out the checks and sealed the envelopes for each bill, she noticed a letter from the welfare agency and opened it. She read the letter twice, but she thought for sure her eyes were playing tricks on her. "That bastard," she said out loud, and then looked over at the children and saw Ashley staring at her with curiosity. She never used profanity in front of them, and she could tell that her daughter was surprised about what she'd heard her say. And while Marcella was livid about the contents of the letter, she had to explain herself. "That's a bad word, and I'm sorry for saying it," she said, looking at them with guilt shielding her face.

"What did Daddy do this time?" Ashley asked.

Marcella wanted to tell her. She wanted to tell both of them how deadbeat and how terrible their father was. But she had vowed a long time ago not to badmouth Tyrone to the children, regardless of what he did. "He didn't do anything. It's nothing," she said, trying her best to convince Ashley that she was telling the truth.

Ashley looked at her in disbelief and then turned her attention back to the television screen. Nicholas didn't seem to care one way or the other and never even looked in his mother's direction. There was a chance that he hadn't even heard what she'd said, since he seemed so caught up in the television set.

She picked up the letter, went into her bedroom, and shut the door. Then she sat down on the side of the bed and dialed Sharon's number. Marcella was so furious, that she could barely wait for her to answer the phone.

"Hello?" Sharon said.

"Girl, you will never guess in a million years what that snake-lowlife has done to me!" Marcella said quickly.

"Who? Tyrone?"

"Who else?"

"What did he do now?" Sharon asked, sounding prepared for almost anything.

"I got a letter from my caseworker today, and it says that my food stamps have been suspended until I report to their office. And that my case will be redetermined after they investigate how much child support Tyrone James has been paying me for his two children."

"What?" Sharon yelled.

"You heard me? Suspended because of the child support *Tyrone* has been paying."

"Where did they get that information from?"

"It's more like *who* did they get it from. He's the only one who would have reported anything like that. I can guarantee you that."

"You think he's low-down enough to do something like that?"

"Of course he is. And the worst part of all is that he barely pays me anyway. He brought over a check yesterday for the first time in three weeks, so I don't know how he had the gall to report any-thing."

"He actually writes you a check?"

"Yeah, he didn't start doing that until I started seeing Darryl, but now I know why. And the only reason he's doing this is because he doesn't like Darryl."

"I don't think it has anything to do with him liking Darryl. More than anything, he's probably pissed off at the fact that you're see-ing someone as intelligent as Darryl. Tyrone is jealous. You can be-lieve that."

"I don't know what for, because he and I were through long before I met Darryl. And he's been going out with Priscilla forever."

"Still. I guarantee you, he's jealous."

"Tyrone makes me so sick till I can't stand it. Wait till I see him."

"If I were you, I wouldn't waste my time arguing with him. And
you know how pissed off Darryl got the last time you had a run-in
with Tyrone."

"I know, but I can't let him get away with this. He's gone too far
this time, and I'm going to tell him about himself. Darryl will just
have to understand."

"But what if he doesn't? I'm telling you, Marcella, you should
leave well enough alone. Tyrone isn't worth it, and he's definitely
not worth losing Darryl over. He's the best thing that has ever happened to you. You said that yourself."

Marcella was becoming more and more furious by the minute,
and while she understood where Sharon was coming from, it didn't
seem to matter to her. She had to set Tyrone straight once and for
all. And she had to do it now. "Hey, let me call you back, okay?"

"Marcella. I know you're not going to confront him, are you?"
Sharon said in a pleading voice.

"I'll call you back, okay?" Marcella said, ignoring Sharon's question as politely as she knew how.

"Look, Marcella, for the hundredth time, he's not worth it."

It felt more like a thousand times, and Marcella was a little fed
up with hearing what Sharon had to say. She'd called Sharon for
one reason, And one reason only: because she needed her support. But this was one time Marcella wished she hadn't. Sharon was
supposed to side with her, but she was acting like she was trying to
take up for Tyrone. The last thing she wanted to do was hang up
on Sharon, so she tried to end the conversation again. "Sharon, I
know you don't agree with what I'm about to do, but you're just
going to have to understand. I have to get this off my chest, and
the only way I can do that is by calling Tyrone," she said irritably.

And Sharon picked up on it. "Look, you're my best friend and
the sister I never had. I love you more than anything in this world,
and there's nothing I wouldn't do for you or Ashley and Nicholas.
All I care about is your happiness. That's all. I'm not trying to tell
you what to do, but I don't want to see you ruin things with Darryl,
either."

Marcella knew Sharon was right, but she still couldn't let Tyrone get away with what he had done. She'd let him practically walk over her for years now, and this was the last time he was going to get away with it. "I know you're just trying to look out for me, but I have to do this. He's pushed me to the limit for the last time."

"I don't know what else to say, except that you're making a big mistake."

"Well, if I am making a mistake, then I'm the one who's going to have to live with it. Right?" Marcella said, surprising herself. She'd never spoken to Sharon in that manner before, but at the same time Sharon should have never tried to tell her what to do, either. And she was so persistent about it.

"Fine," Sharon said in a tone that sounded as though her feelings were hurt. "Do what you have to do."

"I intend to. And I'll talk to you later," Marcella said and pressed the button on the phone. As soon as she set the receiver down on the base of the phone, she cringed. She'd actually hung up on her best friend. She and Sharon had never had an argument. Maybe a disagreement or two, but never a full-fledged argument. But, then lately, whenever the subject of Tyrone and her children came up, Marcella was in the habit of going off on whomever she came in contact with. She'd gotten into it with Racquel last year at the Fourth of July cookout, threatened Tyrone with a baseball bat, embarrassed herself in front of Darryl at the movie theater, and now she'd hurt Sharon's feelings for no reason at all. She didn't know what was happening to her. Sometimes she felt like she was losing her mind. One minute she was happy, and the next minute she was ticked off at the smallest little thing. She wanted desperately to call and apologize to Sharon, but she wasn't sure what she should say to her. Maybe it was better to let things cool down for a while. She'd call her later in the evening or possibly stop by her condo.

As she reached to lift the phone, preparing to dial Tyrone's phone number, it rang. "Hello?" Marcella said, not wanting to talk to anyone.

"Hey, we need to talk," Sharon said and sighed. "I'll be over in an hour or so, okay?"

"Okay, I'll see you then," Marcella said, smiling, and then hung up the phone. She felt better already. She needed Sharon in her life more than ever before, and she thanked God for giving her a best friend who was so loving, so caring, and so understanding. She couldn't wait to apologize to her, and she was never going to treat her this terribly ever again.

Marcella picked up the phone and dialed Tyrone.

"Hello?" his mother said.

"Hey, Ma," Marcella said in a surprised voice. She'd expected Tyrone to answer the phone, and not his mother. "How are you doing?"

"Oh, I'm fine, honey. Working hard every day, but I'm fine. How's my grandchildren?"

"Oh, they're fine."

"And how's your mother?"

"She's fine. As a matter of fact, I just spoke with her earlier this morning, and she asked how you were doing, too."

"You tell her I said hello when you talk to her again."

Marcella didn't want to be rude, but she needed to talk to Tyrone now. "Is Tyrone there, by chance?"

"He sure is. I'll get him for you," Tyrone's mother said and yelled for him to pick up the phone.

He picked up another extension, and his mother told Marcella to take care and that she'd talk to her later.

"Hello?" Tyrone said, sounding sarcastically pleasant.

"All I want to know is one thing. Did you or did you not report your child-support payments to the welfare office?"

"I told you if you kept clownin' me what was going to happen. You thought you were the Queen of Sheba when you had your little boyfriend over, but who's getting the last laugh now. Huh?"

"You no-good snake. You make me sick," Marcella said, tightening her face. "Why don't you just make it easy for everybody and die?"

"I told you to stop messing with me, but you kept talking to me like I was nobody."

"So, because your little ego got hurt, you decided to take food away from your own children?"

"You can manage. You do still work, don't you? And I know the Housing Authority dropped your rent to zero when you went back to school. I mean, I'm not stupid."

"Maybe if you paid your child support like you were supposed to, I wouldn't have to worry about food stamps or anything else."

"You mean so you can spend it on yourself? And for all I know, you might be spending it on your little doctor friend."

"Tyrone, you are really something else. I knew you were a low-life, but I had no idea you would stoop low enough to do something this dirty. But what goes around comes around."

"Oh, so now you're threatening me again. Marcella, please."

She slammed the phone down so hard that she felt a vibration move up her arm. She felt like screaming at the top of her lungs. She took a deep breath and tried to calm herself down. She would get through this. Tyrone was doing everything he could to make her miserable, but she wasn't going to let him succeed at it. She was in love with a wonderful man; she had two beautiful children; she had a mother and sister who loved her; and a best friend who would move mountains if it meant helping her. No, Tyrone wasn't going to bring her down. One day he would regret not spending time with his children the way he should have, but it was going to be too late.

During the next three hours, Ashley and Nicholas cleaned up their bedrooms and did whatever else Marcella told them, while she cleaned up her bedroom, the bathroom, and finished her homework assignment for Accounting II. She'd been working on this same problem set for the last hour, but she just couldn't seem to make it balance. Her eyes were starting to get tired, so she laid her pencil down and pushed the ledger sheets to the side. She glanced at her watch and wondered where Sharon was. She'd said she'd be over in about an hour, but now it was almost four hours since she'd spoken with her. It was unlike her to be late for anything, and if she couldn't help it, she usually called. Maybe she and Marcus had decided to do something at the last minute. It was Saturday, and they did usually spend the whole day together. She wished she could spend time with Darryl, too, but he was pulling a double shift at the hospital. She wondered how Racquel was doing and decided to call her.

"Hello?" Raquel answered.

"Hey, girl. What's up?"

"Not much. What's up with you?"

"The kids have been cleaning up and watching TV, and I've been working on my accounting homework. That's about it. So how are you and Kevin?"

"There's still some distance, but at least he's talking to me again. I guess it'll take some time before things get back to normal."

"I'm so glad to hear that. You two belong together."

"Yeah, I know, and I can't believe we came so close to ending our whole marriage. And you'll be glad to know that I've finally decided to consider adoption. I still don't feel completely comfortable with the idea of it, but I promised Kevin I would think really hard about it."

"That's wonderful. I really think you're making the right decision."

"I sure hope so, because I'm telling you, there's no way we would have made it, if we hadn't come to sort of a compromise."

Marcella heard the call-waiting signal in her phone. "Hey, hold on for a second," she said, pressing the button inside of the phone receiver. "Hello?" she said to whomever was calling.

"Marcella," Darryl said sadly. "I don't know how to tell you this, but . . ."

"But, what?" she said, sounding alarmed.

"Sharon was in a serious car accident."

"Oh, no, Darryl, no. I'll be there in a few minutes."

"Marcella, wait," he said, pausing.

"Wait for what?" she asked, confused.

"She didn't make it."

"Noooo, Darryl. Please," Marcella said, dropping down to her knees on the kitchen floor, still holding the phone, and slowly shaking her head in denial. "Not Sharon, Darryl, please tell me it wasn't her."

"Baby, I'm leaving the hospital right now, and I'll be there as soon as I can. I called your mother, and she should be there any minute."

Marcella dropped the phone to the ground, curled her body in a ball, and cried loudly. Ashley and Nicholas ran to her and kneeled down beside her.

"Mom, what's wrong?" Ashley asked and put her arm around her mother.

"Mom, you're scaring me," Nicholas said with tears in his eyes.

Marcella was crying hysterically, and she felt like her heart had been yanked out. She folded her arms and rocked back and forth. Ashley heard a knock at the door and ran to answer it, while

Nicholas sat next to his mom, trying to hold on to her as best he could. When Ashley opened the door, she saw that it was her grandmother.

"Granny, something's wrong with Mom," she said, leading her over to where Marcella was.

"I know, baby," Corrine said, hugging her granddaughter and walking with her through the living room and then into the kitchen.

"Sweetheart," Corrine said, kneeling down to the floor, pulling Marcella into her arms. "I know it hurts, but you have to believe that everything is going to be all right," she said, stroking Marcella's hair.

"Granny, what's wrong with Mom?" Ashley asked in a worried tone of voice.

Corrine blinked quickly as tears began to fall from her eyes. "Your aunt Sharon was killed in a car accident."

"Oh, God, Mom," Marcella screamed out. "I killed her. I killed her. I killed her," Marcella said quickly.

"No, baby. Don't say that." Corrine tried to calm her daughter down.

"Yes, I did. If I hadn't treated her so badly on the phone, she never would have tried to come over here . . . It's all my fault," Marcella moaned.

"Look, baby, no matter what you think, it's not your fault, and there's nothing you could have done to stop this from happening. All of our times are set, honey, so don't blame yourself. What you have to do now is ask God for strength, so you can get through this."

Ashley and Nicholas looked at their mother and it was obvious that they didn't understand why this was happening. Corrine saw the look on their faces and wanted to console them, but right now she had to do everything in her power to help Marcella. Because if she didn't, there was a chance her daughter might have an emotional breakdown.

Chapter 16

For the next two days, Marcella stayed in bed and refused to discuss anything that had to do with Sharon's funeral. She knew it was her responsibility, since Sharon had no family, but she just couldn't bring herself to make the arrangements. Since the day of the accident, Racquel and Corrine had tried to talk her into it, but she still wasn't ready to face the fact. A part of her wanted to believe that this was all just some horrible nightmare. But the hours and the days were starting to pass by, and she was starting to realize that this wasn't some nightmare at all. That it was as real as the sun rising in the east and setting in the west.

She still regretted that she'd been so rude to Sharon when they'd had the conversation regarding Tyrone, and she kept playing a mental tape of it over and over again. She wanted so desperately to turn the time back, so she could apologize to her and take back everything she'd said, but it was too late. Sharon had said she was on her way over, and Marcella had thought for sure she'd have the opportunity to tell her how sorry she was when she got there. But Sharon had never made it more than a few miles from her apartment when some reckless teenaged driver swerved in front of her on the expressway. She was thrown from her seat, and her head had crashed straight into the front windshield. She suffered severe head injuries and other deep lacerations as a result of the glass shattering all over her body. She'd died on arrival at Covington Park Memorial Hospital. Her car had been totaled, and when they transported her to the hospital, the police had searched through her purse trying to find information concerning next of kin, but they hadn't found anything. That was the reason why it had taken so long for someone to contact Marcella. And if Darryl hadn't just so happened to go down to the ER, there's no telling when Marcella would have been notified. Sharon had always been so well organized and so well put together, and it surprised Marcella that she didn't have something in her wallet or purse to indicate who should be called in case of an emergency. And it surprised her even more when the investigating officer said that Sharon didn't have her seat belt on. It was so unlike her.

Marcella felt numb, and she wished she could close her eyes, fall off to sleep, and never wake up again. This was such a tragedy, and she honestly didn't know how to deal with any of it. Ashley and Nicholas had gone to school today, and she was glad, because it wasn't good for them to see her in such bad shape. She usually tried to be strong in front of them whenever something bad happened, but this was one time she hadn't been able to. She still had her family, but at the same time she felt so alone. So empty. It was a feeling that she hadn't experienced before. She and Sharon had both just turned thirty this year, and she'd thought for sure that they had their whole lives ahead of them. That they had so much more time to spend together. There were still things she needed to tell her. Things she needed to do with her. It just wasn't fair. And while she knew it was wrong to question, let alone blame God for what had taken place, she didn't understand why this had to happen. Sharon was such a wonderful and giving person, and here murderers, drug dealers, child abusers, and the like were running around doing whatever they pleased. Life was so confusing. She'd known all along that no one could live forever, but she never expected that Sharon's life would end before her thirty-first birthday. Tragedies like this only happened in the movies, and even if it did happen in real life, things like this never happened to her. Her grandparents had passed away a few years back, but she'd had plenty of time to prepare because they'd both suffered from long-term illnesses. But Sharon had died almost instantly and without warning.

Marcella lay in the bed for another half hour and then dragged herself into the shower. She stood under the hot water so long, her body shriveled up like a prune. After she dried herself off, she put on a pair of stone-washed jeans and a black wool sweater. She usually lotioned her body down, especially in the fall and winter to keep her skin from becoming so dry, but she didn't care about any of that today. She brushed her hair back and wrapped a thick beige rubber band around it. The people from the funeral home had called the evening before saying she could come to their office around four o'clock, so they could prepare the obituary for the newspaper, pick out the casket, and make the final funeral arrangements. It was now nearly noon, and Corrine had said she'd be by to pick Marcella up at 12:30 P.M. She'd taken off work, so that she and Marcella could go over to Sharon's condo to search for any insurance policies, which she may have had, and to look over her will. Marcella had thought Sharon was too young to make out a will when she'd had her attorney draw one up two years ago, but now she had to admit, it did make things a lot easier when someone died. Tomorrow wasn't promised to anyone, and Marcella was more of a witness to that theory now than she cared to be.

Corrine arrived at Marcella's apartment on schedule, and they immediately drove over to Sharon's. When they entered the condo, they went directly up to the guest bedroom, which Sharon had turned into a home office. Inside the closet was a safe, which Sharon had given Marcella the combination to, so Marcella pulled it out, opened it, and spread all of the documents across the oakwood desk. She and Corrine sat facing each other. The first item she noticed was Sharon's will. She skimmed through the first page of it, which was mostly a bunch of legal jargon, and finally turned to the second page, which began to list her assets and who she'd left them to. Marcella hated doing this. Two weeks ago, she would have liked nothing more than for someone to leave her some luxuries or money in general, but now she didn't care about any of that. As a matter of fact, she was starting to realize how messed up her priorities had been over the last few years, because what good was money if you didn't have the people you loved to share it with?

She moved her finger down the page and read through the paragraphs carefully. From the looks of it, Sharon had made her executor, which she already knew. But what she didn't know, was that she had left everything to her and her family. She knew Sharon didn't have any living relatives, with the exception of her father, but she didn't know where he was anyway. She'd made Marcella, Ashley, Nicholas, and Corrine the beneficiaries on the life-insurance policy provided by her employer, which was worth one times her base salary. And Marcella was sure that Sharon earned just over sixty thousand dollars annually.

"Mom, can you believe this?" Marcella said, teary eyed.

"Sharon loved you so much," Corrine said, smiling at her daughter.

"She loved all of us," Marcella said, turning her attention back to the will.

"She left twenty-five percent to each of us. There's a lot of legal terms here, but it basically says that Ashley's and Nicholas's portions are to be placed in trust and used to pay toward their college expenses, but should they decide not to attend college, the monies will be kept in trust until they reach twenty-one years of age. And should something happen to Ashley, then her money would transfer to Nicholas for his education, and vice versa," Marcella said and paused for a moment. "But it also says that if her death results from an accident, the policy will pay two times her salary. And it sounds like we'll each still get twenty-five percent of the first fifty percent, or fifteen thousand dollars, but the remaining amount will also go toward the children's education. Except, if they don't go to college, then that portion of their money will revert back to me."

"What does all that mean?" Corrine asked, obviously confused by what Marcella had just said to her.

"I'm not completely sure, but I think it means that since she died accidentally, her policy will now pay one hundred twenty thousand dollars. Which means that we'll all still get twenty-five percent of the first sixty thousand, but the other sixty thousand will be divided equally between the children. But, if they don't go to college, then that portion of their money will revert back to me. So, from the way it looks, they each have forty-five thousand for school."

"It sure sounds like she really thought this all out, doesn't it?"

"That's just how Sharon was, and she knew that one of my main worries was how I was going to put Ashley and Nicholas through college."

"Is there a policy for her funeral and burial expenses?" Corrine asked. "That's what we need more than anything else."

Marcella searched through the pile. "I don't see anything. Maybe there's something else in the will," Marcella said, turning the page. She scanned down the page until she came to the word "burial." "Here it is. It says that her savings account at Bank First is to be used for her funeral and burial expenses."

"Did you see any bankbooks or statements?" Corrine said, gazing down at all of the paperwork.

Marcella shuffled through the documents again and found a bank statement. She opened it and then reviewed the information contained in it. "She has a little over five thousand dollars in the account, but if that's not enough to cover it, I'll pay the difference from what she left me."

"No," Corrine said. "You have two babies to take care of, and you know that car of yours isn't going to outlast these winter months. I'll pay the funeral home and the cemetery, and whatever else they need. And we still have to go by the flower shop to order the blanket for the casket."

Marcella knew she should be happy to have such an inheritance, but suddenly, she felt sad again. She just couldn't shake this, and it felt strange sitting inside of Sharon's condo when she wasn't there. And even worse, knowing that she wasn't coming back. And it seemed wrong to be sitting here discussing what she'd left for everyone else, but Marcella knew it couldn't be helped. Her grandmother had made sure that all of her burial expenses had been taken care of before she passed away, too, and when her grandfather had died, she had even purchased a headstone with both of their names on it. Her grandfather's birth year and the year he died were engraved under his name, and her grandmother's birth year was printed under hers with a dash after it. It was almost like she was waiting to die. Marcella had thought putting your own name on a headstone while you were still living was the weirdest thing she'd ever heard of, but now she realized how much stress it took off the family. It was hard enough trying to come to terms with the loss of a loved one, but it would be an even greater disaster if the family didn't know where they were going to find the money to pay for a decent funeral. Marcella could still hear her grandmother's words: "Baby, we all have to leave here one day, so we might as well get ready for it. And there's no sense in leaving a burden on the family, when we can help it."

Marcella gathered together all of the documents from the safe and placed them in a large envelope. She went to turn off Sharon's computer, which must have been running since Saturday afternoon. When she moved the mouse by accident, the screen saver vanished, and she saw a document that Sharon obviously had been working on. The heading said "Five-Year Goals," and she'd listed two of them. The first said that she wanted to find out who her father was, and the second said that she wanted to meet the perfect guy and get married to him. Marcella had thought Marcus was the man of Sharon's dreams, and she was sure that Marcus thought the exact same thing, or at least had been hoping he was.

She exited WordPerfect without saving the document, because the last thing she wanted was for Marcus to find out that Sharon hadn't *ever* planned on marrying him. Chances were, he'd never go through her computer files anyway, but Marcella still didn't want to take the risk. He loved Sharon more than anything, and it wasn't worth hurting his feelings.

Marcella and Corrine walked back down the stairs, checked things over, and then left.

"You do know that we're going to have to clean all of her belongings out, don't you?" Corrine asked Marcella.

"Yeah, I know. But I don't even want to think about any of that right now. Maybe in a couple of weeks."

"I'm sure Marcus will want to help, and there might be some things he wants to keep."

"I'm sure there will be. He's supposed to meet us at the funeral home and then come by my apartment later this evening, so maybe I'll mention it to him then," Marcella said, sliding into her mother's car.

Corrine turned the ignition and drove away from the condo.

It was nine o'clock, Ashley and Nicholas had just gone to bed, and Marcella was lying in Darryl's arms on the sofa with her head against his chest. She was glad that the day was finally coming to a close, and with the exception of a couple of items, all of the funeral arrangements had been made.

She, Corrine, and Marcus had decided to have the funeral on

Wednesday, with a three-hour visitation prior to service time. The funeral director had shown them each of the caskets that he had in stock, and they'd all agreed on the deep cobalt-blue one, which had mixtures of silver in it. He'd also informed them that they needed to select something for Sharon to wear, so Marcella told him that she would bring everything he needed by the funeral home tomorrow morning. And the only thing they had left to do was deliver a photo of Sharon, and the order of service information, to one of the local desktop publishers, so the programs could be printed.

Marcella closed her eyes.

"What's the matter, baby?" Darryl asked.

"I feel so exhausted, and I can't knock this guilty feeling that I have."

"What do you feel so guilty about?"

"If I hadn't spoken to Sharon so rudely, she never would have gotten in her car to drive over here. I should have apologized to her when she called back, but I didn't, and I'll never forgive myself for it."

"You never told me that you guys were upset with each other, so what happened?"

Marcella opened her eyes immediately, and it was a good thing Darryl couldn't see the expression on her face. She'd never told him about the argument because she hadn't wanted to explain why she and Sharon had been exchanging words in such a disagreeing manner. He'd made it pretty clear that he didn't want her confronting Tyrone anymore, and she wasn't sure how he was going to react if he found out that she'd gone against his wishes. But there was no sense in keeping it from him now. "I found out on Saturday that my food stamps have been suspended, until the welfare office determines how much child support I receive from Tyrone, so I called Sharon to tell her about it. And then one conversation led to another."

"But why would something like that cause you and Sharon to get into an argument?"

Marcella paused for a second. Maybe it would be better if she told him something other than what really happened. But, on the other hand, they had a truthful and trusting relationship, and she didn't want to jeopardize it by lying to him now. It wouldn't be fair to him or her, and she knew one lie always led to another. And then it usually got to the place where a person couldn't keep track of which lie he or she had told last. As far as she was concerned, it wasn't worth all of that. Besides, she felt bad enough as it was for not being truthful with him about their sex life. And anyway, she'd only called Tyrone, which was a lot different than seeing him in person, so Darryl probably wouldn't be nearly as upset as he was that evening they'd taken the children to the movie theater. "Because I wanted to call Tyrone and tell him off about what he did, and she kept telling me I shouldn't."

"What do you mean, what he did?" he said, lifting her upper body away from him.

"He's the one who called my caseworker to report his child-support payments."

"How do you know that he's the one who did it?"

"Because I just know, and anyway, he admitted it when I called him."

"So, even though you knew how I felt about these run-ins between you and Tyrone, you called him anyway?"

"Baby, I was upset, okay? I know how you feel, but I just couldn't help calling him," she said with an innocent look on her face.

"When is this going to end, Marcella?" he asked, staring at her angrily.

"There's nothing *to* end," she said nervously, because the only time he called her by her first name was when he was extremely serious or wasn't happy with her about something.

"You know, I'm getting real sick of hearing about Tyrone. And why can't you just leave him alone? I mean, he's never going to change, and you know that."

"I know, baby, but when I read that letter from the agency, I lost it. I know I shouldn't have called him, but I just couldn't help it. Tyrone knows that I depend on those food stamps, and he only did it because I'm seeing you. I just couldn't let him get away with doing that."

"Well, after you called him, did that change anything?" he asked sarcastically. "I mean, come on."

"That's not the point."

"Then, what is the point?" he asked, folding his arms and waiting for an answer.

She was at a loss for words, and decided not to answer him.

He shook his head in confusion. "Look, Marcella. I love you and I want to be with you, but I can't keep dealing with this Tyrone situation. I told you before that the best way to handle Tyrone is by ignoring him. He only pays you child support when he feels like it anyway, and it's not like you need him for anything else. This is going to have to stop, and that's all there is to it."

"How can you expect me to cut off all communication with Tyrone, when he's the father of my children? You know that's not possible."

"What do you need to talk to him about, Marcella?" he asked, raising his voice. "He doesn't do a thing for Ashley and Nick, and he treats you like a dog."

"I know that, but there are still going to be times when we have to cross each other's paths."

"Why? Just give me one good reason why."

"You just don't understand," she said, rising from the sofa.

"I just don't understand what?" he asked, moving his body to the edge of the sofa.

"He calls over here to talk to Ashley and Nicholas, and he comes by to pick them up from time to time, so there's no way I can avoid seeing or talking to him completely."

"I never said that. What I'm saying is that you don't have to keep arguing back and forth with him. Ashley and Nick are old enough to talk to their father without your help, and when he comes to pick them up, the most he should be doing is honking his horn for them to come out. He doesn't need to be coming in here for any reason I can think of."

"I don't see why you're so upset, because it's not like I went to his house and confronted him."

"If you don't see why I'm upset, then we have a bigger problem than I thought," he said, standing up.

"Darryl, you knew I had two children when we met, and you had to know that there would be times when I would have to talk to their father."

"Yeah, when it came to their well-being, or something like that. But I'm not about to keep putting up with these arguments you and he keep having. It's almost like the two of you still have feelings for each other, or something."

"Darryl, please. You know good and well that I don't have those kinds of feelings for Tyrone. I'm in love with you, and I've told you that over and over again."

"I'm really starting to wonder if, in fact, you do, and it's getting to the point where I feel like I'm in some sort of competition with Tyrone."

What was he talking about? She loved *him,* and she couldn't care less whether Tyrone lived or died. And she couldn't understand at all why he was so upset about something so petty. He was acting like he was jealous of Tyrone, and that didn't make any sense to her. She spent all of her time with him, not Tyrone, and that was the only thing that should have mattered. She couldn't just pretend like Tyrone didn't exist. Like they didn't share two children together. So what was she supposed to do? "I don't know what to say," she finally said.

He stood in front of her. "Look. I don't want to upset you any more than I already have, and I don't want to keep arguing with you about Tyrone, so maybe I should leave."

"Darryl, my best friend just died, and I need you now more than I ever have. So, can't we just put this Tyrone thing behind us? At least until after the funeral?"

"I'll tell you what. I'll come by after work tomorrow afternoon. Maybe by then, both of us will have cooled down," he said, pulling her into his arms.

They hugged, but it didn't feel the same. He was more distant than he usually was, and she could tell that he'd only made the effort to hug her because he thought she expected it. And not at all because he wanted to.

"I'll talk to you tomorrow," he said, and kissed her on the forehead. Then he turned and walked out the front door.

First, she'd lost her best friend, and now it felt like she was losing Darryl. She felt like her whole world was crumbling into a million pieces, and her heart ached violently. For once, she wished it could rain without pouring when it came to the problems in her life.

She turned off the television set, switched off the lamp on the faded brass end table, walked into her bedroom, dove facefirst on her bed, and wished for this night to be over.

Chapter 17

"It's hard to believe she's gone, isn't it?" Marcus said to Marcella. It had been four weeks since the funeral, and they'd both chosen today as the day to sort through Sharon's condo. They'd already packed up the office, and now they were in her bedroom.

"It really is. But it does seem like it's becoming more and more of a reality as the days continue on. At first, I didn't think I would ever accept the fact that she was gone, because I depended on her for just about everything. She always gave me a shoulder to lean on whenever I needed it, and a lot of people wouldn't have done half the things she did for my children."

"But she loved those kids like they were her own, and every time she referred to Ashley and Nicholas, she would always say her 'niece and nephew.'"

"I know, and they loved her like she was their biological aunt," Marcella said, taking some of Sharon's suits from her closet and laying them on the oversized wrought-iron canopy bed.

"Hey," Marcus said, unplugging the off-white floor lamp. "Do you mind if I ask you something personal?"

"Go ahead," Marcella said, wondering if he wanted to know something about her, or something about him and Sharon.

"Do you have any idea why Sharon wasn't that thrilled about marrying me?"

Oh, no! She'd been afraid that the subject of his and Sharon's relationship might come up, and she had no idea how she should respond to him. Especially, since she *did* know why Sharon didn't want to marry him. Or at least part of the reason why anyway. "I think maybe she just wanted to be sure that getting married was the right thing for her to do. I mean, I know she loved you, because she told me so on more than one occasion, but you know how careful she was when it came to making major decisions," Marcella said, hoping she had convinced him that Sharon really did adore him.

"But what could have made her second-guess whether marrying me was the right thing to do? I mean, she knew how much I loved her and how dedicated I was to our relationship. So that's why I don't understand it."

Now what was she supposed to say? He was making her feel uncomfortable, and she wished he would change the conversation to something else; something that had nothing to do with him and Sharon. "Well, all I know is that she loved you, Marcus, and no matter what, you should never think differently."

"Look, Marcella, you and Sharon were like sisters, so I know she confided in you about everything. And if you know something more, then I wish you'd tell me. Even if it's something you don't think I want to hear. Because at least then maybe I can add some closure to all of this," he said, leaning against the wall with his arms folded.

Why did he want to know about this so badly? And why was he acting like his life depended on it? She wanted to help him, because she knew how hurt he was over losing the woman he practically worshiped, but she just couldn't hurt him, and she didn't want to betray Sharon's confidence in her, either. "Sometimes people love each other more than anything else in the world, and still never get to the point of wanting to get married. It doesn't mean that there's something wrong with you, or that there was something she didn't like about you. But it simply means that she wasn't ready to take such a huge step in her life," Marcella said, standing in front of the armoire with a pile of sweaters draped over her arm.

"Yeah, maybe," he said doubtfully.

"You've got to get on with your life, Marcus. I know it's hard, but you have to do it. You're intelligent, you're an attractive guy, and you have your whole life ahead of you."

"You're right, but just answer me this one question."

"What's that?" Marcella asked curiously.

"Did it have anything to do with our sex life?"

"What do you mean?" Marcella asked, trying to sound surprised about the question.

"Was she happy with it? Did I satisfy her? You know, did she enjoy making love to me?"

Marcella couldn't believe what she was hearing. She'd always felt like she and Marcus were pretty close because of Sharon, but not once had she ever imagined him asking her something so personal. Something so embarrassing. She'd thought asking Marcus over to help clean out Sharon's belongings was a great idea, but now she wasn't so sure. As a matter of fact, she was starting to see just how much of a mistake it had been. "As far as I know, everything was fine," Marcella said and was sure she was going to be struck down with lightning any minute now.

"You're sure?" he asked, staring straight into Marcella's eyes.

"Really, I am."

"Well, if there wasn't a problem with that, then I don't know what was wrong with us."

"Nothing was wrong with either one of you, and who knows, maybe Sharon would have married you in time."

"I really doubt that, because whenever I brought the subject up, she always tried to avoid talking about it. She just wasn't interested in making a commitment to me," he said, pulling out each of the drawers to the dresser and placing them on the floor one by one.

"Well, like I said, you have your whole life ahead of you, and as time goes on, you'll be fine."

"I know, but it's hard when you love someone as much as I loved Sharon, and then you start to realize that the person obviously didn't feel the same way about you."

Marcella didn't know what else to say, but she couldn't help but wonder if maybe Darryl was suspecting the same thing about her. She never gave him any reason to believe that he wasn't satisfying her, but now after listening to Marcus, she really couldn't be sure.

She pulled two handfuls of lingerie out of one of the drawers Marcus had set on the floor and then placed them inside one of the cardboard boxes. For a while she and Marcus worked in silence, then they reminisced about all the good times they'd shared with Sharon. Over the next few hours, they finished packing everything in every room. Then they walked outside to their respective automobiles.

"Well, I guess this is it, until Kevin and Racquel pick up the U-Haul truck tomorrow morning," Marcus said, pulling the collar up on his brown leather jacket.

"Yeah, I guess it is," Marcella said and then turned back to look at the beautiful brick building they'd just exited.

Marcus did the same, took a deep breath and looked back at Marcella. "Marcella, if you ever need anything for the children, yourself or anything at all, I hope you know that you can call me the same as you would if you had a brother."

"I know that," she said, smiling at him. "And I will. I promise."

"Now, don't just say that and then don't do it, because I'm serious."

"I'm telling you, I'll call you if I need you. And you do the same. Even if you just need someone to talk to."

"Okay, then, I'll see you guys in the morning," he said, hugging Marcella.

"We'll see you then, Marcus. And thanks for coming over to help me with all the packing."

"No problem. No problem at all," he said.

They sat in their cars, and shortly after, they both drove off.

Chapter 18

It was one week before Christmas, so Racquel and Marcella decided to drive downtown on Michigan Avenue to do some last-minute shopping. It had always been sort of a tradition for the two of them to spend the last Saturday before Christmas strolling the busy streets, admiring all the fancy decorations, but this year they'd changed the traditional day to Friday, since they both were on Christmas break; Marcella from the university and Racquel from the elementary school that she taught at. It was so beautiful this time of year, especially with the newly fallen snow, that they both hated when the holiday season ended.

They'd just left Filene's Basement, where they'd found some wonderful bargains, and were headed South on Michigan Avenue searching for a cafe that wasn't too crowded. When they found one, they went inside. The instrumental version of "Santa Claus Is Coming To Town" was playing, and a petite Italian-looking hostess seated them near the front window. After she advised them of the day's specials, she handed each of them a menu and asked if they wanted to start with something to drink. They'd gotten kind of cold from all of the walking, so they each ordered a cup of hot chocolate.

"Who would have ever thought that Sharon would never see another Christmas?" Marcella said, gazing out the window toward the

sidewalk, where a group of happy-looking senior citizens was passing by.

"I know," Racquel said, switching her attention to the direction
Marcella was looking.

"I get so sad every time I think about her. And even though I finalized the sale of her condo last week, it still doesn't seem real.
She had so much promise, and she was such a good person."

"They always say that the good die young, and with the way this
world is nowadays, you have to wonder if maybe she isn't in a much
better place than we are, anyway."

"You do have a point there. Life is so strange. It seems like you're
up one minute and down the next. And based on the way my life
has been going, I don't think there's ever going to be a time when
everything is going good all at the same time," Marcella said, scanning the menu.

"I've always wished for that, too, but to tell you the truth, I don't
think it's possible. It seems like the things we want the most, are
the things we can't ever have."

"All I've ever wanted was a decent job, and even though I'm
about to start the second semester of my sophomore year, it seems
like I'm never going to finish."

"Well, you wanted a good man, too, and Darryl is all of that and
then some."

"Yeah, but things haven't been the same since we had that argument about Tyrone two months ago. He still calls and comes by,
but not nearly as often as he used to. And he seems distant."

"Well, I'll tell you like you told me when Kevin and I were having all those problems. You need to sit down and have a serious
talk with him. Because if you don't, things will get worse before
they get better."

"I don't even know if it will do any good. I think the idea of having to deal with a woman who has children by another man is a bit
more than he's willing to put up with. He doesn't have a problem
with Ashley and Nicholas, but he can't stand the sight of Tyrone."

"Forget Tyrone. What you need to do is cut that jerk off completely. He doesn't mean the children or you any good anyhow.
And he sure as heck isn't worth losing Darryl over."

"I know, but you know I can't do that. Ashley is getting to the
point where she could live with or without him because he's always

lying to her, but Nicholas adores everything about him. Regardless of what he does or doesn't do for them."

"Good it's you. Because I'm telling you, men like Darryl are hard to find. And on top of that, he's a doctor, too? There's no way, Marcella."

"You're only saying that because you've never had to be in this situation. It's just not that easy," Marcella said, closing her menu.

"I don't understand you and Mom. It's almost like Tyrone has some spell over both of you. First, Mom accepts his apology for showing out on her in her own house, and now you're prepared to give up Darryl for him."

Marcella didn't say anything.

The waitress set down two cups of hot chocolate and two glasses of water, and then prepared to take their orders. "So, have you decided on what you're going to have?" Racquel asked Marcella, realizing that she'd crossed the line with her previous comment.

"Yes, I'll have the bacon, cheddar, and onion quiche," Marcella answered and watched the waitress jot her selection down.

"And you?" the waitress said, smiling at Racquel.

"I'll have the California pie," Racquel responded.

"Is that it?" the waitress asked, reaching for their menus.

"I think that'll be it for now, but we might want dessert later," Racquel said.

"That'll be fine," the waitress said and then left the table.

"So, have you decided what you want for Christmas?" Racquel asked Marcella.

"No. Not really. And anyway, you've already bought most of Ashley's and Nicholas's gifts, and that's enough."

"Well, that's the least I could do. I know Sharon had planned to buy some of them, but I'm their aunt, and I wanted to get them some things, too. But that still doesn't have anything to do with you."

"I know, but I got the biggest gift ever last month when I bought that Grand Am. It was a couple of years old, but it feels like a new car to me."

"That was so wonderful of Sharon to leave her insurance policy to you, Mom, and the kids, especially since you've been needing another car for a long time now."

"I know. That Cutlass was on its last leg, and I don't know how much longer it was going to be before it gave out. And there's no way I could have gotten to work and school without a car. It was such a blessing."

"Yeah, it really was. So, since it was totaled, what happened with Sharon's car?"

"Her insurance company paid it off because the boy that caused the accident didn't have any insurance on his car."

"That is so ridiculous. And I can't believe people actually ride around here without insurance. It's so inconsiderate to everybody else."

"It really is," Marcella said, looking toward the kitchen of the restaurant, checking to see if their food was coming.

"That's a cute gold bracelet," Racquel said, admiring what she saw on Marcella's wrist.

"Oh, thanks. This was Sharon's. And so was this sweater I've got on. She willed all of her personal items and furniture to me, too. Plus, we got both of her TV's and her entertainment center."

"Girl, you have really been blessed. I mean, you have nice furniture in your apartment, you're two years away from getting your degree, you're driving a nice car, and you've got money in the bank."

"Yeah, my life is a lot better in some ways, but not much better financially because I spent almost ten thousand on the car. And I put the other five thousand in the bank for living expenses and my auto insurance."

"But at least you have more things than you had before. I know Sharon is gone, but I'm so grateful that she loved you enough to do what she did. Friends like her don't come along every day, because I know I've never had a friend like that. Of course, you're my best friend, but I still don't have one that I'm not related to," Racquel said as the waitress set their entrees down on the table. She asked if she could get them anything else, they both said no, and then she turned and left.

"This is so good," Marcella said in the middle of chewing a forkful of the quiche.

"They have a different type of quiche daily, and they're always real good," Racquel said, sprinkling pepper inside of her California pie. "So how's Marcus doing?"

"I spoke with him two days ago, and he seems to be doing okay, but he really misses Sharon a lot. He was so in love with her."

"Gosh, it's a good thing he never found out that she didn't feel the same way about him, because I remember when you told me about what she'd written on her computer."

"Yeah, I know. It's hard when you love someone, and then you find out they don't feel the same way. He would have been devastated."

"I was so shocked when you told me she wasn't happy with the sex, because not only does Marcus look good, but he also has a decent job."

"I know," Marcella said, sipping some water from a long-stemmed glass. "And she told me more than once that she really loved him. But, regardless of how good someone looks or how much money he has, if he's not the one, he's just not the one."

"You know I know that better than anyone. Remember Cecil from high school. He used to hound me every day during my entire senior year. Actually, he was one of the nicest guys I ever met, but I just couldn't make myself like him."

Marcella laughed. "Maybe he was *too* nice, because those are the guys nobody ever wants for some reason or another. It's stupid, but that's usually how it is."

"Maybe. But I still did okay by marrying Kevin. He's always treated me one hundred percent, and we never had any real problems until this thing with me trying to get pregnant came about. He was downright cruel with some of the things he said to me, and he walked out on me practically every time we had an argument. All of that really took a toll on our marriage, and I wish none of it had happened."

"But all that matters now, is that you finally got things worked out."

"Somewhat. Because we still aren't the same, and I'm starting to wonder if we ever will be. He spends a lot of time at work and at the 'Y,' so we haven't spent a whole lot of time together during the past two months. I mean, it doesn't seem like he has an attitude, or like he doesn't love me, but he just isn't the same as he used to be. I can't put my finger on it, but something's different. And we only make love once or twice a week."

"Maybe you need to ask him what's wrong."

"I've wanted to, but I don't want to stir things up if I don't have to."

"Well, making love once or twice a week is a milestone compared to what's going on with me. It's been over a month since

Darryl and I have done anything like that. He's usually working, and if he's not, the kids are always around."

"Well, that's no reason. Because you know Ashley and Nicholas can always spend the night with us."

"I know, but I've been trying to spend as much time as I can with them. They miss Sharon almost as much as I do. She did a lot for them, and they loved her like she was their blood aunt. Plus, Darryl loves being with them, too."

"But, still, you need to spend some time alone with him. I'm sure he doesn't mind being around Ashley and Nicholas, but you can bet he'd like to spend at least some of his time with *just* you. Every relationship needs that. I know you have a responsibility to your children, but you have to balance your time between doing things with them and doing things with him. That's the very reason why most married couples grow apart after they have children. They don't spend enough quality time together. I mean, how romantic can you be when two crumb snatchers are looking directly in your face."

They both laughed.

"I know. I know. But it's just that they don't have anybody else. Tyrone is never there for them, and I hate putting them off on you and Mom all the time."

"Putting them off?" Racquel asked, frowning. "Please. We love those children, and we love you."

"I know you do," Marcella said, smiling.

"Look at those cute little twins," Racquel said excitedly as she looked out the window and saw two adorable little girls dressed in red wool coats and matching hats.

Marcella smiled.

"What I wouldn't give to have two beautiful little girls like them."

Marcella wasn't sure what to say. Racquel was so wishy-washy when it came to the subject of having babies, and she didn't want to say the wrong thing. Maybe she should say something encouraging about adoption. "So what have you finally decided as far as trying to adopt a baby?"

"I've thought about it objectively, and we've met with a lady from the adoption agency once, but I haven't decided for sure. Kevin thinks it's a great idea, so I'm sure we'll go forward with it, if . . . ," Racquel said, cutting the sentence off.

"If what?" Marcella asked curiously.

"My mouth is so big. I promised myself that I wouldn't say anything to you, Mom, or Kevin, and now look," Racquel said with disappointment.

"Racquel. The cat is out of the bag now, so you might as well tell me whatever it is you're trying to hide," Marcella said, laughing, but deep down she felt uneasy. She hoped Racquel hadn't gone and done something behind Kevin's back. She didn't know what it could be, but what if she'd bypassed Kevin and used some donor's sperm? It sounded far-fetched, but Racquel was so desperate, there was no telling what she'd done.

"You promise you won't say anything to anybody?"

"Do I ever?"

"Girl, I'm serious. You can't tell anybody."

"Okay, what?"

"I missed my period at the beginning of this month."

"You what?" Marcella said, smiling.

"At first, I thought I was late, but then when three weeks passed by, I started wondering if maybe I might be pregnant. So this morning I took a sample of urine to the infertility clinic."

"Girl, that's great news. I can't believe you didn't tell me."

"I didn't want to get anyone's hopes up. Especially Kevin's. And there's a chance he would have gotten angry if he thought I was still holding on to some fantasy."

"Why didn't you just go and buy one of those home pregnancy tests? Because I don't know how you can stand waiting."

"I don't trust those. I know it's silly, but I feel more comfortable when it's done professionally. Not that it's ever helped me in the past, though."

"Girl, I am so happy for you," Marcella said, grabbing her sister's hand.

"Don't get too happy, because we don't know anything yet. It could be just another false alarm. Lord knows, I've gotten enough negative pregnancy results to last a lifetime."

"Kevin will be so excited. And Mom will be thrilled when she hears about it."

"Marcella, what did I tell you?" Racquel asked, squinting her eyes.

"I mean, after you find out."

"Okay. Because you did give me your word that you wouldn't say anything."

"How come you're so calm about all of this? You've wanted this for as long as I can remember, and now you're acting like it's no big deal."

"Because I've been disappointed too many times. So if I am, I'll be happy; but if I'm not, then that's fine, too."

"When will they have the results?"

"Later this afternoon, I'm sure."

"Why don't you call the nurse on your cellular phone right now?"

"No, I'm not going to worry about it until I get home, and if she hasn't called me by then, I'll give her a call."

"I don't believe you," Marcella said, shaking her head.

"When I was overly obsessed with the idea of getting pregnant, you guys didn't understand, and now that I'm nonchalant about it, you don't get that, either. How can a person win?" Racquel said, laughing.

"I know, but it's just that I'm so excited, and I don't understand why you're not."

"I am excited, but not to the extent that I used to be. I mean, even though it took me forever, I do finally realize that it's time for me to stop being so selfish and to just be thankful for all the good things that I do have in my life."

"I guess," Marcella said. Actually, she was glad that Racquel had come down to reality and was willing to accept whatever the outcome was, because it was better for everyone involved. Especially, when it came to Kevin. At first, she'd thought Racquel was just pretending when she said she'd given up on trying to get pregnant and was considering adoption, but now Marcella was starting to believe that she was telling the truth. Marcella hoped that Racquel was pregnant, but more than anything, she was glad to know that if she wasn't, her sister wasn't going to crack up over it.

They finished their lunch, ordered two slices of chocolate cheesecake, which was too rich in taste, and chatted a little while longer. When they'd eaten the last of their dessert, Racquel left money on the table to cover the check and tip, and soon after they left the cafe. They went to a couple of department stores, a number of specialty stores, and then headed back home.

As Racquel pressed the garage-door control, she turned into the driveway and saw Kevin's truck already parked inside. More than anything she'd wanted to beat him home, just in case the nurse called from the clinic, but the backed-up traffic on the expressway had made it virtually impossible. She turned the ignition off, gathered together the shopping bags in the backseat, stepped outside the car, and then pressed the garage door control a second time. She opened the door leading to the kitchen as best she could, since both of her hands were full, and then stepped inside the house. She dropped all of the bags on the floor, removed her black wool hooded jacket, matching scarf, and black leather cowboy boots. Kevin was nowhere in sight, and since he usually never played the messages on the answering machine, she figured she'd ease into the bedroom and play them herself. He was probably already lying on the sofa in the family room watching television, so she doubted that he would notice anything. This was good, because that way, if the results were negative, she'd have plenty of time to settle herself down before going in to speak to him. She'd thought this was no big deal like she'd told Marcella, but her nerves had been running wild ever since they started on their way home two hours ago. She'd tried not to get her hopes up, but the truth was, she was more excited this time than she ever had been before.

She walked up the stairs as quietly as she could, and then slipped into the bedroom. She could hear the theme music from *Family Matters* playing, so she quickly stepped into her bedroom and shut the door. But to her surprise, Kevin was sitting in the plush-textured lounger over in the corner by the window with his legs crossed masculine-style. She jumped when she saw him.

"What are you so jumpy for?" he asked with a serious look on his face.

"Nothing really, I just wasn't expecting you to be in here, since I heard the TV playing in the other room," she said, trying to play off the fact that he'd caught her trying to sneak into the bedroom.

She walked over to him and they kissed.

"So how was work?" she asked, glancing on the sly at the answering machine, praying to God that it wasn't blinking. When she saw that it wasn't, she felt relieved. It was too late to find out now, but at the same time, it was much better to wait until Monday, when Kevin would be at work.

"Almost everybody took the afternoon off since it's so close to the holiday, so I took off the last two hours, too."

She felt like suffocating. What if he'd gotten home in time to answer the phone call from the clinic? Maybe that was the reason the answering machine wasn't blinking in the first place, and even worse, maybe that's why he'd been sitting in the bedroom waiting for her to get home. He didn't look upset, but he was probably going to confront her any minute now. She breathed deeply, pretended like she was searching for some important item on the dresser, and waited for him to say something. Anything.

"So when were you going to tell me?" he finally asked.

Her body felt like it was on fire, and while she tried, she couldn't look at him. He'd known about this from the very beginning, and he'd done nothing more than string her along. She could kill him for doing this to her, and she was never going to forgive him for being so cruel. Especially about something like this. She was pissed off now, and decided to play right along with the program. "When was I going to tell you what?"

"That you were pregnant. That's what," he said, rising from the chair.

What was he talking about? She just knew she hadn't heard him right. There was no way. She didn't know what to say, but babbled out something off the top of her head. "I didn't know."

"Well, I know you didn't know, but you had to think you were, or you wouldn't have taken a pregnancy test. Why didn't you tell me?"

She could feel her pulse beating faster and faster and faster, and she felt the same as John Amos had in *Coming to America:* like break-dancing. *Could it actually be true?* she thought. "Are you telling me the test was positive?"

"The nurse called a couple of hours ago, and said that you were definitely pregnant."

"Oh, Kevin, can you believe this?" she said, and then did what she always did when something major happened. She cried. Except, this time, it was because she was happy.

He grabbed her, laid his cheek against hers, and it wasn't long before she felt tears dropping from his face and onto her neck. This was the happiest day of their lives, and she couldn't believe it had actually come to pass. God was good, life was great, and America was a wonderful place to live as far as she was concerned. She wasn't sure what living in America had to do with any of this, but for some reason she was thinking it. But right now a thousand thoughts were cruising through her mind, and she didn't know what to do next.

"Baby, I'm so sorry for the way I've been treating you," he said, crying louder and louder.

"I know, sweetheart," she said, caressing his back as they continued holding each other. "But we've been under so much stress because of all of this."

"I know, but I had no right treating you so badly," he said, and then cried so hard that if they'd been in public, it would have been humiliating for both of them.

She pulled him over toward the bed and sat down on the edge of it. He kneeled in front of her, laid his head to the side on her lap, and then wrapped both of his arms around her waist. Usually she was the one who always needed consoling, but here she was having to comfort Kevin for the first time since they'd been together.

"Baby, it's okay," she said, trying to convince him that everything was going to be fine.

He cried for a few minutes longer and then raised his head up. He stared at her in the same manner that he used to, before all the arguing and confusion had started. "Baby, I love you so much, and I promise you, I'll never turn against you like I did ever again. I mean that," he said, and kissed her passionately. She felt chills shooting through her entire body, and wanted him as badly as she could tell he wanted her. She'd promised Marcella that she would call her as soon as she found out whether she was pregnant or not, but that particular phone call was going to have to wait. Because nothing, absolutely nothing, was going to interfere with the feelings she and Kevin were experiencing at this very moment.

Chapter 19

MAY 1995

"Okay, now, it's time to settle down," Racquel said to her extremely active, and rather loud, second-grade class. It was 8:35 A.M., and time for the day to begin. The children were always hyped up when they entered the classroom, but it was even worse when they came in on Monday because they were always so excited about the items they'd brought in for show-and-tell. Even Racquel enjoyed this part of the class period because she knew her students were liable to bring in anything, from household gadgets to vacation souvenirs. One never could tell, and anything at all was possible.

"One . . . two . . . three," Racquel said in a serious tone, so they knew she meant business. Which worked, because now they were all sitting in their seats giving her their total attention.

"So who wants to go first?" Racquel asked, smiling, because she knew everyone's hands were going to rise at the same time. It was the one time when they all longed to go first. But, of course, the response was just the opposite when it came to answering questions in relation to their main subjects.

"Pick me, Mrs. Wilson, please," most of them begged, waving their hands through the air.

"Why don't we start with Jeremy this time," she said.

Jeremy left his seat and walked on his heels to the front of the class, licking his tongue out at the rest of his classmates on the way. He was going first and was proud of it.

"That's enough of that, young man," Racquel said to Jeremy in response to his tongue problem.

"These are the two Power Rangers that my foster dad bought me this weekend," Jeremy said, holding one in each hand.

"So what," Christopher said. "My mom bought me *all* the Power Rangers a long time ago. So what's so big about that?"

"Christopher!" Racquel yelled. "You know better than to say something like that, and I've told you over and over again that it's not nice to be rude. Now tell Jeremy you're sorry."

"Sorry," Christopher said as low as he could but still loud enough for the class to hear him. And of course now he was pouting.

Racquel saw the sad look on Jeremy's face and felt bad for him. He wasn't as fortunate as most of the kids in the class, and he didn't get toys on a weekly basis, like some of the other children. He didn't even wear clean clothes all the time, for that matter. But it wasn't his fault, and Racquel wasn't about to allow any of his classmates to hurt his feelings. It wasn't right, and she wasn't going to have it.

None of her students came from wealthy homes, but most of their families were considered middle class. Jeremy, however, fell in a different category altogether. He lived in the projects not too far from the school, and his mother was barely able to put food on the table, let alone buy extras like toys and clothes. Not to mention the fact that he'd been taken away from her and placed into a foster home on two separate occasions, thanks to her leaving him at home for days all by his lonesome. So, Racquel understood exactly why Jeremy was proud of his Power Rangers, but at the same time she also understood clearly that seven- and eight-year-olds really didn't know any better.

"Those are very nice, Jeremy. Aren't they, class?" Racquel said, trying to smooth Christopher's comments over.

"Yes, Mrs. Wilson," they all said in unison.

"Okay, Jeremy, you can have a seat. Tiffany, you can go next, please."

Tiffany skipped from her desk in the last row all the way to the front, but didn't have anything in her hand to show the class. She stood there smiling at first, and then began speaking. "This is my new jean outfit that my mom bought me," she said, grinning from ear to ear.

Most of the boys frowned at her, and some of them watched her with no expression at all. But the girls pursed their lips together and then rolled their eyes at her because they couldn't stand her. Tiffany was a beautiful little girl with a light-chocolate complexion, who wore two thick jet-black braided ponytails, with a part down the center of her head to separate them. And really the fact that she was beautiful wouldn't have been so bad, but the problem was, she knew it. The rest of the girls in the class always complained that Tiffany thought she was cute, and that she bragged too much. And while Racquel would never have agreed with them openly, she knew exactly what they were talking about. She was only a second-grader, but she hardly ever wore the same thing twice. Which was ridiculous, because that was the very reason her attitude was so messed up. She didn't have any values, and it was obvious that her parents weren't making the slightest effort toward teaching her any. And there was only so much Racquel could say and do. So mostly she just put up with her, so long as she wasn't criticizing any of the other children about what they didn't have.

"That's very nice, Tiffany," Racquel said, hoping she'd take her seat immediately. But she didn't.

"It's made by Guess?, and my mom bought it from Marshall Field's," she said boastfully.

"Okay, Tiffany. Thank you," Racquel said as politely as she could, but the rest of the children still laughed out loud. They hated Tiffany's guts. That was for sure.

Tiffany strutted to her seat with her head high in the air, ignoring all of them. She didn't have any friends, and from the way she acted, it didn't seem like she really cared one way or the other. She'd cried a couple of times at recess when some of the other girls wouldn't let her play hopscotch or jump rope with them, but her feelings didn't stay hurt for too long. This girl was something else, and Racquel didn't even want to think about how sad her life was going to be once she became an adult.

Racquel chose the rest of her students one by one, so they could each have a turn showing and telling, and then she had them take out their spelling workbooks. After that, they saw a science film about birds, went to lunch, did their math, worked on their reading assignments, and then prepared to go home.

"Tonight, I want you all to start studying your spelling words, so you'll be ready for the test on Friday," Racquel said, leaning her behind against the front of her desk. She set both of her hands on top of her stomach, and after a few seconds she felt the baby moving. She continued holding her stomach because the baby was kicking in an extremely rough manner. "Whoa," she said before she realized it.

"What's the matter, Mrs. Wilson?" Christopher asked with concern in his voice.

"Mrs. Wilson, what's the master with your tummy?" Cynthia wanted to know.

Miss Tiffany sucked her teeth the way people do when they're irritated about something. "Don't you know anything? It's the baby kicking. My mom's stomach used to do that all the time before she had my baby brother, and she used to let me and my dad touch it."

Miss Thing was way too grown, and too far beside herself, and Racquel just looked at her. "Yes, it's just the baby kicking," Racquel confirmed for the rest of the class.

"Now, when did you say it was coming again?" Brianna, a cute little biracial girl wanted to know.

"In August, while you guys are enjoying your summer break," Racquel said and then felt a little awkward. Nowadays the whole concept of getting pregnant was discussed with children a lot more openly than it had been when she was growing up. She could still remember overhearing her grandmother whispering to her mom whenever they discussed the fact that someone had gotten pregnant or was just about to deliver a baby. Her grandmother didn't think that that particular "grown folks" topic should be brought up in front of anyone who wasn't over sixteen years of age, and her mother pretty much still felt the same way today. But Racquel had learned early on in her teaching career that these little elementary-school students knew so much that they could almost teach their elders a thing or two.

After the explanation of her due date, the bell rang, and the students grabbed their spring jackets, and hurried outside into the hallway. Racquel sat down at her desk and took a deep breath. Teaching second grade had always been a challenge—an enjoyable one, but still a challenge. But now that she was six months pregnant, it really wore her out. But on the other hand, since she had already gained thirty pounds, maybe that had more to do with her being tired than anything else. She couldn't believe she still had three months to go and was already wobbling around like she was ready to deliver at any time.

She leaned back in her chair and closed her eyes, trying to relax her mind, but it wasn't long before she started thinking about the baby and everything that had to do with it. The ultrasound had shown almost conclusively that she and Kevin were having a little girl, and she couldn't have been happier. Especially, since she'd bought tons and tons of pink clothing. She'd even decorated the nursery in pink and mint green. She'd bought everything from cloth diapers, Pampers, and receiving blankets to crib sheets, stuffed animals, and sleepers. She'd even purchased the car seat, stroller, and baby monitor. She hadn't missed a beat, and that was the main reason she didn't see a reason for her mother and Marcella to waste money on giving her a baby shower. She didn't know what people could bring that she didn't already have. She'd bought most of it over the last few years, but the day after she'd found out she was pregnant, she'd shopped for the baby every single weekend thereafter. And sometimes she shopped on weekdays, if she felt good and was in the mood for it.

She opened her eyes and turned to the next day's lesson plan, so she could mentally prepare herself for what the class would be covering. As she started to review it, she remembered that she was supposed to remind Kevin to pick the clothes up from the cleaners. Some of the cleaning was his, but most of it was hers, and since she only had a few professional-looking maternity outfits, she was almost out of things to wear. She pulled out her cellular phone and dialed his work phone number.

"Kevin Wilson speaking," he answered.

"Hi, baby. How's it going?"

"I'm fine. And how are you and my daughter doing?"

Racquel loved when he said that. His daughter. It had sort of a nice ring to it, and it made her feel good all over. "We're both fine. I'm about to get out of here after I finish up a couple of things, but I wanted to call and remind you about the cleaning."

"And it's a good thing you did, too, because I definitely hadn't thought about it anymore."

Of course he hadn't. How many men remembered any of what they were supposed to? Unless, of course, it had something to do with what time and what day of the week the football, basketball, or baseball games came on. But she was used to his forgetfulness, and after all these years it really didn't phase her.

"Okay, then I guess I'll see you at home in a couple of hours," she said, holding the phone with her shoulder so she could arrange the piles on her desk.

"I love you, baby," he said in a caring voice.

"I love you, too."

After she finished organizing her desk, she turned the lights out and left the room. As she drove along in her car, she passed Ashley and Nicholas's school and smiled. Usually she picked them up on the way home, but after Sharon died, Corrine switched her job from the night shift, so she could work days instead. She had wanted to leave that shift for a long time, and there was no better time than now, when Marcella needed all of their help the most. So, Corrine and Racquel shared the responsibility of keeping them every other week, but this week just so happened to be her mother's.

She continued driving down the road and felt a sharp cramp in the lower part of her stomach. *Shoot!* She could just kick herself for eating those leftover baked beans at lunchtime. But they were so good that she couldn't help herself. As a matter of fact, she couldn't help herself when it came to eating anything. She practically ate and drank everything she came in contact with, and she couldn't think of too many foods that she didn't like. Everything tasted good so long as it filled her stomach up, and lately, that's all that mattered to her.

The pain was slowly starting to subside, and she felt a lot more at ease. She drove down the street that led to her subdivision, entered it, and then drove into the driveway. After she pulled into the garage, she pressed the control to close it, swung her legs outside the car, closed the door, and then inserted her key inside the lock of the door leading into the kitchen. Once she was in, she set her purse down, kicked off her one-inch pumps, proceeded through to the living room, opened the front door, and grabbed today's mail. But, when she went to close the door, she felt another sharp pain in her stomach, except this time it was ten times sharper than the one she'd experienced earlier. She held her stomach and made her way to the plush chair to sit down. She'd thought it was just gas again, but now she was doubling over with excruciating pain, and it didn't seem like it was going to let up. She'd never felt pain like this before, and it sort of scared her. She was only six months along, but based on what Dr. Reed had told her, and what she'd learned in Lamaze class, she knew a baby could come at any time; even if it was way too early. She struggled to stand up, forced herself into the kitchen, and pulled the cordless phone down from the wall. Her first instinct was to call Kevin, but for some reason she didn't think she had time to wait for him to drive all the way home and then take her to the hospital, so she dialed 911 and waited for them to answer. She moaned and groaned, and the pain was getting worse instead of better.

"Nine-one-one. What's your emergency?" a lady answered.

"I think I'm going into labor," Racquel said, straining to get the words out.

"Okay. Is anyone there with you?"

"No, my husband is still at work," Racquel said, breathing harder.

"Do you have any idea how far apart your contractions are?"

"No. My stomach started cramping a few minutes ago, and it still hasn't stopped."

"I think we'd better get an ambulance over to you right away," the 911 lady said without delay. "Is your address 2222 Holly Lane?"

"Yes," Racquel said, tightening her face with pain.

"I'm dispatching an ambulance to you right now, but I want you to stay on the line with me until the paramedics arrive, okay?"

"Can you call my husband?" Racquel asked with a groan in her voice.

"I sure can. What's his number?"

Racquel recited Kevin's work number to the 911 representative and then waited for the ambulance to get there.

Kevin had been sitting and waiting on pins and needles for what seemed like ten hours, and he felt like he was about to go insane. He'd paced up and down the hallway next to the surgical waiting area more times than he cared to think about, and his nerves were running wild. Corrine and Marcella had tried to settle him down, but nothing they said to him seemed to make a bit of difference. He couldn't understand why it was taking so long. Dr. Reed had come out close to an hour ago saying that they were going to perform an emergency C-section, but he hadn't given any specific details as to what was going on. Kevin was starting to get worried, and while Corrine and Marcella had been trying to hide their fears, he knew they were just as concerned as he was. He tried to be positive about the whole situation because lots of babies were born when the mother had only carried them for six months. They were usually premature, but with time, they turned out just as healthy as normal children.

He sat down across from Corrine, Marcella, and her children, but it wasn't more than sixty seconds before he'd stood up again and walked back out into the hallway. Corrine and Marcella looked at each other.

"Mom, what's going to happen to Racquel if she loses her baby?" Marcella asked Corrine in a whisper.

"I really don't know, but I do know that we have to keep our faith strong."

"I'm trying to, but you know she already had one miscarriage."

"I know, but that time she only carried the baby three months."

"Maybe you're right," Marcella said, glancing across the room at Nicholas, who was sitting at a small round table trying to put a jigsaw puzzle together. Ashley was doing her math homework.

Kevin walked slowly back into the waiting room, sat down in the chair closest to the doorway, and laid his head back with his eyes closed. But right when he did, Dr. Reed walked in and closed the door.

"Is everyone in here part of your family?" Dr. Reed asked and sat down in the seat adjacent to Kevin.

"Yes, this is Racquel's mother and sister. And her niece and nephew," Kevin responded nervously. "Is Racquel okay?" he asked fearfully.

"Racquel is fine. It took a while for us to get her stabilized because her blood pressure shot up so high, but she'll be fine."

"And how's the baby?"

"I'm sorry, Kevin, but she didn't make it. Her lungs just weren't strong enough to survive such an early delivery."

Kevin gazed at him without any movement, tears slowly streamed down his face.

"Lord. Lord. Lord," Corrine said, making her way across the room to Kevin. She sat down in the chair next to him, rubbing his back.

"No," Marcella said in a grunting voice with her hand over her mouth.

Ashley looked at her mother, set her math book down in the next chair, and walked over to sit with her. Nicholas followed behind her.

"Your wife is in recovery right now. You should be able to see her in about an hour or so. Someone will let you know when she's been moved to a private room," Dr. Reed said and stood up. "I'm really sorry," he said again, and patted Kevin on his knee. Then he left the room.

Tears were flowing from Kevin's face at a more rapid pace, and both of his hands were balled into tight fists. They'd gone through all of this for nothing, and he couldn't understand why things had turned out the way they had. He tried hard to think back to what he might have done to deserve such harsh punishment, but he couldn't think of anything. He had always tried to lead a decent life ever since he could remember, and he went out of his way to treat people with the utmost respect. This whole ordeal had turned into a complete disaster, and he wanted to run outside the hospital, so he could scream in peace with no one around so he wouldn't have to feel embarrassed. But he knew he had to be strong for Racquel because she was going to need him more now than she ever had before. She was going to need all of them. He sniffled a couple of times and wiped the wetness from his face with the two tissues Corrine had given him.

"Everything will be all right," Corrine said, trying to convince Kevin, but more than anything, she was trying to convince herself.

"I know, Mom," Kevin said. "But you know how badly we wanted this baby. And how am I going to tell Racquel?"

"Racquel will be fine. It will take some time, but she'll be fine," Corrine said, trying to give him peace of mind, and she hugged him. "It might not seem like it now, but God knows best."

Marcella wiped the tears from her face and walked across the room to where her mother and brother-in-law were sitting. She sat down on the other side of him. "We *will* get through this, Kevin."

Kevin closed his eyes and thought a thousand thoughts. But there was one thought that stuck out in his mind the most: What was going to happen to their marriage now?

Chapter 20

A whole month had passed since they'd buried their beautiful daughter, Karlia Renee Wilson, but Racquel was still acting as if her own life was over. She really didn't see a reason for living, and she did nothing except mope around the house day after day. And sometimes she didn't even bother to do that.

She'd gone into total hysterics when Kevin had told her the news about the baby, and for a while the nurses had thought for sure they were going to have to sedate her and strap her down to the bed. Everyone in the family had known that the loss of the baby wasn't going to be easy for her to deal with, but they'd never guessed that her reaction was going to turn out as bad as it had. Dr. Reed had kept her in the hospital for three days; partly because of the C-section, but mostly because of her extreme emotional state. Corrine and Marcella had been worried sick the entire time. When she finally did come home, she walked straight through the front door and into the bedroom without saying anything to anyone. It was almost like she was a zombie and had lost her mind. And the most she'd said during the ride home from the hospital was that she wanted to go up to her own bedroom and not the guest bedroom on the first floor. But eventually Corrine convinced her that it wasn't good for her to climb stairs so soon after having surgery. Racquel hadn't argued with her about it, but it was obvious that she wasn't happy about it, either. And to prove it, she hadn't spoken to any of them the rest of that afternoon.

Racquel dragged her legs out of the bed and started toward the master bathroom until she heard the phone ringing. Her first thought was to ignore it, but since it might be Kevin, she decided to answer it.

"Hello?" she said in a monotone voice.

"Hey," Kevin said enthusiastically. "Are you up yet?"

"If that's what you want to call it," she said dryly.

"So how are you feeling?"

"Okay, I guess."

"Do you feel well enough to meet me for lunch?" he asked optimistically.

Racquel hated going through this with him every day, and he was starting to get on her nerves. Couldn't he see how hurt she was? She hadn't even gone back to work before the school year ended, like he'd suggested, so she couldn't understand at all why he thought she wanted to go out to some restaurant. "I don't feel like it today. But maybe some other time."

"Okay, then when?" he said irritably.

"I don't know, but not today."

He paused for a minute and then spoke. "What do you want me to do, Racquel?"

"What do you mean, what do *I* want you to do?"

"Exactly what I said. I've gone out of my way to try and help you overcome the loss of the baby, and I don't know what else to do."

"Overcome the loss of the baby? Is that what you're waiting for? Well, I'm sorry to disappoint you, because that's never going to happen. I don't know how you can expect something like that. I don't even know how you can just pretend like nothing happened. Just because you've been waltzing around here like everything is back to normal, I hope you don't think I'm about to do the same thing."

"I didn't say everything was back to normal, but, Racquel," he said, pausing, "life goes on."

"Maybe for you it does, but not for me."

"I knew this was going to happen. We're back in the same old rut we were in before you got pregnant, aren't we?"

"Look, Kevin. My baby just died, and regardless of how you feel, I can't just sit here and pretend that she never existed."

"I'm not pretending, either, but maybe if you at least try to put forth some kind of an effort, we might be able to get through this a lot easier."

"Kevin, who are you to tell me about putting forth an effort, when you never even so much as said hello to your mother when she came here for the funeral?"

"Racquel, you know the situation with my mother, and you know why I don't have anything to say to her. And I didn't invite her to come here in the first place. You did."

"She had a right to be here the same as your father did because Karlia was her granddaughter, too. At least she thought enough of us to come. Something my own father didn't even have the decency to do."

"Racquel, what does all of this have to do with us?" Kevin said in a fed-up tone.

Racquel was steaming and felt like slamming the phone on the hook, but she didn't.

"So, you don't have anything else to say?" Kevin asked angrily.

"As a matter of fact, I don't."

"Well, then, I guess this conversation is over."

"Whatever, Kevin," she said and slammed the phone down. And for some reason, she didn't feel bad about it, because right now she was pissed off at everyone involved. Her mother had been coming by every single day trying to get her out of the house; Marcella had been talking some crazy mess about adoption; and Kevin was acting as if he didn't care whether Karlia had lived or died. And she was never going to show her face back at Westside Missionary Baptist Church for as long as she lived. Those women at the church had come over each day claiming to bring food for the family and to pay their respects, but all Racquel saw them doing was filling up their own plates and spreading a lot of gossip. It was almost as if they were celebrating the fact that someone had died. She'd heard one of the deacons' wives saying, "We've got it backward. We're supposed to be sad when a child is born into this sinful world, and happy when someone passes on to their glory." The fact of the matter was: Nobody understood how she felt. *They* hadn't lost their own flesh and blood. *They* hadn't lost the only thing that mattered to them the most. And she could bet *they* didn't feel like dying the way she did.

She walked into the master bathroom, pulled out a medicine

bottle, opened it, and dumped two sleeping pills into her hand. She ran some water in a paper cup, threw the tablets in her mouth, and swallowed two gulps of water behind them. Then she crumpled the cup up, threw it in the forest-green wicker wastebasket, and walked back out to the bedroom.

She picked up her purple satin robe from the chair, tied the belt, and walked over to the dresser. She pulled the top-right drawer open, pulled out an envelope, and sat down on the bed. When she turned the envelope upside down, a stack of photos came tumbling out. They were the photos that the church photographer had taken at the funeral. Her mother and Marcella hadn't thought it was a good idea for her to have pictures of the baby lying in a casket, but Racquel had made it clear that her mind was made up, so they'd had no choice except to go along with it.

She gazed at the first one, and then moved it to the bottom of the pile. Then she did the same with the second, third, and fourth. But when she came to the fifth one, she paused for a minute and then dropped the rest down on the bed. Most of the photos were similar to each other, but for some reason this one stood out in the crowd. And now she knew why. Karlia was smiling at her. Or at least it looked like she was. And it seemed like she was trying to say something to Racquel.

"What is it, sweetie?" Racquel asked, smiling at the photo.

"It's scary in here, Mommy," Racquel heard Karlia say.

"I know, honey. Mommy's going to come get you from that dreary old funeral home just as soon as she can get dressed," she said in baby talk. "Your daddy is going to be so happy when he gets home from work," she said joyfully.

Racquel closed her eyes tight and held the photo against her chest with both hands. Maybe Karlia wasn't dead after all. Maybe Kevin had made a huge mistake when he'd told her that the baby's lungs hadn't been strong enough for her to survive. Yeah, that had to be it, she thought with a smile.

She opened her eyes and pulled the photo away from her body, so she could tell Karlia that everything was going to be fine. But what she saw this time, was her worst nightmare. It was her beautiful baby girl lying in a gory-looking, miniature off-white casket. And she wasn't smiling, and her eyes were no longer open.

Racquel dropped the photo on the floor and screamed at the top of her lungs.

"I don't know what we're going to do with that girl," Corrine said to Marcella, and then folded the last of Nicholas's underwear.

Corrine had worked ten hours at the factory and had decided to stop by Marcella's for a little while to see the children. But since the children were occupied with their usual summer-evening activities, she was helping Marcella fold the clothes that she'd washed at the Laundromat earlier that afternoon.

"Kevin called me this afternoon at work saying that Racquel hung up on him. And I'm telling you, Mom, he sounded like he was completely fed up with her," Marcella said, folding Ashley's red short set.

"If she doesn't stop this, he's going to leave her. I just know he is," Corrine said worriedly.

"And then she'll really lose her mind."

"Maybe you can try to talk to her again."

"Every time I try to talk to her, she makes an excuse to get off the phone, and if I drop by the house, she pretends like she's sleepy or doesn't feel well. And the few times she has talked to me, she usually says something like 'You don't understand' or 'You're just taking Kevin's side.' And to tell you the truth, I'm getting a little sick of it. Racquel's my sister, and I love her, but she's taking this too far."

"Maybe she needs to see a psychiatrist or something. Maybe this is worse than we thought."

"Even if we found one for her and made the appointment, she'll never go."

"No, she probably wouldn't," Corrine said disappointedly. "I'm telling you the truth—if it's not one thing, it's another."

Marcella didn't say anything because she knew her mother was worried sick about Racquel. And who could blame her? Racquel was her daughter, and she had a right to be concerned about her well-being. But Marcella was starting to wonder just how long Racquel was going to carry on like this, because enough was enough.

"I called her this morning when I took my first break, and she sounded okay," Corrine continued.

"Well, I didn't call her today at all. I thought about it, but I knew she was going to have the same attitude, so I didn't. And when Kevin called and said she'd hung up on him, that *really* made me not want to call her."

"I know you're a little irritated, but she's still your sister, and she's still my daughter. And it's up to us to try and understand what she's going through."

"But that's just it, Mom. We *don't* understand what she's going through. I mean, we both know what it's like to have children, but at the same time we've never lost any. And that's why when I talk to her, I don't know what to say. So, I don't know, maybe you're right. Maybe we really should try to get her some professional help."

"But it's like you said before, she probably won't go." Corrine patted down the stack of Nicholas's T-shirts that she'd just finished folding.

"Well, at this point I don't think we have a choice because Kevin isn't going to put up with her too much longer. Their marriage was barely hanging by a thread before she found out she was pregnant, and I don't think he's going to keep putting up with all this rejection from her."

"You know what? I'm going over to talk to both of them right now, because this doesn't make any sense at all," Corrine said, picking up her purse and standing up.

"I really hope you can talk some sense into her. Because if you don't, she and Kevin don't have a chance."

Shortly after Corrine left Marcella's apartment, Darryl showed up. With all the crazy hours he'd been working at the hospital over the last two months, they'd hardly spent any time together, and she missed being with him. And this was as good a time as any, since Ashley was in Marcella's room on the phone with her little girl-friend, and Nicholas was playing with the Nintendo that Tyrone had bought for him two weeks ago. A purchase that had surprised everyone. And to top it all off, he had even bought him a remote-controlled television set to go along with it. Nicholas wasn't turning eleven for three months, but Tyrone claimed that since Nicholas had been begging for it for so long, he wanted to give him his birthday present early. And that was the main reason why Marcella hadn't gone off on him for not paying his child support for the last two weeks. She knew he still had a responsibility to pay her, regardless of what he bought extra, but for some reason she didn't mind going without it, after she saw that huge smile on her baby's face. He'd never had anything that expensive before, and his happiness was important to her.

She walked into the living room and sat down next to him.

"So what's up for this weekend?" she asked, caressing his fade haircut.

"Work, of course."

"Not again," she said with a disappointed look on her face.

"I know, but I really don't have a choice."

"Well, when are you going to have a day off again?"

"I barely glanced at the schedule on the way out, but probably next Monday and Tuesday," he said, staring straight at the television.

He was acting strange, and Marcella was starting to feel uncomfortable. "Well, maybe I can get the partners to give me one of those days off, so we can do something. Shoot, we haven't gone anywhere together in months." Or made love, either, for that matter. At least that's what she wanted to tell him because truth was, she had needs just like every other woman in America, and it was time he realized it. But she didn't want him to think she was some sex-craved animal, so she kept her thoughts to herself.

"Hey, Nick," Darryl said, ignoring what Marcella had said.

"Hi, Darryl," Nicholas said, smiling and giving him a high five. "You wanna play a game with me on the Nintendo?"

"You mean, do I want to beat you at a game on the Nintendo?" he said, standing up.

"No way. Nobody can beat me at any of the games. Not even you," Nicholas said excitedly.

"Well, we'll see about that," Darryl said, dragging him playfully into his bedroom.

What, Marcella thought. They hadn't seen each other in over a week, and now he was going to play some game with Nicholas? None of this added up, and she was starting to get upset. She'd known for a while now that their relationship wasn't the same as it had been in the beginning, but she'd thought things had gotten a lot better since the Tyrone situation. But maybe it had just been her imagination. And just maybe she'd been fooling herself, because now he was acting like he didn't want to be with her at all.

And if he didn't, then why did he bring his tired behind over to her apartment in the first place? She wasn't going to be treated like this without some sort of an explanation.

"Darryl," she said, standing inside Nicholas's doorway.

"Yeah," Darryl said, keeping his attention on the game. Nicholas was so engulfed that he didn't hear a word she said.

"Can I see you for a minute?" she said without smiling. The last thing she wanted was to clown him right in front of her children. But, if he didn't have a good reason for acting the way he was, all sorts of fireworks were about to shoot off.

"Let me finish this game, and I'll be in there."

She wanted to tell him to put the stupid game control down now, but she decided to stay calm. She walked into her bedroom.

"Ashley, you're going to have to switch to the kitchen phone or call your little girlfriend back."

"Girl, hold on a minute," Ashley said, blowing with disgust.

"I just know you're not blowing because I told you to get off my phone, are you?" Marcella asked, raising her eyebrows as high as they would go.

"I wasn't blowing at you," Ashley said, lying as best she could.

"Of course you were. Just for that, I want you to hang that phone up and stay off of it for the rest of the night."

"What did I do?" Ashley asked, raising her voice. She was clearly irritated.

"Get out of here, Ashley, before I make it a whole week."

"Dog," Ashley said under her breath while storming out of the room.

"What did you say?" Marcella said, walking behind her daughter.

"Nothing," Ashley said fearfully because she knew she'd gone too far.

Marcella grabbed her by her collar. "I don't know who you think you're playing with, but I'm the mother in this house," she said, pointing her finger so close to Ashley's nose that she almost touched it.

Tears were rolling down Ashley's face, but she didn't dare say anything.

"You can just sit in here for the rest of the evening, and I don't want you using that phone until I tell you to. Even if it's next year.

With your little fast self," Marcella said, angrily slamming Ashley's bedroom door.

"What's going on with you two?" Darryl asked, following Marcella back into her bedroom.

Marcella ignored his question and slammed the door as soon as they both entered the room. She'd planned on talking to him in a decent manner, but she was too fired up now to control herself. "So what's up, Darryl? I mean, why are you acting like this?"

"Acting like what?" he asked.

"You know exactly what I mean. A few months ago, you told me that you were in love with me, but now I hardly see you at all."

"That's because I've been working so much. And until this past month, you were going to school and working a lot of hours yourself."

"So what? I've been doing that the whole time that we've been dating, and it's never been a problem before."

Darryl sat down on the bed and took a deep breath. "Sit down."

"Sit down for what?" she asked angrily.

"Marcella, please sit down."

She finally did what he wanted, but she sat as far away from him as she could.

"I've been trying to say this for the longest, but I didn't know how."

She didn't like where this conversation was going, but she didn't have a choice now except to hear it.

"I've been offered a position in California when my residency is up next month, and I've decided to take it."

She was stunned. "You're what?"

"I'm taking a position in California."

"Did it ever once occur to you that maybe we should discuss a decision as important as that?" she said, raising her eyebrows.

"No, because you and I both know our relationship hasn't been working out the way we thought it would. In the beginning, things were great between us, but Tyrone was always in the background. And you allowed him to be."

"Tyrone? You know good and well Tyrone doesn't have anything to do with this."

"Maybe not as far as you're concerned, but I told you from the start that I couldn't deal with my woman continually getting into heated arguments with some guy she used to go with."

"But you knew what those arguments were about, and it wasn't like we still had feelings for each other."

"To be honest, I didn't know what was going on between you and him."

He was pissing her off more and more by the minute, and she was close to kicking him out. "So, then, that's it? You're moving away, just like that?"

"I really don't have a choice. It's the best offer that I have, so have to take it."

"It wasn't more than a year ago that you said you were pretty sure Covington Park Memorial was going to offer you a good position. So what happened to that?" she asked, crossing her arms.

"Their offer wasn't even close to the one I'm taking in California."

"You really had me fooled, Darryl. You know that?" she said, standing up.

"Look. I hope there're no hard feelings behind this, because I really think this is better for both of us."

"How can you say this is better for me? Because I don't see how I'm going to benefit from any of this."

"But it's still better, because you deserve someone who can spend more time with you. Someone who can deal with your particular situation."

"What do you mean *my* particular situation?" she asked, placing her right hand on her hip.

"You know how it is, Marcella, when a woman has children by another man. It takes a very special person to deal with that, and I just don't think I could ever handle it. I love Ashley and Nicholas, but I think we'd both be fooling ourselves if we started thinking that we could all live happily ever after. And even if we tried, Tyrone would find some way to mess everything up."

Tyrone. Tyrone. Tyrone. She was sick of all of his whining about Tyrone. Here he was supposed to be a doctor, but he was acting like a jealous schoolboy who was having problems with his first teenaged girlfriend. This was ridiculous, and while she hated not having anyone in her life, she didn't need someone consumed with all these insecurities. And if she'd said it once, she'd said it a thousand times. She, Ashley, and Nicholas were a package deal, and any man who couldn't deal with that might as well move onto his next victim.

"I'm not even going to acknowledge that stupid comment you just made, because if I do, I'll end up cussing you out in a way like you never have been before. So, just get out," she said, opening the bedroom door.

"Marcella . . . ," he said. "I don't want to leave until you calm down. I mean I wouldn't want you to slice my tires over something like this," he said, laughing.

This idiot was something else. And she couldn't believe he had the nerve to actually be standing there laughing in her face. Like this was some joke of the week. And who did he think he was anyway? Denzel Washington or somebody? Please, he wasn't *that* good. And now that he was rising so far above himself, she decided that this was the perfect time to fill him in on a few things. "Slice your tires?" she said, closing the bedroom door, hoping her children wouldn't hear what she was about to say. "First of all, I wouldn't even stoop low enough to do anything like that, and secondly, you're not worth it, anyway. And the sex wasn't that great, either. Oh, I know you thought you were really doing something whenever we supposedly made love, but I've got news for you, sweetheart. You need to buy some books, watch some videos, take some classes, or do whatever it is men do when they can't satisfy a woman. And while you're learning how to do that, I suggest you grow something big enough between your legs to back up all of that huffing and puffing you used to be doing."

He laughed, but she could tell from the strange look on his face that he was embarrassed. Still, he tried to pretend like this newfound information wasn't fazing him the least little bit. "Yeah, right, Marcella. You sure weren't saying all of that a few weeks ago."

"Oh, you mean a few weeks ago when you went down on me? Yeah, you're right, that was good, but the rest was just as pitiful as it's always been. I just never told you because I didn't want to hurt your feelings. But now I couldn't care less."

"Women always get like this when they get dumped," he said, opening the bedroom door.

"I've never had a reason to tell any other man how terrible he was in bed, because I've never experienced anyone as pathetic as you. Truth be told, you're in a class all by yourself, and I feel sorry for you. And I'll tell you another thing, if someone does marry you, it'll be for one reason, and one reason only. That medical degree that you have, and the salary that goes along with it," she said, following him to the front door.

"Well whoever it is, it won't be you," he said, walking out the door.

"You worthless ingrate," she yelled and slammed the door.

What nerve. When she'd first met him that day at church, she'd felt like melting. He was gorgeous, polite, and intelligent. Shoot, by her standards he was everything a woman could hope for, and then some. She'd been thinking all along that someone like him wouldn't be with her forever, but in the back of her mind she'd been hoping that things just might work out. She wasn't even that in love with him anymore, but he was good with her children. And until lately, he treated her like royalty. And she was even willing to accept the terrible sex he was dishing out as a trade-off for all of his other good qualities. And the fact that he was going to earn over one hundred thousand dollars a year had made him a lot more attractive than any other man she knew, too. She never dated men for their money, but at the same time it didn't hurt when they had it.

She didn't want to be alone, but for the first time ever, she'd been "dumped" by a man and wasn't the slightest bit hurt over it. Well, maybe a little hurt, but not to the extent where she couldn't get over it. And one thing was for sure. If she'd survived all the other trying times in her life, this one wasn't going to be any different.

Chapter 21

"Kevin, what am I supposed to do for money?" Racquel asked, following behind him from one room to the next.

"I'll help you out until the divorce is final, but after that, I suggest you go back to work like everybody else does when they need money," he said sternly.

Kevin had begged and pleaded with her in every possible way he knew how, but it hadn't made any difference, and nothing had changed between them. She refused to go out of the house, she still didn't want to make love to him, and she'd made it clear that she wasn't going back to work at the elementary school when classes started at the end of this month. Her mother and sister had tried to convince her that she needed professional help, but in so many words, she'd told both of them to mind their own business. And they'd done just that.

But now Kevin had waited as long as he could, and since another month had passed since the death of the baby, he decided that their marriage was over. Racquel didn't seem to care about anything but herself anyway, and he had to move on. Even if it meant without her.

"Kevin, why can't you understand what I've been going through? I'm your wife, and you're supposed to be here for me—no matter what."

"That's the whole problem. I've been here for you all along, but you've been so caught up in your own little selfish world, that you couldn't see it. We've been together, what? Five years? And we've done nothing except try to have a baby. And now I'm emotionally drained from all of it," he said, carrying another load of suits down the carpeted stairway.

She followed behind him out to his utility vehicle. "If we talk this over, I know things will get better," she said, looking around the neighborhood. From what she could see, there was no one in the vicinity standing outside or peeking out their window. She was glad it was dark outside. Because the last thing she wanted was for her neighbors to see Kevin moving his things out of the house.

"I'm all talked out. And even when I did have something to say, you allowed it to go in one ear and right out the other. Even when your mother came over here last month to talk to both of us, you pretty much ignored everything she had to say. And you've gone out of your way to hurt her and Marcella every time they've called or come by to see you."

"I lost my little girl, Kevin. How many times do I have to keep saying that, and when are you going to understand how painful that was for me?" she asked as they both walked back up to the bedroom.

"Why is everything always about you?" he yelled. "I lost my little girl, too, Racquel. But life doesn't end just because something bad happens. I mean, just look at you. You've been off work all summer, and you've barely been out of the house more than ten times in the past two months. I remember when getting your hair and nails done was one of your top priorities, but now you don't even do that anymore. And worse than that, it's pretty obvious that you don't even take a bath or get into the shower on a daily basis. You're a complete mess, and I hope for your sake that you do something about it."

"How can I worry about any of that when I'm still mourning the loss of my child?"

"You just don't get it, do you?" he asked, shaking his head. "You really don't."

"I can't believe after all we've been through, you're going to just walk out on me like it's no big deal."

"But that's just it. We've been through too much, and I'm tired of going to hell and back every time something doesn't turn out the way you want it to."

She leaned against the wall by the armoire and looked on as he continued packing his underwear, socks, and ties in the black nylon suitcase. He'd been threatening to leave her for the longest time, but she had to admit, not once had she ever believed he would actually go through with it. It crossed her mind from time to time, but that was pretty much it. And he was right when he said she'd hurt everyone else's feelings, because she could still remember every single one of the times that she'd been downright rude to her mother and sister. And now she realized that all they'd been trying to do was help her; but to her, they'd gone about it the wrong way. And that was the very reason why she'd reacted the way she had. They'd tried to force her into seeing some psychiatrist, but she didn't see a reason to waste money on something that she didn't need. She'd had a few hallucinations about the baby being alive, but that had only happened a couple of times, and she'd tried to tell them that. But they hadn't listened and still insisted that she needed to talk to someone about her emotional well-being and her very serious marital problems. But she tried to make them see that all of her problems would eventually work themselves out without the help of some overpriced shrink. Her mother had warned her time and time again that one day Kevin was going to do more than just talk about leaving and was actually going to do it. And while Racquel really hadn't paid much attention to her advice before, right now, that's all she could think about. She had to stop him. That was all there was to it. Even if it meant she had to pretend about how she really felt.

"Okay, okay, okay. You win. I'll go to a counselor, I'll go back to work next month, and I'll make love to you every night if that's what you want," she proclaimed.

"What do you think this is, some kind of game? It's too late for a bunch of promises that we both know you're not going to keep. I've given you chance after chance to come to your senses, but you never took me seriously. And now nothing, and I mean nothing you say, is going to stop me from moving out."

She couldn't believe what she was hearing. She'd said all of the right things, and she'd thought for sure he'd change his mind about leaving. It had always worked in the past whenever he talked

about ending their marriage, but this time he didn't seem to care
about what she had to say. "But, Kevin, how can you just throw
away five years of marriage?" she asked fearfully.

"It was more like five years of hell. Things were good the first
year, but you and I both know it's been tumbling downhill ever
since. You didn't care, and now I feel the same way," he said, zip-
ping the suitcase.

"Are you saying you don't love me anymore? Because you know
I love you more than anything in this world." Tears were rolling
down her face.

At first, he tried to ignore what she'd just said, but it was obvious
that he felt sorry for her just the same. "Racquel. Sit down," he
said, sitting on the side of the bed.

She sat next to him.

"I do still love you, but the problem is, I don't know if I'm *in*
love with you. We've had a lot of problems, and our relationship
has been terribly damaged because of them. When you found out
you were pregnant this second time, I thought for sure our marriage was going to get back on track. But when you lost the baby,
things got worse than they had been before. Instead of just accepting things the way God obviously meant for them to be, you became more and more obsessed with chasing this fantasy of yours.
And although I wish I could look at you and say that we can work
this out, I can't. Too much has happened, and I doubt very seriously if we can do anything to fix it," he said holding her hand.

"But, Kevin . . . ," she said bawling.

"I'm sorry, Racquel, but that's how I feel." He gazed at her for a
few seconds and then stood up. "If you need me for anything, I'll
be at The Waterstone. Their number is in the phone book." He
picked up his suitcase and then walked over to the doorway. She
sat on the bed staring at him, and although he stared back at her,
neither of them said a word. Finally, he walked down the stairs,
and it wasn't long before she heard him drive off.

Kevin had actually left her. She kept playing the whole idea of it
over and over in her mind, but it didn't seem real. All she'd ever
wanted was a family, but now she had nothing. She didn't have a
baby, and now she didn't have a husband to love her. She felt like
the walls were closing in on her, like she was cracking up. And how
on earth was she going to face her mother and Marcella when they

found out about all of this? They'd both seen this coming for some time now, and the last thing she needed to hear were a bunch of I-told-you-so's. Especially since they'd tried to warn her on more than one occasion. But what hurt her the most was that she hadn't paid enough attention to her own situation to foresee any of what was happening. She knew they had problems and that Kevin was unhappy with the way their marriage was going, but she never thought things were bad enough to cause a separation. Or even worse, a divorce. But then, he would never go as far as filing for a divorce. Not Kevin, the man who said he would always love her, no matter what. But on the other hand, she hadn't thought he would just walk out on her like he had, either, so she really couldn't be sure of what he was going to do.

She sighed deeply and swallowed hard. She had to figure out a way to get through to him. She had to make him see that this could all be worked out. Because if she didn't, there was no doubt that she was going to lose the best thing that had ever happened to her.

As soon as Racquel opened her eyes, she shut them quickly, trying to avoid the sunlight that was beaming down from her bedroom window into her face. She'd tossed and turned most of the night, hadn't dropped off to sleep until around 5 A.M., and she felt like she'd been run over by a train. Her whole life was in a rut, and she honestly didn't know what to do to make things better. She'd wanted to call Kevin last night, but since he probably needed some time alone, she'd decided against it. But now she needed to talk to him. She needed to hear his voice. She picked up the phone on the nightstand and dialed his number at work. It rang four times and then finally his voice mail answered. "Hi, this is Kevin Wilson at Whitlock Aerospace, and I'll be out of the office until Monday, August twentieth. However, if you have a situation that needs immediate attention, please press zero when you hear the tone, and someone will help you. Thank you."

Racquel waited for the tone, but didn't see any sense in leaving a message since he was going to be out for a whole week. Which sort of surprised her because he hadn't mentioned one thing about taking time off from work. And she couldn't help but wonder what was going on.

She reached inside the bottom drawer of the nightstand, pulled out the phone directory, searched through the Yellow Pages for the number to where Kevin was staying and dialed it. The phone rang five times before there was an answer.

"Thank you for calling The Waterstone. How may I direct your call?" answered a Black woman with a very distinctive voice.

"Could you please ring Kevin Wilson's room?"

"One moment," the woman said and then transferred the call.

After three rings Kevin picked up. "Hello?"

"Hey," Racquel said softly.

"How are you?" he asked in a groggy tone of voice, sounding like he'd just woken up.

"As well as can be expected, I guess, considering the fact that you left me the way you did."

He didn't say anything.

"I didn't wake you up, did I?" she continued.

"As a matter of fact, you did. I didn't get to sleep until sometime early this morning."

"Is that why you missed work today?"

"No. I decided to take the rest of the week off yesterday."

"Well, I didn't know what was going on when I called your number at work because you never said anything about taking a vacation."

"This whole thing with us has taken a toll on me, and I needed a break. That's all."

"I can understand that, but why did you have to move out?"

"I explained that to you last night."

"But I still don't understand it. I mean, I know we've been going through a rough time, but I never thought you would actually walk out on me like this."

"I didn't want to, but things were getting worse every day. And for three months you've acted like I don't even exist. And I couldn't take that anymore."

"I realize that now, and I know I was wrong for treating you the way I did. But I swear if you give me another chance, I'll do everything in my power to make this all up to you," she said pleadingly.

"But just last night, you were still trying to make it seem like I was wrong for having a problem with the way you've been acting. So how can you just change your whole way of thinking in one night?"

"Because I had all night to think about it. And regardless of what I said, or how I may have been acting the last couple of months, I know now that you're the most important thing in this world to me, and I'll die if I lose you," she said, stroking her hair.

"But it's not just the things that went on over the last couple of months. It's all the crap that I had to put up with for the last five years. I mean I went out of my way to make you happy, and I gave you all the love that I knew how to give. And it still didn't make a difference to you because all you ever cared about was making a baby. I don't think you ever went one day without mentioning it, and that's not normal. And all of this is partly my fault, because I never should have let it go on for as long as I did."

"But we loved each other, and that's all that mattered."

"No, that's not all that mattered to *me*, because a marriage is based on a lot more than just feelings. What about trust?"

"What do you mean, trust?" she asked, frowning. "Racquel, you know what I'm talking about."

"No, I don't," she said, knowing good and well that he was referring to the abortion issue.

"I'm talking about those abortions you had."

"All of that happened before I met you, and since I knew how you felt about abortions, I was afraid to tell you. Can't you understand that?"

"No, because I asked you if you'd ever done anything like that, and you flat out said no."

"But you wouldn't have understood then, just like you don't understand now."

"How do you know? I mean, I could have gotten over the fact that you had two abortions, but what really pissed me off was the fact that you lied to me. And on top of that, you slept with a married man for money. To me, that's no different from being a prostitute, if you ask me," he said angrily.

She couldn't believe he was actually comparing her to a prostitute. Her relationship with Tom hadn't been anything like that because they'd had real feelings for each other. They hadn't been in love. Or at least she hadn't. But they still enjoyed being together. And while she knew they were wrong for playing around behind his wife's back, not a day went by when she didn't feel sorry for it. But there was nothing she could do to change it now, and she wished Kevin would stop harassing her about something that had nothing to do with him.

"It wasn't like that, Kevin," she said, trying to convince him.

"Whatever," he said, sounding irritated. "And regardless of what that doctor said, I'd be willing to bet that those two abortions are the real reason you can't carry a baby to full term."

"Oh, so now you're the doctor, right?" she said furiously. She'd tried to be nice ever since the conversation started, but now he was tapping into the wrong subject.

"No, I'm *not* the doctor, but I do know that having two abortions at such a young age couldn't have helped you any."

"Kevin, if that had been the problem, Dr. Reed would have figured it out when he ran all those tests on me. There was nothing wrong with me, and you know it."

"See," Kevin said, laughing sarcastically. "You're still obsessed with that same old madness."

"You're the one that brought it up. Not me."

"Look, I'm not even going to keep arguing with you about this. And anyway, I need to get ready for an appointment, so I'm going to have to talk to you later."

"What appointment?" she asked with deep curiosity.

"With my attorney."

Attorney? Why did he need to talk to an attorney so soon? Surely not about divorce proceedings. He just couldn't be. She dreaded asking him what this was about, but she had to know. "What are you seeing an attorney for?"

"I'm filing for a divorce."

"You're what?"

"I've thought about it from every angle, and I just don't see any chance of us working this out."

She wanted to beg him not to do it, but she could tell that his mind was already made up. "Well, I guess there's nothing else I can say."

"Look, no matter what you think, I never wanted things to end this way. And to be honest, I thought being in love with you was enough, but I realize now that love doesn't mean anything if your wife doesn't appreciate you."

"But I did appreciate you. I might not have shown you as often as I should have, but I did appreciate you. And I loved you."

"But you didn't love me or make love to me the way your sister Marcella does now."

Racquel sucked her breath in as hard as she could, popped her eyes open, and sat straight up in her bed all at the same time. She moved her eyes back and forth around the room trying to familiarize herself with the surroundings, and then it finally dawned on her that she was sitting inside of her own bedroom. Her face was covered with thick layers of sweat, her heart beat rapidly, and her nightgown was soaked to no end.

She peeped over at Kevin, who was still asleep, and closed her eyes for a few minutes. Then she smiled when she realized that this marital separation had been nothing more than a terrible dream.

Chapter 22

"Mom, my head hurts," Nicholas said, walking into his grandmother's kitchen.

"It's probably just from all the excitement, because I know you hardly slept a wink last night, and you don't feel like you have a fever or anything," Marcella said, removing her hand from his forehead. "The party isn't going to start for another two hours, so maybe you should go lie down for a while." Marcella hugged him close to her.

"You can go get in my bed if you want to," Corrine said, smiling at him, because she knew how much her grandson loved lying in her bed.

Nicholas left the room without any argument.

Marcella was sitting at the kitchen table trying to figure out which games the children were going to play; Racquel was mixing some pop and punch together; Corrine was finishing the hors d'oeuvres for the adults who were coming; and Ashley was in the dining room setting up the paper products on the table. Nicholas was turning eleven today, and the family was giving him a birthday party. He'd had small ones before at Chuck E. Cheese, and places like that. But this year they'd decided to give him one at home, so they could invite all of his little friends from school, as well as all their relatives. Which was sort of a tradition, since they'd done the same thing for Ashley when she'd turned eleven two years ago. Marcella wasn't sure why they'd chosen such an oddball year like eleven to give the children their first family birthday party, but for some reason that's just the way it had turned out.

"Has Nicholas been complaining about any headaches before?" Corrine asked.

"Last week, he said he had one, and I gave him some children's aspirin. He was fine after that, though," Marcella said.

"Well, if it keeps up, maybe you should take him to the doctor," Corrine said.

"I know. And I should probably go ahead and make an appointment now because his pediatrician only takes welfare patients on certain days."

"But you're not on welfare, are you?" Racquel asked, looking at Marcella.

"Well, not really, since I don't receive any cash, but we're still covered by the medical card," Marcella said.

"But what does that have to do with what days you can see the doctor?" Racquel asked.

"I don't know, but there are a lot of doctors that do that."

"That's stupid, and it's almost like they're discriminating against people who don't have some high-class insurance carrier."

"That's a shame," Corrine commented.

"So whatever happened with your food stamps getting cut off?" Racquel asked.

"They're deducting ten percent from my allotment every month until the overpayment has been recouped. But I thought I told you that already," Marcella said.

"You might have, but you know how out of it I've been for the last few months. Sometimes it feels like I lost a whole year of my life," Racquel said shamefully. "And I never did apologize to either of you for acting the way I did," she said, looking from Marcella to her mother.

"Baby, don't even worry about that," Corrine said. "We know you were going through a hard time, and all that matters now is that you and Kevin are trying to work things out, and that you're getting on with your life."

"That's right," Marcella said, looking up from the game materials. "Nobody's even thinking about any of that."

"I know. But I don't know what I would have done if both of you hadn't been there for me, because I really was about to lose my mind. Having those hallucinations and all those nightmares was starting to scare me," Racquel said.

"Yeah, they were starting to scare me, too, when you told me about that crazy dream you had," Marcella said, laughing.

"Oh, don't even bring that up," Racquel said, feeling a little embarrassed because it was that very dream that made her realize she couldn't live without Kevin. She hadn't been the least bit worried that her sister was really having an affair with him, but it definitely had painted her a vivid picture of how awful it would feel losing him to some other woman. And it was the reason why she'd taken a semester's leave of absence from work, so she could be the wife she should have been to him a long time ago.

"I mean, just think. Kevin and I in love with each other," Marcella said, cracking up.

"Girl, I don't even know what made me dream some crazy mess like that," Racquel said.

"I don't know, either," Corrine said, laughing.

"I mean, don't get me wrong, I would love to find someone like Kevin, but that's about as far as it goes," Marcella said.

"You will," Racquel said.

"I doubt it. When I first started seeing Darryl, I thought he was the perfect guy, but you see how that turned out. And the worst part about it was that I really wasn't expecting it when he broke up with me that night, and some of the things he said really hurt me."

"Poor man," Racquel said. "I don't even want to think about what you said to him."

"You know how it is when your feelings get hurt," Marcella said. "A person is liable to say anything."

"Oh my goodness," Corrine said, laughing.

"Shoot, you'd have thought I wasn't raised very well, because I really went off on him," Marcella said.

"I can only imagine . . . because I know *you* when someone treats you badly; we *all* know," Racquel said, and the three of them laughed.

"You're terrible," Racquel said, and they all laughed.

Ashley stuck her head into the kitchen and shook her head at all of them. Marcella looked at her and felt guilty, because even though Ashley's and Nicholas's bedroom doors had been closed, she knew the children had heard almost everything she'd said that night. And the last thing she'd wanted was for them to hear her arguing with a man she'd been sleeping with. Or anyone for that matter. But Darryl had hurt her, and she hadn't been able to help it.

"Oh, shoot," Marcella said, covering her mouth. "I forgot to bring the cake."

"I thought you picked it up this morning from the bakery?" Corrine asked.

"I did, but it was so early that I put it in my refrigerator and then forgot about it," Marcella said, standing up from the table. "I'd better run home real quick and get it."

"You want me to ride with you, Mom?" Ashley asked.

"Only if your aunt and your granny don't need you to help with anything else."

"We've just about got everything done, so go on ahead, baby," Corrine said to Ashley.

"We'll be right back," Marcella said, heading out the back door with Ashley following behind her.

"I'd better go and check on Nicholas to make sure he's all right," Corrine said, placing the last appetizer on one of her silver relish trays.

"He's probably long gone to sleep by now," Racquel said, pulling four packages of hot dogs from the refrigerator.

Corrine walked through the dining room to the hallway that led into her bedroom and saw Nicholas tossing from side to side like he couldn't get comfortable.

"Baby, what's the matter?" Corrine asked him.

"My head hurts, Granny. It hurts bad," he said, holding his head on each side with both of his hands.

"Where is it hurting?" she asked, sitting down beside him on the bed.

"It hurts all over," he said, still curling his legs up to his chest.

"Racquel," Corrine yelled into the kitchen.

Racquel dropped the hot dogs on the counter and rushed into her mother's bedroom. "What is it, Mom?"

"There's something wrong with Nicholas, and I think we need to take him somewhere."

"Owwwww," Nicholas said, screaming and crying as loud as he could. "Owwwww."

"Honey, call an ambulance," Corrine told Racquel.

Racquel grabbed the phone and dialed 911 as fast as her fingers allowed.

"Nine-one-one. What's your emergency?" a man answered.

"We need an ambulance right away. My little nephew is complaining of a severe headache, and he's in a lot of pain."

"When did this start?"

"What?" Racquel said angrily. "It started earlier, but there's no time for all of that. We need an ambulance, and we need one right now because he's about to go into a fit."

"Is your address 3331 Hampton Avenue?"

"Yes, it is."

"An ambulance will be there shortly."

"Nicholas!" Corrine yelled as she watched him stop moving.

"Mom, what's wrong with him?" Racquel said, dropping the phone to the floor and leaning her head down to his chest to see if his heart was still beating.

"Oh Lord have mercy, I don't think he's breathing!" Corrine said loudly and grabbed him into her arms.

"Nicholas?" Racquel called to him. "Nicholas?"

But he didn't answer, and he didn't move.

"Lord have mercy on this child," Corrine said, rocking him back and forth.

Racquel picked the phone back up. "Hello?"

"Yes, I'm still here," the man said.

"He's not moving, and he's barely breathing."

"But he is breathing, though?"

"Yes, I think so," she said nervously.

"Okay, just stay on the line until the paramedics arrive. They should be there any minute."

Racquel watched her nephew in terror.

"Nicholas is going to be so happy when he sees that new bike his aunt Racquel and uncle Kevin bought him," Marcella said, turning down Baxter Avenue, which was about three miles from the apartment.

"They got him a bike?" Ashley asked in amazement.

"Yep, they sure did."

"That same dirt bike he's been looking at in that catalog?"

"Uh-huh," Marcella said, pulling up to a four-way stoplight.

"Are Uncle Leroy and Aunt Clara coming?"

"You know they wouldn't miss a family get-together for nothing in the world."

"Mom, is Aunt Racquel ever going to have a baby?" Ashley asked hesitantly, because even though she was thirteen, it was obvious that she didn't know if she should be asking such a grown-up question.

"Probably not, but why are you asking?" Marcella asked, wondering why Ashley had brought this subject up out of nowhere.

"Because she seems so sad all the time, and Nicholas and I hardly ever get to spend the night with her and Uncle Kevin anymore."

"They've been through some really rough times trying to have a baby, and now they're trying to spend as much time together as they possibly can. I know it might be hard for you to understand, but sometimes when a husband and wife have problems, they grow apart and need to spend time alone with each other."

"Is that why you and Darryl broke up?"

"What do you mean?"

"Because you hardly ever got to spend time alone together."

Marcella wasn't sure where Ashley was going with all these questions, but she had a feeling she wasn't going to like it. "We spent lots of time together when he wasn't working."

"I know, but I heard him say that it takes a special man to deal win a woman who has children by someone else. Or something like that."

"When did you hear him say that?" Marcella asked, knowing exactly when Ashley had heard him make those horrible comments.

"That night you and him got into that argument, and he walked out."

Marcella pulled into the parking lot, parked the car in front of their apartment building, turned the ignition off, and turned toward her daughter. She'd already figured that Ashley had heard some of the argument between her and Darryl, but she had no idea that Ashley had heard his comments about her and Nicholas.

"Darryl and I broke up for one reason, and one reason only. We weren't right for each other. So don't you think for one minute that you and Nicholas had anything to do with it. And if he had had a problem with either one of you, I would have stopped seeing him a long time ago. You and Nicholas mean everything in this world to me, and the three of us will always be together no matter what. I know since I started school, I haven't been able to spend as much time with you like I used to, but it's only because I'm doing everything I can to make a better life for all three of us."

"We know that, Mom," Ashley said, like Marcella had told her all that a hundred times before. "I missed you a lot when you first started, but now I understand why you have to work and go to school at the same time."

"We owe your granny, your aunt Racquel, and your uncle Kevin a lot for taking care of you guys the way they do, and I promise when I graduate a year and a half from now, we'll spend a lot of time together, and we'll do all the things normal families get to do."

"It would be even more normal if Dad could be with us, too," Ashley said, looking straight ahead.

Marcella felt her stomach turn, because lately she'd been under the impression that it didn't matter to Ashley one way or the other if her father came around or not, but apparently that wasn't so. "I know, sweetheart, but sometimes things don't work out like that for every family. And that's why I struggle every day trying to be a mother and a father for both you and your brother. Someday when you and Nicholas are older, you'll understand better why people can't be together when they're not right for each other. Now do you have any other important questions before we get out of the car?" she asked, smiling at Ashley.

"Nope. That was all," Ashley said in a mature tone of voice.

When they walked into the apartment, Ashley headed straight for the bathroom, and Marcella made her way into the kitchen. She set her purse down on the table, pulled the cake out of the refrigerator, and set it on the counter. Then the phone rang.

"Hello?" Marcella answered.

"Marcella," Racquel said in a shaky voice.

"What's wrong?" Marcella asked worriedly.

Racquel tried to speak but couldn't. And after a few more seconds, she broke down in tears.

"Racquel, what's wrong?" Marcella asked swiftly.

"Baby?" Corrine said to Marcella after taking the phone from Racquel.

"Mom, what's wrong with Racquel?" Marcella asked anxiously.

"Honey, it's Nicholas."

"What about him? Is he all right?" Marcella asked nervously.

"Kevin is on his way over, so he can bring you to the hospital."

"Why, Mom? What's wrong with my baby?" Marcella said, clamp-ing the phone in her hand as tight as she could.

"He had an aneurysm."

"I'm on my way, okay?" Marcella said, preparing to hang up the phone.

"No, baby. You wait for Kevin because you're too upset to be driving anywhere."

"But he needs me, Mom. What are the doctors saying? Are they going to do surgery? What?"

As Ashley walked out of the bathroom, she heard a knock at the door and looked at her mother to see if she wanted her to answer it or not.

"Mom, that must be Kevin at the door, so I'll see you in a few minutes," Marcella said and hung up the phone. She walked swiftly through the living room and opened the front door. Ashley followed behind her, trying to figure out what was going on.

"I'm ready, Kevin," Marcella said, ready to walk out of the apart-ment without her purse, keys, Ashley, or anything except herself.

"Marcella, wait," Kevin said, stepping into the apartment.

"There's no time for that. Mom said Nicholas had an aneurysm, and we have to get over there right now."

"Marcella, I promise you I'm going to take you to the hospital, but I need to tell you something first."

"What?" she said impatiently.

Kevin hesitated and took a deep breath.

"What?" she said frowning at him.

"Nick passed away a little while ago."

Marcella felt a knife slice through her heart. "What do you mean he passed away a little while ago?" she asked in disbelief.

"He's gone, Marcella." Kevin stared at her with tears rolling down his face. "Little Nick is gone."

Chapter 23

Marcella gazed out the window of the black limousine as it cruised down Orchard Avenue behind the hearse. They'd just left the funeral and were on their way to the cemetery for the burial services. Marcella's eyes were bloodshot red from all the crying that she'd been doing over the last five days, and the pounding in her head was unbearable. She was numb and heartbroken, but more than anything, she felt guilty, because she was convinced that Nicholas would still be alive if she hadn't spent so much time away from him. He'd had a couple of headaches, but she hadn't paid much attention to them until the day of his birthday party. And not once had she even considered that he might have something as serious as an aneurysm. Especially since he was just turning eleven years old and had never been sick with anything except maybe the flu or a cold.

And it had all happened so fast. One minute she was picking up his cake, and the next minute Kevin was at her door telling her he was dead. She hadn't even gotten a chance to say goodbye or to tell him how much she loved him, and she was never going to forgive herself for that. Her mother and sister had been with him right up until the moment he took his last breath, but she was his mother, and it was her responsibility to be there for him whenever he needed her. If it hadn't been for her stupid goals and selfish determination to succeed, she never would have spent all that time taking classes at the university and then working all those hours at the accounting firm in the evening. She tried to be with him and Ashley as much as she could during the summer, but that hadn't been enough, and now she knew it. And what right did she have anyway going back to school at twenty-eight? She had two small children who depended on her, and it was her duty to take care of them until they became adults. She'd made her bed, and it was her responsibility to lie in it. When Sharon had suggested that she go back to school to get her degree, she'd thought it was a wonderful idea, but now she could clearly see how big a mistake it had really been.

Marcella looked across the limo and saw Ashley buried deep inside her father's arms. She cursed the ground that Tyrone walked on, but she was glad he'd been there to comfort Ashley over the last few days when she couldn't. Especially since he'd practically bawled his eyes out when they'd called him to the hospital. And while she couldn't believe it, it was because of him that Nicholas had a decent life-insurance policy. It wasn't like he had gone out and purchased one on his own, but it was his company's policy to cover all employee dependents, and it had made a world of difference as far as the funeral costs. As a matter of fact, if it hadn't been for that policy, she and her family would have had to scrounge up the money to cover whatever the welfare department wouldn't.

When they arrived at the cemetery, they parked and then walked over to the tent that hovered over the burial site. Marcella, Corrine, Ashley, Tyrone, and his mother sat down in the five chairs positioned directly in front of the body, and Racquel and Kevin stood behind them. Marcella saw her father and his wife standing to the side and tried to force a smile on her face. Everyone else gathered around them accordingly.

When the pastor had finished with the prayer and announced that food was being served back at the church for the family, the funeral director removed roses from the bed of flowers covering the casket and passed one to each of the immediate family members. After that, everyone except Marcella stood up. She knew it was time to go, but she couldn't stop staring at the monstrous-looking hole that the yard men had dug for Nicholas. And the thought of them lowering him down into it made her skin crawl. She just couldn't bear the idea of leaving him out there all by himself, and she wanted to take him back home where he belonged.

After Corrine shook hands with a few people, she gently pulled Marcella up from the chair and started walking her in the direction of the limo. But as soon as she did, Marcella pulled away from her.

"What am I going to do without you, Nicholas?" Marcella said, leaning over the casket, crying. "What am I going to do?"

"I know, baby," Corrine said, trying to ease her away from the tent. "You don't have to worry about him because he's resting now."

"Oh, God, Mom, why?" she said, laying her head against her mother's chest with her hands balled up in front of her face.

Her father and Kevin noticed Corrine struggling with Marcella and rushed over to help her. Both of the men held Marcella on each side and escorted her over to the limo. When everyone was seated and the doors had been shut, the driver headed back to the church.

A couple of hours had passed since they'd arrived back at Corrine's house from the church. She, Ashley, Racquel, and Kevin were now sitting in the den watching a moment-of-truth movie on Lifetime. Marcella hadn't felt too good on the way home and was now lying down in the bedroom.

"Ashley, you can go lie down, too, if you want," Corrine said.

"I'm fine, Granny," she said, sadly leaning back in the cocoa-brown recliner.

Corrine's heart went out to her granddaughter because she could tell that Ashley was in a lot of pain. But she also knew that there wasn't a whole lot she could do, and that only time could improve the way she was feeling.

"Granny, do we have to go back home tonight?" Ashley asked.

"Not if you don't want to. You and your mom can stay here as long as you need to," Corrine said, wondering why she didn't want to go back to the apartment. She figured it was probably because they'd spent every night with her since the day Nicholas passed away, and Ashley was starting to get used to it.

"If we are, then we need to go get some more clothes," Ashley said.

"You're not going to school tomorrow, are you?" Corrine asked.

"I might," Ashley said, looking at her grandmother.

"Maybe we can go get them when your mom wakes up," Racquel said, looking over at Ashley.

Ashley nodded in agreement and turned her head back toward the television. Then the doorbell rang.

"I wonder who that is?" Corrine said, preparing to stand up from the love seat.

"I'll get it, Mom," Racquel said, rising from the sofa.

"It's probably your dad," Kevin said, glancing at Racquel.

Corrine looked at Racquel, but didn't say anything.

Racquel strutted through the living room, pulled the front door open, and smiled when she saw her dad standing on the steps.

"Hey, Daddy," Racquel said, hugging him.

"Hi, pumpkin," he said, hugging her the way distant relatives do when they haven't seen each other in a long time.

"So how come you and Theresa didn't come back to the church for dinner?" she asked, referring to her stepmother as she closed the door.

"We were kind of exhausted from the flight this morning, so we went back to the hotel to get some rest."

"Why didn't she come with you over here?"

"She doesn't feel comfortable around your mother, so she decided not to. You know how that is."

"Oh, she could have come," Racquel said, knowing good and well she was glad the witch hadn't. Because the last thing she wanted to see was her hanging all over him like some teenager. And that was the same reason she hadn't offered for them to stay with her and Kevin when she'd found out they were flying in for the funeral.

"I'm really glad you came, Daddy," Racquel said and then hugged him again.

"I know, pumpkin, and I'm sorry I wasn't here for you when you lost the baby a few months ago," Mitchell said, kissing her on the forehead.

"Oh, I understand," Racquel said, trying to pretend that his not coming hadn't bothered her, when in reality, it had practically killed her. But she wasn't about to give him the satisfaction of knowing it.

"Where's everybody at?" Mitchell asked.

"Marcella is lying down in Mom's bedroom, and everyone else is in the den," Racquel said, heading down the hallway. Mitchell followed behind her.

"How's it going, son-in-law?" Mitchell said, extending his hand to Kevin.

"Fine, Mr. Jones. How are you?" Kevin said, standing to his feet, shaking his father-in-law's hand.

"And how's my favorite granddaughter?" Mitchell said, grinning at Ashley, obviously wanting to hug her.

But Ashley remained seated because she'd only seen this man two other times in her life, and she really didn't know him all that well. "Hi," she said, smiling the way people do when they first make an acquaintance.

"Corrine," he said acknowledging his ex-wife after he saw that Ashley wasn't interested in hugging him.

"Mitchell," Corrine acknowledged in a cool tone and then switched her eyes back to the tampon commercial on the television screen.

Racquel noticed it and spoke up. "Sit down, Daddy."

"Well, maybe just for a little while," he said and then hesitated when he realized that the only seat available was the one next to Corrine on the love seat.

"You can sit down," Corrine said surprisingly.

Mitchell grinned a funny grin and sat next to her.

"So how long are you here for?" Kevin asked.

"Until tomorrow morning," Mitchell answered.

"How come you're leaving so soon?" Kevin asked. "I thought we would at least get to take you out to dinner or something."

"We've got some things to take care of at home, so we have to get back."

Racquel looked at her father and thought, Yeah, right. Because she knew the real reason they were leaving was because his wife hadn't wanted to come in the first place.

"You mean to tell me, you only flew in here for one day, knowing full well that your daughter just lost her child?" Corrine asked him.

Racquel didn't like the look on her mother's face, and she prayed that she wasn't about to go off on him. They'd gotten into it during every other one of his visits, but she'd thought for sure that things would be different this time, given the circumstances.

Mitchell looked at Corrine and pretended like he hadn't heard her, obviously not knowing what to say.

"I'm telling you the truth, some things just never change," Corrine said, standing up and walking out of the den.

Ashley watched her grandmother leave the room, glanced at her long, lost grandfather, and then looked over at her aunt Racquel, waiting for her to say something.

"She's just under a lot of stress right now, Daddy," Racquel said, trying to butter her mother's comment. "That's all."

"Maybe I should go," he said.

"But you just got here," Racquel said, partly wanting him to stay and partly wanting him to go before her mother blew up completely.

"I know, but I really should be getting back to the hotel."

Her mother was right, Racquel thought. Some things *didn't* ever change. Or some people for that matter. Here her father had messed around with one woman after another the entire time she and Marcella were growing up, and now that they were older, he still didn't see a reason to spend any quality time with them. It just didn't seem to be the most important thing on his agenda, and it was starting to piss Racquel off.

"Well, at least look in on Marcella before you leave," Racquel said as nicely as her emotions allowed her to.

"Oh, definitely," he said, standing up and walking toward Corrine's bedroom. He opened the door.

"Baby girl?" he called out to Marcella, checking to see if she was asleep.

"Hi, Daddy," Marcella said, raising up in the bed. "I thought I heard your voice in there. Come on in and turn on the light."

Mitchell flipped the light switch on and shut the door halfway. "How's my baby girl doing?" he asked, leaning down to hug his youngest daughter, and then sat down beside her.

"It hurts so bad, Daddy. And I miss him so much."

"I know you do, but you'll get through it."

"I don't know if I can or not, and I wish I never had to leave this house ever again. I know it sounds strange, but every time I think about him taking his last breath in this room, I feel so close to him when I'm in here."

"It might not seem like it right now, but things will get better as time goes on. You'll see," he said, rubbing her back. "And you've got a beautiful little daughter out there who needs you more than anything."

"I know, Daddy," she said sadly.

"And while I'm not a churchgoing man, the best advice I can give to you is to pray for strength."

"I have been, but the pain isn't getting any better."

"But it will in time," he said, smiling at her.

"Well, I'm going to be leaving out first thing in the morning, so I'd better get back to the hotel."

"I thought you were going to stay until the weekend?" she said, obviously disappointed.

"I wish I could, but I've got some things I need to take care of at home," he said, barely able to look her straight in her eyes.

"Well, I guess if you have to go, you have to go."

"I'll try to get back here to see you around Christmas, if I can," he said, hugging her again and then kissing her on her cheek.

"Thanks for coming, Daddy," she said, feeling like she was talking to some stranger.

"You take care of yourself, and I'll call you this weekend." He eased out the door.

"Bye, Daddy," she said, smiling with tears in her eyes because she knew it was going to be a very long time before she saw him again.

Mitchell stepped back into the den, shook Kevin's hand, and hugged Ashley whether she wanted him to or not. Racquel walked him to the front door and hugged him. She watched as he drove the black rental car out of the driveway.

Right after their father left, Racquel finally convinced Marcella to take a ride with her so she could get some fresh air. Marcella still wasn't happy about leaving the house, but since Ashley needed a change of clothing for the next day, she reluctantly agreed to it. She couldn't care less if they went to pick up a change of clothing or not, because she wasn't going anywhere anyway. But Ashley was acting like she was going to have a fit if they didn't. Kevin was still at Corrine's watching some special on ESPN.

"I never had a full understanding of how you felt when you lost Karlia back in May, but if it's anything like the way I feel now, I don't know how you survived it," Marcella said, leaning her head back against the headrest.

"It was one of the hardest things I ever had to go through, and I wouldn't wish it on even the most terrible person," Racquel said, pressing on the accelerator, leaving a four-way stop sign.

"My heart aches so bad."

"And it will for a long time, but I promise you, it will get better."

"It just doesn't seem fair. First it was Sharon, then Karlia, and now Nicholas. I mean, if anything else happens to me, I'll probably go insane."

"Believe me, I know exactly how you feel," Racquel said, slowing down at the stoplight. "And I want you to know that I'm here for you day or night, and that I'll always be here for you and Ashley, no matter what," she said, squeezing Marcella's left hand with her right one.

Tears streamed down Marcella's face, and Racquel did everything she could to hold hers back. Because for the first time in her life, she wasn't so concerned about her own problems, and she knew she had to be strong for her sister. The sister that meant everything to her.

"Mom?" Ashley said when she thought her mother had settled down. "Can we stop at Henry's to get a hamburger?"

"I know you're not still hungry after eating all that food at the church," Marcella said, turning to look at Ashley.

"I felt sick, and I didn't eat that much."

"I guess we can stop on the way back to Mom's if your aunt Racquel doesn't mind."

"You know I don't mind," Racquel said. "We can stop wherever she wants to. So how long are you planning to be off work?"

"I don't know. To tell you the truth, that's the last thing on my mind," Marcella said, gazing out the window.

"Well, I'm sure they'll understand, and since you're only working part-time because of school, they can probably make it without you for a while."

"Who knows?" Marcella said like she had no interest in the conversation.

"I know you probably don't feel like it, so if you want, I can call your professors to find out what your assignments are. At least that way you won't get so far behind."

"I have a course syllabus for every class, so all I have to do is follow that. But I'm not going to worry about school anyway until sometime next week, because I'm just not in the mood for it right now," Marcella said and then leaned her head back on the headrest and closed her eyes.

Racquel knew it was too soon for Marcella to think about anything or anybody except Nicholas, but at the same time she was trying to keep the conversation on a more positive level. Because if she didn't, not only was Marcella going to break out in tears again, but she was going to do the same thing herself. But since she could tell Marcella wasn't interested, she figured it was better to drop the school and work subject altogether.

"Ashley, have you decided whether you're going to school tomorrow?" Racquel asked.

"I still don't know if I want to or not," Ashley said.

"Tomorrow is already Friday, so you might as well wait until Monday," Marcella commented.

Ashley didn't say anything and continued looking out the window.

They drove the rest of the way in silence, and when Racquel turned into the apartment complex, she parked. Then they all stepped out of the car and walked inside the building. But as they approached Marcella's apartment, they noticed that the door was cracked partially open.

"Did you forget to close the door?" Racquel asked.

"No, I don't think so," Marcella said as they walked closer to it.

"Mom, what if somebody's in there?" Ashley said, staying close behind her mother.

They moved closer to the door and stood there for a minute trying to see if they could hear any noise or movement going on inside. And then finally when Marcella saw that all the lights were on, she pushed the door open slowly. But when they walked in, all three of their mouths fell wide open. Everything was gone. Sharon's navy-blue leather furniture. Sharon's brass and glass coffee tables. Sharon's twenty-five-inch color television. Sharon's glass dinette set. Sharon's Pentium computer. And from the way it looked, the list was only going to continue, once they made their way through the rest of the apartment.

Marcella stood in a complete daze. Racquel and Ashley did the same.

Chapter 24

"I know I asked you this last night, but do you have any idea who could have robbed you like this?" Corrine asked. She'd just dropped Ashley off at school, and now she and Marcella were sitting at the kitchen table having coffee.

"No, I don't have the slightest idea," Marcella said, shaking powdered creamer into her cup. "But with all the thugs and delinquent boys that live in the complex, it could have been anybody. And that's the very reason why when we moved my old furniture out and Sharon's in, we did it late at night. But apparently that didn't make any difference."

"I think it would be better if you and Ashley stay here for a while. At least until you're able to get back on your feet."

"I really hate to burden you like this."

"Honey, you and Ashley are not bothering me one bit by staying here, and as long as I have a place to stay, so do the both of you."

"I can't believe the only thing they left were our bedroom sets, and that was probably only because they didn't want to bother with taking the beds apart. And to think that they took my living-room furniture and my dinette set. I mean, it had to have taken a lot of time to do that, because it's not like you could just move all of that out of the apartment and out of the building in a few minutes."

"Yeah, but thieves have been known to rob people when they

know a funeral is going on because they know more than likely no one will be home."

"It's just not right, though. Sharon worked hard to buy those things, and now they're gone. And it just doesn't make sense."

"I know, but you know how roguish some of these fools can be here in Covington Park. Some of them would steal the clothes off a dead man if they thought it would benefit them in some way."

Marcella glanced at her mother with a hollow look on her face. She knew her mother's reference to a dead person was just a figure of speech, but it still reminded her of just how lost she felt and how depressed she was over losing Nicholas.

As soon as Corrine realized what she'd just said, it was obvious that she regretted it. But she didn't say anything.

"Mom, why did I have to lose my baby like this? I've always tried to be a decent person, and I've always tried to be a good mother. So, why did God just take Nicholas the way He did? I keep trying to understand it, but I can't."

"Honey, God has His reasons for doing the things He does, and even though we might not understand them, He doesn't make mistakes. And He never burdens you with any more than you can bear."

"I've been struggling all these years trying to take care of two children all by myself, living in a low-income housing complex, and trying to go to school. And then on top of all that, I lost the best friend I ever had, watched my sister almost have a nervous breakdown, lost my little Nicholas, and now practically everything I owned is gone, too."

"Things will get better. You may not think so right now, but they will."

"But things aren't getting better, they're getting worse!" Marcella yelled. "So why does everyone keep telling me that?"

Corrine stared at her daughter, but didn't speak.

"I'm sorry, Mom," Marcella said, pushing her chair back from the table with tears streaming down her face. She walked out of the kitchen without looking back.

Corrine watched her until she was out of sight and wondered what was going to happen next.

*   *   *

At twelve o'clock Marcella woke up, left her childhood sleeping quarters, and strutted into the den hoping to find her mother. But when she arrived, Corrine wasn't there. She continued through the house, calling out her mother's name, but there was no answer. Finally, she walked into the kitchen and saw a note lying on the counter next to the microwave oven. It was from her mother saying she'd stepped out to the grocery store, needed to run a few errands, and would pick Ashley up from school on the way home.

Now Marcella felt even worse about the way she'd yelled at her mother. She hadn't meant to, but it was just that she was fed up with hearing about how everything was going to be all right. How everything happens for a reason. And how things get better with time. They were all nice words of encouragement, but at the same time they weren't making her feel any better. As a matter of fact, she was starting to see exactly why people committed suicide. Before last Saturday when Nicholas had passed away, she'd thought it was the sickest thing a person could do to themselves, but now the whole idea of it didn't sound so bad. Especially now when she really didn't have anything to live for. And she could kick herself a thousand times over for not understanding what Racquel was going through when she'd lost Karlia. She'd known that losing a child had to be painful, but never in her wildest imagination had she thought it would hurt this severely.

She paced back and forth through the house, sat down for a minute in the den, stood up again, and paced the floor some more. She was a nervous wreck, and she wanted this day to end. She wanted all this suffering to go away. Some of the women at the church had promised her that things would start to look up after the funeral, but now that it was one day past, she felt worse. And she was starting to realize that it wasn't ever going to get better.

And she couldn't understand at all why Ashley had gallivanted off to school the first day after her brother's funeral, like nothing had happened. Like it was just another normal event that had taken place and wasn't a big deal. Didn't she know that Nicholas was her brother? Didn't she know how much he loved his big sister? And even worse, didn't she love him back?

Marcella decided that she needed to lie down again and headed into the bedroom. But as soon as she stretched out across the bed, the doorbell rang.

Who could that be, she thought and frowned. She hoped it wasn't someone from the church dropping by for a friendly visit because she wasn't in the mood for it. She went into the living room and peeped out the window. It was Tyrone.

She opened the door wide enough to speak through it. "Ashley decided to go to school today, so she won't be home for at least another three hours or so," she said, wishing he'd go away.

"Well, is it okay if I come in and talk to you for a few minutes?"

About what? He'd never wanted to talk to her about anything before. And whenever they did try to communicate with each other, they always ended up arguing. And she wasn't about to go there with him today. "This really isn't a good time, and I was just about to lie down. Maybe I'll feel better later, and you can call me then."

"I know things haven't been the greatest between us, but all I'm asking is that you let me come in for a few minutes. That's all," he said sincerely. Or at least it sounded sincere to Marcella.

"I'm really having a hard time dealing with everything that has happened, and I'm just not in the mood for any heated debates," she said, stroking her hair from front to back. "I just can't handle anything like that right now."

"I'm having just as hard a time dealing with this as you are, and that's why I want . . . no, that's why I need to talk to you," he asked with both his hands stuck inside the pockets of his black leather jacket. It was barely the second week in October, but it was already windy and starting to get a little nippy outside.

Marcella wasn't sure what to do now. His words seemed genuine, and he'd never been this cordial with her for as long as she could remember, but she just didn't know if it was a good idea to let him in or not. Plus she didn't feel right inviting him into her mother's house knowing how horribly he'd disrespected her two years ago. But on the other hand, she needed to be with someone, or there was a chance she was going to lose her sanity. And as much as she hated to admit it, she really didn't mind if that someone was Tyrone. "Come on in," she said, holding the door open so he could pass through it. Then she closed it and they walked into the den.

"So what did you want to talk to me about?" she asked, sitting down in the recliner.

He sat on the edge of the love seat. "To tell you the truth, I really don't know where to begin. I guess the first thing I want to say is that I'm sorry."

"Sorry for what?" Marcella asked, staring at him. He'd never apologized for anything before, and she couldn't wait to hear this.

"For treating you the way I have for the past few years, and for not being there for Ashley and Nick the way I should have been."

Marcella couldn't believe what she was hearing. Tyrone James was actually sitting there saying the words "I'm sorry." Now that was a new one. And she couldn't help but wonder what the catch was. There had to be something. She was sure of it. "So why are you telling me this now?" she asked curiously.

"Because I woke up this morning feeling like I owed you an apology, and I've been thinking about our situation a lot lately. Maybe it's because of what happened to Nick," he said sadly.

Oh, that's exactly what the reason was. And the only reason he'd come over to talk to her was because he was feeling guilty. The kind of guilt that adult children feel when their elderly parents die and they haven't done one single solitary thing to help take care of them. But now that he'd made this wonderful discovery, she wondered what he wanted from her. Surely not her sympathy. She was becoming slightly miffed at the whole idea of him apologizing because really, it was too late for any of that. And since she was starting to become a little irritated, it was probably better if she didn't make any comments. So she didn't.

"Don't you have anything to say?" he asked, gesturing with his hands, almost begging for her input.

"What is it *for* me to say? I mean, I never did anything to cause you to treat me the way you did, and I never kept Ashley and Nicholas away from you. You had every opportunity to be with them whenever you wanted, but you didn't. And on top of that, you wouldn't even pay your child support the way you were supposed to or watch them in the evenings while I worked."

"I know. I know. I know, but I promise you, things are going to be different now. You can believe that."

Promises, promises, promises. He'd made a lot of promises to her when they were in high school, too, but he hadn't made good on any of them. So why on earth should she believe any of what he was saying now? "Well, for Ashley's sake, I hope you do start acting like her father, because she needs both of us."

"I'm telling you, Marcella, things are going to be different. I swear they are."

She gazed at him doubtfully.

And he obviously picked up on it. "I'm serious. Things are going to be different. And to tell you the truth, the situation never would have gotten like this in the first place if it hadn't been for me messing up my knee the way I did."

Why did the father always have an excuse when it came to the reason why he didn't spend time with his children? Mothers were never allowed any privileges like that. And if they did neglect their children to that extent, they were labeled unfit. And it wouldn't be long before Children and Family Services came knocking at their door snatching the children away so they could place them in some foster home. No, he could believe what he wanted, but the truth of the matter was, his knee injury had little, if anything, to do with him being irresponsible. But she still wanted to see what his reasoning behind all of this was. "What did your knee injury have to do with anything?"

"You know how bad that messed me up. My whole life depended on football, and when I lost my scholarship, I couldn't afford to go to college."

"But you still got a high-paying job through that apprenticeship program. So it's not like you haven't been making good money. Some people who have college degrees don't even make the kind of money you make."

"But playing college ball was my dream, and you know I had a good chance of going to the Pros, too."

"So what are you saying? Because you didn't get to live out your dream, you thought it was okay to take your frustrations out on everybody else?"

"No, that's not what I'm saying at all, but I did build up a lot of anger because of what happened, and I've wanted to blame everyone except myself. I've been talking to my mother about it a lot lately, and she thinks I should talk to someone professionally."

"Well, all I can say is that I hope you start trying to build a better relationship with Ashley as soon as possible because she seemed so distant this morning, and she's acting as if none of this has really affected her, but I know it has."

"I want to start building a better relationship with you, too," he said seriously.

She wasn't sure where he was going with that comment, but she hoped he wasn't thinking that there was some small chance for them to get back together, because there wasn't. "If you had paid your child support and spent time with Ashley and Nicholas like you should have, we never would have had any problems with each other. And this thing with you trippin' out whenever I date some-one has got to stop, too. I don't have a problem with your and Priscilla's relationship, and I think it's only fair that you give me the same respect with mine."

"I know, but it just makes me crazy when I see that you have feel-ings for someone else. I know I don't have a right to get angry, but I do."

"But why? You and I broke up for good over eleven years ago."

"I know, but it still bothers me. I guess I'm just jealous," he ad-mitted.

"Well, my main concern is not about me dating anyone, it's about Ashley's welfare," she said, changing the subject.

"Maybe we should spend time with Ashley together. Maybe we should try to be more like a family."

After all those times he'd called her out of her name? After all those times he'd missed paying his child support? After all those times he'd tried to cause problems with her and Darryl and any other guy she'd ever dated? He couldn't have been serious. She could never fall in love with him again, and the only feelings she had for him were the kind a woman has for a man when she has children by him. And that was it. "I really wish things could have worked out between us years ago, but now too much has been said and too many incidents have taken place."

"So, you don't think there could ever be a chance with us get-ting back together?" he said regretfully.

"No, I don't," she said and actually felt sorry about it because he seemed so humble. She wanted to know what had happened with Priscilla, but since it wasn't her business, she shied away from asking him about her.

He looked at her and forced a partial smile, obviously trying to pretend that he was okay with her response.

"I don't know when I'm going back to school or work, but I do know that Ashley and I will be staying here with Mom for a while, so this is where you'll have to come see her or pick her up," she said, trying to steer clear of the getting-back-together subject.

"Why are you going to stay here?"

"Somebody came into the apartment yesterday and took almost everything we had."

"No way," he said in a surprised manner.

"Yeah. They did."

"Did you report it to the police?"

"Yeah, but you know they'll never find out who did it."

"Well, if you need anything, let me know."

With Tyrone acting this nice, the world was definitely coming to an end. Marcella just knew it. "If you really pay your child support and spend more quality time with Ashley like you said earlier, we'll be just fine."

"I'll be by to get her this evening," he said, standing up.

"Okay," she said, rising from the recliner. They walked into the living room.

"When are you going back to work?" he asked, opening the front door.

"I don't know. One minute I'm having a normal conversation with someone the way we are right now, and the next minute I'm crying my eyes out, or feeling like I want to die," she said, leaning against the entryway wall. "I'm just not ready yet."

"I can understand that. Well, I guess I should go. Tell Ashley to call me, alright?" he said, gazing at her.

Marcella gazed back at him, examining his face. She hadn't paid much attention to his physical characteristics in years, but today she couldn't help but notice his gorgeous hazel-brown eyes. The same eyes that her sweet little Nicholas had been blessed with. And while she'd always tried to convince herself that Nicholas hadn't resembled his father in the least, now she could no longer deny the fact that he was his father's son. He was the spitting image of him. And she wished she could stand there admiring Tyrone's face for the rest of all eternity. She missed Nicholas so much, and the only connection she had with him was Tyrone. She felt weak and she could feel the pressure building inside her eyes as she tried to resist shedding any more tears. She'd wept so much over the last few days that her eyes felt permanently swollen. She felt so alone, and she wanted to beg Tyrone to stay with her until her mother came back home. She knew it wasn't the logical thing to do, but she needed someone to hold her. Someone to make her feel safe. "Tyrone," she said, swallowing hard while tears rolled down her cheeks. "What am I going to do without my baby?"

Tyrone closed the door and pulled her into his arms.

Chapter 25

Racquel sprayed Windex across the dining-room table, and then cleaned it with the front section of yesterday's newspaper. It seemed strange using something other than a paper towel or a rag of some kind, but the newspaper kept the glass spotless and left no smearing. When she finished with that, she pulled out black linen place mats, matching linen napkins, two off-white plates and placed them at each end of the table. Then she wrapped the silverware inside the napkins, inserted black candles inside each of the two brass candleholders, and placed everything on the table the way she wanted it for dinner. She and Kevin hadn't shared a romantic dinner like this one all year. And she couldn't wait to see his face when she surprised him with his favorite dish, broccoli-and-cheese lasagna.

Their marriage was still on shaky ground, but she was hoping that after tonight, things would start looking up. She'd neglected him in every way, and it was time to do something about it. She'd thought for sure that things would return back to normal when she'd finally given up on trying to have a baby, but it hadn't. And when her nephew passed away, their love for each other had seemed like it was becoming stronger. But now that the funeral was over, Kevin was distancing himself from her again, and it was obvious that he'd only been affectionate with her, trying to make it easier for both of them to deal with Nicholas's death.

She left the dining room, walked back into the kitchen, washed the glass-cleaner residue from her hands, lifted the covered lasagna-filled baking dish from the counter, and set it inside the preheated oven. Then she removed the lettuce, cucumbers, and tomatoes from the refrigerator, sliced them, mixed everything together, and poured a mixture of oil and vinegar over the entire salad.

She glanced at her watch and saw that she still had plenty of time to shower and get dressed before Kevin got home from work. She wasn't sure what she was going to wear, but she wanted it to be something sexy. Something that would make him stand up and take notice. Something that would complement the elegant after-five hair-style she'd received at the hair salon earlier that morning. Something that would make him lose all control the minute he saw her. Especially since they rarely made love anymore, and when they did, Kevin no longer bothered with any foreplay and simply went straight for the kill. And it was clear that all he was interested in was satisfying himself. He'd never been like that before, but Racquel knew that his actions had a lot to do with the fact that making love had become nothing more than a dreadful routine. He'd told her that months and months before, but she hadn't listened, and now she was paying for it.

After Racquel showered, smoothed lotion on her body, and rolled deodorant under her arms, she went into the kitchen and removed the lasagna from the oven. It had taken an hour to bake, but now she needed to let it cool for at least a half hour. When she returned back to the bedroom, she slipped on a black lacy bra, matching bikini panties, and ebony-black pantyhose. Then she pulled a black sleeveless crêpe-wool dress from the closet, stepped into it, and zipped it. She replaced the makeup that she'd washed off before showering, stepped in front of the mirror attached to the dresser, and smoothed the sides of her hair with both hands. Kevin was going to be there any minute, so she slipped on a pair of plush black slippers and went into the kitchen so she could warm the garlic bread. When the bread was ready, she went into the dining room, pulled out two wineglasses from the server, and lit the candles. Then she dimmed the dining-room lights and flipped on the CD player so she could listen to some jazz while she waited.

She sat patiently for ten minutes and wondered if maybe she should call to check on Marcella. She hadn't sounded like she was doing too well when Racquel had spoken with her this morning, and she was hoping that things might have gotten better for her as the day went on. Their mother was starting to become worried, but it had only been a week since the funeral, and Racquel knew better than anyone that it took time to overcome the loss of a child. And in all honesty, one never overcame it, but simply learned to live with it.

When Racquel heard Kevin enter the house, she went to meet him in the kitchen.

"What's all this for?" he asked, dropping his black leather brief-case down on the kitchen table.

"It's for you," she said, kissing him.

"I know that's not my lasagna over there?" he said, looking in the direction of the stove.

"As a matter of fact, it is," she said.

"What's the occasion? And why are you all dressed up?"

"There's no occasion really. I just thought it would be nice to surprise you with dinner."

"Well, is it ready? Because I'm starved," he said, slipping off his suit jacket, laying it on the back of the chair. Then he loosened his tie and opened the top button of his shirt.

"It's ready, but I want us to have a drink first so we can talk."

"Baby, I don't mean to mess up what you have going here, but if it's okay with you, I'd rather we talk while we're eating. I haven't had anything to eat since noon," he said, grabbing an everyday plate from the dish rack.

No. No. No. This wasn't at all how she'd planned for the evening to turn out. He was supposed to walk through that door, grab her into his arms, kiss her erotically, and then sit down with her for a glass of wine. And couldn't he see that she'd already set plates on the table from their good china set? And she could just kill him for loosening his tie and undoing the button on his shirt like they were sitting down to eat pizza. What did he think she'd gotten all dressed up for anyway? She wanted to yell at him, but since she didn't want to argue, she decided against it. "I already have plates on the table," she said, moving the bowl of salad to the dining-room table.

"Oh," he said, replacing the plate back in the rack.

When they sat down in the winter-white high-back chairs, Kevin forked a hefty amount of salad onto his plate, and Racquel poured herself a much-needed glass of dinner wine.

"So how was work?" she asked.

"Okay," he said, chewing a mouthful of lettuce, and didn't elaborate any further.

"Kevin, what's wrong with us?" she asked, setting the empty wineglass down on the table.

"What do you mean?" he asked, looking at her.

"I mean, what's wrong with our marriage?"

"It's not so much what's wrong with our marriage, but more like what happened to it than anything else," he said, sipping some wine.

"But we've gotten past all those problems."

"But it still caused a lot of distance between us."

"Well, what do you think will make it better? I mean, tell me what you want me to do."

"To be totally honest with you, I really don't know what you can do. I used to think that all our problems had to do with the infertility situation, but now . . . now I don't even know if I'm in love with you anymore," he said, taking another sip of wine.

She swallowed hard and stared at him. She'd heard him say those same exact words in her dream, but this time she was wide awake, and the pain was much more real than it had been then. "So what are you saying?" she asked hesitantly.

"Hey, why don't we finish eating first, and then we can talk after that," he said, scooting the high-back chair away from the table.

She wanted to object, but she was hurting so bad that she decided to go along with his idea of delaying the conversation.

When Kevin chewed the last forkful of lasagna, he leaned back in his chair. Racquel sat in her chair waiting for him to speak.

"That was good," he said, referring to the meal.

She didn't acknowledge his appreciation and continued to wait for him to resume their discussion.

"Look," he said, pausing. "It's not that I don't love you, but it's just that we don't have that same passion between us like we used to. And I know it's because of all the problems we've had."

"Well, I don't know what to do to make things better. I mean, I took a leave of absence from teaching with the hope that I could spend more time trying to satisfy you. But that doesn't seem to be making any difference at all."

"I know you did, but something still isn't right. And the last thing I want to do is end our marriage without trying to make it work, but it seems like the more we try, the worse things get."

"Is there someone else?" she asked and regretted it as soon as she closed her mouth. Because if there was, his confession was going to kill her.

"No. There's not. You know I'm not like that, Racquel. Or at least you ought to know by now."

"Kevin, I don't know what to think with you sitting here saying that you're not in love with me."

He sighed intensely. "Maybe that wasn't the right choice of words."

"Well, that's what you said."

"And I also said that I do still love you, but it's just that the passion isn't there."

"Well, what do you suggest we do?" she asked disgustedly.

"Maybe what we need is some time apart," he said, clasping his hands together on the table.

"You're not serious?" she said, frowning.

"It's not what I want, but maybe a separation would allow us to rethink our priorities."

"*My* priorities are straight," she said, elevating the sound of her voice.

"But they weren't always," he said matter-of-factly. "I suggested a long time ago that we give up on trying to have a baby because I knew how much tension it was causing between us. And although you said you would consider adopting a child, you haven't said much else about it."

Is that what this was all about? Adopting a baby. She'd said she would consider it, but this was a very serious move, and she needed to be sure that this was the right thing for them to be doing. "So, are you saying that adopting a baby will solve all our problems?"

"No, I'm not saying that at all because now I'm not sure if it would be smart bringing an innocent child into our lives when we're having all these problems, anyway. So, I guess what I'm trying to say is that I don't think it's doing either one of us any good to keep living the way we're living. I'm not saying that we should just separate and cut off all ties, but I do think we need some time apart so we can try to work this out."

"You sound like you've been thinking about this for some time now, so when were you planning to tell me?" she asked and pursed her lips because she was sick of hearing those same romantic jazz songs playing repeatedly on the CD player. Especially since there wasn't anything romantic about what was going on with her and Kevin.

"I hadn't thought about it seriously until the last couple of weeks."

"Well, is that what you're going to do? Move out?" she asked nervously.

"I really think it would be best."

"What about seeing a marriage counselor?" she said hastily.

"I don't know, because the last thing I want to do is blow a bunch of money on something that isn't going to help."

"You didn't think it was a waste of money when you and my family tried to get me to see a psychiatrist after the baby passed away."

"But that was different."

"How was it different, Kevin?" she asked, leaning back in her seat.

"I don't know," he said, obviously confused about his feelings. "Okay, maybe we *should* see a marriage counselor."

"Well, if that's the case, I think we should see one before you move out. I mean, maybe moving out isn't the right thing to do, because it might push us further apart instead of closer together."

He didn't say anything.

"I'll call your benefits office tomorrow to see if your insurance covers seeing a counselor," she said, ignoring the fact that he hadn't fully agreed on not moving out.

"Fine," he said, rubbing his hands down the front of his face like he was exhausted. "Make the appointment."

Racquel stared at him with tears in her eyes, not knowing what to say or what move to make next. Her romantic, candlelight dinner had pretty much been ruined with all this talk about separation, but she still wanted to make love to him. Because strangely enough, it seemed like she craved him more after they argued, or like now, when she was sad about something. It didn't make much sense, but that's how she always felt. And she had a feeling that Kevin felt the same way, because it was during those times that they made the best love of all. Although now, he was just sitting there watching her without any expression on his face, and she couldn't tell if he desired her, or if he was dwelling on the problems in their relationship. She wanted to seduce him but decided that it wasn't worth risking the chance of him rejecting her.

She slid her chair back, stood up, lifted her partially empty plate and wineglass from the table, and walked toward the kitchen trying hard not to look in his direction. But he stopped her as she passed by him.

"Hey," he said, smiling at her. "Set that down for a second, and come here."

She did what he asked and sat on his lap. "What?" she asked, trying to appear emotionally grounded, but knowing full well that what she really wanted to do was burst into tears.

"You know, I do really love you," he said, wrapping his arms around her waist. "And whether you believe it or not, I do want us to work all of this out."

She rested her hands on his shoulders and cried silently.

"And regardless of what I said about us separating or me moving out, it's not what I want. But it's just that I get so frustrated when I think about how in love we were when we first met and how good we were together. And for the longest time, you didn't seem to care about what happened between us one way or the other, so I decided that I might as well take the same attitude."

"I know, but I promise you, all of that is over," she said, placing both of her hands on the sides of his face. "And all I want to do is show you how much I love you and how much I need you in my life," she said and pecked him on his lips.

He wiped the tears from her face and kissed her fiercely. And her heart felt like it was going to explode. Then without even realizing it, she pulled off his tie, removed his dress shirt and then his undershirt. She kissed him passionately around his neck and on his chest. He unzipped her dress and pulled it over her head. Then he unsnapped her bra and tossed it on the carpet. Racquel dropped her head backward and screamed with enjoyment.

But when the foreplay was over, they both stood up. Then he removed his trousers and undershorts and sat back down in the chair. She stepped out of the rest of her undergarments, and they made beautiful love the way Racquel had hoped.

Chapter 26

"Hello?" Marcella answered in a groggy voice, her eyes still closed.

"Hi, I'm looking for Marcella Jones, please," the voice said on the other end of the phone line.

"This is she" Marcella said, raising up in the bed when she realized the voice sounded like Bob's, one of the partners at the accounting firm.

"Marcella, this is Bob Jenkins."

"Hi, Bob, how are you?" she asked, wondering why he was calling her.

"Did I wake you?"

"No," she lied. "I'm not feeling well." She realized that today was the day she'd told him she'd be returning to work.

"Oh, I'm sorry to hear that. Are you back in school yet?"

"Yes," she lied again. And she couldn't help but wonder if he knew she was lying, since he was calling her at a time when he knew she should be at school.

"So, are you still planning to come back to work this week?"

"To be honest with you, Bob, I'm still not feeling up to it." Although she didn't dare tell him, she didn't know when she was going to be ready.

"Well, I know you're going through some difficult times right now, but we've been without a part-time clerical person for over two months, and we really need you to come back this evening."

Now what was she going to do? She'd put them off for more than eight weeks, and they'd been more than understanding about her situation. But now it sounded like he was giving her an ultimatum, and she wasn't sure how to respond to his request. "I missed almost two whole weeks of school, and it's been hard these last couple of months trying to get back into it. But I really think I'll be ready to come back to work by next week or the one following. Especially since by then, I'll almost be finished with my semester course work, and I'll be getting ready to take my finals." She hated lying to Bob the way she was, but there was no way she was going to tell him that she'd withdrawn from all her classes.

"Well, we've got some extremely important projects that we're working on, and as much as I hate saying this, we're going to have to hire someone in your place if you're not able to come in."

Hire someone in her place? Was this some nice way of telling her that she was going to be fired? It was only a part-time position, so why couldn't they simply hire someone through one of those temporary agencies until she returned? She'd been with the firm for over five years, and she couldn't believe they'd get rid of her just like that. "Do you think you could give me until next week?" she asked fearfully, because she really needed her job, but at the same time she wasn't ready emotionally or physically to go back, either.

Bob paused for a few seconds and then spoke. "Although I know Martin isn't going to be too happy about me doing this, I'll give you until day after tomorrow."

What good was two more days going to do for her? "Thank you, Bob," she said, pretending to be relieved. "And I really appreciate you doing this for me."

"Well, I hope you feel better, and I'll see you on Wednesday."

"Okay, I'll see you then," she said, preparing to hang up the phone until she heard him say something else.

"Marcella?"

"Yes."

"If for some reason you don't make it in on Wednesday evening, we'll have no choice but to let you go. We'll still consider hiring you when you graduate, but we won't be able to keep you on part-time or pay any more of your tuition," he said regretfully, and Marcella could tell that his decision was strictly business, and nothing personal.

"I understand," she said, moving her legs from under the comforter to the side of the bed.

"Take care."

"Thanks for calling," she said, hanging up the phone.

She'd known for some time that this day was coming. She'd tried to force herself into going back to school two weeks after Nicholas's funeral, but it hadn't worked out. No matter how hard she tried, she just couldn't grasp onto what her instructors were trying to teach, and most of the time her mind drifted off in a thousand directions. Which is why she'd finally gone to the admissions and records office and had withdrawn from all her classes. She hated doing it, but she promised herself that it was only for this term and that she would reenroll next semester. Of course when her mother and Racquel had found out about it, they'd thrown a complete fit. That is, until she informed them that *her* life was *her* business, and that her dropping out of school really didn't concern either one of them.

But if she lost her job—well, that was going to be a whole different story. Because then she'd have no choice except to surrender her apartment, and she'd be forced to move in with her mother on a permanent basis. The Housing Authority had already dropped her rent to zero due to her part-time employment, but without a job at all, she wouldn't have nearly enough money to pay her utility bills. As a matter of fact, the only money she would have to depend on was Tyrone's child support. The same child support that he'd so conveniently gotten lax with again.

She could kill herself for sleeping with him that afternoon he'd come by her mother's house to see her, but for some stupid reason, she hadn't been able to resist him. She was lonely, and she'd allowed him to play on her vulnerability to the fullest extent. She'd always known that he couldn't be trusted, but he sounded so sincere when he said he wanted to do right by her and Ashley, and that he wanted them to be a family. But now he spent even less time with Ashley than he had before Nicholas passed away. Marcella didn't now—and wasn't ever going to—have any genuine feelings for him again because there was far too much history between them, but a part of her had wanted to believe that he was still in love with her. Not because she wanted a relationship with him, but because she needed to be loved. She needed to be loved by a man.

But, then, who was she kidding? Because Tyrone was far and apart from even resembling a real man, let alone actually being one. He acted more like an immature little boy than anything else. So she knew all those thoughts about needing to be loved were basically just a bunch of excuses and a bunch of wishful thinking. And while she hated admitting it, she could no longer deny the fact that she'd had sex with him for one reason and one reason only: He knew how to rock her world. As a matter of fact, she'd never even been with another man who could compare to him. He was that good, and she hated him for it.

The more she thought about Tyrone and how trifling he was, the more she despised herself for allowing him to skip payment after payment. She should have turned him in right after he caused that reduction in her food stamp allotment, but whenever she thought about it, it reminded her of the day Sharon was killed in that car accident. Because it was that whole Tyrone incident that had caused them to disagree in the first place. She had wanted to tell Tyrone off, and Sharon kept advising her not to.

"Well, I'll tell you one thing, you didn't die for nothin'," Marcella said out loud to Sharon, picked up the beige receiver and dialed 411.

"Directory assistance, what city, please?" the directory operator answered.

"Covington Park. Could you give me the number for Child Support Enforcement, please?" Marcella asked, waiting to take a mental note of the phone number.

"Thank you, here's that number," the operator said and played a computerized announcement.

Marcella pressed the button inside the phone and dialed the number.

"Good morning, Child Support Enforcement, how may I help you?" a younger woman, probably in her early twenties, answered.

"Yes, I'd like to speak to someone concerning the issuance of a child-support order," she said, switching the phone from her right ear to her left.

"Do you know where the father lives and where he works?"

"Yes, he lives and works right here in Covington Park," Marcella said guiltily because she'd always known where he was, but she'd told her caseworker from the very beginning that she didn't, so they wouldn't cut her money off when she'd first gotten on welfare and wasn't working.

"Good, because that'll make the process go a lot faster. Now what I'll need to do is take your name and phone number, so that I can assign you to a caseworker, and then he or she will call you back with a time to come in for your initial intake interview."

Marcella told the woman her name and recited her mother's phone number instead of her own, because she knew her telephone was on the verge of being shut off. Plus, she probably wasn't going to be moving back to her apartment any time soon, anyhow. "How long will it take to get into court once I have my interview?"

"Oh, probably anywhere from six months to a year. It just depends on your particular case."

"Six months to a year? But that's such a long time."

"I know, but with the number of cases we have in this county, compared to the small amount of caseworkers, it's the best we can do."

"Okay. When do you think someone will call me to schedule my appointment?"

"Probably sometime this week, but if not, definitely by the first of next week."

Marcella felt like telling her to just forget the whole thing, but she knew she needed this money more than ever, since there was a good chance she might be losing her job. And she'd spent the rest of the money from Sharon's insurance policy on miscellaneous bills. "Well, thank you for your help," Marcella said.

"Goodbye," the woman said and hung up.

It just wasn't fair for her to have to wait this long to get what was rightfully hers, and now she wished she'd taken him to court a long time ago. Everyone had begged her to, but she just hadn't been motivated enough to do it. And she wasn't sure why she hadn't, except that back when she wasn't working, she'd been worried about them cutting her check off completely. And even now, she wondered just how long it was going to be before they calculated an overpayment for that. Then when she'd started working, she had become worried about them eliminating her food stamps. She knew she'd been cheating the government by concealing Tyrone's whereabouts, but it was the only way she had sort of made ends meet.

Marcella stood in front of the old-style wooden dresser and stared at herself in the mirror. Her hair was wild and scary and she hadn't done anything with it in over a week. And she wasn't going to do anything with it today, either. She walked outside the bedroom, went into the kitchen to find a few snacks, and looked up at the clock on the wall. It was almost ten o'clock, so she had to hurry if she wanted to get back into the bedroom before *The Price Is Right* came on. She pulled down an unopened bag of tortilla chips from the cabinet, pulled out a jar of medium salsa and a can of Coke from the refrigerator, and grabbed a partially filled bag of Chips Ahoy. Then she headed back into the bedroom, set the phone down on the floor, and piled all of her food on top of the nightstand. She picked up the remote, turned on the twenty-inch color TV set, and turned it to the network hosting her favorite game show. As the commercials flashed across the screen, she positioned a deep-turquoise backrest against the wooden headboard, leaned back on it, and then opened her chips and salsa dip.

Her day began and ended pretty much the same way every day. First, she watched *The Price Is Right, The Young and the Restless,* then the area news, followed by *The Bold and the Beautiful, Days of Our Lives,* a local talk show, and then *Sally,* and finally *Oprah.* And it was these television shows that allowed her to keep at least some sanity because she really didn't care about anything else. And it was fine with her if she never left the house ever again. Her mother was taking care of Ashley and was doing a good job with her. And since it seemed like Ashley enjoyed spending all this time with her grandmother, Marcella really didn't have any important responsibilities anymore. And why should she care about anything anyhow? She'd tried to do all the right things, she'd tried to treat people the way she wanted to be treated, but where had all of that gotten her? From what she could see, nowhere.

She watched all of her programs as planned, and with the exception of a few sales calls over the phone, there hadn't been any other interruptions. But now she heard her mother laying her keys down on the kitchen counter, and Marcella knew it was just a matter of time before she burst into the room with her usual fussing.

"Have you been sitting in this room watching TV all day?" Corrine asked as soon as she stepped inside the doorway.

"Pretty much," Marcella said nonchalantly.

"Where's Ashley, and why isn't she home yet?" Corrine asked with her hand on her hip.

She's gone, and that's why she's not home *yet*, Marcella thought sarcastically, but didn't dare say it. "She's probably over at that Patrice's house," Marcella said without taking her eyes off Oprah and her guests.

"Ever since the school district switched her bus route to the one over here, she's been going somewhere else every day after they drop her off," Corrine said, pausing. Then she continued. "You know, I've been taking care of Ashley like she's my own child for weeks now, and even though I don't mind it, she's your daughter and it's time for you to start acting like it."

Marcella looked at her silently and wished her mother would stop drowning out the talk show.

"Don't you have anything to say?" Corrine asked irately.

"Mom, what do you want me to say? I'm barely taking care of myself, so how am I going to take care of Ashley? She acts like she prefers being around you instead of me anyway."

"That's because you don't give that girl the time of day. You don't say more than two words to her when she's here, and you don't do anything with her."

"I don't have any money to do things with her."

"I'm not talking about those kinds of things. I'm talking about sitting down with your daughter to see how she's doing in school, or even just to see how she's dealing with her brother's death."

"She's barely even shed any tears since the day of the funeral, so I'm sure she's fine."

"Marcella, I don't know what's gotten into you, but this isn't like you at all. You used to be such a good mother, and I was always so proud of that."

"Well, if I was such a good mother, then why did God take Nicholas away from me? Huh, Mom? Tell me that?" Marcella said, slightly raising her voice.

"Girl, we've been through that over and over again, and I'm tired of trying to explain the facts of life to you. And whether you understand what happened or not, that still doesn't give you the right to just give up or to neglect your daughter the way you're doing. She's thirteen years old, and a girl that age needs her mother."

"Ashley knows that I'm here for her if she needs me."

"No, she doesn't. And what type of an example do you think you're setting for her by lying up in this filthy room like you've been doing?" Corrine asked, shifting her eyes around the room.

"Mom, I'm depressed. Why can't you understand that?" Marcella said, trying to make her mother comprehend.

"Do you remember when Racquel kept singing that same song when she lost her baby, and you told her that it was time for her to accept what happened so she could get on with her life? Do you?" Corrine asked, folding her arms.

"This is different."

"Different how, Marcella?" Corrine asked sternly.

"Racquel never even got to know her baby, and she only held her for a few minutes. But I was with Nicholas for eleven years."

"Losing a baby is losing a baby, and it doesn't matter how much time you got to spend with it. And I sure hope you don't say anything like that to Racquel."

"Mom, why are you doing this?" Marcella asked, wishing she would leave her alone.

"Because I want you to get up off of your behind and start living again. I've tried to be as patient with you as I can, but enough is enough. And it doesn't make any sense how you just dropped out of school in the middle of your third year. All that time and work for nothing."

"Mom, how do you expect me to go to class or study feeling the way I do?"

"Because you're strong. I raised both you and Racquel to be strong Black women, and I refuse to accept anything less than that. I went through a lot with your father. Lord knows I did. But I started on my job when Racquel was barely two months old, and I've been there ever since. And even when your father left, I took care of you girls, and I made sure the bills were paid. So, you tell me what would have happened to you if *I* had fallen into some deep state of depression. What would you and Racquel have done then? Both of you were a lot older than Ashley, but you were still only teenagers."

"Mom, losing a husband is not the same as losing a child. You have to know that."

"I'm not saying it is the same, but what I am saying is that life has to go on. And you need to go back to work before those people end up firing you."

Marcella looked straight at the television set because the last thing she wanted was for her mother to find out that she was only two days away from losing her job with the firm. "What sense does it make for me to go back to work when I can't even concentrate on anything else for more than two minutes."

"You at least have to try," Corrine said, and then the phone rang.

After the second ring, Marcella reached down to the floor to pick it up. "Hello?"

"Ms. Jones?" a woman said.

"Yes, this is," Marcella said, trying to figure out the voice.

"This is Mrs. Johnson, Ashley's counselor at Covington Park Junior High."

"Yes, what can I do for you?" Marcella asked curiously.

"Ashley seems to be having some problems with not getting her homework done in just about every one of her classes, and a couple of the teachers have reported that she's been sassing them whenever they ask her a question or tell her to do something."

"When did all this start?" Marcella said, glancing at her mother reluctantly and wishing she would I go away.

"It started about a month or so ago, and we've mailed a couple of letters to your house. I even tried to call you a couple of times, but I didn't get an answer."

Marcella wasn't surprised about the unanswered phone calls, because there were lots of days when she didn't even bother to look at the phone, let alone answer it. But she did think it was strange that she hadn't gotten the letters, since she'd had all her mail forwarded to her mother's address. "Well, I'll have a talk with her as soon as she gets home this evening," Marcella said in a frustrated manner.

"We just wanted to let you know because Ashley was a model student when she started here last year in seventh grade, and she always got straight As, but this year, things aren't going well for her at all. I don't know if it has something to do with her brother's death or if something else is bothering her."

"Well, as I said, I'll speak with her this evening, and I'll try to give you a call sometime tomorrow afternoon."

"That will be fine."

"Thank you for calling," Marcella said and hung up the phone.

"What was that all about?" Corrine asked without delay.

"That was Ashley's counselor calling to say that she hasn't been turning in homework, and that she's been sassing some of her teachers."

"Mmm. Mmm. Mmm. See, that's exactly what I've been trying to tell you. That girl needs you, and it's your responsibility to know what's going on with her."

"She always says that she doesn't have any homework, or that she did it at school. So what am I supposed to do?"

"You're supposed to be her mother, Marcella," Corrine yelled.

Marcella was getting fed up with all this harassment, and she wished her mother would stop it before this whole conversation turned uglier than it already was.

"The next thing you know, she'll be sneaking around here seeing some little mannish boy, and I'd hate to see her end up pregnant."

"Pregnant?" Marcella said, frowning. "Mom, Ashley is only thirteen years old. And she's way too smart to let something like that happen anyway."

"Nowadays, these girls are getting pregnant earlier and earlier, and being book smart doesn't mean she won't get caught up with some boy."

"Ashley is not messing around with some boy."

"How do you know?"

"Because I do," Marcella said and heard the back door shutting.

Corrine looked at her and walked out of the bedroom without saying anything else. Marcella followed behind her. When they arrived in the kitchen, Ashley was setting her book bag down in a chair.

"Ashley, what is this I'm hearing about you not turning in your homework assignments?"

"I don't know," Ashley said, shrugging.

"What do you mean you don't know?" Marcella said, raising her voice.

Ashley stared at her with an I-don't-see-why-you're trippin' look on her face.

"Your counselor called here this afternoon, and not only did she say you weren't doing your homework, but she also said that you've been talking back to a couple of your teachers. So is that true, too?"

"No," Ashley said, looking at her grandmother.

"Oh, so what you're saying then, is that your teachers are lying on you," Marcella said in an I-know-better-than-that tone of voice.

Ashley looked at her grandmother again, like she was expecting Corrine to defend her.

"Don't look at me," Corrine said. "It's your mama who's talking to you."

"I'm really disappointed in you, Ashley. You know I've been going through a rough time, so why are you trying to do things to worry me like this?"

"You don't care about me, anyway, so why should I waste my time doing some stupid homework?"

Marcella raised her eyebrows in shock. "What do you mean I don't care about you?"

"You don't. And all you ever talk about is how much you miss Nicholas."

"That's because I do miss him."

"But he's *dead*, Mom," Ashley said in a hostile tone. "And *I'm* still here."

"Ashley!" Marcella said, shaking her head in disagreement.

"Can I be excused now?" Ashley asked, looking away from her mother and folding her arms.

"Ashley, what's gotten into you?" Marcella asked, realizing for the first time that something was seriously wrong with her daughter.

"Nothing," Ashley said, scowling.

"What I want you to do is go to your room," Marcella said, feeling angry and hurt at the same time.

"You're just like . . . ," Ashley mumbled as she left the room.

"What did you say?" Marcella yelled out, walking behind her.

"You're just like my no-good daddy."

Marcella's heart fell to the floor.

Chapter 27

"I just don't understand what's gotten into Ashley," Marcella said, leaning back on the sofa in her sister's family room. "She's so ornery and disrespectful."

"For one thing, she's hurting over Nicholas," Racquel said, curling her legs under her behind.

"I realize that, but I'm not going to keep putting up with that little attitude of hers. And do you know what she said yesterday before she stormed her little self out of the room?"

"What?"

"That I was just like her no-good daddy. And if I hadn't caught myself, I would've strangled her."

Racquel looked away from Marcella like she was suddenly interested in what was on TV.

"Can you believe that?" Marcella continued.

"Maybe she didn't mean it exactly like it sounded."

"How else could she have meant it?"

"Maybe it's because you haven't spent as much time with her lately. I know you've been going through a hard time, but she probably needs you right now more than she ever has before."

"But I *have* been there for her, and so has Mom," Marcella said defensively.

"I know, but I'm telling you from experience. Sometimes we get so caught up in ourselves that we forget about the needs of everyone else. I mean, take me for example. I was so obsessed with getting pregnant, that I neglected the most important person in my life. And I almost lost him because of it."

"I'm not obsessed with Nicholas's death, I'm just having a hard time accepting it."

"I know you don't see it that way, because I didn't, either. But it does seem like you've gotten to the point where you don't care about anything or anybody."

"That's not true, and I love Ashley more than anything else."

"I know you do, but since Kevin and I have been going to see that marriage counselor, I'm finally able to see how selfish I was. All I cared about was having a baby, and everything else was second. Including my marriage. So, I'm telling you, Marcella. Don't make the same mistakes did."

"Well, I don't know what to do."

"Do exactly what you used to do before Nicholas passed away. Even though you were in school and working, you still used to spend a lot of time with them when you could, and I'm sure Ashley misses that."

"Maybe if I hadn't started school in the first place, none of this would be happening."

"What does your going back to school have to do with anything?"

"It kept me away from them so much. I was so busy worrying about how much more money I could make by going back to school, that I didn't even notice how sick Nicholas was."

"Marcella, I know you're not still trying to blame yourself for Nicholas's death, because there really weren't any warning signs, so there was nothing you could do."

"But maybe if I had been around him more, I would have noticed something out of the ordinary. Something that would have made me take him to the doctor."

"Mom and I watched Ashley and Nicholas all the time when you worked, and we never noticed anything. As a matter of fact, until you said he'd had a couple of headaches, we weren't even aware of that. So you have to know that there wasn't anything any of us could have done. God knows, I wish we could have, but there wasn't."

Marcella acknowledged her sister's comments with a slight nod.

"I know losing a child is difficult," Racquel said. "Believe me, I do. But you have to move on. Not just for your sake, but for Ashley's. Because if you don't, she's going to end up in trouble. And you know what kind of trouble I'm talking about."

"Mom was saying the same thing yesterday, but I really doubt it because Ashley is too sensible for that," Marcella said and then suddenly remembered what Ashley had done to that little Jason when she was just eleven years old. But Racquel still didn't know about that.

"Well, just the same, you'd better watch her a lot more closely than you have been. Especially since she's got that I-don't-care attitude and thinks that nobody cares about her. Because believe it or not, your childhood can affect you for the rest of your life. That's part of the reason why I have such a huge desire to have children."

"What do you mean?" Marcella asked in a confused tone.

"Because with Daddy and Mom arguing all the time and then getting a divorce, it's almost like I'm wanting to give my child the type of home I thought I should have had. It's almost like I'm hoping that I'll be able to relive my childhood the right way through my own son or daughter. At least that's what the counselor has been saying."

"You were having those same thoughts yourself two years ago. Remember when we talked about it that day we were driving home from Michelle's baby shower?"

"I know, but I still couldn't change the way I was feeling. So, maybe I needed to hear it from a professional before I could finally do something about it."

"Well, if that's what it took, then that's all that matters," Marcella said, glancing at the television.

"I'm just glad for Kevin's sake, because I was really taking him through a lot of changes."

"So, are you guys doing okay?" Marcella asked, leaning the side of her head into the palm of her hand, and resting her elbow on the back of the sofa.

"A whole lot better than we were, that's for sure. And it seems like we've both benefited from the counseling sessions, because we've learned more about each other in the last two months than we have the whole time we've been married. And even though we still have a long way to go, it seems like we're a lot closer. Almost closer than when we first met."

"I'm really glad to hear that, because you and Kevin deserve to be happy," Marcella said, smiling at her sister.

"You and Ashley deserve to be happy, too, and you will be as soon as you two start doing more things together," Racquel said, gazing directly at Marcella.

"Well, now that I have to go back to work tomorrow, it's going to be even harder for me to spend time with her."

"I thought you said you were going back in a couple of weeks?"

"That's what I wanted, but one of the partners called me yesterday and said that if I don't come in tomorrow evening, they're going to replace me."

"It's probably a good idea for you to get back to work anyway, but maybe they'll let you work during the day now that you're not in school."

"That's just it, they don't know about me dropping out of school, and I don't want them to. Especially since they paid half of my tuition, and I withdrew from my classes too late to get a refund back."

"But maybe you should tell them anyway, because there's a chance that they'll understand."

"I don't know. And to be honest, I really don't feel mentally or physically ready to go back to work anyway. It took everything I had just to take a shower, get dressed, and drive over here after I dropped Ashley off for school. And if I hadn't needed to talk to you so badly, I'd probably still be in bed."

"I know how you feel because the main reason I took this leave of absence from teaching was so I could concentrate on Kevin, but part of it was because I was still so messed up emotionally and didn't feel comfortable being around my students."

"All I know is that things have got to get better," Marcella said with a deep sigh.

"They will," Racquel said, smiling and rubbing Marcella's back in a circular motion. "Don't even worry about it."

"So how was school?" Marcella asked Ashley as she walked through the back door.

"Okay," Ashley said with no enthusiasm.

"What homework do you have for tonight?" Marcella asked, removing a package of ground beef from the refrigerator. Since Corrine had gone directly to the salon after work to get her hair done, Marcella had decided to cook some spaghetti.

"Algebra."

"Well, I think you should start working on it now, while I'm cooking dinner."

Ashley blew her breath louder than usual and headed toward her bedroom with her book bag hanging from her shoulder.

"Why don't you sit in here and do it at the kitchen table?" Marcella asked, wanting to keep her in the same room with her so she could make sure she was really doing her schoolwork.

"It's more comfortable if I do it on Granny's desk in the bedroom," Ashley said, looking at her mother.

"Fine, but if you have any trouble with those math problems, I want you to come out here and ask me."

Ashley left the room.

After about thirty minutes the phone rang. Marcella knew it was for Ashley, but she decided to pick it up anyway to tell whoever it was to call back later when she was finished with her homework. But when she lifted the receiver, she heard Ashley saying hello and some boy asking her what was up. Marcella's first instinct was to hang up, but instead of doing that, she reached her finger toward the base of the phone on the wall and pushed the mute button.

"Hi, Jason," Ashley said in a cutesy voice.

"So when did you move in with your grandmother?" Jason asked, sounding like a twenty-year-old.

"A couple of months ago after my brother died."

"Oh, yeah. I heard about that when we moved back in with my mom."

"You and your brothers live across from our apartment again?"

"Yeah. We moved back right before your brother died, but I never did get a chance to see you."

Marcella felt her blood pressure skyrocketing. She wanted to go off right then and there, but she had to wait a few minutes longer to see where this ghetto-boy conversation was going.

"What were you doing up at our school today?" Ashley continued.

"Me and my boys hang out at a lot of different schools every day."

"What high school do you go to?"

"I don't. I threatened to beat down this teacher if she didn't raise up off me about some crazy homework assignment, and when the principal told me to apologize to her, I told him I wasn't hearing that noise, and that I wasn't tellin' her nothin'. So they suspended me, and I never went back."

"Man. So you don't go to school at all?" Ashley asked in a shocked tone of voice.

"Nope. And my uncle says it's a waste of time for any Black person to go to school anyway because no matter what you learn, the White man is still going to keep you down."

"Not if you get a college education, he can't."

"Girl, that piece of paper doesn't mean anything. You'll see."

Ashley didn't say anything, and Marcella was getting more upset by the second.

"So when are you and me gonna hook up? With your fine self."

"I don't know. We hardly ever come back over to the apartment since all of our stuff got stolen," Ashley said, sounding sad.

"Well, why don't you skip school tomorrow so we can hang out?"

"Skip school?" Ashley said, sounding confused.

"Yeah. You ride the bus to school like you always do, and then I'll meet you on the school grounds."

"I don't know, Jason . . . I mean, sometimes my mom takes me and drops me off."

"So what. She doesn't sit there watchin' you until you get inside the school, does she?"

"No, but if she finds out, she'll kill me."

"How is she going to find out? Look, Ashley, I know you're not going to start acting like a little girl, are you? Because I really like you a lot. Shoot, ever since we were together that one day in your apartment, I haven't wanted to be with anyone else but you. And I cried when your mother threatened to call the police on me if I kept messing with you. I wanted to be with you so bad."

"I don't know, Jason," Ashley said, sounding scared.

"Look, Ashley, I'm fifteen, and I have certain needs."

Marcella released the mute button. "I'll tell you what you need, you little low-life thug, you need to be locked up in jail somewhere. And if you ever call this house again, you'll live to regret it."

"Aw, man, Ashley. I just know your moms isn't threatenin' me again," Jason said, laughing.

"No, I'm not threatening you. I'm telling you exactly what I'm going to do if you ever contact my daughter or go near her again."

"Look, trick, my *mama* don't even tell me what to do, so who actually do you think you are?"

"Just call back over here again, and you'll see," Marcella said and then wondered why she was actually sitting there arguing back and forth with some illiterate fifteen-year-old.

"That's why all your precious little stuff got stolen out of your apartment."

"Boy, what are you talking about?" Marcella asked, scrunching her face.

"You heard me. And if you keep messing with me, more than that is gonna happen to your smart tail."

"Ashley, hang up the phone!" Marcella yelled, waiting to make sure she did, and then she slammed the kitchen phone on the hook as hard as she could.

"Ashley! Get out here!" Marcella screamed.

Ashley dragged into the kitchen as slowly as she could.

"Are you crazy, giving that boy this phone number?"

"I'm sorry, Mom," she said, trembling.

"Don't you remember the talk we had when you snuck that little mannish boy into our apartment two years ago? Huh?"

Ashley shook her head yes, but didn't make a sound.

"Well, what were you thinking now? That since you were two years older, it was okay to see him?"

"I just wanted to talk to him. That's all."

"I told you that you could talk to boys on the phone when you turned thirteen, but I think you know I didn't mean somebody like Jason. That boy is headed for trouble, and anybody that has anything to do with him is headed in the same direction," Marcella said, pausing. "Ashley, what am I going to do with you? I mean you're messing up in school and now you're giving out your grandmother's phone number to some thug. For all you know, he could be in some Chicago gang, or something."

Ashley stood in front of her mother, looking as if she was holding her breath, and her eyes were filled completely with water.

Marcella took a deep breath. "Ashley, don't you know how much I love you? Don't you know that you're the only thing I have left in this world besides your granny, your aunt, and your uncle?"

Tears gushed down Ashley's face, and her feet stayed glued to the floor.

"Honey, I know I haven't been myself lately, but when Nicholas died, I just didn't know how to deal with it. Sometimes I still don't know how to deal with it, but I'm going to try a lot harder to. I know it wasn't fair for me to ignore you the way I have, but I really wasn't able to see it, until your granny came down on me yesterday. And I'm sorry. But at the same time, you're old enough to understand some of these things, and just because I'm going through some changes, doesn't mean you should stop doing your schoolwork, or that you have the right to talk back to your teachers. Because you know I didn't raise you that way," Marcella said, pulling her daughter into her arms.

Ashley sniffled continuously with her eyes closed and hugged her mother like it was her last opportunity. Marcella held her until she calmed down.

"You do know that I love you, don't you?" Marcella asked, looking down at her.

Ashley looked up at her and said, "Yes."

"And you do understand how important it is for you to do well in school, right?"

"Yes."

"Well, then, why did you suddenly think it wasn't worth doing your schoolwork anymore?"

"Because *you* didn't. I heard you telling Granny one night that you just couldn't go to your classes anymore, and that it wasn't worth all the trouble."

Marcella paused, closed her eyes for a few seconds, and then spoke. "But I was wrong, honey. And don't you ever let anyone lead you to think that it's not worth getting an education. Okay?"

"Yes," Ashley said, laying her head back on her mother's chest.

Marcella hadn't held her daughter this much since Ashley was a toddler, and she couldn't remember the last time Ashley had ever wanted to hug her as tight as she was right now. And she felt a closeness with her, like she never had before. The kind of closeness every mother and daughter alive needed to have if they wanted to survive all the troubles in this world.

And it was at that moment that she knew she was going to work tomorrow, that she was going back to school in January, that she was going to graduate from college, and that she was going to be the best role model and mother she could be for Ashley.

And that's all that really mattered.

Epilogue

Not once will I ever forget that day I found Ashley's diary, and not once will I ever forget what I read in it. It's been years now, but it still makes me cringe whenever I think about it. And while I thought the whole idea of writing my thoughts down on paper was kind of silly, for some reason I purchased this journal and decided that this would be the day I made my first entry. I'm not really sure where to begin, except with what's going on today. I'm actually graduating from the university! And on top of that, I'm graduating with high honors. I mean, who would have ever thought it? If only Sharon and Nicholas could be here to witness the ceremony, or just to even share this special time in my life. It's been almost three years since I lost Nicholas and almost four since Sharon passed away, but I still have a hard time accepting any of it. Well, maybe I have accepted it, but I still have my days when I can't help but shed a few tears. It seemed so unfair to lose both my child and my best friend in the same twelve-month period. But I do realize that that's just how life is, and that we weren't put here to stay here forever. But at least I have my little Ashley. Although since she's turning sixteen next month, I guess she's not really all that little anymore. But no matter how old she gets, she'll always be my baby. And I couldn't be prouder when it comes to all of her accomplishments. She's a straight-A student in the college preparatory program at Covington Park High, a member of the cheerleading squad, vice-president of the Afro-American Club, and from the way it looks, she'll be graduating a whole semester early. She's such an intelligent young lady, and I couldn't be happier that she's decided to pursue a medical degree and wants to specialize in infertility. At first I wasn't sure why she chose that particular field to go into, but then I realized that it probably had something to do with Racquel and Kevin not being able to have a baby. And I don't think it made things any easier for her when she saw how many changes they went through because of it. But, thank God, their marriage is finally back on track and couldn't be better. And on top of that, they became foster parents to a beautiful two-year-old little girl. A little girl whose mother dropped her off at the nursery one morning and never came back to pick her up. She's been with Racquel and Kevin for some time now, and we all love her to death. She's such a little sweetheart, and Racquel and Kevin are planning to adopt her just as soon as the agency allows them to. And I really hope that the adoption agency doesn't take as long as the Child Support Agency took when it came to ordering Tyrone to take care of Ashley. It took a little over a year, but instead of sixty dollars a week, that wonderful female judge ordered him to pay me one hundred forty dollars a week. Of course, he started his usual slacking on the payments, and it wasn't long before I had to take him back to court. And this time the judge ordered that the money be taken directly from his paycheck. Needless to say, he barely speaks to me now, but he has been spending a fair amount of time with Ashley. Which is all I want from him anyway. It's amazing how things work out, though. Once upon a time, I didn't know how I was going to put food on the table, or how I was going to keep the electricity on in my apartment. And all I ever dwelled on was what I didn't have and how I was going to get it. But now things have finally changed. I'm getting over five hundred dollars a month from Tyrone; the partners at the accounting firm are starting me off with thirty-five thousand dollars a year as an accountant, and the thirty thousand dollars that Sharon left for Nicholas was issued to me a few months after he passed away. Which will make all the difference in the world when I make the down payment on the house Ashley and I have been looking at. It's been wonderful living with Mom, and even though we're closer than we've ever been before, it's still not the same as having my own place. Plus, now that she's dating a really nice guy from church, I'm sure she needs more privacy. She'll never admit it, but I know she does just the same. And Mom isn't the only one who met someone recently, because Marcus told me that he thinks he's met the woman of his dreams, and he's bringing her to my graduation today, so I can meet her.

I'm really looking forward to it, and I'm extremely happy for him. So anyway, that's pretty much it for now, except I do have one last thing to say. Life wasn't always good for me, but right now I truly couldn't be happier. And if I never learn another lesson for as long as I live, I've definitely learned this: When it rains, it pours; but when the sun does shine, it really shines brightly.

Don't miss

Casting the First Stone

the first Reverend Curtis Black novel

available everywhere books are sold.

Chapter 1

Tanya crossed her legs for what seemed like the hundredth time and gazed at her husband in disgust. She'd been sitting as patiently as she possibly could, pretending to pay attention to what he was saying. But the more she listened to his pathetic observations, the more annoyed she became. And just looking at the eight-hundred-dollar suit, the overpriced dress shoes, and the expensive gold watch he was wearing was enough to make any human being puke. She couldn't believe he actually had the audacity to stand before his three thousand-plus congregation, practically demanding that they give more money. Exactly how much more *money* did he think these people could afford anyway? The majority of them were already obeying God's word by paying ten percent of their weekly incomes to the church, and to suggest that they should be giving anything more than that was simply ridiculous. That is, unless there was a reason for it. An important reason, such as one of the families being left homeless due to a fire or flood. Or one of the less fortunate members needing assistance with emergency medical bills or help with burying their deceased loved ones. As far as Tanya was concerned, situations like those were fine, but anything else just didn't seem justified to her. Every Sunday Curtis laid down the same wretched guilt trip, and she was sick of it: "You are robbing God if you don't pay your tithes, and He will bless you even more if you give an additional offering."

It was so hard to believe that this was the same man she'd married eight years ago. She'd thought for sure that Curtis Black was the man of her eternal dreams. He was intelligent, responsible, attractive, and, without a doubt, the most spiritually grounded man she'd ever made acquaintance with. They'd met during her junior year at Spelman, his senior year at Morehouse, and had fallen hopelessly in love with each other immediately. He pursued his bachelor's degree in business, and she worked hard on her degree in psychology. Then, shortly after they'd each completed their graduate studies in counseling, Curtis announced that God had called him to preach, and that he wanted her hand in marriage. And for the first six years, they'd been happier than any married couple could have thought possible. Everyone said they were a perfect match, and their friends and family members always raved over how attractive the two of them looked together. Curtis with his tall, broad-shouldered body and deep-mocha complexion, and Tanya with her black, bobbed hairstyle and medium-cocoa skintone. But what all their admirers didn't know was that not everything that looked good was, and that her and Curtis's model marriage had long since turned into something very ugly and dreadfully different.

If they all only knew about the horrible rumors that had started only weeks after Curtis was installed as pastor of Faith Missionary Baptist Church, which was located on the south side of Chicago, and how Tanya had purposely tried to ignore each and every one of them—hoping these rumors were nothing more than vicious lies. That is, until those lies began floating in a mile a minute, from every possible direction, and she'd had no choice except to believe that at least some of what she was hearing had to be true.

The thought of Curtis sleeping with another woman had always made her cringe, but now Tanya's pain was slowly turning to rage. She hated the ground that he walked on and everything he stood for. She wished him dead on almost every occasion, and she wasn't sure just how much more of this facade of a marriage she could actually take. She was sick of him and sick of pretending that they were this perfect couple who loved each other more than life itself. And even worse, she hated him for not spending any time with their six-year-old daughter, Alicia—the same daughter who still worshipped everything that had to do with her father. She didn't deserve to be neglected by him that way, and just thinking about how he treated her pissed Tanya off.

Oh, but enough was enough. And as soon as they arrived back at their South suburban home in Covington Park, wife of a pastor or not, she was going to show him a side of her that he'd never seen before.

Tanya snapped out of her daydream and watched her husband step away from the podium. She couldn't believe he was still begging for more money.

"We as black people have little, because we think little, and I want you all to know that it's up to you and I to take care of Faith Missionary Baptist Church," Curtis said, walking down the center aisle of the beautiful sanctuary, just past the second pew where Tanya was sitting. "If you want me to take you places that you've never gone before, then we are going to have to get rid of these stingy attitudes. I can feel them throughout the entire congregation, and it ain't nothin' but the devil who is trying to convince you to hold on to those purses and those wallets. Who gave you those purses and those wallets in the first place? And who gave you those good jobs that most of you go to every day? And who gave you a roof over your head, clothes on your back, and food on your table? I'll tell you who. God did."

Curtis paused for a moment and shut his eyes. Then he opened them. "God has laid an important message on my heart. He wants me to ask every adult who is here right now to give an extra twenty dollars this morning."

Tanya noticed some of the members looking around at each other. Some even whispered to the person sitting next to them. And it was obvious that most of them were sick and tired of dealing with this same old Jim-Jones-Jim-Bakker-Jimmy-Swaggert-need-more-money sort of mentality. She couldn't help but wonder just how far Curtis was actually willing to go when it came to getting what he wanted from these innocent people. But the more she thought about it, the more she realized that her husband really didn't have any limitations when it came to anything.

And that was the one thing that frightened her the most.

Right after the Black family changed out of their Sunday-go-to-meeting attire, they each sat down at the kitchen table to eat the barbecued rib dinners they'd picked up on the way home from church. Usually they sat in the dining room for Sunday dinners, but sometimes when they ordered take-out, they ate in the kitchen instead.

"So, baby girl," Curtis said to his daughter, "did you enjoy the service today?"

"Yes. You preached really good, Daddy," she said, smiling.

Tanya smiled too, but only to pacify Alicia.

"And *you* sounded real good yourself when you led that song today," he complimented her. Alicia was a member of the children's choir.

She beamed. "Thanks."

"What about you, baby?" He turned his attention to Tanya. "Did you enjoy the service?"

"It was fine," she said, trying to keep her composure, because she didn't know how much longer she was going to be able to control herself.

"The spirit was really moving through the church today, wasn't it?" he continued.

"Yeah, I guess it was," she answered.

"Mom?" Alicia said. "Can I go next door to Lisa's?"

"I guess, but if they're in the middle of eating dinner, then I want you to come right back home."

"I'll bet they already ate, because they get out of church way earlier than we do," Alicia offered.

Hmmph, Tanya thought. Everybody got out of church earlier than they did. She didn't know a lot of African-American Catholics, but their next-door neighbors never missed Mass on any week she could think of. And they were always home before noon every Sunday.

"Okay, but make sure you wash your hands before you go," Tanya instructed.

Alicia did what her mother told her, and then left the house in a hurry.

However, as soon as Alicia had barely darkened the front doorway, Tanya lit into Curtis like a madwoman.

"You know, Curtis, I don't know who you think you are, but you are not God's gift to this earth," she said, shoving the wooden chair that she was sitting on up to the table as hard as she could. She'd tried to calm herself down during the drive home and then again when they first started eating dinner, but now she felt like she was going to explode.

Curtis frowned. "What are you talking about?"

"You know exactly what the hell I'm talking about."

"No. I don't. And I'd appreciate it if you wouldn't use that kind of language in my house," Curtis said, spooning up a helping of peach cobbler.

Tanya glared at him and wanted to slap that dessert right down his throat. "What do you mean, *your* house?" she asked, folding her arms, staring at him. "This house is just as much mine as it is yours. And you'd better get this through your head, too: I'll say whatever I feel like saying. Whenever I feel like it. You might control those tramps you sleep around with, but you don't control anything that has to do with me."

"Lord have mercy," Curtis said, squinting at Tanya. "This ain't nothin' but the devil tryin' to come between us, because Lord knows I haven't been sleeping around with any women."

"Curtis, please. I mean, why is the devil always responsible for everything when it comes to you getting caught up in your mess? And, if that's the case, then let me ask you this. Is he responsible for you laying up with practically every woman at the church who will have your little jack-leg preachin' ass?" Tanya said and was shocked at her own words. She hadn't spoken so profanely since college, and even more so since she became a minister's wife, and she wasn't proud of it. But it was just that she'd had it up to here, there, and everywhere with Curtis's sleeping around. She didn't have one ounce of proof, but that was only because he was always so smooth, slick, and secretive with his wrongdoings. But she knew what he was up to, because he'd long stopped satisfying her in bed, and, to tell the truth, their lovemaking was nonexistent. And no man, especially one who was as high-natured and passionate in bed as Curtis, could go without sex week after week, and, lately, month after month. No. Pastor Curtis Jasper Black was definitely getting his needs fulfilled somewhere else. She was sure of it.

Curtis looked at his wife as if she was crazy. "Why are you doing all that cursing?"

"Now, which do you think is worse, Curtis? Me using the word hell and a-s-s or you running around all over town committing adultery? See, that's the thing with you, you're always pointing out what everyone else is doing wrong when all along, you're doing something much worse. And to think you're the head of a prominent Baptist church. Please."

Curtis shook his head in confusion. "I don't know what's gotten into you, but I'm going to pray for you. Maybe we need to pray together, so the devil can loosen his hold on you."

"What's gotten into me is that I'm sick of hearing all these rumors about you and these women, and I'm sick of you coming into this house sometimes as late as midnight and one o'clock in the morning. Claiming that you've been doing the work of the Lord. Claiming that you were at some Baptist ministers' meeting. Claiming that so-and-so needed you at the hospital all evening to pray for their dying soul. Or that Mary, Sue, and Jane needed you to pray for their gangbanging son. Yeah right," she said, throwing the last of the dinner dishes into the dishwasher.

Curtis sighed deeply and then stood up from the table. "Look, I've had enough of this. And I won't be spoken to this way in my own house. I'm the head of this house, and you *will* respect me whether you want to or not. A wife has a place, and she should stay in it. And I'm only going to tell you this one last time. I'm not sleeping around with any women. I love you and Alicia, and I would never betray my family, regardless of what you and any of the rest of those gossipy women at church think. They're just jealous, and the sooner you figure that out, the better off we'll be."

"Jealous of what, Curtis?"

"Jealous of the way you dress, the kind of house you live in, and that brand-new Lincoln Navigator you drive around in every day. The ones who are talking are the ones who wish they were in your shoes."

She couldn't believe how shallow and superficial he was. And what did material things have to do with anything anyway? And since she didn't know, she decided to ask him. "What do material things have to do with you sleeping around, Curtis?"

"Look!" he yelled at the top of his lungs. "I've already told you a hundred times. I'm *not* sleeping around with anybody."

"Well, then, why don't you make love to me anymore? Huh? Explain that."

"Look, I'm under a lot of pressure and that being pastor of a church as large as Faith Missionary involves a lot of hard work. You know how tired I am every evening when I get home. But I promise, things will get better."

"Maybe when hell freezes over, but then, I don't plan on staying around long enough to see if things will get better or not," she said, wiping the kitchen table.

Curtis laughed sarcastically and shook his head. Then he grabbed his car keys. "I'm out of here. And I hope the devil has turned you loose by the time I get back, because I really don't want to hear any more of these paranoid accusations."

As he turned to walk out of the kitchen, Tanya threw the wet dishcloth and hit him in the back of his head.

"See, that's why I'm never here. And for the record, maybe I don't make love to you anymore, because you're always doing all that nagging, and it really turns me off."

"If you were being the faithful husband that you're supposed to be, then I wouldn't have anything to nag about. And on top of that, what about Alicia? You hardly spend any time with her, and I'm sick of you neglecting her the way you do," Tanya said, and wanted to cry her eyes out. Partly because of how Curtis was ignoring their daughter, but mostly because he'd actually admitted that she turned him off sexually.

"Alicia knows how much I love her, and she also knows how busy I am with church business. As a matter of fact, she seems to understand that more than you do. And you're my wife."

"She's only a child, Curtis. And she'll believe anything you tell her because you're her father. But I'm not six years old like her. And I know for a fact that there isn't that much church business going on anywhere."

"Whatever, Tanya," he said, and opened the door leading to the garage.

"Where are you going?" she yelled behind him. "To lay up with Adrienne Jackson?"

"To lay up with who?" he said, laughing in denial.

"You heard exactly what I said. To lay up with Adrienne Jackson," Tanya repeated, becoming more angry by the second. She'd heard that Deacon Jackson's wife was Curtis's prime-cut mistress, and although Tanya didn't have proof of it, she couldn't dismiss what she'd been hearing.

"If you must know, I'm going out to visit some members on the sick list," he said without looking back at her.

"Liar!" Tanya shouted. But Curtis shut the door. And it wasn't long before she heard him driving down the street.

Tanya sat down at the kitchen table and clasped her hands together under her chin. A thousand thoughts circulated through
her mind. A part of her wanted to believe that her marriage had a
chance, but things were so awful between her and Curtis that she
was starting to seriously doubt it. He didn't seem to care about her
at all anymore, and it had gotten to the place where he found any
and every excuse in the book to spend time away from her and Alicia. She was so tired, and even though she was angry, she was hurt,
too. And she was ashamed of the way she had spoken to him. He'd
deserved every bit of it, but that wasn't her usual way of handling
things. Her parents hadn't raised her that way, but as of late, she
hadn't been able to control the way she felt, much less the things
she said. Not to mention the violent and conniving thoughts she'd
been having. The kind of thoughts that were totally against any-
and everything she believed in. She'd been sure that marrying a
minister would guarantee her complete happiness, because it certainly had for her Aunt Margaret in Memphis, but now she knew
that not *every* minister was sincere, and that some were merely playing with God. She regretted ever going out on a first date with Curtis. As a matter of fact, the only positive thing she'd gotten out of
this whole ordeal was her sweet little innocent Alicia. And as much
as she wanted to divorce Curtis, she knew she had Alicia to consider. She didn't know how much longer she could sleep in the
same bed with Curtis, but she knew she had an obligation to her
daughter. Which meant she had no choice except to continue living a life of complete turmoil until Alicia turned eighteen. Which,
unfortunately, wasn't going to be until twelve years from now.

Tanya grunted at her last thought, and then heard the phone
ringing.

She glanced up at the Caller ID box, and saw that it was Curtis
calling from his cellular phone. She wasn't in the mood for any
more arguing, and she definitely didn't want to hear any more of
Curtis's lying. But she reached and picked up the cordless phone
just the same.

"What?" she said in a nonchalant tone of voice.

"Tanya. Look. I'm really sorry for arguing with you, and I'm
even more sorry for not spending any quality time with you and
Alicia. But I'm telling you. From this day forward, things are going

to be different," he said, and paused. The continued. "You sound like you're ready to divorce me, and that's not what I want."

Tanya listened, but she was leery. Especially since Faith Missionary's bylaws specifically stated that in order for a minister to keep his position as pastor of the church, he had to be married. So, she couldn't help but wonder if that was his real reason for calling—the real reason he was sounding like he was in beg mode. A mode that the Reverend Curtis Black never thought he needed to shift into for anyone.

She switched the phone from one ear to the other, but didn't say anything.

"I know you're upset," he continued. "But we can work this out. I'll be home in a couple of hours or so, and we can talk then. All right?"

"I don't know that talking is really going to change anything. It's not like you can take back what you've been doing."

"Tanya. I'm telling you. No matter what you've been hearing, I'm not messing around with other women. I admit that I have purposely tried to find things to do just so I wouldn't have to spend so much time at home, but that's only because you and I have been having so many arguments. But for the millionth time, I would never sleep with another woman. You and I took vows before God, and I have a commitment to Him, you, and our daughter."

"Mmm. Hmm," Tanya said, rolling her eyes toward the ceiling in disbelief.

"I'll talk to you when I get home, okay? And . . . Tanya?"

"What?" she answered irritably.

"I love you."

Tanya didn't say anything.

"Did you hear me?"

"I heard you," she said in a so-what tone of voice.

"You're not going to say it back, though. Right?"

"Curtis, I think you and I are much too old to be playing these little teenage phone games, and if you want to talk to me, I'll be here when you get home."

"Okay, okay. I'll see you later."

Tanya hung up the phone and walked outside to check on Alicia.

HERE AND NOW

KIMBERLA LAWSON ROBY

ABOUT THIS GUIDE

The suggested questions are intended to enhance
your group's reading of Kimberla Lawson Roby's
Here and Now. We hope these ideas will increase
your enjoyment of a powerful book centered on
the high price we pay when we believe the grass is
greener on the other side.

DISCUSSION QUESTIONS

1. Why do you think Racquel was so obsessed with trying to conceive a baby?

2. Do you think Kevin should have been less tolerant of Racquel's obsession?

3. Should Marcella have reacted in a more severe manner after reading Ashley's diary?

4. Do you think many women feel the same way Sharon felt about Marcus and the way Marcella felt about Darryl in terms of sexual compatibility?

5. Do you believe Marcella and Racquel's relationship with each other is comparable to the relationship between most sisters?

6. Prior to reading *Here and Now*, were you aware of the trials and tribulations that couples sometimes endure when dealing with infertility?

7. In your opinion, when do you think Marcella and Racquel each realized that the grass is not as green as most people think on the other side?

8. Have you ever thought that you wanted to walk in someone else's shoes, were able to do it, and then regretted it afterward?

9. Do you believe Marcella did the best she could with what she had?

10. Do you think Darryl was fair to Marcella?

11. Do you think the Fourth of July cookout was typical of most family get-togethers?

AN INTERVIEW WITH KIMBERLA LAWSON ROBY

Q: Your first book was self-published and rode the BlackBoard Bestseller list for months. What do you think accounts for that?

A: It had a lot to do with the fact that I researched the publishing industry months and months before making the decision to self-publish, and then I created an extensive marketing and promotional plan. Since my novel was being geared towards a black female audience, I mailed marketing packages to over 250 black bookstores throughout the country. It didn't hurt that so many black women seemed to be able to relate to the story-line of *Behind Closed Doors*.

Q: What do you think are the major issues facing black women in America today?

A: Most of the major issues facing black women in America today are also common issues with women of all colors, and include finding and sustaining healthy, loving relationships with men, raising their children as single parents and proving to corporate America that they are just as qualified as any of their colleagues, regardless of sex or race, in terms of holding top management positions.

Q: How did you address them in your book?

A: Well, in *Behind Closed Doors* the two female characters find that their marriages are falling apart, and that they must do everything necessary to try and put their lives back into perspective. In *Here and Now*, Marcella struggles to raise her two children by way of a seven-dollar-an-hour job, and receives sporadic child support payments from the father only whenever he feels like paying it. Racquel causes major upsets within her marriage because of an obsession with not being able to have a baby, and both women threaten their relationship with each other.

Q: Marcella rides in an old Cutless, shops at discount stores, takes care of her decidedly undesigner clothes—this is a far cry from the territory of women's commercial fiction as defined by Joan Collins and even Terry McMillan—what made you decide to create a life that is not defined by glamour?

A: I decided on these particular lifestyles, because most women don't have thousands and thousands of dollars in the bank, a five-bedroom home, or a Mercedes Benz to drive around in. So, what I wanted to do was write something that most women could relate to themselves. Of course, in my first novel, the two female protagonists have great careers, a home in the suburbs and drive above-average vehicles, but their marital problems still parallel those of any woman at any income level. These women were not handed anything on a silver platter, they simply went to college and did all the things necessary to reach their goals. In *Here and Now*, all women will be able to relate in one way or another—whether they are struggling to raise their children in a public housing project, or living a middle-class lifestyle.

Q: The women in your novel, the two sisters Marcella and Racquel, the best friend, and even the mother, have had their share of difficulties with the men in their lives. What is happening in America that makes it so hard for the sexes to work things out between them?

A: It seems as though people don't have the same moral values as say our parents and grandparents had years and years ago. We live in a world where people have become impatient and they seem to be looking for lots of conveniences. This means that a good number of people have become selfish and are more apt to care about themselves before thinking of anyone else. It also doesn't help that the male/female ratio in this country is completely out of proportion, which means a lot of men don't see a real reason to commit to an exclusive relationship. Finally, although it is extremely positive that women have become so much more independent over the years (especially in the nineties), this sometimes causes conflicts as well.

Q: Racquel, Marcella's successful and married sister, can't conceive and the difficulties of it and her obsession over becoming a parent threaten her marriage. Is her reaction a common one? What

does it mean to her not being a parent versus Marcella who has two children and who has trouble making ends meet?

A: Yes, based on my research, her reaction is common. There are some women who want children more than anything in this world and at any cost. Some women who experience infertility problems feel as though their femininity has been violated and that they are failures as women. Racquel is willing to do whatever it takes to conceive a baby, regardless of the consequences, and that is where her conflicts begin with her husband, Kevin, who believes they can live happily ever after whether they have a baby or not.

Q: You deal with a pretty explosive issue when Marcella realizes her ten-year-old daughter has been coaxed into having a very dangerous and inappropriate sexual experience with a neighbor's child. What led you to write such a controversial subplot?

A: Whenever I am outlining a novel, my imagination usually runs pretty wild, but I have to say that this particular issue evolved during the actual writing of the book. While it is pretty explosive, my message here is that lots of problems and misfortunes can arise with young children when they are being raised in single-parent households and sometimes left alone. We can't overlook the fact that there are far too many girls getting pregnant and having babies at very early ages. Most parents would prefer to believe that their twelve- or thirteen-year-old daughter still has her virginity and would never have the audacity to think about sexual relations, but in reality, statistics are showing us otherwise.

Q: You have another scene in the book where a household robbery takes place during a funeral. What do you think has happened to our communities that makes such an occurrence possible?

A: My grandmother used to always say that charity begins at home, and in my opinion, the home is where most of our problems are originating. Family values and the discipline of children in this country have broken way down, and I am amazed at the number of parents who allow their children to tell them what they are and are not going to do, not to mention the number of parents who haven't the slightest idea where their children are most of the time or what it is they are doing. Of course, the children who weren't taught any morals and weren't disciplined properly back in the seventies and eighties are now the teenagers and adults who make up our communities.

Q: Marcella's best friend supplies the Christmas presents and other financial assistance for Marcella and her children—what is the sustaining power of women's friendships?

A: Women are strong, independent and dependable creatures and always have a tendency to stick together and be there for one another, no matter what. I always say that there is no stronger friendship than the one between two women. By instinct, women tend to have very caring, sensitive and nurturing personalities, and that seems to make all the difference in the world.

Q: What was the most important aspect of these women's relationship to you? When you sat down to write the book what did you most want to say about what women mean to each other across generations and blood lines?

A: The most important aspect was dependability and the staying power of their relationships. Marcella and Racquel have their differences as sisters, but through it all, they remain in each other's corner. Their mother, Corrine, encourages both daughters to lead decent lives and has clearly taught both of them the importance of family values. This means that it is probably safe to assume Corrine's mother and grandmother more than likely were of the same thinking. A good example is my grandmother and the way she raised my mother and her three sisters, and then how my mother taught me those same morals and family values when I was a child, as well as during the early stages of adulthood.

Q: Do you think novels that are as realistic as yours are helping to redefine and reshape women's popular literature?

A: Yes, I do. What I hear consistently is that my novels are stories that women can relate to. In some cases, I've been told that the stories made them re-think their own situations, and it was the reason they eventually decided to do something about them. I've even had women tell me that reading my novels gave them hope and showed them that they can overcome many different obstacles. This, of course, gives me the best feeling of all.

Q: Who do you see as influences? What inspired you to start writing novels? Where do you find inspiration now for your work?

A: My influences are my mother, my maternal grandmother (who is deceased), and my husband. My mother and grandmother because they always insisted that I could do anything I set my mind to, that I should never give up, and that I should always keep my faith in God. And my husband, because he appreciates me as a woman, loves and respects me as his wife, and encourages me to move mountains. As far as my inspiration to begin writing novels, I always knew that I was supposed to be doing something other than working in a business, corporate setting. I would work for a company for one or two years, and although I'd love my job in the beginning, eventually, I would become bored, and then move on to another. And then finally when I made a decision to sit down and take a long hard look at what it was I really wanted to do, it didn't take me very long to realize that it was writing novels.